An Introduction to
English Legal History

An Introduction to English Legal History

Third edition

By J. H. Baker, LL.D., F.B.A.

Professor of English Legal History and
Fellow of St Catharine's College, Cambridge;
Honorary Bencher of the Inner Temple

Butterworths
London, Boston, Dublin, Edinburgh, Hato Rey,
Kuala Lumpur, Singapore, Sydney, Toronto,
Wellington
1990

United Kingdom	Butterworth & Co (Publishers) Ltd, 88 Kingsway, LONDON WC2B 6AB and 4 Hill Street, EDINBURGH EH2 3JZ
Australia	Butterworths Pty Ltd, SYDNEY, MELBOURNE, BRISBANE, ADELAIDE, PERTH, CANBERRA and HOBART
Canada	Butterworths Canada Ltd, TORONTO and VANCOUVER
Ireland	Butterworth (Ireland) Ltd, DUBLIN
Malaysia	Malayan Law Journal Sdn Bhd, KUALA LUMPUR
New Zealand	Butterworths of New Zealand Ltd, WELLINGTON and AUCKLAND
Puerto Rico	Equity de Puerto Rico, Inc, HATO REY
Singapore	Malayan Law Journal Pte Ltd, SINGAPORE
USA	Butterworth Legal Publishers, AUSTIN, Texas; BOSTON, Massachusetts; CLEARWATER, Florida (D & S Publishers); ORFORD, New Hampshire (Equity Publishing); ST PAUL, Minnesota; and SEATTLE, Washington

All rights reserved. No part of this publication may be reproduced in any material form (including photocopying or storing it in any medium by electronic means and whether or not transiently or incidentally to some other use of this publication) without the written permission of the copyright owner except in accordance with the provisions of the Copyright, Designs and Patents Act 1988 or under the terms of a licence issued by the Copyright Licensing Agency Ltd, 33-34 Alfred Place, London, England WC1E 7DP. Applications for the copyright owner's written permission to reproduce any part of this publication should be addressed to the publisher.

Warning: The doing of an unauthorised act in relation to a copyright work may result in both a civil claim for damages and criminal prosecution.

© Butterworth & Co (Publishers) Ltd 1990

A CIP Catalogue record for this book is available from the British Library .

First edition 1971
Second edition 1979

ISBN 0 406 53101 3

The cover shows the Court of King's Bench in the 1450s, when it was presided over by Sir John Fortescue. A trial is about to take place in banc: the long-haired prisoner at the bar, escorted by the marshal with his long wand and flanked by two serjeants at law in parti-coloured robes, holds up his right hand on arraignment; the jury is being sworn in by one of the criers. Around the table sit the clerks with their rolls, and in the foreground a bedraggled group of prisoners await their turn. (By kind permission of the Treasurer and Masters of the Bench of the Inner Temple.)

Printed by Billings Bookplan, Worcester

Preface

When I began this revision, ten years had passed since the second edition and I was soon forced to concede to myself that further major changes were inevitable. Of course, improvements to such a book as this cannot easily be made without using more words, and I can only hope that the slightly larger bulk of this edition does not detract from its avowed purpose of providing an elementary introduction to the subject. The increase in length is due partly to the fuller explanations given of some topics, and partly to the need to take some account of the extensive literature which has been published in the field since 1979. The explosion of interest has been remarkable, and is signalled by the appearance of three new journals and a growing corpus of conference-papers. Much of the new learning is reflected in the lengthened reading-lists at the end of each chapter; even so, I have not tried to take account of everything written in the last ten years, which would fill many volumes. Although the property and contract chapters have been further divided for convenience, I have generally preserved the structure and coverage of the previous editions. In particular I have not attempted to expand very far the treatment of those nineteenth-century reforms which start new stories rather than round off the old; they are in any case now the subject of two separate textbooks, each longer than this, to which the reader is referred. There is only one completely new chapter, dealing with villeinage and personal liberty; but several new sections have been fitted within the old framework. Another inevitable increase since the second edition is visible in the footnotes. References to the relevant sources in Baker and Milsom, *Sources of English Legal History*, have been added throughout, and this has required a general revision of policy with respect to citations. References are generally given to sources of special importance or instructional value, sources of quotations, recently published sources, and other materials relied on but not to be found in the further reading. I have nevertheless continued to assume that readers seeking further information or enlightenment will venture into the contents of these reading lists, and especially Professor Milsom's *Historical Foundations of the Common Law*.

J. H. Baker

January 1990

Preface to the second edition

Some might think a second edition of a textbook on legal history more in need of justification than a new edition of a textbook on some rapidly developing branch of modern law. Surely, they will ask, legal history does not go out of date? The straight answer to their question is that all history, meaning history as we see it rather than the bare facts of the past, is subject to change: and in the last eight years original research has revealed so many new facts that our interpretations of English legal history are having to change as fast as the modern law does. The more honest answer to the question is, alas, more subjective. When the first edition was written the author saw things with a clarity given only to those who have not come fully to appreciate the extent of their own ignorance. No doubt that defect gave the book an illusory strength from the point of view of the groping student, but equally it must have caused widespread irritation among the more discerning readers. Many shortcomings, ranging from undue compression to manifest error, became apparent as the years passed, through further reading and research, and through trying to make sense of the subject to successive generations of students. In the optimistic belief that slightly more comprehensiveness is not incompatible with comprehensibility, I have made numerous additions throughout and have rewritten most of the first part. No doubt in eradicating the more obvious shortcomings I have introduced others. I have, nevertheless, tried hard not to alter the character of the book as an elementary historical introduction to English law, through which the reader may find his way to more substantial works. Perhaps the most formative influence on the shape and content of this edition has been the experience of lecturing on the history of English law to the inns of court, a yearly task which I was pleased to attempt six times; and I wish to record my gratitude to the Council of Legal Education for providing me with the opportunity of reconstruction. Among the many influences on the substantive rethinking behind this edition the foremost have been my Cambridge colleagues; to them, and indeed to all who have helped me, knowingly or otherwise, my gratitude knows no bounds.

JHB
Cambridge
December, 1978

Contents

Part two

Appendix I

Appendix II

Table of Statutes

Note: the best printed text of the statutes from 1236 to 1713 is *The Statutes of the Realm* (1810–27). For Magna Carta in its various issues, see the appendices to J.C. Holt, *Magna Carta* (1965).

Table of Cases

Cases cited by name

Kings and Queens of England since 1066

with the dates of their accession

House of Normandy
William I, 25 Dec. 1066–1087
William II, 26 Sept. 1087–1100
Henry I, 5 Aug. 1100–1135
Stephen, 26 Dec. 1135–1154

Angevins (*House of Plantagenet*)
Henry II, 19 Dec. 1154–1189
Richard I, 3 Sept. 1189–1199
John, 27 May 1199–1216

Plantagenets (*continued*)
Henry III, 28 Oct. 1216–1272
Edward I, 20 Nov. 1272–1307
Edward II, 8 July 1307–1327
Edward III, 25 Jan. 1327–1377
Richard II, 22 June 1377–1399

House of Lancaster
Henry IV, 30 Sept. 1399–1413
Henry V, 21 March 1413–1422
Henry VI, 1 Sept. 1422–1461

House of York
Edward IV, 4 March 1461–1483
Edward V, 9 April 1483
Richard III, 26 June 1483–1485

House of Tudor
Henry VII, 22 Aug. 1485–1509
Henry VIII, 22 April 1509–1547
Edward VI, 28 Jan. 1547–1553
Mary I (alone), 19 July 1553–1554
Philip and Mary, 25 July 1554–1558
Elizabeth I, 17 Nov. 1558–1603

House of Stuart
James I, 24 March 1603–1625
Charles I, 27 March 1625–1649
[Interregnum, 1649-60]
Charles II, 30 Jan. 1649 (de jure); restored 29 May 1660–1685
James II, 6 Feb. 1685–1688
William & Mary, 13 Feb. 1689–1694
William III (alone), 28 Dec. 1694–1702
Anne, 8 March 1702–1714

House of Hanover
George I, 1 Aug. 1714–1727
George II, 11 June 1727–1760
George III, 25 Oct. 1760–1820
George IV, 29 Jan. 1820–1830
William IV, 26 June 1830–1837
Victoria, 20 June 1837–1901

House of Saxe-Coburg and Gotha
Edward VII, 22 Jan. 1901–1910

House of Windsor
George V, 6 May 1910–1936
Edward VIII, 20 Jan. 1936
George VI, 11 Dec. 1936–1952
Elizabeth II, 6 Feb. 1952–

Table of Abbreviations

CPMR	*Calendar of Plea and Memoranda Rolls Preserved among the Archives of the City of London* (A. H. Thomas and P. E. Jones ed., 1926-61), 6 volumes covering the period 1323-1482.
CUL	Cambridge University Library.
EELH	S. E. Thorne, *Essays in English Legal History* (1985). Collected essays.
EHR	English Historical Review.
Essays AALH	Association of American Law Schools, *Select Essays in Anglo-American Legal History* (1907-09), 3 volumes.
Fifoot HSCL	C. H. S. Fifoot, *History and Sources of the Common Law* (1949).
Fitz. Abr.	A. Fitzherbert, *La Graunde Abridgement* (1577 ed.). [1st ed., without title, 1514-16.]
fo.	folio.
Glanvill	*The treatise on the laws and customs of England commonly called Glanvill* (G. D. G. Hall ed., 1965).
HLR	Harvard Law Review.
HLS	Harvard Law School.
Holdsworth HEL	W. S. Holdsworth, *History of English Law* (1922-66), 16 volumes.
IJ	Irish Jurist (new series).
JLH	Journal of Legal History.
KB 27	Public Record Office, plea rolls of the Court of King's Bench.

Kiralfy SB — A. K. R. Kiralfy, *Source Book of English Law* (1957).

Law, Litigants and the Legal Profession — A. H. Manchester and E. W. Ives ed., *Law, Litigants and the Legal Profession* (1983). Conference papers (Birmingham).

Law-making and Law-makers — A. Harding ed., *Law-making and Law-makers in British History* (1980). Conference papers (Edinburgh).

Laws and Customs — M. S. Arnold et al. ed., *On the Laws and Customs of England. Essays in Honor of S. E. Thorne* (1981).

Law and Social Change — J. A. Guy and H. G. Beale ed., *Law and Social Change in British History* (1984). Conference papers (Bristol).

Legal History Studies 1972 — D. Jenkins ed., *Legal History Studies 1972* (1975). Conference papers (Aberystwyth).

Legal Record and Historical Reality — T. G. Watkin ed., *Legal Record and Historical Reality* (1989). Conference papers (Cardiff).

Legal Records and the Historian — J. H. Baker ed., *Legal Records and the Historian* (1978). Conference papers (Cambridge).

Legal Theory and Legal History — A. W. B. Simpson, *Legal Theory and Legal History. Essays in the Common Law* (1987). Collected essays.

LHR — Law and History Review.

Lib. Ass. — *Liber Assisarum* (1679 ed.).

LPCL — J. H. Baker, *The Legal Profession and the Common Law. Historical Essays* (1986). Collected essays.

LQR — Law Quarterly Review.

LTLH   A. W. B. Simpson, *Legal Theory and Legal History. Essays on the Common Law* (1987). Collected essays.

Manchester MLH   A. H. Manchester, *A Modern Legal History of England and Wales 1750-1950* (1980).

Manchester, *Sources*   A. H. Manchester, *Sources of English Legal History. Law, History and Society in England and Wales 1750-1950* (1984).

Mansfield Notebooks   Judicial notebooks of Lord Mansfield as CJKB (1756-88), belonging to the present Earl of Mansfield, Scone Palace, Perthshire, MSS. TD 80/52.

Milsom HFCL   S. F. C. Milsom, *Historical Foundations of the Common Law* (2nd ed., 1981).

OJLS   Oxford Journal of Legal Studies.

pl.   placitum (case-number within a term).

Plucknett CHCL   T. F. T. Plucknett, *Concise History of the Common Law* (5th ed., 1956).

Pollock & Maitland   F. Pollock and F. W. Maitland, *History of English Law before the time of Edward I* (1895; 1968 ed.), 2 volumes.

repr.   reprinted.

Rot. Parl.   *Rotuli Parliamentorum* (1783), 6 volumes.

R.S.C.   Rules of the Supreme Court.

SHCL   S. F. C. Milsom, *Studies in the History of the Common Law* (1985). Collected essays.

Simpson, *History of the Land Law*   A. W. B. Simpson, *A History of the Land Law* (2nd ed., 1986).

sjt   serjeant at law.

SS   Selden Society (annual volumes, 1887-).

SS Supp. Ser.   Selden Society Supplementary Series.

Stat.   Statute.

TRHS   Transactions of the Royal Historical Society.

Wentworth   J. Wentworth, *System of Pleading* (1795-98), 10 volumes.

Y.B.   Year Book. References to Ric. II are to the Ames Foundation editions. References to 11-20 Edw. III are to the Rolls series editions unless otherwise stated. Other citations are to the old black-letter editions (reprinted 1679-80), cited by term, regnal year, folio, and placitum.

Printed law reports are cited by the references currently in use. They may also be found in the *English Reports* reprint.

Part one
1. Law and Custom in Early Britain

When, in 1470, an English serjeant-at-law maintained that the common law had been in existence since the creation of the world,[1] it is not improbable that he believed it literally. There was even a veneer of truth upon the notion, inasmuch as English law represented an unbroken development from prehistoric time. There had been no conscious act of creation or adoption. What the serjeant did not perceive was that there had been a time, not so many centuries before his own, when there was no law at all as he understood it. For him, as for ourselves, the law consisted of a body of known and uniform rules, with their own rational coherence. But four centuries before 1470, at the time of the Norman conquest, England had neither judicature nor legislature in any developed sense. There were decision-making bodies, from the king's council down to the village meeting; but decisions can be made without following or making fixed rules, and in these ancient assemblies no distinction could have been made between the processes of adjudication, administration and legislation. Decisions settled the matter in hand and were not expected to do more; they were not constrained by the past and did not fix rules for the future. That is not to suggest that law was immediately preceded by despotism or anarchy. Good decisions are guided by custom and wise counsel as to what is reasonable. Even so, good order, custom and due deliberation are not quite the same as 'law'.

VARIETY OF CUSTOMS IN EARLY BRITAIN

One feature of custom which distinguishes it from the later common-law tradition is its variability from one people to another, or from one area to another. Uniformity was hardly to be expected when social habits and attitudes varied widely with race and geography. Given the many vicissitudes of the tribes and races which inhabited the British Isles before the Normans, any search for the laws or customs of England before the emergence of the nation itself is bound to fail. To the extent that common features may be discerned in the customs of different

[1] *Wallyng v. Meger* (1470) 47 SS 38, per Catesby sjt.

people and places, the unifying force is not a common law but the general social and moral assumptions of the age, or even the natural instincts of mankind at particular stages of development: the parallels are often found to transcend national and geographical boundaries.

Our first glimpses of ancient British customs are through Roman eyes, because the learned men among the Britons preferred to pass on their traditions by word of mouth rather than commit them to writing. Julius Caesar described the native priest-judges, called druids, who preserved and enforced the Celtic religion and customs; but of those customs he related very little, save that they involved human sacrifice. The Romans themselves had a sophisticated jurisprudence, and to them the usages of the British had little more than anthropological interest. Whether their colonisation of Britain made any lasting impact on native traditions is doubtful. Roman law was certainly enforced, at least on Roman citizens. The famous jurist Papinian is known to have heard cases in the forum at York, and the first reported English case was heard before Javolenus Priscus, as *legatus juridicus* of the province of Britannia, around 85 A.D.[2] Yet, in the confusion which followed the Roman withdrawal at the beginning of the fifth century, the Celts were left to pursue their tribal customs without impediment. The chief enduring survival was the Christian Church, which lingered to vie with the druidical order for spiritual authority and ultimately to prevail. During the next two centuries the British mainland was subject to constant invasion from across the North Sea. The conquering Angles and Saxons pushed the Celtic people back into the west of the island, into Wales, Cornwall, and south-west Scotland. The invading races differed from the Celts in religion, language and physical appearance; and they brought with them Teutonic customs which even the Romans had noticed as being different from those of Britain and Gaul.

The Anglo-Saxons are the first inhabitants of whose legal usages anything is known, because they were the first to introduce written laws. The earliest surviving English legislation,[3] that of King Aethelberht I of Kent, appeared in about 600 A.D. and has traditionally been associated with the supposed conversion of that king to Christianity by St Augustine. The early Christian kings relied on the counsel of their bishops in temporal as in spiritual affairs, and the clergy had the literary skill to initiate the technique of government through the written word. Bede wrote, two centuries later, that the new

---

[2] D.36.1.48. For law and government in Roman Britain, see S. Frere, *Britannia* (2nd ed., 1978), ch. 10.

[3] It is also the earliest surviving Germanic legislation, and the first text of any kind written in English.

laws had been made 'according to the Roman example', and many were indeed taken up with ecclesiastical matters: the laws of Wihtred (*c.* 700 A.D.) were even stated to be the outcome of a clerical assembly. Recent research has raised the contrary possibility that Aethelberht's laws were those of the last pagan king. They were written in Anglo-Saxon, not in clerical Latin, and it may be that Bede retrospectively overemphasised Augustine's influence. Whatever the inspiration may have been, it is clear that the Anglo-Saxon codes did not 'codify' existing customs, let alone make new law. They were directed at readers who could be presumed to know the customs already, and offered fixed rules to govern situations which must previously have rested on discretion. Prominent in them, as in other codes of later date, was the fixing of the blood-money payable in lieu of feuding. It is easy to imagine how arbitration failed to assuage the passion for retribution: honour demanded full satisfaction. But the Church taught that it was honourable to be merciful and accept monetary emendation; and the pre-ordained scales of penalties which peace and pride alike required seem closely associated with the disciplinary codes (called 'penitentials') which the northern Church devised to regulate spiritual emendation for sins. The influence of the Church in thus discouraging blood-feuds seems very likely.

The Danish invasions of the ninth century subjected the eastern parts of the island to new Scandinavian influences. Where the Danes conquered, their 'Danelaw' prevailed. The very word 'law' is believed to have been given to the English language by the Danes. The struggle between the Anglo-Saxon peoples and their common enemy gave King Alfred of Wessex (d. 899 A.D.) his opportunity to begin the unification of the former into the single kingdom of England: a process which was completed in the tenth century. King Alfred is reputed to have taken a deep interest in justice, and to have taken on himself the occasional review of decisions made by subjects. In the prologue to the code which he promulgated for the West Saxons in the 880s (or perhaps slightly later), he is reported as claiming[4] that he and his advisers studied the laws of Aethelberht of Kent, Ine of Wessex, and Offa of Mercia,[5] together with the Bible and the penitentials of the Church, before embarking on their task. This may have been the first attempt to compare the miscellaneous customs of the English. But Alfred's written laws were still far removed from anything like comprehensive common law. They were an attempt to impose uniformity in certain limited fields, and as such set a constitutional precedent for legislation

---

[4] It is not clear whether the preamble is to be taken as historical truth, or how much Alfred personally contributed to the exercise.

[5] The laws of Offa (d. 796 A.D.) have not survived.

by the kings of England. The precedent was followed by nearly all of Alfred's successors, including the Danish King Cnut (1016-35), whose laws were composed in 1018 by Archbishop Wulfstan (d. 1023) of York, and enlarged in the 1020s. The laws of Cnut and of King Edward the Confessor (1042-66) were the main sources of old English usages for writers after the Norman conquest. Nevertheless, despite all this legislative activity, England was still governed rather by unwritten and variable custom than by uniform law. The principal reason for the absence of common law at this stage was the absence of any judicial machinery to require it.

'Communal' Justice

Societies are slow to recognise legal authority as now understood. Custom and religion are forces in the community to be upheld and maintained as a matter of tradition, or social obligation, or to earn eternal salvation; but legal sanctions necessitate the imposition of forces which the early community is unready or even unable to wield. Force belongs in the state of nature to individuals who have the power to use it, and the suppression of private force by investing the community at large with a greater force required a degree of social organisation which it must have taken countless dark and forgotten centuries to achieve. If one man takes something from another, the most obvious remedy is for the victim to try to take it back; and when it was also the only remedy, no man had any rights beyond those which he was physically able to protect for himself. In the absence of strong government or judicial control, people administered their own justice by self-help: by forcible entries, reprisals and family feuds. One of the first causes of a legal system is the desire to prevent or discourage feuding and private warfare, by offering some peaceful alternative. Here the community could assist, as a body in public meeting, by encouraging the parties to settle their differences or submit them to honourable arbitration. If the parties could not agree, the community did not decide between them as a court would decide today; but it might press on them, or one of them, an oath or supernatural test which could not be disputed.

PROCEDURE AND PROOF

Very little is known of the growth of communal organisation in England. The 'moot' or folk-assembly, first mentioned in the Kentish laws of the eighth century, was of prehistoric origin. It would be unrealistic to regard it, even when the dim rays of history first fall upon its outlines, as a court of law. It was an open-air meeting of the populace to discuss local affairs. It had no judge, and there were no lawyers. The principal men of the locality were gathered under the presidency of a 'doomsman' or 'shire-man', but acted as a community. The community issued no writs and kept no records: which is why we know so little about it. Our knowledge is based on a small number of brief allusions in written documents, cautiously augmented by what we know of survivals in later periods or parallels in other countries.

The procedure in contentious matters was calculated to avoid reasoned decision-making. If the parties could not be persuaded to make a 'love-day' – to settle amicably – then resort could be had to proof by oath, which might have to be backed up by a physical test. In order to put the defendant to this hazard, the plaintiff was required to establish a prima facie case; and this was the purpose of his 'suit' (*secta*), the group of followers whom he brought with him to back him up on oath. The suit had some affinity with witnesses, and they may have been subject to examination as to competence, but their testimony was only part of the interlocutory process and did not dispose of the matter.[6] If the defendant was allowed the benefit of proof by oath, he proceeded to swear on the holy evangels to the truth of his case, in very general terms and without possibility of cross-examination. In the form of proof known to later generations as wager of law, he was expected to bring with him some neighbours as 'compurgators' or 'oath-helpers' to back up his word. If this lesser kind of proof was deemed inappropriate, usually because of the gravity of an accusation and the unreliability of the party's word, the oath might have to be proved by the physical test of an ordeal. Ordeals involved an appeal to God to reveal the truth in human disputes, and they required priestly participation to achieve this rapport with the Deity. Several forms of ordeal were recognised by the early Christian Church, but in England they usually took the form of fire or water. In the former, a piece of iron was put into a fire and then in the party's hand; the hand was bound, and inspected a few days later: if the burn had festered, God was taken to have decided against the party. The ordeal of cold water required the party to be trussed and lowered into a pond; if he sank, the water was deemed to have 'received him' with God's blessing, and so he was quickly fished out.

There was a prolonged intellectual debate about the legitimacy of the ordeal. It was not clear how man could expect God to answer human

---

[6] Suit was absorbed into common-law procedure, and until 1856 plaintiffs in many actions had to make a formal proffer of 'good suit' (e.g., p. 629, post). By 1343, however, it was decided that the suit could not be examined (see B. & M. p. 212); and it therefore became fictitious (except in the action of neifty: p. 535, post).

questions: might He not, for instance, choose to absolve men who had broken the law but repented? And what if He decided not to intervene at all, but to leave the matter to be settled by His ordinary laws of nature? Could one be sure in a given case whether He had intervened? There is some evidence that those who administered ordeals, perhaps because of such doubts, began to feel a responsibility to facilitate the result they considered right: for instance, by letting the iron cool in cases where suspicion was weak, or by interpreting a burned hand liberally. In the last days of the ordeal, the acquittal-rate was surprisingly high. Above all, it was not clear that humans had any right to invoke God's miraculous intervention in mundane affairs: indeed, the Church taught that it was wrong to tempt the Almighty. In 1215, the Lateran Council, after discussing these problems, took the decisive step of forbidding clergy to participate any more in ordeals.[7] This led in England to the introduction of the criminal trial jury.[8] It did not affect wager of law, which did not require a priest and did not depend on instant divine revelation. Proof by simple oath and compurgation therefore survived, and passed into the common law.[9] But it worked on the same inscrutable system as the ordeal. There was no question of going behind it into the facts of the case, let alone of having to weigh whether the oath was true, since that was settled conclusively by the compurgators. The oath, like the ordeal, was intended to obviate formal enquiry into the factual merits of the case. This is commonly summarised by saying that, under this old system, judgment preceded proof: once it was adjudged that one of the parties should swear or perform a test there was no further decision to make, except whether he had passed it. The wise men of each community needed to know how to regulate disputes, when and how proofs should be imposed on disputants, and what should be done when the result was known. Here was room for argument and human discretion, and perhaps even for the evaluation of testimony.[10] If the case was pressed to 'law', the real decision on the merits was taken by the compurgators. This was a workable method of resolving disputes, and we should not dismiss it as irrational simply because the

---

7   The ordeal of water survived much longer in folklore in the custom of 'swimming' alleged witches; this illegal form of ordeal was used near Chelmsford as late as 1863.

8   See p. 579, post. The ordeal was not much used, if at all, in 'civil' cases.

9   It was not formally abolished until 1833. The 1215 measure did not affect trial by battle either; but that was probably a Norman innovation.

10   Such evaluation, however, was of the witnesses rather than of their 'evidence', because the latter was only given in general terms and was not subject to dissection. For an illuminating contemporary account of this kind of trial in early Welsh law, see *The Law of Hywel Dda* (D. Jenkins ed., 1986), pp. 83-98.

critical decision was not made by a court applying legal rules to established facts. However, the proof was the end rather than the beginning of the process of resolution: there was no thought of developing principles to accommodate the endless variety of factual situations. And in the absence of any centralisation to ensure uniformity from place to place, or of records to ensure consistency over time, the old way of doing things could never have generated a body of law comparable to that of ancient Rome or Plantagenet England. Rights and liabilities could not be worked out in detail, because law stopped short at what we now call procedure.

THE OLD ENGLISH ASSEMBLIES

Of the structure and distribution of communities in the Britain of the Dark Ages we have but a faint picture, based largely on archaeology and the study of place-names. There were at one time at least a dozen kingdoms, some large and some small. Even when powerful kings in the ninth and tenth centuries began to unify and dominate the greater part of what is now England, we need not suppose that the average inhabitant thought of himself as English or had much consciousness of anything beyond the little closed world of his own village.

By the tenth century a single kingdom of England was virtually established, and with an increasingly effective monarchy came a more homogeneous scheme of local government. The whole country was divided by this period into 'shires' (counties),[11] which have remained substantially the same in name and shape down to the present day.[12] Their origin is obscure, and probably not uniform. Some of the shires south of the Thames, and also Essex and Middlesex, correspond to old Saxon kingdoms, while names such as Norfolk and Suffolk suggest ancient tribal communities. But most of the shires derive their names from a borough at or near the centre, and it is likely that these represent a northward extension of the shiring system from Wessex for military and tax purposes. The boroughs themselves had been established as royal strongholds against invasion, and in some cases by capture had become the strongholds of invaders; they were therefore suitable centres for a defensive system under which, in the tenth and eleventh centuries, the shires were assigned to provincial royal commanders called 'ealdormen' or earls. The shire had an assembly, which by the time of

---

[11] The word 'shire' was used in Wessex as early as the 7th century, but possibly in a different sense; there is no evidence of wider use at that date.

[12] The principal changes were made in 1972, when a number of smaller counties were abolished and a few new ones created.

King Alfred (959-975 A.D.) met twice a year, attended by the ealdorman and bishop, to discuss the more important affairs of the region. The laws of Ine of Wessex (*c*. 690 A.D.) refer to justice (*riht*) being demanded before the shire-man – perhaps the ealdorman's deputy – and it seems that the shire moot, like all other assemblies of that period, combined judicial, administrative and legislative functions.

The laws of Athelstan (d. 939 A.D.) mention smaller units called 'hundreds' into which the shires were divided.[13] Each hundred was under the responsibility of a hundredman. The hundreds were subdivided into 'tithings', which were notionally groups of ten families under the responsibility of a tithingman. The sorting of the population into hundreds and tithings was a means of maintaining good order and raising taxes to support the king. The hundreds also met monthly to transact the ordinary judicial and administrative business of the community; and twice a year, at what was later called the 'view of frankpledge', the tithings were reviewed to make sure that every free man was 'in borh' (pledged to good behaviour) and that crimes were being duly presented for investigation. Although most hundreds fell exactly within the bounds of a shire, there was no hierarchic relationship between the two institutions;[14] both, within their geographical limits, were sovereign, in the sense that they followed their own customs without interference. It is likely, however, that only the more important or troublesome disputes were reserved for the infrequent and solemn shire moots.

The boroughs likewise had assemblies, variously called burghmoots, portmanmoots, or (when held indoors) hustings. In medieval times these would develop into busy courts for merchants: despite the ancient character of their procedures (including wager of law), they were expeditious and fulfilled the needs of the mercantile community.[15] They flourished into Tudor times, and in some cases beyond. The borough performed similar functions for townspeople, both administratively and judicially, as the hundred performed for country folk; borough and hundred were therefore reckoned to be mutually exclusive. In London, however, the husting was really the equivalent of a shire, and it came to displace the old shire moot. The London equivalent of the hundred was

---

13   In some northern parts the Scandinavian word 'wapentake' was used instead; it is said to derive from the practice of taking up and brandishing weapons to signify assent at a meeting.

14   In some parts of the country there were intermediate units: the ridings of Yorkshire (meaning 'third'-ings), the similar 'parts' of Lincolnshire, the lathes of Kent, and the rapes of Sussex.

15   For the codification of their customs in medieval times, see M. Bateson, *Borough Customs*, 18 and 21 SS.

the 'ward', and the division into wards has continued largely unchanged to the present.

The smallest assembly was that of the village. Although it may often have coincided with a tithing, it was not a subdivision of any of the other units but simply a conglomeration of dwellings corresponding in many cases to the later ecclesiastical and administrative unit of the parish. The settlement of a group of families in a village, with open-field farming, must have necessitated at least a communal agricultural policy, and it is possible that village meetings were once the place to settle it. Of the village moot, however, we find little or no trace in early history. In the centuries after the Norman conquest the wider community of the vill continued to exercise police functions, independently of manorial feudalism; but its role as a forum for small-scale decision-making was taken over by the manor,[16] and (much later) the parish, and it did not survive.

From Communal to Personal Authority

The earliest form of justice was not conceived of as emanating from a ruler or from a ruler's learned judges. We do not hear of the king's law, or of a lord's law, but of communal justice or the custom of the people. This 'folk-right' (*folcriht*) is frequently mentioned even in the royal legislation of the Anglo-Saxon period, and King Alfred's last will mentions an instruction to his own council to apply folk-right in a particular matter. In the ancient assemblies there was no 'judge' as such. The business was transacted by those attending as 'suitors', under the chairmanship of the ealdorman, or his deputy. Yet such is the dependence of good administration and effective justice upon the energy of the elders or leaders of a community that, almost as soon as these institutions are noticed in written sources, jurisdiction seems to be a duty vested in individuals rather than in the community at large. The origins of this aspect of lordship are difficult to trace. Eventually it would merge with feudal lordship, but it seems to be present before any definitely feudal characteristics can be identified. Some ealdormen may have represented earlier royal families. In some cases lordship may have evolved from prehistoric traditions of chieftainship, in others by delegation from the king. The roots of such authority were not in political theory, for there was none, but in the fact of power and personal leadership. What may seem to us to be a shift of authority from the community to lordship was in fact probably no more than a

[16] See p. 10, post.

failure to conceptualise the 'community': authority was identified with people, not with constitutional theories. The old way of thinking is most apparent in the sphere of public order, where what is protected is not the safety of the community but the peace (*grith*) of particular persons. In this concept of peace, what we regard as public and private rights are indistinguishable; the peace of a churl was simply his right to compensation for wrongs done to him and his family, but the peace of a lord included the protection of his vassals and was a right more akin to jurisdiction than a cause of action.

The notion of seignorial authority, the authority which went with being a lord,[17] gave rise to a separate system of courts existing alongside the counties and hundreds.[18] Every lord, from the upper levels of tenure down to the lowest, in theory held court for his 'men'. At the lowest level, peasant communities were organised into 'manors', which were the estates surrounding a lord's mansion house or 'hall',[19] small units of feudal government often coterminous with a village but sometimes smaller. The lord's court, or hall-moot, in some places made bye-laws, dealt with disputes about contracts and torts, and punished minor crimes, in addition to despatching the agricultural and feudal business. For many, perhaps most, Englishmen it was the only authority that impinged on their daily lives. The manorial court belonged partly to the feudal and partly to the 'communal' scheme of things; although the lord (or his steward) presided, the free men had a voice, and the court was the means whereby the customs of rural communities were put into effect.

By far the most important consequence of the personalisation of authority was the constitutional ascendancy of the king, especially once England became a single kingdom in the tenth century. The king had been responsible for establishing the borough, hundred and shire, and in all of them he placed his own officials called 'reeves' to watch over their operation. The laws of Edward the Elder (d. 925 A.D.) and Athelstan (d. 939 A.D.) make plain the duty of the king's reeves in borough and hundred to see that all men received the benefit of the customary law (folk-right) and the 'doom-book' (presumably Alfred's code) in those assemblies. Some hundreds were allowed to fall under the control of lords, and some parcels of hundredal jurisdiction came to belong to lords

---

17 For feudal lordship, see p. 256, post.

18 It is not known how common seignorial courts were before the Norman period. Since the Domesday commissioners reported of a particular manor that it 'has its pleas in its lord's hall', perhaps in 1087 this was still unusual: Maitland, *Domesday Book and Beyond*, p. 91.

19 The Latin word *manerium* originally denoted residence, probably the lord's house itself.

of manors; in such cases, the lords were said to possess *sake* and *soke*, the right to hold court and to compel suitors to attend it. Even in these cases, however, the king retained some supervisory control and might deprive a lord who abused his authority. The shire remained more closely in the king's control; and the shire-reeve (or sheriff), whose duties extended to visiting the hundreds twice yearly for the view of frankpledge, soon became one of the most important officials in the country.

Before the Norman conquest of 1066, therefore, the constitutional theory that justice is a prerogative of the Crown was beginning to have some foundation in fact, though it was not yet expressed in words. The king's peace was a concept wide enough to bring many disputes between subjects within the purview of the king's own court, his council of wise men or *witan*. Since at least the time of Alfred, kings had undertaken the responsibility of looking into disputes, and by the 1020s so many were the complaints received by King Cnut that he found it necessary to confine recourse to his court to those who had already sought a remedy in the hundred. Failure of justice elsewhere provided the basis for a nascent royal jurisdiction over civil causes, while the concept of the king's peace provided the basis for a parallel jurisdiction over crime. The king was also a feudal lord, and like other lords was expected to do justice to his tenants.[20] The other most significant innovation was the employment of writing in the business of government. As an outward manifestation of their royal authority, the Anglo-Saxon kings were (as we have seen) issuing codes declaring the law or containing general directions to reeves and lords. The later Anglo-Saxon kings were also using written instruments under impressive seals to confer or define jurisdiction: charters granting *sake* and *soke*, criminal jurisdiction,[21] or borough status, and writs referring disputes or declaring rights to assemblies of the shire.[22] Still, be it noted, there was no king's law, as distinct from the folk-right which varied from place to place. But the seeds of the common-law system which flowered in the twelfth century had been sown and were starting to grow.

---

[20] Before William I, however, it was not settled that *all* land was held ultimately of the king.

[21] Each crime seems to have needed a separate grant: e.g., *grithbryce* (breach of the peace), *infangenetheof* and *utfangenetheof* (theft), *hamsocn* (housebreaking), *forsteal* (ambush), *flymenafyrmth* (harbouring fugitives).

[22] Writs have been traced back to the time of King Ethelred (d. 1016); whether they were used earlier is a matter of dispute. See G. Barraclough, 39 *History* 193.

Further reading

Pollock & Maitland, vol. I, pp. 1-63
Holdsworth HEL, vol. II, pp. 1-118
Plucknett CHCL, pp. 3-10, 83-100
Milsom HFCL, pp. 11-23
J. E. A. Jolliffe, *The Constitutional History of Medieval England* (4th ed., 1961), pp. 1-128

ANGLO-SAXON LAW

T. P. Oakley, *English Penitential Discipline and Anglo-Saxon Law* (1923)
H. G. Richardson and G. O. Sayles, *Law and Legislation from Aethelberht to Magna Carta* (1966), pp. 1-29, 157-169
D. Whitelock, *English Historical Documents 500-1042* (2nd ed., 1979), part II
P. H. Blair, *An Introduction to Anglo-Saxon England* (2nd ed., 1977), ch. IV
P. Wormald, 'Aethelred the Lawmaker', in *Ethelred the Unready* (D. Hill ed., 1978), pp. 47-80
A. W. B. Simpson, 'The Laws of Ethelbert' (1981), *Laws and Customs*, pp. 3-17 (repr. in LTLH 1-15)
A. J. Frantzen, *The Literature of Penance in Anglo-Saxon England* (1983)
H. R. Loyn, *The Governance of Anglo-Saxon England 500-1087* (1984)

EARLY METHODS OF PROOF

J. W. Baldwin, 'The Intellectual Preparation for the Canon of 1215 against Ordeals' (1961) 36 *Speculum* 613-636
P. Hyams, 'Trial by Ordeal: the Key to Proof in the early Common Law' (1981), *Laws and Customs*, pp. 90-126
R. Bartlett, *Trial by Fire and Water* (1986)

THE OLD ASSEMBLIES (INCLUDING THEIR LATER HISTORY)

Pollock & Maitland, vol. I, pp. 527-688
F. W. Maitland, *Domesday Book and Beyond* (1897)
S. B. Chrimes in Holdsworth HEL, vol. I (7th ed.), pp. 1*-24*, 5-24
W. A. Morris, *The Frankpledge System* (1910)
W. O. Ault, *Private Jurisdiction in England* (1923)

H. M. Cam, *The Hundred and the Hundred Rolls* (1930); *Law-finders and Law-makers in Medieval England* (1962), chs. I, III-V; *Liberties and Communities in Medieval England* (1963)

J. P. Dawson, *A History of Lay Judges* (1960), pp. 178-286

A. Harding, *The Law Courts of Medieval England* (1973), pp. 13-31

R. B. Palmer, *The County Courts of Medieval England 1150-1350* (1982)

2. Origins of the Common Law

The conquest of England by William Duke of Normandy in 1066 was described by Maitland as a catastrophe which determined the whole future of English law.[1] Yet such legal changes as are ultimately attributable to this event did not occur suddenly or through deliberate Norman policy. William claimed to be king by lawful succession, and one of his first acts was to promise the English that they could keep their old laws. The Norman invaders were warlike, uncultured and illiterate. Whether they appreciated it or not, they found in England a system of law and government as well developed as anything they had left in Normandy. Certainly they had no refined body of jurisprudence to bring with them. Those changes which were immediate and deliberate tended rather to divide than to consolidate: new racial discriminations between French and English, a new and seemingly barbaric addition to the ordeals (trial by battle),[2] the separation of ecclesiastical courts from the shires and hundreds, the subjection of the vast tracts of forest land to an alien and oppressive 'forest law' protecting the royal hunt, and a brand of military feudalism which gave seignorial jurisdiction a new basis and probably in its initial workings also divided sharply the French and English. None of this helped produce a common law; if anything the reverse.

The common law emerged in the twelfth century from the efficient and rapid expansion of institutions which existed in an undeveloped form before 1066. England, unlike Normandy, was already a unified nation with a central government ruling through sheriffs answerable to the king, and it had the beginnings of a bureaucratic administration operating through written instruments under the king's seal. To this the Normans, and their Angevin successors, brought a taste for strong government and a flair for administration, so that within a century after the conquest the rudimentary court of the Anglo-Saxon kings had grown to produce two great departments of state (the Exchequer and the Chancery) and a judicial system whereby the king's justice was dispensed regularly by members of the king's household.

The effect of these changes on legal administration can be understood by comparing two twelfth-century law books. The state of things in the

---

[1] Pollock & Maitland, vol. I, p. 79.
[2] See p. 87, post.

first half-century after 1066 was described in the compilation known misleadingly as the *Leges Henrici Primi* (*c.* 1118), which was probably the private work of a continental observer. There were three distinct systems of law in England: the law of Wessex, the law of Mercia, and the Danelaw. But there were differences of detail, particularly in procedure, in each of the thirty-two counties. There were the courts of shires, hundreds and boroughs, the courts of lords, and the courts of the king. Trial by oath, ordeal or battle was universal; but the details varied from place to place and according to the status of the parties. Proceedings were oral, and therefore legal tradition was unstable. Litigation, according to the author, was as uncertain as a game of dice.[3] The uncertainty is well illustrated by the confusion in the book itself, which collects ill-digested Anglo-Saxon laws with scraps of Canon law and personal observations. The writer did, nevertheless, perceive the paramount position of the king, whose enormous power (*tremendum regiae majestatis imperium*) placed him above all other laws. The king's court, for this reason, enjoyed a special position: 'over and above everything stand the pleas of the royal court, which preserves the use and custom of its law at all times and in all places and with constant uniformity'.[4]

This last statement may seem more significant in retrospect than a contemporary could have understood. The financial records of Henry I show that his court was indeed regularly resorted to by suitors, but such was the price of royal justice that it was doubtless beyond the reach of most people. The regularity of procedure which characterised the common law was already discernible, but royal justice was not yet the common property of all subjects. During the disorders of Stephen's troubled reign (1135-54) it almost slipped away. The foundation of the common law has commonly been traced to the reign of Henry II (1154-89), who succeeded in restoring the firm government of Henry I's days. It may be that the appearance of greater legal activity during his reign is distorted by the increased use of written records; but almost certainly there was a dramatic increase in property litigation as a result of the preceding anarchy, and to the same period apparently belongs the settling of the courts and the writ system.

The second of our books illustrates the nature of the change.[5] It was a treatise 'on the laws and customs of England', based solely on the workings of the royal court. The treatise, traditionally but questionably

---

3   *Leges Henrici Primi*, vi.6 (Downer ed., p. 98): 'incerta penitus alea placitorum', the utterly uncertain dice of pleas.

4   Ibid., pp. 97, 109.

5   The transformation is also visible in the slightly earlier *Dialogus de Scaccario*.

attributed to Sir Ranulf de Glanvill (justiciar of England 1180-89), gives the impression that the variety of local customs had not diminished; and so the book avowedly presents only one aspect of the law of the time. The great step forward was in the author's treatment of the fixed customs of the king's court as constituting *jus et consuetudo regni*, the law and custom of the realm. Whether Glanvill and his contemporaries could actually foresee that the law of the realm would in due course virtually displace local custom does not affect the significance of the twelfth-century jurisprudential advance. Just as the monk Gratian, a generation earlier at Bologna, had produced from the confusion of ecclesiastical laws a coherent system of Canon law deriving ultimate authority from the pope,[6] so Glanvill and his fellow councillors under Henry II produced a coherent system of English law deriving ultimate authority from the king. Against that uniform system, local custom would thereafter be seen at best as exceptional and at worst as exceptionable.

Unlike Gratian, who resolved discrepancies in the canonical sources by means of a 'concordance of discordant canons' which amounted to a system of legal theory, the author of *Glanvill* isolated the law of England by focusing on the work of the king's courts to the exclusion of all else. His laws and customs of the realm were primarily about how to gain access to those courts and what do when there.[7] Both the organisation of the courts, and the formulae to be used in them, may have been regulated by royal legislation since lost: *Glanvill* itself refers to 'assizes' and 'constitutions' of this nature, and also to unwritten laws promulgated by the king's council. Some such laws may have been decisions reached in considering specific disputes, like case-law, though a distinction between adjudication and legislation at this period would still be anachronistic. Moreover, few decisions were embodied in authoritative texts or records, and so the steps by which the common law of England was brought into being are largely untraceable. It is possible, nevertheless, to sketch in broad outline how the institutions of the common law emerged from the bold experiments of the twelfth century.

Regional and Itinerant Royal Justice

If the main consequence of the spread of royal justice was to be intellectual, its causes were more mundane. The Crown's first object

---

[6] See p. 146, post.

[7] For the history of the writ system, see ch. 4, post.

was to develop the scope of breach of the king's peace in order to preserve public order. Effective criminal justice is the first prerequisite of good government, and the Normans took up and strengthened the Anglo-Saxon system of communal responsibility, introducing safeguards to counterbalance the growing power of sheriffs. Henry II was especially concerned to restore order after the civil war, and the extension of litigation about land doubtless had the same ultimate object, since lordship over land carried power over men. There was an added financial incentive, in that the pursuit of law and order was profitable. Some pleas of the Crown were indeed purely fiscal, but criminal justice also bore golden fruit in fines and forfeitures. The rolls of the Exchequer testify to the steady revenue from judicature; the itinerant royal justices in 1218-19 raised over £4,000,[8] and even under Edward I it did not seem incongruous for the government to raise 'great treasure' for the war in Scotland by 'causing justice to be done on malefactors'.[9] The people are said by chroniclers to have groaned under the burden of royal investigations and money-raising judicial expeditions; and yet they apparently flocked to the same judges for the recovery of their possessions, and were prepared to pay money for royal justice. The main attractions for the private litigant were no doubt the effective process and enforcement which royal writs procured, and the availability from the late twelfth century of a central written record which would end dispute for all time. To squabble about weighty matters in local courts was often to waste time to no purpose, because even if a fair hearing were obtained the judgment might be unenforceable, and there was always the risk that it would be reopened before the king. The king's law was not yet universal; but the king's judgments could not be questioned or ignored. Royal justice therefore triumphed because it suited both Crown and litigants that it should do so. Yet it could not have undergone its tremendous expansion if it had continued to depend on the king's personal involvement. The means by which the king's commands could reach far and wide, in a suitably impressive and imperious form, was the writ. And the means of extending the king's direct control of justice throughout the length and breadth of the realm was the practice of delegating royal authority to trusted members of the king's own court. It was this innovation, as much as any other achievement of the Norman period, that made possible the common law. Again there is a parallel with the Church, since the pope introduced delegates at the same period and for the same

---

[8] B.E. Harris, 46 *Pipe Roll Soc* (new ser.) xvii. This represented over 7,000 amercements.

[9] *Croniques de London* (Camden Soc., 1844), pp. 28-29.

reason. The Anglo-Norman equivalent of the judge-delegate was the *justiciarius*.[10]

The twelfth-century chief justiciar was really a viceroy, a deputy of the king empowered to act in royal affairs, and as such was concerned with all matters of state, administrative and judicial. The first and greatest justiciars,[11] notably Roger of Salisbury (d. 1139) and Sir Richard de Lucy (retired 1178), were what we should call prime ministers; and their principal monument was the elaborate revenue system centred on the Exchequer. In addition to these justiciars of England, Henry I appointed local justiciars to attend to Crown business in particular counties or groups of counties. This enabled an extension of royal justice without extending the powers of sheriffs. But the idea of locally based justice was short-lived, probably because viceregal power was politically dangerous if severed from the central court. In Stephen's reign it threatened the monarchy itself. Geoffrey de Mandeville (d. 1166) provided kings with a warning of the power which subjects could acquire if unchecked; he became not only earl and sheriff of Essex, but also chief justiciar of Essex and other counties. By Glanvill's time, county justiciars had disappeared. Justiciars of England were likewise discontinued. They were not regularly appointed after 1234, and the last was Hugh le Despenser (d. 1265).

Another method of delegation which appeared at the same time, and was to prove more enduring in a subsequent form, was to send justices out on an ad hoc basis from the royal household. The travelling justices would form a nucleus of *justiciarii totius Angliae*, who had no local roots, and who would remain members of the king's council and transact national business when required. Still this did not constitute a regular system of courts, and one litigant who sought royal justice in 1158 has left a detailed picture of the expense and trouble involved in pursuing the king or his justiciars in various parts of the country.[12]

Following these experiments, Henry II proceeded a step further. In 1166 he appointed Geoffrey de Mandeville and Sir Richard de Lucy as justices to tour the whole of England, with a particular view to enforcing the new legislation ('assizes') concerning criminal law and disseisin.[13] Mandeville's death in October 1166 ended the exercise, but

---

[10] The same Latin word continued to be used for the 'justices' of the superior courts of law long after the disappearance of the great justiciars to be mentioned here.

[11] The function is older than the title, since Bishop Odo of Bayeux filled a very similar role in the 1070s: see D. Bates, 4 *Anglo-Norman Studies* 1-12. Roger of Salisbury, though usually reckoned among the justiciars, was actually styled *procurator regni*.

[12] For the Anstey case, see P. M. Barnes, 36 *Pipe Roll Soc.* 1.

[13] See pp. 86, 266-268, 576, post.

the experiment was frequently repeated between then and the end of the century with notable success.   In 1176 the itinerant justices were organised into six circuits, though the number was to fluctuate before six became the settled number for the assize circuits.[14]   The justices assigned to these circuits, who numbered as many as twenty or thirty at a time in the 1180s, were known as *justiciae errantes* (later *justiciarii in itinere*, justices in eyre); and the French word 'eyre' became the name of one of the most prominent forms of royal justice until the time of Edward III.[15]   Every so often a 'general eyre' would visit a county, bringing the king's government with it.   Large throngs of people attended, to account for themselves or to seek justice; special regulations were required to control the rates of board and lodging during the crowded sessions; the writs were read and the justices' authority publicly proclaimed, local officials delivered up their insignia of office as if to the king in person, and the justices started into their long agenda (the 'chapters of the eyre'), investigating crimes and unexplained deaths, misconduct and negligence by officials, irregularities and shortcomings of all kinds, the feudal and fiscal rights of the Crown, and private disputes.   The general eyres were not merely law courts; they were a way of supervising local government through itinerant central government.   They begat fear and awe in the entire population.   The justices did not always proceed according to modern standards of probity or fairness: contemporaries complained that the justices were apt to be *errantes* metaphorically as well as literally.   Indeed, we read of complaints that the eyre of 1198 reduced the whole kingdom to poverty from coast to coast,[16] and we learn of Cornishmen fleeing to the woods to escape the eyre of 1233.[17]   Counties might pay heavy fines for lenient treatment, or even buy off an eyre altogether.   Popular reaction to such heavy-handedness was to kill the general eyre before the middle of the fourteenth century.[18]   Yet it was the strength, the severity even, of Angevin government which incidentally gave England a body of national law unique in Europe.

JUDICIAL COMMISSIONS

The usual means of transmitting authority from the king to his itinerant justices was a commission under the great seal.   The justices in general

---

[14]   See pp. 24-25, post.

[15]   *Eyre* derives from the Latin *iter*, a journey or circuit.

[16]   *Chronica Rogeri de Hoveden* (Rolls ser.), vol. IV, p. 62.

[17]   *Annales Monastici* (Rolls ser.), vol. III, p. 135.

[18]   See p. 23, post.

eyre acted under commissions to try 'all pleas whatsoever', and were regarded as belonging to the permanent judicial establishment.[19] But a wide range of more limited and temporary commissions developed in the thirteenth century. On the civil side, among the most popular remedies in the later twelfth century were the 'petty assizes' introduced by Henry II, which ordered an enquiry into the facts in dispute. Each suit in effect required a separate judicial sitting to hear the result of the enquiry; justices in eyre took assizes on their way, but it was also convenient for special justices to be commissioned to take them between eyres. To authorise the holding of pleas of the Crown two principal types of commission were issued: those of oyer and terminer (to enquire into, hear and determine the offences specified) and gaol delivery (to try or release the prisoners in the gaol specified). Such commissions could be general, extending to all or most offences committed within a named county or group of counties, or special, extending only to named persons or particular events. We shall see later in this chapter how such commissions governed the administration of criminal justice, both by assize judges and by justices of the peace, down to the present century.

Central Royal Justice

The focal point of royal government was the *curia regis* (king's court), the body of advisers and courtiers who attended the king and supervised the administration of the realm. It was not a specific court of law,[20] any more than the eyre was, but rather the descendant of the Anglo-Saxon *witenagemot* (meeting of the *witan*, or royal advisers) and the ancestor of the king's council which later subdivided into parliament and the privy council. The justices in eyre were usually members of this focal *curia regis*, to which they returned when their itinerant duties were performed, besides being in themselves a *curia regis*. But the eyre system did not exhaust the judicial resources of the king's central court, which continued to attract suitors who could not await the next eyre or who wanted the king's personal attention. To the extent that the king delegated this central business, there emerged yet another way of employing justices: instead of sending them round the country, they could remain at the centre to hear suitors coming to them from all parts.

---

[19] Thus *Bracton*, vol. II, p. 307, distinguishes permanent justices (either 'residing in a certain place, such as the Bench' or 'wandering from place to place') from justices of assize, who held temporary office.

[20] For the development of the notion of a 'court' see LPCL pp. 153-169.

When we speak of the *curia regis* as the 'centre' of royal administration, we should remember that the centre was not static. The king himself was given to peripatetic rule, for to stay in one place for too long was not sound policy; and the king's court followed the king. Nevertheless, even in the twelfth century there was a tendency for a corps of administrators to settle in one place, usually the palace of Westminster, while the king was away. The Exchequer was the first department to be deposited; the king's treasure and the elaborate revenue service which controlled it were too cumbrous to keep constantly on the move. The department took its name from the place where it settled, a room where accounts were reckoned at a chequered table (the *scaccarium*, or Exchequer[21]) and where the *curia regis* met annually from the time of Henry I. The Exchequer was also the first department to keep a written record, the great roll of the pipe, which was started in 1130. During the long absences from the realm of Henry II and Richard I in the second half of the twelfth century, the 'central' judicial business of the *curia regis* also found a regular home at Westminster, and this required another written memory (the *curia regis* rolls).

THE TWO BENCHES

The establishment of a stationary royal court, functioning independently of the king's personal presence, marks the origin of the traditional judicial system of England. It is impossible to say precisely when it happened, because (in the absence of continuous surviving records before the 1190s) the evidence is fragmentary. Abbot Benedict of Peterborough recorded in his chronicle that in 1178, after complaints that the people had been vexed by the number of the eyres, Henry II ordered that five judges from his household were to remain *in curia regis* and not to depart therefrom, and that they should refer only difficult cases to himself.[22] There was once a controversy as to whether this ordinance established the King's Bench or the Common Pleas, as the two principal royal courts were later called. The better view now is that it established neither, but was one of Henry II's experiments with the judicial system. What is clear is that under Henry II a central royal court, called 'the Bench', began to sit regularly at Westminster. *Glanvill* refers to a *capitalis curia* (chief court), and also contrasts the justices staying in the Bench (*in banco residentes*) with those wandering

---

[21] The name for a chess-board. Before the introduction of arabic numerals and arithmetic, accounts were generally reckoned by moving counters on partitioned boards.

[22] *Gesta Regis Henrici Secundi* (Rolls ser.), vol. I, p. 207.

about on eyre. In an expanded but early version of the incipit, the subject of the treatise is defined as being the laws and customs used *in curia regis ad scaccarium et coram justiciis ubicumque fuerint.*[23] This passage has been taken by some to indicate three institutions: 'in the *curia regis*, at the Exchequer, and before the justices wheresoever they may be'. But it is more likely that it refers only to two: 'in the king's court at the Exchequer, and before the justices wheresoever they may be'. The *curia regis ad scaccarium* was probably the same as the Bench, the reference to the Exchequer being to the place of meeting rather than the institution. The Exchequer department did develop its own judicial side, with the 'barons of the Exchequer' as the judges, in the 1190s; but that was a revenue court.[24]

The distinction in *Glanvill* between the justices who went on circuit and those who stayed behind is a very simple one. It does not imply any difference of jurisdiction, or even of personnel. It was simply a difference in the manner of employing the king's justices. By about 1200, however, a new distinction is perceptible. The typical justices of the Bench, or in eyre, were no longer politicians and men of public affairs, but professional judges spending most of their time on the administration of the nascent common law. By way of contrast with this ordinary system, the king and his greater advisers entertained suits of particular royal interest *coram rege seipso* (before the king himself). From 1200 some of the business *coram rege* was recorded separately (on *coram rege* rolls). King John (1199-1216) spent more time in England than his predecessors, especially after the loss of Normandy in 1204, and seems to have been chiefly responsible for encouraging such proceedings before himself. So far did this trend proceed that in 1209 the Bench at Westminster was completely discontinued.

The brief suspension of the Bench cannot be regarded as the abolition of a court. There was still only one kind of royal judge, and all John did was to rearrange the sittings of his judges so that none remained at Westminster save when he was there himself. Perhaps, in the sense that the moving king was the administrative centre of the kingdom, he saw it as a form of centralisation. The measure was not, however, popular. The need to seek out the king for routine cases was a hardship to plaintiffs and defendants alike. In 1214 the Bench was revived, and the following year it was agreed in Magna Carta that 'common pleas should not follow the king but should be held in some certain place'.[25] This

---

23 *Glanvill* (Hall ed.), p. 1, note *b*.
24 For its history, see p. 56, post.
25 Magna Carta 1215, cl.17 (1225, c.11).

provision did not refer to any specific court, and it did not mean the 'certain place' to be a fixed geographical location.[26] Almost certainly it did not have the Bench exclusively in mind, because in 1215 the itinerant judges represented the ordinary system of royal justice, and their sessions were sufficiently certain in location to fall outside the mischief.[27] The practice after 1215 was indeed to suspend the Bench when the judges were sent out on eyre. The purpose of the statute was not, therefore, to create or entrench any particular tribunal, but to ensure that litigation in respect of common pleas – those not involving the king – was conducted in courts which did not follow the king to uncertain places. In fact sittings *coram rege* were in abeyance during the minority of Henry III and were not revived until 1234. During that period the Bench acquired a professional bar, the counters of the Bench,[28] and before the end of Henry's long reign its business had become so important and sophisticated that the very arguments of the counters and judges were being reported in books.[29]

After proceedings *coram rege* recommenced in 1234, it is possible to perceive the origins of the two principal courts of common law, the Common Bench and the peripatetic court *coram rege* (or King's Bench). From 1234 there were two distinct series of plea rolls, called *coram rege* and *de banco*, and within a generation there were two fully distinct institutions, each with its own judges and officials. By the end of the century the two benches had replaced the eyres as the ordinary source of royal justice. The normal interval between eyres had become far too long for them to provide justice on a regular basis in any particular county, and in any case their unpopularity led to their complete demise in the early years of Edward III.[30] As a consequence the Bench became, by accident rather than design, the principal court for common pleas.[31]

---

[26] Even in later practice it meant only that writs summoned defendants to answer common pleas in the Bench at a specified place. This was usually Westminster, but it could be changed: under Edward I and Edward III the Bench sat for several years at York. See further p. 46, post.

[27] Magna Carta 1215, cl.18, said assizes should be taken in the counties, though the 1217 version (c.12) added the proviso that they could be adjourned into the Bench. The county was probably deemed to be 'a certain place': Clanchy, 'Magna Carta and the Common Pleas', p. 223. But by 1500 assizes were not regarded as common 'pleas' at all: see 102 SS 113.

[28] See p. 179, post.

[29] See pp. 204-205, post.

[30] See D. Crook, 97 EHR 241. They were not formally abolished. Eyres were still occasionally held for specific purposes, such as *quo warranto* proceedings: p. 167, post. Chief justices in eyre of the forests were indeed appointed until 1817, but their offices (at any rate after Charles I) were purely honorific.

[31] Already by 1290 it was associated with Magna Carta, cl.17: 57 SS 11.

The later history of these courts, which remained in being for over six centuries, will be traced in the next chapter.

The establishment first of eyres and then of the two benches still left a major practical problem. The eyres had brought central royal justice into the counties, but at a considerable cost in terms of delay. The same work could be done in the interim by the county and hundred assemblies on their own, but to the extent that royal justice was desired in the county on a regular basis the eyres did not provide it. Litigation in the Bench, on the other hand, could be expensive and impracticable if all the persons involved had to attend court outside their county. The difficulties of personal attendance were solved for the parties by the appearance around 1200 of a class of professional attorneys, who were allowed to represent their absent clients through all the stages of a lawsuit. The chief difficulty, however, was that both the presentment of crimes and the conduct of trials by assize or jury – which rapidly became a common feature of royal justice[32] – required the presence of twelve or more men from the vicinity where the matter in question occurred. To have required the presence at Westminster, or before the king's person, of juries of presentment or trial would soon have brought the system to the point of collapse. In fact the system was soon modified so that it did not have to work that way. By a combination of miscellaneous expedients, which were eventually brought together to form another enduring institution of the common law (the assizes), the centralisation of royal justice was reconciled with the need for local investigation and trial.

The means of achieving this reconciliation was the frequent issue of commissions to perform judicial functions in the country. We have already noticed how ad hoc commissions were increasingly issued between eyres in the thirteenth century, and this had the result that routine criminal cases and petty assizes were not normally initiated in the central courts. The very same system was used to solve the problem of litigation in the benches themselves. Although juries were always summoned to appear on a certain day at Westminster, or before the king himself, it became the practice to add 'unless before then (*nisi prius*) the king's justices should have come' into the county.[33] In truth no one expected the jurors to obey the principal summons, because it was usually arranged that the king's justices would come into the county

---

[32] See pp. 86-90, post.
[33] For a specimen entry, see p. 630, post.

first (as commissioners of assize and gaol delivery), so that in addition to their other functions these commissioners could receive jury verdicts for transmission to the bench on their return. The nisi prius system may have originated in the twelfth century; and it was placed on a regular footing by legislation beginning in 1285.[34] The theory behind it always remained different from that of the assizes. Whereas assize commissioners had original jurisdiction to hear a case from beginning to end, with power to give judgment or to refer difficulties to the Bench, the justices at nisi prius had only a delegated power to proceed on issues referred to them from the benches and could not give judgment. Unlike the other powers of circuit justices, it was not conferred by commission; it was a delegated power tacked on by parliament to the functions of judges already commissioned to go on circuit for other purposes.

Despite the variety of these activities, they were all welded together in the thirteenth century into a single and regular system known later as 'the assizes'. During that century it became usual for the active members of commissions to be men of law, often including the justices of the benches; and after 1340 the assize commissioners were required by statute to be justices of either bench or serjeants at law. In 1293 the commissioners were organised into four circuits, rearranged into six in 1328. By statutes of 1299 and 1328 it was ordained that assize commissioners should stay to deliver the gaols in the counties where they sat, and – much later – it became usual for them to be given commissions of general oyer and terminer as well.[35] All this settled into a seasonal cycle. Twice a year two judges or serjeants would be assigned to each of the six circuits, through which they rode with their clerks and records during the vacation. At each county town, or other appointed place, the commissions would be read out in public and the justices would proceed to take the assizes, deliver the gaol, and try the nisi prius cases. But the assizes, though moulded into a regular routine, never became a distinct 'court' in the permanent sense. The jurisdiction of the judges rested entirely on the commissions which issued for each circuit: the judges could therefore be regularly interchanged, and after 1340 it was quite normal for a Common Pleas case to be tried at nisi prius by a King's Bench judge, and vice versa. The nisi prius proceedings, being simply an extension of the work of the benches, were recorded in the rolls of those courts. The other assize business was, however, completely divorced from the central system; no central

---

[34]   Statute of Westminster II 1285, c.30. Another expedient (used until 1285) was to direct that the verdict be taken by the sheriff himself in the county court: Palmer, *County Courts*, p. 287.

[35]   This enabled them to try accused persons who were not in the gaol.

record system was devised, and many assize and gaol delivery rolls have been lost. For all its oddities, the assize system proved so useful and adaptable that it remained part of the English way of life until its abolition in 1971.[36] Even since 1971, it is a feature of the English legal system that judges from the central courts may be sent to various parts of the country to try the more important cases; but their disposition is once again a matter of administrative discretion.

Effects on Local Justice

It would be agreeably neat if the progress of royal justice could be regarded as the result of a predetermined campaign to replace the older order of things by the common law of the king's courts. That such was the inevitable consequence was not necessarily intended or foreseen, and it is doubtful whether at any stage in the process kings or their advisers had such a sweeping plan in mind. Throughout the period when the greatest advances were made, kings seemed more concerned to assert their grip on existing jurisdictions than to lessen them. Henry I ordained that men should litigate in the shires as they had done before the conquest. The twelfth-century justices in eyre sat in the county court, and took over its proceedings in the king's name, so that in furthering the king's power they also enhanced the authority of the older institution. The justices of assize, too, were enjoined by Magna Carta to sit on the day and at the place of the county court.[37] The central courts depended on the sheriff to execute writs; and they made use of the county for some of their other procedures, such as the declaration of outlawries. Communal justice and its ancient methods of proof were too deep-rooted for anyone to think of abolition; they were simply absorbed into the new system. Neither was there any deliberate attack on feudal jurisdiction. Fear that the royal courts might encroach too far on lords resulted in another provision of Magna Carta, that no free man should be deprived of his court by the writ *praecipe*: the king's court thereafter would entertain writs of right for land held of subjects only if the lord had waived his court or failed to do justice.[38] The thirteenth-century royal courts discouraged minor litigation, and came generally to

---

[36]　Courts Act 1971 (c.23), s.1(2), which restrains commissions of assize, but not commissions of oyer and terminer or gaol delivery. But since 1914 there had been a short-form composite commission of assize, oyer and terminer and gaol delivery.

[37]　Magna Carta 1215, cl.18-19 (1225, cc.12-13). This was doubtless connected with the 'certain place' policy: see p. 23, ante.

[38]　Magna Carta 1215, cl.34 (1225, c.24); but see pp. 269-270, post.

exclude claims under forty shillings, a principle confirmed for trespass actions by a statute of 1278 .[39] Whereas we, in looking back, find it so easy to assume that the common law was intended from the start to be universal and paramount, contemporaries saw it quite differently. In the twelfth century the common law was relatively new and exceptional, to be called into operation only for good reason, with the king's consent, and at a fee. As late as 1278, plaintiffs were being directed to sue in the counties as had been accustomed; and for small claims there were advantages in doing so. We shall see later how this restrictive attitude resulted in some curious distortions of the common law, particularly in the sphere of contract and tort, when the king's law ceased to be exceptional and had to take on work it had previously excluded.[40]

Although there was no policy of attacking the ancient assemblies, there was a continuing policy under the Normans and their successors of harnessing the power of sheriffs. The Crown's 'incurable fear of the sheriff'[41] was no doubt well founded, for the potential power of the sheriff – as continental experience of analogous officials showed – was such as to challenge the king's own authority. The Crown reduced the tenure of office to one year, and subjected sheriffs to stringent financial supervision at the Exchequer. As early as the 1120s we learn of a sheriff, fearsome and mighty in his own county, trembling in his boots when the time came for his reckoning at the chequered table.[42] By reducing the judicial power of sheriffs, however, the Crown indirectly struck at the ancient bodies over which sheriffs had assumed control. The greatest blow was the removal from sheriffs of pleas of the Crown, a process which began de facto with the eyres and was completed de jure by an absolute prohibition in Magna Carta.[43] The prohibition was taken to exclude from the sheriff's cognisance not only prosecutions upon communal accusation but also actions for trespass against the king's peace. Even where the county retained jurisdiction it lacked finality, because parties could remove cases into the central courts by writ of *pone*, or (after judgment) by writ of false judgment. The governmental work of the county suffered a similar decline. Where once the king had visited the counties, in person or by his justices in eyre, by the end of the thirteenth century the more convenient practice had begun

[39] Statute of Gloucester 1278, c.8.
[40] See pp. 52-53, 73-75, ch. 19, post.
[41] Plucknett CHCL, p. 105.
[42] J. H. Round, *The Commune of London* (1899), p. 123.
[43] 'No sheriff . . . may hold pleas of our Crown': Magna Carta 1215, cl.24 (1225, c.17).

of summoning the counties, by their representatives, to the king in parliament.

These changes left the county, the greatest of the local assemblies, bereft of most of its jurisdiction and power. For the remainder of the middle ages it exercised a minor civil jurisdiction in contract and tort. Even in that sphere, the absence of jury trial and the lack of effective final process, coupled with the fifteenth-century interpretation of the 1278 legislation which limited county jurisdiction generally to forty shillings,[44] kept litigation in the county at a low level. The actual decline was intentionally slowed in the thirteenth century by conferring greater jurisdiction on sheriffs by writ. Such writs were called 'viscontiel' (that is, shrieval),[45] and the commonest was the *justicies*;[46] but these were original writs initiating specific cases, and they emphasised that the jurisdiction was controlled by the king.[47] The inherent jurisdiction of the community of the county had been largely taken away. Even the jurisdiction conferred by writ seems to have been on the wane by the early fourteenth century, no doubt because of its vulnerability to *pone*. The later medieval county court thus became a court for small claims only; and it survived thereafter mainly because of its exclusive non-judicial functions, particularly in relation to parliamentary elections and the pronouncement of outlawries. When John Wilkes was outlawed at the Middlesex county court held at the Three Tuns inn in Holborn[48] it was a far cry from the old grand assembly of magnates, bishops and leading county figures. It was no longer even a court of law. So ancient as to be uncertain in its origins, its end was abrupt and ignominious. Shorn of all remaining functions in the nineteenth century, on 17 October 1977 the old county court ceased to exist.[49]

PEACE-KEEPING AT LOCAL LEVEL

Even though the king's eyres and assizes could strike terror into the hearts of malefactors, they could not police the countryside; and without

---

[44]   94 SS *51*. That this was not the original position is shown by J. S. Beckerman, in *Legal History Studies 1972*, pp. 110-117.

[45]   The French word for sheriff was *visconte*.

[46]   For a specimen, see p. 614, post.

[47]   It used to be thought that they also diminished the position of the county court by conferring jurisdiction on the sheriff personally. That is how they read; but the jurisdiction was in fact exercised by the county court: Palmer, *County Courts*, pp. 189-198.

[48]   *R v. Wilkes* (1770) 4 Burr. 2527 at 2530.

[49]   See p. 33, post.

an efficient system for bringing crimes to their attention they would have made little impact. The old system of communal responsibility was therefore continued and reinforced. The hundreds remained responsible for presenting crimes, and could be collectively punished for failing to discover the perpetrators of known crimes.[50] The representatives of hundreds and vills who were bound to attend and present crime before the royal judges became the institution known as the grand jury.[51] Twice a year the sheriff visited each hundred to hold the 'sheriff's tourn', to review the frankpledge or tithing system and to process pleas of the Crown. The system appears neat in theory, yet it broke down in practice as a result both of the curtailment of shrieval power and the fragmentation of jurisdiction in private hands. After Magna Carta the tourn could not 'hold' pleas of the Crown – that is, try them – and was confined to making preliminary enquiries with a view to presentment before the royal justices. Many hundreds fell into private hands, and lords of hundreds often claimed to oust the tourn and to hold their own 'courts leet' in its stead. The view of frankpledge, or oversight of the tithing system, was kept up by lords possessing leets chiefly as a source of small income from 'head money'; but as a means of preserving order its only lasting consequence seems to have been the election of constables, a practice maintained with varying degrees of effectiveness until the establishment of a professional police force in the last century.

The policing problem was solved by yet another innovation. As early as 1200 the practice had begun of appointing a number of knights in each county to 'keep the peace', which seems to have imported a militia or police function rather than one of judicature. As the most reliable segment of the county establishment, these conservators of the peace were frequently employed on special commissions of oyer and terminer and gaol delivery, to relieve the load on the justices of assize between circuits; and by a series of statutes in the reign of Edward III (1327-77) the judicial functions of these officials were increased and regularised, so that they became 'justices of the peace'. The principal safeguard against excessive local power, from the king's point of view, lay in the use of commissions. Not only was authority distributed, but it was easily revocable: without a commission the justices could not act, and every new commission (whatever changes it contained) superseded the last. At intervals a commission of the peace was drawn up for each county, listing the substantial knights and gentry of the area

---

[50] The main legislative provision was the Statute of Winchester 1285, c.2, making the people of the hundred answerable for robberies.

[51] See p. 576, post.

and taking care to include the *sages et apris de la leye*,[52] charging them both to keep the peace and 'to enquire into, hear and determine' a long list of crimes, ranging from felonies to economic offences and sorcery. The first of these 'charges' imposed an individual police responsibility on each justice; justices could arrest suspects and commit them to gaol, and could require anyone to give surety for keeping the peace – a realistic substitute for frankpledge. The second was in effect a general commission of oyer and terminer to any two or more of the justices (with a 'quorum' of lawyers[53]) and empowered the justices collectively to hold their sessions of the peace.[54] Directed by statute to be held at four seasons (Michaelmas, Epiphany, Easter and the Translation of St Thomas), these were known as the general quarter sessions of the peace. The jurisdiction of quarter sessions was in theory virtually coterminous with the criminal side of the assizes, but in practice inferior. For six centuries until their abolition in 1971, the quarter sessions provided a mixed tribunal of lawyers and laymen to deal with those serious pleas of the Crown which were not reserved for the assize judges. And until the reorganisation of local government in the nineteenth century, the justices were also responsible for the administrative duties of the county, such as provision for the poor and orphans and the maintenance of highways and bridges. Some of this administrative business, together with the pre-trial police work of the justices, was transacted in private between quarter sessions; and some was transacted in the intermediate 'petty sessions', as they were later called, which became minor courts by virtue of legislation giving the justices powers of summary conviction.[55]

The rise of the justices of the peace corresponds very closely with the demise of the county and hundred as institutions for the despatch of public judicial and administrative business. Soon after the hearing of pleas of the Crown was taken from sheriffs, it was handed directly to the justices; and in 1461 many of the remaining powers of sheriffs' tourns followed suit.[56] Parliament repeatedly ignored the existence of the old county assembly as it heaped new duties of all kinds upon the commissioned magistrates. It might be said that in reality the Crown

---

52　The requirement of Stat. 18 Edw. III (sess.ii), c.2.

53　*Quorum* means 'of whom'; in the judicial part of the commission the list of justices was followed by a *quorum* clause ('of whom A., B., or C. shall be one').

54　The commission of the peace still has two 'assignations', but since 1973 it has been addressed generally to such persons as may from time to time hold office as justices; new justices are no longer appointed by inserting their names in the commission, but by instrument under the hand of the Lord Chancellor.

55　See p. 583, post.

56　Stat. 1 Edw. IV, c.2. The tourn was not abolished till 1887.

had taken the county from the sheriff and put it into commission. The greater men of the shire – the *buzones* (as *Bracton* called them), on whose nod the decisions turned – still served the shire, but in new roles. As knights of the shire they represented the county in parliament, which was itself a triumph of centralisation. And as justices of the peace they continued the judicial and administrative work of the shire, but now under commissions through which alterations in personnel and duties could be made at will. The reality of this continuity was such that the old assembly did not need abolition. The leaders of the county could afford to ignore it. What had once been the privilege of attendance at the shire moot became an unwelcome burden cast off on to tenants of certain pieces of land; and a combination of exemptions, powers of attorney, and evasions, enabled the effective withdrawal of those who now wielded their influence at Westminster or in the sessions. The multifarious county customs mentioned almost with despair by the eleventh-century writers had, of course, disappeared in the process. Once again, no one had decreed that the common law should prevail; but a stream of expedients had gradually produced a situation in which the old ways of doing things faded away.

LOCAL CIVIL JUSTICE

The communal jurisdictions endured longest at the level of borough and manor, perhaps because at that level they were independent of the sheriff. Ironically, these courts in many cases outlived even the King's Bench and Common Pleas, which were abolished in 1875. But here, too, the nominal continuity concealed another victory of the common law.

Most city and borough courts continued unabated until Tudor times, and many a good deal longer; a few flourished until the axe of uniformity cut them down in 1971.[57] For most of this period they were patronised by mercantile litigants, for whom they offered speed and procedural advantages. In Tudor times, however, merchants began to transfer their allegiance to the King's Bench, and the King's Bench encouraged them by upsetting judgments of municipal courts on technical grounds. It was possible to challenge a borough record by writ of error, on the grounds that the law and custom of the realm had not been complied with.[58] Although the King's Bench distinguished

---

[57] Courts Act 1971 (c.23), ss.42-43, abolished the Mayor's and City of London Court, the Norwich Guildhall Court of Record, the Salford Hundred Court of Record, and the Tolzey Court of Bristol.

[58] See 94 SS *51-52, 258,* 324-325; B. & M. 286.

substantive common law from procedural customs, the threat of reversal must have persuaded borough courts to assimilate their practices as far as possible to those of the central courts; and so these valuable small-debt jurisdictions, invariably from the fifteenth century presided over by recorders bred in the inns of court, became urban courts of common law.

The higher feudal courts, those of baronies and honours, disappeared at an early date; but manorial courts flourished well beyond the middle ages. By royal grant, or (more usually) immemorial usage, many manorial courts enjoyed 'franchises' giving them jurisdiction in non-feudal matters such as contract and tort; and some, as we have seen, claimed to have the public jurisdiction of hundred and tourn within the precincts of their leets. These franchises varied almost infinitely from one manor to another, but they were eaten into by all the trends mentioned in this chapter, and were subjected to royal control. Even the feudal jurisdiction over land, the right apparently assured to lords by Magna Carta, was overtaken by the common law.[59] The royal courts assumed jurisdiction over the writ of right either through lords failing to claim their courts or by the allegation (increasingly unchallenged, and therefore fictitious) that they had waived them. A wide range of remedies, notably the petty assizes of Henry II and the writs of entry, curbed the suzerainty of lords to such an extent that they became free to decide only as the king's law allowed them, with the result that, at a very early date as regards free tenants, the 'feudal' land law became the cornerstone of the common law. Feudal control, tempered by manorial custom, was imposed for rather longer on the unfree tenant; but royal justice reached him in the fifteenth and sixteenth centuries,[60] when 'tenancy according to the custom of the manor' became a tenancy at common law. Although manorial courts retained some importance until 1925, they did so not as deliberative tribunals but as providing the only machinery for conveying copyhold land. As courts of law their day was long gone.

By the nineteenth century the accidents of history had left a very uneven pattern of local civil jurisdiction across the country. The counties palatine were still to some extent miniature kingdoms, immune to the changes affecting ordinary counties; Durham and Lancaster had their own regalian courts (with benches, exchequers, chanceries and commissioners) until 1875, when they were merged with the High Court.[61] In some towns, borough courts or municipal courts

---

[59] See pp. 264-271, post.

[60] See pp. 349-350, post. For villein status and manorial custom, see p. 534, post.

[61] The Chester courts went first; they were abolished in 1830 with the Great Sessions in Wales: pp. 38, 60, post.

leet continued to provide speedy justice; in others all semblance of judicature had ceased. In rural areas the chances that a court leet or franchisal court had survived were slender, and in any case few of them offered civil remedies. A number of statutory experiments with 'courts of requests' had been made in the larger towns, with varying success;[62] and in 1846 a nationwide system of 'county courts' was established, under which small civil claims could be tried by professional judges. The new county courts bore no relation to the old shire moot, save that their jurisdiction in 1846 was similar to that still possessed in theory by the latter. Their jurisdiction has been steadily extended since then, and all competitors swept aside. The manorial courts, counties, hundreds, leets, courts of pie poudre,[63] and various other obsolete jurisdictions were finally put down in 1977.[64]

The Isolation of English Law

The common law of England proved remarkably durable. It survived civil wars and changes of dynasty. At various times it was claimed to have superiority over the king, parliament and the Church. Both the Reformation and the growth of constitutional monarchy were assisted by the common lawyers' ways of thinking. And, with few outward signs of struggle, the common law withstood two waves of Romanist influence which swept across the Continent. The rediscovery of Justinian's *Digest*, and the consequent explosion of Roman legal studies in the universities of the twelfth and thirteenth centuries, made Roman Civil law the common currency of European lawyers, including the doctors of law at Oxford and Cambridge.[65] Early royal judges were in touch with that new learning, and may have injected some of it into the early chaos; but the effect was prophylactic, and served to immunise English law against fatal infection later.[66] Compared with the rest of Europe, England and its system of government and law were precocious. The scheme of writs described in *Glanvill* and the attendant procedure and terminology, the developed notion of pleas of the Crown with all the machinery for the discovery and trial of criminals, the existence of central and itinerant royal courts capable of subjecting the whole nation to the king's law and government: all these things were in being long

---

[62] See W. H. Winder, 52 LQR 369; M. Slatter, 5 JLH 97; H. W. Arthurs, 5 JLH 130.
[63] Fair courts, originally for deciding disputes between merchants.
[64] Administration of Justice Act 1977 (c.38), s.23, Sch.4; S.I. 1977 No. 1589.
[65] For their professional position in England, see pp. 193-194, post.
[66] Brunner's metaphor: *Essays AALH*, vol. II, p. 42.

before the university law schools were founded. And so, 'while the other nations of Western Europe were beginning to adopt as their own the ultimate results of Roman legal history, England was unconsciously reproducing that history; it was developing a formulary system which in the ages that were coming would be the strongest bulwark against Romanism and sever our English law from all her sisters'.[67] The second wave of Romanism struck at the end of the middle ages, when Renaissance humanism drove out older methods of proof and encouraged the application of rational legal principles based on the Civil law. But once again England had anticipated the rest of Europe without recourse to scholastic learning. Through the process called 'pleading' the common lawyers had built their own elaborate and rational system of law around the writs which governed the business of the royal courts.[68] England's lawyers had their own law schools, located not in the universities but between London and Westminster Hall, where the chief study was not classical texts but writs and pleading and feudal land law.[69] Not that England in any way escaped the rapid social and legal changes of the Renaissance period; but the common-law system was sufficiently adaptable to accommodate them without importing foreign ideas.[70]

Having stood its ground in the land of its birth, the English common law became a force to rival the Civil law beyond the seas. The men who sailed for the new world in the seventeenth and eighteenth centuries, and those who built the British Empire in the eighteenth and nineteenth centuries, took the common law with them as a matter of course. By a breath-taking twist of fate, the insular and arcane learning of the small band of lawyers who argued cases in a corner of Westminster Hall became the law by which a third of the people on the earth were governed and protected, the second of the two great systems of jurisprudence known to the world. Within Europe, however, England remained an island in law as well as in fact. There are obvious reasons why this should have been so, despite extensive travelling and trading contacts. The common lawyers had virtually no intellectual rapport with their Continental counterparts, and their law-French dialect would not have been understood in Paris. Their system of law was so embedded in the procedure of the king's courts as to be largely

---

67   Pollock & Maitland, vol. II, p. 558. For the extent of Roman influence on the English formulary system, see D. J. Seipp, in *Legal Record and Historical Reality*, p. 9; 7 LHR 175.

68   See pp. 90-94, post.

69   See pp. 182-185, post.

70   See further 94 SS *23-51*; and pp. 47-48, post.

incomprehensible outside them. Even its more abstract doctrines were not easily transportable to countries which had different systems of courts and knew nothing of writs or juries. And so English law flourished in noble isolation from Europe, and even (as we shall now see) from parts of Britain

NORMAN LAW AND THE CHANNEL ISLANDS

After 1066 the kings of England were also dukes of Normandy, and both countries were subject to common influences. Many of the legal developments and experiments mentioned in this chapter were also parallelled in the ducal court of Normandy. Nevertheless, the customs of Normandy were recognised to be different from those of England, and sometimes the same institutions and procedures developed in different ways in the two countries. The very process whereby the common law was crystallised through the formulary system brought about a similar crystallisation of Norman law, and sharpened the distinction between the two systems. Not long after the laws and customs of England were summarised in *Glanvill*, a Norman counterpart was written, *Le Très Ancien Coutumier de Normandie* (c. 1199-1220), followed in the middle of the thirteenth century by *Le Grand Coutumier*.

Despite the loss of Normandy to the king of France in 1204, the kings of England maintained their claim to the duchy,[71] though only the Channel Islands remained loyal to the English Crown. The islands have continued since then to be annexed to the Crown in right of the duchy of Normandy, with the legal result that, although their inhabitants are British subjects, the islands themselves are not part of Great Britain or subject to English common law. Their customary law is still Norman, though since 1204 it has developed independently from the law of mainland Normandy, and (like the common law) it has become heavily overlaid by legislation.

Although most lawsuits in the Channel Islands were heard by the local courts, where decisions were made by lay jurats, a few eyres were held between 1299 and 1331, and a handful of early cases were taken to the King's Bench. By the time of Edward I there was a legal profession in the islands, though there is no evidence of training in England. The visiting English judges applied Norman customs rather than the common law of England, though assimilation might eventually have occurred if extensive supervision by the common-law judges had continued. That was not to be. The eyre system collapsed at the same time as in England; and in 1368 the King's Bench decided that it could

---

[71] Possession was actually recovered in 1419 and retained until 1450.

not hear writs of error from the islands' customary courts. The king nevertheless retained ultimate judicial authority; and, since there was no duchy council, the King's Council in 1495 assumed an appellate jurisdiction, providing a model in later times for the more distant dominions. This jurisdiction is still exercised by the Privy Council.

WALES AND THE COMMON LAW

The kingdom to which the Normans succeeded in 1066 did not in fact include the Celtic strongholds which have become Wales, Ireland and Scotland. The Celts in Wales had defiantly preserved the titular kingship of Britain until the death of King Cadwaladr Fendigaid ('the Blessed') in 664 A.D., and all the Celtic peoples preserved their language, culture and customs once they had been driven back into the western and northern extremities of the islands. It is tempting to think that the Welsh bards and Irish 'brehons' who preserved the Celtic customs by memory and verse represented a continuation of the druidical tradition noticed by Caesar. Although the earliest extant manuscripts of the Irish and Welsh laws date from the twelfth century, the contents are of much earlier origin, and provide a link between prehistoric Britain and known civilisation. The Welsh customs which were codified in medieval times as the 'laws of Hywel Dda' [72] superifically resemble the Anglo-Saxon codes in their use of compensation payments to discourage feuding; but they stressed the ties of kinship more prominently than those of community or homage, and there is no mention of ordeals.[73] Early Welsh law was not a law of counties, hundreds and feudal lords, but of tribes and families and chieftains. Yet the customs were not static. The codes themselves were agglomerations of matter from different periods, and Welsh kings altered some of the rules within historical memory.

Wales was still not unified in the thirteenth century. The princes of North Wales enjoyed a dominant position, and owed homage to the king of England; but the lords of the marcher territories, on the borders with England, retained independence. By 1258 Llewelyn ap Gruffudd claimed to be prince of all Wales, and it was this principality which was confiscated by Edward I in 1283, for an alleged breach of fealty, and annexed to the English Crown. The English affected to regard Celtic

---

[72] Hywel Dda ('the Good') was king of most of Wales by the time of his death in 949 or 950 A.D. How much of the redaction occurred in his time is uncertain, but it is possible that he was inspired by Alfred's code for Wessex to initiate a similar work for Wales.

[73] Mr T. G. Watkin has suggested (in an unpublished lecture) that this may reflect lingering Roman influence.

custom with contempt, and Archbishop Pecham advised Edward I that the laws of Hywel Dda were irrational and came directly from the Devil. Accordingly in 1284 the English system of counties, sheriffs and justices was extended by statute to Wales, and an attempt was made to codify some of the principles of English law for the use of Welsh officials.[74] The statute did not apply to the marcher lordships, which were not forfeited to the king but claimed to possess the regalian rights of the old Welsh rulers as independent territories. When in 1354 the marches were made attendant to the English Crown,[75] they still kept their own customs, which varied from one lordship to another.

The statute of 1284 also omitted to extend the jurisdiction of the English central courts to Wales. The English courts declined to try any dispute arising there, so that even the most serious crimes were outside their jurisdiction.[76] Welsh customs therefore continued, although there was increasing English influence on the modes of tenure of land.[77] Indeed the influence of English law was such that by the sixteenth century the Welsh laws seemed to some of the inhabitants themselves to be outmoded, perhaps even a mark of inferiority. There was no outcry when, in 1536, 'the sinister usages and customs' of the Welsh were abrogated and Welsh subjects were granted the same laws and liberties as the English.[78] This measure accompanied the final act of union of Wales with England. The last marcher lordships were done away with, and five new counties introduced. A new system of courts, called the Great Sessions in Wales, was set up. The courts were to sit twice a year in four circuits, each comprising three counties, and to each circuit were appointed justices 'learned in the laws of this realm'. These courts operated alongside the English courts, and they had the same jurisdiction in Wales as the King's Bench and Common Pleas had in England. A further statute of 1543 gave the king power to legislate for Wales without the consent of parliament, the so-called 'Henry VIII clause'. The thinking behind it was not the creation of a wide new legislative power, but a confirmation of the old tradition of prerogative legislation in Wales; in the event it was not used, but it required a great effort to repeal it (in 1624).

---

[74] Statute of Rhuddlan [or, of Wales] 1284, 12 Edw. I. For a specimen (dealing with the law of contract), see B. & M. 281.

[75] Stat 28 Edw. III, c.2.

[76] See *R v. Owain Glyn Dwr* (1401) 88 SS 114; *Dolbyn v. Ap Tudor* (1534) Spelman Rep. (93 SS) 156, 94 SS 340.

[77] Welsh custom generally favoured coparcenary among males: pp. 303-304, post.

[78] Stat. 27 Hen. VIII, c.26. The effect was not to abolish reasonable local customs, which could be proved in the same way as in England: Dyer 363 (1579).

Writs of error, and certiorari in criminal cases, lay after 1536 to remove Welsh cases into the King's Bench at Westminster. The problem of venue continued to prevent a Welsh cause of action being tried by an English jury, but after 1543 it was always accepted that the process of the English Chancery and Exchequer would run into Wales, and eventually (after much controversy) it was established that King's Bench process would run there also.[79] In 1830 the Great Sessions were abolished, and by complete procedural assimilation England and Wales became at last one unified jurisdiction, two extra circuits being added to the English assize system.

IRELAND AND THE COMMON LAW

Ireland was never incorporated into the English court system, but the common law was gradually absorbed there and administered in courts closely analogous to their English counterparts. The old Irish laws were already of great antiquity when the English came in the late twelfth century. The principal law text was the *Senchas Már* ('Great Tradition'), which contains material from as early as the eighth century, and there are glosses and commentaries suggesting that it was studied and taught over many generations. The English settlers, however, at first treated the Irish as being of inferior status, akin to aliens, and took little interest in their customs. In the early 1200s the common-law writ system was introduced in the Dublin courts. Then, by means of general charters and specific grants of denization, and by the direct application of English statutes to Ireland, the privilege of English justice was extended to most Irishmen who sought it. By 1300 the king's courts had branched out, as in England, into a 'Chief Place' (or Justiciar's Bench, presided over by the king's lieutenant or justiciar), a Common Bench, an Exchequer and a Chancery. The jurisdictional boundaries were not as distinct as in England, because the 'common pleas' provision of Magna Carta did not extend to Ireland; but by 1500 the 'Four Courts' in Dublin operated in a similar way to their Westminster namesakes. Their judges were lawyers who had studied in the English inns of court, and occasionally under the Tudors and Stuarts they were Englishmen. After 1541 Dublin had its own society of lawyers, called the King's Inns, though it offered no educational facilities and Irish barristers were required to learn their law in England. In 1615 the first Irish law reports were published in Dublin, being the work of the Englishman Sir John Davies who had been posted there as attorney-general. It was a long

---

[79] *Whitrong v. Blaney* (1677) 2 Mod. Rep. 10, Vaugh. 395; *Lampley v. Thomas* (1747) 1 Wils. 193; *Penry v. Jones* (1779) 1 Dougl. 213.

time, however, before any more Irish reports appeared in print. There was little need. The establishment of royal courts on the English pattern, with judges and advocates bred in the common law, had resulted in an effective transplantation of English law without the need for the kind of legislation used to achieve that result in Wales. The native Irish customs, or 'brehon law', continued in some areas until the seventeenth century; but, like English local custom or Welsh local custom after 1536, such customs could be rejected by the Dublin courts if they offended common-law standards of reasonableness.[80] The full details of the history of royal justice in Ireland nevertheless remain obscure, because in 1922 the Four Courts in Dublin were blown up and centuries of legal records were destroyed.

The four Dublin courts were never wholly independent, for they were the king's courts and, the king being absent, their decisions were subject to review by the king. Error therefore lay to the King's Bench in England, and from thence (at any rate after 1719[81]) to the English House of Lords. The jurisdiction to hear error from Ireland was taken from the King's Bench in 1783, and after the Act of Union 1800 (which abolished the Irish parliament) appeal lay directly to the House of Lords of the United Kingdom parliament. When Ireland was divided in 1920, new courts for the province of Northern Ireland were set up in Belfast, with appeal to the House of Lords.

THE LAW OF SCOTLAND

Although the Scots were Celts, and may be supposed to have followed customs similar to those of Ireland and Wales, the percolation into Scotland of Anglo-Norman feudalism, together with sheriffs, justiciars and the writ system, gave Scotland the framework of another common-law jurisdiction akin to those of England and Ireland. But close liaison was ended by war; throughout medieval times, the Scots were alien enemies in England, and Scotsmen who read law did so in their own universities, or on the Continent, where Roman law prevailed. Scots law therefore, unlike the law in Ireland, developed in a distinctively different way. A prominent feature of the system after 1426 was the reference of petitions to a royal council called the Session. This at first paralleled the development of conciliar and Chancery jurisdiction in England; the medieval Session had a less formal procedure than the

---

[80] *Case of Tanistry* (1608) Dav. Ir. 78. Modern scholarship suggests that the court failed to understand the custom under review in this case.

[81] The doubt was ended by Stat. 6 Geo. I, c.5. The occasion was a recent case in which one party had appealed to the Irish House of Lords and the other to the English House.

regular courts, and (as in England) it could not deal with cases of serious crime or freehold property. In 1532, however, the Session was refounded as the College of Justice, and given jurisdiction over all civil actions.[82] The effect was rather like that of the English Judicature Act of 1873, which fused the old common-law courts and the Chancery, though in Scotland it occurred early enough to prevent the development of separate law and equity jurisdictions and led Scots law still further away from its Anglo-Norman roots. Soon after 1532 the lawyers practising before the Court of Session formed themselves into a Faculty of Advocates, and they began to generate a professional literature in the form of law reports and treatises on practice. In view of their Roman law training, it was natural that, when refined procedures began to call for legal doctrine, these men should have followed Continental practice by drawing on the intellectual legacy of Rome rather than of Westminster. But Roman law was not treated as authority in itself; it was a framework upon which the unwritten customs of Scotland could be systematised. In the two centuries after the refoundation of the Court of Session, a coherent and autonomous body of Scots law was perfected, in large measure through the efforts of the 'institutional' (text-book) writers of the seventeenth century. The classic *Institutions of the Laws of Scotland*, by Lord Stair (written in the 1660s, published in 1681) and the more compact *Institutions* of Sir George Mackenzie (1684), were founded on Scots practice and case-law and betray no hint of English influence.

The merger of the crowns of Scotland and England in 1603 might have led to a merger of laws. James I said in 1604 that he wished to leave 'one country entirely governed, one uniformity in laws'. But the English lawyers, championed by Sir Edward Coke, were fearful of Roman infiltration, not least because of the unlimited power which Roman law gave the king, and the king's scheme for legal union soon foundered. Further proposals for unification in 1670 were successfully resisted from north of the border. When full political union between England and Scotland took place in 1707, there was no question but that Scots law should be preserved, subject to any future alterations by the parliament of Great Britain.[83] Since 1707 appeals have been allowed from the Court of Session to the House of Lords, but the decisions in such appeals are treated in England as foreign law if the matter is one where Scots and English law differ.

---

82   The old justiciar's court continued to deal with criminal cases, and is now the High Court of Justiciary.

83   Act of Union 1706, 6 Ann. c.11 [= 5 & 6 Ann., c.8, in *Statutes at Large*], art.18-19.

Further reading

Pollock & Maitland, vol. I, pp. 64-110, 136-173
Holdsworth HEL, vol. I, pp. 24-193, 264-298
Plucknett CHCL, pp. 11-26, 101-105, 139-156, 165-169
Milsom HFCL, pp. 25-36
J. E. A. Jolliffe, *The Constitutional History of Medieval England* (4th
    ed., 1961), esp. pp. 139-331
H. G. Richardson and G. O. Sayles, *Governance of Medieval England*
    (1963), esp. pp. 173-215; *Law and Legislation from Aethelberht*
    to Magna Carta (1966), pp. 30-154
D. Stenton, *English Justice between the Norman Conquest and Magna*
    Carta (1965), esp. pp. 54-114
R. C. Van Caenegem, *The Birth of the English Common Law* (1973)
P. Hyams, 'The Common Law and the French Connection' (1982) 4
    Anglo-Norman Studies 77-92
M. Clanchy, *England and its Rulers 1066-1272* (1983), esp. chs. 3, 6
J. A. Green, *The Government of England under Henry I* (1986), esp. pp.
    78-117
M. Chibnall, *Anglo-Norman England 1066-1166* (1986), esp. Part III

THE EARLY ROYAL COURTS
W. C. Bolland, *The General Eyre* (1922)
A. Harding, 'The Origins and early History of the Keeper of the Peace'
    (1960) 10 TRHS (5th ser.) 85-109; *The Law Courts of Medieval*
    England (1973), pp. 32-85
W. T. Reedy, 'The Origins of the General Eyre in the Reign of Henry I'
    (1966) 41 *Speculum* 688-724
C. A. F. Meekings, *The 1235 Surrey Eyre*, vol. I (31 *Surrey Rec Soc*,
    1979), introduction
R. V. Turner, *The King and his Courts 1199-1240* (1968); 'Origins of
    the Common Pleas and King's Bench' (1977) 21 AJLH 238-254;
    The English Judiciary in the Age of Glanvill and Bracton (1985),
    esp. pp. 17-25, 65-74, 126-138, 191-205
M. T. Clanchy, 'Magna Carta and the Common Pleas' in *Studies in*
    Medieval History presented to R.H.C. Davis (H. Mayr-Harting
    and R. I. Moore ed., 1985), pp. 219-232

NORMANDY
M. Hale, *History of the Common Law* (C. Gray ed., 1971), pp. 118-
    121
C. H. Haskins, *Norman Institutions* (1918; repr. 1960)

J. H. Le Patourel, *The Medieval Administration of the Channel Islands 1199-1399* (1937); *The Norman Empire* (1976), pp. 261-278; *Feudal Empires Norman and Plantagenet* (1984), chs. II-III

D. Bates, 'Normandy and England after 1066' (1989) 104 EHR 851-876, esp. at pp. 873-874

WALES

Holdsworth HEL, vol. I, pp. 117-132

R. R. Davies, 'The Twilight of Welsh Law, 1284-1536' (1966) 51 *History* 143-164; 'The Law of the March' (1970) 5 *Welsh History Rev* 1-30; 'Law and National Identity in 13th-Century Wales' in *Welsh Society and Nationhood* (R. R. Davies et al. ed., 1984), pp. 51-69

D. Jenkins, 'Law and Government in Wales before the Act of Union' in *Celtic Law Papers* (D. Jenkins ed., 1971), pp. 23-48; (ed.) *The Law of Hywel Dda* (1986), and the bibliography there

J. B. Smith, 'The Legal Position of Wales in the Middle Ages' (1980), *Law-making and Law-makers*, pp. 21-53

P. Roberts, 'Wales and England after the Tudor Union' , in *Law and Government under the Tudors* (C. Cross et al. ed., 1988), pp. 111-138

IRELAND

D. A. Binchy, *Studies in early Irish Law* (1936); *Corpus Iuris Hibernici* (1978) in six volumes

G. J. Hand, *English Law in Ireland 1290-1324* (1967), esp. pp. 172-213; 'English Law in Ireland 1172-1351' (1972) 23 N. Ireland Legal Qly 393-422

F. Newark, *Elegantia Juris* (F. J. McIvor ed., 1973), pp. 185-228 (for later period)

H. H. Pawlisch, *Sir John Davies and the Conquest of Ireland* (1985)

F. Kelly, *A Guide to early Irish Law* (1988), which has a full bibliography

SCOTLAND

G. C. H. Paton (ed.), *An Introduction to Scottish Legal History* (Stair Soc., 1958), esp. pp. 1-43

P. G. Stein, *Roman Law in Scotland* (1968), Ius Romanum Medii Aevi, V, 13b, and the works there cited

B. P. Levack, 'The Proposed Union of English and Scots Law' (1975) 20 *Juridical Rev.* (New ser.) 97-115; *The Formation of the British State* (1987), ch. 3

A. J. MacLean, 'The 1707 Union: Scots Law and the House of Lords' (1983) 4 JLH 50-75

O. F. Robinson, T. D. Fergus and W. M. Gordon, *An Introduction to European Legal History* (1985), chs. IX, XIV

D. M. Walker, *A Legal History of Scotland* (1988-), in progress

W. D. H. Sellar, 'The Common Law of Scotland and the Common Law of England' in *The British Isles 1100-1500* (R. R. Davies ed., 1988), pp. 82-99 (with a valuable survey of recent scholarship)

J. W. Cairns, review of vol. I of Walker's *Legal History of Scotland* (1989), 9 *Legal Studies* 189-213

3. The Superior Courts of Common Law

Westminster Hall, built for William Rufus in about 1099 and enlarged under Richard II around 1395, was the home of the superior English courts until they moved to the Strand in 1882. The interior of the hall is still best viewed from the great north door. On the far side is a flight of steps which used to divide the Court of King's Bench from the Court of Chancery. On the west side of the hall, near the door, was the Court of Common Pleas. The Exchequer was a large chamber which connected with the hall through a passage. Each court occupied a space marked out by a wooden bar at which counsel stood, and in the centre was a large table covered with green cloth[1] at which court officials sat and spread their records. Against the wall, on a raised platform or bench beneath tapestries with the royal arms, sat the judges. Until the eighteenth century there were no seats for counsel, nor any screens to divide the courts from the open thoroughfare; each court was scarcely out of earshot of the others, and speakers had to compete with the noise made by the throng of suitors, lawyers, shopkeepers, cutpurses and sightseers in the body of the hall. This arrangement, seemingly impracticable to modern eyes, was a feature of English public life for five centuries. It survived two civil wars, and even in times of rebellion the judges and counsel kept up their attendance, sometimes with armour beneath their robes. Only in times of plague or flood did the courts leave Westminster Hall, and then only after a formal adjournment by proclamation. A story, doubtless apocryphal, is told of Sir Orlando Bridgman, chief justice of the Common Pleas in the 1660s, that he would not have his court moved back a few feet to avoid the draught from the north door, lest the relocation infringed Magna Carta.[2]

The conservative attachment of lawyers to all the old forms gave them the appearance of complete immunity to change. Yet, beneath this timeless exterior, there occurred between the thirteenth and the seventeenth centuries changes in the common-law system as far-reaching

---

[1] Or a chequered covering in the case of the Exchequer.

[2] R. North, *The Life of Francis North* (1742), p. 97. In fact the old court was demolished and rebuilt in 1741. For the procedure on flooding, see *Memorandum* (1629) Hutton 108.

as any brought about by the Norman conquest or the procedural reforms of the nineteenth century.

MAGNA CARTA AND COMMON PLEAS

We have seen that the result of clause 17 of Magna Carta was the establishment of the two benches. The Court of King's Bench was in law held 'before the lord king wheresoever he should be in England' (*coram domino rege ubicumque fuerit in Anglia*), and was therefore excluded from hearing 'common pleas'. Common pleas for this purpose were all suits in which the king had no interest. As a corollary, the Common Bench (or Court of Common Pleas)[3] had an exclusive jurisdiction over such suits; and they included all *praecipe* actions[4] to recover property or debts, the greater part of all civil cases. The petty assizes[5] were not caught by Magna Carta, and could in proper cases be brought in the King's Bench,[6] but they were more usually brought before commissioners and in case of difficulty adjourned into the Common Pleas for argument. Actions of trespass and replevin[7] were shared with the King's Bench. There was nothing in Magna Carta to prevent the Common Pleas from sharing pleas of the Crown as well, since the prohibition was in one direction only, and in its early days it did indeed sometimes entertain appeals of felony; but its traditional jurisdiction, as settled in the fourteenth century, excluded felony. It nevertheless continued to be used by the king for his own civil actions. It also had a supervisory jurisdiction over inferior courts.

By the fourteenth century the jurisdiction of the King's Bench was equally settled. The Crown side had unlimited criminal jurisdiction throughout the realm, either as a court of first instance or as a forum into which indictments could be removed from other courts for legal discussion. The 'plea' side was occupied mainly with actions of trespass, appeals of felony, and suits to correct errors by courts of record (including the Common Pleas). By comparison with the Common Pleas, the jurisdiction of the King's Bench before Tudor times was

---

[3] It was usually called 'the Bench' or 'the Place' in medieval times. The name Court of Common Pleas, presumably alluding to Magna Carta, was not used until Tudor times. It avoided the confusion which still sometimes arises from such expressions as 'the king's justices of the bench' (which means the Common Pleas, not the King's Bench).

[4] See p. 68, post.

[5] See p. 23, ante; pp. 86, 266-268, post.

[6] But only for property in the county where the court was sitting: 57 SS xliii.

[7] According to *Bracton*, vol. II, p. 439, replevin was a plea of the Crown.

slender. Its records filled only a few hundred skins of parchment a year, whereas those of the Common Pleas filled a thousand or two.

The Common Pleas was the court which more than any other made the medieval common law. It had usually four or five judges, a select bar of serjeants at law, and a large staff of officers: the keeper of the writs (*custos brevium*), the prothonotaries and filazers (who kept the rolls and files), and numerous other clerks and under-clerks. It was the place where the young students attended to learn their law, huddled in a wooden box or gallery.[8] What a judge or serjeant said in the Common Pleas was likely to be remembered or written down for future reference; the year-books were taken up almost exclusively with the debates in this court, and it was not until the sixteenth century that the work of other courts was regularly reported.[9]

CHANGING FUNCTIONS OF THE MEDIEVAL KING'S BENCH

This uneven sharing of business made sense while the King's Bench was literally *coram rege*, since it was in effect a meeting of the king's council for occasional business of importance.[10] But under Edward I the king's personal presence ceased to be usual,[11] and in 1305-18 the court settled down in Westminster Hall. In the century after 1318 it was often sent out on judicial expeditions: at its 'trailbaston' sessions[12] in the country it investigated pleas of the Crown, assizes and private complaints (brought by bill) in the counties where it stopped, with all the energy of an eyre. The unequal distribution of business (as compared with the Common Pleas) still continued to make some sense in this peripatetic phase of the court's history, since it left the King's Bench free to fill part of the gap left by the demise of the eyre system. But the need for moving royal justice of that irregular kind was fast being removed by the regularisation of the assizes, and most of the court's time in the fourteenth century was in fact spent at Westminster. For the whole of Henry IV's reign (1399-1413) it was stationary, and its last local visitations were in 1414 (Leicestershire, Staffordshire and

---

8   See p. 182, post.

9   See pp. 207, 210-211, 466, post.

10   During the king's personal absence in 1253-54 its style did become *coram consilio* (before the council): the word *coram* still indicated the literal truth.

11   At first the *coram rege* formula was modified to indicate his absence, but by the 14th century it was routinely fictitious: 57 SS lxiii-lxv. Cf. *Articuli super Cartas* 1300, c.5, which required the court to follow the king's person; this seems to have been ignored, except in time of parliament.

12   So named from the club-wielding gangsters (*trailbastons*) whom they were primarily appointed to suppress: see 74 SS liv-lxvi.

Shropshire)[13] and 1421 (Northamptonshire). Thereafter the King's Bench settled down in Westminster Hall for good, and its first-instance criminal jurisdiction became confined to Middlesex cases and other cases removed by *certiorari*. De facto it had come to rest in a certain place, and the spirit of Magna Carta would hardly have been infringed had it then assumed a share of the work of the Common Bench; yet the fact of its domicile was one of which the law took no notice whatsoever. The style of the court remained *coram rege*; its process continued to be returnable 'before the lord king wheresoever he should be in England', and until 1876 the full designation of a judge of the court was 'one of the justices assigned to hold the pleas before the queen herself'. Whatever the reality, therefore, the King's Bench was not in law held in a certain place and was therefore still restrained by Magna Carta from hearing common pleas.

THE COMMON-LAW COURTS CHALLENGED

During the fifteenth century the superiority of the ancient common-law courts was challenged by the jurisdictions associated with the king's council and the chancellor. Some have seen these rising jurisdictions as threats to the common law itself. The medieval chancellors were doctors of law from Oxford, and in the later fifteenth century most of the masters in Chancery and officials of the council were also doctors of law. Could not these courts have done the Romanising which in Germany was carried out by the equivalent Reichskammergericht?[14] Yet the real threat was not of a 'Reception of Roman Law', any more in England than in Germany.[15] The newer courts were as English as the two benches, and did not administer foreign law. The practitioners in them were common lawyers, who resorted to them because of the attraction of their relative informality, the ease with which defendants could be arrested, and the inquisitorial method of investigation which by-passed the sheriff and the jury. In the procedures, Roman influence is clearly visible; but it was embodied in an English form, the bill of complaint and subpoena. The reason for intruding mention of these

---

[13] Leicester because a parliament was held there, Shropshire because of reports that it had the highest homicide rate in the country.

[14] The question put, and tentatively answered, by F. W. Maitland in *English Law and the Renaissance* (1901).

[15] Since 1901 the so-called Reception of Roman Law on the continent has been reinterpreted; it now seems not to have been an importation of Roman law so much as the introduction of Roman legal method by university-educated judges. See also 94 SS *23-51*.

courts and procedures here[16] is that their initial success may have had an adverse effect on the business of the common-law courts.

   Cause and effect are difficult to establish in such matters. Between 1460 and 1540 there was certainly a steady downhill slide in the number of cases in the older courts, coinciding with a steep climb in the number of cases going to the newer; but modern research has shown that the climb of the latter was nowhere near matched in quantity by the decline of the former.[17]   A threat was nevertheless perceived by some contemporaries. The judges and officers of the benches recognised that to meet the challenge there would have to be reforms both in law and procedure which would win back the patronage of litigants, through the lawyers who advised them. The problem would have seemed most acute to those dependent on the fortunes of the King's Bench, which lacked the staple business of debt and the real actions to support them; certainly the rolls of that court grew very thin during the fifteenth century. In 1481, Fairfax J urged pleaders to develop remedies which would maintain the jurisdiction, so that 'subpoenas would not be used as often as they are at present'.[18]   By 1500 the process of reform was well under way, and by 1550 the tide was beginning to turn, swelled by an unprecedented flood of litigation in the Tudor period. The King's Bench developed its own bill system, with swift process and procedure to vie with that of the Chancery, and acquired a jurisdiction over most common pleas by a combination of procedural devices. After a good deal of skirmishing, the old and new courts adjusted themselves to a more stable division of business between themselves. By that time, however, the Common Pleas had grown suspicious of the explosion of activity in the King's Bench, and for the second half of the sixteenth century adopted a reactionary approach to the changes which the King's Bench was trying to introduce into the legal system. The legal disputes of the later sixteenth century then took on the appearance of an internecine struggle for business between the common-law courts themselves, in which Magna Carta might seem to be the charter of liberties of the disgruntled officers of the Chancery and Common Pleas. The outward appearance, however, should not deceive us into forming an exaggerated impression of hostility. The principal competitors were not the judges or officers themselves but the litigants and their lawyers, shopping for the most advantageous forum. If the King's Bench personnel had a private stake in furthering this amplification of their

16   For their history, see chs. 6 and 7, post.
17   See Brooks, *Pettyfoggers and Vipers*, pp. 85-87.
18   *Sarger's Case* (1481) B. & M. 513 at 515.

jurisdiction, they were at the same time meeting strong popular demands.

The Resurgence of the King's Bench

BILL PROCEDURE

The recovery of the King's Bench was effected by the exploitation of its bill procedure. A bill, in this sense, is a petition addressed directly to a court in order to commence an action. Procedure by bill was more convenient for litigants than writ procedure, since the latter required the first complaint to be made in Chancery so that an authorising writ could be addressed to the court where proceedings were to be taken.[19] There was nothing new about procedure by bill when it blossomed in Chancery and council – and parliament – between 1350 and 1450.[20] It had an older history in eyre, and had been taken over by the King's Bench in its first trailbaston sessions of 1305-07. When an eyre, or the King's Bench, sat in a county, the sheriff of that county was personally attendant and there was no need to apply to the Chancery for a writ ordering the sheriff to initiate proceedings. When the King's Bench settled at Westminster, the bill procedure remained available for Middlesex cases, and was commonly so used by 1420; cases from other counties required writs.

Bills could also be used in the King's Bench, as in the other superior courts, to commence actions against its personnel and prisoners. Such persons were deemed to be already present in court, and therefore no process was needed to bring them in. For that reason, Magna Carta did not apply; and so a clerk of the King's Bench, or a prisoner in the custody of the marshal of the Marshalsea,[21] could be sued in personal actions such as debt or covenant. Wise attorneys kept a careful watch on the gaol calendar, because they might be able to save their own clients' time and money by taking advantage of process commenced by someone else.[22] Plaintiffs could also combine the procedures themselves. If A wished to sue B for trespass and debt, he need only sue a writ of trespass, upon which B would be arrested and committed to the

---

[19] For original writs, see pp. 67-75, post.

[20] See further p. 113, post.

[21] The marshal was the gaoler to the court, appointed by the earl marshal of England. The Marshalsea Prison was in Southwark, but the marshal attended the court and his prisoners were deemed to be always 'before the king himself'.

[22] Thus in 1442 a creditor brought a bill of debt against a prisoner who had been arrested in another suit brought by Fortescue CJ: 6 JLH 91.

marshal; *A* could then start his debt action by bill, avoiding the expense of a writ.   Around the middle of the fifteenth century attorneys discovered that the like advantage could be obtained even if there was no genuine complaint of trespass: the writ secured the arrest, whatever the facts.   Some encouragement for the use of a fictitious action may have been taken from decisions under Fortescue CJ around 1450, that a bill lay against anyone in de facto custody, and that the court would not enquire into the reason why the defendant came to be there.[23]   The custody was secured by an unsworn ex parte complaint in Chancery of an imaginary trespass; once the defendant was in custody – which included being out on bail[24] – and had been impleaded by bill, the action of trespass could be quietly discontinued before it came to trial.   The falseness of the complaint of trespass was therefore never officially discovered.[25]   By the 1480s the practice, if ethically questionable, had become common form, and had given the King's Bench a jurisdiction over common pleas such as debt.

In order to utilise this jurisdictional dodge, the defendant had to be put into the Marshalsea.   A writ of trespass would do it, but there was a means of short-circuiting the Chancery altogether, a procedural dodge which followed from the jurisdictional.   Since the alleged trespass was fictional, the plaintiff might as well make it a trespass in Middlesex, the county in which Westminster Hall was situated and in which the court now invariably sat.   The defendant could then be arrested on the mere presentation of a bill of trespass, known as the bill of Middlesex.[26]   By the use of two bills, the first alleging an imaginary trespass to secure arrest, the second a genuine complaint against the person arrested, the King's Bench litigant could thus sue in debt without writ.[27]   This device was coeval with the other, as is evident from the disproportionate

---

23   *Kempe's Case* (1448) Y.B. Mich. 27 Hen. VI, fo. 5, pl.35 (a bill lies against a prisoner unlawfully arrested); *Anon.* (1452) Y.B. Mich. 31 Hen. VI, fo. 10, pl.5 (a bill lies against a prisoner bailed from the Marshalsea, even if there is no record of his first committal).

24   Bail were people who took the party into their custody and gave surety for producing him when required. In most civil actions a defendant was entitled to 'reasonable bail'. In minor cases the sureties became fictitious (John Doe and Richard Roe), and release was therefore automatic. In many cases, however, the plaintiff could hold the defendant to 'special bail', and if he could not find real sureties he remained in gaol.

25   Some plaintiffs even sought to cover their traces by bringing the fictitious suit in the name of someone else: an abuse ended by Stat. 8 Eliz. I, c.2.

26   When the court adjourned to Hertford or St Albans in time of plague, the invented trespass was set in Hertfordshire.

27   Note that this second dodge had no bearing on geographical jurisdiction: the court always had jurisdiction throughout England, but the bill procedure was only available for actions laid in Middlesex.

number of filed bills alleging trespasses to land in Westminster (later Hendon). It mattered not whether the plaintiff or defendant had ever set foot in Hendon, or even Middlesex; yet the logic which required the first writ for arresting the defendant to go to the sheriff of Middlesex necessitated one further rigmarole. In the common case of a report that the defendant 'is not found' (*non est inventus*) in Middlesex, the plaintiff had to inform the court that the defendant 'lurks and roams about' (*latitat et discurrit*) in some other county, say Yorkshire; the court then issued a writ called a *latitat* to the sheriff of that county, who was able to effect the arrest.

The new King's Bench bill procedure offered the plaintiff some of the advantages of Chancery bill procedure, particularly in that the latitat (unlike an original writ)[28] did not tie the plaintiff to any particular cause of action, and so defendants could be arrested to answer whatever kind of complaint the plaintiff chose to put into his ti ͻ bill, or even a multitude of complaints. The principal benefit was that 'money need not be spent upon advice till it appeared upon the arrest that the defendant would stand suit'.[29] As one attorney put it, 'the latitat is like to Doctor Gifford's water, which serves for all diseases, and so it holds one form in all cases and actions whatsoever'.[30] Well might a Common Pleas attorney associate the latitat disparagingly with quack medicine, for it had made the King's Bench almost as popular a tribunal for common pleas as the Common Pleas itself. The Common Pleas litigant still needed an original writ from the Chancery, for which he paid a fine proportional to the debt claimed; when the defendant was in court, more ink and parchment was required than in the other court, and technical slips more often threatened disaster. The King's Bench wooed litigants with competitive costs, and sometimes even lowered its fees in order to increase the overall takings. By 1600 the effect on its jurisdiction was dramatic. From a trickle of latitats at the end of the fifteenth century, and a few hundred rolls a year, within a century the court was issuing – according to a contemporary estimate – 20,000 latitats a year and filling 6,000 rolls. Between 1560 and 1640 the increase in King's Bench suits was particularly dramatic, perhaps as much as tenfold.

[28] In suits by writ, any 'variance' between the writ and the plaintiff's subsequent pleading was fatal, because the writ was the only warrant for the subsequent litigation and had to be followed to the letter.

[29] North CJCP in Yale, *Lord Nottingham's Two Treatises*, p. 171.

[30] T. Powell, *The Attourneys Academy* (1623), p. 166.

SUBSTANTIVE REFORMS IN THE KING'S BENCH

In conjunction with the procedural campaign to redistribute business in its own favour, the King's Bench also improved and broadened the range of substantive remedies available at common law. This was the technique which Fairfax J had recommended in 1481; and, as he had also suggested, the main vehicle of reform was the action on the case.[31] Actions on the case were extended by 1499 to enable the enforcement of parol promises. Fyneux CJ, in announcing this reform, stressed that it rendered unnecessary a Chancery suit by subpoena.[32] Also in the time of Fyneux CJ were developed the action on the case for not paying debts, which had procedural advantages over the older action of debt,[33] and another for defamatory words, which had previously been remedied only in the ecclesiastical courts.[34] In the 1530s came the action on the case for trover and conversion, which replaced for most purposes the action of detinue.[35] The court even overcame the major limitation of bill procedure, that it could not be used for real actions to try title to land. It achieved this by developing a species of trespass, called ejectment, to allow recovery of the land, a fundamental change in the law made in 1500; its full exploitation followed the introduction of a fiction in the later sixteenth century.[36]

It can hardly be coincidence that so much of the reform was initiated under Sir John Fyneux, who presided over the court from 1495 to 1525 when its fortunes were at their lowest ebb. He appointed his son in law John Rooper as chief clerk in 1498, and the Rooper family made its fortune from the office between then and its retirement in 1616. Cynics might criticise the judges and clerks for making the court a family business; they undoubtedly had more than a professional interest in the success of the procedures under their control. But they had no monopoly, and they thrived only by satisfying litigants and the profession at large. They were not accused at the time of disingenuous behaviour, and it is a fact that most of the innovations made during this period were accepted and became embedded in the law thereafter. Moreover, neither the substantive nor the procedural reforms had immediately visible consequences. It was nearly a hundred years before the fictitious bill of Middlesex helped reverse the decline of business, a

---

[31]   For the development of actions on the case, see pp. 73-75, post.
[32]   Dictum in Gray's Inn, Fitz. Abr., *Accion sur le case*, pl.45; B. & M. 401; p. 385, post.
[33]   See pp. 384-385, post.
[34]   See pp. 479-498, post.
[35]   See p. 449, post.
[36]   See pp. 341-342, post.

reversal which neither Fortescue CJ nor Fyneux CJ lived to see. Nor did Fyneux CJ see the triumph of ejectment over the old real actions, which began in the reign of Elizabeth I. Even the innovative development of actions on the case had only a slight effect on the overall profits of the court, because the massive increase in lawsuits occurred largely in actions of debt, presumably reflecting an increase in dealings on credit. That was how the bill of Middlesex and latitat helped turn the tide when the new business came. However, the debt-collecting side of the courts was largely a routine business, only bail applications normally coming to a hearing. In the contentious business which occupied the time of judges and counsel with motions and trials, the transformation was of a different nature and owed much to the triumph of trespass. The recasting of the common law which occurred in the sixteenth century seems at the very least to have been speeded, if it is too much to say caused, by the attitudes of those who hoped to restore the fortunes of a court which had temporarily lost its sense of purpose.

REACTION BY THE COMMON PLEAS

While the King's Bench saw itself and came to be regarded as a fountain of new legal remedies, the Common Pleas took an increasingly conservative, and for a time distinctly jaundiced, view of such novelties. When the latitat was first extended by fiction, the Common Pleas officials had little cause for concern. They had up to ten times the business of the King's Bench, probably more than they could easily cope with, and could afford to share some of it: especially since the work of trying the same cases at nisi prius was shared between the judges of both benches. In any case, the Common Pleas did not lose business in an absolute sense, because increased litigiousness and dissatisfaction with local courts were bringing plaintiffs in their droves to Westminster; and if much of that new work was diverted to the King's Bench, there was still no loss of profit to the other court. In fact the business of the Common Pleas increased considerably during the sixteenth and early seventeenth centuries, albeit at a slower rate than that of the King's Bench. Nevertheless, the jurisprudence of the Common Pleas began in the 1530s to diverge from that of the King's Bench, particularly in relation to the development of actions on the case,[37] probably indicating the onset of a conservative reaction to the substantive reforms under way in the latter; and by the end of the century these differences had turned into open hostility. The warmest

---

[37] E.g. *Anon.* (1542) B. & M. 415; and perhaps *Anon.* (1535) B. & M. 447; *Anon.* (1535) B. & M. 626 (cf. p. 627 endnote).

quarrel over substantive law took place in the context of contract, where after years of dissension the King's Bench won a marginal victory in 1602.[38] The same period brought opposition to the procedural and jurisdictional reforms in the King's Bench. The Common Pleas attorneys could not simply copy the tricks, because their court had no trailbaston power to hear bills of Middlesex and could not order arrests without the prior authority of a Chancery writ. There was, however, a similar bill jurisdiction against personnel and prisoners. The best they could do therefore was to sue fictitious *writs* of trespass to land, so as to secure the arrest of the defendant on a cause which could be dropped. This gave them the same advantage of flexibility, avoided the poundage on writs of debt, and enabled multiple actions to be commenced on a single process; but the Common Pleas could not escape from the need for a writ, and it failed to make substantial reductions in its own scale of costs, allegedly because the three prothonotaries could never reach agreement on any specific proposal for cuts.[39] Given its disadvantages with respect to costs and procedure, it is remarkable that the Common Pleas overcame the competition at all. The chief reason for its so doing was that it continued to have at least ten times as many attorneys as the King's Bench, many of whom practised in the country and brought in clients to whom King's Bench attorneys were inaccessible or unknown.

During the Interregnum the Common Pleas received a welcome boost from the abolition of fines upon original writs; but ironically this was to precipitate the final collision of jurisdictions when in 1660 the fines were revived, for 'then the very attorneys of the Common Pleas boggled at them and carried all their finable business to the King's Bench'.[40] The immediate solution was an act of parliament in 1661,[41] designed to discourage latitats based on fictions by denying special bail in any action where 'the true cause of action' was not expressed in the process.

The King's Bench was shaken by this attack, which had an immediate adverse effect on its jurisdiction.[42] By the 1670s, however, it had devised an ingenious evasion. The statute said only that the true cause of action had to be disclosed in the process, not that the complaint in the process had to be true. The clerks therefore added a dash of truth

38   *Slade's Case* (1602) B. & M. 420; pp. 390-393, post.
39   Although the chief prothonotary of the Common Pleas had some special prerogatives, there was effectively a triumvirate of chief clerks. In the King's Bench there was only one prothonotary or chief clerk.
40   North CJCP in Yale, *Lord Nottingham's Two Treatises*, p. 172.
41   Stat. 13 Car. II (sess. ii), c.2. A similar measure had been proposed in 1549: Blatcher, *King's Bench*, p. 105.
42   Even in 1668 a reporter noted that the court had little to do: 1 Sid. 365.

to the bill and latitat: the defendant would now be arrested to answer a fictitious complaint of trespass in Middlesex, 'and also (*ac etiam*) to a separate bill of debt to be exhibited according to the custom of the court'.[43] The bill of Middlesex with *ac etiam* did not actually complain of debt, which would have infringed Magna Carta; but it did make mention of the true cause of action to follow, thus satisfying the 1661 statute and enabling the plaintiff to hold the defendant to bail.[44] The effect on the distribution of business is said to have been dramatic.[45]

The *ac etiam* clearly defeated the intention of the 1661 legislation, but who was to correct the King's Bench? The obvious solution was for the Common Pleas lobby to enlist the support of the Lord Chancellor, whose officers were losing their share of the fines for writs. There were precedents from as far back as the time of Elizabeth I for injunctions, or writs of *supersedeas*, to stay latitats on the ground that they were intended to defraud the Crown of such fines. In the 1660s Lord Clarendon C was persuaded to sanction a general form of *supersedeas* to stay latitats containing the *ac etiam* clause in delusion of the statute.[46] But Lord Nottingham C in the early 1670s saw that this policy would not work. The officers' objections were not to the bill procedure on its merits, only to alterations of jurisdictional boundaries which had long outlived their original purpose. The King's Bench, to avoid extinction, might ignore the *supersedeas* and punish sheriffs who tried to execute it; even if the *supersedeas* was obeyed, there was no guarantee that the Common Pleas and Exchequer might not develop similar practices; and if all the courts were stayed, ostensibly for the profit of the Chancery, there would be an embarrassing public outcry. The Chancery therefore decided to remain aloof. As a consequence, the *ac etiam* threatened the Common Pleas with extinction, especially in a period when litigation had begun a decline. There were estimated in the 1670s to be twenty latitats for every original writ issued, and the loyalty of the attorneys – the only protection of the Common Pleas – was breaking. Sir Matthew Hale, chief justice of the King's Bench from 1672 to 1676, conceded that the Common Pleas would be 'in effect destroyed', and that this would be too drastic a turn. When Sir Francis North became chief justice of the Common Pleas in 1675 he found the

---

43 For a specimen latitat with *ac etiam*, see p. 622, post.
44 The *ac etiam* was not used where special bail was unavailable. The only legal consequence of its omission was the defendant's release on the security of John Doe and Richard Roe.
45 See R. North, *The Life of Francis North* (1742), pp. 99-101.
46 'Reasons against the Latitat', Hertfordshire Record Office, Verulam MS. XII.A.30 (from the papers of Sir Harbottle Grimston MR).

court unable to occupy more than a quarter of its sitting time, and he sensed impending disaster. Having failed to persuade Lord Nottingham C to help directly, he adopted the only remaining solution and reluctantly sanctioned the use in his own court of *ac etiams* in conjunction with fictitious writs of trespass; to which compromise Lord Nottingham and the Chancery assented. A century of competition was thus ended. The bizarre legacy of fiction, though requiring plaintiffs to assert untruths as a matter of routine in every civil case, had at least brought improvements in procedure which might not otherwise have occurred.

The Exchequer of Pleas

Although the Exchequer was the oldest of the three common-law courts, it was the last to achieve the position of a regular court for common pleas. Something should now be said of its development. The author of the twelfth-century *Dialogue of the Exchequer* praised the new department not only for its advanced accounting methods, but also for its power to conduct judicial enquiries when needed; and we have seen that by the 1190s there was a distinct judicial function, with judges called barons.[47] In the following century the Exchequer divided into two 'sides', corresponding to the work of the two principal clerical officers, who kept separate records. The lord treasurer's remembrancer was concerned with the fixed revenue of the Crown and with routine auditing and debt-collecting. His side was called the 'Exchequer of Receipt'. The king's remembrancer was concerned with casual revenue, and therefore with litigation by the Crown. His work divided into two parts: purely Crown business, and actions by subjects who enjoyed the privilege of suing in the Exchequer. This division was sharpened in 1236 by the appearance of a new series of rolls (the plea rolls) to record the second class of business, as a supplement to the memoranda rolls which recorded the Crown business. The court whose business they recorded, the Exchequer of Pleas, was quite independent of Chancery control, and could summon defendants by original and judicial writs under its own seal, kept by the chancellor of the Exchequer. Suits were commenced by a writ of *venire facias ad respondendum* or a writ of subpoena; officers and prisoners could be sued by bill.

The attraction of the court to private litigants needs little explanation: the methods used by the king to collect his own revenue

---

[47] See p. 22, ante.

must be the best. Plaintiffs therefore sought to harness its procedures for their own purposes, and by 1290 the court even styled itself a court for common pleas: *communia placita coram baronibus de scaccario.*[48] But attempts were already being made to stop it from developing too far in that direction, probably because private litigants were impeding the king's business. Whether anyone in 1215 had thought that clause 17 of Magna Carta would reach the Exchequer is doubtful; it was not then an issue. By 1280, however, appeals were being made to the clause on the ground that the Exchequer (like the King's Bench) was in law held *coram rege* and not in a certain place. In view of the doubts, legislation was passed making it clear that the court was not for common pleas. On one view it was not even a court of common law.[49] As a result, the Exchequer of Pleas throughout the fourteenth, fifteenth and early sixteenth centuries was a relatively minor civil jurisdiction limited to actions by or against Exchequer personnel, sheriffs, and a few other officers who were bound to render accounts at the Exchequer. By the mid-fourteenth century, actions could also be brought by debtors to the Crown, who were allowed to recover their own debts or damages in order to be able to satisfy the king. The writ used in such cases was called *quominus*, because it alleged that by reason of the debt or damages due to the plaintiff he was 'so much the less able to satisfy [the king] of the debts which he owes at the Exchequer' (*quo minus nobis satisfacere valeat de debitis quae debet ad scaccarium*).[50]

These were the ground rules of jurisdiction, which did not change. But the actual jurisdiction proved no more constant than that of the two benches. The first means of evasion was to bring suit as the servant of an Exchequer official; the number of merchants claiming in the fourteenth century to be such servants raises a strong suspicion that the claims were being made fictitiously.[51] This device seems to have been stopped, and it was to the *quominus* that thoughts turned when other jurisdictions came under stress in the Tudor period. Suppose a plaintiff wishing to sue in the Exchequer alleged fictitiously that he was a debtor to the king: was that a refutable assertion, or would the assertion itself be sufficient to give the court jurisdiction? There is evidence that the fiction had been tried out in the time of Henry VII, and that it became common form in the mid-sixteenth century, its chief use being to

---

48   E.g. 48 SS 123.
49   57 SS lix (1340).
50   For the form of writ in full, see p. 622, post.
51   See Ball, 9 JLH at 310.

provide a remedy against executors for their testator's debts.[52] But it did not at first lead to the kind of expansion which took place in the King's Bench, because the barons long obstructed the fiction by allowing the defendant to challenge it.[53] The court also refused, in 1588, to allow a lessee of the queen's lessee to sue there, 'or else by such means all the causes of England might be brought into the Exchequer'.[54] However, what was still unthinkable in 1588 became daily practice in the course of the next century, perhaps during the Interregnum. Sir Matthew Hale, as chief baron in 1665, scrupulously attacked the fiction and also the assumption that a man could recover the whole of his demand even if it exceeded his liability to the Crown: 'to make the king's prerogative a stale to satisfy other men's debts would be unreasonable, inconvenient and mischievous to the subject'.[55] But by then it was too late, and this particular prerogative had become common property. Despite Magna Carta and subsequent legislation, and despite the better judgment of some of the barons, the Exchequer of Pleas had been turned by litigants into a third court for common pleas. No sooner had this development occurred, however, but the writ of *quominus* itself went largely out of use; plaintiffs found it easier and less expensive to use the Exchequer *subpoena*,[56] albeit still on the supposition that they were Crown debtors.

Meanwhile the status of the barons had advanced. Until 1550 only the chief baron was usually a serjeant at law. The junior barons were commonly chosen from among the remembrancers and clerks steeped in Exchequer practice, and until the fifteenth century were often clergymen; by 1500 they were mostly benchers in the inns of court, but still revenue specialists. After 1579, however, nearly all the barons[57] were appointed from the serjeants at law, which qualified them to belong to one of the Serjeants' Inns and to be assize judges, often trying cases

---

52 B. & M. 218 n.10, 426, 448. Executors could not be sued elsewhere in debt on simple contracts, because they could not wage law; but wager of law was not allowed in *quominus*.

53 *Ragland v. Wildgoose* (1581) Sav. 11, at 15. But the assertion went merely to jurisdiction, and so the fiction could not be objected to once the defendant had pleaded in bar: *Jervas' Case* (1582) Sav. 33.

54 *Calton's Case* (1588) BL MS. Hargrave 12, fo. 238v.

55 *A.-G. v. Poultney* (1665) Hard. 403 at 404. Cf. *King v. Lake* (1667) Hard. 470; Hargrave, *Law Tracts*, p. 278.

56 Although Bl. Comm., vol. III, p. 46, says the *quominus* was still the basis of all Exchequer proceedings in the 1760s, the guides to practice state clearly that it was disused much earlier: *The Compleat Sollicitor* (1668), p. 417; *The Compleat Clerk in Court* (1726), p. 193.

57 With the exception of the 'cursitor baron', who occupied an inferior place in the court. The office was abolished on the death of Bankes B in 1856.

from the King's Bench and Common Pleas. From being experts in the mysterious 'course of the Exchequer' they had become fully fledged common-law judges, equal partners with the justices of the two benches.

Uniformity and Abolition

The outcome of these developments was that by the end of Charles II's reign the three central courts of law had acquired comparable jurisdiction over most common pleas and had developed procedures which, though divergent in outward forms and in costs, worked very much alike in practice. Each court nevertheless retained some specialist functions. The King's Bench still had its supervisory role, through error and *mandamus* on the civil side and *certiorari* on the Crown side, and occasionally entertained criminal trials at bar. The Exchequer continued its proper revenue jurisdiction. The Common Pleas kept a monopoly of the true real actions, because the King's Bench bill procedure was confined to personal actions, and the *quominus* was appropriate only to claims for money which could be applied in paying a notional Crown debt. In reality, however, this restriction had come to mean very little, because the real actions had been replaced for most purposes by ejectment. Even the Exchequer could hear ejectment, although its main object was to recover land, because the damages claimed would support a *quominus* clause. The only actions, therefore, in which the Common Pleas retained a true monopoly were real actions for those types of property not recoverable by ejectment: principally *quare impedit* (for an advowson), and the writ of right of dower *unde nihil habet* (for a widow's unassigned third share of her husband's land).

By the eighteenth century it was customary to speak of the 'twelve judges' (of the three courts) as a body equal in status and authority and function, and to regard their assignment to three separate tribunals as little more than an accident of history. The burden of trying cases was shared equally and indiscriminately between them as assize commissioners. Only questions of law arising after the trial would normally reach one or other of the courts sitting at Westminster in term time. The prospect of a legal difficulty might have influenced the plaintiff's choice of court; but probably the choice more often depended on the sphere of practice of the attorney consulted, on subtle differences in costs, and procedural advantages.

Despite the parity of jurisdiction, the business was still not equally distributed. Litigation in Westminster Hall declined steadily between the 1680s and the 1750s, and when it began to pick up in the second half of the eighteenth century the King's Bench captured the lion's share. Again we may suspect the force of personalities: Fyneux's successor, Lord Mansfield, chief justice from 1756 to 1788, responded creatively to the needs of an active commercial community, and the vitality of his court contrasted dramatically with the 'sleepy hollow' of the Common Pleas. In 1828, Henry Brougham MP complained in the House of Commons that, so long as there were three courts, unevenness was inevitable: 'it is not in the power of the courts, even were all monopolies and other restrictions done away, to distribute business equally, as long as suitors are left free to choose their own tribunal'; there would always be a favourite court, the business would draw the best lawyers and judges, and this would entrench its favoured position.[58] That was an uneconomic use of judicial resources. After Brougham's exposure of various defects in the system, a commission was appointed to enquire into the practice and procedure of the courts of law. The most immediate reforms were the abolition of the Welsh courts in 1830, and the introduction of uniform process, in place of the latitat and *quominus* and Common Pleas *capias*, in 1832.[59] The division of work between the central courts was left for another generation to tackle. In 1867 a Judicature Commission was appointed to enquire into that division with a view to ascertaining whether improvements could be made, and the outcome was the Judicature Act 1873, under which the central courts were abolished and their jurisdiction transferred to a single High Court.[60]

The High Court of Justice which came into being on 1 November 1875 was composed of five divisions, three of which corresponded to the Queen's Bench, Common Pleas and Exchequer. That was not part of the permanent plan, but was an expedient to avoid the compulsory retirement or demotion of the chief justice of the Common Pleas (Coleridge) and the chief baron of the Exchequer (Kelly), which would have broken the constitutional principle that superior judges were irremovable. By chance, Cockburn CJ (of the Queen's Bench Division) and Kelly B both died in 1880, and on 16 December 1880 the Common Pleas and Exchequer Divisions were abolished by Order in Council.[61] The Queen's Bench Division became the sole representative of the old courts of common law, and Lord Coleridge thereupon became Lord

---

58   H. Brougham, *Present State of the Law* (1828), p. 10.

59   Uniformity of Process Act 1832, 2 & 3 Will. IV, c.39.

60   36 & 37 Vict., c.66. This established the Supreme Court of Judicature (s.3), divided into the Court of Appeal and the High Court (s.4). It came into force on the same date as the Judicature Act 1875, which made some further provisions.

61   The Order was unsuccessfully opposed in both houses of parliament.

Chief Justice of England.[62] The irony of the resulting situation is preserved to this day, in that common pleas are tried by the judges of the Queen's Bench Division, an irony compounded in 1971 by the creation of a new Crown Court to do the work which had once been appropriate to the King's Bench. But the irony is superficial. There is, once more, a single *Curia Regis*.[63]

Further reading

Holdsworth HEL, vol. I, pp. 194-264, 633-650

Milsom HFCL, pp. 52-55, 60-70

Manchester MLH, pp. 125-135

Cornish & Clark, pp. 23-26, 38-45

G. O. Sayles, 'The Evolution of the King's Bench before 1272' (1936) 55 SS xi-xl; 'The Jurisdiction of the King's Bench' (1938) 57 SS xxxiv-lxxii; (1955) 74 SS xxvi-lxvi

M. Hastings, *The Court of Common Pleas in 15th Century England* (1947)

A. Harding, *Law Courts in Medieval England* (1973), pp. 86-123; 'Plaints and Bills in the History of English Law ... 1250-1350' (1975), *Legal History Studies 1972*, pp. 65-86

J. S. Cockburn, *History of the Assizes 1558-1714* (1972)

J. H. Baker, 'The Court of King's Bench' (1978) 94 SS *23-51*; 'The Changing Concept of a Court' (1986) LPCL 153-169

COMMON PLEAS AND KING'S BENCH

Tract by Sir Francis North in *Lord Nottingham's 'Manual of Chancery Practice' and 'Prolegomena of Chancery and Equity'* (D. E. C. Yale ed., 1965), pp. 179-174 (and Lord Nottingham's response, pp. 158-159)

Tract probably by Sir Matthew Hale in F. Hargrave (ed.), *Law Tracts* (1787), vol. I, pp. 357-376

C. A. F. Meekings, 'King's Bench Bills' (1977), *Legal Records and the Historian*, pp. 97-139; 'A King's Bench Bill Formulary' (1985) 6 JLH 86-104

---

[62] This title had been used informally for chief justices of the King's Bench. Since 1875 it has been the statutory title of the president of the Queen's Bench Division.

[63] This was Lord Selborne's observation in introducing the Judicature Act 1873: *Parliamentary Debates* (H.L.), vol. 214 (3rd ser.), col. 336-337. The Crown Court was established by the Courts Act 1971 (c. 23).

J. H. Baker, 'The Court of King's Bench' (1978) 94 SS *53-63*
M. Blatcher, *The Court of King's Bench 1450-1550* (1978)

FLUCTUATIONS IN BUSINESS
M. Blatcher, 'The Great Depression', in *The Court of King's Bench 1450-1550* (1978), pp. 10-33
E. W. Ives, *The Common Lawyers in pre-Reformation England* (1983), pp. 199-207, 212-216
C. W. Brooks, *Pettyfoggers and Vipers of the Commonwealth* (1986), pp. 48-111; 'Civil Litigation in England, 1640-1830', in *The First Modern Society* (A. L. Beier et al. ed., 1989), pp. 357-399

EXCHEQUER
H. Jenkinson, *Select Cases in the Exchequer of Pleas* (48 SS, 1932), introduction
H. Wurzel, 'The Origin and Development of Quominus' (1939) 49 *Yale Law Jo.* 39-64
D. J. Guth, 'Notes on the early Tudor Exchequer of Pleas' in *Tudor Men and Institutions* (A. J. Slavin ed., 1972), pp. 101-122
J. H. Baker, 'The Exchequer of Pleas' (1978) 94 SS *63-64*
R. M. Ball, 'Exchequer of Pleas, Bills and Writs' (1988) 9 JLH 308-323

4. The Forms of Action

In the mind of the modern lawyer pleading and procedure are ancillary to the substantive law, and a law student may complete the academic stage of his studies without reading the *Supreme Court Practice* or becoming immersed in precedents of pleading. Law is treated as a body of abstract rules which are applicable to given factual situations. The rules under which litigation is initiated and pursued are of great practical importance but are generally treated for educational purposes as separate from the substantive rules which the courts apply once the facts are before them. In real life the relationship between law and fact may not be as clear cut as that, but it is true to say that large parts of the law have achieved an intellectual existence independent of the legal system.

Much of our legal history will defy comprehension unless this separation of law from procedure is put out of mind. The learning about writs, forms of action and pleading was fundamental to the common law, not simply because lawyers were more punctilious about form than they now are, but because the procedural institutions preceded the substantive law as now understood. The principles of the common law were not laid down in the abstract, but grew around the forms through which justice was centralised and administered by the king's courts. There was a law of writs before there was a law of property, or of contract, or of tort.

Originating an Action

Legal proceedings are commenced, or 'originated', when a plaintiff makes his complaint or demand in due form. In the local courts the plaint itself was enough to set the process of justice in motion, and it did not have to be written. When, in the early days of itinerant royal justice, complaints were laid before the justices in eyre or justices *coram rege*, orally or by informal (French) bill, the royal courts were merely taking over existing procedure. Where, however, a plaintiff wished to originate a suit in the Common Pleas, or in the King's Bench when sitting in another county, he had to purchase a royal writ from the king's Chancery[1] to authorise the commencement of proceedings. The

---

[1] For the secretarial role of the Chancery, see p. 114, post.

reason is that these royal courts, although they rapidly became the ordinary and regular courts of law, were at first exceptional. The king was not here merely taking over a traditional system, but was offering a new and separate justice of his own. This alternative justice was a royal favour before it became a right. In the case of the court before the king himself, and the eyre with commission to entertain all pleas, the favour was soon extended generally to all comers. But those who wanted the additional advantage of suing outside the itinerant system had to seek and pay for a grant of that favour in the form of an 'original writ'. The writ worked like a pass admitting suitors to the kind of justice for which they had paid, and there were different kinds of pass for different purposes. By 1200 many types of writ had become common form in the Chancery, and were issued on payment of a standard fee; but the writ remained a normal prerequisite to litigation at Westminster.

It has been suggested that original writs evolved from writs containing executive commands to sheriffs to do justice between the parties in the county or to take some specified action. Such writs were in use in Anglo-Saxon times, and the pipe rolls of Henry I show them still in regular use at the beginning of the twelfth century. The writ of right patent retained this form, being a command to the feudal lord of whom the plaintiff claimed land; and the viscontiel writs similarly conferred judicial authority on the sheriff.[2] Some other writs, such as habeas corpus, prohibition, and mandamus, also used this executive form and became known as 'prerogative writs'.[3] The development which turned other executive writs into originals was the introduction of an option; the addressee, invariably the sheriff, was to convey a command to the defendant, coupled with the alternative of coming before the king's court to explain why it was not obeyed. The failure to obey royal writs was itself a plea of the Crown,[4] and so long as there was no limitation on what might be commanded any matter could be brought within the scope of royal justice by first issuing a writ. This form of original writ, a command with an 'or else' clause, was established in the twelfth century. Another kind of formula, slightly later in date, ordered the sheriff to take pledges from the defendant to appear in court to explain himself. This appears to represent a further stage in which the option of carrying out a royal command has been removed; it was appropriate for dealing with allegations of wrongs already committed. Of these two principal classes of writ there will be more to say

---

2   Both were in the form *praecipimus tibi*: for specimens, see pp. 612-614, post.

3   See pp. 164-172, post.

4   *Leges Henrici Primi*, x.1 (Downer ed., p. 108).

presently. A third formula, associated with the petty assizes, was to order the sheriff to summon men of the vicinity to answer a question framed in the writ, and to summon the defendant to be there to hear the answer[5]

These writs addressed to the sheriff did not, like an eyre or assize commission,[6] confer jurisdiction on the court by direct grant, but authorised the initiation of proceedings in the court mentioned. The words 'and have there this writ' made an original writ 'returnable' into a specified court: that is, the sheriff had to send the writ to the court, endorsed with a report (called the 'return') on the action he had taken. On receipt of the returned writ, the justices had jurisdiction over the matter to the extent mentioned in the writ, and could themselves issue further returnable writs (called 'judicial writs') to secure the attendance of the defendant and continue the action through its further stages. Each returned writ was placed on file, by the keeper of the writs (*custos brevium*), as the court's warrant for the next step taken.

The original writs were designed to regulate justice, not to limit it. According to *Bracton* there were as many writ formulae as there were types of action,[7] and well into the thirteenth century new forms could be drafted when need arose by the chancellor and his masters, perhaps in consultation with the king's council and judges. In this formative period, we find writs in use which did not survive into later practice, and there is no need to suppose that those who first drew up new formulae intended them to last unalterably for centuries. What caused the original writs to become fundamentally important to the common law was the early tendency for the formulae to become fixed. Once a writ had been issued it became a precedent for the future, and there was a reluctance to change the formula if it was found serviceable. A plaintiff did not, therefore, concoct his own writ, in the way that he was free to formulate his plaint or bill when approaching a court directly. He had either to find a known formula to fit his case, or apply for a new one to be invented. By the time of *Bracton* there were substantial collections of precedents (called 'registers') to guide the Chancery clerks and the emerging legal profession,[8] and by the middle of the thirteenth century

---

[5] See pp. 86, 266, post. For specimens, see pp. 616-618, post. The assize of novel disseisin seems to have undergone a transformation from executive to original writ: it began as a simple command to the sheriff to reseise the plaintiff (*praecipio ut resaisias P*), which came to be 'judicialised', first by adding the word *juste* (*juste resaisias P*), and then by adding the explicit direction to investigate the question asked.

[6] These were also issued under the great seal: p. 19, ante.

[7] *Bracton*, vol. IV, p. 286.

[8] See p. 202, post.

the complete register of formulae was so great that the uninhibited invention of new writs was seen as something of a grievance. Some check was felt necessary. *Bracton* recognised this in stating that new forms of writ must be consonant with law and approved by the council. That is tantamount to saying that royal jurisdiction could not be extended without legislative and judicial sanction. This position is confirmed by complaints in 1244 that the chancellor was often issuing writs against justice or contrary to law;[9] and in 1256 a defendant asked the court to quash a writ as 'novel, unheard of, and against reason'.[10] What seems, then, already to have become the orthodoxy was voiced two years later in the Provisions of Oxford 1258, under which the chancellor was to be sworn to issue no unprecedented writs without the consent of the king's council.[11] After this period, although occasional innovations were sanctioned by parliament, the categories became more or less closed. The effect was momentous. Finding the right formula was no longer simply a matter of consistency and routine. If a would-be plaintiff could not find a writ in the register he was without remedy as far as the two benches were concerned. That is not to say that he was without remedy at all. The benches did not have exclusive or even comprehensive jurisdiction, and the denial of access to them in particular cases was often deliberate policy. Indeed, it was feared that if the old system of justice broke down the royal courts would be swamped with business they were not equipped to dispatch: a fear amply borne out by the fate of the general eyre. Nevertheless, as the common law administered in the two benches gradually became the regular law of the land, so the law of the land came to be dominated by the range and wording of the original writs. Formulae which had been drafted for more or less administrative purposes, to authorise the impleading of an adversary before an exceptional royal tribunal, were seen as defining the rights and remedies recognised by the common law, and thus as fixing the common law within an immutable conceptual framework.

The choice of original writ governed the whole course of litigation from beginning to end, and the plaintiff selected the most appropriate writ at his peril. Procedures and methods of trial available in an action commenced by one kind of writ were not necessarily available in another. The classification of writs was therefore more than just a convenient arrangement for reference purposes; it was a classification of actions, and in course of time a map of the substantive outlines of the

---

9   M. Paris, *Chronica Majora*, vol. IV (Rolls ser.), pp. 363, 367.

10   *Abbot of Lilleshall v. Harcourt* (1256) 96 SS xxix, 44. The case was settled.

11   *Annales Monastici*, vol. I (Rolls ser.), p. 448.

common law.[12] The original writ, said Stonor J in 1315, was the basis of the law.[13] Later lawyers referred to the compartments of law and practice associated with different writs as the 'forms of action'. These forms of action were the first object of legal study. The two earliest treatises on the common law, *Glanvill* and *Bracton*, were essentially books about writs and the procedures generated by them. And we know that the first stage in a medieval law student's training was to learn the writs, doubtless by rote. The medieval *Natura Brevium* (The Nature of Writs) was the students' primer; and when the renowned legal author and judge Sir Anthony Fitzherbert published a new *Natura Brevium* in 1534 he wrote in the preface that the writs were the 'fundamentals on which the whole law depends'.[14]

Types of Original Writ

A writ (*breve* in Latin, *brief* in French) was a thin strip of parchment containing a letter in the name of the king, usually written in Latin,[15] and sealed with the great seal. That is as much as can be said by way of generalisation about the nature of writs, because the contents of the letters varied from one form of action to another. After 1833 there was only one type of original writ, and the plaintiff filled his own particulars into a stereotyped form. But the common-law writs were different in form from each other, and some of the deeper divisions of form reflect different approaches to litigation. The classification of original writs for present purposes begins with the rudimentary distinction between a right and a wrong. The assertion of a right – a *demand* – received different treatment from the complaint of a wrong – a *plaint*.[16] A right was continuous, even eternal, and it was necessary that its vindication be accomplished with care and caution; the highest solemnities of royal justice were accordingly lent to the protection of rights, especially those of a proprietary nature, for the decision would bind the parties and their successors in title for ever. A wrong, on the other hand, was something

---

[12] See Table A on p. 83, post.

[13] *Horthwait v. Courtenay* (1315) 45 SS 5, per Stonor J ('bref original est fondement de ley'); repeated in 104 SS 142 (1320), per Stonor J.

[14] For these works, see also pp. 214, 216, post.

[15] Early privy-seal writs were sometimes in French. For the conversion to English, see p. 103, post.

[16] A similar division is seen in viscontiel writs (p. 28, ante) between the *justicies* (to order the defendant to do something) and the *audias* (to hear a complaint of misconduct).

past, beyond undoing, and something which at first concerned the royal courts only in so far as it infringed the king's peace. The consequences of serious wrongs, in terms of life and property, might be just as grave as in actions about rights, but the philosophy with which they were approached was necessarily different. Enquiries into misdeeds were usually less perplexing than enquiries into rights, and were peculiarly appropriate for the jury. Minor wrongs were not at first within the ambit of the king's justice at all.

PRAECIPE WRITS

The forms of action for pursuing demands belonged to the category of writs which it was suggested above may have developed from executive commands. The sheriff is told to command (*praecipe*) the defendant to do what is demanded by the plaintiff or demandant, or else to come before the king's justices to explain why (*ostensurus quare*) he will not. The king's court acquires jurisdiction in default of restitution of the supposed right by the defendant. Presumably at some stage the option of performance had been real; but it became fictional.[17] The disappearance of the reality of the option made the *praecipe* writs truly original, in that they were conceived of as originating an action from the time of their issue rather than from the moment of non-compliance; there was no need to prove a refusal before process could issue.

The classical *praecipe* formula was settled by 1150, and there were soon a number of different species. The principal type, perhaps the prototype, was used to claim land; the sheriff was to command the defendant to 'render' or yield up to the demandant the land which the latter claimed as his right.[18] There were variants of this formula for claiming kinds of real property as diverse as advowsons and easements, and derivatives (such as writs of entry and formedon) for claims under differing kinds of title. The *praecipe quod reddat* formula was also used to claim chattels or debts which the defendant unjustly withheld, or the performance of a covenant, or to obtain an account of moneys received. And there was a negative version, *praecipe quod permittat*, under which the defendant was to be ordered to allow the demandant to have or to do something: to have an easement or profit (*quod permittat habere*), to knock down a nuisance (*quod permittat prosternere*), to present a

17   For an explicit statement from the 1480s, see the Inner Temple moot in Keil. 116, pl. 57.
18   This was addressed to the sheriff only where land was held in chief, or where the lord waived his court: pp. 265, 270, post. But the writ of right patent to the lord contained a similar 'or else' clause: p. 612, post.

clergyman to a benefice where there had been an obstruction (*quod permittat presentare*, usually called *quare impedit*), or to grind corn without paying toll. What is interesting about this *quod permittat* group is that four different kinds of legal claim were linked by a common formula: the form preceded any legal analysis. These writs also mentioned wrongdoing, and yet they were actually demands of right, the rights being such as required exercise by the demandant's action rather than the defendant's. All the *praecipe* actions have this in common, that they look not to compensation for misconduct but to the restoration of some right; they are prospective rather than retrospective, in the subjunctive mood rather than the active, and in the present tense rather than the past. Where possible they resulted in recovery of the right, enforced by a writ to hand over the thing in demand or to do what was asked.[19]

As these were the oldest and most solemn of actions, the procedure which accompanied them was archaic and solemn, and slow. Much parchment and wax was needed to secure the appearance of the defendant, who could safely ignore several initial stages in the process against him, and even at later stages was allowed various excuses (called 'essoins') for not appearing. In the writ of right, trial was originally by battle, the judgment determined by God. In debt and detinue, and to begin with in covenant, trial was by oath-taking (wager of law), the most familiar mode of proof in the old communal courts. The *praecipe* writs were therefore closest to the old ways of doing things and the first to seem outmoded. One course might have been to modify the procedures to bring them into line with current notions of efficacy. In the twelfth century that was still thinkable, and in 1179 Henry II did indeed introduce the 'grand assize', a form of jury, as an alternative to battle at the option of the defendant. By Edward I's time, however, the conservatism which accompanied the rise of the legal profession, and which had frozen the writ system, put paid to radical procedural change. As neither their wording nor the concomitant procedures could be modified, the *praecipe* writs became less and less usable; and their fate was to be gradually superseded by whatever newer and more effective remedies could be found. One solution was found in the bill procedure of the Chancery and conciliar courts. But alternatives existed within the common-law forms of action, and principally in the second main class of writs, those concerned more with wrongs than with rights.

---

[19] This was once possible even in covenant, though here the usual remedy came to be damages.

PLAINTS OF WRONG

The petty assizes, already noticed, fall between the two classes. But one of them, novel disseisin, was effectively an enquiry into wrongdoing; the bringer of the action was a 'plaintiff' – an 'appellant' in *Glanvill* – rather than a 'demandant', the general issue was 'No tort', and damages could be recovered for the wrongdoing. At the same time as novel disseisin was introduced to deal with a particular form of disorder, we find other procedures (one of them likewise attributed to an 'assize') to deal with what we call crime. Complaints of violent wrongs could be made either by the community, through the grand jury, or by the victim or his next of kin.[20] The latter made an 'appeal', originally oral, upon which the accused was arraigned and tried. The most serious appeals were those alleging felony, and the appeal of felony was the only kind of appeal to survive into the later common law. But there were once appeals of trespass for other breaches of the king's peace; and these gave way on the one hand to actions of trespass,[21] and on the other to indictments for misdemeanour. Although the appeal did not require a writ for its commencement, it became increasingly common to use a writ of attachment to produce the defendant in court to answer the charge against him.

A third mode of proceeding against a wrongdoer was by a writ in the form *pone*,[22] whereby the sheriff was ordered to 'put the defendant by gage and safe pledges' to come before the king's justices and show why (*ostensurus quare*) he had committed some specified misdeed. It will be remembered that the *ostensurus quare* formula had been used in the 'or else' clause of the *praecipe* writs, where the defendant was to come and explain his disobedience of the command; but here it was elevated into a direct command to come and explain the matter alleged against him. The direct *ostensurus quare* formula possessed various subspecies: a form of replevin,[23] the writ of waste,[24] the writ of deceit (for misconduct

---

20 See further pp. 573-577, post.

21 See p. 71, post. In 1241 an appeal for carrying away hay was quashed on the ground that an action by writ was available: *Crown Pleas of the Wiltshire Eyre 1249* (Meekings ed.), p. 83. And in 1321 knocking a door down was said to be too 'simple' a trespass for an appeal on the crown side of the eyre: 85 SS 93.

22 Another kind of *pone* was used to remove cases from inferior courts: p. 265, post. This was in the form *pone ad respondendum*. The *pone* formula also occurs in novel disseisin.

23 See pp. 271-272, post. For the notion that replevin was a plea of the Crown, see p. 45, ante. In 1310, Bereford CJ said replevin was a writ of trespass: 22 SS 195.

24 Waste (and a number of other writs concerning property, such as *quare ejecit* and ravishment of ward) were not in the form *pone*, but contained a summons *ostensurus quare*: see the form, p. 620, post.

in legal proceedings), and – the broadest category of all – the writs of trespass.

TRESPASS

'Trespass', the law-French word for *transgressio* or wrongdoing, was not in the beginning a term of art. In the 1525 translation of the Lord's Prayer – 'forgive us our trespasses' – the word is used both for the *peccatum* (sin) and *delictum* (wrong) of the Vulgate.[25] Trespass was a broad enough category at one time to embrace felony, criminal misdemeanour and disseisin as well as those wrongs remedied by the later actions of trespass and trespass on the case. It acquired the narrower meaning because it became the name of a great family of original writs. None of these writs actually employed the word 'trespass',[26] but they were related by the *ostensurus quare* formula and eventually by common procedures. They were also linked by an approach which distinguishes them from the *praecipe* actions. Whereas a *praecipe* writ ordered the defendant to accede to a demand or justify himself, a trespass writ brought the defendant directly to court to explain why he had done wrong. Trespass writs were therefore not concerned with the vindication of rights, but with punishment and amends for past transgression. A writ of trespass offered no option, even fictitious, of doing right: as Blackstone put it, while a *praecipe* writ was 'optional', trespass was 'peremptory'. It embodied a complaint rather than a demand. As with the assize and the appeal, trial was by jury. And the outcome of a successful suit was damages, with a fine to the king in serious cases.

The *ostensurus quare* formula appeared in the decades before 1200, though trespass writs are uncommon before the middle of the thirteenth century. It seems highly probable that such actions developed in tandem with the appeal, in which the writ of attachment to answer an accusation mirrored the *ostensurus quare* formula but included words alleging felony. Appeals of felony continued in use as a means of recovering stolen goods, or of achieving the execution of an aggressor; but the appellor ran the risk of having to fight a battle, or of being severely punished if the appeal failed. The appeal of death apart, most appeals could be converted into actions for damages by omitting the words of felony.[27] This may be why most of the earliest writs of trespass contain

---

[25] Matthew, vi.12, 14 (1525 and 1611 versions; but 'wrong' in the *New English Bible* of 1961). Cf. Luke, xi.4 (sin).

[26] The word sometimes occurs in the pleadings: e.g. in the 14th-century form of general plea, *Non fecit transgressionem*.

[27] *Bracton*, vol. II, p. 411, explicitly says this.

the phrase 'with force and arms and against the king's peace', a phrase taken from the appeal. The writ of trespass for taking and carrying away goods (*de bonis asportatis*) was closely similar to the appeal of larceny, and that for assault and battery was similar to the appeal of mayhem. However, the writ was not as restricted as the appeal, and could also be brought for trespass to land (*quare clausum fregit* and ejectment).[28]

It was settled in the course of the thirteenth century that writs of trespass – in whichever bench they were returnable – could only be issued in respect of wrongs committed 'with force and arms' (*vi et armis*) and 'against the king's peace' (*contra pacem regis*), or which infringed royal franchises.[29] Only such wrongs were suitable for the attention of the king's justices. Other wrongs were more appropriate for local jurisdictions, and there was a policy of discouraging private disputes in the highest courts about mere passing wrongs. Thus in 1278 it was enacted that actions of trespass should be brought in the county as in the past, and that no one should have a writ of trespass unless he swore that the claim was substantial.[30]

The limitation of writs of trespass to wrongs *vi et armis* and *contra pacem* did not reflect any narrow understanding of the nature of 'trespass'; it was merely a fetter on the jurisdiction of the central courts. But the desire for remedies in those courts soon came into conflict with this limitation, which in the fourteenth century was increasingly felt to be an inconvenience with little purpose. Since local courts were generally forbidden to entertain suits for more than forty shillings without royal sanction,[31] there would have been a failure of justice if non-violent trespasses involving a greater sum were excluded from the king's courts as well. The pressure for change is first seen in attempts to use *vi et armis* writs fictitiously, smuggling in actions under the pretence of force in the hope that no exception would be taken. A series of actions for injuring horses with force and arms, brought against defendants identifiable as smiths, suggests irresistibly that the complaints were really of shoeing accidents;[32] and doubtless there were other fictions which are no longer capable of detection. If the truth

---

28   As in the case of the woman whose door was knocked down: p. 70, note 21, ante.

29   The writ of deceit might also be considered a species of trespass: here the king's interest was in the integrity of his justice.

30   Statute of Gloucester 1278, c.8.

31   This was a common-law rule, the date of which is uncertain: see J. S. Beckerman, in *Legal History Studies 1972*, p. 110.

32   See Milsom, 74 LQR at 220-221, 586. For selling contaminated wine *vi et armis*, see *Rattlesdene v. Grunestone* (1317) B. & M. 300.

came out, some plaintiffs met with a helpful court,[33] but others did not, especially where the non-violent nature of the wrong appeared from the plaintiff's own count.[34] The necessity for the plaintiff to make out some royal interest had become an embarrassment.

TRESPASS ON THE CASE

The *vi et armis* restriction was openly abandoned in the 1360s, when the Chancery clerks began regularly to issue writs of trespass in which the phrase was omitted.[35] Orthodox teaching from the sixteenth to the present century was that the innovation was sanctioned by a statute of 1285, which provided that the clerks of the Chancery should draw up a new writ 'whenever henceforth it should happen in the Chancery that a writ is found in one case but none is found in a like case (*in consimili casu*) falling under the same law (*cadente sub eodem jure*) and requiring a like remedy'.[36] But no such connection was explicitly made in medieval times, and historians now disagree as to the role of the statute. It was eighty years before the abandonment of the *vi et armis* requirement in practice, and the fictions resorted to in the interim would have been unnecessary and absurd if the statute had already authorised the change. It may be that the statute simply removed the need for an exact precedent when issuing new writs, and that by a process of accretion the corpus of trespass formulae grew little by little until eventually the force and arms could be dropped. However, the facts suggest a more sudden change of policy around the mid-1360s;[37] and it is difficult to see how a writ for a non-forcible wrong could have been thought 'in like case' to a writ for a forcible wrong, or as 'falling under the same law', when it had already been held that the writ *vi et armis* did not lie for the non-forcible wrong.

The new writs differed from the vast run of *vi et armis* writs. They embodied the same *ostensurus quare* formula; but whereas the *vi et*

---

[33] E.g. *Anon.* (1304) B. & M. 297; *Petstede v. Marreys* (1310) B. & M. 298.

[34] E.g. *Anon.* (1313) B. & M. 300 (deceit in selling); *Toteshalle v. Orfevre* (1321) 86 SS 149, B. & M. 301 (conversion by a bailee); *Houton v. Paston* (1321) 86 SS 282, B. & M. 302, per Herle J (accident). Cf. *Anon.* (1374) B. & M. 304 (negligence). See also *Anon.* (1390) B. & M. 305 (horse overworked by bailee).

[35] The relaxation began earlier with bills: e.g. *The Oculist's Case* (1329) B. & M. 340 (eyre of Nottingham); *Bukton v. Tounesende* (1348) B. & M. 358 (King's Bench at York); p. 375, post.

[36] Statute of Westminster II 1285, c.24 (*in consimili casu*). The statute also says that if the clerks cannot agree, they are to refer the problem to parliament. A 15th-century reader on this provision said it was 'to no effect': BL MS. Lansdowne 1138, fo.104.

[37] Perhaps involving the king's council, who certainly considered and sanctioned the action against innkeepers: B. & M. 554, per Knyvet CJ.

armis writs were mostly 'general', accommodating wide spectra of facts in simple stereotyped forms,[38] all other writs of trespass had to set out the plaintiff's cause of action with some particularity in what was called his 'special case'. The special facts were recited in a *cum* (whereas) clause, following immediately after the words *ostensurus quare*, and preceding the direct assignment of wrongdoing.[39] The *cum* clause is first found in *vi et armis* writs, in the thirteenth century, as a way of adding aggravation or explanation; and there were precedents long before the 1360s of *cum* clauses showing the breach of some royal interest, such as a franchise, in lieu of force.[40] There was also a line of cases in which special writs were brought for flooding through non-repair of sea-walls, culminating in a leading case of 1344 in which the writ was described as being 'a formed writ conceived on his case' (*in suo casu conceptum*); it is difficult to account for this exception to the *vi et armis* rule, except as an analogue of the *praecipe quod reparari facias*, but here the extension occurred before 1285.[41] When writs without *vi et armis* became more common in the 1360s, introducing actions for negligence and breaches of contract, for deceit by sellers, for damage caused by dangerous animals, for the loss of goods from inns, and for misconduct by bailees, the *cum* clause (setting out the special facts) was indispensable. Early descriptions of such writs, for instance 'a writ according to his special case', betoken formulae specially created for individuals.[42] As they became more common, the whole family of non-forcible trespass actions was given the generic name of 'trespass on the case' or of 'actions on the case'.[43]

This difference of form seems to represent no more than an accident of history. The general *vi et armis* writs came first, and the plaintiff who could not find one suitable for his purpose had to have a special one drawn up for him with an explanatory clause. At first any other differences were minimised, perhaps at first by retaining the *contra pacem* formula, though this soon ceased to be necessary. The conceptual unity is in fact more striking than the differences. For

---

38   Thus the battery formula (p. 618, post) could embrace wrongs as diverse as shooting or running down with a horse and cart. See p. 456, post.

39   For specimens, see pp. 618-622, post; B. & M. 343-344, 385.

40   E.g. *Prior of Coventry v. Grauntpie* (1309) B. & M. 611 (franchise of market).

41   Milsom, 74 LQR 430-434; *Bernardeston v. Heighlynge* (1344) B. & M. 338.

42   E.g. B. & M. 358 ('special writ according to the case', 1369), 341 ('writ according to his case', 1372), 378 ('writ formed on his special case', 1400), 381 (trespass '*sur le matter monstré*', i.e. on the facts set out, 1425). (Similar expressions were used for writs other than trespass.)

43   'Trespass on the case': B. & M. 367 (1441), 554 (1443). 'Action on the case': B. & M. 613 (1410), 397 (1449).

instance, it might have been supposed that trespass on the case was a common plea and therefore outside the jurisdiction of the King's Bench; but the point was not pressed and had no practical effect.[44] It was also arguable that jury trial was not de rigueur in trespass on the case, as it was in trespass *vi et armis*, and in 1374 the argument nearly prevailed;[45] but by the 1380s it was settled that wager of law was not acceptable in any writ of trespass.[46] Another difference concerned mesne process; but in 1504 any previous doubts were settled by the enactment that the same process was available in case as in trespass.[47] As late as 1610 it could be said that trespass was a collective name, including the two species trespass *vi et armis* and trespass *super casum*.[48] Such, however, became the dominance of form over substance that in later ages lawyers convinced themselves that the species 'trespass' and 'case' must have been distinct entities for a reason, and that they ought not to be confused. Suing by the wrong writ was fatal; and so different did trespass and case become in the legal mind that they could not even be joined in one action.[49] Eighteenth-century rationalisation made the test one of directness. An action of trespass for fixing a spout so that it directed rainwater onto the plaintiff's house was on this basis struck down in 1725 because the proper action was case. Fortescue J put the distinction between a man who threw a log into the highway and hit someone (trespass), and one who left a log in the highway and someone tripped over it (case).[50] Such distinctions might be rather scholastic; but, as Lord Raymond CJ remarked in the same case, 'we must keep up the boundaries of actions, otherwise we shall introduce the utmost confusion'. The accident of history had been elevated into a principle of law, a rule which would require much effort and learning to avoid.[51]

---

[44] 94 SS 57-59.

[45] *Stratton v. Swanlond* (1374) B. & M. 360 at 361, per Cavendish CJ ('This writ does not suppose force and arms, or *contra pacem*, and so it seems wager of law is quite acceptable'). However, the defendant withdrew the wager of law and accepted a jury.

[46] *Rempston v. Morley* (1383) Y.B. Mich. 7 Ric. II, p. 30, pl.11, at p. 301. In *Garrok v. Heytesbury* (1387) B. & M. 507 at 508, the point was again raised, but not pressed.

[47] Stat. 19 Hen. VII, c.9; B. & M. 342.

[48] *Cox v. Gray* (1610) B. & M. 351. In the 15th-century actions on the case were often referred to simply as 'trespass': e.g. B. & M. 380, 508, 581, 611, 613.

[49] See this argued in *Haukyns v. Broune* (1477) B. & M. 629 at 630, per Townshend sjt.

[50] *Reynolds v. Clarke* (1725) B. & M. 354; quotation from 1 Stra. 634.

[51] See further p. 467, post.

Judicial Writs

Process is the name given to that part of the machinery of justice whereby persons are brought to justice and judgments enforced. The details of the process available in different forms of action are points of practice which have little fascination for posterity; but historians must not forget that such things were of immense importance to litigants, and may often have affected their choice of action and the development of the law. Process was governed by writs, but not from the Chancery: they were issued under the seal of the court, and were called judicial writs.

Since a suit could not proceed in the absence of a defendant, the first stage was to secure the defendant's appearance: or, if he would not appear, to outlaw him. This was called the 'mesne' process, because it was intermediate between the original writ and the judgment. As soon as an original writ was returned into the Common Pleas or the King's Bench it was taken to an officer of the court called a 'filazer' who thereupon issued all the writs of mesne process until the appearance of the defendant or the commencement of outlawry. The principal forms of mesne process were the writ of attachment (under which the defendant had to provide sureties for his appearance), the *distringas* (under which the defendant was distrained by seizure of his property), and the *capias ad respondendum* (under which the defendant was arrested). The *capias* was the most effective, but it was limited at common law to suits for breach of the king's peace; gradually by statute it was extended to other personal actions.[52]

Judicial writs resembled originals in that they too were addressed to the sheriff and were returnable in court. The effectiveness of process therefore depended on the sheriff. Unable as he was to claim expenses, and liable in damages if he made mistakes, the temptation for him to do nothing was considerable. The sheriff could return to a *distringas* that he could find nothing to distrain, or to a *capias* that the defendant was ill or not to be found. Whether he had looked was a question one was not allowed to ask, and so these returns became common fictions for use by under-sheriffs who could not be persuaded to take positive action or who hoped by delay to prise some gift from the plaintiff. There was, in any case, a succession of judicial writs to be issued in due sequence before any real sanctions began to operate. Even where *capias* was available, three successive writs went out before further steps were taken, and notwithstanding them the plaintiff still could not seek judgment by

---

52   In 1285 to account, in 1351 to debt, detinue and replevin, in 1504 to case, and in 1531 to covenant: B. & M. 342.

default but had to resort to outlawry. Outlawry was an elaborate rigmarole, requiring the sheriff to 'exact' the defendant by calling upon him to come forth at five successive county assemblies. But it was not as terrible as it sounded. It could easily be reversed for formal slips, and technical escape routes seem to have been left almost as a matter of course; if all else failed, an outlawry could be pardoned on payment of a pound or two to various officials. The Robin Hood legends have preserved an image of outlaws as desperate outcasts; but by 1400 outlawry was not usually much of an inconvenience, and even royal officials could continue in office while outlawed.[53]

Moderate delay in litigation was often defended as a desirable feature of royal justice in an age when communications were slow. Certainly the common-law system had ample opportunities for delay built into it at many points. One contributing factor was the division of the legal year into terms during which formal business had to be transacted. These originated in the twelfth century, when the Exchequer began to hold its major accounting sessions at Easter and Michaelmas. The council was assembled for these sessions, and the justices stayed afterwards to dispose of judicial business. Two further terms were probably added in the 1190s when the Bench became firmly established. The terms were separated by four vacations, periods when the Church prescribed holidays, when the king's justices took time to make their circuits, or when everyone went home. All Sundays and certain saints' days were non-juridical (*dies non juridici*) at common law. The three religious seasons of Christmas (with Advent and Epiphany), Lent (with Easter) and Trinity (with Whitsun and Corpus Christi) account for three of the vacations; while the fourth, the 'Long Vacation', kept the summer months free for home pursuits when weather could make town life unsafe. Thus was the legal year divided into the four terms during which the courts sat at Westminster: Michaelmas (in October and November), Hilary (in January and February), Easter (in April and May), and Trinity (in May and June). The total number of working days in the year, in Elizabeth I's time, was only 99;[54] later reforms took away about ten more days, so that for as much as three quarters of the year there were no common-law courts sitting at Westminster.

Each term was divided into four or more 'returns', each return-day being a week apart. All writs were made returnable at one of these days, and at that stage the plaintiff had to take his next step. There were three days of grace at each return, and a provision for late entries on payment

---

[53] Elizabeth I is said to have complained at the number of outlaws sitting as members of parliament.

[54] Meekings, in *Legal Records and the Historian*, p. 111 n.1.

of a fine after the fourth day; but if the plaintiff missed the return altogether, his action was 'discontinued' and he had to give up or start again. If the sheriff or the defendant defaulted at the return, then the plaintiff would ask for the next judicial writ to be issued, returnable after a prescribed interval at another return-day, often the next term. It was the function of the attorneys to watch their clients' causes to make sure that steps were taken at the proper days. The system was typified by delay. It was not uncommon for a year or two to pass before a defendant appeared. This was one of the main reasons why, if there was any choice, plaintiffs preferred those forms of action which needed the fewest writs to procure an appearance.

If the parties pleaded to an issue of fact, further judicial writs were required to produce a jury: first the *venire facias juratores*, repeated if it had no effect, then the *distringas juratores* (to distrain recalcitrant jurors), and finally the *habeas corpora juratorum* (to produce their bodies).

FINAL PROCESS

Execution of a judgment was likewise obtained by judicial writs addressed to the sheriff. The choice of writ depended on the form of action and the nature of the judgment. In real actions the judgment was usually to recover seisin of the land demanded, and the writ of execution was then the *habere facias seisinam* in which the operative words were 'cause A to have seisin'.[55] A judgment for money, whether for a debt, damages, or costs,[56] was primarily enforced at common law by the writ of *fieri facias* (commonly called fi. fa.), which ordered the sheriff to seize the defendant's chattels[57] and cause the sum to be 'made up' (that is, raised by sale). Freehold land was not liable at common law to execution for a money judgment, except in the case of the king or a recognizee.[58] In 1285, however, parliament introduced an alternative procedure called *elegit*, under which a judgment creditor could elect instead of fi. fa. to have the defendant's goods and a moiety of his lands

---

[55]   In ejectment, when a term was recovered (see p. 340, post), the writ was *habere facias possessionem*.

[56]   A plaintiff was generally entitled to costs in all cases where he recovered damages: Statute of Gloucester 1278, c.1. (Later statutes provided that in certain cases costs should not exceed the damages: e.g., p. 465, post.) The defendant was first given costs in 1531: 23 Hen. VIII, c.15.

[57]   This included leaseholds: see B. & M. 191.

[58]   In these cases a *levari facias* was used, allowing the profits of land to be taken as well as chattels. For recognizances, see p. 354, post.

delivered to him as a passive security.[59] In practice it came to operate like a mortgage, the debtor remaining in possession and paying an assessed rent until the debt was paid off. In those actions where mesne process was by *capias*, the plaintiff had the further option of suing execution against the debtor's person by the writ of *capias ad satisfaciendum* (ca. sa.), under which the debtor was incarcerated until the debt was paid: a technique which depended for its limited success largely on the hope of intervention by friends.

These writs proved remarkably durable, and were unaffected by the Common Law Procedure Acts. The abolition of imprisonment for most civil purposes in 1869 put a virtual end to the fearful ca. sa., though it remained available in rare cases until 1981.[60] *Elegit* was actually enlarged in scope in 1838, so that *all* the defendant's lands were made liable to execution; only in recent times has it been replaced by the more flexible charging order.[61] Fi. fa. and writs of possession are still in common use, and (retaining their common-law form) have turned out to be the principal survivors of the medieval writ system.[62] More modern forms of execution – designed chiefly to reach a wider range of assets than tangible property – derive either from statute[63] or from Chancery procedure.[64]

End of the Forms of Action

Much of the variety described in this chapter came to an end as a result of the triumph of trespass and case, which shared a common procedure from beginning to end, over most other actions.[65] Debt remained numerically the most important action, but (as was seen in the last

---

59 Statute of Westminster II 1285, c.18. The tenancy was a freehold protected by novel disseisin; but it was treated as a chattel for succession purposes, so that it went to personal representatives together with the debt itself.

60 Supreme Court Act 1981 (c.54), s.141. Imprisonment in civil cases was generally abolished by the Debtors Act 1869, 32 & 33 Vict., c.62.

61 Judgments Act 1838, 1 & 2 Vict., c.110, s.11; Administration of Justice Act 1956 (c.46).

62 In 1988 alone, 65,811 writs of fi. fa. and 2,861 writs of possession were issued to enforce Queen's Bench Division judgments: *Judicial Statistics for 1988* (Cmd 745), p. 34.

63 E.g. charging orders, introduced by the 1838 Act as a means of levying execution against stocks and shares; and attachment of debts (including bank accounts and earnings), introduced in 1854.

64 E.g. sequestration (see p. 120, post) and receivership.

65 In one form of trespass (ejectment), mesne process was altogether dispensed with by the use of fictions: see pp. 341-342, post.

chapter) the usual mode of suing in debt by 1700 depended on fictitious actions of trespass to land. The expansion of trespass, and especially of the flexible action on the case, provided the common law with a temporary escape from the formulary system, an opportunity to melt down the medieval law and recast it in new moulds. Most of the law as we know it was shaped by this process. After the redistribution, the commonest types of trespass and case became the basis of a new scheme of actions: *assumpsit* (for breach of parol contracts, and restitutionary claims), trover (for interference with personal property), actions on the case for torts (such as defamation and negligence), and ejectment (to recover real property). But the flexibility inherent in trespass and case prevented any recurrence of the restrictiveness and procedural nicety which beset the *praecipe* actions. For most purposes the new remedies were but subdivisions of one form of action.

This progress towards uniformity was carried to a conclusion by nineteenth-century legislation. Most of the forms of action, as distinct procedures, were abolished in 1832 and 1833. Actions were thereafter commenced by one same form of writ, in which the kind of action was merely inserted in the space provided. After 1852 it became unnecessary even to state the 'form of action' in the uniform writ,[66] and different causes of action could now be joined in one writ.[67] The reforms extended also to mesne process. The assimilation and simplification of mesne process in all the superior courts was mentioned in the last chapter; the 1852 legislation went further by introducing the possibility of judgment in default of appearance.[68] The return-days were abolished,[69] and eventually the services of the sheriff were dispensed with for all preliminary stages, so that parties served their own writs and pleadings within set time-limits. In 1875 the form of the original writ was again changed, principally by adaptation of the Chancery subpoena which it also replaced; the substance of the claim was endorsed on the back, but not in any technical phrases. In 1980, the immemorial writ formula itself was finally abandoned, Lord Hailsham C having formed the view

---

66   Uniformity of Process Act 1832, 2 & 3 Will. IV, c.39; Real Property Limitation Act 1833, 3 & 4 Will. IV, c.27, s.36; Common Law Procedure Act 1852, 15 & 16 Vict., c.76, ss.2-3. For the new form, see p. 626, post.

67   Common Law Procedure Act 1852, s.41.

68   Ibid, s.27. Since there would in such cases be no pleadings, it was necessary for the plaintiff to endorse the writ with particulars of his claim; the procedure was only appropriate for debt and liquidated money-claims. This system was preserved in R.S.C. 1875, Ord. XIII (later Ord. XIV).

69   The terms were also abolished by Judicature Act 1873, 36 & 37 Vict., c.66, s.26. Curiously, the vacations were not abolished; the periods of business between vacations are now called sittings.

that sending a command from the queen herself was too awe-striking and might dismay a layman. What now originates proceedings, though called a 'writ', is in fact a simple notice to appear. The last original writ in the queen's name was issued on 2 June 1980.

These changes were procedural, and were not intended to alter any of the substantive law which was enforced through the forms of action. Yet the law was so inseparable from the writs that the disappearance of the latter left conceptual problems. The chief problem arose from the fact that so many of the writs had come to overlap. Since 1833, for example, there had been an election between trespass and case, so long as the wrong complained of was not wilful.[70] But what is the substantive distinction, if any, between trespass and case?[71] The election between conversion and detinue remained important until a statute of 1977 declared curtly that 'detinue is abolished'. But what exactly was thereby abolished?[72] There may be a similar distinction between debt and *indebitatus assumpsit*, though its subtleties seem to be appreciated only in the Antipodes.[73]

'The forms of action we have buried,' said Maitland at the turn of the century, 'but they still rule us from their graves'.[74] The passage of years has only gradually diminished their influence. If occasionally the ghosts are reproached for 'clanking their spectral chains',[75] one learned judge has asserted that 'if one is not unduly timorous one may find that they are waving one along the path of justice'.[76] Yet the posthumous rule of the forms of action has tended towards a tyranny which in life they were never permitted. The categories of common-law thought were in a way closed in 1832, and where once the law might have developed through the recognition of new writs it is now left at the mercy of commissions and an overworked parliament. Law reform is no longer subject to judicial review.

---

[70] *Williams v. Holland* (1833) 10 Bing. 112; p. 467, post.

[71] Until 1959 there was thought to be a remaining procedural distinction: *Fowler v. Lanning* [1959] 1 Q.B. 426, [1959] 1 All E.R. 290.

[72] See p. 452, post.

[73] *Young v. Queensland Trustees* (1956) 99 C.L.R. 560; *Pavey & Matthews Pty Ltd v. Paul* [1985] 3 N.S.W.L.R. 114, (1987) 69 A.L.R. 577, on which see Ibbetson, 8 OJLS 312.

[74] *Forms of Action*, p.2.

[75] *Leakey v. National Trust* [1980] 1 All E.R. 17 at 26, per Megaw LJ, echoing *United Australia Ltd v. Barclays Bank Ltd* [1941] A.C. 1 at 29, per Lord Atkin. For the continuing influence of forms of action in public law, see p. 175, post.

[76] *Sir Robert McAlpine & Sons Ltd v. Minimax Ltd* [1970] 1 Lloyd's Rep. 397 at 422, per Thesiger LJ.

Further reading

Pollock & Maitland, vol. II, pp. 558-597

Milsom HFCL, pp. 33-38, 243-246

F. W. Maitland, *The Forms of Action at Common Law* (1909, repr. 1962)

R. C. Van Caenegem, *Royal Writs in England from the Conquest to Glanvill* (77 SS, 1959)

D. Sutherland, 'Mesne Process upon Personal Actions in the early Common Law' (1966) 82 LQR 482-496

G. D. G. Hall and E. de Haas, *Early Registers of Writs* (87 SS, 1970)

J. H. Baker, 'Original Writs and Mesne Process' (1978) 94 SS 85-92

TRESPASS AND CASE

H. G. Richardson and G. O. Sayles, 'The Writ of Trespass' (1941) 60 SS cviii-cxxxiv

A. K. R. Kiralfy, *The Action on the Case* (1957), pp. 1-54

S. F. C. Milsom, 'Trespass from Henry III to Edward III' (1958) 74 LQR 195-224, 407-436, 561-590 (repr. in SHCL 1-90)

M. J. Prichard, 'Trespass, Cases and the Rule in Williams v. Holland' [1964] CLJ 234-253

T. G. Watkin, 'The Significance of "In Consimili Casu"' (1979) 23 AJLH 283-311

A. Harding, 'The Origins of Trespass, Tort and Misdemeanour' (1981) 96 SS xxxii-lviii

Table A. Principal types of original writ

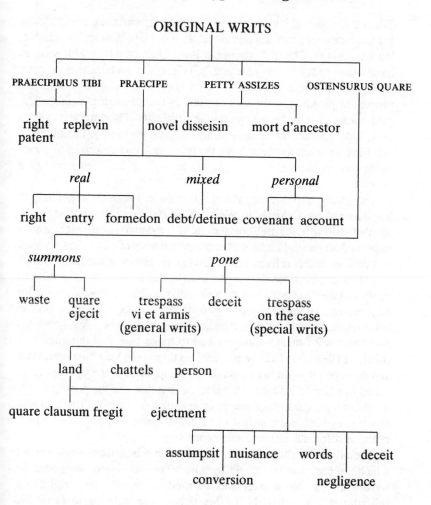

5. The Jury and Pleading

When the medieval law student had learned the writs, the next stage of his education was to learn pleading. 'It is one of the most honourable, laudable and profitable things in our law,' Littleton advised his son, 'to have a knowledge of fine pleading.'[1] This was an understatement, even in the fifteenth century. The common law had developed through the process of pleading, and was embodied in the forms of pleading. The year-books seem to be occupied with little else. Pleading was not, as now, a preliminary exercise in draftsmanship pursued in chambers; it was the core of the advocate's art, the prime task undertaken by a lawyer in open court, the end to which legal training was for several centuries directed.

The occasion for the creation of this science, a science taught only in England and used chiefly in Westminster Hall, was the appearance of another English institution, the jury. Systems of justice which depended on general oaths, and supernatural tests of oaths, had no need of pleading in any refined sense; God could not be interrogated. God would choose between the parties, but He could not be told the rules to apply or asked to reveal His reasons. Divine intervention by its nature stopped short of finding facts or making law. Juries, too, would choose between parties, and often inscrutably; but they could be asked questions and could raise them. Lawyers had to make sure that the questions referred to these 'lay folk' were questions they could least misunderstand; and questions thought to be outside the competence of the jury had to be raised in advance before the judges. At first this was the principal way in which legal questions came to be considered in court. The common law was refined and clarified in medieval times in discussions which occurred before the jury was summoned.

The original writs provided no more than a bare framework around which the common law might be built. The wording of the *praecipe* writs showed that a man was entitled to recover his 'right and inheritance', his chattels, or his debts, was entitled to have his covenants performed, and so on. The trespass writs showed that a man was entitled to redress for being beaten or imprisoned, or for having his goods taken or his land trodden on, and so forth. But the writs did not

---

[1] *Tenures*, s.534. This was printed in 1481, but written in the 1450s or 1460s.

say, and it was not their business to explain, what an inheritance was, let alone a 'right'; they did not indicate what circumstances made one person 'owe' money to another, or what constituted a covenant; they did not hint at whether a man might be beaten or imprisoned lawfully (as, by process of law), whether his goods might be taken lawfully (as, by distress for rent), or whether there might be justifications for going on his land (as, by invitation). Until such questions could be raised and answered in a systematic way, there could be no body of law in anything like the modern sense. Yet before the introduction of juries and pleading, such questions were not formally askable. So long as procedure inhibited the rational analysis of disputes into their component elements, the key words of litigation – words like 'inheritance', 'owe', 'covenant', 'force and arms' – remained innocent of legal meaning and incapable of technical definition or refinement. Inheritance can only become a legal concept when the pedigree can be discussed, and someone can be asked to rule whether one descendant or another has the right to succeed. Owing can only become a legal concept when the details of a transaction can be looked into, and someone asked to rule whether they result in a debt. And this is true of the whole law. 'Legal development consists in the increasingly detailed consideration of facts.'[2]

From 'Proof' to 'Trial'

The older methods of ending disputes are better referred to as methods of 'proof' than of 'trial', because trial suggests the weighing up of evidence and arguments by a tribunal acting judicially. Supernatural proofs and the oaths which they tested were absolute and inscrutable; no legal questions were asked, no reasons given, no facts found, no rules declared. This, together with the absence of records, explains why early law and custom is so elusive. The advent of royal justice in itself made little difference, because decision by proof was not confined to the ancient local courts. It was the only system anyone knew. The king's judges did not start out in the twelfth century with an inspired vision of things to come; they simply took over and continued what had gone before, what must have seemed part of the natural order of things. The ordeals of fire and water, wager of law, and the Norman judicial combat, thus became part of the procedure of the royal courts in their earliest phase. Nevertheless a different, more investigative approach began to

2 Milsom, 17 *Univ. Toronto Law Jo.* 1.

appear in the twelfth century in certain kinds of case, and its advantages very soon made the older ways obsolescent.

THE RISE OF THE JURY

A jury was a body of men sworn to give a true answer (*veredictum*, verdict) to some question. Now, the idea of swearing men to furnish true information was very old and not peculiar to England. It was the only way of collecting data needed for fiscal or administrative purposes: God could not be asked to produce suspects or count sheep. The inquest had roots in Scandinavia and in the old Carolingian empire. It may have been used before 1066 in both England and Normandy, though not for settling private disputes. Certainly the Norman kings used sworn inquests to uncover information of use to the Crown, an early instance being the enormous Domesday survey of the country in the 1080s. Much use was made of juries of accusation, sworn to inform the king's justices of suspected criminals without hiding anything;[3] once the suspects were produced, they were tried in the old way, by water or fire. Under the Normans the jury might rather have been seen as a technique for relentless government prying than as the bastion of liberty which later theory made it. Yet what was found effective for kings was soon demanded by subjects, and kings were willing to provide it, at a price. Under Henry II the petty assizes and the grand assize each provided an escape from battle, an institution already losing favour in the twelfth century;[4] the assize in this sense was simply a form of jury, taking its name from the ordinance ('assize') under which it was introduced.[5] The twelve free and lawful men mentioned in the writ were summoned to 'make recognition' of the facts, and were sometimes called recognitors. The classical form of 'petty jury' appeared first in criminal suits, where its use was warranted by the complaint of a breach of the king's peace; when appeals of felony and actions of trespass separated in the thirteenth century,[6] the mode of trial remained closely similar in each kind of proceeding, and it was also used upon indictments for crime. In a trespass action, when parties pleaded to issue – nearly always by the

---

3 This became the 'grand jury', a permanent institution from Henry II's time until the present century: p. 576, post.

4 *Glanvill*, ii.7. *Glanvill* refers to both kinds of assize as royal favours (*beneficia*). The grand assize (1179) was the later and more solemn of the two procedures: four knights were first summoned to elect the twelve knights who were to give the verdict.

5 For the petty assizes, see pp. 149 (utrum, 1164), 267 (novel disseisin, 1166 or late 1170s), 267-268 (mort d'ancestor, 1176), post. For the grand assize, see p. 266, post.

6 See p. 70, ante.

defendant simply pleading Not guilty – a writ of *venire facias* was sent to the sheriff commanding him to cause twelve men of the neighbourhood, unrelated to the parties, to come before the court to 'make recognition': that is, to enquire into the matter and state the truth therein. This body of twelve was called a jury (*jurata*), because it was put on oath before giving its verdict; its members were jurors (*juratores*), persons who have been sworn.

From the time of its introduction the province of the jury steadily increased, as the old forms of proof were laid aside. Its prominent place in criminal procedure was a direct result of the decision of the Church in 1215 to stop ordeals.[7] Judicial combat was not affected by that decision; although the Church disliked it, the procedure was less mystic and required no clerical participation. Battle therefore remained available in appeals of felony; but it was distrusted by complainants and judges alike, and it soon went out of general use.[8] Battle survived also in writs of right; but there too demandants were driven to alternative remedies to avoid it.[9] Its disuse enabled battle to survive in retirement until the nineteenth century; it was abolished only after a gauntlet was thrown into a startled Court of King's Bench in 1818.[10] The one archaic method of proof which survived to any consequential extent in the royal courts was wager of law,[11] or compurgation, which was regularly used in actions of debt and detinue until the beginning of the seventeenth century. The defendant took an oath that he did not owe the money, or withhold the goods, and produced eleven compurgators to testify to his credibility. The system had made good sense when the compurgators had been neighbours acting, in effect, as judges of fact. But a system which worked in local courts, and in the eyre, did not survive the centralisation of royal justice in the two benches. The nisi prius system was not extended to compurgation, and it was unrealistic to expect eleven men to be brought from far afield in routine cases. At Westminster, therefore, the procedure became partly fictionalised. The defendant could hire professional compurgators to help him out, and by

---

[7]   See p. 6, ante; p. 579, post.

[8]   See p. 14, ante; pp. 574-575, post.

[9]   See p. 266, post. For a minute description of the procedure, see *Staunton v. Prior of Lenton* (1330) 98 SS 546; M. J. Russell, 1 JLH 111.

[10]   *Ashford v. Thornton* (1818) 1 B. & Ald. 405; Stat. 59 Geo. III, c.46. The last previous wager of battle in a writ of right was in 1638, but the fight was stopped at the last minute: *Claxton v. Lilburn* (1638) Cro. Car. 522. See also 94 SS *116*. In 1985 a defendant in the High Court of Justiciary in Scotland tried unsuccessfully to wage battle against the lord advocate, claiming that the 1819 statute applied only to England.

[11]   Originally the 'lesser law', the greater being the ordeal.

the end of the sixteenth century it was part of the official duty of the court porters to provide them, for a fee. Wager of law thereupon became, in reality, the single oath of the defendant, coupled with a ceremony for which the defendant paid; and this led to its decline even before 1600. Its complete avoidance was made possible by the extension of actions on the case to enable the recovery of debts.[12] During the seventeenth century it became obsolete and the procedures were forgotten; by 1680 it could be noted with satisfaction, in an unusual case when law was waged, that 'none could be persuaded or hired' to act as compurgators.[13] Wager of law had become a complete anachronism and was permitted to linger until the last century, alongside battle, only as a disused relic.

The story would have been rather different if the 1374 opinion had prevailed which allowed wager of law in actions on the case;[14] the opinion was rejected because of a preference for the jury in all cases of wrongdoing. That rejection was to facilitate great and unforeseen changes in later centuries, because plaintiffs over the course of time would exercise much ingenuity in expanding artificially the concept of trespass to secure jury trial. The popularity of the jury therefore provides the explanation for the eventual triumph of trespass over the older actions.

TRIAL BY JURY

It was obvious from its inception that the jury was to operate very differently from an ordeal. The jurors were independent neighbours, summoned by the sheriff, who were to search their memories and use their minds. What may not have been so obvious was how differently they were to function from the party's own suit or compurgators.[15] The jurors' oath to say the truth is not greatly different from that of a witness, or even from that of a compurgator who swears to his belief in the truth of an oath. Certainly, like witnesses and compurgators, their chief qualification was that they were supposed to know somewhat of the truth before they came to court; hence the rules requiring them to be drawn from the vicinity where the facts were alleged. But were they to speak collectively and inscrutably, like compurgators, or were they to be

---

12   See pp. 389-394, post.

13   *Cristy v. Sparks* (1680) B. & M. 223. A practical manual of 1623 said 12 oath-helpers were needed, while one of the 1650s (printed 1694) said 6: B. & M. 222, 224. The true number was 11.

14   See p. 75, ante.

15   Cf. *R v. Wight* (1321) 85 SS 76 at 77, per Passeley J.

examined individually like witnesses? *Bracton* was quite clear that, in criminal cases (where they were then chiefly used), the judges should examine the jurors one by one and evaluate their answers.[16] The early records occasionally show judges putting questions to different jurors and even to different juries in the same matter, reserving to themselves the final decision. Those judges did not see a clear distinction between finding the facts and applying the law. Yet they did perceive some difference between jurors and witnesses; we hear of evidence being given to the jurors, and *Bracton* speaks of jurors as having a judicial function.

By the late fourteenth century, however, it was obvious that the collective, judicial character of the jury was going to prevail. Juries were being summoned not merely to answer questions, but to try sworn evidence in court. Although jurors were still allowed, even expected, to inform themselves before coming to court,[17] by the 1380s it was clearly an irregularity to communicate with them once they were sworn other than by giving evidence in open court.[18] If the jurors were spoken to, or treated to food and drink, by either party, their verdict could be quashed and a new trial ordered. The sequestration of the jury became a regular practice as improper influence grew rife, and it was enforced with such rigidity that its members became as prisoners to the court. After their charge, the jurors were confined 'without meat, drink, fire or candle', or conversation with others, until they were agreed; and if they could not agree they were supposed to be carried round the circuit in a cart until they did. The merest suspicion of misbehaviour was punishable, and we read of Tudor jurors being fined for eating sweets.[19] So far was the quasi-judicial theory of jury trial carried, that by the middle of the sixteenth century it was irregular for jurors even to inform each other of facts without giving formal evidence.[20] The constraints of discomfort were primarily intended to encourage unanimity; for, although traces are still found until 1346 of the earlier view that the judges were to resolve

---

[16] *Bracton*, vol. II, p. 404. There is a mordant allusion to Pontius Pilate, who accepted a verdict without satisfying himself as to the facts.

[17] In 1427 it was agreed in parliament that parties in assizes should be given the names in advance so that they might inform them of their titles: Rot. Parl., vol. IV, p. 328, no.30.

[18] See *Griffith v. Weston* (1387) Y.B. Trin. 11 Ric. II, p. 29, pl.10, at p. 35; *Anon.* (1389) 100 SS xxviii-xxix; *Raynell v. Cruwys* (1388) Y.B. Pas. 12 Ric. II, p. 182, pl.21, at p. 185; *Pole's Case* (1391) 88 SS 64; *Wantley v. White* (1391) ibid. 80. The critical moment was the taking of the jurors' oath.

[19] E.g. *Earl of Arundel's Case* (1500) 94 SS *113*; *Mucklowe's Case* (1576) Plowd. at 519. In 1587 four jurors were fined merely for being in possession of raisins and plums: HLS MS. 16, fo. 253v, pl.85.

[20] *Anon.* (1557) Dyer's circuit reports, Inner Temple MS. Petyt 511.13, fo. 36; *Graves v. Short* (1598) Cro. Eliz. 616.

any disagreements, if necessary taking majority verdicts,[21] all the verdicts in the rolls were (or were recorded as being) the unqualified verdicts of twelve. A leading case of 1367 put the matter beyond doubt; rejecting the earlier precedents, the court held a majority verdict to be void.[22]

Maitland thought the judges had adopted the unanimity requirement as 'the line of least resistance';[23] it saved them from having to make awkward decisions. But the consequences ran deeper than they knew: the trial of the facts had become procedurally isolated from the application of the law. It was to become a constitutional principle sacred to generations of Englishmen, and later to a new world as well,[24] that men should be tried by their peers, and that judges should not meddle with questions of fact. But perhaps the most far-reaching effect was that it resulted in the elaboration of substantive law. The decision as to what were material questions of fact for the jury necessitated a decision as to what the law was. However, such questions of law were not in medieval times raised after the facts had been ascertained by trial, but in the course of deciding what the jury was to be asked to try. This is where we must return to the history of pleading.

Medieval Pleading and Legal Development

Pleading began when the defendant appeared at the bar of the court, in person or by attorney, and the plaintiff stated his demand or complaint. In the royal courts the plaintiff's opening pleading was called a 'count', the French word for a tale or story. Its main object was to amplify the matter outlined in the writ, and to reveal the details of the cause of action. Before the middle of the thirteenth century a profession of counters had emerged,[25] whose business was to compose counts and pronounce them before the judges in the French set forms of the royal courts. Numerous written collections of precedents of counts (the *Narrationes* and *Novae narrationes*) were produced in the thirteenth and fourteenth centuries.

---

21   E.g. Fitz. Abr., *Verdit*, pl. 40 (eyre of Nottingham, 1329); *Anon.* (1346) Y.B. Mich. 20 Edw. III, pt ii, p. 555, pl.110.

22   Y.B. Mich. 41 Edw. III, fo. 31, pl.36; also in Lib. Ass. 41 Edw. III, pl.11.

23   Pollock & Maitland, vol. II, p. 627.

24   The United States Constitution (1787), art. 3, required crimes to be tried by jury, and the 7th Amendment (1789) required 'the right of trial by jury' to be preserved in civil actions for more than $20.

25   The counters of the Common Bench became in the 14th century the 'serjeants at law': see p. 180, post. The term was dropped in the other courts, where pleading could be performed by apprentices.

In earliest times, drawing the count correctly was the hardest part of pleading. The defendant had merely to deny ('defend') everything in the count to reach the proof stage. Alternatively he could take 'exception' to the count for insufficiency, or variance from the writ, or for want of capacity to sue. Neither the general defence nor the exception raised substantive points of law, so long as the count was in a regular form. The rise of the jury changed the old order of things completely in civil cases.[26] The counters no longer went away when they had recited their counts, but stayed to help formulate the question for the jury. This was called producing the 'issue', which was the question on which the dispute turned. The general denial remained the defendant's usual course; it produced the 'general issue', under which the truth of every material allegation in the count was put in question. But a more precise issue could be produced if the parties agreed to stake everything on a more specific point. This was pleading, properly so called. Bracton referred to such a move as a jeopardy (*jocus partitus*), a chess term meaning a set problem; and in the earliest year-books it is called a 'peremptory exception', because it bound the party whatever the outcome.[27] The compilers of the year-books were greatly interested in the problems of pleading, which had become the main preoccupation of the Bar and the focus of study in the law school which attached itself to the inns of court in the mid-fourteenth century. Bracton's chess metaphor was well chosen. Whereas the twelfth-century *Dialogue of the Exchequer* had referred to litigation as a game of hazard, it had become a game of skill, played out by the masters of pleading at the bar of the Common Pleas.

REACHING THE ISSUE

The issue (*exitus*) was the end and object of pleading, and the way out into the country where the answer would be found at nisi prius. A case only reached this stage when the parties had fixed on a point which would settle the matter one way or the other; and logic taught that this occurred as soon as some affirmative proposition was met by a direct negative. The logic worked very simply. The plaintiff narrated his facts. The defendant had only two logical courses open to him: he had either to deny those facts (or one of them), or admit them and show that they did not entitle the plaintiff to succeed. This provided him with four possible pleas. A denial of all the facts was a general traverse, and it

---

[26] The general denial remained the norm in criminal trials, to which the system of pleading about to be described had no application. See p. 594, post.

[27] The procedural exception was called a 'dilatory exception' (later a dilatory plea), because it merely delayed proceedings.

produced the general issue. The denial of one material fact was a special traverse, and it put that fact in issue. If the defendant admitted the facts, he might deny that in law they amounted to a case against him; this was a demurrer, and it produced an issue of law, no facts being in dispute. Or he might admit the plaintiff's facts but introduce further facts to explain them away; this was a confession and avoidance. This fourth kind of plea did not produce an issue, because it did not indicate any dispute; the plaintiff had to reply to the avoidance, the defendant's new facts, using the same four logical choices. The pleadings continued in this way until a fact was denied, or a party demurred; since a party could not vary from anything he had previously pleaded, or plead more than one matter,[28] only a few moves were usually necessary.[29]

An example will illustrate the various possibilities. Suppose the plaintiff brings an action of trespass for beating his servant so that he lost her services. The defendant may tender the general issue by pleading Not guilty, which puts on trial every allegation in the count. Or he may traverse a single point, for instance by denying that the person allegedly beaten was the plaintiff's servant. Or he may admit that he beat the plaintiff's servant, and allege new facts: perhaps that he was a sheriff arresting her by virtue of a *capias*. Only in this third case is there no issue, because nothing is as yet contested. In that case the plaintiff must answer the new facts. He may reply generally, so that every new allegation in the plea may be disputed at the trial: for instance by showing that the sheriff was not acting as a sheriff but was brawling. Or he may traverse a single point, perhaps by denying that he was sheriff when the beating occurred. Or he may confess and avoid: for instance, by admitting that the sheriff had a *capias* to arrest the servant but asserting that he had used excessive violence. And so on, until an affirmative is negatived. All assertions which are not denied have to be treated as if they are true, because their truth cannot come into question if the parties do not make an issue of them.[30] A fortiori, the court has no judicial knowledge of anything which is not pleaded, nor can such a thing be put to the jury. The pleadings, therefore, define conclusively what is in dispute.

---

[28]   See p. 104, post.

[29]   The names of the stages in pleading were: count *or* declaration (plaintiff), plea *or* bar (defendant), replication (plaintiff), rejoinder (defendant), surrejoinder (plaintiff), rebutter (defendant), surrebutter (plaintiff).

[30]   E.g. *Dunman v. Weldon* (1329) B. & M. 210 at 211, per Scrop CJ.

ORAL AND 'TENTATIVE' PLEADING

When the science of pleading was at its zenith, pleadings were exchanged orally by counsel at the bar. After the clerk had enrolled them on the parchment record, turning the words into Latin, they became binding and unamendable.[31] Until that happened, oral pleas were flexible and hypothetical, advanced tentatively for discussion rather than peremptorily laid down. The possibility of making tentative pleas,[32] with a view to possible withdrawal after discussion, enabled questions of law to be raised in court at the pleading stage. Suppose in our example of battery that the plaintiff wishes to question the amount of force which may be used in effecting an arrest. Is it for the defendant to say that he used no more force than was necessary, or for the plaintiff to reply that the force was excessive, and what precise words should be used? In deciding such questions, the serjeants and the court were primarily thinking ahead to the trial and the practicalities of proof; but they would inevitably have to make assumptions of law. The wording of pleas reflected the state of legal thought. Suppose, again, that our plaintiff wishes to plead that the *capias* was improperly obtained; in deciding whether he may do so, someone may have to decide whether in law process can be invalidated by extrinsic circumstances, whether sheriffs are excused even if they execute invalid process, and whether sheriffs must verify their authority at their peril. These are sophisticated questions of a kind which could never have been contemplated in the days of ordeals. They came to be asked because they were beyond the knowledge of common jurors, who were summoned to speak to the facts, not to state the law.

Instead of continuing the pleadings in this way, a party had the option of demurring in law: that is, admitting all the facts alleged by his opponent and saying that the law did not compel him to respond to them because they amounted to nothing.[33] That raised an issue in law for the court alone to decide. Demurrers were sometimes entered of record; but in medieval times the judges were extremely reluctant to decide them, and the usual effect of a formal demurrer was to confirm

---

[31] The critical moment was not the writing down, but the handing in of the rolls at the end of term.

[32] This helpful expression was coined by Maitland: 20 SS lxvii.

[33] *Demurrer* in law French meant to abide or dwell, and the original sense in the context of tentative pleading was that of sticking to one's pleading instead of moving on. In later usage, however, it was the opponent of a pleading who demurred, and the proponent 'joined in demurrer'.

and perpetuate the uncertainty which had occasioned it.[34] What happened more often in practice was that the demurrer was made tentatively, so as to generate the kind of unrecorded discussion just mentioned. If opinion seemed against the demurrer, it would be withdrawn and a plea pleaded; if in favour, the disputed plea would be withdrawn and another plea tried out. Discussion was never of the verified facts, only of formulations of supposed facts which could be tried later.[35] And the system did not usually require the judges to give reasoned judgments disposing of the case, as they did in later times; their role was more that of umpire and adviser. The judgment pronounced at the end of the case followed automatically from the verdict; it required no reasons, and could be entered up in chambers. Law reporters had no interest in such judgments, because they threw no light on the law. They wanted to know what happened to tentative pleas when they were tried out before the assembled legal expertise of Westminster Hall. It is from these rambling, technical, and often inconclusive, debates about hypothetical situations, distorted by the French shorthand of the reporters, that we have to extract the developing assumptions of the common lawyers.

JUDGE, JURY, AND MEDIEVAL LEGAL DEVELOPMENT
If we can view the process just described as making law, then any law which resulted was made informally, off the record, and in a way which did not bind anybody; but perhaps we should do better not to view the system as regularly making law at all. Certainly legal development was not the chief concern of the lawyers who took part in it. Counsel were retained to win cases, not to advance jurisprudence. Judges seem to have been as embarrassed by new questions of law as they were by questions of fact, and did what they could to avoid making decisions if there was a division of opinion on the bench. How far it was appropriate to delve into the facts of particular cases in order to make new distinctions was not predetermined; and on the whole the judges preferred, in the interests of clarity and certainty, not to allow it. It was better, said the judges, to suffer a mischief in an individual case than the 'inconvenience' (inconsistency or unpredictability) which would follow from admitting

---

[34]   Arnold estimates that only 1 in 3 were decided in 14th-century trespass cases: 100 SS xxvii. A rough analysis of the 12 rolls for 1493-95 gives a similar figure for all cases (4 out of 13): CP 40/923-934. In 1517-23, the proportion had risen to 35 out of 77: LPCL 475.

[35]   For a modern analogy, see *Donoghue v. Stevenson* [1932] A.C. 562, where the appeal was on the pleadings. No one will ever know whether there really was a snail in the ginger-beer bottle, but this factual uncertainty makes no difference to the force of the precedent.

exceptions to general rules.[36] Special pleading was therefore restricted, and wherever possible parties were driven to plead the general issue, leaving all to the jury. The jury were expected to do substantial justice, and of course they could do so without altering the law. Exceptions were made only when it was clear that the 'lay folk' ran the risk of error through ignorance of the law, where the merits were more technical than factual, or where the issue was properly narrowed by a justification.[37] Thus, if a defendant in battery wished to plead self-defence, he had to plead it specially, because on a general plea of Not guilty the jurors would only be expected to investigate the fact of beating: indeed, in 1321 Stanton J rebuked members of a jury as 'wicked rascals' for seeking to return a verdict of self-defence on a plea of Not guilty.[38] Similarly, if a defendant in trespass to land sought to rely on some property right, it had to be pleaded specially, to divert the jurors' attention from the physical act complained of in the count to the real question of title. Such exceptions were made for practical reasons, not on the ground that it would be useful to know the law. In time, special pleading found its own standard forms, such as the plea of self-defence, and attempts to raise new kinds of question by special pleading were warmly contested. The longest survival of the old attitude is in the criminal trial, where to this day special pleading is forbidden. The prisoner always took the general issue, Not guilty, leaving everything to the jury; as a consequence criminal law could not be revealed or refined through tentative pleading.[39]

It was all very well to cast the burden of decision as far as possible on to the jury, and to bury legal questions, but what if the jurors themselves demanded to know the law? They had every moral right to do so, at least in those actions where they were liable to serious penalties if they gave a false verdict. 'We are not men of law,' bemoaned a jury in 1314 who had been asked to find whether land granted by an abbot to a layman was 'free alms' or lay fee.[40] They might ask to give a 'special verdict'; that is, to state the facts in detail

---

36   See 94 SS *38*; and the quotation on p. 369, post. For a modern analogy, see *The Chikuma* [1981] 1 All E.R. 652, [1981] 1 W.L.R. 314, per Lord Bridge (urging the courts in commercial cases to follow 'clear and consistent principles and steadfastly refuse to be blown off course by the supposed merits of individual cases').

37   That is, where the defendant admitted the act complained of but justified it.

38   *Lacer v. John, servant of Serjeant Cambridge* (1321) 86 SS 142 at 143; they then found the defendant guilty of battery. See also 100 SS xiii-xv.

39   See pp. 594-596, post.

40   *Abbot of Tewkesbury v. Calewe* (1314) 39 SS 158 at 161. After a mystifying discussion, Bereford CJ told them, 'Say what you feel'.

and 'pray the discretion of the court' as to the result. A statute of 1285 made it the right of jurors in an assize of novel disseisin to refuse to give a general verdict 'so that they do show the truth of the deed and pray aid of the justices'.[41] There was a particular reason for allowing this latitude in novel disseisin: the issue was fixed by the words of the writ. In other actions, however, the special verdict was virtually stifled by the middle of the fourteenth century.[42] If jurors were given complete freedom to throw questions back at the court, the courts would have been forced into making formal legal decisions, on the record, which they preferred not to make. A compromise solution, which may have been in use in the fourteenth century, was to allow tentative special verdicts, so that after legal direction the verdict could be entered generally one way or the other; this kept the question off the record, and therefore away from the court at Westminster. But this practice gave way to the trial judge's direction as to the law, a statement which similarly escaped the record and avoided becoming a source of later argument in the same case or a precedent in future cases. Directions were to become, in much later times, subject to scrutiny after trial,[43] and in the sphere of criminal law the principal vehicle for legal development. In medieval times, however, the machinery for such scrutiny did not exist; nothing said at the trial, either by the judge or the witnesses, was part of the record, and trials were seldom reported.

Under this regime, formal questions of law arose only from pleadings, the hypothetical formulae advanced before trial, rather than from the facts as found. In those actions where juries were not used, pleading remained at its primeval stage, and the law stood still. Thus, in actions of debt on a contract, defendants invariably pleaded the general issue and often waged their law; for centuries this unchanging procedure prevented questions about the law of contract from being asked. The medieval law of debt was a law of procedure and little more, because it was a survival of the ancient pattern of lawsuit.[44] Even in jury cases, if special pleading was outlawed, questions could similarly be kept away from legal consideration; that is why, for instance, questions of fault in trespass remained largely unexplored before the nineteenth century.[45]

---

41   Statute of Westminster II 1285, c.30.

42   See Arnold, 18 AJLH 270-274; Baker, 94 SS *158*. See also Rot. Parl., vol. II, p. 203, para. 22 (rejection in 1348 of petition to allow special verdicts more widely).

43   See p. 100, post.

44   See p. 367, post.

45   See pp. 456-459, post.

The System Transformed

In the sixteenth century profound changes occurred in the common-law system, and especially in the procedures associated with judicial law-making. The most visible result was that pleading became, as now, the beginning of the litigation lawyer's task rather than the end. We now take this for granted. It has been widely accepted since Tudor times, and recently declared on high legal authority,[46] that it is generally a more economical arrangement to try the facts first if they are unclear. This particular result has often been linked with the introduction of paper pleadings during the fifteenth and sixteenth centuries. Paper drafts saved trouble when common forms were used, and aided the memory when complex matter was pleaded; moreover they focused attention on the Latin words, as they would be entered, rather than on the French as spoken. But the practice can be traced back as far as the thirteenth century,[47] and it has no bearing on the change under consideration because the paper plea was no more binding than the oral plea, and did not preclude discussion in court. The real change came when paper pleas could no longer be debated in court with the possibility of amendment, so that tentative pleading went out of use. This occurred during the sixteenth century, and one cause may have been the Statute of Jeofails of 1540.[48] The Act had been passed in the hope of preventing objections to trivial errors of form in pleading, by providing that formal exceptions could only be taken on demurrer. The party disposed to quibble about form therefore had to admit all the facts and stake his case on the technicality, and it was thought this would seldom be risked. But the measure backfired, and led to an increase in formal demurrers. The courts then decided that it would prejudice any decision they might have to make as judges if they gave opinions on pleading before demurrer, and so tentative pleading was disallowed. Elizabethan courts were still asked on occasion to allow tentative debates, but they normally refused; and by Charles I's time the year-book type of discussion was a thing of the past.[49] Had this happened in isolation, the result would have been to stifle the principal means of legal discussion in court. In fact it was only made possible by other changes in the conduct of litigation. The sixteenth century saw a new judicial confidence, a willingness to make authoritative decisions, and a

---

[46] *Tilling v. Whiteman* [1980] A.C. 1 at 17, 25; *Allen v. Gulf Oil Refining Ltd* [1981] A.C. 1001 at 1010, 1022.

[47] See 57 SS ci-cii (1290s).

[48] Stat. 32 Hen. VIII, c.30.

[49] *Anon.* (1641) March N.C. 156, pl.224. See also 94 SS *156.*

corresponding desire in the legal profession and its clientele to have the law clearly stated upon known or admitted facts. The formal demurrer was one way of achieving that result, but it was not the best way for a party with a meritorious case, since it involved abandoning any case he might have on the facts;[50] the important change lay in finding ways of discussing the legal effect of facts after they had been found by the jury.

MOTIONS IN BANC

The procedure whereby questions could be raised after the trial, by motions 'in banc' to the court at Westminster,[51] existed in medieval times, but was limited to badly joined issues (jeofails) or formal defects in the trial, such as misconduct by jurors. From the late fifteenth century, however, it was extended to enable substantive questions of law to be argued after verdict. There were three basic forms of motion in banc: the motion in arrest of judgment, the motion for judgment *non obstante veredicto*, and the motion for a new trial.

The motion in arrest of judgment was at first the commonest. It was made by the defendant after a verdict for the plaintiff, on the ground that, even though the facts alleged by the plaintiff had been conclusively found to be true, they disclosed no cause of action on which the plaintiff could succeed. Such a motion would have been of no use in connection with the old actions of debt or trespass *vi et armis*, because the facts were stated in the count in general words and in common form, so that unless a plaintiff had experimented with some fanciful novelty there was nothing new to argue about. A motion in arrest depended on special facts, which had to be on the record. Two developments brought the procedure into its own. One was the rise of actions on the case, for in them the plaintiff's 'special case' was infinitely variable and bursting with legal questions. In medieval times a new action on the case had been assailable either by a 'plea in abatement' to quash the writ as invalid, or by a demurrer to the count;[52] but by 1500 the more convenient procedure was to take the objection by motion in arrest of

---

50   Coke learned the lesson in his first case, *Lord Cromwell's Case* (1581) 4 Co. Rep. 12 at 14 ('never at first demur in law when after the trial of the matters in fact the matters in law will be saved to you').

51   For the mechanics of the procedure, see p.159, post.

52   E.g. *Waldon v. Mareschal* (1369) B. & M. 359 (plea in abatement); *Somerton v. Colles* (1433) B. & M. 385, 388 (plea in abatement); *Shipton v. Dogge* (1442) B. & M. 391 (demurrer to bill).

judgment, so that the defendant could have a trial first.[53] Much of the modern common law arose from such arguments, as actions on the case gradually replaced those *praecipe* actions in which tentative pleading had made little impact. The second development was the resurgence of the special verdict. When the policy had been to refuse to accept such verdicts, lawyers had sometimes achieved the same object by means of a 'demurrer to the evidence'; this meant in effect that the parties agreed on the facts as disclosed by the evidence at the trial, and had them entered on the record in Latin, discharging the jury and leaving the decision to the court.[54] By the middle of the sixteenth century, however, the courts relented and began to allow special verdicts to be given in special actions, such as actions on the case, and on issues raised by special pleading.[55] By Coke's time it was a rule that the court could not refuse a special verdict in any action. The terms of the verdict were settled by counsel and entered on the roll, to be argued in banc on motion; this permitted a consideration of more detailed problems than appeared from the pleadings.

After the mid-seventeenth century, a similar result was commonly obtained by persuading the trial judge to reserve a point of law for the court in banc. A general verdict was then taken for the plaintiff, but with leave to set it aside if the court decided in the defendant's favour. If the point arose on facts not of record, the parties settled a 'special case' or 'case stated' for the opinion of the court. This was an agreed statement of the facts, signed by opposing counsel; it operated in practically the same way as a special verdict, but was less expensive since the case was not entered on the record.[56] It later became common for the judge to put specific questions to the jury in order to ascertain the factual basis of their verdict; the answers were not part of the verdict, which was still recorded in general terms, but could be used in banc.

---

[53] E.g. *Sarger's Case* (1481) B. & M. 513; *Johnson v. Baker* (1493) B. & M. 399 at 400; *Pykeryng v. Thurgoode* (1532) B. & M. 411.

[54] See 100 SS xxvii (rare in 14th century); 94 SS *111-112, 158* (slightly more common in early Tudor period). An example, the object of which is unclear, is *Orwell v. Mortoft* (1505) B. & M. 406.

[55] *Anon.* (1553) Benl. 37, pl.69 (only on general issue); *Burgh v. Warnford* (1553) Dalison Rep., BL MS. Harley 5141, fo. 12; *Panel v. Moor* (1555) Plowd. 91; stated as a general rule in *Dowman v. Vavasor* (1586) 9 Co. Rep. 7 at 11-14. Cf. *Anon.* (1531) Bro. N.C. 187 (denied).

[56] See Prichard, [1960] CLJ at 92-95; and p. 160, post. Special verdicts remained in use where parties wished to reserve the possibility of a writ of error by having the facts recorded.

A motion for judgment *non obstante veredicto* was made by the plaintiff after a verdict for the defendant.[57] Its scope was far more restricted than the motion in arrest, because the only situation where the plaintiff was entitled to judgment despite an adverse verdict was where the defendant had confessed a good cause of action and pleaded an avoidance which was bad in law. Moreover, it was not allowed where the defect in the plea could be rectified by amendment; in that case, a 'repleader' was ordered, leading to a fresh trial of the correct issue.

The court could not upon motion increase or mitigate the damages awarded by the jury, since the award was based on facts not on the record; though there was an exception in the case of mayhem, where the personal injury was apparent to the sight.[58] Nevertheless, the rolls show that plaintiffs often remitted part of their damages, and it has been shown that before the seventeenth century this may reflect pressure from the court in banc to mitigate awards considered excessive.[59]

The motion for a new trial was the last and most extensive of the methods of raising questions of law after verdict. Its medieval purpose of upsetting verdicts by reason of procedural defects on the face of the record, such as recorded misconduct by jurors,[60] remained its principal purpose until the later seventeenth century. And it was limited by the judges' insistence that a verdict could not be set aside unless the invalidity of the trial appeared on the record.[61] But in the Restoration period the courts edged back from this principle by allowing motions, first on the basis of affidavits of misconduct,[62] and then on the trial judge's certificate that he considered the verdict contrary to the evidence.[63] This permitted control both of the substantive finding and of the award of damages. By the eighteenth century a new trial could be obtained on the further grounds of misdirection by the trial judge, or a

---

[57]   For a rare case of a plaintiff moving in arrest of judgment, on the grounds that his own count was bad, see *Blyth v. Topham* (1607) B. & M. 570. This was done to save costs.

[58]   Even then the court would only intervene if all the material facts were available: *Burford v. Dadwel* (1669) B. & M. 334. For the general rule, see *Bonham v. Lord Sturton* (1554) 1 Dyer 105; *Hawkins v. Sciet* (1622) Palm. 314.

[59]   R.H. Helmholz, 103 LQR at 629-634.

[60]   E.g. the cases cited on p. 89, ante. In such cases the facts were recorded in the *postea*, the document containing the verdict sent back to Westminster.

[61]   *Hall v. White* (1607) 1 Bro. & Goulds. 207; *Martyn v. Jackson* (1674) 3 Keb. 398.

[62]   *Goodman v. Catherington* (1664) 1 Sid. 235.

[63]   *St Bar v. Williamson* (1674) 3 Keb. 351. Cf. *Slade's Case* (1648) Style 138, where Bacon J said the Common Pleas had already begun to allow such motions, but the King's Bench thought it 'arbitrary'.

mistaken ruling as to the admission of material evidence.[64] It became the regular practice in such cases to require a report from the trial judge to the court in banc, and this accounts for the judges beginning in the eighteenth century to take notes of evidence. The judge's views were generally followed as to whether a verdict was against the weight of the evidence, though the full court could refuse a new trial at its discretion. The new procedure was not confined to questions of fact, but also enabled legal discussion in banc of matters outside the record; and this technique was perfected by Lord Mansfield CJ, particularly as a means of refining commercial law. Mansfield would state 'very particularly and minutely, from his own notes taken down at the trial, (which he read to the audience verbatim,) the exact state of the facts as they came out upon the evidence', so that the question could be argued in banc.[65] Mansfield's techniques were not without contemporary controversy,[66] especially when he tried to extend them to the control of criminal juries.[67] Like the priests who had tinkered with ordeals in which they had lost faith, the judges had begun to impose strict limits on the authority of the jury; jurors no longer had 'an absolute despotic power', but their worst mistakes could be put right.[68] The motion for a new trial went much further in this direction than the other procedures, by throwing the whole case before the court and not merely the formalised phrases of the record; and, since the judge's version of the facts sometimes carried more weight than the verdict, it prepared the way for the demise of the civil jury.

Decline of the Common-Law System

By the seventeenth century the science of pleading had begun to degenerate from its original simplicity 'and to become a piece of nicety and curiosity'.[69] Hale CJ attributed the decline to the end of oral pleading: 'anciently pleading was at the bar, and then it did appear

---

[64] E.g. *Anon.* (1702) 2 Salk. 649, 6 Mod. Rep. 242.

[65] *Sanderson v. Rowles* (1767) 4 Burr. 2064 at 2067. Cf. Lord Mansfield's own remarks in *Bright v. Eynon* (1757) 1 Burr. 390. For his notebooks, see E. Heward, 92 LQR 438.

[66] Eldon also attacked Mansfield's use of the special case procedure as effectively stifling the possibility of appeal: p. 161, post.

[67] LPCL 311-312.

[68] *Ash v. Ash* (1696) Holt 701 at 702; Comb. 357, per Holt CJ, adding, 'for the jury are to try cases with the assistance of the judges, and ought to give reasons when required, that if they go upon any mistake they may be set right'.

[69] M. Hale, *History of the Common Law* (1971 ed.), p. 111.

plainly what was stood upon; and if the party did demur, he knew what he did. But pleading is now got all into paper and since that, of late, men make it but a snare and trap and piece of skill.[70] The reports amply bear him out. In the year-book period difficulties were eradicated before issue joined, and cases were rarely lost beyond salvation on points of mere form. It was indeed ironic if the result of the Statute of Jeofails 1540 had been to increase the use of catching demurrers and to accelerate the end of special pleading. No doubt the line between form and substance was not easy for a lawyer to see. There is a safety in forms and precedents which readily commends itself to any professional man who has to advise clients, and the judges who were responsible for the state of affairs lamented by Hale had conceived it their duty to maintain the forms of law. Coke CJ, writing in 1628, observed that 'more jangling and questions grow upon the manner of pleading, and exceptions to form, than upon the matter itself, and infinite causes [are] lost or delayed for want of good pleading'. But the lesson he drew was not that there should be a return to informality; rather that lawyers should be more precise. If form were neglected, he wrote elsewhere of writs, 'ignorance, the mother of error and barbarousness, will follow, and in the end all will be involved in confusion and subversion of the ancient law of the land'.[71]

The inflexibility of special pleading after the sixteenth century was one of the chief reasons for the decline which we must now trace.

LATIN AND COURT-HAND

When the plea rolls first started it was unthinkable that they should be in any language but Latin, the learned language of all Christendom, a language of certainty and elegance used for records of every kind. Their physical construction was designed to last: a clear, formal hand written on good parchment. Many of the earliest rolls have survived in almost pristine condition, a feat which will not be repeated by the flimsy records of our own day. Both the language and the set hand became immutable requirements of the common law. In 1588 a sheriff was fined for returning a writ in ordinary handwriting. The judges had good reason: court-hand can be read when very worn, whereas plain writing 'would be so worn in a dozen years that no man can read it'.[72] Proceedings in English could be reversed for error.[73] The language

---

70 *Anon.* (1672) Treby Rep., MS. in Middle Temple, 717.

71 Co. Inst., vol. I, p. 303; *Blackamore's Case* (1610) 8 Co. Rep. 156 at 159.

72 Goulds. 111.

73 E.g. *Grisling v. Wood* (1588) Cro. Eliz. 85.

requirement was attributed to the loose wording of a statute, but the need to render forms and statements into a dead language had the advantage of encouraging economy of words and precision of thought. Such features of the common-law system nevertheless tended to alienate the lay public, and they were carried too far.

The preciseness of Latin meant that the omission of a single down-stroke or contraction sign, or an error of Latin accidence, were fatal mistakes in a writ. Even the learned author of the new *Natura Brevium* once brought a writ which turned out to contain a grammatical error.[74] The slightest slip could affect the sense: thus in 1533 a convicted murderer was saved from the gallows by a single letter in the indictment.[75] The rendering of post-classical concepts into Latin was an endless source of trouble. English words could be used in conjunction with an *anglice* ('in English . . .') or *vocatus* ('called . . .'). The former was used to clarify an equivalent word: for instance, *tres argentei pixides pro nicotiano anglice* 'tobacco boxes'. The latter was used if there was no exact equivalent: for instance, *duo pocula vocata* 'tea pots'. In cases of real difficulty, the two were combined, as in *quatuor pocula more Japanie picta duplicatis marginatis anglice vocata* 'Japanned double tipped mugs'.[76] The clerk's worst headaches were eased by the publication in 1685 of a useful manual of 'words Latinised which you cannot find any Latin for in any dictionary', such as football-match (*pilae pedalis lusus*), cork-screw (*cochlea suberea*, which surely suggests a screw made of cork) or spatterdashes (*lutosae caligae amphibularos ex panno vulgari factae*).[77] A dead language, for all its virtues, imposed real practical difficulties on the living.

When eventually, in 1731, parliament abrogated the use of Latin and court-hand,[78] the remedy hurt as much as the disease. Pleaders thought it unsafe to depart from the grammatical constructions of the past, and so English pleadings read like schoolboy translations. The Latin names of writs had to be restored by amending legislation, because writs of 'he lurks' (*latitat*) or 'wherefore he impeded' (*quare impedit*) sounded ridiculous. More seriously, the literacy of attorneys declined, and many lawyers were cut off from any real understanding of the precedents on

---

[74] *Fitzherbert v. Welles* (1532) Spelman Rep. (93 SS) 15.

[75] *R v. Rogers and Walker* (1533) Spelman Rep. (93 SS) 52; LPCL 307 (*quidam* for *quidem*).

[76] Examples from *A Treatise on Trover* (1721), pp. 398-399. For an objection to arabic numerals, see *Hawkins v. Mills* (1674) 2 Lev. 102.

[77] G. Meriton, *Nomenclatura Clericalis* (1685).

[78] Stat. 4 Geo. II, c.26. There had been a similar measure in 1650, but it was disregarded at the Restoration.

which they remained vicariously dependent. One pleader saw such a decline that 'if our laws, pure and unsullied in themselves, receive many more changes, our properties will be as precarious in the hands of the most skilful lawyer as our lives are in the hands of the physician'.[79]

DOUBLE PLEADING

It was an axiom of the common law that a special plea could only be taken on a single point, so that one issue resulted.[80] Numerous explanations have been offered. In the quaint language of 1667 it was alleged to be 'pur avoider le stuffing del rolls ove multiplicity de matter'.[81] Another view was that it kept the laymen's task within their frail comprehension. Another was that it deterred liars. None of these is wholly convincing. The parties paid for the parchment. The jurors were often asked to try the general issue, and would then need to understand every facet of the case. And it was not always the case that double defences were mutually inconsistent: the buyer of a horse might honestly say that he was an infant, that the debt was statute barred, and that he had given something in satisfaction. The chief reason why the common law set its face against double pleading is that it was the only logically certain way of bringing the parties to a decisive issue. If there were two issues, there would be a problem if each party won one of them. Moroever, to each of two pleas a plaintiff might make two replications, and then in theory the pleadings might multiply in geometric progression. The single-point rule prevented this nightmarish possibility; and when it was first established, by the early fourteenth century, it may also have met the technical point that complex issues could not be tried at nisi prius.[82] Even so, the rule could sometimes work injustice if it prevented consistent defences from being raised, especially hard when plaintiffs were able to frame their declarations in several alternative ways.[83] In 1705, therefore, legislation was passed to enable defendants to plead several distinct pleas to the same cause of action with leave of the court.[84] The statute was widely used, and leave seems rarely to have been refused. It was even possible to plead

---

79   J. Mallory, *Modern Entries*, vol. II (1735), fo. 367v.

80   The rule only applied to each cause of action. In trespass to three cows the defendant could plead a different plea as to each cow; but not that he had distrained the three cows and also that he had bought them.

81   *Churche v. Brownewick* (1667) 1 Sid. 334.

82   Statute of Westminster II 1285, c.30. See 100 SS xii.

83   The practice of framing multiple 'counts' in a single declaration seems to have begun in the 17th century: B. & M. 473 n.17.

84   Stat. 4 & 5 Ann., c.3 [= c.16 in *Statutes at Large*], s. 4.

generally and specially in the same action, or to plead mutually inconsistent pleas. But the statute did not extend to plaintiffs' replications, and it did not allow a party both to plead and to demur. Neither did it, in strictness, permit double pleas; it permitted several pleas, and doubleness in one of several pleas remained demurrable.

GENERAL AND SPECIAL PLEADING

Pleading had originated as a means of controlling juries, by narrowing their terms of reference and excluding problems of law from their consideration. The new procedures, however, and especially motions for new trials, enabled juries to be controlled after they had pronounced, or even made them practically redundant (as where a formal verdict was taken subject to a point of law, or a special verdict was drawn up by counsel). Special pleading then became less necessary, and there was a resurgence of the general issue. The courts encouraged this by relaxing earlier rules of evidence which had restricted the defences which might be proved under the general issue. Under the new dispensation, a defendant in trespass could plead Not guilty and show in evidence what amounted to a confession and avoidance (such as self-defence).[85] And in ejectment, which had replaced the old real actions, the defendant was actually obliged to plead the general issue, so that questions of title, long enmeshed in the intricacies of archaic rules of pleading, became a matter of evidence to the jury.[86] During the Interregnum there was even a move to enable the general issue to be pleaded in all cases. That was not to be, for the present, but parliament recognised and assisted the trend, making provision for pleading the general issue in over a hundred statutory actions introduced between 1600 and 1750. The change is manifestly apparent in the Georgian precedent books, which reveal a preoccupation with declarations in actions on the case and contain very few special pleas. As the general issue returned to favour, the reasons for pleading specially changed. A special plea might alter the order of speeches at the trial; it might restrict the evidence which could be given by narrowing the issue; or it might simply be used to confuse or delay an opponent. The expression 'special pleading' passed into the layman's vocabulary as a synonym for the deployment of technicalities to perplex an adversary. Some lawyers, notably Mr Serjeant Runnington (d. 1821), argued that the ends of justice would best be served by ending special pleas altogether.

---

85 Cf. p. 95, ante.
86 See p. 341, post.

Against this trend there came a reaction, headed by Mr Serjeant Stephen (d. 1864), in the early nineteenth century. Stephen considered the principles of pleading to be one of the finest products of the human intellect, and demonstrated the thesis by writing the first reasoned treatise on them. He did not justify special pleading on historical grounds, but on the practical requirements of the day as he saw them. The general issue failed to define the dispute before trial, and consequently added to expense by compelling parties to come armed for all eventualities; and it failed to separate points of law and fact, so that points of law arose at nisi prius where there were no library facilities. Stephen wished the general issue to be abolished. And so the serjeants joined issue between themselves as to the purpose and utility of the science created by their predecessors five centuries earlier.

In 1830 the vexed question was referred to the Committee on Courts of Common Law. Stephen was a member, and carried persuasion to his fellows. They admitted that special pleading still exhibited too many bad qualities, but thought the advantages were of superior weight.[87] Parliament thereupon empowered the judges to make rules of court implementing the spirit of the report; and soon afterwards the judges promulgated the New Pleading Rules of Hilary Term 1834.

The 'Hilary Rules', which were said to have been the brainchild of Stephen's judicial ally Baron Parke, drastically restricted the availability of the general issue. For instance, Not guilty in trespass was limited to a denial of the breach of duty or act complained of; once again, as in the fourteenth century, justifications (such as self-defence) and titles had to be specially pleaded. There was thus a forced revival of special pleading. But the consequences were less salutary than Stephen and Parke had envisaged. One loophole was that defendants, prevented from pleading generally, tried to obtain the same result by traversing specially every single allegation in the declaration.[88] But the greatest snag was that it resurrected all the ancient learning in the state in which it had been abandoned, without modification of its purely formal technicalities. It proved to be a Baroque revival. Pleaders scuttled back to the old blackletter books, and legal history for a while became a vocational subject. But it was imperfectly grasped history, misapplied to unworthy ends. Demurrers on points of form flourished; practising counsel were more concerned to trip up adversaries than to perfect Stephen's science in all its intellectual purity. The judges must bear some of the blame for this turn of events. A generation later Lord Coleridge reminisced about their

---

[87]   *Parliamentary Papers 1830*, vol. XI, p. 45.
[88]   *Cooling v. Great Northern Rly Co* (1850) 15 Q.B. 486, per Lord Campbell CJ.

'idolatry of Baron Parke', whose undoubted learning and intellect 'were devoted to heightening all the absurdities, and contracting to the very utmost the narrowness, of the system of special pleading', so that the merits of cases took second place to the forms of procedure.[89] The attitude of the early Victorian judges was summed up by the fictional Mr Baron Surrebutter, who, having failed to explain the system to an uncomprehending litigant, loftily suppressed his complaints by saying, 'I do not conceive that laws ought to be adapted to suit the tastes and capacities of the ignorant'.[90] They were not, however, behaving irresponsibly by the lights of their age. Imposing precise formal discipline on the Bar has always been a strong judicial temptation, and the Victorian judges had inherited a tradition that lawsuits were akin to a sporting contest; a participant who deserved to win on merit but failed to observe the rules of the game could not in fairness be declared the winner.

END OF THE COMMON-LAW SYSTEM

The experiment with special pleading went so badly wrong that within twenty years parliament began, with judicial help, to rebuild the system from first principles. The Common Law Procedure Act 1852[91] and the consequent Trinity Rules of 1853 retained much the same choice between the general issue and special pleading as before; but special traverses were abolished, and pleadings were to omit all immaterial statements, fictions, and legal or formal phrases (such as 'force and arms' and 'against the peace of our lady the queen'). No demurrers or motions in arrest of judgment were to be allowed for lack of form in pleading. It even became possible by mutual consent to proceed to trial without pleadings at all, either by stating a question of fact in the form of an 'issue' or by stating a question of law in a 'special case'. This possibility was used to good effect when the Commercial Court was established in 1895.[92] Another major procedural reform of the 1850s concerned the admission of evidence. At common law the testimony of

---

[89] 'The Law in 1847 and the Law in 1889' (1890) 57 *Contemporary Rev.* 797 at 799-801.

[90] G. Hayes, *Crogate's Case: A Dialogue in the Shades on Special Pleading Reform* (1854); reprinted in Holdsworth HEL, vol. IX, pp. 417-431. This lampoon, written by a serjeant, is still amusing reading.

[91] Stat. 15 & 16 Vict., c.76.

[92] This was not a new court, but a separate listing of commercial cases in the Queen's Bench Division before a specialist judge; the court soon attracted specialist leading counsel. The streamlining of procedure was introduced by the first judge, Mathew J: E. Parry, *My Own Way* (1932), pp. 80-81; 60 LQR 324 at 325; 86 LQR 313 at 314.

the parties and interested persons had been excluded, on the grounds of bias, and this frequently made it impossible to prove a just cause of action or defence.[93] In 1843 persons with an interest, and in 1851 the parties themselves, were enabled to be competent witnesses.[94]

The Judicature Acts 1873-75, and the new rules of court appended in the schedule to the latter, carried the reforms further. The plaintiff was to begin with a 'statement of claim' stating briefly the facts on which he relied and what relief he claimed.[95] The defendant was then to make a brief statement of his defence (which could include a set-off or counterclaim), provided that he did not merely deny generally all the facts in the statement of claim. Beyond the defence, the parties could either plead new facts (by way of confession and avoidance) or join issue on the whole or part of the previous pleading. Each pleading was to contain, in numbered paragraphs, 'as concisely as may be a statement of the material facts on which the party pleading relies, but not the evidence by which they are to be proved'.[96] Prolixity was to be punished with costs. These provisions stifled the general issue[97] and reduced special pleading to its most basic premises. The demurrer was swept away in 1883, and parties were then enabled instead to raise points of law by pleading, or by applying to have a pleading struck out as disclosing no reasonable cause of action or answer.[98] An objection in point of law could be pleaded in addition to a denial of the facts; and points of law could be taken at the trial even if not pleaded. Moreover, the rules of court themselves were to be subject to regular revision by the judges. The resulting system is that still in use, subject to a few modifications made in the present century. Pleading is still conducted with care; parties may be held to their pleadings if amendment would cause injustice to their opponents, and may have to pay for their errors with costs. But it is now the substance of the pleading, never its form,

93 'Nonsuits were constant, not because there was no cause of action, but because the law refused the evidence of the only persons who could prove it': Lord Coleridge, 57 *Contemporary Rev.* at p. 798. The defendant's predicament was brought to general notice by the fictional *Bardell v. Pickwick*: C. Dickens, *The Posthumous Papers of the Pickwick Club* (1837), ch.33 (ch.34 in later editions).

94 Lord Denman's Act 1843, 6 & 7 Vict., c.85; Lord Brougham's Evidence Act 1851, 14 & 15 Vict., c.99.

95 Common-law declarations had not included a 'claim'; the relief was fixed according to the form of action. The statement of claim was an amalgam of legal and equitable traditions.

96 Supreme Court of Judicature Act 1875, 38 & 39 Vict., c.77, Sch. I, Ord. XIX, r.4.

97 Something very similar crept back into use, in the form of a general traverse to each and every allegation in the statement of claim: *Supreme Court Practice 1988*, vol. I, p. 305.

98 R.S.C. 1883, Ord. XXV.

which governs the outcome. As an appellate judge observed with pride in 1887, 'law has ceased to be a scientific game that may be won or lost by playing some particular move.'[99]

Even more drastic in its effects than the abolition of the old system of pleading has been the virtual disappearance in England of the civil jury. The possibility of trying facts by judge alone was introduced by the Common Law Procedure Act 1854. There were at that date already many inferior courts in which juries were not used; and in the court in banc, on motions for new trials, it was the trial judge's treatment of the facts which really mattered. All the experience suggested that judges were more likely to understand the factual issues than laymen, and were as competent to assess evidence. The 1854 Act therefore enabled parties, by consent, to leave issues of fact to a judge; and this was so often done that by the end of the century only half the civil trials in the High Court were by jury. The 1854 Act said that the 'verdict' of the judge was to have the same effect as the verdict of a jury; and the rules made under it show that the verdict was to be drawn up and entered in the same way. Yet, if the judges had taken to finding general verdicts without directing themselves, it would have become difficult to raise questions of law and evidence in banc. Some judges were indeed bewildered by the dual role imposed on them,[100] and for some years it was possible to speak of a judge 'misdirecting himself'. In the course of the twentieth century, however, the alternative of jury trial has largely disappeared. The very existence of the option made the decision to ask for a jury suspicious: it suggested the hope of confusion in a weak case, or the expectation of exorbitant damages in cases involving distressing details or high feelings. When wartime conditions led to temporary prohibitions of civil jury service, this was a further blow from which the civil jury never recovered. Since 1933 parties have been allowed juries only with leave of the court, except in cases of libel and a few other matters; and in recent years the courts have indicated their unwillingness to give such leave.[101]

As jury trial became exceptional, and then virtually extinct, so trial by judge alone became a process different in nature and result. English judges did not in the end adopt the practice of giving general verdicts, nor even, as in some American states, of making separate 'findings of

---

99   Lord Justice Bowen, repr. in *Essays AALH*, vol. I, at p. 541.

100   J. A. Foote, *Pie-Powder* (1911), pp. 84-85, tells an amusing story of a judge who was unsure whether he should find the facts as he himself thought or as he thought a common jury would have found.

101   *Ward v. James* [1966] 1 Q.B. 273, [1965] 1 All E.R. 563; *Williams v. Beesly* [1973] 3 All E.R. 144, [1973] 1 W.L.R. 1295.

fact'. Motions for new trials were not allowed in respect of trials without a jury. The notion of a verdict thus completely disappeared in civil trials. Instead, the English trial judge delivers a discursive 'judgment' in which findings of fact are intermingled with comment. What is now called the 'judgment' combines in one piece the trial judge's notes on the evidence, a 'direction' in law, a special verdict, and the court's decision, often adding for good measure the arguments of counsel as well. In a sense the trial judge is still stating a case, for potential use on appeal,[102] but he is now doing more than was permissible under common-law procedure. The substitution of one man for twelve, and the surreptitious disappearance of the formulaic concept of a verdict, have left the judge free to publish his ruminations on the evidence in a way which the common law in its wisdom forbade to juries. The effects of this change have gone far beyond procedure. We have seen how the emergence of the jury, by forcing a separation of fact and law, led to the refinement of substantive principles of law. The disappearance of the procedure which separated fact and law has put the development of the common law into a kind of reverse. So long as questions of law arose upon pleadings intended to define the issue for the jury, or upon directions to the laymen by the judge, they could remain relatively clear and simple. Now that fact and law are no longer decided separately, it is never certain to what extent judgments turn on the facts and to what extent the judge's comments on particular facts are intended to create legal distinctions. In theory every case now establishes some new point, however minute. Moreover, the tendency to minimise the importance of pleadings means that cases may change direction during the trial, and yet again in the course of an appeal, so that issues are not always formulated with the precision necessary to establish what principles of law are applicable.[103] Coke and Mallory were right in their predictions of a slide into uncertainty, but for the wrong reasons. The flight from formality and from the common law has brought a retreat from clear principles into a myriad of particular instances. Equity, in the old sense of deciding every case on its own facts,[104] has begun to replace and not merely to supplement the law.

102 For the replacement of the procedures in banc by appeals, see pp. 159, 164 post.

103 See *Banbury v. Bank of Montreal* [1918] A.C. 626 at 709, per Lord Parker; *Farrell v. Sec. of State for Defence* [1980] 1 All E.R. 166 at 173, [1980] 1 W.L.R. 172 at 180, per Lord Edmund Davies.

104 See pp. 117-120, post. It will be noted that the equity of the medieval Chancery was administered by a judge sitting alone without a jury.

Further reading

Pollock & Maitland, vol. II, pp. 574-674

Milsom HFCL, pp. 38-50, 70-81; 'Law and Fact in Legal Development' (1967) 17 *Univ. Toronto Law Jo.* 1-19 (repr. in SHCL 171-189)

E. M. Morgan, 'A Brief History of Special Verdicts' (1923) 32 *Yale Law Jo.* 575-592

R. Sutton, *Personal Actions at Common Law* (1929), pp. 72-204

M. S. Arnold, 'Law and Fact in the Medieval Jury Trial: Out of Sight, Out of Mind' (1974) 18 AJLH 267-280; 'The Control of the Jury' (1985) 100 SS x-xxxi

J. H. Baker, 'Trial of the Issue' (1978) 94 SS *103-116*

DEVELOPMENT OF THE JURY

J. P. Dawson, *A History of Lay Judges* (1960), pp. 118-129

R. V. Turner, 'The Origins of the Medieval English Jury' (1968) 7 *Jo. British Studies* (pt ii), 1-10

R. C. Van Caenegem, *The Birth of the English Common Law* (1973), pp. 62-84

J. Oldham, 'The Origins of the Special Jury' (1983) 50 *Univ. Chicago Law Rev.* 137-221; 'Special Juries in England: 19th Century Usage and Reform' (1987) 8 JLH 148-166

J. M. Mitnick, 'From Neighbor-Witness to Judge of Proofs: The Transformation of the English Civil Juror' (1988) 32 AJLH 201-235

For reading on the criminal jury, see pp. 592-593, post

PLEADING

Holdsworth HEL, vol. III, pp. 627-656

H. J. Stephen, *A Treatise on the Principles of Pleading* (1826)

J. H. Baker, 'Joinder of Issue: the Mechanics of Pleading' (1978) 94 SS *92-103*; 'Pleading and Litigation as Sources of Law', ibid. *142-163*

M. S. Arnold, 'The Medieval Rules of Pleading' (1985) 100 SS x-xx

REFORMS

Holdsworth HEL, vol. IX, pp. 262-335

6. The Court of Chancery and Equity

The courts and procedures described in the preceding chapters embodied the regular 'course of the common law'. Although the courts altered their jurisdictions, and the procedures were distorted and evaded in different periods, the essential premises and outward forms of the common-law system went almost unchanged between the thirteenth and the nineteenth centuries. It came to be thought an Englishman's birthright to be subject to this system rather than to any other, and a steady stream of medieval statutes from Magna Carta onwards guaranteed that no free man should be deprived of life, liberty or property save by 'due process of law'.[1] These statutes were intended as legal restraints on the power of the Crown to erect new jurisdictions, restraints on the very power which had earlier introduced the common law and its due process as an extraordinary alternative to regular local justice. And they were not just abstract theory. In 1368 the justices at Chelmsford held void a commission to seize a man and his goods without due process.[2] In 1406, Gascoigne CJ declared that 'the king has committed all his judicial powers to various courts',[3] and in the same year the King's Bench declared unconstitutional the courts of Oxford University which by royal charter proceeded according to the Civil law of Rome.[4] Expansion of the conciliar jurisdiction under Henry VIII led to actions founded on the medieval legislation.[5] Under the Stuarts the due-process principle became of even greater constitutional significance. The notion that the king had exhausted his judicative powers by creating the common-law courts was pressed to its limit by Coke CJ when in 1608 he told James I that he had no authority to participate in the

---

[1] Stat. 28 Edw. III, c.3; 42 Edw. III, c.3. For Magna Carta 1215, cl.29, see pp. 537-538, post.

[2] Lib. Ass. 42 Edw. III, pl.5. See also Co. Inst., vol. IV, p. 163.

[3] *Chedder v. Savage* (1406) Y.B. Mich. 8 Hen. IV, fo. 13, pl.13.

[4] *Peddington v. Ottworth* (1406) 88 SS 166. In 1388 it was held in parliament that 'the realm of England never has been and never shall be ruled or governed by the Civil law': Rot. Parl., vol. III, p. 236.

[5] See pp. 135, 537, post.

judicial decisions of his own courts.[6] And in 1641 the principle was invoked by parliament in abolishing the Star Chamber.[7]

The statutes of due process were provoked by a series of experiments with the judicial system; if litigation had become a game of skill, it was not fair to change the rules at random. Yet, despite their lofty phrases, they represented a departure from constitutional orthodoxy. The king could hardly have lost his sovereignty by exercising it. He was sworn 'to do equal and right justice and discretion in mercy and truth',[8] and so if the regular procedures proved deficient it was his royal duty to furnish a remedy. The king therefore retained an overriding residuary power to administer justice outside the regular system; but the important limitation imposed on that power by the due-process legislation was that it could be invoked only where the common law was deficient, and not in matters of life, limb or property. By the end of the thirteenth century numerous petitions (or 'bills') were being presented to the king, asking for his grace to be shown in respect of some complaint. The usual royal answer was 'let him sue at common law', which in suitable cases could be achieved simply by sending the bill to justices in eyre or trailbaston. Sometimes a petitioner complained of misconduct by litigants or officials in frustration of the common law; such bills were in the time of Edward III commonly passed on to the judges of the courts concerned, with a covering letter commanding them to do right.[9] In the exceptional cases where the king took some direct action, we can see the beginning of the newer jurisdictions which came to be associated with the king's council.

Already in the fourteenth century the petitioning of the king by bill, seeking a remedy as of grace, was so common that such business had to be referred to special sessions of the council or parliament; and in hearing these petitioners the council directly continued the role of the Anglo-Saxon *witan* and the Norman *Curia Regis*. By the middle of the century only petitions of special importance, such as those seeking a general and permanent change of law or procedure, were reserved for parliament, where, if the bills were assented to, they became statutes. Private suits were more often dealt with by the council, or delegated to individual councillors such as the chancellor, admiral, or marshal; and

---

6 *Case of Prohibitions del Roy* (1608) 12 Co. Rep. 63.
7 See pp. 135, 540, post.
8 Coronation oath of Edward II, *Statutes of the Realm*, vol. I, p. 168.
9 The plea rolls do not usually give any hint of such intervention, but the recently released *Recorda* files of the King's Bench (KB 145) include a number of such bills and writs, in French. The use of informal letters was probably introduced in cases where the king's own interests were involved: for an enrolled example, see *R. v. Bishop of Lincoln* (1320) 104 SS 105 at 110-111.

petitioners took to addressing the appropriate individual or body directly. Out of the council's arrangements for dealing with these cases grew several distinct courts;[10] but the most important, because it ultimately developed a jurisprudence of its own, was that of the chancellor.

The Chancery

The Chancery (*cancellaria*) began as the royal secretariat, housed in the king's chapel.[11] In origin it was no more a court of law than the Exchequer, but was a department of state descended from the Anglo-Saxon scriptorium where royal writs and charters were drawn and sealed.[12] The head of the department, the chancellor, had the custody of the great seal of England, which was used to authenticate the documents which his clerks prepared. Royal grants of property, privilege, dignity or office, charters, writs and commissions, all had to 'pass the seal' in Chancery. The original writs of the common law emanated from the same department, and through them the chancellor was associated with the ordinary administration of justice.

The chancellor has always been primarily an officer of state and a minister of the Crown. Most medieval chancellors were also bishops, or even archbishops. Some chancellors, notably Cardinal Wolsey (1515-29) and Lord Clarendon (1658-67), were prime ministers in all but name. Appointments to the office, which still takes ceremonial precedence over the newer rank of prime minister, are made on political grounds. Yet the majority of chancellors have been lawyers[13] and until 1875 spent most of their time sitting in court. The anomaly that a politician should hold the highest judicial office in the land was compounded by the undefined nature of the chancellor's jurisdiction. The chancellor received no patent or commission defining his office, which he held at the king's pleasure, and took no part in the ordinary administration of justice as an assize judge. His powers derived from

---

10 See ch.7, post.

11 The word *cancellaria* derives from a lattice or screen, but there is no evidence of such an arrangement in the English Chancery; the name was imported from the continent, probably in the 1060s.

12 For the origins of this department, and the case for an Anglo-Saxon 'chancellor', see S. Keynes, *The Diplomas of King Aethelred 'the Unready'* (1980), pp. 134-153. For the case against, cf. P. Chaplais, in *Studies in Medieval History presented to R.H.C. Davis* (1985), p. 41.

13 This is true even of the medieval episcopal chancellors, who were mostly graduates in Civil or Canon law and in many cases former practising advocates.

his custody of the great seal and from his pre-eminent position in the king's council.

THE GREAT SEAL

The great seal has been since the eleventh century the most important mark of authentication in the realm. The silver seal matrix, bearing the sovereign's effigy, was in later times carried by the chancellor on formal occasions in an embroidered purse and set before him in court. Whoever was appointed to keep the seal necessarily possessed the authority which the seal conveyed. 'Keepers of the seal' were originally appointed on a temporary basis, between chancellors, but in later times the office of lord keeper of the great seal was sometimes granted permanently; though of slightly lower status, a lord keeper had legally the same authority as a lord chancellor. When the seal was placed temporarily in the keeping of several commissioners of the great seal, they too had the same powers as a lord chancellor. After the union with Scotland in 1708, there was no longer a great seal of England alone, and no chancellor of England; but the Chancery, and the court of the lord high chancellor of Great Britain, remained purely English institutions.[14]

THE CHANCERY CLERKS

The medieval chancellor had a large staff of clerks, who were reckoned of his own household and were therefore distinct from other branches of the *Curia Regis*. The first grade of clerks were the twelve *clerici ad robas*, so called because they received liveries of robes; they were known by Tudor times as the masters of the Chancery, and during the Tudor period were often doctors of law. They deputised for the chancellor in both administrative and judicial affairs. A late thirteenth-century writer describes them as hearing petitions and complaints, which they determined by issuing writs; though by that time the discretion to invent new remedies was severely curtailed.[15] After the middle of the fourteenth century their main task was to assist the chancellor in dispatching litigation in the Chancery itself. The foremost of these senior clerks was the clerk (or master) of the rolls, who kept the records of documents authenticated in Chancery (such as the patent rolls, close rolls, and treaty rolls) and appointed the lesser clerks. The second grade of clerks were known in medieval times as 'bougiers' and were also twelve in number. The chief officers in this grade were the clerk of the Crown in Chancery, who controlled grants under the seal, and the clerks

14 *R. v. Hare and Mann* (1719) 1 Stra. 146.
15 *Fleta*, ii.13 (72 SS 123); p. 66, ante.

of the Petty Bag, who controlled much of the administrative business of the Chancery. The third grade were the cursitors (or *clerici de cursu*) who wrote out the standard form writs 'of course'. The development of the chancellor's jurisdiction, shortly to be outlined, led to the growth of many new offices, particularly the department of the six clerks, who were originally deputies to the master of the rolls and who acted the part of attorneys; so much did their work expand that eventually the six clerks had their own deputies, the sixty clerks.

The first signs of judicial activity in the Chancery began in connection with its specialised administrative work. Questions relating to royal grants could be raised there. The Chancery also controlled inquisitions relating to the Crown's property rights. For instance, on the death of a tenant in chief a writ of *diem clausit extremum* issued from the Chancery commanding a local official to hold an inquisition post mortem to discover exactly what lands he held, of whom, and on what day he died, and who and how old was his heir; this information would enable the seizure of whatever was due to the king as feudal lord. Such inquisitions were frequently 'traversed' by interested parties, thus raising legal questions for the Chancery. The chancellor in addition had an exclusive common-law jurisdiction in personal actions involving his staff. All such proceedings were conducted on the Petty Bag side of the Chancery, called the 'Latin side' because the records were kept (as in the other central courts) in that language. The Chancery was held 'before the king', and in this aspect of its jurisdiction bore a close resemblance to the medieval King's Bench, with which it worked in close cooperation; issues of fact were regularly sent to be tried on the Crown side of the King's Bench as if it were part of the same court.

The Chancery also received petitions seeking redress against the Crown; the king could not be sued by his own writ in the other courts. The determination of 'petitions of right' was obviously a function of the king's residuary jurisdiction to do justice to his subjects rather than of the regular common law. To that extent it foreshadowed the growth of bill procedure which brought the Court of Chancery into prominence. But the connection between the Latin and 'English' sides was minimal. The development of a new kind of bill procedure made the court in effect an extraordinary court for common pleas, but unlike the King's Bench (which achieved a similar feat) it was not tied to the forms or language of the common law and was arguably not even a court of record.

THE ENGLISH SIDE

The chancellor's English jurisdiction, so called because the bills and pleadings were written in the vernacular tongue,[16] grew not from the departmental work of the Chancery but from the jurisdiction of the king's council to deal with bills of complaint. We have seen that in the fourteenth century bills addressed to the king in council, complaining of interference with the common law, were passed on to the judges. Some cases of this kind passed through the Chancery, as 'a convenient clearing-house for all kinds of business transacted elsewhere'; but before 1350 its function in such cases was not to dispense justice so much as to facilitate its achievement in other courts.[17] In the second half of the century, however, bills were increasingly referred to the chancellor himself, so that a specific remedy could be provided by the Chancery irrespective of whether proceedings were pending at common law; and by 1400 petitioners had begun to address their complaints directly to him. The Chancery may have been thought an appropriate place to discuss new remedies because of its traditional supervision of the issue of original writs. A plaintiff applying for an original writ was in a sense making a petition in Chancery;[18] and in that context it became a common saying that no deserving plaintiff would be sent out of the Chancery without a remedy: *nullus recedat a curia cancellariae sine remedio*.[19] In the thirteenth century one possible response to a petition had been to allow a new form of original writ; when that power was curtailed, the bill might be referred to parliament for a legislative solution. But often the redress sought was ad hoc, arising from the special facts of the particular case, and here it was appropriate to make a decree which bound only the parties to the suit. Decrees were at first made in the name of the king in council, and then by the 'court', sometimes reciting the presence of the judges and serjeants, councillors and advisers; during the fifteenth century the chancellor came to issue decrees in his own name. In making such decrees, medieval councillors or chancellors did not regard themselves as administering a system of law different from the law of England. They were reinforcing the law by making sure that justice was done in cases where shortcomings in

---

[16] Some of the earliest were actually in French. The 15th-century court used Latin for its endorsements on documents; but the decree books, beginning in 1544, were in English.

[17] Sayles, 76 SS lxxi, lxxix.

[18] *Fleta* ii.13 (72 SS 123).

[19] *Anon.* (1489) Y.B. Hil. 4 Hen. VII, fo. 5, pl.8, per Moreton C, quoting the words of the Statute of Westminster II 1285, c.24, *in consimili casu* (p. 73, ante). Cf. Y.B. 21-22 Edw. I, 323, per Bereford CJ ('no one should leave the Chancery in despair').

the regular procedure, or human failings, were hindering its attainment by due process. They came not to destroy the law, but to fulfil it.[20]

The previous two chapters have shown why it was difficult to conceive of the common law apart from the procedures through which it operated. In the King's Bench and Common Pleas it was circumscribed by the writ system. Its mesne process was dependent on the good will of sheriffs. It was further constrained by the forms of pleading, by the rules of evidence, and by the uncertainties of jury trial. The possibilities of mechanical failure were legion. And the growing strength of the substantive law could also work injustice, because the judges preferred to suffer hardship in individual cases than to make exceptions to clear rules.[21] The stock example was that of the debtor who gave his creditor a sealed bond, but did not ensure that it was cancelled when he paid up. The law regarded the bond as incontrovertible evidence of the debt, and so payment was no defence.[22] Here the debtor would suffer an obvious hardship if he was made to pay twice; but the mischief was a result of his own foolishness, and the law did not bend to protect fools. It was in the interests of certainty that deeds should prevail over mere words. Likewise, if a man made an oral contract where the law required written evidence, he would find himself without remedy. Again, if someone granted land to others on trust to carry out his wishes, he would find that at law the grantees were absolute owners who could not be compelled to obey him.[23] Now, it was not that the common law held that a debt was due twice, or that a promise or trust could be broken; such propositions would have been dismissed as absurd. Yet those were the results which followed from observing strict rules of evidence, rules which might exclude the merits of the case from consideration but which could not be relaxed without destroying certainty and condoning carelessness. For a creditor, promisee or trustee to take unfair advantage of those strict rules was without question wrong; but it was a matter for their consciences rather than for the common law.

The chancellor was free from the rigid procedures under which such injustices sheltered. His court was a court of conscience,[24] in which defendants could be coerced into doing whatever conscience required in the full circumstances of the case. Such a court obviously proceeded in a very different fashion from the Common Pleas.

---

[20] F. W. Maitland, *Equity* (1909), p. 17.

[21] See pp. 94-95, ante.

[22] See p. 369, post.

[23] See p. 286, post.

[24] This term was in use by the early 15th century: 10 SS 121.

EARLY CHANCERY PROCEDURE

The early history of the Chancery is difficult to uncover for want of full documentation; the procedure was informal, and for the first century little has survived beyond the files of bills. It seems probable that the English jurisdiction was established in its distinct form during the reign of Richard II, since already by 1393 there were complaints of its abuse. It was perhaps firmly settled while John of Waltham was master of the rolls (1381-86), a period when Canon lawyers dominated the staff.[25] The procedure clearly owed something to the inquisitorial procedure of the canonists, and may have been modelled on the canonical *denunciatio evangelica*,[26] though the Chancery never became a court of Canon law and its practitioners were always members of the inns of court.

No original writ was necessary, and all actions were commenced by informal complaint, either by bill or by word of mouth.[27] Process in most actions was begun by writ of subpoena, a simple summons to appear in Chancery or else forfeit a penalty;[28] in practice the penalty was not enforced, but a disobedient defendant was subject to proceedings for contempt.[29] Pleading was in English and relatively informal. Evidence was taken by interrogation or written deposition. There was no jury; the court assembled a dossier of information until it saw fit to take action. The Chancery was always open; it was not tied to the terms and return-days, though for convenience it observed them as far as possible. It could sit anywhere, even in the chancellor's private house; and causes could be tried out of court by commission of *dedimus potestatem* to country gentlemen. These advantages enabled medieval chancellors to provide swift and inexpensive justice, especially to the poor and oppressed. Sheriffs and juries could be bypassed where undue pressure was feared; corruption could not prevent a fair hearing. The chancellor's eyes were not covered by the blinkers of due process, and he could go into all the facts to the extent that the available evidence permitted. He could order bonds and other writings to be cancelled where they would

---

[25] Stat. 17 Ric. II, c.6 (authorising the chancellor to award damages at his discretion for false suits in the council or Chancery by *subpoena*); Rot. Parl., vol. IV, p. 84 (complaint in 1415 of canonical procedure introduced in the time of Waltham).

[26] This was a suit brought to admonish a party to act conscionably, which could result in redress to the complainant. See H. Coing, 71 LQR 223; J. L. Barton, 'Equity in the Medieval Common Law' (p. 133, post).

[27] This makes it impossible to measure the quantity of business in Chancery: the increase in the number of bills during the 15th century may be due simply to a decline in oral complaints.

[28] For a specimen, see p. 624, post.

[29] First by attachment, and then by a 'commission of rebellion' empowering laymen to arrest the defendant and bring him to the Chancery.

only serve unjust ends; and, conversely, he could order the discovery of documents which were needed to enforce legal rights. He could order parol contracts to be performed, and fiduciary obligations discharged. He could ensure that unfair advantage was not taken of the weak and foolish. And defendants could not easily evade this new and powerful justice; for contumacy they could be imprisoned, or their property sequestered.[30]

By exercising this jurisdiction in conscience, the chancellor was nevertheless not causing any of the 'inconvenience' which the law eschewed. In Chancery each case turned on its own facts, and the chancellor did not interfere with the general rules observed in courts of law. The decrees operated *in personam*; they were binding on the parties in the cause, but were not judgments of record binding anyone else.

BUSINESS OF THE CHANCERY 1400-1600

The difficulty of measuring business in the early Chancery accounts for inconsistencies between writers on the subject.[31] It seems nevertheless to be generally agreed that business was steadily increasing towards the end of the fifteenth century, and that it increased dramatically during the sixteenth, until the court became so flooded with suits that it could scarcely cope. This expansion turned the Chancery into the third major court in Westminster Hall, but it was accompanied by a change in the general run of its business. At the beginning of the fifteenth century, the typical petition complained of weakness or poverty, or the abuse of position by an opponent. Throughout that century tort and commercial cases feature as prominently as property disputes, and there was also a substantial appellate jurisdiction over inferior urban courts. Frequently the relief sought related to an action at law: a plaintiff at law might need discovery, a defendant at law might need the action stopped. When the tide of business swelled, however, the greater part of it was in the sphere of real property. Some of this was attributable to the growing practice of creating uses or trusts of land;[32] but there were many other ways of getting property cases into Chancery, and the work was by no means dominated by uses. Although the Chancery could not in theory interfere with the legal title, it could decree possession and could ensure

---

30   A commission of sequestration enabled property to be seized and the profits sequestered until compliance. This was in use by the 1530s: Guy, *Career of More*, at pp. 58, 59. Decrees were also widely enforced by making the parties execute penal recognizances, payable to the chancellor or masters: e.g. 94 SS 349.

31   Miss Avery (p. 133, post) thought the main burst came during the chancellorship (1432-50) of John Stafford; Dr Pronay (p. 134, post) put it in the 1470s.

32   See pp. 284-287, post.

that a successful party was put in possession; the procedure as settled in Tudor times was to issue a writ of execution, and if that was disobeyed a writ of attachment, an injunction to deliver possession, and a writ of assistance to the sheriff.[33] It could also make decrees to 'quiet' possession, either to protect the party in possession or to restore possession wrested by force until the merits were tried.[34] As the property jurisdiction waxed, the other aspects waned. The tort jurisdiction was largely given up. In the sphere of contract, the most important business came to be ordering the completion of conveyances, and relief from mortgages and penal bonds. A reason for this change we have already seen. The popularity of the Chancery in the later fifteenth century had been perceived as a challenge to the courts of law to change their ways, and was one of the spurs which goaded the King's Bench into extensive reforms in the law of contract and tort through actions on the case, and into adopting a bill procedure.[35] Moreover, much of the business with which it had started had gone elsewhere. The kind of unusual violence or abuse of power which the regular system was powerless to redress needed attention at the highest level; complaints of this nature were increasingly diverted to the full council and became the foundation of the Star Chamber jurisdiction.[36] The council also found new ways of dealing with poor men's causes.[37] By Elizabethan times the Chancery was too busy to concern itself with petty matters, and in 1579 sent away a plaintiff who claimed a right of entry to hang washing in his neighbour's yard.[38] The Chancery had ceased in reality to be an extraordinary court. Although it retained procedures which were extraordinary in the sense that they were outside the common law, and was beginning to develop principles of its own, it had become a court of constant resort.

---

[33] It was also possible to put a plaintiff in possession by means of a commission: *Boles v. Walley* (1559) Cary 38. For the mid-16th century jurisdiction over title, see E. Henderson, 26 AJLH 97.

[34] E.g. *Eland v. Savile* (1530) Guy, *Career of More*, p. 57 (possession restored pending suit); *Warnes v. Burwell* (1530) ibid. 56 (possession protected); *Sapcote v. Newport* (1560) Cary 47 (possession protected).

[35] See pp. 47-53, ante.

[36] See p. 136, post.

[37] See p. 138, post.

[38] *Hamby v. Northage* (1579) Cary 76. By this time there was also a rule of court forbidding claims for less than £10.

Law and Equity

Despite these changes in business, it continued to be a trite saying that the Chancery was not a court of law but a court of conscience. Developments in the system of pleading and discussing cases in banc had by Elizabethan times fostered the modern conception of law as a body of rules applicable to given sets of facts.[39] The chancellor, by way of contrast, was less concerned with rules than with individual cases. He combined the role of judge and jury, and in delving as deeply as conscience required into the particular circumstances before him he did not make such a definite distinction between fact and law. That in itself explains the slow development of Chancery jurisprudence; in most cases the court's object was to tease out the merits of a case on the facts, in the manner of a jury, rather than to apply legal rules. It also explains why the chancellor's justice was seen as something superior to the less flexible justice of the two benches. Indeed, if proceedings in other courts were in themselves unconscionable, the chancellor would enjoin plaintiffs to cease them: this was called the 'common injunction'.

The chancellor's transcendant form of justice acquired the name 'equity'. But equity was nothing new. Aristotle had written of it as a means of correcting general laws which in their nature could not provide for every eventuality; in particular it required written laws to be interpreted according to the intention rather than the letter.[40] The notion was well known to medieval lawyers. *Glanvill* mentions it as a feature of the common law,[41] and throughout the year-book period it was applied to the interpretation of statutes.[42] What was new was its application to the extraordinary jurisprudence of the chancellor, for which it seemed an especially apt term when it came to be seen as distinct from common law.[43] In a celebrated case of 1615, Lord Ellesmere C explained that the reason why there was a Chancery was 'that men's actions are so diverse and infinite that it is impossible to make a general law which may aptly meet with every particular and not fail in some circumstances. The office of the chancellor is to correct men's consciences for frauds, breaches of trust, wrongs and oppressions

---

[39]   See pp. 97-101, ante.

[40]   Aristotle, *Ethica Nichomachea* (W. D. Ross ed., 1925), v.10.

[41]   *Glanvill*, prologue; ii.7; vii.1. The equity of the law is frequently mentioned in the earlier year books.

[42]   See p. 240, post.

[43]   It had been applied to his common-law jurisdiction in *Anon.* (1328) Y.B. Hil. 2 Edw. III, fo.20, pl.5, per [Hotham] C ('this is a place of equity').

of what nature soever they be, and to soften and mollify the extremity of the law.'[44]

The shift from 'conscience' to 'equity' was more than a change of vocabulary. It is not certain how medieval chancellors arrived at their decisions, but the word 'conscience' has an ad hoc, subjective ring to it. The clerical chancellors were guided no doubt by their training in theology and Canon law, but they were also driven back onto their own consciences, exercising the temporal counterpart of the confessional. They even referred occasionally to the law of nature. Certainly they did not apply the technical learning of the Canon law, or the doctors of law would have been brought in as practitioners before them; but there were occasional complaints of overreaching.[45] The complaints loudened as a result of Cardinal Wolsey's chancellorship (1515-29). Wolsey had no legal training of any kind, and delighted in putting down lawyers; his arrogant confidence in his own untutored common sense, and his desire to please plaintiffs, left in some minds an impression of arbitrariness. The chancellor's jurisdiction had visibly become another system of secular justice, sharing all the failings of human institutions; and the decisions of an unlearned chancellor easily offended at least the lawyers' sense of fairness. A strong reaction appeared in a treatise written by an anonymous 'serjeant-at-law' shortly after Wolsey's death. The writer 'marvelled' that the chancellor should presume to interfere by subpoena with the king's law, which was the inheritance of the subject. Conscience was a variable standard, for 'divers men, divers consciences'; and it offended the rule of law. The 'serjeant' went so far as to assert that the chancellor's jurisdiction was founded on ignorance of the merits of the common law, and that it was contrary both to reason and the law of God.[46]

It could fairly be said in response that the 'serjeant' was equally ignorant of the true basis of Chancery jurisdiction; his argument was certainly intemperate and exaggerated. But the rift was largely closed by Wolsey's successor, Sir Thomas More (1529-33), the first chancellor since the fourteenth century to have been educated in the common law. More had earlier written that to allow a judge, even a good judge, to follow his own whim would defeat the principle that justice must be

---

[44] *Earl of Oxford's Case* (1615) 1 Rep. Ch. 1 at 6.

[45] E.g. Stat. 4 Hen. IV, c.23 (forbidding interference after judgment at law); Rot. Parl., vol. IV, pp. 84 (n. 25, ante), and 189 (unsuccessful petition of 1422, that no one should sue in Chancery unless a judge certified there was no remedy at law).

[46] *Replication of a Serjeant at Law*, in Guy (ed.), *St German on Chancery and Subpoena*, pp. 99-105. It is not certain that the author really was a serjeant.

seen to be done.[47] He nevertheless believed that the common law was too 'rigorous', and he not only exercised the equitable jurisdiction as fully as his clerical predecessors but continued the practice of inhibiting common-law actions by injunction. When the judges complained, he invited them to dinner and told them that it belonged to their own discretion to 'mitigate and reform the rigour of the law'; if they would do that, he promised he would issue no more common injunctions. The judges declined the offer, because, as More later told his biographer, 'they may by the verdict of the jury cast off all quarrels from themselves upon them, which they account their chief defence'.[48] The judges had no wish to become involved in decisions of fact, and therefore could not tackle questions of conscience. In truth the judges did introduce more flexibility into the common-law remedies by allowing a wider range of actions on the case; but their flat rejection of More's proposal destined equity to develop in England as a system separate from the common law. Until More's time it could still be argued that equity or conscience operated in all courts, albeit to an extent which varied with the degree to which individual circumstances could be revealed to the court. As late as 1550 it was said by the King's bench that 'conscience is *aequum et bonum*, which is the basis of every law'.[49] But thereafter equity would increasingly be regarded as the peculiar prerogative of the Court of Chancery. As a consequence, equity itself became a kind of law, in the sense of a body of coherent principles, and the original rationale of the chancellor's bill jurisdiction faded into history.

CHANCERY AND THE COMMON-LAW COURTS

Before the distinction between law and equity hardened in this way, the Court of Chancery and the law courts enjoyed a harmonious relationship. The judges of the two benches frequently attended in Chancery to give legal advice, and seem to have had no difficulty in reconciling the different roles of the two jurisdictions. In a Chancery case of 1452, Fortescue CJ countered a legal argument with the words, 'We are to argue conscience here, not the law'.[50]

The harmony gave way briefly to discord under the Tudors. Wolsey's disdain for the common law has been mentioned; and

---

[47]   From *Responsio ad Lutherum*, as translated in 94 SS *81*. Cf. Audley's reading on uses (1526) B. & M. 103 at 104.

[48]   W. Roper, *The Lyfe of Sir Thomas Moore* (E. V. Hitchcock ed., 1935), pp. 44-45.

[49]   Bro. Abr., *Estates*, pl.78. Cf. speech on installation of Anderson CJCP (1582) Moore K.B. 116 at 117, per Bromley C ('*aequum et bonum*, which are the life of the law').

[50]   Mich. 31 Hen. VI, Fitz. Abr., *Subpena*, pl.23.

prominent judges were among those who brought about his downfall. Another temporary eruption of discontent occurred during the chancellorship of Sir Thomas Wriothesley in 1546, when some common lawyers petitioned the council complaining of attempts to introduce Civil law into the Chancery. The petitioners claimed that their profession was jeopardised, and Wriothesley was soon afterwards deposed for abuses 'to the great prejudice and utter decay of the common laws'.[51] The regular appointment of legally trained chancellors[52] ended further fears of that nature; but there was an explosion of a different kind in 1616.

The trouble in 1616 was largely caused by a clash of strong personalities. Lord Ellesmere, the chancellor (1596-1617), was an able common lawyer by training; but as he grew older his political and personal prejudices gained the better of him, and he repeated Wolsey's error of antagonising the judges. He particularly annoyed them by entertaining suits in Chancery after judgment had been given at common law, and also allowed a backlog of thousands of cases to pile up. Any criticism of himself he represented as an attack on the monarchy as established by God. The appointment of a doctor of Civil law, Sir Julius Caesar, as Master of the Rolls in 1614 was perhaps the final straw. In 1613 Sir Edward Coke had been made chief justice of the King's Bench, and he joined battle with Ellesmere over the Chancery's claim to reopen cases after judgment at law. Coke had the law on his side; the procedure was an irregular appeal, contrary to statute and to a decision of all the judges in the Exchequer Chamber in 1598.[53] He began to release, by habeas corpus, prisoners committed by Ellesmere for contempt of injunctions;[54] and he encouraged such prisoners to prosecute their opponents for the crime of impeaching the judgments of the king's courts. Unfortunately for Coke, his hints were taken up by the unworthiest of litigants; and, after a misguided attempt by a crank to indict various officials including Ellesmere, the dispute was referred to James I in 1616. Coke was by then in political disfavour for other reasons, and Ellesmere combined with Francis Bacon and the Duke of Buckingham to engineer his downfall. Coke was dismissed from office

---

[51] *Acts of the Privy Council*, vol. II, p. 48.

[52] There were three more episcopal chancellors in the 1550s, but the only non-lawyers thereafter were Sir Christopher Hatton (1587-91), Dr John Williams, bishop of Lincoln (1621-25) and Lord Shaftesbury (1672-73).

[53] Stat. 4 Hen. IV, c.23; *Finch v. Throgmorton* (1598) LPCL 208-209. Cf. p. 155, post.

[54] See p. 168, post.

the same year.[55] The weakness of Coke's personal position at that moment enabled Ellesmere and Bacon to persuade the king to issue a royal decree confirming the chancellor's jurisdiction to entertain suits after judgments at law. But in 1617 Ellesmere died, and Bacon on succeeding him took pains to restore good relations with the profession and with the judiciary. Once the dust had settled, the 1616 decree would be seen as illegal;[56] but never again did the relations with other courts become so strained that the division of functions led to any hostility. The lawyer chancellors from that time onwards concentrated on refining equity as a body of principles, and any remaining jurisdictional hardships resulted from the procedural inconvenience of having to seek equitable and legal remedies in separate courts.

EQUITY ACCORDING TO RULE

The essence of equity as a corrective to the rigour of laws was that it should not be tied to rules. If, on the other hand, no consistent principles whatever were observed, parties in like cases would not be treated alike; and equality was a requisite of equity. As John Selden quipped in the mid-seventeenth century, if the measure of equity was the chancellor's own conscience, one might as well make the standard measure of one foot the chancellor's foot.[57] The conundrum was an old one. St German, the anonymous 'serjeant', and Sir Thomas More, had all agreed that subjective equity had no place in a legal system. The chancellor, argued St German, must order his conscience after the common law. He could not attempt to enforce the finest dictates of conscience, for at some point litigation had to be final. Thus the Chancery did not always undo the results of deceit: it did not upset a false verdict in an attaint, or a wager of law tainted by perjury. On the other hand, many of the rules applied to uses by the Chancery had no moral content; the trustee was bound by them in conscience merely because they were positive law. A case of 1522 showed that a trustee was not to follow his own conscience, but was to obey his beneficiary; his conscience, like the chancellor's , was ordered by law.[58] Moreover, the acts of a supreme legislature could not be upset by recourse to conscience; statutes might be construed equitably, but they could not be disregarded in Chancery on the grounds that they were unconscionable or

55 See p. 191, post.
56 *R. v. Standish* (1670) Treby MS. Rep., LPCL 438.
57 *Table Talk of John Selden* (F. Pollock ed., 1927), p. 43.
58 *Gresley v. Saunders* (1522) Spelman Rep. (93 SS) 22-23.

because a party was unaware of their effect. In all these cases the only 'court of conscience' was the party's own soul.[59]

Another factor which compelled chancellors to regulate their supreme power was the sheer success of the equity jurisdiction in terms of the number of petitioners which it attracted. Faced with so many thousands of petitions, they were obliged to develop routine attitudes to commonly recurring cases. There had always been a procedural *cursus cancellariae*, a common 'course' of the court; by the mid-sixteenth century the *cursus* was coming to embrace substantive doctrine as well.[60] In the 1590s lawyers were beginning to take notes of what the chancellors said in court, and Bacon C in 1617 even appointed an official reporter to sit at his feet.[61] After 1660 Chancery cases were regularly reported. The enunciation of general reasons for decisions, with a view to their being reported, completed the reduction of equity to a system of principles. By 1676 a chancellor could repudiate the idea that equity had any dependence on his own inner conscience: 'the conscience by which I am to proceed is merely *civilis et politica*, and tied to certain measures'.[62]

Thus equity hardened into law. Trusts and mortgages were governed by rules as clear as any rules of common law. In matters of contract and tort, the Chancery normally followed the law. There were few equitable torts,[63] nor would contracts be amended to make them less harsh: 'the Chancery mends no man's bargain'.[64] It could be said in 1675, without a hint of paradox, that a contract without consideration was binding in conscience but not in equity.[65] Precedents were as binding in equity as at law, and now even the Chancery would sooner suffer a hardship than a departure from known rules.[66] It is true that

---

59 Cf. Y.B. Hil. 4 Hen. VII, fo. 5, pl.8, per Fyneux sjt ('many things are to be sued here which are not remediable at common law, but some are in conscience between a man and his confessor').

60 See *Bartie v. Herenden* (1560) B. & M. 121.

61 26 SS xxii; *Legal History Studies 1972*, p. 17. Some dicta by Ellesmere survive in manuscript, and there are unpublished reports from the 1630s onwards; but the Bacon reports have not survived.

62 *Cook v. Fountain* (1676) 3 Swan. 585 at 600, per Lord Nottingham C.

63 An exception is equitable waste, for which damages were occcasionally given: *Brown v. Lord Bridges* (1589) Tothill 51. But Chancery generally refused to award damages.

64 *Maynard v. Moseley* (1667) 3 Swan. 655. An exception was the relief given against penalties: pp. 370-371, post.

65 *Honywood v. Bennett* (1675) Nottingham Rep. (73 SS) 214.

66 *Galton v. Hancock* (1743) 2 Atk. 427 at 439, per Lord Hardwicke C. Cf. Bl. Comm., vol. III, p. 440.

equity has remained more flexible than the common law, because it can take greater account of individual circumstances; for instance, remedies can be lost by delay, by the intervention of third-party interests, or by a lack of complete probity on the part of the plaintiff. Guidelines seemed more helpful than rigid rules: the first published book on equity was arranged around fourteen general principles of the very broadest nature, such as 'Equality is Equity', and 'Equity prevents Mischief'.[67] But the preoccupation of the court with matters of property, the high intellectual capacities of many chancellors and leaders of the Chancery Bar, and the superior quality of the later reports, all combined to render equity as certain and scientific as law. The process may even have gone too far. *Rigor aequitatis* set in,[68] and equity almost lost the ability to discover new doctrines. 'Nothing would inflict on me greater pain in quitting this place,' said Lord Eldon C in 1818, 'than the recollection that I had done anything to justify the reproach that the equity of this court varies like the chancellor's foot'.[69]

Practical Defects of the later Chancery

It is the height of irony that the court which originated to provide an escape from the defects of common-law procedure should in its later history have developed procedural defects worse by far than those of the law. For two centuries before Dickens wrote *Bleak House*, the word 'Chancery' had become synonymous with expense, delay and despair. That the court survived at all owed something to the vested interests of its officials but still more to the curious fact that expense and delay do not extinguish hope. Those landed families, if any there were, who escaped the throes of Chancery litigation were fortunate indeed.

The root of much of the trouble was the principle that ultimate responsibility for everything done by the court rested on the chancellor's shoulders. Had he been a full-time judge the strain would have been enormous; but the situation was worse, because for much of his time he was engaged on affairs of state, administrative matters, and the business of the House of Lords. Not until 1885 was the heavy administrative burden recognised and eased by the creation of the Lord Chancellor's Department, headed by a principal secretary who also holds the ancient office of clerk of the crown in Chancery.[70] Inevitably the routine

---

[67]   R. Francis, *Maxims of Equity* (1727).

[68]   Allen, *Law in the Making*, p. 416.

[69]   *Gee v. Prichard* (1818) 2 Swan. 402 at 414.

[70]   See Lord Schuster, 10 CLJ 175. There have subsequently been proposals for a Ministry of Justice to relieve more of the load.

judicial business was widely delegated. Some of it was transacted before the master of the rolls; yet, as there was but one court, he could only sit when the chancellor was absent – often in the evening – and his decisions were subject to review by the chancellor. Enquiries into facts were either referred to masters of the court or to laymen in the country. In Tudor and Stuart times the latter was commonly effected by reference to lay commissioners appointed to 'hear and end according to equity and good conscience', in effect a form of arbitration; in later periods the court directed the issue to be tried by jury at the assizes.[71] Even these devices made little impact on the ever increasing lists of unheard and part-heard cases. Chancellors were unwilling to give equitable relief until all the relevant facts were ascertained, especially since their decisions were usually final; and yet they never had the benefit of a trial from beginning to end. If some fact were wanting, the only course was to adjourn; and perhaps when the cause came on again there would be more time wasted in reconstructing arguments, not to mention the possibility of new insights and doubts to cloud the issue. Throughout the seventeenth and eighteenth centuries the estimates of causes depending reached figures like 10,000 to 20,000, and the time taken to dispose of them could be as long as thirty years.

The second main cause of the trouble was the dependency of the Chancery officials on the fee system. Most of the hundreds of clerks were remunerated not by salary but by fees, paid for each task they performed. Many of the fees were extortionate, if assessed objectively, and the standards of morality in taking them were somewhat flexible. Two distinguished chancellors (Francis Bacon and Lord Macclesfield) were dismissed for accepting 'presents'; but for their subordinates gifts were almost respectable. Gold or silver could open paths through the Chancery morass, and by long usage many 'presents' became fees which could be demanded as of right with an untroubled conscience. The masterships had become so valuable that in the early 1700s they could be sold for as much as £5,000. Since every step in litigation attracted more fees, there was no incentive to expedition, let alone procedural reform. One typical innovation was that which enabled masters' reports to be lengthened by reciting the whole of the previous proceedings verbatim in a 'whereas' clause before starting on the substance of the report. The masters were not accountable for funds in court, and when the South Sea Bubble burst in 1725 it was found that over £10,000 was missing; it had been borrowed for investment by some of the masters. The six clerks received £2,000 a year for two months' work filing

---

71 This was achieved by bringing a collusive action at law on a fictitious wager concerning the fact in dispute.

documents and signing copies, a labour which they delegated to others. Litigants were obliged to order, and pay for, copies they did not want and which were sometimes never made. The sixty clerks were paid by the page for drawing documents; and so they developed such large handwriting, and used such wide margins, that it was said a skilful clerk could spread six ordinary pages into forty. Attempts to reform these abuses were met with hostility and almost complete failure. Offices were property, and reform was resisted as being tantamount to arbitrary confiscation.

A few good words should be said of Chancery procedure, most of which ultimately prevailed over 'due process'. The process of the present High Court is closer to that of the Chancery than to the writ system of the common law. Interlocutory proceedings before masters, the availability of discovery, the use of affidavits and interrogatories, trial by judge alone, most forms of relief other than damages, and the use of sequestration and receivership, all derive from Chancery procedure and were unobtainable at common law. By the eighteenth century, however, the advantages were offset by the abuses. Chancery pleadings had become verbose and complex, and the use of minutely drafted interrogatories served often to hinder rather than advance the progress of a suit. The documentation produced in most Chancery suits was elephantine, and by Lord Eldon's time the work seemed to be grinding to a halt. Eldon was Lord Chancellor from 1801 to 1827, and has borne much of the blame for the conditions over which he presided. He was so renowned for procrastination that his court was said to be a court of 'oyer sans terminer'. He had by no means created the mess, but his very exacting judicial standards were incompatible with the load of work thrust upon him. He admitted on retirement that he had 'somewhat of the cunctative' in his character; he had been against giving extempore judgments at the conclusion of arguments, because he thought that as Chancery litigation had increased counsel had become less well prepared, and therefore it fell to him to satisfy himself that nothing had been overlooked. He also disliked the semblance of dispatch which could be created by delegating issues to masters and juries; he felt this usually led to appeals and ultimately to more delay than a trial in Chancery.[72] But a one-man court could not possibly cope with all the business on this basis. When, in 1824, Eldon was appointed to head a commission of enquiry into the causes of delay, the state of affairs could hardly have been worse. Even a simple matter could take five years to determine, and vast funds – £39 million, it appeared – mouldered in court, out of human dominion, the remains of undecided cases and wrecked fortunes. Appalling instances were mentioned to the commission. The case of *Morgan v. Lord Clarendon*, commenced in 1808, was still in its interlocutory stages; sixteen years had been spent on routine work, no counsel had been briefed, and yet the costs had already reached £3,719. Eldon was too resigned to the situation to perceive any obvious remedy; his report found little fault with the system, and attributed most of the delays to the carelessness or obstinacy of the parties.

Reform and Abolition

Perhaps the most drastic of the nineteenth-century reforms of the judicial system, and certainly the most pressing, were those which attacked the practical evils in Chancery.

The problem of judicial manpower was tackled by appointing a vice-chancellor in 1813 and two more in 1842, and by increasing the jurisdiction of the Master of the Rolls. After 1833 the Master of the Rolls was empowered to sit concurrently with the chancellor in a separate court. Still the chancellor had the final say, until in 1851 a Court of Appeal in Chancery was established, comprising in addition to the existing Chancery judges some additional 'justices of appeal in Chancery'.

The deeper problems were tackled by the gradual abolition of most of the offices in the court. The six clerks went in 1842, the masters in 1852; care was taken to buy out vested interests using public funds, so that no individual was harmed. These officers gone, business in chambers could be streamlined; after 1852 it was conducted, according to new rules, before the master of the rolls or the vice-chancellors and their 'chief clerks'.[73]

These measures encouraged talk of fusion between law and equity,[74] and they prepared the way for still more sweeping reforms. Under the Common Law Procedure Act 1854 the Chancery was empowered to decide questions of law, to try issues of fact by jury, and to award damages; courts of law were empowered to compel discovery, to grant injunctions, and to a limited extent to allow equitable defences to be pleaded. The work of the various courts being thus to a greater extent assimilated, the process of fusion was a relatively slight step. The step was taken in 1865 for the county courts and in 1875 for the superior

---

[73] The title 'master of the Supreme Court' was substituted for 'chief clerk' in 1896. Analogous officers in other divisions of the High Court had the same title.

[74] E.g. the proposal of 1851 discussed in 47 *Law Magazine & Rev.* (3rd ser.) 82.

courts.[75]   But was fusion procedural or substantive?   And, if there was to be no distinction between law and equity, should the resulting system be regarded as equity or law?

Procedural fusion was the main object of the Victorian legislation. All the judges of the Supreme Court were empowered to administer law and equity, and both the Chancery and the common-law courts were abolished.   The establishment of a Chancery Division of the High Court merely reflected the convenience of specialisation, not the nature of the remedies available.   But the promoters of the legislation also envisaged fusion at a deeper level.   The only direct enactment was that 'in all matters . . . in which there is any conflict or variance between the rules of equity and the rules of common law with reference to the same matter, the rules of equity shall prevail.'[76] The precise meaning of this subsection proved elusive.   Some lawyers at first thought the distinction between law and equity had been obliquely abolished, and that there was, for instance, no longer any distinction between legal and equitable estates in land.   Sir George Jessel MR, the first to preside over the Court of Appeal, was inclined to incorporate equitable doctrines into the common law, and once suggested that damages could be given for innocent misrepresentation prior to a contract.   His successor, Lord Esher MR, is said to have complained openly that Jessel 'had been sent to dragoon the Court of Appeal into substituting equity for Common Law, but that he (Esher) and his Common Law colleagues would not have it'.[77] At any rate, by 1897, when Lord Esher retired, it was plain that the effect of the section had been minimal.   No new remedies had been created.   Indeed, as Maitland pointed out, the section had been based on a misapprehension.   Law and equity were never in 'conflict or variance', because equity was not a self-sufficient system; at every point equity presupposed the existence of common law.[78]

Attempts have been made in the present century, particularly by Lord Denning MR, to banish the distinction between law and equity.   To the extent that they have succeeded, equity has taken on a new meaning.   If, for reasons of history, equity had become the law peculiar to the Court of Chancery, nevertheless in broad theory equity was an approach to justice which gave more weight than did the law to particular circumstances and hard cases.   The abolition of the historical, procedural distinction gave new emphasis to this broad view of equity.   The

---

[75]   Stat. 28 & 29 Vict., c.99; Supreme Court of Judicature Act 1873, 36 & 37 Vict., c.66.

[76]   Judicature Act 1873, s.25(11).

[77]   A. Underhill, *Change and Decay* (1938), p. 87.

[78]   F. W. Maitland, *Equity* (1909), pp. 16-17.

survival of a distinct Chancery Bar, still largely domiciled in Lincoln's Inn, where Lord Eldon's court used to sit in vacation, has ensured the continuance of the specialist traditions of the Court of Chancery in property matters. But those traditions are no longer so closely related to equity as distinct from law; in fact Chancery judges are the least likely to administer equity in the broader sense, because the type of work they do demands as much certainty as clear rules can provide. The Queen's Bench judges, on the other hand, in dealing with agreements and accidents, are more given to the equitable approach, having inherited it from the jury. Paradoxically, as the equity of the Chancery has hardened into law, so the law has been dissolving into something like abstract equity, with a consequent loss of clarity and certainty.[79] Today, therefore, the Chancery Division is not a court of conscience; and 'it is the common lawyers who now do equity'.[80]

Further reading

Holdsworth HEL, vol. I, pp. 395-476; vol. V, pp. 215-338; vol. IX, pp. 335-408; vol. XII, pp. 178-330, 583-605

Milsom HFCL, pp. 82-96

Manchester MLH, pp. 135-143

W. P. Baildon, *Select Cases in Chancery 1364-1471* (10 SS, 1896)

J. F. Baldwin, *The King's Council in England during the Middle Ages* (1913), ch. X

A. D. Hargreaves, 'Equity and the Latin Side of the Chancery' (1952) 68 LQR 481-499

J. P. Dawson, *A History of Lay Judges* (1960), pp. 145-172

D. E. C. Yale, *Lord Nottingham's 'Manual of Chancery Practice' and 'Prolegomena of Chancery and Equity'* (1965), esp. pp. 1-80; *Lord Nottingham's Chancery Cases* (73 SS, 1954; 79 SS, 1962)

W. J. Jones, *The Elizabethan Court of Chancery* (1967)

M. E. Avery, 'History of the Equitable Jurisdiction of the Chancery before 1460' (1969) 42 BIHR 129-144; 'An Evaluation of the Effectiveness of the Court of Chancery under the Lancastrian Kings' (1970) 86 LQR 84-97

J. L. Barton, 'Equity in the Medieval Common Law' in *Equity in the World's Legal Systems* (R. A. Newman ed., 1973), pp. 139-155

---

[79] See pp. 109-110, ante.

[80] *Hill v. A. C. Parsons Ltd* [1971] 3 All E.R. 1345 at 1359, per Lord Denning MR. See also p. 233, post.

N. Pronay, 'The Chancellor, the Chancery, and the Council at the End of the 15th Century' in *British Government and Administration* (H. Hearder and H. R. Loyn ed., 1974), pp. 87-103

W. H. Bryson, *The Equity Side of the Exchequer* (1975)

F. Metzger, 'The Last Phase of the Medieval Chancery' (1980), *Law-making and Law-makers*, pp. 79-89

J. B. Post, 'Equitable Resorts before 1450' (1983), *Law, Litigants and the Legal Profession*, pp. 68-79

J. A. Guy, *The Public Career of Sir Thomas More* (1980), pp. 35-93; 'The Development of Equitable Jurisdiction 1450-1550' (1983), *Law, Litigants and the Legal Profession*, pp. 80-86; *St German on Chancery and Statute* (SS Supp. Ser. 6, 1985)

W. M. Ormrod, 'The Origins of the *Sub pena* Writ' (1988) 61 BIHR 11-20

THEORY OF EQUITY IN CHANCERY

W. H. D. Winder, 'Precedent in Equity' (1941) 57 LQR 245-279

C. K. Allen, *Law in the Making* (7th ed., 1964), pp. 383-425

J. L. Barton, *St German's Doctor and Student* (91 SS, 1974), pp. xxix-li

D. E. C. Yale, 'St German's Little Treatise concerning Writs of Subpoena' (1975) 10 IJ 324-333

J. H. Baker, (1978) 94 SS *37-43, 74-83*

Z. Rueger, 'Gerson's Concept of Equity and Christopher St German' (1982) 3 *History of Political Thought* 1-30

J. A. Guy, 'Law, Equity and Conscience in Henrician Juristic Thought' in *Reassessing the Henrician Age* (A. Fox and J. Guy ed., 1986), pp. 179-198

C. Croft, 'Lord Hardwicke's Use of Precedent in Chancery' (1989), *Legal Record and Historical Reality*, pp. 121-155

THE CLASH OF 1616

J. P. Dawson, 'Coke and Ellesmere disinterred: the Attack on the Chancery in 1616' (1941) 36 *Illinois Law Rev* 127-152

J. H. Baker, 'The Common Lawyers and the Chancery: 1616' (1969) 4 IJ 368-392 (repr. in LPCL 205-229); *Legal History Studies 1972*, pp. 3-4

G. W. Thomas, 'James I, Equity and Lord Keeper John Williams' (1976) 91 EHR 506-528

L. A. Knafla, *Law and Politics in Jacobean England* (1977), pp. 155-181

7. The Conciliar Courts

We have now seen how the common-law courts were derived from the early king's council or *Curia Regis*, and how at a later stage the Court of Chancery separated from the council as an extraordinary jurisdiction to be invoked where the ordinary course of law failed to provide justice. Still there remained a residuary royal prerogative of justice. Petitions which were not thought appropriate for the chancellor alone to deal with were retained in the king's council, to be considered at its judicial sessions, or were delegated to other, more appropriate officials. In the mid-fourteenth century there was no clear distinction between these jurisdictions, and it could be said that the English bill jurisdiction of the Court of Chancery was not wholly distinct from that of the council until some time in the fifteenth century. In the case of the other conciliar courts, rigid distinctions were not made until the sixteenth century.

It was both the strength and the ultimate downfall of conciliar jurisdiction that it depended on close connection with the king's chief ministers. A principal justification for its existence was that extraordinary action by the king himself and his magnates sometimes offered the only escape from the kind of undue influence which could corrupt sheriffs and juries. But the absolute power needed to check abuses in due process was itself open to constitutional objection. In 1510 a wave of reaction to Henry VII's avaricious ministers Empson and Dudley very nearly carried away conciliar jurisdictions; a bill for abolition was rejected only at the new king's personal insistence. In 1511 two plaintiffs recovered damages against opponents who had sued them before Empson, contrary to the statutes of due process; and there was a flood of less successful actions in respect of conciliar jurisdiction in various forms. By the end of the century the vehicle of attack had become the prohibition, which brought about further clashes in the seventeenth century. In 1641, after an unfortunate decade in which the Star Chamber became too closely involved in politics, conciliar jurisdiction in the old sense was swept away for ever.[1] Despite these drawbacks, however, conciliar justice was a regular feature of the English legal system for nearly three centuries.

---

[1] 94 SS *70-74*; Stat. 16 Car. I, c.10.

The Court of Star Chamber

The best known of the conciliar courts was the Court of Star Chamber. It used to be thought that the court was established by the so-called Star Chamber Act of 1487,[2] but that statute in fact set up a special tribunal to deal with particular problems of law and order; its jurisdiction seems later to have been absorbed into that of the Star Chamber, which was much older. The starred chamber (*camera stellata*), so called from the gilded stars on the ceiling, was a room built within the palace of Westminster in 1347 and thereafter used for judicial sessions of the king's council.[3] For over a century the 'council in the Star Chamber' was nothing other than the council meeting in a particular place; it dealt with state affairs as well as petitions for justice. During the chancellorship of Thomas Wolsey (1515-29) its civil jurisdiction increased dramatically, even to the extent of becoming a grievance; but it was not until 1540 that the Court of Star Chamber and the Privy Council were sufficiently distinct for separate records to be kept; and even after that the membership of the two bodies was almost identical.[4] The Privy Council which then split from the Star Chamber was a smaller body than the earlier council, meeting in secret to discuss government policy and administration; its only jurisdiction from the seventeenth century was of an appellate nature.[5]

At the beginning of the sixteenth century the council in the Star Chamber exercised a predominantly civil jurisdiction. Like the Chancery it was concerned mainly with real property, but petitioners usually complained of riot, unlawful assembly, perjury, forgery, forcible entry, or some other form of oppression, and it was this allegation of misdemeanour which gave the council its theoretical interest in such business. Probably the allegations were often fictitious or exaggerated, and the council was being asked in reality to try title: a task it could not in theory undertake because of the statutes of due process.[6] The formal jurisdiction of the court was nevertheless at first indistinguishable from

---

2 Stat. 3 Hen. VII, c.1. The Star Chamber did not itself rely on the statute: *Chambers' Case* (1629) Cro. Car. 168; Co. Inst., vol. IV, p. 62. The marginal title *pro camera stellata* seems to have been an interpolation.

3 A meeting of 1366 for legal business is mentioned in *Calendar of Close Rolls 1364-68*, p. 237.

4 The chief difference was that the chief justices of the two benches also attended the Star Chamber. Until Elizabeth I's time peers who were not privy councillors also claimed the right to sit, but this was denied.

5 See pp. 161-162, post.

6 Stat. 25 Edw. III (sess. v), c.4, prohibited the council from meddling with freeholds.

that of the Chancery, and the procedure was closely similar. Although it did not become a court of conscience in the same way as the Chancery, and did not develop an equity jurisprudence on the civil side, it was an extraordinary or supplementary court of law, particularly for cases with a criminal element. No clear distinction was drawn between civil and criminal procedure; damages and a wide range of punishments could be given in the same action.[7]

By Stuart times the criminal aspect was more to the fore, because the court was increasingly used by the law officers of the Crown to bring prosecutions. The advantage to the Crown was that proceedings were begun by information and tried summarily: there was no need for a grand jury or a trial jury. There was also an imaginative range of punishments to be imposed, including the slitting of noses and severing of ears. The Star Chamber offered the government a convenient forum for prosecuting sedition and ecclesiastical offences, when juries might not co-operate, though it was always subject to the constitutional limitation that a man could not be tried for his life except by a jury of his peers at common law. The association of the Star Chamber with unpopular prosecutions and vindictive punishments in the 1630s was its undoing. But its true achievement lay in the previous century, when it often provided access to justice unavailable elsewhere. Its principal effect on the law, on the other hand, was in the development of the law of misdemeanours. Criminal libel, forgery, perjury, subornation of perjury, conspiracy, and attempts to commit crimes, were largely the creation of the Star Chamber. It is tempting to characterise this activity as criminal equity; but in this instance 'equity' was an integral part of the common law, because the offences cultivated in the Star Chamber could be prosecuted on indictment in the regular courts.[8] The abolition of the court in 1641 did not, therefore, leave any gap in jurisprudence; the creative work on the criminal side was simply channelled elsewhere. Misdemeanours of a political character could still be prosecuted on information, but in the King's Bench, where they were triable by jury. And the King's Bench claimed to have inherited the equitable function of developing the criminal law to meet new circumstances.[9] This equitable

---

7   See, e.g., *Edwardes v. Wootton* (1607) B. & M. 648 at 649 (fine, damages, penance, imprisonment and binding over, all in one suit).

8   Thus, Popham CJ was reported in 1598 to have started trying prisoners on circuit for attempted felonies: *Wilbraham's Diary*, Camden Soc., vol. IV (3rd ser.), p. 20.

9   E.g. *R. v. Edgerley* (1641) March N.R. 135 at 137 (damaging highway with large vehicles); *R. v. Sidley* (1663) 1 Sid. 168 (indecent exposure). For informations, see p. 578, post. Although punishments for misdemeanour were not fixed at common law, the more extreme Star Chamber punishments were abandoned.

jurisdiction was later supposed to have been abandoned, or rather surrendered to the legislature, in the interests of certainty.[10]

The Court of Requests

The early Tudor council found itself as over-pressed by suitors as the Chancery and relied similarly on delegation and reference. Indeed, conciliar proceedings often had the appearance of a compulsory arbitration process, in which parties were hauled before single councillors or referees, the adjudication being embodied in a conciliar decree. Sub-conciliar agencies of this kind were busy under Henry VII, but fell under the odium attaching to Empson and Dudley and were curtailed in the first years of Henry VIII. Wolsey revived experiments with 'under courts' to relieve himself of minor causes when he grew weary of them; but they were not a lasting success.

The most enduring of the sub-conciliar tribunals was the Court of Requests. As a distinct department of the council, it may be traced to the promotion in 1483 of an official who had been dealing with the 'bills, requests and supplications of poor persons' to be a 'clerk of the council of the requests'.[11] Nevertheless there was not in the fifteenth century a court distinct from the council. In 1519 Wolsey established the 'king's council in the court of requests' as a regular tribunal, meeting in the White Hall and functioning independently of the rest of the council. After the emergence of a separate and more select Privy Council in 1540, it lost any direct connection with the council; the work was then dispatched by the appointment of two masters of requests, followed in 1562 by two 'extraordinary masters of requests'.

The Requests came to be regarded as the court of the lord president of the privy seal; but it was originally the special responsibility of the king's almoner and dean of the chapel royal, which indicates its charitable nature. It had in effect taken over from the council that aspect of early Chancery jurisdiction which had given relief on grounds of poverty, and it emulated Chancery practice to the extent of becoming a court of equity. The court soon felt the effects of the surge in popularity of all the central jurisdictions in the Tudor period, and the

---

10 Bl. Comm., vol. I, p. 92; *Shaw v. D.P.P.* [1962] A.C. 220 at 268, 273; *Knuller v. D.P.P.* [1973] A.C. 435 at 471, 473.

11 *Calendar of Patent Rolls 1476-85*, p. 413. The office may have existed since the 14th century. A 'refrendarie' of the council is mentioned in 1387: Rot. Parl., vol. III, p. 233.

allegation of poverty became increasingly disingenuous as men of substance sought to take advantage of the simple procedures. But the Court of Requests had less constitutional foundation than the Chancery, especially when formal links with the council were severed, and it was frequently complained of as an encroachment on the common law. Towards the end of the sixteenth century the common-law judges began restraining it by prohibition; and in 1598, despite a learned historical essay in defence of the court by Sir Julius Caesar (then one of the masters of requests), the Common Pleas delivered the astounding pronouncement that the court simply did not exist and that its proceedings were *coram non judice*.[12] The hostility was relaxed in the seventeenth century, and the Requests came to be acknowledged as a court of record separate from the council; prohibitions were sent only if the court interfered with the common law. Its new status enabled it to survive briefly the abolition of prerogative tribunals in 1641;[13] but, though never abolished, it was stifled during the Civil War when the privy seal was withdrawn. Since it had developed no distinct equity jurisdiction of its own, nothing substantial was lost. The provision of small-claims courts was more sensibly tackled at a local level, since litigation at Westminster was inevitably more costly.[14]

Regional Conciliar and Equity Courts

In addition to the council which followed the king, there were in the early modern period two regional councils which exercised similar jurisdiction to the Star Chamber and Chancery in certain parts of the country. The Council in the North Parts (meaning Yorkshire and all the counties beyond) originated in the time of Edward IV as the Duke of Gloucester's council, but went into abeyance for some time before it was revived as the Duke of Richmond's council in 1525. The Council in the Principality and Marches of Wales began as the Prince of Wales's council in the time of Henry VII, and was confirmed by statute in

---

[12] *Stepneth v. Lloyd* (1598) Kiralfy SB, p. 301, 12 SS xxxix, Cro. Eliz. 647. The ratio decidendi was narrower than Coke (Co. Inst., vol. IV, p. 97) stated it to be.

[13] Records ceased in 1642, but the power to imprison was upheld by the King's Bench in *Ex parte Howsden* (1645) HLS MS. 113, p. 229. Masters of requests were appointed at the Restoration, but they exercised no jurisdiction.

[14] For urban courts of requests, see p. 33, ante.

1542.[15] Each council met under a lord president and, by devolution from central government, transacted both judicial and administrative business. For a short time after 1536 there was also a Council in the West Parts, but it proved so unpopular that it was suspended.

The common-law courts kept a suspicious eye on these prerogative tribunals to ensure that they did not act *ultra vires* by meddling with the common law. The surveillance, by means of prohibition, became hostile under Coke CJ, who even denied the jurisdiction of a court of equity to grant specific performance of contracts, on the ground that a defaulting party had the right to pay damages if he chose.[16] The lords president complained of Coke CJ's attempts to control them, but the Privy Council ruled that both councils 'should be within the survey of Westminster Hall'. The lord treasurer said there was no reason why Yorkshire should be less free than, say, Cornwall; and yet there was the most miserable slavery when the law was vague or uncertain, and men's fortunes decided by discretion.[17] The councils functioned until the Civil War, when they went into disuse. Only the Council in Wales was resurrected in 1660, by reason of its statutory foundation; but its second life was short, since in 1689 parliament dissolved it as being 'contrary to the Great Charter, the known laws of the land, and the birthright of the subject, and the means to introduce an arbitrary power and government'.[18]

Equity jurisdiction was also exercised in the palatinates, where the equity courts were not related to the king's council but followed a similar course.[19]

---

[15] Stat. 34 & 35 Hen. VIII, c.26. Until 1604 it exercised jurisdiction in England, but in that year it was held that Herefordshire, Worcestershire, Shropshire and Gloucestershire were outside its bounds: Co. Inst., vol. IV, p. 242.

[16] *Bromage v. Genning* (1616) 1 Rolle Rep. 368. The decision was overturned later in the century.

[17] *Case of the Lords President of Wales and York* (c. 1608) 12 Co. Rep. 50, per Lord Salisbury T.

[18] Stat. 1 Will. & Mar. (sess. i), c.27, s.2. Cf. Wales Act 1978 (c.52).

[19] There were four equity courts: the Chancery of Durham, the Duchy Chamber of Lancaster (presided over by the chancellor of the duchy), the Chancery of the County Palatine of Lancaster (presided over by the vice-chancellor), and the Exchequer of Chester (presided over by the chamberlain). The last was abolished in 1830; the Duchy Chamber was not abolished, but has not sat since 1835; the remaining two flourished until 1971 (Courts Act 1971, c.23, s.41).

The Courts of the Admiral and Marshal

The courts of common law could not properly entertain causes of action arising outside the realm, because of the rule that an issue of fact had to be tried by a jury from the place where it was 'laid'; a jury could not be summoned from outside an English county. Ordinary justice ended where the power of the sheriff ended. This gap in the system of justice was closed by the king in council. The council needed no juries, its jurisdiction was *in personam*, and the speed of its process made it easier to deal with transient parties such as seamen or foreign merchants. By the middle of the fourteenth century the council had allowed its extraterritorial jurisdiction to be exercised in all but the most difficult cases by the two sister courts of the admiral and of the constable and marshal. Some foreign causes were retained in the full council,[20] or in the Chancery – where from the seventeenth century equitable relief was sometimes given in respect of land outside the realm.[21]

The two specialised tribunals became courts of regular resort, both following Civil law procedure, and under the influence of the doctors of law they enjoyed a history quite distinct from that of the other conciliar courts. The jurisdiction was nevertheless not as exclusive in practice as the theory of venue dictated, because even in medieval times overseas actions were occasionally tried at law by means of a fictitious supposition that the foreign place was in England. If the plaintiff said that Harfleur was in Kent, or that Hamburg was in London, and the defendant joined issue on the substance of the matter, the jury would be summoned from Kent or London and the place would be immaterial. The common law therefore acquired concurrent jurisdiction in some cases, and in others it even claimed an exclusive jurisdiction which it defended by prohibition.

THE COURT OF THE EARL MARSHAL

The Court of the Lord High Constable and Earl Marshal of England came to prominence in the middle of the fourteenth century[22] as a court having jurisdiction over military matters as diverse as treason, prisoners of war, ransom, contracts with sutlers, and disputed coats of arms. Its

---

[20] The best-known instance is the *Carrier's Case* (1473) Y.B. Pas. 13 Edw. IV, fo. 9, pl.5; 64 SS 30; p. 607, post.

[21] E.g. *Arglasse v. Muschamp* (1682) 1 Vern. 75 (land in Ireland); *Penn v. Lord Baltimore* (1750) 1 Ves. Sen. 444 (land in America).

[22] It had antecedents in the military courts which followed the king's host on active service and held 'pleas of the army' (*placita exercitus*). For the history of martial law, see J. V. Capua, [1977] CLJ 152.

attempts to assert a wider common pleas jurisdiction were restrained by statutes of Richard II, after which it was confined to 'deeds of arms and war' and appeals of treason or felony committed overseas. Because of these strict limitations, and because for political reasons the high office of constable of England was suppressed in the sixteenth century, the court went into abeyance. In 1582 Elizabeth I refused to appoint a constable ad hoc so that an appeal could be brought against Sir Francis Drake,[23] and the court rarely sat again.[24] But the court has understandably been confused with that belonging to the earl marshal alone. This *Curia Marescalli*, or High Court of Chivalry, was revived by James I as a court of honour, which not only tried the right to distinctions of honour and coat armour but also redressed affronts to honour such as slander. The slander jurisdiction was later denied,[25] leaving it with a jurisdiction probably confined to disputes over armorial bearings, which are determined according to the law of arms. The court, which has only sat once since 1737, is the last English court to use the procedure of the Civil law.[26]

THE HIGH COURT OF ADMIRALTY

The Court of the Lord High Admiral of England appeared at the same period as its terrestrial counterpart, to deal with matters arising on the high seas. It was not restricted to causes connected with naval warfare, and was much resorted to by merchants. Like its sister court, it encroached in its early days upon the common law and had to be restrained by statute from hearing matters arising within the realm, whether or not they concerned the sea.[27] The court was presided over by a judge of the Admiralty, usually a doctor of law, and proceeded according to the Civil law, under which process could issue against ships and goods as well as against persons. The law which it applied was based on the *jus gentium*, or universal law of the sea, which was derived from the ancient Rhodian sea law and the 'customs of Oleron'.

The Admiralty was watched by the common-law judges with that jealousy and suspicion which they bestowed on all jurisdictions tainted with Romanism. In the fifteenth century actions were allowed in the

---

[23] *Doughtey's Case* (1582) Coke's MS. Rep., BL MS. Harley 6687, fo. 311v; LPCL 202.

[24] A notorious exception was *Lord Rea v. Ramsey* (1631) 3 St. Tr. 483, in which battle was waged.

[25] *Chambers v. Jennings* (1703) 7 Mod. Rep. 125.

[26] *Manchester Corporation v. Manchester Palace of Varieties Ltd* [1955] P. 133, [1955] 1 All E.R. 387.

[27] Stat. 13 Ric. II, c.5; 2 Hen. IV, c.11.

two benches against adversaries who sued in Admiralty contrary to statute,[28] and during the sixteenth century a torrent of prohibitions rained on those who chose the Civil law. In 1536 the criminal jurisdiction was by statute turned over to the common law, so that pirates and other marine criminals could be tried by jury under special commissions of oyer and terminer. By 1600 the admiral's jurisdiction was at a low ebb. According to the Elizabethan judges, he could not try causes arising on land beyond the seas, but only causes arising on the sea; and the sea for this purpose ended at low water-mark, except when the tide was in.[29] This extremely restrictive view excluded charterparties and foreign maritime contracts, which the common law had taken over by means of fictions.[30] The admiral was left to deal with seamen's wages, which were earned at sea, collision and salvage, and prize.[31] The Civilians, of course, took a wider view of their jurisdiction, and retaliated with their own fiction: that contracts were made 'upon the high seas' when in truth they were not. In 1633 the Privy Council directed a settlement of the dispute, under which the Admiralty was to be allowed actions for freight and actions to enforce charterparties relating to overseas voyages and maritime contracts made on foreign soil.[32] This settlement did not last, however, and by the end of the century the common law had succeeded in depressing the Court of Admiralty to a worse condition than it had enjoyed in Tudor times.

The court revived somewhat during the Napoleonic wars, when the prize jurisdiction benefited from British naval successes. A number of statutes after 1840 extended the Admiralty's competence to include all maritime matters except charterparties, and the value of the specialised tribunal was recognised in 1875 when it was incorporated into the Probate, Divorce and Admiralty Division of the High Court. The president of that division used to sit with the silver oar of the Admiralty before him when trying maritime cases. Coke's final victory came in 1970, when the division was abolished and admiralty business transferred to the Queen's Bench Division.[33]

---

[28] 94 SS 73 n.4.

[29] *Constable's Case* (1601) 5 Co. Rep. 106.

[30] Indeed the common law assumed a concurrent jurisdiction over causes arising on the sea: e.g. *Anon.* (1542) Bro. N.C. 5 (action on the case for goods lost on high seas).

[31] Prize, from the French verb *prendre*, is the right to a share in the proceeds of enemy ships and cargoes seized at sea.

[32] *Memorandum* (1633) Cro. Car. 216.

[33] Administration of Justice Act 1970 (c.31). The oar, however, remains in use for admiralty sittings.

Further reading

Holdsworth HEL, vol. I, pp. 477-580

J. F. Baldwin, *The King's Council in England during the Middle Ages* (1913)

C. G. Bayne and W. H. Dunham, *Select Cases in the Council of Henry VII* (75 SS, 1956)

G. R. Elton, 'Conciliar Courts' in *The Tudor Constitution* (2nd ed., 1982), pp. 163-217

C. M. Gray, 'The Boundaries of the Equitable Function' (1976) 20 AJLH 192-226

J. A. Guy, 'Wolsey, the Council and the Council Courts' (1976) 91 EHR 481-505; 'The Privy Council: Revolution or Evolution?' in *Revolution Reassessed* (C. Coleman and D. Starkey ed., 1986), pp. 59-85

J. H. Baker, 'The Conciliar Courts' (1978) 94 SS 70-74

STAR CHAMBER

W. Hudson, *The Court of Star Chamber* (1621), printed in F. Hargrave (ed.), *Collectanea Juridica*, vol. II (1792), pp. 1-240

J. Hawarde, *Les Reportes del Cases in Camera Stellata, 1593-1609* (W. P. Baildon ed., 1894)

I. S. Leadam, *Select Cases before the King's Council in the Star Chamber* (16 SS, 1902)

T. G. Barnes, 'Star Chamber and the Sophistication of the Criminal Law' [1977] *Criminal Law Rev* 316-326; 'Star Chamber Litigants and their Counsel' (1978), *Legal Records and the Historian*, pp. 7-28

J. A. Guy, *The Cardinal's Court: the Impact of Thomas Wolsey in Star Chamber* (1977); *The Court of Star Chamber and its Records to the Reign of Elizabeth I* (1985)

COURT OF REQUESTS

I. S. Leadam, *Select Cases in the Court of Requests* (12 SS, 1898)

L. M. Hill (ed.), *The Ancient State Authoritie and Proceedings of the Court of Requests by Sir Julius Caesdr* (1975)

CONSTABLE AND MARSHAL

G. D. Squibb, *The High Court of Chivalry* (1959)

M. H. Keen, 'The Jurisdiction and Origins of the Constable's Court' in *War and Government in the Middle Ages* (J. Gillingham and J. Holt ed., 1984), pp. 159-169

ADMIRALTY

F. Wiswall, *The Development of Admiralty Jurisdiction and Practice since 1800* (1971)

T. J. Runyan, 'The Rolls of Oleron and the Admiralty Court in 14th Century England' (1975) 19 AJLH 95-111

D. E. C. Yale, 'A View of the Admiral Jurisdiction: Sir Matthew Hale and the Civilians' (1975), *Legal History Studies 1972*, pp. 87-109

8. The Ecclesiastical Courts

At much the same time as the common law of England was being fashioned through the centralisation of royal justice, the universal law of the Church was developing as a parallel (but wider) system of jurisprudence through the centralisation of ecclesiastical authority in the pope at Rome. By the twelfth century there was a mass of rules and pronouncements circulating in collections of 'canons', many of which were purely theological in content, such as creeds and doctrinal statements. Canon law became a scientific system, distinct from theology and ecclesiastical history, largely as a result of the work of the Bolognese monk Gratian. Gratian's *Decretum* (*c.* 1140) set out to systematise the canons in accordance with a hierarchical scheme of authority with the pope at the earthly summit: whatever the pope decreed was to be obeyed, however intolerable or wrong; if the pope erred, the punishment would be his, and the obedient would be released. The study of this new Canon law became all the rage in medieval European universities; a system of courts developed to cope with the litigation which its study fuelled; and numerous questions found their way to the popes for decision. The papal answers to these forensic questions, contained in letters called 'decretals', provided additional material for study. By the fourteenth century there was a substantial body of Canon law (the *Corpus Juris Canonici*) comprising Gratian's collection, the Decretals of Pope Gregory IX (1234),[1] the Sext (1298), and the Clementine Decretals (1305-14); to which were later added the *Extravagantes* of Pope John XXII (1316-34) and the *Extravagantes Communes* (c. 1300-1480).[2]

As far as England was concerned, there had been a time, before the twelfth century, when bishops wielded their spiritual authority without the aid of a distinct system of courts, and without appeals to the bishop of Rome; ecclesiastical matters were dealt with in the old local assemblies. In the shire court the bishop presided with the sheriff, and it

---

[1] This was a retrospective collection going back to the 12th century, and including some English cases from the time of Pope Alexander III.

[2] The *extravagantes* were unofficial collections, and there was no standard text until they were printed at the beginning of the 16th century. The Roman Church made substantial alterations to the *Corpus Juris Canonici* at the Council of Trent in the 1560s, and abandoned it altogether in 1918. Ironically, the medieval *Corpus Juris Canonici* still has a residuary authority in England.

seems that spiritual matters were placed first on the agenda.[3] William I ordered in the 1070s that pleas of bishops and archdeacons should not be heard in the hundred courts, but that the power of the king and the sheriff should be available to compel appearance before the bishop. This was an attempt to prevent the corrective jurisdiction of the Church, which generated a monetary income, from passing with the hundreds into lay hands. The separation of ecclesiastical and lay pleas at county level probably did not occur until the next century. As with the royal courts of the same period, there is no distinct event to record; bishops exercised their authority in different ways, and one intermediate stage between the county and the settled courts of later times was the synod.[4]

By the end of the twelfth century, however, the Church and its legal administrators had constructed a transnational hierarchy of tribunals, with the pope at its apex, and the English courts were accommodated in this new system. The archdeacons, at the lowest level, had criminal courts for the correction of moral and disciplinary offences; appeal lay from archidiaconal courts to episcopal 'courts of audience'. The bishops also had their 'consistory courts', presided over by chancellors learned in Canon law, which heard lawsuits such as matrimonial and defamation cases. From bishops appeal lay to one of the two archbishops: in the province of York to the Chancery Court of York, in that of Canterbury to the Court of Arches.[5] From these provincial courts, appeal lay to the pope: either to papal delegates (the equivalent of commissioners) or to the papal audience court, usually known from the fourteenth century as the Rota.[6] The Rota was reconstituted under Pope John XXII in 1331, when it was composed of doctors of law, selected from all over Europe, sitting in the palace at Avignon. A prominent papal auditor in the formative years was William Bateman, bishop of Norwich and founder of a law college at Cambridge; either he or his Cambridge protégés in the Rota began the tradition of reporting cases there, thereby adding to the decretal and academic literature of the Canon law a body of judicial case law.[7]

---

3 William of Malmesbury tells of a famous bishop who used to doze off once the Church business was concluded: *Gesta Pontificum* (Rolls ser.), p. 282.

4 See C. Morris, 82 EHR 449.

5 So called because it sat in the church of St Mary-le-Bow, in London, which is built over arches.

6 So called from the wheel-shaped arrangement of the lords auditors' benches in the hall of justice at Avignon.

7 The earliest rotal reports in print are those of Dr Thomas Fastolf, taken in 1336-1337, published in 1475: see [1986] CLJ 84.

CANON LAW AND COMMON LAW

The Canon law of the Western Church was taken to apply to all Christians in all places, and nearly all people in England were (or were deemed to be) Christians;[8] but its enforcement in the temporal world depended on the co-operation of temporal authority, and the degree of co-operation varied from one country to another. No English king, or royal judge, would have dreamed of disputing the spiritual authority of the Canon law as an abstract proposition. Papal authority was more difficult to accept absolutely, especially since some popes had laid claim to temporal as well as spiritual authority, and there was considerable room for argument as to what matters were spiritual and what temporal. The conflicts of jurisdiction were not typically disputes between an embattled Church and a hostile royal power; there was rather a conflict of laws, caused by the existence of two systems of equal validity which claimed to operate within the same geographical territory.

The first major clash arose in the 1160s over the immunity claimed by the clergy from secular criminal jurisdiction. After stormy scenes, the council at Clarendon in 1164 agreed to a compromise. Clerks were to be arraigned before the temporal court; if they asserted and proved their clerical status, they were to be handed over for trial to the bishop; if convicted of a serious crime, they were to be degraded from their orders and returned to the lay court for punishment as laymen. This sensible settlement, which was consistent with current Canonistic teaching, fell foul of a personal dispute between King Henry II and Thomas Becket, the archbishop of Canterbury, who argued that the procedure resulted in double punishment. That the Church should have sought privilege for murderers and felons now seems shameful, but Becket's assassination by a covert military operation earned him a martyr's crown and the Church succeeded in making him England's most popular saint. The papal view on clerical immunity hardened after this episode, and the clergy won their privilege; it was later to play a bizarre role in the history of English criminal law.[9] Nevertheless, Becket's posthumous victory was limited to capital charges against clergymen and did not give the Church priority in other disputes. Popes who wanted temporal power had to descend to human politics; and, on a more practical plane, bishops needed temporal co-operation to enforce their own judicial authority by imprisonment. On the other hand, kings did not like to incur the wrath of the Church. For the rest of the middle

8 The only exceptions of any significance in England were the Jews, until they were expelled in 1290. (They were readmitted by an Order in Council of 1674.)

9 See pp. 586-589, post.

ages, therefore, most conflicts were fought out between private litigants in particular cases. The means was the royal writ of prohibition, whereby a party could seek to prevent litigation in an ecclesiastical court. His opponent might retaliate by setting in motion the process of excommunication. But these weapons were wielded by subjects, not by Church and State; and among the keenest seekers of prohibitions in the early days were the clergy themselves.

The issue of writs of prohibition as a matter of course, on a bare application being made, was much complained of by bishops in the thirteenth century. The constitutional wrangle over their use was won by King Edward I, who nevertheless conceded a procedure (called 'consultation') by which the prohibition could be withdrawn if an adversary satisfied the king's judges that the cause was spiritual. The decision as to what matters were spiritual was therefore reserved to the king and his judges. Attempts to clarify existing boundaries were made in the writ *Circumspecte agatis* (1285),[10] and the *Articuli cleri* (1315), as follows: the Church courts had an unquestioned jurisdiction over marriage and bastardy,[11] testate and intestate succession to personal property,[12] and punishment of mortal sin, such as fornication, adultery or gluttony. Church land was only excluded from temporal jurisdiction if it had been given 'in free, pure and perpetual alms', without any form of feudal service to the lord; if the status of land was in dispute, it was tried in the royal court by the assize *utrum*.[13] The appointment of clergy to benefices was for the bishop; but the right to nominate a clerk for such appointment was a temporal right (an 'advowson') which was justiciable in the royal courts; questions as to tithes, the principal income of benefices, were subject to a troublesome division of authority. Contracts were for the temporal law; but 'breach of faith' was a sin which could be corrected by penance in the spiritual courts.[14] Two torts were allowed to the Church courts: laying violent hands on a clerk,[15] which was concurrently a breach of the king's peace, and defamation, which was not actionable at common law until the

---

[10] This was later called a 'statute' and generally treated as such, though it merely embodied existing practice in a letter of guidance to the judges.

[11] See pp. 545-548, 557-562, post.

[12] See pp. 435-436, post.

[13] Also introduced by the council at Clarendon in 1164. For *utrum*, see E. G. Kimball, 43 EHR 341; A. W. Douglas, 53 *Speculum* 26; for free alms, see Douglas, 24 AJLH 95.

[14] R. H. Helmholz, 91 LQR 406.

[15] R. H. Helmholz, 8 *Monumenta Iuris Canonici* (Series C: Subsidia) 425.

sixteenth century.[16] In each case the remedy was penance, not civil compensation; but in practice a civil remedy was achieved by allowing commutation of the penance on terms.

This settlement gave the Church a pervasive jurisdiction over the lives of most ordinary people: over family matters and wills, sexual offences, defamation and breach of faith. The king's courts, on the other hand, retained a complete control over temporal property, including advowsons and some of the land owned by Church institutions; they accordingly enjoyed the extensive patronage of bishops, monasteries and other ecclesiastical bodies when pursuing their not inconsiderable temporal rights.

In case of conflict, the king's law prevailed. This principle was applied even to limit papal authority. In the fourteenth century the king in parliament legislated against papal interference with advowsons,[17] stating that 'the Holy Church of England' had been endowed with benefices by kings and nobles within the realm, and that these were protected by the law of the land. The same legislation, reinforced by the Statute of Winchester (1393), prescribed severe penalties for drawing out of the realm any plea belonging to the king's court, and this was held to extend to actions in Church courts within England.[18] The courts were also expressing difficulties about the status of the pope: he was recognised as bishop of Rome, but not as a bishop to whom the court could send writs. A papal excommunication was for that reason treated by the English royal courts as invalid.[19]

Effect of the Reformation

By the end of the fifteenth century the uneasy peace between the two jurisdictions was breaking down. The King's Bench was receiving a stream of actions brought on the Statute of Winchester against parties

---

[16] See pp. 495-498, post. The ecclesiastical jurisdiction here was peculiar to England, and was based on a local 'constitution' of the Council of Oxford 1222, which imposed automatic excommunication on those who laid crimes on others. The word *crimen* in the legislation was liberally construed to include all punishable sin.

[17] Statutes of Provisors 1351 and 1353, 25 Edw. III, stat.iv; 27 Edw. III, stat.i. The pope had been taking over church livings to use as rewards, and they were often given to absentees, even foreigners; this was called 'provision'.

[18] Statute of Provisors 1353, c.1; Statute of Winchester 1393, 16 Ric. II, c.5.

[19] *Seton v. Cokeside* (1358) Y.B. 30 Edw. III, Lib. Ass. pl.19 (misdated); *Anon.* (1413) Hil. 14 Hen. IV, fo. 14, pl.4; *Sondes v. Pekham* (1484) Mich. 2 Ric. III, fo. 4, pl.8. The absence of communication by writ would deprive the party of the regular means of absolution.

who had sued in ecclesiastical courts concerning matters which overlapped the jurisdictional boundary.[20] There was frequent complaint of avarice and extortion by officials, of uncertainties and delays, and of the unfairness of the inquisitorial procedure. Pamphleteers such as St German, in the time of Henry VIII, argued that the king's law permitted the ecclesiastical jurisdiction only on trust, and that if the trust was abused the liberty was forfeited like any other. In 1529 the most powerful prelate in England, Thomas Wolsey, Lord Chancellor, archbishop of York, cardinal of St Cecilia trans Tiberim, and papal legate *a latere*, was condemned by the King's Bench on his own confession for improperly using his legatine authority contrary to English law. The precedent enabled the king's advisers to bring the rest of the clergy to heel, and prepared the way for the legal revolution effected by the Reformation parliament. A separate issue of state had occasioned the crisis;[21] but the issue was argued in legal terms, and the manner of its resolution was a culmination of earlier legal developments.

From January 1534 the Church of England was severed from Rome, and appeals to the pope were forbidden.[22] Some common lawyers advocated abolition of the Church courts at the same time, but that would have required fusion of Canon law and common law. Some kind of fusion was seriously contemplated. A law commission was duly appointed to prepare a code of 'the king's ecclesiastical laws of the Church of England', and those canons which they did not approve were to be abrogated. Meanwhile the old Canon law was to continue in force, except where it was contrary to the common or statute law or the king's prerogative. Since the report of the commission was either forgotten or deliberately shelved, the transitional provision slipped into permanence.

Henry VIII suppressed the study of Canon law at Oxford and Cambridge, so that the judges and advocates thereafter were all doctors of Civil law. Nevertheless, the doctors preserved the cosmopolitan learning of the canonists, and the long survival of the wider jurisdiction of the Church may be attributed to the existence of this small but persistent Civilian profession.[23] The English ecclesiastical courts were largely unaltered by the Reformation, the chief effect of which in the juridical sphere was the introduction of two new courts to replace the extraterritorial papal courts. The regular appellate court was to be the

---

[20]   94 SS *66-68*.

[21]   See pp. 562-564, post.

[22]   Stat. 24 Hen. VIII, c.12; 25 Hen. VIII, c.19.

[23]   See pp. 193-194, post.

Court of Delegates, which took over the jurisdiction of papal delegates; the statutory delegates were a mixture of temporal judges and doctors of law, appointed by the Chancery.   In the 1580s a Court of High Commission was set up, to exercise the supreme personal jurisdiction of the Head of the Church, particularly in criminal matters; it was a spiritual Star Chamber, much hated for its proceeding by oath *ex officio*, whereby a man could be driven to condemn himself under questioning.

The Church courts, like all others, experienced a considerable expansion of business in the sixteenth and seventeenth centuries; and towards the end of the sixteenth century their activities (especially in relation to tithes) were increasingly questioned in the King's Bench and Common Pleas by writs of prohibition.   Under Coke CJ various inroads were made upon their jurisdiction, especially in relation to the oath *ex officio*, but in the 1630s the Church establishment became more high-handed and the enforcement of religious policy became a popular grievance.   In 1641 the Long Parliament abolished the High Commission and the criminal jurisdiction of other ecclesiastical courts; much of the civil jurisdiction also disappeared during the Interregnum. The High Commission was never revived, and the punishment of minor offences by archdeacons' courts (though revived in 1661) passed de facto in the eighteenth century to the justices of the peace.   By the middle of the nineteenth century it was felt to be no longer appropriate for the law of one denomination, albeit the Church by law established, to govern the entire population.   The defamation jurisdiction was abolished in 1855; that over marriage, separation and probate, which had been the principal work of the consistory courts, went in 1857.[24]   After that time the jurisdiction of the ecclesiastical courts has been confined to Church matters, such as faculties to alter or sell consecrated property and disciplinary proceedings against clergy.

Further reading

Holdsworth HEL, vol. I, pp. 580-632

Milsom HFCL, pp. 23-25

Vaisey Commission, *Canon Law in the Church of England* (1947)

R. C. Mortimer, *Western Canon Law* (1953)

E. Kemp, *An Introduction to Canon Law in the Church of England* (1957)

[24]   Stat. 18 & 19 Vict., c. 41; 20 & 21 Vict., c. 77 and c. 85.

C. Donahue, 'Roman Canon Law in the Medieval English Church' (1974) 72 *Michigan Law Rev.* 647-716

M. Chibnall, *Anglo-Norman England* (1986), pp. 192-207

R. H. Helmholz, *Canon Law and Common Law* (1989)

JURISDICTIONAL DISPUTES

G. B. Flahiff, 'The Writ of Prohibition to Court Christian in the 13th Century' (1944-45) 6 *Medieval Studies* 261-313, 7 *Medieval Studies* 229-290

W. R. Jones, 'Relations of the two Jurisdictions' (1970) 7 *Studies in Medieval and Renaissance Hist.* 77-210

R. M. Fraher, 'The Becket Dispute and the two Decretist Traditions' (1978) 4 *Jo. Medieval Hist.* 347-368

R. H. Helmholz, 'Writs of Prohibition and Ecclesiastical Sanctions in the English Courts Christian' (1976) 60 *Minnesota Law Rev.* 1011-1033; 'The Writ of Prohibition to Court Christian before 1500' (1981) 43 *Medieval Studies* 297-314

W. Epstein, 'Issues of Principle and Expediency in the Controversy over Prohibitions to Ecclesiastical Courts in England' (1980) 1 JLH 211-261

D. Millon, 'Circumspecte Agatis Revisited' (1984) 2 JLH 105-128

THE COURTS AND THEIR WORK

B. Woodcock, *Medieval Ecclesiastical Courts in the Diocese of Canterbury* (1952)

A. H. Manchester, 'Reform of the Ecclesiastical Courts' (1966) 10 AJLH 51-75

J. E. Sayers, *Papal Judges Delegate and the Province of Canterbury 1198-1254* (1971)

G. I. O. Duncan, *The High Court of Delegates* (1971)

R. Houlbrooke, *Church Courts and People during the English Reformation 1520-1570* (1979)

R. Wunderli, *London Church Courts and Society on the Eve of the Reformation* (1981)

N. Adams and C. Donahue, *Select Cases from the Ecclesiastical Courts of the Province of Canterbury c. 1200-1301* (95 SS, 1981)

THE REFORMATION AND AFTER

R. A. Marchant, *The Church under the Law 1560-1640* (1969)

G. R. Elton, *Reform and Renewal* (1973), pp. 129-139

D. Logan, 'The Henrician Canons' (1974) 47 BIHR 99-103

J. H. Baker, 'Spiritual Jurisdiction' (1978) 94 SS 64-70

R. H. Helmholz, *Roman Canon Law in Reformation England* (forthcoming, 1990)

J. Guy, 'Thomas More and St German: the Battle of the Books' in *Reassessing the Henrician Age* (A. Fox and J. Guy ed., 1986), pp. 95-120

9. Judicial Review of Decisions

The present judicial system recognises that judges and juries make mistakes by providing for redress by way of appeal to a higher court. People have come to regard the right to appeal as an essential requirement of natural justice, and as long ago as 1723 it was said to be 'the glory and happiness of our excellent constitution, that to prevent injustice no man is concluded by the first judgment; but that if he apprehends himself to be aggrieved he has another court to which he can resort for relief'.[1] It was not always so. The machinery of appeals was not built into the common law at the outset, and when the central courts subjected each other and inferior tribunals to judicial review the means were at first limited in scope.

It is easy to understand why the earliest legal systems had no appeal process. There was no possibility of human error in a judgment supported by divine intervention. Even the establishment of juries, and the consequent separation of findings of fact from rulings on law, did not result in the introduction of appeals. Judgments in the superior courts were intended to be final; there was no justification for appealing from the king to anyone else. The only conceivable outside forum would have been the Church; but we have seen that when papal intervention appeared to threaten the authority of royal jurisdiction, parliament legislated to stop 'appeals' from the king's courts to any others.[2] Neither was there any obvious purpose in allowing the decisions of the king's judges to be reopened before different royal judges. The decision of a court such as the King's Bench or Common Pleas was a decision of the whole bench, not of the trial judge alone; and provided such a court kept within its bounds it would have produced unnecessary uncertainty to permit another court to say that its decisions were mistaken. Obviously trial judges in the country cannot give the same detailed attention to legal arguments as can the central judicial bodies, and one of the advantages which would be claimed for an appeal is that it enables greater legal concentration to be brought to bear on a problem once the facts have been ascertained. The trial judge is now regarded as a 'court of first instance', and a review of his decision by a

---

[1] *R. v. Cambridge University, ex parte Bentley* (1723) 1 Stra. 557 at 565, per Pratt CJ.

[2] See p. 150, ante.

panel of judges must therefore be by way of appeal. Under the nisi prius system, however, the trial judge was not a court capable of giving judgment; his task ended when the verdict was given, and the verdict was then returned to the full court of three or four judges so that they could give judgment. The kind of attention now given to cases on appeal was therefore given, under the old system, before judgment was entered. It followed that when judgment was given in banc it should be regarded as final and conclusive. Indeed, the finality of a judgment once entered accounts for the reluctance of the medieval judges to enter a judgment at all if a division of opinion occurred on the bench.[3] In case of doubt, proceedings would be adjourned as often as necessary to enable the doubts to be fully explored and for the judges to deliver their 'arguments' (in effect tentative judgments), which could be reviewed on successive occasions until a consensus of judicial opinion was found. Delays which might now seem intolerable were regarded as acceptable, indeed as essential to the deliberative process. The present system has sacrificed some of this circumspection to speed, but insures against error by providing for an appeal after judgment.

The introduction of the jury nevertheless raised other problems, and procedures were provided for dealing with them. Corruption and misconduct by jurors were undeniable obstacles to justice. An action called 'attaint' could be brought against jurors for giving a false verdict, and if it was successful the verdict would be quashed. But attaint did not permit judicial review of decisions of fact by way of appeal, to determine their substantial correctness, nor of rulings or directions in law by the trial judge. The only question was whether the jurors had perjured themselves, and the only evidence which could be considered in the attaint was that laid before the trial jury.[4] Though not abolished until 1825, the procedure was rarely used even in medieval times, and by Tudor times was virtually obsolete, because the punishment of perjured trial jurors was so severe that attaint juries would seldom find against them. Misconduct by juries was more easily raised by motion;[5] or, in serious cases, by complaint in the Star Chamber. The motion in banc, as we shall see, was to contribute more to the modern notion of an appeal than proceedings in error, which we shall nevertheless consider first. Despite the superficial resemblance between error and appeal, the former made nothing other than the record available for scrutiny, and by

---

3   See pp. 93-94, ante.

4   *Rolfe v. Hampden* (1542) Dyer 53; *R. v. Ingersall* (1593) Cro. Eliz. 309 at 310. Trial in an attaint was by jury of 24.

5   See p. 100, ante.

confining itself to procedural propriety was closer to what is now termed 'judicial review'.

Proceedings in Error

The basis of proceedings in error was the record, or plea roll, which contained a formal minute of all the stages in the action down to judgment. The record was invested with such a sacred finality that it was accepted as conclusive evidence of what it contained; but it could be questioned for mistakes revealed on its face. A writ of error ordered judges to send the record of particular proceedings to a superior court for inspection. The court of error could only concern itself with 'manifest error' revealed by the record itself (as where an essential step was missing), or with new facts (such as the death of a party) not inconsistent with the record but requiring proof by the plaintiff in error. If the plaintiff in error assigned points worth argument, the other party was summoned to hear the alleged errors and dispute them; after argument the court either affirmed or reversed the judgment of the lower court.

The inability of the court of error to go behind the record made it difficult in medieval times to raise questions of substantive law. The formulaic character of the pleadings kept vital facts off the record, and the mode of entering the verdict kept the evidence off the record as well. So long as the proceedings were in common form, and correctly entered, there could be no challenge on the grounds that the judges or the jury had erred in law, because no error by them would ever appear on the face of the record. Before the sixteenth century most writs of error were indeed brought on technical, procedural grounds. The rise of actions on the case, and the revival of special verdicts, in the sixteenth century placed more detail on the record and enabled new points of substance – such as the sufficiency of the consideration for a promise – to be raised by writ of error. Error could be brought whenever a motion in arrest of judgment was appropriate;[6] and so it began in the Tudor period to make a parallel contribution to legal development.

COURTS OF ERROR

Every court of record was subject to the surveillance of some other tribunal to ensure that in giving judgment it did not err on the face of its

---

6 See pp. 98-99, ante; p. 159, post.

record.[7] From local courts of record, such as borough and franchise courts, from the counties palatine, and from the Common Pleas itself, error went to the King's Bench. From the King's Bench and the Exchequer of Pleas, both deemed to be held *coram rege*, error lay in medieval times to the king in council or in parliament. The latter jurisdiction came to be exercised by the House of Lords alone, and was never very effective. In 1357 the Commons prayed that judgments in the Exchequer might be reviewed by the King's Bench, but the king replied that they should instead be referred to a committee consisting of the chancellor, treasurer, and two justices. Ten years later a statutory tribunal, the Council Chamber (subsequently known as the Exchequer Chamber), was established to hear writs of error from the Exchequer. In the case of the King's Bench a like remedy was delayed until 1585, when another statutory court – also called the Exchequer Chamber – was set up because of the difficulties of securing a hearing in parliament.[8] This court consisted of the justices of the Common Pleas and barons of the Exchequer, and was very active from the 1590s. Error still lay from this court – and from the King's Bench as a court of error – to the House of Lords. Such cases became more frequent in later times, and the unsuitability of the Lords for such purposes remained a problem: the shortage of legal expertise was remedied by summoning the judges to attend, but the judges' opinions could be disregarded by lay peers voting against law.[9]

The use of writs of error to question points of substantive law in actions on the case led in Elizabethan times to some unfortunate disagreements between the central courts which were difficult to resolve. In 1602 a law student noted with dismay that if the King's Bench overturned a unanimous Common Pleas by three votes to one, three judges would prevail over five; worse still, as Coke CJ complained in 1611, one third of the judiciary could defeat the majority if the Exchequer Chamber reversed the five King's Bench judges by four to three.[10] Judgment without consensus was a new and unsettling phenomenon, especially when all the judges concerned were equal in rank.

---

7   From courts not of record, such as local and seignorial courts, there was an analogous procedure whereby those courts were ordered to make up an ad hoc record of a case for review by the Common Pleas.

8   Rot. Parl., vol. II, p. 168; Stat. 31 Edw. III, sess.i, c.12; 27 Eliz. I, c.8.

9   An instance of this is *Bishop of London v. Ffytche* (1783) 1 Bro. P.C. 211, 17 LQR 367, where the bishops voted in their own interest against the judges.

10 *The Diary of John Manningham* (R. P. Sorlien ed., 1976), p. 149; *Maine v. Peacher* (1610) B. & M. 454. Cf. *Fossett v. Carter* (1623) Palm. 329; Cro. Jac. 662, where the 1585 Act was construed to require a majority of at least six.

Two major reforms preceded abolition of the procedure in the nineteenth century. In 1830 the error jurisdiction of the King's Bench, Council Chamber and Exchequer Chamber was combined in a new Court of Exchequer Chamber, comprising the judges of all three superior common-law courts; error from any one court was heard by the judges of the other two. In 1852 the writ of error was abolished, and proceedings in error became a 'step in the cause' rather than a separate action. Finally, in 1875, proceedings in error were themselves abolished.[11] They had been rendered otiose by the introduction of an appellate procedure.

Development of the Appeal

The nisi prius system enabled jury verdicts to be taken by assize judges on circuit, and in the absence of any formal defect in the proceedings judgment would normally be entered in the office as a matter of course the next term. But the full court which met in banc at Westminster could stay the entry of judgment if cause were shown. The procedure in banc required one of the parties to make an *ex parte* motion for a 'rule *nisi*', which was an order for the opposing party to show cause against what was sought; if the opponent was successful the rule was discharged, otherwise it was made absolute. If the verdict had been for the plaintiff, the defendant's counsel could move either in arrest of judgment or for a new trial.[12] The motion in arrest of judgment involved showing cause against the plaintiff's rule *nisi* for judgment; it was subject to the same limitations as error, being confined to matter intrinsic to the record. The motion for a new trial could be used from the late seventeenth century to raise matters extrinsic to the record,[13] and therefore gave the court in banc wider powers to consider questions arising from the trial. But all these powers were exercised before judgment, and not by a court of appeal. Once the court in banc had given judgment, the only redress was of the limited kind provided by the writ of error.

---

[11] Stat. 11 Geo. IV & 1 Will. IV, c.70; Common Law Procedure Act 1852, 15 & 16 Vict., c.76, s.48; Judicature Act 1873, 36 & 37 Vict., c.66, Sch. I, Ord. LVIII, r.1. For 'error on the face of the record' in *certiorari*, see p. 171, post.

[12] See pp. 98-101, ante.

[13] See p. 100, ante.

RESERVATION OF POINTS OF LAW

It was common in medieval times for petty assizes to be adjourned 'for difficulty' into the Common Pleas for argument in banc before judgment was given;[14] the adjournment procedure was necessary because assizes did not begin in the central courts and judgment ordinarily belonged to the assize commissioners rather than a court in banc. By the sixteenth century assize commissioners were also reserving difficult questions arising at nisi prius or gaol delivery for discussion at Serjeants' Inn or in the Exchequer Chamber during term time. The judges assembled to consider such reserved cases – usually the twelve or so judges of the three common-law courts – were not acting as a court of record, but as an advisory assembly; nevertheless their opinion was always acted on, and (if reported) would serve as a precedent for the future.

In criminal cases it was usual to take a verdict and respite sentence or execution until the point was resolved;[15] if necessary a pardon would be obtained in accordance with the decision of the twelve judges. From an extremely informal beginning, the procedure became increasingly regularised, the judge stating a written case and counsel being heard; but it was not until 1848 that it was put on a statutory basis, as the Court for Crown Cases Reserved.[16] Even after 1848 the reservation of cases was at the discretion of the trial judge; the defendant did not acquire a right of appeal until the introduction of the Court of Criminal Appeal in 1907.[17]

A comparable civil procedure, which has already been noticed,[18] developed within the nisi prius system in the seventeenth century to replace the informal Serjeants' Inn consultations. With the agreement of the trial judge, points of law could be reserved for consideration by the full court and then argued in banc upon motion. When this procedure was first introduced, a decision to set aside the verdict resulted in a new trial;[19] but an eighteenth-century refinement made the decision of the full court final, so that the plaintiff was nonsuited if the point

---

14 This was provided for by Magna Carta 1217, c.13 (1225, c.12), which said that the assize should then be determined in the Bench. The serjeants' monopoly of audience did not extend to adjourned assizes.

15 See further pp. 595-596, post.

16 Stat. 11 & 12 Vict., c.78. At first all 12 judges sat, but the number was reduced to five in 1875.

17 The Court of Criminal Appeal consisted of the lord chief justice and the judges of the King's Bench Division, with a quorum of three; it was reconstituted as the Criminal Division of the Court of Appeal in 1966.

18 See p. 99, ante.

19 *Noell v. Wells* (1668) 1 Sid. 359; 2 Keb. 337; 1 Lev. 235.

was decided against him. This second change made the procedure more attractive than motions for new trials, which were more sparingly granted and involved the expense of a retrial.[20] On the other hand, the informality of the procedure effectively prevented review by a court of error.[21]

The practice of withholding judgment until points of law could be discussed elsewhere was not confined to trial judges. It was not uncommon for the judges of one bench to send one of their number across Westminster Hall to state a case to the judges of the other. The year-books of the fifteenth century also mention meetings of all the judges in the Exchequer Chamber,[22] or occasionally in a London church, to debate difficult cases or matters of public importance in an informal way. We need hardly doubt that similar discussions occurred over dinner in the Serjeants' Inns; opinions there begin to be reported in the 1520s. At first the Serjeants' Inn meetings were merely professional discussions by members of the particular inn; but during the sixteenth century they became more open, and functionally indistinguishable from the gatherings in the Exchequer Chamber.[23] The Serjeants' Inns were a more convenient venue when the judges were not at Westminster, and may have been considered less formal.[24] The pronouncements of the judges at these assemblies, though not operative as judgments, were keenly reported and were doubtless a better guide to common opinion than the decisions of single courts.

THE PRIVY COUNCIL

After the abolition of the Star Chamber in 1641, the only jurisdiction exercised by the Council in suits of an adversary nature was appellate.[25] It was a royal prerogative to entertain applications for redress in respect

---

[20] *Cox v. Kitchin* (1798) 1 Bos. & P. 338 at 339, per Buller J.

[21] *Lord Eldon's Anecdote Book* (1960), pp. 159-162. Eldon was mistaken in thinking Mansfield had invented the procedure.

[22] An important example is *Shipton v. Dogge* (1442) B. & M. 391 (King's Bench case); p. 383, post. Chancery cases could be referred in the same way: e.g. *Re Lord Dacre* (1535) B. & M. 105 at 110.

[23] Thus, *Slade's Case* was argued in the Exchequer Chamber in 1597, and then at Serjeants' Inn in 1598 and 1602: B. & M. 420, 428, 431. Cf. *Cantrell v. Churche* (1601) ibid. 588 at 591 (motion in Serjeants' Inn after judgment in the Exchequer Chamber). For Chancery cases discussed in Serjeants' Inn, see ibid. 148 (1581), 124 (1596).

[24] Note Walmsley J's retrospective comments on *Slade's Case* (1602): B. & M. 442, 443.

[25] The Privy Council also had, and still has, an authority to advise the Crown on hypothetical questions of law and on constitutional matters. The precedence of king's counsel before serjeants was so settled: p. 189, post.

of the overseas jurisdictions of the Crown, and this was virtually the last judicial prerogative to be retained by the king's council and not delegated to a regular court. The jurisdiction of the council over the Channel Islands had been established since at least 1495,[26] and in the seventeenth and eighteenth centuries it was extended to all the plantations and colonies. Appeals of this kind were usually referred to a standing committee on which legal and colonial expertise was represented. In 1832 and 1833 the appeals committee was placed on a statutory footing as the Judicial Committee of the Privy Council, with a defined membership and a slightly extended jurisdiction: in addition to hearing foreign appeals, it was also to be the final court of appeal for ecclesiastical cases in place of the Court of Delegates, and for admiralty cases (including appeals from colonial vice-admiralty courts).[27] The previous appeals committee had proceeded informally, and it was already settled that appeals were allowed on the substantial merits of the case. Moreover, the Civil law notion of an appeal, as applied to ecclesiastical and admiralty jurisdiction, was closer to review in equity than to error at common law. The Privy Council, then, furnished a model for a court of appeal in the 1830s; but it was limited to matters arising outside the realm.

REVIEW IN CHANCERY

Error lay from the Latin side of the Chancery to the king in parliament. But error was not appropriate for the English side, because there was no record. At first the only way of reviewing a decision in equity was by reopening the matter before the chancellor himself, or his successor, or by obtaining a commission of review. However, after a great deal of argument in the seventeenth century, it was finally decided by the House of Lords in 1675 that it could review decisions on the English side.[28] A review in equity enabled all the available facts to be taken into consideration, since there was no record; and, since juries were not involved, the court of review conducted a rehearing on the merits, a true appeal. In 1851 a Court of Appeal in Chancery was erected for hearing Chancery appeals, and the notion of full-time appeal judges was introduced for the purpose.[29] A final appeal still lay to the Lords.

---

[26] See p. 36, ante.

[27] Stat. 2 & 3 Will. IV, c.92; 3 & 4 Will. IV, c.41.

[28] *Shirley v. Fagg* (1675) 6 State Tr. 1121. The House of Commons opposed the decision and there was a brief constitutional crisis. But the appellate jurisdiction remained: an important early example of its use is *Howard v. Duke of Norfolk* (1685) B. & M. 169 at 176.

[29] They were known as justices of appeal in Chancery.

THE COURT OF APPEAL AND HOUSE OF LORDS

The appeal, having become fully established in respect of admiralty, ecclesiastical and colonial courts, and courts of equity, made its debut in the common-law system in 1854. Legislation of that year provided for an 'appeal' to a court of error from a court in banc against a decision to award or refuse a nonsuit (on a reserved point) or a new trial. Parliament expressly referred to the court of error as a 'court of appeal' for this purpose. When the Exchequer Chamber, and proceedings in error, came to an end in 1875, it was this Court of Appeal (now so named) which passed into the new scheme of things. The system envisaged by the Judicature Commission was that motions 'in banc' would be made to the Divisional Court of the appropriate division of the High Court; and thence an appeal would lie, as it had since 1854, to the Court of Appeal. The common-law Court of Appeal merged at this time with the Court of Appeal in Chancery, acquiring full-time lords justices of appeal.

There had been considerable prior discussion as to whether the appellate jurisdiction of the House of Lords should be retained, or transferred to the Judicial Committee of the Privy Council, but by 1873 it was decided to abolish the second appeal altogether. Under the Judicature Acts as passed, the jurisdiction would indeed have disappeared; but, before the new legislation came into force, conservative opposition from members of Disraeli's government forced a reconsideration of the role of the House of Lords. At the last moment the original scheme was changed, the Lords were given a statutory appellate jurisdiction superior but akin to that of the Court of Appeal, and yet another judicial rank was introduced, the lord of appeal in ordinary.[30] Ironically, the court established under the 1873 Act kept the name *Supreme* Court of Judicature,[31] though its supremacy had been snatched from it before birth. The judicial House of Lords which in truth occupied the supreme position was, however, no longer the same as the upper chamber of parliament, but a court composed of professionally qualified judges sitting independently of the parliamentary sittings of the House. The creation of lords of appeal rendered unnecessary the cumbrous practice of summoning the judges to give advice,[32] and ended the participation of other peers in appeals.

---

[30] Appellate Jurisdiction Act 1876, 39 & 40 Vict., c.59. The lord of appeal was the first statutory life peer.

[31] The expression 'supreme courts at Westminster' had, however, been used generically for the common-law courts before 1875: e.g. 20 & 21 Vict., c.43, s.1.

[32] The practice was not abolished, but has not been used since *Allen v. Flood* [1898] A.C. 1; p. 527, post.

This legislative afterthought led to a more fundamental change than might have been expected from an otherwise conservative saving measure. Since the addition of a further appellate tier might have taken a case before three successive panels of judges after trial, the role of the divisional courts was brought into question; and the chosen solution was to do away with motions in banc. The motion in banc before judgment was transformed into an appeal after judgment, and the post-trial work of the divisional courts in High Court actions was thereby transferred to the Court of Appeal.[33] Some would have abolished the divisional courts at that point; but it was decided to keep them, chiefly so that the Court of Appeal would be protected from hearing cases stated by inferior courts.[34]

The Prerogative Writs

The notion of an appeal by way of rehearing was by these means extended so that the judgments of courts of law could be reviewed in the same way as the decrees of courts of equity. The extension removed the need for proceedings in error, which were narrower in scope. But the notion of judicial review represented by error, though restricted to formal and apparent errors, could be applied to a broader range of decisions than those covered by the writ of error, and in particular to decisions made without the assistance of juries. The broad notion was that the king's courts should keep all lesser authorities within the procedural and jurisdictional bounds set by the law, and provide the subject with a remedy if tribunals or officials exceeded their legal authority or gave orders which were patently contrary to law. The function of controlling authority was regarded as a royal prerogative, and until the sixteenth century it had been primarily the responsibility of the king's council. In Coke's time local authorities, especially the justices of the peace, were supervised directly by the assize judges acting on the council's instructions;[35] but from the middle of the seventeenth century political control passed to the lords lieutenants of counties, and legal control to

33   Motions for new trials were transferred to the Court of Appeal shortly afterwards, by the Judicature Act 1890 (Sir Robert Finlay's Act), 53 & 54 Vict., c.44, s.1.

34   For cases stated by magistrates, see p. 171, post. Under the new scheme, cases were stated to the Queen's Bench Divisional Court, with appeal direct to the House of Lords.

35   This was achieved not by any formal appeal procedure, but by the judges' domination of the commission of the peace (to which they belonged) as representatives of central government. The assizes were given a general superintendence over the justices of the peace by Stat. 4 Hen. VII, c.12. For the methods of control, see Cockburn, *History of the Assizes*, pp. 153-187.

the central courts. The assizes judges were still consulted on sessions questions in the eighteenth century, but became unwilling to give advice which the justices were free to ignore; the proper course was to state cases formally for the King's Bench.[36]

The surveillance of inferior authorities by the King's Bench had begun much earlier. Coke CJ claimed the jurisdiction to correct 'errors and misdemeanours extrajudicial, tending to the breach of the peace, or oppression of the subjects. . . or any other manner of misgovernment'.[37] Thus began one of the most important and distinctive developments of the common law. The principle known as the 'rule of law' treats all exercise of authority as subject to the control of the regular courts of law and furnishes the subject with a legal remedy when any official, however mighty, exceeds the power which the law gives him. Since all power must be warranted by law, it follows that no power is outside the law; moreover any lawful power over the lives, liberty or property of others, even if not conferred on a court, must be exercised in accordance with certain minimum standards of fairness. According to Coke, even a discretionary authority was within the principle: 'although the words of the commission [of sewers] give authority to the commissioners to act according to their discretion, their proceedings ought nevertheless to be limited and bound within the rule of reason and law, for discretion is a science . . . and they are not to act according to their wills and private affections'.[38]

The means whereby the central courts put the rule of law into practice was the adaptation of certain judicial writs so as to extend judicial review to all bodies which exercised judicial or quasi-judicial functions. These writs had been designed for purely routine procedural functions. In their newfound role, they ceased to be obtainable as of course, and the court in granting them had 'a great latitude and discretion . . . not bound by such strict rules as in cases of private rights'.[39] The jurisdiction was, in other words, equitable. But, being exercised by the courts of common law, it was more convenient to attribute it to the royal prerogative; since the time of James I habeas corpus has been referred to as a 'prerogative writ'. The name was not altogether apt, because in the early stages of their expansion these writs were mainly

---

[36] In 1724, at Hereford assizes, Lord Raymond CJ 'did not care to give his opinion where they might choose whether they would stand by it or not, but if they would bring it into the King's Bench he would there give his opinion and make them stand by it': 11 *Law Magazine & Rev.* (3rd ser.) at p. 274.

[37] 11 Co. Rep. 98; Co. Inst., vol. IV, p. 71.

[38] *Rooke v. Withers* (1598) 5 Co. Rep. 99 at 100.

[39] *Lord Montague v. Dudman* (1751) 2 Ves. 396, per Lord Hardwicke C, ruling that the Chancery could not restrain mandamus by injunction.

used to curb prerogative activity by councillors and conciliar courts. Lord Ellesmere C strongly objected on this ground to Coke CJ's usurpation of the conciliar supervisory function: 'in giving excess of authority to the King's Bench he doth as much as insinuate that this court is all sufficient in itself to manage the state . . . as if the King's Bench had a superintendency over the government itself'.[40] Subsequent events have made this a greater dispute between law and equity than that which Coke lost in 1616; for in this context Coke's common-law brand of equity prevailed, and it has in the long term proved as fruitful as the equitable creations of the Chancery.

PROHIBITION

The oldest member of the 'prerogative' class of writs was the writ of prohibition, which was developed in the thirteenth century as a means of restraining ecclesiastical courts from meddling with temporal causes.[41] During the sixteenth and seventeenth centuries it was established that it would lie to all other kinds of judicial tribunal: to the palatinates, to conciliar courts, to courts of Civil law (such as the Court of Admiralty, Court of Chivalry, and university courts), and to all inferior jurisdictions. By virtue of this procedure the boundaries of jurisdictions, and the interpretation of the charters or statutes on which they rested, fell exclusively to the judges of the two benches. Coke CJ claimed that prohibitions might even be sent to the Chancery, but that was never settled; it will be recalled that the dispute between Coke and Ellesmere had to be resolved by James I in person.[42] But Coke CJ and his brethren did prohibit the High Commission and the provincial councils, which were prerogative courts. In later times prohibition did not develop as dramatically as the other prerogative writs, because the Crown made no attempt after 1641 to erect new types of court without parliamentary sanction, and the restraint of non-judicial powers may be achieved in other ways. It was, nevertheless, fully settled in the nineteenth century that prohibition would if necessary lie to statutory bodies and central government departments.

QUO WARRANTO

Whereas prohibition enabled a private party to stop a specific action against him, a general challenge to the existence of a jurisdiction or

---

[40] 'Observations on Coke's Reports', printed in L. A. Knafla, *Law and Politics in Jacobean England* (1977), pp. 307-308 (spelling modernised above).

[41] See p. 149, ante.

[42] See pp. 125-126, ante.

franchise could be made by a writ ordering the sheriff to summon the claimant to show by what authority (*quo warranto*) he exercised it. Extensive use of this procedure was made by Edward I in what was intended to be a comprehensive survey of inferior jurisdictions; the investigation proved too ambitious, but one lasting outcome was a statute which fixed as 1189 the time from which prescriptive claims had to be made.[43] The statute also provided that, to save costs, writs of *quo warranto* should be returnable before justices in eyre. This had the unintended consequence that *quo warranto* disappeared with the eyre system itself. There was a revival under Henry VIII, and three or four special eyres were commissioned for the purpose.[44] At the same time a less cumbrous procedure was devised, in the form of an information laid in the King's Bench by the attorney-general. This 'information in the nature of a *quo warranto*' thereafter completely supplanted the procedure by writ. The Tudor revival was once interpreted as part of a government campaign to suppress private authority, but it now seems that most of the informations were brought on the relation of private suitors; and by the seventeenth century it was a recognised procedure for subjects to promote such informations in the name of the master of the Crown Office. The last major political use of *quo warranto* occurred when Charles II sought to remodel municipal corporations by forcing new charters upon them. The City of London fought this reform to the bitter end, and was called upon by information to show 'by what warrant' it claimed its privileges; in 1683 the King's Bench delivered the shattering judgment against the city that its liberty of being a corporation be seized into the king's hands.[45] The following year, by an equally dramatic use of the analogous procedure of *scire facias*, the charter of the province of Massachusetts was rescinded for encroachment on the royal prerogative in founding Harvard College. After this period, the steady suppression of private and irregular jurisdictions by act of parliament reduced the need for *quo warranto*; but its scope was nevertheless extended to cover all usurpations of public functions of importance, even if they were not judicial.[46] The information in *quo warranto* was abolished in 1938, but the same remedy may still be given by injunction.

---

43 Statute of Quo Warranto 1290.
44 For one held at Lynn in 1522, see Spelman Rep. (93 SS) 199.
45 *R. v. City of London* (1682) 8 State Tr. 1039.
46 *Darley v. Reginam* (1846) 12 Cl. & Fin. 520, reviewing earlier cases.

HABEAS CORPUS

The writ of habeas corpus has become the principal safeguard of personal liberty. It is not a little ironic, therefore, that its original purpose was not to release people from prison but to secure their presence in custody. The words 'habeas corpus' (have the body) occurred in the common judicial writ of *capias*, in the Chancery subpoena, and in the *habeas corpora juratorum* to compel the attendance of jurors. The first use of the writ to challenge imprisonment was in cases of privilege; an officer of a central court, or a litigant there, could be released from imprisonment in another court by writ of privilege in habeas corpus form. The Court of Chancery at the same time developed a similar procedure for reviewing the cause of imprisonment in an inferior tribunal; this species of writ was called *corpus cum causa*, and it became a common remedy against the misuse of borough jurisdiction in the fifteenth century. The King's Bench developed the *habeas corpus ad subjiciendum* in the sixteenth century, chiefly to enable subjects to challenge unconstitutional imprisonment by privy councillors and officers of state; it ordered the person detaining the prisoner to have his body before the court together with the reason for his detention.[47] The judges extended the reach of the writ in the seventeenth century to committals by inferior courts, and in the time of Coke CJ to superior courts such as the High Commission; Coke even released prisoners committed by the Lord Chancellor.[48] Coke's successor Mountagu CJ tried to dispel the feeling that the writ was being used to counter prerogative power by explaining that it was itself 'a prerogative writ, which concerns the king's justice to be administered to his subjects; for the king ought to have an account why any of his subjects are imprisoned'.[49] Only after fierce wrangles in the time of Charles I did the general principle triumph.[50]

The prerogative writ of habeas corpus thus replaced earlier civil actions[51] as the most effective means of challenging a deprivation of liberty. The Habeas Corpus Act 1679[52] improved the procedure in criminal cases, so that the writ could be obtained in vacation; prisoners had to be produced within three days, and any prisoner not tried within

---

47   For a specimen, see p. 626, post.

48   See 4 IJ at 374-378 (repr. in LPCL at 211-215).

49   *R. v. Lord Warden of the Cinque Ports, ex parte Bourn* (1619) Cro. Jac. 543.

50   See pp. 539-540, post.

51   The writs *de homine replegiando* (p. 536, post), *de odio et atia*, and mainprise, enabled release in certain cases. Most disputes about imprisonment before 1600 were tried in actions of false imprisonment; but these lay only to recover damages after the event.

52   Stat. 31 Car. II, c.2.

two terms was to be given bail. But the remedy was not confined to persons on criminal charges, for the writ could be addressed to anyone believed to be keeping a subject in improper confinement, to produce the body and the 'cause' for scrutiny. By issuing habeas corpus the King's Bench was able to affirm and protect a wide range of fundamental personal liberties: for instance, by denying the power of parliament to imprison people beyond the period of one session, of courts to coerce jurors by imprisonment after verdict, or of husbands to detain their wives in order to exact their conjugal rights.[53] It enabled persons committed to madhouses to secure a proper medical review of their condition.[54] It brought questions as to the custody of children before the courts.[55] And it enabled a slave, once landed in England, to resist being sent back into slavery.[56] In recent times its chief use has been to question orders of extradition and deportation, since the writ is available to all persons except enemy aliens who are present within the jurisdiction. Even in its widest application, however, it does not enable an appeal on the merits of a decision to imprison. Its function is to question the lawfulness, not the inherent correctness, of an imprisonment. But courts have extended their powers of review by acknowledging that the lawfulness of imprisonment may depend upon the manner in which a discretion is exercised.[57]

MANDAMUS

A good many writs, including the writ of error, contained the word *mandamus* ('we command'); but the species distinguished by that word was developed only at the beginning of the seventeenth century, as a means of controlling borough and city authorities. It seems that, as with habeas corpus, the original application of the writ was in cases of privilege;[58] but from about 1615 the King's Bench asserted a general jurisdiction to order a local authority to do something or else show cause why it did not.[59] At first mandamus was used as a writ of

---

53 *Streater's Case* (1653) 5 State Tr. 365; *R. v. Sheriffs of London, ex parte Bushell* (1670) Vaugh. 135; 1 Freem. 1; *R. v. Lister, ex parte Rawlinson* (1721) 8 Mod. Rep. 22; 1 Stra. 478; *R. v. Jackson* [1891] 1 Q.B. 671.

54 *R. v. Turlington, ex parte D'Vebre* (1761) 2 Burr. 1115.

55 E.g. *R. v. Johnson* (1723) 1 Stra. 579 (young child delivered to guardian); *R. v. Delaval* (1763) 3 Burr. 1434 (older child to decide for herself).

56 See p. 542, post.

57 E.g. *R. v. Governor of Brixton Prison, ex parte Schtraks* [1964] A.C. 556.

58 *Middleton v. Osborne* (1574) 3 Dyer 332.

59 *R. v. Mayor of Plymouth, ex parte Bagge* (1615) 11 Co. Rep. 93; 1 Rolle Rep. 224.

restitution for those deprived of public offices, such as alderman or constable, recorder or churchwarden; it secured a review of local elections to such offices, when they were alleged to have been corruptly mishandled, and helped to establish democracy as a principle of the common law. Until the last century, the almost invariable purpose of mandamus was the protection of some office or status which could not be recovered by an assize;[60] and this purpose was extended in the eighteenth century to include ecclesiastical benefices such as prebends, and university degrees.[61] In 1763 mandamus was awarded to restore a presbyterian minister, and Lord Mansfield CJ observed that it was a prerogative writ which 'ought to be used upon all occasions where the law has established no specific remedy'.[62] It would not, however, protect a private employment, for there the remedy was to sue for breach of contract;[63] and it could not be used to establish rights of fellowship or membership of colleges or inns of court, because these are domestic bodies under the control of their 'visitors'. Reforms in local government in the nineteenth century, which transferred administrative functions to elected councils,[64] greatly reduced the need for the original use of mandamus; but it has since been turned to the wider use of compelling local and central public authorities or officials to carry out their statutory duties, including the proper exercise of discretionary powers.[65]

CERTIORARI

The writ of certiorari was originally a means of supplying information to a superior court by way of certification, especially from another court of record.[66] For instance, it might be necessary during proceedings in error from the Common Pleas for the King's Bench to inspect the original writ or a warrant of attorney, and in that case a certiorari went to the officer of the Common Pleas commanding him to search his files and certify what he could find to the King's Bench. A different form of

---

60 For the limitations of the assize for an office, see p. 489, post.

61 *R. v. Cambridge University, ex parte Bentley* (1723) 1 Stra. 557.

62 *R. v. Barker, ex parte Mends* (1763) 3 Burr. 1265 at 1267.

63 E.g. *Lord Protector v. Caius College* (1655) Style 457 (headmaster of Perse School).

64 Especially after the Municipal Corporations Act 1835, 5 & 6 Will. IV, c.76, under which borough councils were to be elected by ratepayers and separated from the borough sessions of the peace.

65 *Padfield v. Min. Agriculture, Fisheries and Food* [1968] A.C. 997, [1968] 1 All E.R. 694; *Sec. State for Education v. Tameside M.B.C.* [1977] A.C. 1014.

66 The key words were '*certiorari volumus*' (we wish to be informed). For a specimen, see p. 626, post.

the writ was used to remove records into the King's Bench, so that proceedings could be taken over by the superior court. Until the seventeenth century this procedure was confined to indictments, which could be brought into the King's Bench and either tried there, or quashed, or sent for trial in the country. This gave the King's Bench before 1500 a limited power to review criminal jurisdiction; but review was limited to the wording of the indictment, and most judgments to quash were made on purely technical grounds.[67]

In the reign of Charles I the procedure was extended to administrative orders made by justices of the peace, first as a way of removing recognisances to enforce orders, and then to remove the orders themselves for scrutiny. By the end of the seventeenth century the King's Bench had a flourishing jurisdiction as a court of review for both summary convictions and orders of quarter sessions relating to such matters as public works, licensing, and the settlement of the poor. The essential features of the jurisdiction were settled by Holt CJ: certiorari would lie to any body created by statute which acted judicially, even if it was not a court of common law; statutes creating powers outside the common law were to be strictly construed; and before conviction a man was entitled to be summoned so that he had an opportunity to present his case.[68] Certiorari could not, however, be used to question purely 'ministerial' or administrative decisions. And, as with error, the superior court was limited to an examination of the record to ensure that no order or conviction was *ultra vires*; it could not conduct a new trial or act as a court of appeal.[69]

In the nineteenth century the situations which had occasioned the remedy changed. Summary convictions after 1848 were entered in a form which rendered review of the record unprofitable, and from 1857 doubts in law could be raised by case stated to the one of the superior courts.[70] In 1888 county administration was taken from the justices of the peace and transferred to elected councils which were not regarded as judicial bodies.[71] In the present century the growth of the welfare state has resulted in more and more powers being conferred on administrative bodies, with no statutory appeal to the courts; there are now over fifty

[67] See pp. 594-595, post.

[68] See *Groenvelt v. Burwell* (1700) 1 Ld Raym. 454; *R. v. Chandler* (1702) 1 Ld Raym. 581; *R. v. Dyer* (1703) 6 Mod. Rep. 41; Holt 157.

[69] *R. v. Bolton* (1841) 1 Q.B. 66 at 76, per Lord Denman CJ ('We must not constitute ourselves into a court of appeal').

[70] Stat. 20 & 21 Vict., s.43, ss.2, 6.

[71] Local Government Act 1888, 51 & 52 Vict., c.41, s.3 (administrative functions of quarter sessions transferred to county councils).

categories of administrative tribunal in England. One of the boldest developments of the common law has been the extension of the old remedy of certiorari to these statutory bodies. The courts have achieved this by relaxing the notion of a 'record', so that they may correct 'errors in law' in the certified decisions of any public body which interferes with the rights or obligations of subjects.[72] Even in relation to courts, the notion of a record has been transformed for this purpose; it is no longer the bare minute, setting down the procedural essentials in standard form, but includes the judge's stated reasons.[73]

DECLARATIONS AND APPLICATIONS

A modern remedy which goes further than any of these prerogative remedies is the action seeking a declaration of right from the court rather than specific relief. This started as an equitable procedure, of which an ancient prototype was the petition of right against the Crown; but in private proceedings until 1883 a declaration could only be granted where some specific relief was also available. Since 1883 the action for a declaration has become a remedy in its own right, regularly given by the High Court whether or not other relief is claimed.[74] Although the declaration when given is not directly enforceable, it would be unlawful to act against it; and it may be combined with an injunction or damages. From the 1950s the courts encouraged its use in the sphere of 'public law', because its freedom from technical restrictions enabled gaps to be filled between the prerogative remedies; it could be used, for example, against the Crown, or a professional body, and even to question subordinate legislation; it could be prospective yet not retrospective; and the rules as to *locus standi* were more relaxed than in other actions.

Until 1977, however, a declaration could not be combined with a prerogative remedy, and the prerogative remedies could not be combined with each other. On the recommendation of the Law Commission, this difficulty was overcome by the simple expedient of a new rule of court introducing an 'application for judicial review'.[75] This enables an application for mandamus, prohibition, certiorari, declaration or injunction, separately or in combination, to be made in a summary way; but the new procedure is constrained by a strict time limit, and by

---

72 See *R. v. Local Government Board* (1882) 10 Q.B.D. 309; *R. v. Northumberland Compensation Appeal Tribunal, ex parte Shaw* [1952] 1 K.B. 338, [1952] 1 All E.R. 122.

73 *R. v. Knightsbridge Crown Court, ex parte International Sporting Club (London) Ltd* [1981] 3 All E.R. 417.

74 It was introduced in this form by R.S.C. 1883, Ord. XXV, r.5.

75 R.S.C. 1977, Ord. LIII; Supreme Court Act 1981 (c. 54), s.31.

safeguards to prevent the abuse of the procedure by cranks and busybodies.[76]

Administrative Law

The growth of the prerogative remedies and declarations affords an excellent illustration of the way in which the common law can adapt to new circumstances in order to protect long established notions of justice. The forms of 'oppression and misgovernment' which Coke CJ sought to control sprang chiefly from bodies established under the royal prerogative to administer policy or 'equity' outside the safe framework of the common law. Once the Crown had been painfully brought under the law, it was parliament which began its own democratic form of despotism. Countless statutory bodies have been created over the last 150 years, many of them with sweeping powers to restrict freedom and redistribute private property and money, others empowered to allocate funds raised from subjects by various forms of taxation. In 1978 it was discovered that administrative tribunals dealt with six times as many cases as the High Court and county courts together. These new powers had been introduced by the democratic consent of the governed; but that did not remove the need for fairness in their application to the individual. The power to take away a man's home or his livelihood is a far greater power than that of fining him £5, and it would be a travesty if the latter were subjected to careful judicial review and not the former. Many of the new administrative powers were conferred on non-judicial bodies for the very reason that government departments wished to control the membership of those bodies and the policy which they administered in a way which would not be allowed in the case of a court. The powers conferred on boards, tribunals, ministers and officials were often therefore expressed in absolute terms; their decision was to be final, it was not to be questioned in any court, or it was to be as valid as if embodied in legislation. There is an obvious conflict between the letter of such statutes and the spirit of the common law; but, so far, it is Coke's common law which has prevailed. The legislation cannot itself be set aside;[77] but much can be done by way of interpretation, using the presumption in favour of procedural fairness. Coke had insisted that discretion, even absolute discretion, was a science controlled by law and not an arbitrary power. In the eighteenth century, when parliament purported to give magistrates powers which could not be reviewed, the

[76] Leave of the court is needed to commence proceedings, and to obtain discovery.
[77] Coke's claim that it could was not pursued in England: p. 241, post.

courts held that parliament could not have intended the magistrates' decisions to be regarded as properly made, and therefore beyond review, unless they were made in strict accordance with the legislation and with the principles of natural justice.[78] The same principle was sometimes applied in the nineteenth century.[79] In the earlier part of the twentieth century, however, the courts felt that their armoury was insufficient to cope with the alarmingly absolute discretion conferred by modern legislation on administrative bodies. In place of law there was policy, which was administered not by judges but under the control of civil servants and their masters. In 1929 the lord chief justice himself thought the rule of law had been buried; and the only remedy was to raise the alarm through the press.[80]

The tide has turned since the 1930s to such an extent that 'administrative law' has become one of the most creative and beneficial areas of modern judicial activity. Parliament, though responsible for the spread of tribunals, has itself contributed to the new spirit. Since 1947 the Crown has been made liable to actions in contract and tort. And in 1958 measures were passed to subject tribunals to the rule of law; chairmen were to be appointed by the lord chancellor, and were to give reasons for their decisions, so that certiorari would lie to correct errors; and in some cases an appeal to the High Court was provided.[81] The judges returned to the attack on language purporting to confer absolute power,[82] and began to blur the distinction between administrative and judicial bodies. From the old cases on summary convictions and churchwardens, and the like, have emerged certain broad principles of 'natural justice' to which all decision-making bodies are in some degree subject: those who make decisions affecting others must be free from bias, must be properly informed, must apply the law correctly, must not take account of irrelevances, and must allow those likely to be affected to put their case.

The substantive principles of law may be traced back in a direct line to Sir Edward Coke; yet it is no cause for rejoicing that many of the procedures through which they are implemented are still those of Coke's

---

78   *R. v. Moreley* (1760) 2 Burr. 1040.

79   E.g. *Cooper v. Wandsworth Board of Works* (1863) 14 C.B.N.S. 180 (seemingly arbitrary power subject to implied right to be heard).

80   See the pessimistic reflections of Lord Hewart LCJ in *The New Despotism* (1929).

81   Crown Proceedings Act 1947, 10 & 11 Geo. VI, c.44; Tribunals and Inquiries Act 1958, 6 & 7 Eliz. II, c.66.

82   E.g. *Anisminic Ltd v. Foreign Compensation Commission* [1969] A.C. 147, [1969] 1 All E.R. 208 (provision that determination 'shall not be called in question in any court of law' did not oust jurisdiction to decide whether determination *intra vires*).

day. The prerogative writs were the one group of forms of action left untouched by the reforms of the nineteenth century,[83] and it was necessary to choose the correct remedy at one's peril. There were hopes in 1977 that the application for judicial review would solve that problem. A consequence of the reform, however, has been a new distinction between public law remedies (sought by application) and private law remedies (sought by action). Since the House of Lords has decided that an action is no longer the appropriate way of seeking a public law remedy,[84] there appears to be a new formulary system under which a plaintiff may lose merely because he has chosen the wrong form of action.[85] The parallel with the thirteenth century is instructive for the historian, for in neither legal world was the introduction of newer and better remedies intended to entangle litigants in formalism; but this time the solution will doubtless be found more expeditiously.

Further reading

Holdsworth HEL, vol. I, pp. 213-218, 222-231, 242-246, 368-377, 516-525, 641-645

Milsom HFCL, pp. 55-59

Manchester MLH, pp. 171-188; *Sources*, ch. 8

M. Hemmant, *Select Cases in the Exchequer Chamber* (51 SS, 1933; 64 SS, 1945)

R. Stevens, 'The Final Appeal: Reform of the House of Lords and Privy Council 1867-76' (1964) 80 LQR 343-369

J. H. Baker, 'The Stay and Reversal of Judgments' (1978) 94 SS *116-123*; 'The Correction of Errors', LPCL 298-301; 'Reserved Cases', LPCL 315-318

P. A. Howell, *The Judicial Committee of the Privy Council* (1979)

J. S. Hart, 'The House of Lords and the Appellate Jurisdiction in Equity, 1640-43' (1983) 2 *Parliamentary Hist.* 49-70; 'Judicial Review in the House of Lords, 1640-43' (1984) 5 JLH 64-78

---

[83] In 1938, however, the remedies of mandamus, prohibition and certiorari ceased to be available in the form of writs, and became orders obtained on application by notice of motion: Administration of Justice (Miscellaneous Provisions) Act 1938, 1 & 2 Geo. VI, c.63. (Some confusion was caused after 1854 by the introduction of an *action* for mandamus, now obsolete; but that was really a species of injunction.)

[84] *O'Reilly v. Mackman* [1983] 2 A.C. 237.

[85] See J. A. Jolowicz, [1983] CLJ 15; Sir W. Wade, 101 LQR at 187-188.

PROHIBITION
See p. 153, ante

QUO WARRANTO
D. W. Sutherland, *Quo Warranto Proceedings during the Reign of Edward I* (1963)
J. Levin, *The Charter Controversy in the City of London 1660-88* (1969)
H. G. Goodyear, 'The Tudor Revival of Quo Warranto' (1977), *Laws and Customs*, pp. 231-295

PREROGATIVE REMEDIES
Holdsworth HEL, vol. IX, pp. 104-125
S. A. de Smith, 'The Prerogative Writs' (1951) 11 CLJ 40-56
L. L. Jaffe and E. G. Henderson, 'Judicial Review and the Rule of Law: Historical Origins' (1956) 72 LQR 345-364
E. G. Henderson, *Foundations of English Administrative Law* (1963)

10. The Legal Profession

There is necessarily a close relationship between any system of law and the experts who operate it: the judges who declare what it is, the advocates who present cases in court, the counsellors who advise clients as to its effect, those who expound it by writing and teaching, and all who make it their study. The emergence of the common law of England was more or less coincident with the appearance of professional judges, who were soon followed by practitioners; and its refinement as a body of rational principles in the thirteenth and fourteenth centuries was chiefly the accomplishment of the élite body of judges and advocates who belonged to the order of serjeants at law; a body which, in over six centuries of history, numbered less than one thousand members, less than one fifth of the size of the present practising English bar. Beneath the serjeants was a much larger profession, centred after the middle of the fourteenth century on the inns of court and chancery. The strength and unity of this profession explain how the reasoning of a small group of men in Westminster Hall grew into one of the world's two greatest systems of law. For this peculiarly English professional structure was wholly independent of the university law faculties, where only Canon law and Roman Civil law were taught, and this factor as much as any other ensured the autonomous character of English law and its isolation from the influence of Continental jurisprudence.

ORIGINS OF A PROFESSIONAL BENCH AND BAR

We have seen in previous chapters how the common law evolved from the practices adopted by the twelfth-century *justiciarii*, the members of the *Curia Regis* who toured the country on eyre or sat in the Exchequer and Bench. Had they understood the meaning of our terms, these early *justiciarii* might have considered themselves civil servants rather than lawyers; getting through the workload in an orderly manner was more important than fine learning, and therefore a degree in law – in Roman law – was not required. Some of them were clergy, while others – including some of the most successful (like Lucy and Glanvill) – were knights; but by their uniform administration of royal justice they elevated the judicial role into a distinct and technical profession. They devoted their working lives to the system they were helping to establish, and handed on the traditions of the king's justice to their successors; indeed, by 1200, continuity was facilitated by the practice of appointing to the bench men who had served as clerks to the judges of the previous generation. The appearance in the next few generations of a body of professional advocates and attorneys to mediate between the judges and private litigants added another class of legal expert, a class which soon outnumbered the judiciary. It became obvious that judges needed to be comparable in background and forensic skill with those who appeared before them, and by the end of the thirteenth century it had become a general rule that judges of the two benches could only be appointed from the professional bar. As a result, England possessed from an early date a bench and bar united by their membership of a common profession. This new profession had arisen independently of the Church and the universities, and was rooted in the practice of the law of the land.

The Medieval Profession

This non-clerical legal profession appeared in the course of the thirteenth century. How far litigants would have had access to expert assistance before then is unclear. The clergy were not allowed by Canon law to practise in lay courts for gain, though it is possible that they provided some assistance to litigants until a lay profession came into being. The need for a regular profession must, however, have been pressing once the royal courts were established. Litigation in central courts, often far from home, required management by men who could follow the king's court wherever it might be and who understood its procedures. Moreover, the growing technicality of the oral proceedings in court, conducted in the French tongue, made expert advocacy indispensable. From the very start, those two functions were conceived of as being distinct. The 'forespeaker' (*advocatus* or *prolocutor*) who stood beside a litigant and spoke for him, subject to correction, was quite different from the representative (*attornatus* or *procurator*) who stood in another's shoes and acted on his behalf so as to bind him in his absence. There has therefore never been any question of the English legal profession dividing into two; the division of function preceded the appearance of a profession, though the precise allocation of functions has shifted over the centuries.

We cannot properly speak of a legal 'profession' until such time as men were following the law for a living, and subject to some form of discipline in so doing. The first element was present as early as 1200-10, when the names of certain pleaders, attorneys and essoiners[1] are found to recur in the rolls of the *Curia Regis*; but these habitual practitioners did not act to the exclusion of others, nor were their functions always mutually exclusive. The element of professional regulation was probably added later in the thirteenth century. In 1275 it was enacted that professional lawyers found guilty of deceit should be punished;[2] and in 1280 the city of London made regulations concerning practitioners in the mayor's court, for the administration of an oath to those newly admitted, and for keeping separate the functions of pleader, attorney and essoiner. It is certain that some closely analogous regulation was made for the Common Bench at about the same period, for as soon as there is clear evidence of such matters – in the records of the fourteenth century – it is found that the pleaders in the Bench were selected by the judges there, made to take an oath, and were then expected to remain aloof from lesser practitioners. A study of the names of pleaders in the records and year-books of Edward I's reign establishes that before 1300 a small group of highly skilled advocates dominated the bar. At the same time, the attorneys in the royal courts became a distinct profession. Their role was to represent clients in the formal aspects of litigation, managing suits for absent clients, taking out writs and instructing counsel. They came likewise to be selected by the judges, and sworn to do their duty; as officers of the court they were subject to disciplinary control by the bench. The separation of pleaders and attorneys was a natural separation of different skills, between quick-witted and learned court-room lawyers and managerial, clerkly lawyers.[3] The same distinction between specialists and general practitioners was reproduced much later by barristers and solicitors.

THE SERJEANTS AT LAW

The pleaders in the Common Bench were already, it seems, an identifiable class in 1230, when Matthew Paris referred to them as 'the forespeakers of the Bench, whom we vulgarly call *narratores*'.[4] Their principal job was to recite the plaintiff's count (*narratio*) and engage in any argument which ensued. By the end of the century the identity of these counters or *narratores* is well known from the year-books and plea

---

[1] An essoiner (*excusator*) was employed to make formal excuses for non-appearance in court. In the 14th century the function was absorbed into that of the attorney.

[2] Statute of Westminster I, c.29.

[3] Coke, in the seventeenth century, said it was a distinction between *officium ingenii* and *officium laboris*: Co. Inst., vol. II, p. 514.

[4] *Chronica Majora* (Rolls ser.), vol. III, p. 619. For the count, see p. 90, ante.

rolls; they were the leaders of the profession from whom the judges were invariably chosen, and whose arguments at the bar were noted down by reporters for future learning.

During the fourteenth century this select group of counters in the Common Bench was organised into a fraternity or guild known as the order of serjeants at law. Admission to this body took place every few years, so that (after 1329 at the latest),[5] new serjeants were 'called' in batches of about six to nine. The admission soon became a kind of degree ceremony, or 'creation', conducted by the judges of the Common Pleas, and initiated by the issue of a writ of subpoena to the graduand ordering him to make himself ready to assume 'the estate and degree of a serjeant at law' (*status et gradus servientis ad legem*).[6] This estate and degree was not merely a professional qualification, but a public honour which could compete for status with knighthood and the doctorate. New serjeants took an oath to serve the king's people, gave a sumptuous feast which the king sometimes attended, distributed gold rings with mottoes,[7] and were invested with their hoods and coifs. The coif, originally a white silk or linen head-covering tied under the chin, was the badge of the serjeants until the last century; but it came to be almost covered by a black skull-cap, and by Victorian times it had dwindled into a circular patch on the crown of the wig. The central point of the creation ceremony was the admission at the bar of the Common Pleas; each new serjeant was led up by two senior serjeants and heard to count for the first time. It was this count which made him a serjeant.

The serjeants enjoyed their greatest fortunes in the year-book period, when the bulk of civil litigation passed through the Common Pleas. Sir John Fortescue said in the fifteenth century that the serjeants were the richest advocates in the whole world. They were the leaders of the bar by natural, judicial and royal selection. But their titular distinction outlived their importance, and it was their destiny to decline with the court to which they belonged, though the process was slow and unplanned. Although they had audience in the King's Bench and other

---

5 Nine new counters were admitted in October 1329: Baker, *Serjeants at Law*, p. 155. There had been group calls in 1309 (nine), 1311 (six), and 1318 (five), and perhaps in the 1290s; but before 1329 counters had also been admitted singly.

6 The earliest known writ in this form was used in 1382, but before that an informal privy seal order was employed: Baker, *Serjeants at Law*, pp. 28-29, 254. The use of a subpoena may have been necessary to combat a reluctance on the part of some lawyers to undergo the lavish expense of creation.

7 The giving of gold is first mentioned in 1329: BL MS. Add. 41160, fo. 40v. Cf. 97 SS 13, 14 (eyre of Northants., 1329); Y.B. 16 Edw. III, pt ii, p. 387n (general call of 1342).

courts, the serjeants shared it, to their cost, with the apprentices at law. Furthermore, when written pleadings replaced oral pleading at the bar, and contentious proceedings effectively began with the trial at nisi prius,[8] the pre-eminence of the serjeants as pleaders was undermined. Serjeants retained a monopoly of motions in banc, and of signing special pleas, in Common Pleas cases; but for all other business they had to compete with the lower branch of the bar. The growth of a junior bar also caused the loss of the serjeants' exclusive right to judicial appointments, because from the sixteenth century it became common to appoint judges from outside the order of coif by the expedient of putting new judges through a formal creation ceremony for qualifying purposes only. The first documented instance of this occurred in 1519, when John Ernle, the attorney-general, was made chief justice of the Common Pleas; the precedent was followed in 1545, when Sir Richard Lyster, chief baron of the Exchequer (but not a serjeant) became chief justice of the King's Bench. The practice thereafter became ever more common, so that many eminent judges – Coke, Mansfield and Blackstone among them – were men who had never practised as serjeants in the Common Pleas. The exclusive character of the order was destroyed in the seventeenth century when ministers sold the coif for bribes, and by 1700 there were ten times as many serjeants as there had been in 1500, but with less for them to do. Even the precedence which the serjeants enjoyed over the rest of the bar gave way in the seventeenth century to the new rank of king's counsel. The attractions of the coif waned once it was found to pin men beneath their juniors who attained this newer rank.[9]

The end of the serjeants was finally settled in 1846 when, by a statute passed hurriedly in the long vacation, the Common Pleas was opened to the whole bar.[10] The order of the coif was never abolished, but the last non-judicial serjeants were created in 1868. When the High Court was set up in 1875, its judges were not required to take the coif; and the last judge required to become a serjeant was Lindley J, appointed to the old Common Pleas in May 1875. Although Lord Cairns LC informed the House of Lords that the power to create serjeants remained, it was well known that it would not be used. The serjeants therefore

---

[8] See pp. 97-101, ante.

[9] See pp. 188-189, post.

[10] Stat. 9 & 10 Vict., c.54. For an unlawful attempt by Lord Brougham to achieve this by royal warrant, see *The Serjeants' Case* (1839-40) 6 Bing. N.C. 235; J. Manning, *Serviens ad Legem* (1840).

sold Serjeants' Inn in 1877, and watched their order die away. The last serjeant, Lord Lindley, died in 1921.[11]

APPRENTICES AT LAW

The emergence of a non-clerical literate profession in the thirteenth century necessitated an educational system independent of the Church. By the second half of the century there was indeed some kind of law school, known only from surviving texts of its lectures and disputations, and by the 1280s its students were known as the 'apprentices of the Bench'. There is no evidence that these apprentices were articled to anyone; they were learners attached to the court itself, where a kind of gallery – called the 'crib' or (later) the 'pecunes' – was installed for their accommodation.[12] Not all apprentices could become serjeants; and, since there was no intermediate degree, the designation 'apprentice' continued to attach to them when they entered practice. The fully-fledged apprentices therefore became a junior branch of the profession; and there was plenty for them to do. They might practise as counsel available to the public[13] or as private advisers to great landowners, as attorneys, as clerks and officials, or as advocates in the King's Bench, Chancery and lesser courts, and on circuit. As these functions increased in number and importance the process of judicial control, the process which had produced the order of serjeants centuries earlier, repeated itself. This time, however, the judges could exercise their discretion by reference to an established standard, the status of the individual in the inns of court. By Tudor times, the 'apprentice of the law' was no longer a student, but a senior graduate in one of these inns.[14]

THE LEGAL INNS

The western suburbs of London were filled, by the fourteenth century, with the town houses or inns (*hospicia*) of the statesmen, civil servants and lawyers whose work brought them to London when parliament and the courts were in session. Of these only the inns of court, and the inn

---

11   Serjeant Sullivan (d. 1959), often called 'the last serjeant', was not a member of the English order, but was the last survivor of the king's serjeants in Ireland. The rank of queen's serjeant survives even now in the county palatine of Lancaster; but it has no connection with the order of the coif.

12   'The Pecunes', 98 LQR 204 (repr. in LPCL 171).

13   Before the establishment of the chambers system, lawyers attended in Westminster Hall in the morning and in St Paul's in the afternoon for the purposes of being consulted.

14   It was equated with a readership in an inn: LPCL 88-89, 108.

or palace of the archbishop of Canterbury at Lambeth, have retained their original character and identity. The judges and serjeants usually had houses to themselves before Tudor times, but the apprentices and clerks often found it convenient to live in shared accommodation, sometimes in part of an inn of a magnate who did not need it, occasionally in the household of a judge or senior official. About twenty inns are known to have been used by apprentices of the law, most of them in the parishes of St Andrew Holborn and St Clement Danes. Some were short-lived, others grew into permanence. In no case was there a 'foundation' or incorporation, as with the colleges at Oxford and Cambridge; they were creatures of expediency. By the middle of the fourteenth century, however, some of the inns had taken over the responsibility for educating lawyers; lectures and disputations were held in their halls. In this connection four inns achieved a predominant position; they were known by the 1420s as the 'inns of court'.[15]

The origin of the inns of court is not precisely known. The Temple was the *hospicium* or London residence of the knights Templar until their dissolution, and the Inner Temple hall stands on the site of the refectory of the military order, still linked by cloisters to the round church. It was let to lawyers in the fourteenth century, probably by the 1340s, and before 1388 the legal tenants had formed the two societies of the Inner Temple and Middle Temple. Gray's Inn was the town house of the Lords Grey of Wilton before it was let to apprentices at about the same period. No mention has been found of Lincoln's Inn as a legal society before 1417, and it is not certain whether it is as old as the others. Ancient tradition supposed it to have been the inn of Henry de Lacy (d. 1311), earl of Lincoln, whose arms adorned the Tudor gatehouse; but it seems more likely to have taken its name from Thomas de Lincoln, a serjeant at law in the time of Edward III. The earliest records of any of the legal societies are the Black Books of Lincoln's Inn, which begin in 1422 and show that already by that time there was a settled social and educational routine. By that date, too, the serjeants were drawn almost exclusively from the four inns of court.

The other inns were of lesser status, and by the middle of the fifteenth century were used chiefly by the attorneys and clerks who could not gain admission to one of the greater houses, and by younger students coming to learn to the rudiments of procedure. The number

---

[15] The English expression is found *c.* 1425, in *Arnold's Chronicle* (1811 ed.), p. 291 ('ynnes of courte'). Its Latin forms (*hospicia hominum curiae, hospicia jurisconsultorum*) suggest that it was an abbreviation of 'inns of the men of court'.

fluctuated, but by 1500 had settled at nine, known compendiously as the 'inns of chancery'.[16] The implication that they had a common origin in association with the Chancery is misleading; but some of them had probably been the houses of Chancery clerks who taught the elements of the writ system. In Tudor times they came under the control of the inns of court, the latter sending members to lecture to the satellite societies and in some cases acting as landlords. The educational functions virtually ceased in the middle of the seventeenth century, but the inns of chancery continued to provide accommodation and social facilities for attorneys until they were sold and the societies wound up in Victorian times. Only one of the medieval buildings survives, the hall of Barnard's Inn; but Staple Inn, carefully rebuilt after war damage, still evokes the atmosphere of these forgotten little colleges of law.

The fifteenth-century inns of court and chancery together formed a law school not much smaller in size than the University of Cambridge. It would be called in Tudor times the Third University of England; and with good reason, for it played at least as full a part as the two older universities in the education of laymen destined for high or local office. The academic routine was already ancient when first noticed in the Black Books. After his elementary grounding in an inn of chancery, a student who aspired to the bar would seek admission to one of the inns of court as a student, or 'inner barrister'; he would spend seven years or so attending courts, performing oral pleading exercises (called moots), attending lectures (called readings), and keeping commons with his fellows.[17] After this training he might expect to be called to the bar as an 'utter barrister'. The term 'barrister', found in the Black Books in the middle of the fifteenth century, indicates the status of the member at moots; the inner barristers sat within the bar, like clerks of the court, and the utter barristers stood outside it, like serjeants. There is reason to think that graduation as a barrister originally occurred by performing a pleading at the bar of an inn, just as the graudation of a serjeant took effect by counting at the bar of the Common Pleas. Twice a year, in the Lent and summer vacations, a barrister of at least ten years standing was elected to deliver a reading, or course of lectures, upon a selected statute. After performing this duty he became a bencher, so called because he sat on the bench at moots, taking the part of a judge. The

---

16   The nine were: Barnard's Inn, Clement's Inn, Clifford's Inn, Davies (later Thavies) Inn, Furnival's Inn, Lyon's Inn, New Inn, Staple Inn and Strand Inn.

17   A student was usually admitted to clerks' commons, and progressed after a few years to masters' commons. The significance of this division seems to have more gastronomic than academic.

readers or benchers assumed the task of governing their inns, including the selection of candidates for call to the bar.

The system of readings never provided a coherent course of legal instruction, and readings were not given on the common law except to the extent that it was relevant to the exposition of a statute; but it initiated the student in the intricacies of legal analysis and debate, teaching him skills which he could himself practise in moots. In 1642 the civil war fatally disrupted the educational life of the inns; attempts at revival in 1660 were largely unsuccessful.[18] Law students were thereafter left to fend for themselves.

The New Profession

Since the principal litigation of medieval times was concentrated in the Common Pleas, the serjeants and attorneys were engaged in the most important contentious work of the nation. The attorneys of the Common Pleas were officers of the court who carried on the formal side of litigation, issuing process and authorising entries on the plea rolls. Argument in open court was the exclusive province of the order of the coif. But neither of those old branches of the profession had any monopoly on the new work which flooded into the King's Bench and conciliar courts in the sixteenth century, or on the conduct of cases at nisi prius. In the absence of contrary regulation, and subject to the law of maintenance, this work could be done by anyone who could claim to be a professional man of law.[19] Occasionally the year-books provide glimpses of proceedings outside the Common Pleas, and we can see that the senior apprentices were as busy there as the serjeants were in their own court. It had become possible to earn a living from the law without becoming a serjeant or an attorney; the other 'men of court' thereby grew into a new branch of the profession.

In the sixteenth century attempts were made, both by the judges and by the Privy Council, to impose some control on this new branch. Whether there was any previous definition of rights of audience is unclear, though it seems that in practice they were restricted in the superior courts to benchers of the inns of court. With the explosion of litigation in the Tudor period, however, the benchers were not

---

18 See LPCL 35-38.

19 'Maintenance' was the tort (and misdemeanour) of meddling in someone else's litigation. In 1354 it was a sufficient justification of maintenance that one was a 'man of law': LPCL 124. A century later, membership of an inn was pleaded: ibid. 110-111.

sufficiently numerous to take all the cases, and so the barristers were let in; and this gave rise to the first regulations, which were measures to ensure that only barristers of a certain standing should appear in the superior courts.[20] It was already an assumption that call to the bar of an inn was a sine qua non for practice at the bar of the central courts; no other appropriate qualification existed. The domestic rank of utter barrister thus became a public degree, and to reflect this change it became generally known as the degree of 'barrister at law'.

Contemporaneous with this process of definition was the appearance of yet another kind of legal practice, that of the 'solicitor'. Solicitors are mentioned in the fifteenth century, and were so called from the function of 'soliciting causes': that is, helping clients through the jurisdictional jungle, giving general advice, and instructing attorneys and counsel as appropriate. Since the name described the function rather than a specific class of lawyer, solicitors were not at first rigidly separated from barristers or attorneys. Young barristers were expected to gain experience by soliciting causes, while an attorney of the Common Pleas acted as a 'solicitor' when pursuing cases in the Chancery or conciliar courts. Indeed, there was a widespread view that only barristers and attorneys could lawfully act as general solicitors;[21] without such a qualification, to meddle in litigation was to commit maintenance. The judges, with the aid of the Star Chamber, waged a fierce campaign between 1590 and 1630 against 'mere' solicitors; but they proved indestructible, and became in the mid-seventeenth century a fourth separate branch of the profession. Although the attack had proceeded partly on the basis that soliciting was best done by young barristers, the bar became so busy with appearances in court, giving opinions, and settling pleadings, that they did not press their case to be solicitors as well. Barristers found it more convenient to leave preliminary dealings with clients, and the preparation of briefs, to attorneys and solicitors, and thereby reinforced their claim to be specialists to whom cases were referred by the latter.

The new callings of barrister[22] and solicitor thus came to mirror the older callings of serjeant and attorney, of *advocatus* and *procurator*. The barristers were conscious of their status as specialists sharing the learned

---

[20] *Tudor Royal Proclamations* (P. L. Hughes and J. F. Larkin ed.), vol. I, p. 408, no. 294 (call to the bar, and eight years standing from admission, required in 1547). Call to the bar was not then required for advocacy in local courts, but seems to have become obligatory as a result of *Broughton v. Prince* (1589) LPCL 129-134.

[21] There was no objection to a client's servant or permanent adviser soliciting his causes.

[22] The term is here used to include benchers, who nowadays are regarded as still being barristers; but this usage is anachronistic.

traditions and professional obligations of the serjeants, which gave them superiority over the purely ministerial practitioners and their clerks. Steps were taken to emphasise that superiority by excluding attorneys and solicitors from the inns of court. The bar projected the image of an honourable calling for gentlemen, which, in accordance with classical notions of a liberal profession, was followed from a sense of public duty rather than for lucre. Out of this sentiment was born the rule that barristers cannot sue for their fees, which are regarded as *honoraria* in the Roman sense, that barristers should not court the company of attorneys, and that barristers should no longer undertake the routine work of soliciting causes or attending directly to the everyday affairs of clients. The elevation of the barrister suited the solicitor perfectly well, because it extended his own range of exclusive business. By the eighteenth century, however, the solicitor had become not only acceptable but even respectable. In 1729 attorneys and solicitors were subjected to closer professional regulation, to exclude undesirables; and at about the same time they formed a 'Society of Gentlemen Practisers in the Courts of Law and Equity'. As a result of the professional control imposed by this society, and its descendant the Law Society (incorporated in 1826), the profession of solicitor[23] became in the nineteenth century as respectable as that of barrister. The social differences between the two classes have withered away, and the professional differences are in function and expertise rather than in education or ability.

KING'S (OR QUEEN'S) COUNSEL

The only *degrees* in the common law are that of serjeant-at-law, conferred by the judges upon the nomination of the Crown, and those of bencher and barrister at law, conferred by the inns of court. There have been and still are, however, various *offices* which members of the bar might fill in the course of their profession: an office being a paid public employment rather than a degree. The highest offices open to the bar were judicial, as were some of the lowest – for instance, recorderships of boroughs and stewardships of manors. Of offices appropriate to practising advocates the most rewarding were those relating to the litigation of the Crown. The king retained counsel and attorneys in each central court: the king's serjeants in the Common Pleas, the king's attorneys there and in the King's Bench, and the king's serjeants and

---

[23] The much older title of attorney was abolished with the courts to which the attorneys belonged. From 1 November 1875, all existing attorneys were to be called solicitors: Judicature Act 1873, 36 & 37 Vict., c.66, s.87.

attorneys in the palatinates and in Ireland. In the fifteenth century the single office of king's attorney-general combined the older separate offices in the two benches, and in 1461 the first king's solicitor-general was appointed. Despite their titles, these offices were always held by members of the bar. The king's serjeants were usually between two and four in number, and by virtue of their rank they preceded the rest of the English bar. But in 1623 the attorney-general and solicitor-general were by royal warrant given precedence over all but the two most senior king's serjeants, known thereafter as the king's first (or 'prime') and second serjeants; and by another warrant in 1813 they were given their present pre-eminence over the entire bar.[24] The standing of these two senior law officers had increased steadily since the fifteenth century, when they were already a stepping-stone to judicial office. In Tudor times two serjeants gave up the coif to become law officers, technically a loss of status, because the position was more influential and lucrative. A seventeenth-century attorney-general could earn (besides his modest salary of £81) at least £6,000 a year in fees,[25] while in the eighteenth century several earned over £10,000 a year.

The attorney-general, solicitor-general and king's serjeants together constituted the king's counsel in ordinary. The first king's counsel 'extraordinary' to be granted that office by patent was Francis Bacon. He had been called within the bar in 1594 as Queen Elizabeth I's 'learned counsel extraordinary, without patent or fee'; and in 1604 James I granted him by patent the office of 'one of our counsel learned in the law', with 'place and precedence in our courts or elsewhere and preaudience' and a fee of £40 per annum.[26] Only one other king's counsel was appointed by James I, but Charles I appointed nine and Charles II thirty-one. It is doubtful whether the office was really needed; but this was an age for bestowing, or selling, titles, and the right of preaudience was highly valuable to the recipient. In theory the king's counsel were supernumerary law officers who, in return for a small salary, held permanent retainers which prevented them from appearing against the Crown; until 1920 it was necessary for them to obtain a licence to appear for the defence in a criminal case. In practice, it was the precedence and preaudience which led rising barristers to seek the silk

---

[24] The reasons for these alterations are explained in Baker, *Serjeants at Law*, pp. 58-61, 112.

[25] Sir Francis Bacon estimated his income as attorney-general in 1616 to be £6,000. But it has recently been estimated that Sir Robert Heath's income as attorney-general in the 1620s exceeded £10,000 a year: P. E. Kopperman, *Sir Robert Heath 1575-1649* (1989), pp. 249-250.

[26] The patent is printed in Sainty, *English Law Officers*, p. 294. The 1594 call within the bar is noted in BL MS. Harley 1697, fo. 43.

gown.[27] The institution of the rank of king's counsel proved to be the principal death blow against the order of serjeants. It was unsettled until 1670 whether serjeants took professional precedence of the new officers, but in that year King Charles II in the Privy Council personally delivered the damaging decision that they did not.[28] Thereafter the most junior king's counsel preceded even the most senior serjeant (not being a king's serjeant), and it was the prospect of continuous demotion which deterred the most able lawyers from applying for the coif. A serjeant could, of course, take silk and become a king's serjeant; but this would carry him in one leap over the heads of many of his seniors, and in all but a few cases this would have been unacceptable and professionally dangerous. By the nineteenth century nearly all barristers with high aspirations chose the silk gown in preference to the coif of a serjeant, and this tendency contributed more than anything else to the decline and gradual extinction of the order of the coif.

The Judiciary

We have noticed that an expert judiciary preceded the formation of a profession of private practitioners, but that as soon as such a profession came into existence its most prominent members were the prime candidates for judicial appointments. The first practising lawyer to become a royal judge was perhaps Roger Huscarl (d. *c.* 1230), a justice of the *Curia Regis* from 1210; he had started practice as an attorney in the 1190s. By the end of the thirteenth century nearly all the superior judges had practised as serjeants in the Common Pleas, and in the fourteenth century it became a firm rule that only serjeants at law could be appointed to judgeships in the King's Bench and Common Pleas or to commissions of assize. In the Court of Exchequer, the chief baron was very often a serjeant, but it was not until the last decade of the sixteenth century that the coif became an invariable qualification for the barons.[29] All these judges received salaries and robes from the Crown, but made up much of their incomes from court fees. Permanent judgeships, unlike recorderships and inferior judicial offices, prevented the holders from continuing in private practice at the bar; but in

---

27 The proper dress of all king's counsel was a gown with black lace and tufts; but since the eighteenth century they have worn black silk gowns, and are consequently called 'silks'. Junior barristers wear stuff mourning gowns.

28 The proceedings, and the order in council, are printed in Baker, *Serjeants at Law*, pp. 488-490.

29 See p. 58, ante.

medieval times judges were allowed to give private advice, and habitually acted as arbitrators, in which capacity they accepted fees and alimentary gifts from the public. The judiciary were thus removed from the profession of the bar only by office, and in the two Serjeants' Inns[30] the judges lodged and dined alongside their brethren of the coif. If a judge lost his office, he could return to practice as a serjeant; and this was not an infrequent event in the troubled years of the seventeenth century.

The independence of the judiciary from political control is now rightly regarded as one of the pillars of the constitution, but it was built on an unsure foundation. The judges were servants of the king, appointed and paid by the king, and in theory removable at the pleasure of the king. On paper they were no more secure in office than a government minister, who held office on similar terms. And in reality kings often expected subservience from their judges in matters affecting the Crown. Fourteenth-century courts routinely received direct instructions from the Crown by writs of privy seal requiring favour,[31] and it seems that the judges generally complied. It is difficult to assess how far medieval judges were liable to dismissal for behaving independently. Although there may have been political forces behind the occasional removal from office, for offences not usually specified in detail, the year-books frequently show the judges deciding against the Crown, and a general independence of spirit is assumed. It was the professional training of the judiciary, and the notion of a constitutional monarchy as expounded by Fortescue in the fifteenth century,[32] which transformed the personal loyalty which judges owed the king into a more objective form of loyalty to an impersonal Crown and to the king's common law. The independent stance of particular chief justices may have helped to establish a general principle of independence. The famous story that Gascoigne CJ had committed Prince Henry (later Henry V) for contempt in trying to browbeat the court, whether true or not, was a popular tale in the sixteenth century. Huse CJ provided another instance at the very beginning of the Tudor age; when in 1485 the new king desired the judges to give preliminary opinions in a treason case, the chief justice declined, saying that 'it would come before the King's Bench judicially, and then they would do what by right they

---

30   One was in Fleet Street, and the other in Chancery Lane. In 1730 the former was given up and the two societies merged.

31   For a striking example, see 104 SS 110-111.

32   J. Fortescue, *The Governance of England* (C. Plummer ed., 1885); *De Laudibus Legum Angliae* (S. B. Chrimes ed., 1942). Fortescue was chief justice of the King's Bench from 1442 to 1461.

ought to do'.[33] Under Henry VIII there is a notable contrary instance of judges conforming their opinions to the king's wishes,[34] but it is difficult to gauge how often such situations occurred. There were very few removals from judicial office before the seventeenth century; but that fact alone is as consistent with judicial subservience as with independence. Probably the Crown rarely applied, or needed to apply, extreme pressure on the judges; when it did so, the reaction depended on the quality of the men in office and the extent of their personal agreement with royal policy.

In the seventeenth century the judiciary came into head-on collision with the Crown on several occasions. The first major episode was in 1616, when the judges were summoned before the Council to say whether they would stay a suit if the king so ordered. All the judges submitted except Coke CJ, who answered (doubtless remembering the example of Huse CJ) that 'when that case should be, he would do that should be fit for a judge to do'.[35] A few months later Coke was dismissed, by a writ giving no reasons, despite his reputation as the greatest lawyer of the time. During the next twenty-five years James I and Charles I removed several more judges who refused to behave as the government wished, and judicial office became less secure than it had ever been. The judges who stayed in office were often associated in popular perception with the government of the day, and within a few decades the awesome judiciary which the people had revered at the beginning of the century came to be regarded, rightly or wrongly, as an instrument of prerogative rule. The decision of a majority of the judges in favour of the imposition of ship-money in 1638 brought their reputation for impartiality to its lowest ebb, and in 1641 several of the ship-money judges were impeached.

Contemporaries saw the solution to be life tenure for judges. The appropriate words of limitation in a patent granting office for life were *quamdiu se bene gesserit* (so long as he should behave well). Bryan CJCP had (perhaps uniquely) received such a patent in 1472,[36] and the majority of barons of the Exchequer after 1450 were given tenure on the like terms. In 1642 Charles I was pressured into appointing judges during good behaviour, and the practice was followed under Charles II by Lord Clarendon LC; but from 1668 there was a quiet return to grants

---

[33] *R. v. Stafford* (1486) Y.B. Trin. 1 Hen. VII, fo. 26, pl.1.

[34] *Lord Dacre's Case* (1535) B. & M. 105 at 111; p. 291, post. Cf. 102 SS xvii-xviii.

[35] *Acts of the Privy Council 1615-1616* (1925), p. 607.

[36] His immediate predecessor, Danby CJ, seems to have been dismissed, perhaps for supporting the readeption of Henry VI in 1471.

'during pleasure'. Even judges who had life tenure were insecure, because they could be suspended from sitting; a suspended judge remained technically in office, and received his salary, but took no further part in decisions.[37] Charles II also began the practice of forced retirement. It had been very rare for judges to retire, since there was no right to a pension; usually they served until they died. But there were precedents for permitting judges to retire with a pension on grounds of old age or ill health, by issuing a 'writ of allowance';[38] in 1678 the same writ was used peremptorily to remove Rainsford CJ to make way for a court favourite (Scroggs CJ), and in 1679 to remove several judges for political reasons. These scandals were exceeded by James II, who removed twelve judges in four years, mostly for refusing to recognise his claim to dispense with statutes. The lesson was learned. William III was advised to appoint all his judges during good behaviour, and after 1700 tenure during good behaviour was guaranteed by the Act of Settlement.[39] Yet even tenure during good behaviour ended with the demise of the Crown. Upon the king's death all judicial proceedings ceased, and all judicial authority returned to the new king; one of the first acts of a new king was to deliver the great seal to a chancellor, who could use it to seal patents appointing the judges. On the death of a sovereign, therefore, the Crown had the opportunity to dismiss judges and other officers of state by not renewing their patents. Queen Anne discontinued some judges in this way in 1702. After 1707, however, patents were continued for six months after the demise of the Crown; and since 1760 continuity in office has been secured by statute.

Once judges received security of tenure, the principal form of political influence lay in the choice of new judges. There is no constitutional machinery for reviewing appointments, which are an act of absolute royal prerogative. Until 1946, when Lord Goddard was appointed, it had been a very frequent practice[40] for four centuries to offer chief justiceships when vacant to government law officers. Politics sometimes played a part in the appointment of puisne justices as well, even as late as the turn of this century, when Lord Halsbury LC made

---

[37] *Re Justice Archer* (1672) T. Raym. 217; Lincoln's Inn MS. Misc. 500, fo. 206v.

[38] An early example is that of Kingsmill J (1606). It had been done more recently for Hale CJ (1676) and Twisden J (1678), though Hale had scrupulously advised against his own pension.

[39] Stat. 12 & 13 Will. III, c.2; and see D. A. Rubini, 83 LQR 343. Some modifications have been made in recent times to introduce a retiring age of 75 and a procedure for removal in case of permanent infirmity: Judicial Pensions Act 1959, 8 & 9 Eliz. II, c.9, s.2; Administration of Justice Act 1973 (c.15), s.12.

[40] With two exceptions (Lord Tenterden CJKB and Erle CJCP) all 19th century chief justices had served as law officers. Tenterden had been Treasury counsel.

some nominations which were widely condemned as showing party bias. It has to be said, nevertheless, that most of the judges appointed in this manner after the seventeenth century conducted themselves with complete propriety in office; if judgeships were occasionally given as a reward for past service or friendship, the tradition of judicial independence was strong enough to prevail over party sentiments once the patent was sealed. Lord Ellenborough CJ was (in 1806) the last chief justice to serve in the Cabinet, and his association with the administration was controversial at the time;[41] thereafter judges, excepting the lord chancellor, have remained aloof from party politics.

It may seem strange that the tenure secured, with such a struggle, for judges of the superior courts is not given to other judges. The reason is partly historical. Until 1972 justices of assize were appointed by commission, and until 1973 justices of the peace were appointed in the same way. Commissions were issued ad hoc from time to time, and there was no guarantee that any person would be continued from one commission to the next. Circuit judges are now appointed by royal warrant, justices of the peace by an instrument signed by the lord chancellor; but these documents confer no greater security of tenure than commissions. The majority of judges are therefore to this day removable at the behest of the lord chancellor, who remains an active member of the government. So far the high traditions of their office have restrained lord chancellors from abusing the power, despite occasional pressure from members of parliament to do so.

Civilian Advocates

The practitioners and judges in the English ecclesiastical and admiralty courts were until 1857 wholly separate from the common-law profession just described. There was a parallel division between advocates (corresponding to serjeants) and proctors (corresponding to attorneys), but their training was quite distinct from that provided in the inns of court. Proctors were bred up in the routine of their courts, by a kind of apprenticeship; if they had an academic qualification at all, it would have been as a bachelor of law. The advocates were doctors of law from the universities of Oxford and Cambridge who had been

---

[41] The government answered haughtily, 'we take not our principles of the English constitution from the theories of Montesquieu and Blackstone' but from precedents, and that it was idle to talk of the separation of powers: *Ann. Reg. 1806*, pp. 27-33.

admitted to practise by the ecclesiastical authorities.[42] In medieval times most practising advocates were necessarily canonists; but after Henry VIII's reign, when the schools of Canon law were closed, they were doctors of Civil law (usually abbreviated as D.C.L. at Oxford, LL.D. at Cambridge). From them were appointed the judges in those courts, and the king's advocate, who acted as law officer there. Many, though not all, of the advocates belonged to a society called Doctors' Commons, where they kept common table and built up a precious library of foreign law books. This society was formed by the 'doctors of the Arches' in the fifteenth century, for reasons of social convenience, and never possessed educational functions like those of the inns of court. It was incorporated in 1768 as 'the College of Doctors of Law exercent in the Ecclesiastical and Admiralty Courts'. The doctors' ancient traditions and scarlet robes resembled in some ways those of the serjeants, and they acquired a similar reputation for being a 'cosey, dosey, old-fashioned, time-forgotten, sleepy-headed little family party'.[43] Many of the Victorian advocates were men of learning and distinction; but the institution was out of tune with the Victorian spirit of rationalism. Upon the establishment of secular divorce and probate courts in 1857 the doctors were deprived of their monopoly of audience in those important spheres, and two years later they lost their monopoly in Admiralty. Since it was much easier to become a barrister, no new doctors were expected to be admitted; and so, as a profession, the advocates lost heart. The society of Doctors' Commons sold its library in 1861, and its premises in 1865. The last member of the profession, Dr T. H. Tristram, died in 1912.

Legal Education in the Universities

If the common law sometimes appeared to be an orderless science, it was chiefly because it lacked a comprehensive system of education. No one ever had to attempt to teach or learn the law as a coherent whole, and for most students the sole objective was to obtain a sufficient grounding in practice. The universities had law schools, but taught Civil and Canon law to the exclusion of the law of the land, perhaps because they disdained any subjects which were not expressed in Latin.

---

42 Usually by the dean of Arches upon receipt of a mandate from the archbishop of Canterbury. But there were some advocates who practised exclusively in the northern province, presumably by licence from the archbishop of York; they were not always doctors.

43 C. Dickens, *David Copperfield* (1850), ch.23.

The vast majority of law graduates before Victorian times took Holy Orders and became country parsons; a few chose administrative positions in the Church, or became advocates in Doctors' Commons. The common lawyers with equal insularity rejected any special knowledge of Roman law or its method. In fact the medieval inns of court probably owed a good deal to the university model, with an analogous combination of lectures and disputations. But the lectures did not provide a complete course of instruction, and the exercises were chiefly designed to produce skilful and quick-witted advocates. At its height, the professional law school was tough and effective; but, as we have seen, it came to an abrupt end in the middle of the seventeenth century, leaving self-help as the principal method of legal education. A law student would attend Westminster Hall in term-time, with pen and notebook, to learn legal method; and he would try to obtain a seat in a lawyer's office where he could study the routine of pleading and conveyancing at first hand. His law would be gathered from such books as he could afford to buy or borrow; and the most useful of these owed more to the alphabet than to rational analysis. If he began practice too soon the chances were that he would never learn much law; but if he put it off too long he might confuse himself beyond salvation.

By a strange turn the universities were destined to succeed where the inns of court eventually failed. England was perhaps the last European country to admit the study of the municipal law into its academic curriculum,[44] but the process began in earnest when Dr William Blackstone began to lecture on English law at Oxford in 1753. In 1758 the Oxford lectures were endowed by the foundation of the Vinerian Chair, and within the next fifty years similar chairs were founded at Trinity College Dublin and at Cambridge. Blackstone's lectures were not aimed at professional law students, but at country gentlemen and clergymen who needed an outline knowledge of the legal system; yet his was the first attempt since *Bracton* to expound the whole of the law in a rational, though elementary, method. The publication of the lectures in 1765-69 as the *Commentaries on the Laws of England* provided law students with a primer, and rendered further lectures for the time being less necessary. Blackstone's immediate successors certainly did not attract large audiences; nor did the early Downing professors at Cambridge. Indeed, at times the lectures in English law ceased altogether for want of hearers. But the example had been set.

A new impetus for legal education came from the efforts of Andrew Amos, a practising barrister who accepted the first Chair of English Law

---

44 F. Sullivan, *Principles of Feudal Law* (1772), p. 10.

in the new University of London in 1828. He gave evening classes and lectures in Gower Street for bar students and articled clerks who had spent the day in an office, and his avowed intention was to combine practical observation with academic discussion. His classes were a notable success, and in 1839 the University awarded the first academic degrees in the common law.[45] Again, however, it was a one-man success; and before long legal education returned to the doldrums. There were insufficient endowments to attract professors of distinction, and students preferred to learn their law in the rival professional law schools which were springing up at that time. It is a sad reflection on the status of legal education in those days that most distinguished English lawyers between about 1850 and 1950 were either not university graduates at all or were men who had read subjects other than law. The state of legal education was nevertheless constantly debated. In 1846, and again in 1971, it was recommended that universities should teach the elements of legal science and that professional law schools should teach the practice. The profession responded by establishing the Council of Legal Education in 1852 to serve the inns of court;[46] but lectures were voluntary and came to be virtually superseded by the services of crammers, while examinations for the bar were not made compulsory until 1872.[47] In 1850 Oxford introduced a B.A. course in law and history, and in 1858 Cambridge established a law tripos. Experiments in extending legal education to the provinces began in the same period with the foundation of a law department at Queen's College, Birmingham, in 1850.[48] These measures initially had more impact on the education of prospective solicitors than barristers, because of the engrained notion that the latter, as members of a liberal profession, ought to read arts or greats rather than law. Towards the end of the century, however, the academical study of law revived in the two older law faculties under such brilliant professors as Maitland, Dicey, Anson and Pollock; and by 1933 there were over 2,500 students reading law at sixteen English universities.[49] The study of law at university is now recognised as a liberal education in its own right; and it has also become

45   See [1977] *Current Legal Problems* 1.
46   The school established in 1852 became the Inns of Court School of Law in 1967.
47   The Law Society, which had provided lecture courses since the 1830s, acquired an established School of Law in 1903.
48   See W. W. Pue, 33 AJLH 241. Departments of law were founded at Owens College, Manchester (later Manchester University) in 1880, and at University College, Liverpool (later Liverpool University) in 1892.
49   51 LQR 179.

the normal preliminary to the vocational training required for both branches of the profession.[50]

Further reading

Holdsworth HEL, vol. II, pp. 311-318, 484-512; vol. VI, pp. 431-499; vol. XII, pp. 4-401

Manchester MLH, pp. 50-83

Cornish & Clark, pp. 45-53, 98-110

J. H. Baker, 'Counsellors and Barristers: an Historical Study' [1969] CLJ 205-229 (repr. in LPCL 99-124); 'Solicitors and the Law of Maintenance 1590-1640' [1973] CLJ 56-80 (repr. in LPCL 125-150); 'The English Legal Profession 1450-1550' in *Lawyers in early Modern Europe* (W. Prest ed., 1981), pp. 16-41 (repr. in LPCL 75-98); *The Order of Serjeants at Law* (SS Supp. Ser. 5, 1984)

R. C. Palmer, 'The Origins of the Legal Profession in England' (1976) 11 IJ 126-146

W. R. Prest, *The Rise of the Barristers* (1986); (ed.) *Lawyers in early Modern Europe and America* (1981)

E. W. Ives, *The Common Lawyers of pre-Reformation England* (1983)

D. Duman, 'The Late Victorian Bar' (1983), in *Law, Litigants and the Legal Profession*, 140-154

R. Cocks, *Foundations of the Modern Bar* (1983)

N. Ramsay, 'Retained Legal Counsel, *c.* 1275-*c.* 1475' (1985) 35 TRHS (5th ser.) 95-112

J. Sainty, *A List of English Law Officers, King's Counsel and Holders of Patents of Precedence* (SS Supp. Ser. 7, 1987)

P. Brand, 'The Origins of the English Legal Profession' (1987) 5 LHR 31-50

INNS OF COURT

S. E. Thorne, 'The early History of the Inns of Court' (1959) 50 *Graya* 79-96 (repr. in EELH 137-154)

R. F. Roxburgh, *Black Books of Lincoln's Inn*, vol. V (1968), pp. 448-476; 'Lawyers in the New Temple' (1972) 88 LQR 414-430; 'Lincoln's Inns of the 14th Century' (1978) 94 LQR 363-382

[50] Articled clerkship for solicitors has been compulsory since the 17th century. But pupillage for barristers, though almost universal, was not made compulsory until 1958. More recently, attendance at a vocational law school has also been made compulsory for both branches.

A. W. B. Simpson, 'The early Constitution of the Inns of Court' [1970] CLJ 241-256; 'The early Constitution of Gray's Inn' [1975] CLJ 131-150 (both repr. in LTLH 17-52)

W. R. Prest, *The Inns of Court 1590-1640* (1972)

J. H. Baker, 'The Inns of Court in 1388' (1976) 92 LQR 184-187 (repr. in LPCL 306); 'The Old Constitution of Gray's Inn' (1977) 81 *Graya* 15-19 (repr. in LPCL 39-43); 'The Inns of Court and Legal Doctrine' in *Lawyers and Laymen* (T. M. Charles-Edwards et al. ed., 1986), pp. 274-286

W. C. Richardson, *A History of the Inns of Court* (1978)

ATTORNEYS AND SOLICITORS

R. Robson, *The Attorney in 18th Century England* (1959)

M. Birks, *Gentlemen of the Law* (1960)

C. W. Brooks, *Pettyfoggers and Vipers of the Commonwealth: the 'Lower Branch' of the Legal Profession in early Modern England* (1983)

CIVILIAN ADVOCATES

B. P. Levack, *The Civil Lawyers in England 1603-41* (1973); 'The English Civilians 1500-1750', in *Lawyers in early Modern Europe* (W. Prest ed., 1981), pp. 87-109

G. D. Squibb, *Doctors' Commons* (1977)

C. T. Allmand, 'The Civil Lawyers', in *Profession, Vocation and Culture in Later Medieval England* (C. H. Clough ed., 1982), pp. 155-180

D. R. Coquillette, *The Civilian Writers of Doctors' Commons* (1988)

THE JUDICIARY

A. F. Havighurst, 'The Judiciary and Politics in the Reign of Charles II' (1950) 66 LQR 62-78, 229-252; 'James II and the Twelve Men in Scarlet' (1953) 69 LQR 522-546

W. J. Jones, *Politics and the Bench: The Judges and the Origins of the English Civil War* (1971)

S. F. Black, 'Coram Protectore: the Judges of Westminster Hall under the Protectorate of Oliver Cromwell' (1976) 20 AJLH 32-64; 'The Courts and Judges of Westminster Hall during the Great Rebellion' (1986) 7 JLH 23-52

J. H. Baker, 'The Independence of the Judiciary' (1978) 94 SS *137-142*

D. Duman, *The Judicial Bench in England 1727-1875* (1982)

R. V. Turner, *The English Judiciary in the Age of Glanvill and Bracton* (1985)

LEGAL EDUCATION

S. E. Thorne, *Readings and Moots in the Inns of Court*, vol. I: Readings (71 SS, 1952)

H. G. Hanbury, *The Vinerian Chair and Legal Education* (1958)

J. H. Baker, 'The Education of Lawyers' (1978) 94 SS *125-137*; *Readings and Moots in the Inns of Court*, vol. II: Moots (105 SS, 1989), introduction

P. Brand, 'Courtroom and Schoolroom: the Education of English Lawyers prior to 1400' (1987) 60 BIHR 147-165

11. Legal Literature

The literature produced by a profession is often the clearest guide to the state of its intellectual development. It is, of course, possible for courts and administrative systems to function without books; but it is impossible for a body of law to develop very far without the interposition of writing. Yet even if law may exist, and indeed develop, in an unwritten form, the vision of the historian is necessarily circumscribed by the written word; his knowledge must be derived from those written sources which the accidents of time have preserved, and therefore he needs to be aware of their character and limitations. The ways in which law came to be written about were various. Once the opinions of the courts, and of the serjeants, were recognised as providing good evidence of the law and of accepted practice, it was sensible for someone to note them down for future reference. And when the inns of court organised readings and disputations in which accepted doctrine was tried and tested in the presence of judges and benchers, it was again sensible for those present to keep notes. The forms and procedures followed by the courts called for formularies, first of writs and then of pleadings; and formularies attracted notes of explanation and commentaries, to help the beginner understand as well as learn the forms. The more assiduous medieval lawyers must have spent countless hours writing out their own libraries. Even a century after the introduction of the printing press, the copying or abstracting of legal texts by hand remained a feature of legal self-education. As books became the repositories of legal learning, so lawyers became hungry for books. By 1500 the inns of court all had libraries, and a century later there were over a hundred law books in print. The publication of law books subsequently grew with such rapidity that by 1800 the printed literature of English law extended to over 1,500 separate titles.

Glanvill and *Bracton*

The common law of the king's courts was from the outset embodied in the practice of those courts, and therefore in precedent. Anyone wishing to use those courts needed to know whether an action was available, and if so how to commence it. The first book on the common law was therefore, as might be expected, primarily a compilation of writs with an account of the procedures which they initiated. The treatise called *Glanvill* was written in about 1187-89, probably by one of the royal justices if not by Glanvill himself. We have already noticed its significance in concentrating on the work of the central courts.[1] The decision of the author to concentrate on writs rather than on legislative decrees was equally significant; English law was seen as rooted in the practice of the courts, on the remedies given in particular cases, rather than in juridical abstractions. The forms of action, if not yet carved on tablets of stone, were beginning to dominate legal thinking.

The active life of *Glanvill* was quite short, because it was soon overtaken both by legal change and by a much larger work. The larger treatise with the same title, *De legibus et consuetudinibus Angliae* ('on the laws and customs of England'), appeared in the thirteenth century.[2] It bears in some versions the name of Henry de Bracton (d. 1268), one of the judges *coram rege* in the 1240s and 1250s, and is generally known as *Bracton*. It used to be thought that it was written in the 1250s, using plea rolls of the previous generation which had first been collected into a notebook. Recent scholarship suggests that it was mostly written in the 1220s and 1230s, using current plea rolls, and then mangled by editors who tried to bring it up to date in the middle of the century. Bracton may well have been one of these later editors, but his work was evidently never finished; there are, throughout the text, inconsistencies and broken promises to continue topics later. The treatment is again heavily based on the writ system, but filled out with evidence of judicial practice selected from the plea rolls and with speculative learning derived from Roman and Canon law. The number of surviving manuscripts (over fifty) shows that it circulated very widely in the thirteenth and fourteenth centuries; but it failed to have a deep and lasting impact because it was written too soon. The compiler was able to survey the whole of the common law with confidence only because it had not yet become clogged with sophisticated detail; special pleading had barely begun, and there was probably no law school teaching English law. Had the common law developed in the Continental manner, *Bracton* might have been glossed and then replaced by still more comprehensive Latin treatises in the same genre. But despite the attempts to correct and update the text before circulation, and the

---

[1] See pp. 15-16, ante. The best edition is by G. D. G. Hall (1965).

[2] *Bracton De Legibus et Consuetudinibus Anglie* (G. E. Woodbine and S. E. Thorne ed., 1968-77). It was first printed in 1569.

appearance of Latin epitomes or *summae*,[3] the work of the nascent legal profession soon left this kind of book behind. For background reading, the student of Edward I's time preferred books in French, such as *Britton* (*c.* 1290);[4] while, for full initiation, he attended the lectures given for apprentices of the Bench[5] and studied the oral pleading of the serjeants in open court. The obsolescence of *Bracton* not only left the common law without systematic exposition for the next five hundred years; it was a sign that the common law was coming to be tied more closely to the life of courtroom practice than to expository writing.

Formularies

The elementary need for guidance in the practice of the king's courts explains why compilations of the forms of writs are among the most plentiful of early English legal manuscripts. *Glanvill* and *Bracton* had provided the wording of the most important formulae, but the corpus of available writs was growing too fast for treatises to accommodate them. What was most needed was a comprehensive working formulary of the writs themselves. A bare collection of writ formulae was called a 'register'. Whether there was ever one authoritative Chancery register is unknown, but some of the early manuscripts were owned by Chancery clerks and it seems probable that each master made his own collection, using earlier versions which came to hand. The earliest belong to the first quarter of the thirteenth century, and the latest to the sixteenth century.[6] All registers contain texts of writs, in Latin, but they differ in scope and arrangement. Their size increased enormously during the thirteenth and fourteenth centuries, and they attracted glosses in the form of notes and 'rules' which probably derive from lectures in the inns of chancery; but they reached their final form when the older writs ceased development. The classical register was that printed from a fifteenth-century exemplar as the *Registrum Omnium Brevium* in 1531. It contained only a few early specimens of actions on the case, and no serious attempt was made to update it when those actions transformed the common law in the sixteenth century. That role fell to another type of formulary, the collection of precedents of pleading.

---

3 The most widely circulated were the two attributed to Hengham CJ: *Radulphi de Hengham Summae* (W. H. Dunham ed., 1932); P. Brand, 11 IJ 147. For Gilbert de Thornton's *Summa*, see Thorne, EELH 111.

4 The best text is still the edition by F. M. Nichols (1865; repr. 1983).

5 See p. 182, ante; p. 214, post.

6 *Early Registers of Writs* (E. de Haas and G. D. G. Hall ed., 87 SS, 1970).

The progenitor of this second type had appeared within a generation of the first registers, and was evidently for the use of counters. The books of counts contained specimens, in French, with occasional interspersed instructions for their use. They reached the peak of their development in the fourteenth century, when the manuscripts called *novae narrationes* (or 'new counts') gave a wide selection of counts and also of defences.[7] But the books went out of use, except for educational purposes in the inns of court, when attention shifted from the count to tentative special pleading.[8] The full art of tentative pleading could only be learned by observation, or by the study of verbatim reports of interchanges in open court,[9] since it was a dynamic process and could not be captured in set formulae. In any case, the most important form of special pleading was not the French spoken in court but the Latin formulation entered on the roll; it was the Latin entry which settled what was in issue, which provided the focus for any proceedings subsequent to the trial, and which served as a precedent for the future. It is probable that when paper pleadings were circulated to assist the court they were in Latin, and that by a reversal of earlier practice the oral plea had become merely a French paraphrase of a draft Latin entry. The prime need for access to Latin precedents was that of the clerks responsible for the entries on the rolls, and it was the prothonotaries of the Common Pleas who first compiled 'books of entries' in the late fifteenth century from the records in their custody. The replacement of French *narrationes* by Latin books of entries is in itself clear evidence of the shift from oral to written pleading.[10] By the sixteenth century there was a wider demand for precedents of entries, to assist attorneys and counsel (who did not have ready access to the plea rolls) in framing pleas themselves. The first to be printed was the *Intrationum excellentissimus Liber* (1510), the authorship of which is unknown. The best were compiled by judges: William Rastell's *Collection of Entrees* (1566), based on at least three earlier collections, and Sir Edward Coke's *New Booke of Entries* (1614). Rastell and Coke both included a good selection of actions on the case, and in later books of entries these came to predominate. The later collections of precedents of actions on the case effectively combined the functions of both registers and *narrationes*, and for this reason they continued to be produced from ever more modern precedents until the nineteenth century. The genre

---

7   See *Novae Narrationes* (E. Shanks and S. F. C. Milsom ed., 80 SS, 1963).
8   See pp. 93-94, ante.
9   See p. 205, post.
10 See p. 97, ante.

survives as Bullen and Leake's *Precedents of Pleading* (1st ed., 1860; 12th ed., 1975).

Reports of Cases

A lawyer practising in the king's courts needed to know much more than the bare routine formulae. He needed to know how the courts worked. Although this could only be learned by experience, as early as the 1220s lawyers were extracting interesting cases from the plea rolls as illustrations of the law, and many such cases were used by the author of the treatise called *Bracton*. The rolls continued to be the most authoritative source of precedents into later times, and it was common for counsel to 'vouch the record' when citing a previous case. But the record was highly formulaic, using stereotyped Latin phrases in place of detailed assertions, omitting the evidence, the arguments of counsel, and the reasons for judgments. The debates between the serjeants and judges, the tentative pleading and judicial rulings which obliquely revealed the assumptions of the common law,[11] took place off the record, and only the formalised results went down on parchment. For those learning the law, these forensic exchanges were naturally of greater importance than the bare record. Long attendance in Westminster Hall was therefore an indispensable part of a common lawyer's education. The natural store for such learning was the human mind. Royal judges of the twelfth and thirteenth centuries must have relied heavily on memory and experience, prompted by the rolls. But memory is frail and unsafe, and if continuity was to be preserved from one generation to another, and if legal discussions in the Bench were to reach a wider audience than those who happened to hear them in court, then some additional kind of record was required.

THE YEAR-BOOKS

The first surviving reports of arguments or remarks attributed to named judges are from the 1250s. The earliest are little more than collections of dicta; some are apparently intended to illustrate accounts of procedure; some are found in collections arranged by forms of action; and some, from the 1280s onwards, are the reports of particular eyre sessions or terms at Westminster. The last format was the one that prevailed. Eyres were becoming infrequent, though the last sessions were reported in full; but from 1300 there is a continuous stream of reports of

[11] See pp. 94-96, ante.

arguments in the Common Pleas. The reports were written in Anglo-French, the language of courtly speech. The arguments are given in abridged form, often impenetrably brief, but with the names of the speakers and occasional comments. Their authorship is unknown, and they are referred to by the generic name 'year-books'.[12] Contemporaries called them 'terms', since the only headings in the manuscripts are those of the law terms to which the reports relate.

The first year-books were obviously the creature of the new legal profession which developed in the reigns of Henry III and Edward I, but opinion is divided as to whether they were produced primarily for established practitioners, such as serjeants and court officials, or for young apprentices. A long-standing tradition, beginning in about 1550, firmly attributed the year-books to official reporters, conjecturally identified by some as the prothonotaries of the Common Pleas. But this thesis is no longer accepted; there are no records of the appointment or payment of official reporters, no year-books are preserved with the records and office-books of the courts, and some of the early reports are both informal and inaccurate in matters of factual detail. The purpose of the reports cannot have been to supplement the rolls for official purposes, since they frequently omit the details (such as the names of the parties) which would be needed to identify the entries in the record. The purpose must rather have been to record the intellectual aspect of litigation: to circulate and preserve for future learning, both by students and by their practising elders, the possible moves in the recondite games of legal chess played by the pleaders in open court. If we have to account for their beginning, the most likely explanation is that they arose from a case-method of instruction in the law school which served the apprentices of the Bench before the emergence of the inns of court. This would help to explain the anonymity of the texts; they were not individual compilations, but resulted from the communal interchange of notes generated by the teaching process. For the same reason, the contemporary value of the earliest reports lay not in their historical authenticity as precedents but in the ideas and suggestions which they contained. If one report is very different from another, we should not rush to blame it on carelessness; we may rather be seeing a teacher teasing out the points in a case by varying the facts. If that is so, it mattered little who wrote the manuscripts; any sense they made was

---

12   The name reflects the mode of citation, by regnal year. The later method was to cite by year and folio; but that was unsuitable before the foliation was standardised by the printers. Cases may also be cited by term and *placitum* (the case-number within the term).

self-evident, and any nonsense could be freely corrected or ignored by the owner.

The mystery and anonymity surrounding the year-books of Edward I is almost as deep two centuries later with respect to those of Henry VII and Henry VIII. Nevertheless, it cannot be assumed that they were still being produced in the same way and for the same purposes. Once the age of experiment was over, the reports settled into a more uniform and at times apparently single series. Although it is tempting to associate this continuity with the establishment of the inns of court, no direct link has yet been discovered; and it seems certain that the last year-books were not produced under their superintendence. Law reporting was a matter of private enterprise, and the uniformity is to some extent an illusion produced by the Tudor printers, who made no attempt to distinguish the work of different hands.[13] Yet at any one time there were probably only a few reporters, who supplied the rest of the profession. In the fifteenth century some of them can be identified. The earliest so far discovered was a Wiltshire apprentice (John Bryt), some of whose work is found in the printed year books of Henry IV, but who also reported cases on the western circuit. The first of whom anything much is known was Roger Townshend, admitted to Lincoln's Inn in 1454, created serjeant in 1478, and a justice of the Common Pleas from 1485 to 1493. Since his reports extend from the 1450s to the later 1480s, it is evident that reporting was not confined to a particular class of lawyer but was rather the life-long occupation of individuals. This is true of most of the Tudor reporters whose identities can be established. For instance, John Caryll's reports extend from his student days in the Inner Temple in the 1480s through his time as a prothonotary of the Common Pleas and throughout his career as a serjeant from 1510 to 1523.[14] Other reports of the 1480s and 1490s were the work of an unidentified member of Gray's Inn; and John Spelman of that inn was reporting from about 1502 onwards. If these examples stood alone, it would be an attractive speculation to suppose that there was one reporter in each inn of court; but this does not hold true in the sixteenth century,

---

[13] One exception was the *Long Quinto*, a much longer version of the year 5 Edw. IV (1465-66) than that printed as the vulgate text, and issued separately in 1552. Some of the printed year-books of the 1450s are similar 'long' reports; but the standard versions have never been printed.

[14] About half of Caryll's reports were published in 1602 as 'Keilwey'. Some were printed anonymously in the year-books of Henry VII. The remainder are still unpublished.

and a recently discovered manuscript contains reports written by John Port, a near contemporary of Caryll at the Inner Temple in the 1490s.[15]

In early Tudor times the character of the reports began to change. This was not the result of any breakdown in organisation, but simply a consequence of the transformation of the legal system in the renaissance period. There was actually an increase in the amount of law reporting, and many of the new reports were of cases in the King's Bench, where the most interesting reforms were initiated. With the demise of oral pleading, the reports concentrated more and more on motions in banc raising questions of law after trial; and the direct discussion of substantive law which they contain is therefore more readily within the reach of a modern reader than the inconclusive tentative pleading of the classical year-books. Despite these differences, there was no break in continuity between the year-books and their successors. The year-books did not end at any fixed date. What has usually been taken as their end is the result of two concurrent factors: the advent of printing, and the practice of identifying reports by the name of the author.

THE ADVENT OF PRINTING

Within ten years of the introduction of printing into England in the 1470s, the London printers had found a market in the legal profession. The first printed English law book was Littleton's *Tenures* (1481), and in Henry VII's reign a number of year-books were printed and offered for sale in yearly units at a few pence each. By 1558 the canon of printed year-books was complete; they were reprinted numerous times, still as single years, by the Elizabethan law printer Richard Tottell, and between 1590 and 1610 other printers collected them into eight thick volumes[16] together with the *Liber assisarum* (assizes and circuit cases of Edward III) and the *Long Quinto*. The first attempt to print the whole at once was not made until 1679-80, when what was destined also to be the last edition was produced in tall folio.[17] The effect of printing the year-books was that in time the manuscripts were ousted from practitioners' libraries. The printed version, with all its many defects, had the apparent advantage of providing the profession with a complete

---

15 *The Reports of Sir John Spelman* (93 SS, 1977); *The Notebook of Sir John Port* (102 SS, 1986).

16 1-10 Edw. III; 17-39 Edw. III; 40-50 Edw. III (the *Quadragesms*); Hen. IV and V; 1-20 Hen. VI; 21-39 Hen. VI; Edw. IV; Edw. V, Ric. III, Hen. VII and VIII.

17 The reprint of 1679-80 has been wrongly associated with the name of Mr Serjeant Maynard (d. 1690), who had just promoted the first publication of the year-books of Edw. II (1678). It has been the standard text ever since, though it is arguably the least accurate.

set of reports of accepted authenticity and having a standard method of citation.

Unfortunately for the historian, the magic of the printed word has tended to obscure the underlying textual tradition of the year-books. Many interesting years, including all those of Edward I and Edward II, more than ten years of Edward III, and the entire reign of Richard II, were omitted altogether. In the later reigns a wide variety of texts, no longer recoverable because of manuscript losses, was confused into a deceptively uniform series. Our suspicions are aroused when we find judges speaking after they were dead, and similar chronological impossibilities; moreover, careful investigation shows that what are printed as different but related cases, or as successive arguments in the same case, are sometimes reports of the very same argument by different hands. The last printed year-book of all, ending with Michaelmas term 27 Henry VIII (1535), has been taken to represent some definitive line between old and new; and the cessation of the series was believed by Maitland to be an ominous event which marked the decline of the common law at the zenith of Henrician despotism. In fact law reporting was by then busier than before; it was simply the printing press which had failed to keep up publication. The only surviving manuscript year-book of 1535 continues into the 1540s without any change of style. Indeed, many of the reports of the mid-Tudor period are in general indistinguishable from the 'last' year-books save in the bibliographical particular that no one published them under that name or at all. It is convenient now to confine the term 'year-books' to pre-1535 reports, but necessary to remember that nothing of historical significance is thereby denoted.

NAMED REPORTS

The personalisation of law reports during the Tudor period may have been occasioned by the proliferation of texts and a growing interest in distinguishing the work of different hands; the more uniform jottings of an earlier generation were becoming law books of variable quality and authority. The earliest known reporters of the sixteenth century, such as Sir John Port (d. 1540), Sir John Spelman (d. 1546) and Sir James Dyer (d. 1582), produced reports no different in character from the Tudor year-books; and, like Townshend and Caryll before them, they all began reporting in their student days and continued during their careers as serjeants and judges.[18] *Dyer* was published posthumously in 1585.

---

[18] Port's notes of cases in the King's Bench from 1529 to 1534 (printed in 102 SS 55-76) are the earliest reports in the autograph of an English judge.

Spelman did not reach the press until 1977, followed by *Port* in 1986. There are others still to be printed.

In fact only a minority of the Tudor and Stuart reports were printed, and those usually long after they were written. The profession was accustomed to using manuscript reports of current cases, and they could be obtained in mass-produced copies from law stationers down to the Civil War; even in the eighteenth century it was not uncommon for manuscripts to be cited in court. This explains why some reporters, for instance William Dalison (d. 1559), William Bendlowes (d. 1584), Sir Edmund Anderson (d. 1605) and Sir Francis Moore (d. 1621), were well known and frequently cited long before their work appeared in print. Much of the printing was carried out in the middle of the seventeenth century, when controls on the press were eased, and editing was of a low standard. Some printed reports were mere notes of appallingly poor quality, while the better manuscripts were for reasons of length or unavailability passed by. Unscrupulous publishers placed on title-pages the names of distinguished lawyers of the past, even if the texts were in reality as anonymous as the year-books. The *English Reports*[19] before 1660 present considerable textual problems. At least half of them are wrongly attributed. *Keilwey*, named after an owner, is really a part of Caryll's year-books bound up with Inner Temple moots (probably by Caryll) and fourteenth-century *quo warranto* cases. Parts of *Dalison, New Benloes, Owen, Noy, Popham* and *Winch* are demonstrably spurious in their attribution because they contain cases decided after the alleged reporters' deaths; on page 125 of *Winch* we even find a note of Winch's own death.[20] A glance at the reports called *Dalison, Old Benloes* and *Anderson* will reveal a substantial number of identical texts, albeit in a different sequence in each collection: it was a common practice to collect together cases from borrowed manuscripts without acknowledgment. One case occurs three times, in identical words, in different parts of the collection called *Leonard*.[21]

Of the pre-1660 reports, three series stand out as being of excellent quality. All were seen through the press by their authors, whereas the bulk of the old reports were casual gleanings from dead men's studies. The first, which made the greatest departure from the year-book style,

---

[19] This name was given to the standard reprint of 1900-32, containing the principal pre-1865 reports in 178 volumes.

[20] *Reports of that Reverend and Learned Judge, Sir Humphry Winch* (1657), p. 125. The reports have been attributed, but without any certainty, to Richard Allestree (d. 1655) of Gray's Inn.

[21] *Anon.* (1566) 3 Leon. 13, 4 Leon. 167 and 224. It is identifiable as *Yevance v. Holcomb*, B. & M. 589. Even the publisher did not pretend that these reports were *by* Leonard.

were the *Commentaries* of Edmund Plowden (d. 1585). Plowden reported cases from the 1550s to the 1570s, and took great pains to check details with the counsel and judges and to procure a transcript of the record. He selected for publication only those cases in which questions of law were raised for solemn argument upon demurrer, special verdict, or motion in banc, and edited them carefully with references and comment added. Plowden's conception of a law report as a reasoned exposition of the law, with learned gloss, was taken up by Sir Edward Coke (d. 1634). Coke edited eleven slim volumes of reports between 1600 and 1616, and left further reports in manuscript from which two posthumous parts were printed in 1658 and 1659. He added rather more of his own comment than Plowden had done, often working into one report his own notes of earlier cases, and not distinguishing (as Plowden had) his own views from those he was reporting. Coke's intentions were not dishonest, because like Plowden he still held the medieval view that the correctness of the doctrine reported was more important than the historical precision of the report. His reports were conceived as instructional law books built around actual cases. Coke's personal authority was enough to justify this method, despite strong criticism from contemporaries (such as Lord Ellesmere) who disapproved of his opinions. The volumes have the distinction of being cited simply as *The Reports*, and they have been perhaps the single most influential series of named reports. The third series worthy of mention was that of Edward Bulstrode (d. 1659), a Welsh judge, who in the last three years of his life edited three copious volumes of King's Bench reports taken under James I and Charles I. These reports were not so distinguished as those of Plowden or Coke, but they continued the tradition of careful and detailed reporting into a period better known for books which should never have been printed. Bulstrode's were also the first reports published by their author in English.[22]

The reports of the period 1650-1750 were mostly of an inferior nature, consisting of short notes and scattered arguments intended for private use rather than publication. Some of them were so bad that judges forbade their citation, or resorted to manuscripts to supply their deficiencies: a discipline which the student of legal history must necessarily emulate. For long periods there are no printed reports of what was happening in the Common Pleas. This century did, nevertheless, witness the beginning of continuous if irregular reporting in the Chancery and Exchequer and after 1750 reporting began to

---

[22] Before 1650 all reports were in French. A statute of 1650 required law books to be printed in English. After 1660 some further reports were printed in French, but by 1700 English was invariably used.

improve. Lord Mansfield's distinguished tenure of the office of lord chief justice of England (1756-88) made its impact on the law partly through attracting King's Bench reporters of high calibre, the foremost of whom was Sir James Burrow (d. 1782), master of the Crown Office in that court. Burrow was followed by Henry Cowper (1774-78) and Sylvester Douglas (1778-84), both of whom were writing with a view to publication and maintained the high standards established by Burrow. The appearance of professional reporters[23] such as Cowper and Douglas brought to an end the haphazard phase of law reporting. By the end of the century periodical series were being commissioned for publication in respect of all four superior courts: a venture which, once the profession accepted the high price of the volumes, ensured a steady succession of accurate and recent reports. The first regular series to be brought out almost contemporaneously with the cases reported were Durnford and East's *Term Reports* (King's Bench, 1785-1800), *Henry Blackstone* (Common Pleas, 1788-96), *Vesey Junior* (Chancery, 1789-1817) and *Anstruther* (Exchequer, 1792-97).[24] Thereafter a succession of professional law reporters maintained these and parallel series until 1865, when the Council of Law Reporting was set up to produce the *Law Reports*. With the introduction of shorthand, and the submission of texts to the judges for correction, the identities of reporters have become less important and reports, though not anonymous, are cited as if they were; the most learned lawyer today would not know (or think it useful to know) who reported, say, *Donoghue v. Stevenson*.[25] But the existence of the *Law Reports* has not prevented parallel and specialist series, which continue to proliferate; the courts will allow any report to be cited if it is vouched for by a barrister. Moreover, in modern times it has become increasingly common for verbatim transcripts to be kept of judgments given in the higher courts; and these are available for consultation and citation even though not selected for printing. In consequence, the distinction between report and record has almost disappeared.

ABRIDGMENTS

By the middle of the fifteenth century the bulk of the year-books was so large that lawyers were finding it necessary to compile commonplace

---

[23] Reporting was not undertaken as a permanent profession, but was frequently a means of support for young barristers; Cowper was only 25 when his reports were published.

[24] For nisi prius reports, see p. 466, post.

[25] [1932] A.C. 562. It was Harry Baird Hemming of Lincoln's Inn, reporter in the House of Lords 1911-33.

books or abridgments to help them recover material when they needed it. In commonplaces, points encountered in casual reading were entered up, ideally under pre-ordained titles, for future reference; the reports of Port and Spelman, mentioned above, were entered in books organised in this way. The abridgment was a more systematic and comprehensive product of the same method, perhaps in some cases intended for circulation. A blank volume would be divided into alphabetical titles – say, from *abatement* to *withernam* – and the compiler would work through the year-books, inserting under the appropriate headings a précis or abridged text of major propositions of law and practice or memorable pleading exchanges. The character of these reference works indicates that year-books were already being treated as sources of authority.

Three abridgments of year-books were printed. The first was published in Rouen in about 1490 and has no title-page; the contents seem to date from around 1460, the cases ending in the 1450s.[26] A tradition stretching back almost to the date of publication attributes it to Nicholas Statham (d. 1472), a bencher of Lincoln's Inn. In fact *Statham* is not different in type from several manuscript abridgments of the same period, some of which have almost identical contents: printing, therefore, merely increased the availability of a genre already circulating in manuscript. In the sixteenth century came the larger and more widely used 'grand' abridgments of Fitzherbert and Brooke. Anthony Fitzherbert (d. 1538), who became a Common Pleas judge, owned a large collection of old manuscripts, including many year-books now lost. His *Graunde Abridgement*, first published without title in 1514-16 when he was still a serjeant, was the prime example of this kind of book and had a considerable influence on the techniques of research and citation.[27] It is said to contain 13,845 entries, almost four times as many as *Statham*. The *Graunde Abridgement* of Sir Robert Brooke (d. 1558), printed posthumously in 1573, was in some ways an improvement on Fitzherbert's. It contained more items (over 20,000), with helpful marginalia, but the abridging was more drastic. These two great abridgments relieved the less industrious from having to make their own, and made it unnecessary for law students to read all the year-books through. Many of the cases in the abridgments are unique as printed texts; for instance, those from periods (such as Edward II and Richard II) not included in the vulgate, and those contemporary cases reported by the compilers themselves.[28]

---

[26] E.g. B. & M. 95, 200.

[27] See F. L. Boersma, *An Introduction to Fitzherbert's Abridgment* (1981).

[28] There is more contemporary matter in Brooke; it was printed separately as Bro. N.C. An example of a report by Fitzherbert (1499) will be found in B. & M. 401.

In the seventeenth century attempts were made to abridge the post-medieval reports. Epitomes of Plowden, Dyer and Coke were published as little pocket volumes; and three much larger abridgments were also printed. William Sheppard's *Epitome* (1656), later enlarged into a *Grand Abridgment* (1675) in four volumes, may have resulted from an attempt to survey the law as a preliminary to codification; but it was a muddle, superficially analysed and inaccurate. Of only slightly better quality were William Hughes' *Grand Abridgement of the Law* (1660-63) and Henry Rolle's *Abridgment des Plusieurs Cases* (1668). The latter, published posthumously, had a stormy reception. Its publication was delayed by a lawsuit over copyright, and when it finally appeared it was castigated as a mere student's commonplace book. Vaughan CJ said he wished it had never been printed, since it contained so many conflicting opinions that it made the law ridiculous.[29] Although the contents did little credit to the memory of a distinguished judge,[30] Rolle did at least introduce the improvement of subdivisions which enabled some degree of analysis. Rolle's entries were incorporated in the later abridgments of Comyns and Viner.

Comyns' *Digest*, not printed until the 1760s, was the work of Sir John Comyns (d. 1740), chief baron of the Exchequer, and in its original state was the last English law book written in French. Matthew Bacon's *New Abridgment* (1763-66) contained more connected commentary, including extracts from the unpublished writings of Sir Jeffrey Gilbert. It shared with Comyns a high reputation well into the nineteenth century, and both passed through several editions in England and the United States of America.[31] But the greatest of all the abridgments was the monumental *General Abridgment of Law and Equity* produced in twenty-three volumes between 1741 and 1753 by Charles Viner. It contained nearly all the substantive points of law to be found in the earlier abridgments and later reports, under subdivided titles, with marginal annotations and cross-references. It is the eighteenth-century counterpart to *Halsbury's Laws of England* and the *English and Empire Digest*, and remains one of the first recourses for lawyers searching into pre-1800 law.

Although the abridgments were not of the same intellectual order as reports or textbooks, they began to bridge the gap between the two by systematising the confused mass of ideas in the reports and bringing

---

[29] *Legal History Studies 1972*, p. 7. For the copyright suit, see Carter 89.

[30] Rolle (d. 1656) was CJ Upper Bench 1648-55 and perhaps the most distinguished Interregnum judge. His reports of King's Bench cases (1614-25) were printed in 1675 after enjoying a wide circulation in MS.

[31] An edition of Bacon was printed in Philadelphia as late as 1876.

together for comparison the authorities on particular areas of the law. Their day is by no means past, although their modern successors are issued under a variety of different names.

Treatises

The eclipse of the Latin treatise by the more practical literature described above explains in part why treatises did not occupy the prominent position in English law that they did in most other European legal systems. Nevertheless, the apparent absence of systematic exposition of the law for centuries after *Bracton* does require further explanation. How could students understand what they watched in court if they did not know the underlying premises? It would be worse than trying to understand a chess match without knowing the object of the game or the rules; just such an effort may indeed be required of the historian peeping into the same court through the year-books. The solution to the mystery is almost certainly that there was oral instruction.

Thirteenth-century manuscripts reveal a plethora of short 'tracts', mostly in French, on the choice of writs, on the manner of composing writs, on pleading in abatement of writs, on essoins, and on the elements of pleading.[32] The most enduring of these was the *Old Natura Brevium*, a primer on original writs. It now seems very likely that all of these are derived from lectures given to apprentices of the Bench on common-law procedure. In addition to the course on civil procedure, there seems to have been another on criminal procedure,[33] and an introduction to land law which circulated in writing as the *Old Tenures*.[34] If we knew more about the law school which produced this literature, we should be better placed to assess the impact of the inns of court in the fourteenth century. The ultimate effect, certainly by the mid-fifteenth century, was to replace any coherent instruction in the common law by the system described in the previous chapter: by readings on statute law and by pleading exercises requiring a considerable level of expertise. The explanation is probably that the elementary instruction passed in the first instance to the inns of chancery, where the

---

[32] Collections of these have been printed: e.g. *Four 13th Century Law Tracts* (G. E. Woodbine ed., 1910); *Brevia Placitata* (G. J. Turner ed., 66 SS, 1947); *Casus Placitorum* (W. H. Dunham ed., 69 SS, 1950).

[33] If we may so interpret *Placita Corone* (J. M. Kaye ed., SS Supp. Ser. 4, 1966).

[34] The edition of *c.* 1515 was reprinted in 1974 with an introduction by M. S. Arnold.

Natura Brevium (often bound with the *Old Tenures*) served as a primer into Tudor times,[35] and then disappeared.

The readings to some extent supplied the place of a doctrinal literature of English law. Many of them were taken down in writing and circulated, and it seems possible that the bulk of manuscript readings was once as great as that of the year-books. The earliest seem to date from the late fourteenth century, though a series of *quaestiones* on the statutes, with the names of speakers who flourished in the 1340s, hints at the existence of similar lectures in the middle of Edward III's reign. Medieval readings were nearly all given on the legislation of the thirteenth century, and in treating of such statutes as *De donis* readers were able to embark on minute accounts of the intricacies of the common law of property. If historians have given them less weight than the year-books, that is a reflection of modern assumptions rather than of the contemporary evidence. They contributed to the development of the common law, by systematising and refining doctrine, and in some areas – notably criminal law[36] – they may have been ahead of the courts in developing theory which was later put into practice. The absence of treatises is thus to some extent an illusion. The readings can properly be regarded as anonymous treatises; certainly they influenced the style and content of the books which eventually displaced them.

The first of these new treatises, the books which began life as written texts, was cast in more elementary form than the readings and seems to have been intended to replace the *Old Tenures*, doubtless because rudimentary oral instruction in the land law had ceased. The *New Tenures* (*c*. 1450-60) was the work of Sir Thomas Littleton (d. 1481), a celebrated Common Pleas judge under Edward IV.[37] He claimed to have written it for his son, probably Richard (d. 1518), who later became a bencher of the Inner Temple. Perhaps Richard turned it to profit in a way his father had not intended; but it is possible that manuscripts were already in circulation before the author's death, and that the private purpose was expressed out of professional modesty. From the date of its first publication in print in 1481 it was seized upon by the whole profession as a faithful introduction to the common law of real property. Littleton wrote at a time when the common-law system had reached its

---

35 The first printed edition (1494) was issued at the 'instaunce' of the company of Strand Inn. See also LPCL 18-19. Both treatises were completely rewritten in the 14th century.

36 See p. 595, post.

37 See the entry in *Biographical Dictionary of the Common Law* (Simpson ed., 1984), pp. 317-319. The most recent edition is by E. Wambaugh (1903).

most settled stage of development, and chose to ignore the complications of uses; this, helped by the fluency and clarity of his style, was to give his every word an authority enjoyed by no other legal author before or since. In 1550 *Littleton* had been reprinted more often than the English translation of the Bible, and by 1600 it was 'not now the name of a lawyer, but of the law itself'.[38] With Coke's commentary it was set reading for all law students until the mid-nineteenth century.

THE RENAISSANCE PERIOD

No writer in the sixteenth century applied Littleton's technique with the same brilliance to other branches of the law, but the printing press stimulated the production of more treatises to fill the literary void. The *Natura Brevium* was rewritten by Sir Anthony Fitzherbert, whose *New Natura Brevium* (1534) took account of recent developments and contained references to his *Graunde Abridgement*. Sir William Staunford (d. 1558), another Common Pleas judge, used the latter in compiling his two books on Crown law: *Les Plees del Coron* (1557) on the criminal law, and *An Exposition of the Kinges Prerogative* (1567, but written in 1548). In these works we see already a departure from Littleton, reflecting the shift of emphasis in legal science from common learning to authoritative case-law. No longer, it seems, could a jurist (even if he happened to be a judge) write on his own authority about first principles. He must instead digest written authorities. Style and clarity were, almost unwittingly, sacrificed to a profusion of citations. Staunford expressed the hope that other learned men would digest the whole of the common law, following the titles of Fitzherbert's *Abridgement* but introducing sufficient subdivision to lay bare the principles, so as 'to help the students of their long journey'.[39] Even to the best legal minds, therefore, digesting authorities had come to seem more worthwhile than expounding principles. That was perhaps the worst consequence of the abridgments.

If settled law fared badly, the developing law fared worse. It is only in an advanced state of legal scholarship that nascent ideas find their way into print, and this accounts for the absence of any books about the evolving law of contract and tort or the actions on the case. Those subjects were also largely absent from the inns of court exercises. Christopher St German's *Doctor and Student* (1528-31)[40] was for that

---

38 W. Fulbecke, *Direction or Preparative* (1600), fo. 27v.

39 *The Kinges Prerogative* (1567), preface.

40 The first edition of Part I is dated 1528. Part II came out in 1530, with further additions in 1531. The best edition is now *St German's Doctor and Student* (T. F. T. Plucknett and J. L. Barton ed., 91 SS, 1974).

reason alone a remarkable enterprise. Cast in the form of a dialogue between a doctor of divinity and a student of the common law about the relationship between law and conscience, a debate relevant at that time both to the controversy over the chancellor's jurisdiction[41] and to the extent of the ecclesiastical jurisdiction on the eve of the Reformation, it was not intended as a law book so much as a lawyer's view of moral philosophy written mainly for lay consumption. But it remained popular mainly for its legal content, and the frequency of editions shows that it was second only to Littleton as a standard textbook until the eighteenth century.

The increased printing activity of the seventeenth century brought a torrent of new law books, many of them badly written and of little value, though flowing into new areas such as contract and tort. The best attempt at analysis at the beginning of the century was Sir Henry Finch's *Nomotechnia* (1613), a bold and original essay at methodising the common law by dialectical techniques learned at Cambridge. Finch's scheme influenced later writers, though his book, written in law French and thin in its treatment of individual topics, did not become a standard textbook and was not reprinted.[42] Attempts to expound the personal actions, for instance by William Sheppard in *Marrow of the Law* (1651), *Action upon the Case for Slander* (1662) and *Actions upon the Case for Deeds* (1663), were inferior jumbles of cases and were barely an improvement on the abridgments.[43] The two greatest writers of the seventeenth century, as in the two preceding centuries, were judges.

SIR EDWARD COKE

When Coke was dismissed from office in 1616, and thereby effectively prevented from continuing his *Reports*,[44] he channelled his literary energy into writing his *Institutes of the Laws of England*. Already 64 years of age, and with a heavy parliamentary career still ahead of him, Coke did not live to finish the complete project; but the four parts which he left are a lasting monument to his industry. The first part, published in 1628 and the only part Coke saw in print, was his *Commentary on Littleton*. Coke 'shovelled out his enormous learning

---

41 See pp. 123-124, ante.

42 Finch's *Law or a Discourse thereof* (1627), published posthumously in English, was more successful; but it was based on an earlier version of Finch's scheme. For these books, see Prest, [1977] CLJ 326.

43 See Simpson, LTLH 278-279.

44 See pp. 191, 210, ante.

in vast disorderly heaps',[45] piled around Littleton's *Tenures* to form a phrase by phrase gloss on the text. He delighted in wandering off at tangents, and in doing so covered many aspects of the common law which Littleton's text never hinted at. Coke seems to have been oblivious to the disorder, but the reader can easily forgive him. He wrote like a helpful old wizard, anxious to pass on all his secrets before he died, but not quite sure where to begin or end. The comment on the first section of *Littleton* provides a typical foretaste. The text itself is a definition of 'fee simple'; but the commentary wanders through such disparate topics as etymology, alien status, misnomer in grants, interest rates and usury, the precedence of earth over the other elements, the correct Latin words for ponds, marshes, rushes, willows, elders, and boileries of salt, the Domesday Book, the eight parts of a deed, the styles and titles of the kings of England, the ownership of the Isle of Man, and the legal status of monsters and hermaphrodites. With all its faults, *Coke on Littleton* was the principal textbook on property law until the last century; and the nineteenth edition, encrusted with notes by Hale, Nottingham, Hargrave and Butler, is still much valued. The remaining three institutes comprised a commentary on the older statutes, a treatise on criminal law, and an account of the courts. The manuscripts of these three parts were suppressed by the government on Coke's death in 1634, for fear of any politically dangerous opinions they might contain, but were printed in the 1640s.

SIR MATTHEW HALE

A distinct advance in the quality of English legal literature was made by Sir Matthew Hale (d. 1676), latterly chief justice of the King's Bench. Regarded, like Coke, as an oracle in his own time, Hale has had a more lasting influence and his views on criminal law are occasionally cited in the courts to this day. His are the first English law books to possess a coherence and style with which the modern reader can feel at ease. Yet Hale's influence was delayed, because of his rather singular attitude to publication. Whereas he was quite prepared to unwrap his theological and scientific speculations to the public gaze, he consistently refused to publish what he had written on the subject he knew best, and even forbade publication by his descendants. The legal works were therefore posthumous publications, from his *History of the Common Law* (1713),[46] bound with his *Analysis of the Laws of England*, and the

---

45 F. W. Maitland, *Collected Papers* (1911), vol. II, p. 484.

46 Available as a reprint with an introduction by C. M. Gray (1971). The autograph MS. is in the Clark Library, Los Angeles, but has not received modern attention.

influential *History of the Pleas of the Crown* (1736), to the more recent *Prerogatives of the King* (1976);[47] other works remain unpublished. Hale made considerable use of history, but he was not truly a historian. The old records which he used were a guide to the present, when properly understood. His principal achievement was that he was able to organise and present this arcane material in thoughtful and analytical treatises marked by the clarity of their literary style.

SIR WILLIAM BLACKSTONE

The magnum opus of the eighteenth century was Sir William Blackstone's *Commentaries on the Laws of England* (1765-69), which were based on the lectures he gave as Vinerian Professor at Oxford.[48] Though Blackstone stands in a direct line of succession from Finch and Hale, the succession was broken and imperceptible at the time. The generality of law books in the first half of the eighteenth century were slight in character, and the period was more distinguished by abridgments than textbooks; indeed, by a pleasing irony, the endowment for Blackstone's chair was derived from the profits of Viner's successful abridgment. The only prolific theoretical writer was Sir Jeffrey Gilbert (d. 1726), who wrote clear elementary accounts of most branches of the law while serving as a judge in Ireland; but none of his work was published in his lifetime, and no attempt has ever been made to assemble or assess his voluminous contribution.[49] Blackstone had few printed examples to follow. As with Littleton and St German before him, his success in breaking new ground is attributable partly to the discipline of trying to explain the law to educated laymen. This Blackstone achieved in his lectures with such effect that before long lecture-notes were being passed round by students; and, as he claimed, it was the circulation of corrupt copies which finally induced him to commit the lectures to the press. Blackstone has been accused of blind complacence about the state of the law, and of superficiality in his interpretation of history; but no amount of criticism can destroy the fact that the *Commentaries* were the first connected and reasonably comprehensive survey of English law since *Bracton*, and perhaps the most stylish and readable contribution ever made to English legal literature. Just as Littleton had embalmed the logic of medieval land

[47] *Hale's Prerogatives of the King* (D. E. C. Yale ed., 92 SS, 1976).

[48] See p. 195, ante. The first edition was reprinted in facsimile in 1979, with new introductions. See also G. Jones (ed.), *The Sovereignty of the Law: Selections from Blackstone's Commentaries* (1973).

[49] For a list of printed works, see Simpson, LTLH 295-296. Numerous Gilbert MSS. are in the Hargrave collection (BL), and at the Columbia Law School.

law on the eve of its eclipse, so Blackstone conveyed to a wide readership on both sides of the Atlantic ocean the essential beauty and logic – and occasional absurdity – of a system of law and constitutional theory about to be submerged by a wave of massive reform. Blackstone was at once a final survey of the old common law and the first textbook of a new legal era.

FROM BLACKSTONE TO MAITLAND

After Blackstone, the older kind of law book was dead; but both the professorial[50] and the professional writers proved capable of rising to the high standards which he set. The years immediately following the *Commentaries* saw a number of works of high quality, written outside the universities, but scholarly and reflective rather than strictly vocational. It is enough to mention the remarkable historical and comparative *Observations on the more ancient Statutes* by Daines Barrington (1766); William Eden's *Principles of Penal Law* (1771); and the 'essays' by Charles Fearne on *Contingent Remainders* (1772) and by Sir William Jones on *Bailments* (1781). Lord Mansfield's creative tenure of the chief justiceship of the King's Bench enabled the first textbooks of commercial law to be written in the 1780s and 1790s. Even in 1800, however, the student learned his law from the law reports and by attending court rather than from treatises.[51]

Two distinct schools of legal writer may be identified in the nineteenth century.[52] The first was the young or disappointed barrister producing a standard work of reference. Writing treatises had become a legitimate way of making a professional mark, or of earning a living when fees dried up; and for such writers a full methodical analysis and statement of all the case-law, without too much abstract comment, was the principal end. Some of the practitioners' works of the late Georgian period which have stood the test of time, including complete rewriting by successive editors, are *Woodfall's Landlord and Tenant* (1802; 28th ed., 1978), *Archbold's Pleading, Evidence and Practice in Criminal Cases* (1822; 43rd ed., 1988), *Chitty on Contracts* (1826; 25th ed., 1983), *Byles on Bills of Exchange* (1829; 24th ed., 1979) and *Williams*

---

50   Blackstone's immediate successors at Oxford produced interesting works of some originality, especially R. Chambers, *A Course of Lectures on the English Law 1767-1773* (T. M. Curley ed., 1983).

51   Chief Baron Pollock (d. 1870) recalled that he so learned the law in about 1806: F. Pollock, *A First Book of Jurisprudence* (3rd ed., 1911), p. 314 n.2 ('I myself read no treatises: I referred to them as collecting the authorities').

52   Not much literature in book form was generated by the reform movement. For Stephen's treatise on pleading, see pp. 105-106, *ante*.

on Executors and Administrators (1832; 16th ed., 1982). The second
school of legal writer resulted from the revival of academic law schools
in the later Victorian period, which switched the limelight from the
special pleaders and conveyancers to the universities, where some classic
textbooks – for instance, those of Pollock,[53] Anson[54] and Maitland[55] –
were, like Blackstone's *Commentaries*, being born in the lecture
rooms.[56]

Further reading

P. H. Winfield, *Chief Sources of English Legal History* (1925)

W. S. Holdsworth, *Some Makers of English Law* (1938)

T. F. T. Plucknett, *Early English Legal Literature* (1958)

J. H. Baker, 'The Dark Age of English Legal History' in *Legal History
    Studies* 1972, pp. 1-27 (repr. in LPCL 435-460); 'The Newe
    Littleton' [1974] CLJ 145-155 (repr. in LPCL 231-241)

P. Brand, 'Courtroom and Schoolroom: the Education of Lawyers in
    England prior to 1400' (1987) 60 BIHR 147-165

YEAR-BOOKS

W. C. Bolland, *The Year Books* (1921); *Manual of Year Book Studies*
    (1925)

F. W. Maitland, 'Of the Year Books in General' (1903) 17 SS ix-xx

G. J. Turner, *Year Book 4 Edward II* (1911) 26 SS ix-lxiv

A. W. B. Simpson, 'The Circulation of Yearbooks in the 15th Century'
    (1957) 73 LQR 492-505 (repr. in LTLH 53-66); 'The Source and
    Function of the later Year Books' (1971) 87 LQR 94-118 (repr. in
    LTLH 67-91).

E. W. Ives, 'The Purpose and Making of the later Year Books' (1972)
    89 LQR 64-86

---

[53] *Contract* (1876); *Partnership* (1877); *Possession* (with R. S. Wright, 1880);
Jurisprudence (1882); *Land Laws* (1883); *Torts* (1887); and several others.
Pollock did not move to Oxford until 1883.

[54] *Contract* (1879); *Law and Custom of the Constitution* (1886-92).

[55] *History of English Law before the time of Edward I* (1895); *Constitutional
History of England* (1887, first printed 1908); *Equity* (1888, first printed 1909).

[56] A contemporary wave of scholarship also hit the American law schools,
particularly Harvard, which boasted the presence of Ames, Thayer, Holmes, and
Langdell.

J. H. Baker, 'The last Year Books' (1978) 94 SS 164-170; 'John Bryt's
Reports (1410-1411) and the Year Books of Henry IV' [1989] CLJ
98-114; 'Records, Reports and the Origins of Case-law in
England' in *Judicial Records, Law Reports, and the Growth of
Case Law* (Baker ed., 1989), pp. 15-46

NAMED REPORTERS

J. W. Wallace, *The Reporters arranged and characterized* (4th ed., 1882)
L. W. Abbott, *Law Reporting in England 1485-1585* (1973)
J. H. Baker, 'Coke's Note-books and the Sources of his Reports'
[1972A] CLJ 59-86 (repr. in LPCL 177-204); 'The unprinted
Reports of Henry VIII's Reign' (1978) 94 SS 170-178; 'Sir
Thomas Robinson (1618-83), Chief Prothonotary of the Common
Pleas' (1978) LPCL 243-256; 'Early Tudor Reports and the Plea
Rolls' (1987) 18 *Cambrian Law Rev.* 25-33

TREATISES

B. H. Putnam, *Early Treatises for Justices of the Peace* (1924)
H. Kantorowicz, *Bractonian Problems* (1941)
H. G. Richardson, *Bracton: the Problem of his Text* (1965)
D. E. C. Yale, *Hale as a Legal Historian* (SS Lecture, 1976)
S. E. Thorne, introduction to Bracton, vol. III (1977), pp. xiii-lii
S. F. C. Milsom, 'The Nature of Blackstone's Achievement' (1981) 1
OJLS 1-12 (repr. in SHCL 197-208)
A. W. B. Simpson, 'The Rise and Fall of the Legal Treatise' (1982) 48
Univ. Chicago Law Rev. 632-679 (repr. in LTLH 273-320)
M. Lobban, 'Blackstone and the Science of Law' (1987) 30 *Historical
Jo.* 311-335
A. Watson, 'The Structure of Blackstone's Commentaries' (1988) 97
Yale Law Jo. 795-821

BIBLIOGRAPHICAL REFERENCE

J. H. Beale, *Bibliography of Early English Law Books* (1926; Supp.
1943)
J. D. Cowley, *A Bibliography of Abridgments* (1932)
W. H. Maxwell and L. F. Maxwell, *English Law to 1800* (1955)
J. N. Adams and G. Averley, *A Bibliography of 18th Century Legal
Literature* (1982)
J. H. Baker, *English Legal Manuscripts* (1975-78); *English Legal
Manuscripts in the U.S.A.* (1985-90)
Centenary Guide to the Publications of the Selden Society (1987)

12. Law Making

Common lawyers in most centuries before the last liked to think of their law as an unchanging body of common sense and reasoning which was part of the heritage of the English people. If man's reason does not change, the law cannot change; it is only the application of old ideas to new social circumstances which creates the appearance of change. The function of judges is not to change the law: 'their office is *jus dicere*, and not *jus dare*'.[1] Judicial decisions, on this view, do not make law but merely declare what it is; and the progress of legal history is a slow revelation and refinement of essentially immutable ideas. Change when it comes must be imposed from without, by the legislature. And legislative changes, almost by definition, are at odds with natural reason. Sir Edward Coke wrote that it was 'a maxim of policy, and a trial by experience' that the alteration of any fundamental point of the common law was dangerous, 'for that which hath been refined and perfected by the wisest men in former succession of ages, and proved and approved by continual experience to be good and profitable for the common wealth, cannot without great hazard and danger be altered or changed'.[2] Sir John Davies, in the same vein, wrote that 'the customary law of England ... doth far excel our written laws, namely our statutes or acts of parliament; which is manifest in this, that when our parliament have altered or changed any fundamental points of the common law, those alterations have been found by experience to be so inconvenient for the common wealth as that the common law hath in effect been restored again'.[3] Sir Matthew Hale, looking back over the preceding centuries, was not even convinced that there had been any fundamental changes in the law, because 'the mutations hath not been so much in the law as in the subject matter of it'.[4]

This view of the common law and its relation to legislation is a reflection of lawyers' attitudes rather than of historical fact. The notion

---

[1] F. Bacon, *The Essayes* (1625), p. 316.

[2] *Le Quart Part des Reportes* (1604), sig. B2ᵛ. Cf. Co. Inst., vol. I, p. 379: 'Commonly a new invention doth offend against many rules and reasons of the common law, and the ancient judges and sages of the law have ever ... suppressed innovation and novelties in the beginning.'

[3] *Le Primer Report des Cases en Ireland* (1615), preface.

[4] Preface to H. Rolle, *Abridgement des Plusieurs Cases* (1668).

that the principles of the common law are somehow in existence before anyone has discovered what they are is a convenient figure of speech but not a statement of reality. At no time has the common law stood still. If it had not changed it would have no history. Changes in the law have sometimes come about through barely perceptible modifications and clarifications from case to case; at other times they have occurred swiftly and deliberately, through bold judicial decisions or reforming legislation. But never has the law been exempt from the ceaseless alteration to which all human creations are subject. Even the distinction between judicial and legislative change has not always been as fundamental as modern theory supposes. It is one of degree. The courts do make new law, but they do so within the framework of common law reasoning, whereas a sovereign legislature may legislate irrationally or unreasonably. Yet parliament has not usually acted in a despotic manner. Few legislative acts before the last century could be regarded as radical departures from the common-law tradition, and some lawyers even regarded the acts of the medieval high court of parliament as the decisions of a supreme court of law, a court untrammelled by forms.

The Common Law

In considering the techniques of law-making, it is convenient to have in mind the thesis put forward by Sir Henry Maine (d. 1888) in his treatise on *Ancient Law*. Referring to early societies in general, Maine advanced what he called a 'general proposition of some value' regarding the agencies by which law could be brought into harmony with the current needs of a changing society: 'These instrumentalities seem to me to be three in number, Legal Fictions, Equity and Legislation . . . Their historical order is that in which I have placed them. I know of no instance in which the order of their appearance has been changed or inverted.'[5] The thesis implied a natural progress from making changes while pretending not to (fictions), through making exceptions in particular cases (equity), to direct change by virtue of authority or power. Nevertheless, in so far as it imposed an historical sequence on the harmonising influences, it is difficult to square with the English experience. To be fair to Maine, he used the terms 'fiction' and 'equity' in broad senses and not in the technical senses familiar to English lawyers. But, in focusing on English law, we shall be less liable to confusion if we separate fictions in the technical sense from the

---

5 *Ancient Law* (1861), pp. 24-25.

development of case-law, and if we separate the equity of the Court of Chancery from the equitable spirit which inheres in the common law.

CASE-LAW AND PRECEDENT

There was probably never a time when the common law was not in some sense 'case law', the result of solutions found in real cases. In the twelfth century dialogue on the Exchequer, the student cites the Roman maxim that one should follow reasons rather than precedents; but the master qualifies this by saying that where the reasons for things are obscure it is enough to follow precedent.[6] *Glanvill*, it is true, only once refers to a specific case; but the writs on which his account was based were very likely devised in specific cases after argument in council. By the time of *Bracton* (*c*. 1220-50), the influence of judicial decisions is clear on the face of the text. The author of the preface stated that he had written the book in order to prevent the newer generation of judges from unwittingly leaving the right course settled by their wise predecessors. The law made by those predecessors was preserved in their enrolled judgments. By the 1260s the very words of judges and pleaders were being taken down in writing,[7] and before the end of the century the year-books show counsel citing earlier cases. When a judge of Edward II's time remarked, 'one may safely put that in his book for law',[8] he may even have been addressing the reporters. As we read the year-books, we find the judges openly admitting that their decisions will be taken as precedents in future ages. and we find it maintained that a clear line of precedents should be followed even if the reason was not immediately apparent, for otherwise the 'young apprentices' would lose faith in their books of 'terms'.[9]

On the face of it, the present notion that cases are a source of law might seem to have been always the first principle of English jurisprudence. In truth, the medieval notion of precedent was considerably different from that of the present day. The strict meaning of 'precedent' was a judgment entered on the roll, and a proper citation in court would require voucher of the record. But the formal entry of judgment gave no reasons, and in the majority of cases no law was made on the record by a judgment.[10] Moreover, records were not always what

---

6 R. FitzNigel, *Dialogus de Scaccario* (C. Johnson ed., 1983), p. 59.
7 See p. 204, ante.
8 *Midhope v. Prior of Kirkham* (1313) 36 SS 178, per Stanton J.
9 *Wyndham v. Felbrigge* (1454) Y.B. Mich. 33 Hen. VI, fo. 38, pl. 17, at fo. 41, per Prysot CJ
10 See pp. 94-96, ante.

they seemed; at worst they were bedevilled by fictions, but at best one could not be sure what had actually been argued, or whether there had been argument at all.[11] Where a novel point was explicitly raised by demurrer, the medieval judges were notoriously reluctant to enter judgment at all if there was any disagreement among themselves; and so the plea rolls contain mostly common-form entries, with the occasional interesting question raised by the appearance of a new form. To the extent that new forms of pleading raised questions of law, they hardly ever settled them in a definitive way. If the parties went to issue without demurring in law, the record did not reveal whether the court had given the pleading its approval, or whether a serjeant had decided not to stake his case on a doubtful point, or whether no one had thought the point worth arguing. The development of legal principles, in so far as it occurred in court, therefore belonged to the oral part of the legal process which attracted the reporters. Yet we have already noticed that in this period much of the debate was tentative, extempore and inconclusive.[12]

Any law which emerged in the course of tentative pleading was not law laid down by way of judgment, but accepted learning within the profession: 'common learning', as it is called in the old books. No single precedent could be taken as common learning; it was evidence of practice and professional opinion but no more, because serjeants in pleading made tactical decisions for reasons known only to themselves, or even mistakes. Long usage was more sacrosanct, and the courts were most unwilling to depart from settled precedents. Although the judges were the chief repositories of common learning, their collective declarations were law not just because of their judicial office but because they conformed to the established wisdom of the little intellectual world of Westminster Hall. The common opinion of all the judges and serjeants in the Exchequer Chamber was the highest authority there could be.[13] But if the judges could not agree on the law, the point under discussion could hardly be soluble by common learning, and no majority judicial decision could turn doubts into certainties; judgment was accordingly withheld. This explains the seeming paradox that counsel's decision to withdraw a point from argument, by reframing his plea, sometimes indicated the state of the law more clearly than the pressing of doubtful points on the court by demurrer. It also explains why there could have been no suggestion that a court was bound by a

---

11 This seems to be the point in *Anon.* (1319) 81 SS 131, per Denom sjt ('Cite law and not precedents, for it may be the party wanted to plead and lose').

12 See pp. 93-94, ante.

13 See pp. 160-161, ante.

previous decision. To that extent it was true that judges did not make law. Their opinions were not sources of law, but simply evidence as to what the law was. Legal learning and reasoning transcended single instances.

Increased emphasis on the single decision came in early Tudor times, as a result of the Renaissance emphasis on judicial positivism. New procedures for raising questions of law were developed because lawyers and their clients wanted more definitive rulings from the bench.[14] Then, as more law came to be settled by decisions upon demurrers, special verdicts, or motions after trial, the courts began to look at old precedents in a new way and to belittle the authority of those in which no considered decision was reached. Moreover, the publication of abridgments, coupled with the printing of the year-books, facilitated the use of specific citations in argument. Fitzherbert, in his *New Natura Brevium* (1534), was the first writer to make a practice of discussing earlier cases critically.[15] At the same time, the courts took to a more methodical evaluation of precedents; cases could now be dismissed as out of date, or as aberrations, or as mere exchanges of opinion. The result of these changes was that the formal, deliberate judicial opinion was becoming a distinct source of law, to be distinguished from the passing opinion or obiter dictum. By Plowden's time, the distinction was fully recognised. Earlier reports had mostly been based on 'the sudden speech of the judges upon motion of cases of the serjeants and counsellors at the bar', whereas Plowden claimed of his own reports that 'all the cases here be matter in law tried upon demurrers, or be special verdicts containing matters in law, of which the judges had copies, studied them, and in most of them argued, and after great deliberation have given judgment. And so (as I think) there is most firmness and surety of law in this report.'[16] By 1600 even a majority opinion would have this effect of settling the law.[17]

Notwithstanding this fundamental change of attitude, the doctrine of the binding force of precedent did not appear for another three centuries. Vaughan CJ explained that, since judges sometimes made mistakes, precedents might be wrong. And, although error in a particular case could only be corrected by a court of error, because of the principle of

[14] See pp. 97-98, ante.
[15] See also p. 216, ante. No cases are cited in Littleton's *Tenures*, except in some interpolated passages.
[16] *Les Comentaries* (1571), prologue.
[17] *Slade v. Morley* (1602), p. 392, post, is a good example. See also LPCL 167-169, 472-475.

res judicata,[18] judges were not bound to repeat the error in similar cases. If a judge considered a previous decision to be wrong, then, being sworn to do justice according to law, he ought not in conscience to follow it: 'for that were to wrong every man having a like cause, because another was wronged before'.[19] The desire for certainty was the chief restraining factor; but it could not be assured by rigidity. A strict adherence to precedent can actually increase uncertainty, because it encourages over-subtle distinctions between cases essentially alike.[20]

It is sometimes suggested that the tide turned in the early nineteenth century, and that the principle of *stare decisis* was then elevated into inflexible dogma by conservative judges such as Lord Kenyon CJ and Parke B (later Lord Wensleydale). The *locus classicus* of the new thinking is said to be the latter's opinion in 1833 that rules derived from precedents were applied for the sake of uniformity and consistency even when they were 'not as convenient and reasonable as we ourselves could have devised'.[21] But the learned judge only said that precedents were to be followed 'when they are not plainly unreasonable and inconvenient'. Pollock CB later recalled that 'even Parke, Lord Wensleydale (the greatest legal pedant that I believe ever existed), did not always follow even the House of Lords; he did not over-rule ... but he did not act upon cases which were nonsense'.[22] There was nothing new in the sentiment that long accepted principles ought to outweigh individual opinions; it had often been said in the year-books. The truth is that, from the earliest period, there have been on the bench both 'timid souls' and 'bold spirits';[23] and that to seek a uniformity of judicial philosophy at different periods may be to seek what never existed. It has also been a constant tendency for judges to treat rules of property law – including in due course the principles of equity relating to property – as standing in greater need of certainty than matters of contract and tort. Coke CJ, who spoke frequently of the need for certainty in the land law and strove to banish all the new-found conceptions which had crept in since the Statute of Uses, promoted with equal vigour new developments in the law of contract and in the prerogative remedies of the subject against

[18] The principle that parties are estopped from denying the correctness of a final judgment. There would otherwise be no end to a lawsuit.

[19] *Bole v. Horton* (1673) Vaugh. 360 at 383.

[20] See *Darley v. Reginam* (1846) 12 Cl. & Fin. 520 at 544, per Lord Brougham.

[21] *Mirehouse v. Rennell* (1833) 1 Cl. & Fin. 527 at 546.

[22] Lord Hanworth, *Lord Chief Baron Pollock* (1929), p. 198 (citing a letter of 1868).

[23] See *Candler v. Crane, Christmas & Co.* [1951] 2 K.B. 164 at 174, per Denning LJ..

administrative bodies.[24] Lord Mansfield CJ, one of the boldest of judicial spirits, often acted on the principle that 'as the usages of society alter, the law must adapt itself to the various situations of mankind'.[25] Yet in property matters he accepted the need for fixed rules; so much so that 'if an erroneous or hasty determination has got into practice, there is more benefit derived from adhering to it, than if it were to be overturned'.[26] In 1834 a barrister called Ram published a large collection of interesting but conflicting judicial pronouncements on the subject of precedent. He concluded that a court could be bound by a previous decision, but only if it was 'wholly unimpeachable' or if the objection to it was insufficient to shake its authority.[27] The judicial approach to precedent, far from being inflexible in the 1830s, could only be summarised by drawing a vicious circle.

The duty of repeating errors is a modern innovation, and one which many have come to regret within a generation or two of its introduction. It may have resulted from the improved quality of law reports following developments in shorthand techniques, which made the *ipsissima verba* of the judges available as an authentic text and made bold distinguishing more difficult. But it was more likely a result of the hierarchical system of appellate courts established in the last century. It is obviously a sensible discipline to require lower courts to abide by the rules settled by their superiors. Nevertheless, the hierarchical logic did not require any courts to be bound by their own decisions, or by those of courts of comparable authority. That was settled for the House of Lords only in 1898, and for the Court of Appeal not until 1944, earlier opinions to the same effect having been the subject of disagreement.[28] The theory apparently also requires the Court of Appeal to follow decisions of the Exchequer Chamber and Court of Appeal in Chancery, since those were courts of coordinate authority.[29] The House of Lords in 1966 freed itself

---

[24] See pp. 165, 173, ante; pp. 324-326, post.

[25] *Johnson v. Spiller* (1784) 3 Doug. 371 at 373. The remark prompted Lord Kenyon CJ to respond, 'I confess I do not think that the Courts ought to change the law so as to adapt it to the fashions of the times': *Ellah v. Leigh* (1794) 5 Term Rep. 679 at 682.

[26] *Hodgson v. Ambrose* (1780) 1 Doug. 337 at 341.

[27] J. Ram, *Treatise on Legal Judgment* (1834).

[28] E.g. in *Bright v. Hutton* (1852) 3 H.L.C. 341 at 391, Lord Campbell said that a decision of the House of Lords could only be altered by act of parliament; but Lord St Leonards (p. 388) said every court had an inherent jurisdiction to correct its previous errors.

[29] *Drive Yourself Hire Co. (London) Ltd. v. Strutt* [1954] 1 Q.B. 250 at 272, 274; *Beswick v. Beswick* [1966] Ch. 538 at 552; *Tiverton Estates v. Wearwell Ltd.* [1975] Ch. 146, [1974] 1 All E.R. 209.

from the self-imposed fetter,[30] leaving only the Court of Appeal (Civil Division), and in some situations the divisional courts, subject to such restraint. There was some controversy in the Denning era as to whether the Court of Appeal should not emulate the House of Lords and declare itself once more free; but since 1969 there has been a procedure for by-passing the Court of Appeal where the House of Lords is to be invited to overturn a decision binding on the trial judge.[31]

After 1972 all English courts have been bound by statute to follow decisions of the European Court of Justice in matters of community law; but that court does not regard itself as bound by its own decisions, and an English court which has doubts may reopen a point by making a reference.[32] This radical innovation has started a new chapter of legal history.

FICTIONS

Maine used the term Legal Fiction in its widest sense, 'to signify any assumption which conceals, or affects to conceal, the fact that a rule of law has undergone alteration, its letter remaining unchanged, its operation being modified'.[33] The reason for resorting to pretence for this purpose is that it satisfied the desire for improvement without offending what Maine called 'the superstitious derelish for change'. An example of a fiction in Maine's wide sense is the extension of benefit of clergy to enable courts to avoid imposing the death penalty, first by treating as a 'clerk' anyone who could read, and then by allowing clergy to persons who could not read or who were disqualified from being clergymen.[34] Another was the fictitious finding of bastardy to free a man from villeinage.[35] These were fictitious decisions by the court itself in order to achieve extensions of existing principle. The more usual sense of the term is that of the Roman *fictio*, a false averment of fact by a party which could not be traversed and so could not be shown to be false. We have seen how several English courts in the fifteenth and sixteenth centuries were given enlarged jurisdictions by means of fictitious

---

30 *Practice Note* [1966] 3 All E.R. 77.

31 Administration of Justice Act 1969 (c.58), ss.12-16. The wording of s.12(3) recognises, perhaps for the first time in a statute, that a decision may be 'binding'.

32 European Communities Act 1972 (c.68), s.3(1); *Bulmer Ltd. v. Bollinger S.A.* [1974] Ch. 401 at 419-420, per Lord Denning MR.

33 *Ancient Law* (1861), p. 26.

34 See pp. 568-569, post.

35 See pp. 535-536, post.

allegations.[36] Fictions were also used to extend substantive remedies, the most familiar examples of such false allegations being the deceit commonly laid in *assumpsit* and other actions on the case,[37] the loss and finding in trover,[38] the lease and ouster in ejectment,[39] the collusive common recovery,[40] and the implied promise in *indebitatus assumpsit* for quasi-contractual claims.[41] In all these cases the pretence was of a fact which, if true, would have led to the desired result under pre-existing forms of action. If the untrue fact was not substantially material to the cause of action, but merely satisfied some jurisdictional or procedural requirement which was not essential to achieving justice, then no harm was done by pretending it to be true. Some fictions seem to go further than that, in working substantive changes by implying facts which do seem to be material, such as the implied promise in *indebitatus assumpsit*; and these had a more lasting effect on legal thought, since the implication of a material fact is tantamount to a conclusion of law. The line between fiction and implication is still blurred in the law of contract.[42]

Fictions of whatever kind, even if they encouraged looseness of thought, were not intended to mislead anyone.[43] It is doubtless wrong to lie; but no one was harmed by fictions, and they were only allowed where their operation was fair and the effect desirable in the eyes of the court. In the seventeenth century they were even rationalised as a form of equity: *in fictione juris semper est aequitas*.[44] Nevertheless, once they had done their work of bringing about a change in the operation of the law, their continued repetition as common form added unnecessary mystery if not absurdity to the law. Later writers urged procedural reforms which would render them unnecessary, and one of the achievements of the nineteenth century was indeed to end fictions in the

---

36 See pp. 50-51 (bill of Middlesex and *latitat*), 57 (*quominus*), 136, 139 (conciliar courts), 141, 143 (admiralty), ante.

37 See p. 384, post.

38 See pp. 449-450, post.

39 See pp. 341-342, post.

40 See pp. 319-320, post.

41 See p. 417, post; and also P. Birks, 'Fictions Ancient and Modern' in *The Legal Mind* (P. Birks and N. MacCormick ed., 1986), pp. 83-101.

42 E.g. if a purchaser of goods is given too much change, a modern lawyer would no longer imply a promise to repay the surplus, because that would be a fiction. But he will not hesitate to imply a promise that the goods are merchantable.

43 Cf. Milsom, 74 LQR at 223: 'The aim of fictions is not deception; it is to keep records straight.'

44 Co. Inst., vol. I, p. 150. Cf. *Treatise concerning Estates Tayle* (1641), p. 19 (of common recoveries): *Lex fingit ubi subsistit aequitas*.

classical sense of the term. Such fictions belong to the formulary stage of a legal system; now that emphasis is placed on the facts rather than the forms, it is no longer permissible to make a false assertion in pleading, whatever the purpose. But fictions in Maine's wider sense are by no means defunct, and are frequently combined with legislation in the form of conclusive presumptions, 'deeming' provisions, and terms implied into contracts by law.

Equity and Legal Change

The equity of the Court of Chancery, like the fictions of the common-law courts, proceeded from the premise that the course of the common law was immutable. The just remedy was provided in Chancery, not by changing the law, but by avoiding its effect in the special circumstances of particular cases. So long as chancellors were seen as providing ad hoc remedies in individual cases, there was no question of their jurisdiction bringing about legal change or making law. When, however, equity was regularised and reduced to known principles and rules, the overall content of English law could be said to have been thereby changed. The use and the trust, the equity of redemption, the principles of relief against forfeitures and penalties, and the equitable remedies of discovery, injunction and specific performance, were permanent additions to the substantive law which survived the abolition of the court.

Equity also affected the law independently of the Chancery. It played a role in certain branches of the common law, such as the action for money had and received;[45] this was openly acknowledged under Lord Mansfield CJ, who 'never liked common law so much as when it was like equity'.[46] And some equitable doctrines were received into the law as a result of legislation. The trust, for instance, which began as a mere trusting of someone, with no prospect of legal protection, came first to be upheld by the Chancery in individual cases, then to be a regular species of property, and finally (under the legislation of 1925) the sole means of creating future interests in land.[47] Another example is the will, which was not allowed under the feudal land law. Leaving land by will was made possible by means of the use, an arrangement recognised only in equity; the legal power to devise land was not introduced until

---

45 See pp. 417, 424, post.

46 *Lord Eldon's Anecdote Book* (1960), p. 162. Eldon adds that the attitude was reversed under Lord Kenyon CJ.

47 See pp. 284-287, 328-331, 350-352, post.

1540.[48] Married women were given the capacity to own separate property in equity centuries before they were given legal capacity in 1882.[49] Other new kinds of property, such as copyright and trademarks, were recognised in equity before parliament took them over.[50] And, in the last century, equity was moving towards the recognition of joint-stock companies with limited liability before the statutory foundations of modern company law were laid in 1844 and 1856.[51]

After the Judicature Acts there was some talk of equity being presumed to be past the age of childbearing,[52] but in fact it has continued to bear offspring. One of its more recent progeny, the deserted wife's interest in the matrimonial home, was judicially exterminated; but its demise led to a statutory change in the law.[53] Still more recently, the courts have extended the scope of interlocutory injunctions and orders, first to restrain the removal of assets outside the jurisdiction in order to frustrate litigation in England (the 'Mareva injunction'),[54] and secondly to preserve documentary evidence in danger of removal or destruction before trial (the 'Anton Piller order') .[55] It is true that neither development was attributed to equity as now understood: Mareva injunctions were fathered on a statutory power to grant injunctions when it appears 'just or convenient',[56] Anton Piller orders on the 'inherent jurisdiction of the court'. But both devices are equitable in the original sense of the term; they are new procedures devised by judicial discretion, without precedent, to make the regular law function more effectively.

---

[48] See pp. 284-285, 286, 293, post.

[49] See pp. 553-554, post.

[50] See pp. 516, 522-523, post.

[51] C. A. Cooke, *Corporation, Trust and Company* (1950), pp. 86-88. For a short history of company law, see L. C. B. Gower, *Principles of Modern Company Law* (1969), pp. 22-64.

[52] Harman J said in 1951 that 'Equity is not to be presumed to be of an age past childbearing': R. E. Megarry, *A Second Miscellany at Law* (1973), p. 293.

[53] *National Provincial Bank Ltd v. Ainsworth* [1965] A.C. 1175; Matrimonial Homes Act 1967 (c.75).

[54] *Mareva Compania Naviera S.A. v. International Bulk Carriers* [1975] 2 Lloyd's Rep. 509.

[55] *Anton Piller K.G. v. Manufacturing Processes Ltd* [1976] Ch. 55.

[56] Supreme Court of Judicature (Consolidation) Act 1925, 15 & 16 Geo. V, c.49, s.45.

Legislation

Maine regarded legislation as working in a completely different way from fictions and equity, because it changes law directly as an exercise of authority, whereas the other two media of improvement rest on the assumption that the law does not change. Nevertheless, although it is doubtless correct to regard all forms of royal legislation as an exercise of sovereign power, it may be going too far to suppose that the earliest legislation was primarily intended to alter the substance or the course of the law. The Anglo-Saxon codes, as we have seen, were intended to declare and perhaps unify what had previously been uncertain or variable customs; they were not obviously intended to replace old rules with new. The Normans and Angevins produced a good deal of legislation, variously known as assizes, constitutions and charters, or even *statuta*,[57] though they were omitted from the later canon of statute-law as dating from before the time of legal memory. These enactments, however, and doubtless many more that have been lost, were not changing the common law; they were, in a sense, making it. It is not even to be assumed that contemporaries thought of this kind of law-making as different in character from the function of the judges. What in later times were seen as two distinct branches of the constitution – the legislature and the judicature – had their origins in a less sophisticated notion of kingship in which legislation and adjudication were not distinguishable. The courts and parliament both had their origins in the same royal council which advised the early kings. Even when the courts began to separate from government, the judges could reserve cases of difficulty for the king to decide in person or in council, and conversely the king in council could issue general or specific directions to the judges. The attendance of common-law judges in the medieval Chancery and Tudor Star Chamber, and the presence of today's judges sitting on the woolsacks before the throne at a state opening of parliament, hearken back to a distant age when the king's justices were part of an undivided royal council.

'The statute book' was no more a historical entity than 'the' register of writs, but it was settled in medieval times that the notional canon of statutes began with the confirmation of Magna Carta in 1225. The line was arbitrary, and many statutes after 1225 were not in the same form as later acts of parliament; indeed it is often difficult before the time of Edward III to distinguish parliament and council, the names being used interchangeably to indicate ad hoc advisory assemblies rather than settled

---

[57] For a *statutum decretum* of Henry I which settled the doctrine of coparcenary, see p. 306, post.

institutions. A comparison of the enacting words found in legislation during the first century after 1225 shows no consistency. The charter itself was issued in the name of the king alone; the Provisions of Merton (1236) were made *in curia regis*; the Statute of Marlborough (1267) mentions the presence and agreement of 'men of higher and lower estate'. The Statute of Westminster I (1275) provided a model for the future by reciting the consent of the lords and commons ('the commonalty of the realm').[58] These latter were knights of the shires, citizens, and burgesses, summoned to attend by writs sent to sheriffs, though not as yet constituting a distinct 'house'. It was nearly a century, however, before this became the common form, and parliaments were sometimes summoned without the commonalty being represented at all. The Statute of Westminster II (1285) mentions 'parliament', but the legislation is attributed to the king without any reference to consent; the Statute of Winchester (1285) is also attributed simply to the king; yet the statute *Quia emptores* (1290) is attributed to the king in parliament 'at the instance of the great men of the realm'.

In the reign of Edward III the commonalty began to meet as a separate house, to initiate legislation, and to assert a constitutional role. In 1340 the king conceded the principle that no taxation should be imposed without their consent,[59] and in 1348 it was said that laws were made by the king with the assent of the peers and commons;[60] but the need for consent by the House of Commons to all legislation was not established beyond doubt until after 1400, in that it remained possible for the lords to introduce variations when assenting to commons' petitions.[61] In 1407, Henry IV recognised that the proper legislative procedure was for the lords and commons to debate propositions as separate houses, and only when they were both agreed should the matter be submitted to the king for his assent.[62] From then until the present, parliamentary legislation has required the separate consent of king, lords and commons.

These constitutional developments inevitably led to an increased concentration on the text of bills, as containing the propositions to

---

[58] The opening words are: 'These are the enactments [*establissementz*] of King Edward, son of King Henry, made at Westminster at his first parliament . . . by his council, and by the assent of the archbishops, bishops, abbots, priors, earls, barons, and the commonalty of the land, summoned thither . . .'.

[59] 14 Edw. III, stat. ii, c.1.

[60] *Hadelow v. Regem* (1348) Y.B. Hil. 22 Edw. III, fo. 3, pl.25.

[61] The need for amendments to be resubmitted to the Commons was established in 1414: Rot. Parl., vol. IV, p. 22, no.10; and see *Pilkington's Case* (1455) Y.B. Pas. 33 Hen. VI, fo. 17, pl.8.

[62] Rot. Parl., vol. III, p. 611.

which each house in turn was asked to give its assent. In the fifteenth century the practice arose of inserting in the bill the exact wording of the proposed legislation, and since Tudor times this has been the universal practice. But it is important to remember that medieval legislation was not produced in the same way. It was written law indeed, but not a text which had been pored over word for word by the lawmakers, with debates upon the wording. In the case of some early statutes, the drafting was carried out by the clerks and judges after assent had been given. A statute then represented the terms of a decision upon a generally worded complaint or petition; a decision of the highest authority in the land, but not different in kind from decisions by inferior branches of the *Curia Regis*, which were likewise entered up in writing by the clerks. This accounts both for the freedom with which the older statutes were interpreted and for the otherwise incomprehensible lack of contemporary definitive texts. Until 1299 there was no official procedure for enrolling parliamentary statutes; from that year an official, but still incomplete, roll was kept in the Chancery. Statutes were also registered in the Exchequer, in book form. A parallel record, the rolls of parliament (beginning in 1290), contained only part of the legislation together with non-legislative 'acts' of parliament such as decisions in litigation. Thus the medieval courts had no authentic texts available to them, and argument in court rarely turned on the precise wording of a statute. In the absence of official records, the public and their legal advisers relied on private collections of statutes; hundreds of examples survive, hardly any two of them the same. These manuscripts were never wholly complete. There was no definitive guide to what should be included, and the occasional statute may have escaped notice altogether.[63] They often contained writs, ordinances, procedural directives, and even passages from *Glanvill* and *Bracton*, masquerading as statutes. By professional usage, some of these spurious texts were treated as 'statutes' for practical purposes, although (in so far as it mattered) they were properly to be regarded as evidence of the common law rather than of legislation.[64] It was these private statute-books rather than the public records which formed the basis of the series of printed statutes which began to appear in 1481 and were frequently re-edited in successive centuries as the 'statutes at large'. Not until 1810-22 was an official edition of the old statutes (down to 1713) published; but even

---

63 E.g. the Royal Marriages Act 1428, which was rediscovered in 1977: R. A. Griffiths, 93 LQR 248; G. O. Sayles, 94 LQR 188.

64 *Re Sir John Skrene* (1475) Y.B. Mich. 15 Edw. IV, fo. 13, pl.17, per Littleton J (who also points out that Magna Carta was not a parliamentary statute); *Swaffer v. Mulcahy* [1934] 1 K.B. 608.

the impressive elephant-folio volumes of the *Statutes of the Realm* were acknowledged to be incomplete and to contain apocrypha. In the case of medieval legislation, then, sovereign authority was in practice considerably modified by the vagaries of tradition.

By Tudor times the character of parliamentary legislation had undergone a significant change. The reason was partly procedural, for the result of the changes in bill procedure during the fifteenth century was that legislation was 'no longer the Government's vague reply to vaguely worded complaints, but rather the deliberate adoption of specific proposals embodied in specific texts'.[65] And it was partly political, in that parliament was extending its sphere of activity. The Tudors exalted parliament, and expected somewhat in return. King Henry VIII in parliament was prodigiously industrious, passing some 677 statutes which occupy almost as much space as all the preceding legislation from Magna Carta onwards. Many of these statutes were of immense political significance. The achievements of the Reformation Parliament in spiritual matters established the legislative supremacy of parliament against its only remaining rival, the once universal Church. And in the temporal sphere parliament ventured to the limits of legal possibility: entailing the Crown, fictional livery of seisin,[66] new treasons of appalling width, even boiling in oil as a punishment. Attempts were made to control the environment and the economy by legislation. The changes wrought by parliament in the Tudor period were no more significant than those effected by the courts, but they were seen as conscious changes, the work of humanist legislators confident in their ability to improve things by the right use of power. With this new concept of legislation came a new reverence for the written text. Legislative drafting was now carried out with such skill by Crown lawyers, the legislative purpose being explained in such extensive and explicit preambles, that the judges were manifestly being discouraged from the creative exegesis they had bestowed on medieval statutes. There would always thereafter be a sharp division between the two functions of legislature and judicature, with serious consequences in the future for the vitality of judge-made law.

ACTS OF PARLIAMENT AS JUDGMENTS

The changes in the character of legislation were disguised by constitutional theory. In the thirteenth century, parliament had been

[65] Plucknett, 60 LQR at 248.
[66] For the Statute of Uses 1536, see p. 292, post.

nothing other than a grand meeting of the king's court; and even if by court we mean a judicial body, the term was quite appropriate on account of the volume of contentious business.[67] But, long after most of that business had been directed elsewhere, parliament continued to be regarded as a 'high court', distinguished from other superior courts chiefly in that its acts were not tied to the course of the common law and were not reversible for error. Sir Henry Finch wrote of parliament as having 'absolute power in all cases, as in making laws, adjudicating upon matters in law, trying capital cases, and reversing errors in the King's Bench, and especially is this the proper court where there is some common mischief which the ordinary course of the law has no means to remedy. And all things that they do are like judgments.[68] Its judgments were not *inter partes*, but they bound everyone, on the medieval principle that since all the estates of the realm were represented in parliament, every person was 'privy' to its acts. By Finch's time, however, there were obvious procedural differences between the legislative side of parliament and the judicial side. Half a century later, Sir Matthew Hale pointed out the ambiguity of the phrase 'high court of parliament', which had borne different senses in different periods. Most of the judicial work had long been appropriated to the House of Lords; for, 'although in truth the king and both houses of parliament make the entire supreme court of this kingdom; yet very often, in parliamentary records of writs, *curia nostra in parliamento*, and *curia parliamenti*, is applicable to the lords' house'. Hale therefore found it necessary to distinguish the legislative or 'deliberative' function of parliament from the contentious or 'judicative'. The former looked to the future, the latter to things already done. Even so, Hale treated the functions as being of like nature. The House of Lords, he argued, could not be the supreme court of final appeal because, if it were, 'then is the legislative power virtually and consequentially there also'. The test was whether the house could give judgment against an act of parliament. Hale said that it could not, and therefore it was not supreme. The argument now seems rather academic; but it shows that, as late as the seventeenth century, analytical legal writers saw no fundamental difference between judicial and parliamentary law-making. For Hale, the supreme power of

---

67 Cf. *Fleta* (*c.* 1290) ii.2 (72 SS 109): 'The king has his court in his council in his parliaments . . . where doubts concerning judgments are determined, new remedies devised for wrongs newly brought to light, and justice dispensed'.

68 *Nomotechnia* (1613), ff. 21v-22 (translated).

making laws and the supreme power of deciding cases had to reside in the same body.[69] *Jus dicere* was *jus dare*.

STATUTE LAW AND THE COURTS
From the time of Edward I, English lawyers never doubted the authority of parliament to make new laws or clarify old ones, and in so doing to bind all courts, with the exception only of future parliaments. In 1334, Herle CJ said the judges would not change a particular rule, which was law before they were born, but that the party if he wished could 'sue in parliament to make a new law'.[70] A century later, Fortescue CJ declared that 'this high court of parliament is so high and so mighty in its nature that it may make law, and that that is law it may make no law'.[71] There was therefore nothing particularly new in Sir Thomas Smith's assertion in 1565 that 'the most high and absolute power of the realm of England consisteth in the parliament', as a body representing every Englishman; 'the parliament abrogateth old laws, maketh new, [and] giveth order for things past and for things hereafter to be followed'.[72] Coke CJ was likewise merely paraphrasing these older views when he wrote, in the time of Charles I, that the power of parliament in making statutes 'is so transcendant and absolute as it cannot be confined either for causes or persons within any bounds'.[73] Nevertheless, when supreme power is exercised through the written word, it is always subject to interpretation by those who have to enforce it; and in the application and interpretation of the legislative innovations of the supreme court of parliament, medieval judges enjoyed the like freedom as they had in applying and interpreting the common law of their own courts. This was because, as we have seen, the texts had no special authority in themselves. In the early days when judges helped to draw statutes in parliament, and were therefore closely acquainted with underlying policy, it is not surprising to find them applying that policy rather than the letter of the text. Hengham CJ once cut short a serjeant who was attempting to expound a statute of 1285 with the remark, 'Do not gloss the statute, for we

---

[69]   *The Jurisdiction of the Lords House, or Parliament* (F. Hargrave ed., 1796), esp. pp. 17, 85, 205-207; *The Prerogatives of the King* (D. E. C. Yale ed., 92 SS, 1976), p. 181.

[70]   Y.B. Mich. 8 Edw. III, fo. 69, pl.35. A statutory change is referred to as 'novel ley' in 1304: Y.B. Trin. 32 Edw. I (Rolls ser.), p. 259.

[71]   *Re Thomas Thorp, speaker-elect* (1453) Rot. Parl., vol. V, p. 239.

[72]   *De Republica Anglorum* (1583), pp. 34-35 (written in 1565).

[73]   Co. Inst., vol. IV, p. 36.

understand it better than you; we made it'.[74] Even judges who had not been personally involved might lay claim to a knowledge of the makers' intention which was at odds with the wording: for instance, in 1312 Bereford CJ interpreted a statute by reading in words which were not there, on the footing that the draftsman had negligently omitted to express what was meant.[75] It was thus possible to enlarge a statute by the 'equity': as where a statute providing a remedy against the warden of the Fleet Prison was interpreted to apply to all gaolers.[76] Equity in this sense was the Aristotelian concept of interpretation according to the spirit, general words being necessarily deficient to cover every case.[77] The equitable approach survived into the Tudor period, when Plowden explained: 'It is not the words of the law but the internal sense of it that are the law; for our law, like all other laws, has two parts, the body and the soul: the letter of the law is the body of the law, but the sense and reason of the law is its soul . . . and often when you know the letter you do not know the sense, for sometimes the sense is not as large as the letter and sometimes it is larger.' The test which Plowden advanced for finding the equitable construction of a statute was remarkably like the 'officious bystander' test familiar to modern students of contract law: 'Whenever you read the letter of statutes, imagine that the lawmaker is present, and that you have asked him about the equity; then give yourself that answer which you imagine the lawmaker would have given if he had been present.'[78] It was to take advantage of this approach that Tudor draftsmen began elaborating the explanatory preambles in statutes, so as to frustrate any attempt to assert a legislative intent contrary to that expressly declared.[79]

Some medieval lawyers may have taken the equitable approach to the extreme of believing that an unreasonable or absurd statute could be disregarded entirely. There are a few signs of this happening in the early year-book period,[80] but little in the way of theoretical justification. One possible approach might have been that the statute was vitiated by mistake, in that the lawmaker would not have wished the statute to be

---

[74] *Aumeye's Case* (1305) Y.B. 33-35 Edw. I, p. 82; Plucknett, *Statutes and their Interpretation*, 183-184 (and see pp. 49-50, for further examples).

[75] *Belyng v. Anon.* (1312) B. & M. 52 at 53; p. 318, post.

[76] Port Nbk (102 SS) 115, pl.62; *Plat v. Sheriffs of London* (1550) Plowd. 35 (following earlier cases).

[77] See p. 122, ante.

[78] Commentary to *Eyston v. Studde* (1574) Plowd. 459 at 465, 467.

[79] Port Nbk (102 SS) 115, pl. 59, says (c. 1495) that a statute may not be construed contrary to its recited intention. But the preamble was not always conclusive as to the mischief: *Discourse upon Statutes*, pp. 114-117.

[80] Plucknett, *Statutes and their Interpretation*, pp. 66-71.

put into effect had the full consequences been apparent to him.[81] Another approach, suggested by a fifteenth-century reader, was that, if no parliament could be taken to have intended what the words said, the clerk of parliament must be presumed to have made a mistake.[82] Neither of these approaches could have survived the tightening of bill procedure, with its greater emphasis on the written formulation. St German in the 1520s put into the mouth of his Doctor a third but narrower theory, that a statute against natural law (or the law of reason) was not law at all, but void.[83] Such abstract statements bore little fruit in the practice of the courts. The boldest assertion, which had some influence on the establishing of judicial review of legislation in America,[84] was that of Coke in his report of *Bonham's Case* in 1610: 'it appears in our books that in many cases the common law will control acts of parliament and sometimes adjudge them to be utterly void; for when an act of parliament is against common right and reason, or repugnant, or impossible to be performed, the common law will control it and adjudge such act to be void.' There is no doubt that this was Coke's considered opinion at the time, for the passage has been found written out twice in his own autograph.[85] There is some doubt, however, as to whether anything was made of the opinion by Coke CJ in court or whether it reflected the views of his brethren. It seems better to view it more as a last stand than as a statement of orthodox doctrine. Lord Ellesmere C reacted sharply, saying it was more fitting 'that acts of parliament should be corrected by the same pen that drew them than to be dashed in pieces by the opinion of a few judges'.[86] In his speech to Coke's successor as chief justice, Ellesmere inveighed against the view that judges 'have power to judge statutes and acts of parliament to be void if they conceive them to be against common right and reason', which was for the king and parliament to judge.[87] The context of Coke's remark was a statute which appeared to infringe a principle of natural justice;

---

81 This seems to be the sense of Herle J's remark in *Tregor v. Vaghan* (1334) Y.B. Pas. 8 Edw. III, fo. 30, pl.26 ('There are some statutes made which even he who made them would not wish to put into effect').

82 94 SS *44* n.10. No court, however, could question the record of parliament for error.

83 *Doctor and Student*, 91 SS at p. 15. A similar view was advanced by Sir John Fortescue in *De Natura Legis Naturae*.

84 See Plucknett, 40 HLR at 61-68.

85 *Dr Bonham's Case* (1610) 8 Co. Rep. 114; CUL MS. Ii. 5. 21(2), fo. 93v; Yale Law School MS. G.R24.1, fo. 157v.

86 'Observations on Coke's Reports', printed in L. A. Knafla, *Law and Politics in Jacobean England* (1977), p. 307.

87 *Speech to Sir Henry Montague* (1616) Moore K.B. 826 at 828. He added, however, 'I speak not of impossibilities or direct repugnancies'.

and at least one contemporary, Hobart CJ, shared Coke's view that 'even an act of parliament, made against natural equity, as to make a man judge in his own cause, is void in itself, for *jura naturae sunt immutabilia*'.[88] It seems from the *Fourth Institute*, however, that after further consideration Coke himself abandoned his opinion. As to natural justice, he recounted a story that Henry VIII had asked his judges whether an attainder in parliament could be called in question if the person attainted had been denied an opportunity to defend himself; they had replied that they hoped parliament would never do such a thing, but if it did the act could not be questioned. Coke then listed some oppressive statutes, and drew a lesson which was moral rather than legal; they were 'a good caveat to parliaments to leave all causes to be measured by the golden and straight metwand of the law, and not to the incertain and crooked cord of discretion'.[89] Little more was heard in England of judicial review of statutes, and Coke's doctrine of 1610 was whittled down into a presumption to be applied only where a statute was ambiguous or in need of qualification by necessary implication.[90] The moral proposition alone has remained intact. Parliament cannot make bad good, nor can it make possible the impossible. But it has the power to make bad law, to deem the impossible to have occurred, or to prescribe a punishment for those who fail to do the impossible.

Blackstone said that to permit judicial review of unreasonable legislation 'were to set the judicial power above that of the legislature, which would be subversive of all government'.[91] This principle has in modern times been carried so far in England as to eliminate the equitable approach to construction almost completely. It gained added weight after the 1830s, when reforming legislation was often based on detailed factual enquiries formally unavailable to the courts, and frequently involved a deliberate decision of policy to depart from common-law reasoning.[92] When in 1950 Denning LJ tried to find the intention of parliament in a particular statute and give effect to it by filling in gaps in the wording, Lord Simonds rebuked him for 'a naked usurpation of the legislative function under the thin guise of interpretation'.[93] The last remnant of the equity of a statute is the 'mischief rule', also

---

88 *Day v. Savadge* (1614) Hob. 85 at 87. Cf. *Doctor and Student*, 91 SS at p. 15 ('jura naturalia immutabilia sunt').

89 Co. Inst., vol. IV, pp. 37, 41.

90 Bl. Comm., vol. I, p. 91. Necessary implication can, nevertheless, achieve all that Coke probably intended: see pp. 173-175, ante (natural justice).

91 Bl. Comm., vol. I, p. 90.

92 See Atiyah, *Freedom of Contract*, p. 384.

93 *Magor and St Mellons R.D.C. v. Newport B.C.* [1952] A.C. 189 at 191.

formulated by Coke, which permits ambiguous legislation to be interpreted in such a way as to suppress the mischief which it was designed to eliminate.[94] Even in that attenuated form, it is not much heard of today.

Law Reform Movements

The many reforms effected by judicial decision and statute before the nineteenth century were sometimes sweeping but rarely if ever radical, and seldom the result of a planned programme of change. They usually presupposed and followed established reasoning and known concepts. The resulting legal edifice was likened by Blackstone to a medieval castle, an amalgam of different styles of architecture, full of venerable but disused monuments alongside modern embellishments, always in need of repair, but nonetheless a pleasing and serviceable structure with a continuous history.[95] The legal profession in general would have relished such a metaphor. Practising lawyers well know the danger and uncertainty attending drastic changes in the law. Coke, who effected many moderate and lasting reforms himself while on the bench, wrote repeated warnings against 'innovations and novelties'.[96] Hale, a notable law reformer, thought that much of the 'itching' for change among the people at the time of the Interregnum was caused by ignorance, fear, and envy of the lawyers; and it was as necessary to avoid 'error in the excess, the over-busy and hasty and violent attempt in mutation of laws' as it was to avoid 'error in the defect, a wilful and over-strict adhering in every particular to the continuance of the laws in the state we find them'.[97] The sword of justice must be kept free from rust, but it cannot be brandished at random without doing untold harm. Professional conservatism is, however, a virtue easily misunderstood by the lay public. In a world of *latitats* and demurrers and surrebutters, when lawyers wrote notes in French and submitted their bills in Latin, and when every lawsuit followed a labyrinthine path strewn with parchment and ink and fictions and fees, laymen could be forgiven for suspecting that the whole system had been designed to increase the income of lawyers. History does not generally bear out such suspicions: the

---

[94] *Heydon's Case* (1584) 3 Co. Rep. 7; Bl. Comm., vol. I, p. 87.

[95] Bl. Comm., vol. III, p. 268. Cf. his more peevish metaphorical reference to modern architects who had pulled down 'some of its most useful parts' and left a 'huge, irregular pile': 32 HLR at 975.

[96] See, e.g., B. & M. 68.

[97] 'Considerations touching the Amendment of Laws' in *Law Tracts* (F. Hargrave ed., 1787), vol. I, pp. 249, 253.

abolition of fictions, for instance, does not seem to have resulted in any marked savings in cost or time. But at two periods of history, more than others, dissatisfaction with the state of the law reached such a peak that parliament initiated extensive programmes of reform. Both movements were concerned mainly to improve the procedure and institutions of the law rather than its substantive doctrines. In more recent times, planned law reform has spread to every branch of the law and has become an endemic if unsettling feature of the legal system.

THE CIVIL WAR AND INTERREGNUM

The period from 1640 to 1660 is usually characterised as an age of revolutionary reform. In 1640 there had not been a parliament since 1629 and dissatisfaction with the common law had reached a climax following the *Case of Ship-Money* in 1638. The Long Parliament which first met in November 1640 lost no time in starting; away went the Star Chamber, High Commission, and conciliar courts in 1641, to be followed in a few years by the House of Lords and all the ecclesiastical courts. Then there was the 'Norman yoke' to be cast off, first by the abolition of military tenures and the Court of Wards in 1645, and then by banning the use of Latin and law-French in 1650. In 1649 the king was executed and the monarchy itself displaced. What was to be done next? If kings could be done away with, no other legal institution could be sacrosanct, and in the years that followed there was protracted discussion of legal reform. The initial impetus in the Long Parliament may well have been conservative: a desire to put the clock back to the days before Stuart tyranny began to whittle down the subject's fundamental rights. But ideas for reform soon knew no bounds. The withdrawal of press licensing brought hundreds of printed pamphlets advocating changes which ranged from the mild to the extreme. The revolutionary voices were the loudest, and they did not spare law or lawyers. The Levellers wanted to abolish the whole of the common law, including its courts and practitioners, and replace it by a pocket-book code in plain man's English. Their law would be administered by select laymen who conformed with party standards. This was not to be, save at the level of the county magistracy.[98] The questioning spirit did, however, enter more moderate hearts, and it was the reforming lawyers who achieved the most in practice. The weightiest proposals were those produced by Sir Matthew Hale's law commission of 1652, which contained a few radicals but was dominated

---

[98] Revised guides to the law of justices, for the use of the party men now placed on the bench, were produced at government instigation by William Sheppard.

by lawyers who laboured to keep discussion on a technical plane. A central figure subsequently was William Sheppard (d. 1675), a country lawyer who became enthused by what he naively believed was the start of a great social and moral transformation, and from 1653 to 1657 was employed in London as a draftsman, pamphleteer and co-ordinator of ideas. In 1656 he published an impressive array of proposals for reform: fusion of law and equity; county courts for small claims; a hierarchy of appellate courts; abolition of the forms of action; uniformity of process; the end of special pleading and fictions; trial without jury for small claims; registration of title and simplified conveyancing; abolition of primogeniture; abolition of imprisonment for debt; secular probate courts; survival of causes of action on death, and death to be a cause of action for dependents; abolition of benefit of clergy (with more rational restrictions on the death penalty); abolition of the *peine forte et dure*; prison reform; and also a mass of social reforms, including the introduction of banks and an income tax.[99] Few of these were Sheppard's own ideas, and some were far from new; but as a coherent programme of reform the book seems remarkably prophetic and might have served well enough as a guide for the reformers of the nineteenth century.

In so far as these proposals were acted on in the 1650s, which was not very far, all was undone in 1660.[100] With the Restoration of King Charles II the old forms of law were restored, not excepting even the use of Latin in records, and fictions.[101] The disinclination to sever the good from the bad was an understandable reaction to the repressive illiberality of the preceding regime. Military dictatorships are not renowned for their jurisprudence, and the unlearned members of parliament had not known when to stop. Their High Court of Justice was a worse infringement of liberty than the Star Chamber had ever been, since it could inflict the death penalty without the safeguards of indictment or jury trial; it was the most fearsome political tribunal ever suffered in England. The religious zealots proved more extreme in their way than Archbishop Laud. The Blasphemy Act of 1648 had made it a capital offence to deny the Trinity, or the authority of the scriptures, or that the bodies of men rose again after death, or that there would be a last judgment. Two years later, fornication (on a second conviction) and adultery were made punishable by death, a measure more symbolic than

---

[99]   *England's Balme* ('1657', but issued in 1656).

[100] The conciliar courts and feudal revenue abolished by the Long Parliament were not, however, resurrected.

[101] For an unsuccessful attack on the fictitious bill of Middlesex in 1661, see p. 54, ante.

effective.[102] Actors and popular musicians were to be punished as rogues and whipped. The licentiousness of Charles II's court was an overreaction against this state of opinion; but it is hardly a wonder that the legislative reaction was equally blind. Reform was not killed stone dead; many of the ideas continued to be discussed later in the seventeenth century. But 1660 marked the end of a powerful, and to many rather frightening, movement for law reform. England would be free of law commissions for centuries to come.

THE NINETEENTH CENTURY

The second wave of systematic reform hit the English legal system in the second quarter of the nineteenth century, and we have already noticed many of its effects. The changed intellectual climate which brought it about is often associated with the name of Jeremy Bentham (1748-1832), an eccentric genius who strived to reduce jurisprudence to the principles of a natural science. Bentham had attended Blackstone's lectures at Oxford in 1763 and had been called to the bar, but he regarded the common law with contempt and was particularly offended by Blackstone's eloquent defence of the decidedly quirky status quo. He set himself the life-long task of constructing a rational system of law from first principles. To this end he evolved a method which he called 'deontology', the logic of the will, the science not of what is but of what ought to be. The basic premise to which this method was to be applied was the principle of utility which Bentham had distilled from the works of Beccaria and Priestley. The end of all law should be the greatest good of the greatest number, the optimum balance between pain and pleasure. Bentham proceeded to try the 'whole province of jurisprudence' by this test of expediency, setting pleasures against pains and reconciling conflicting human interests in minute detail by applying his 'felicific calculus'.

The peculiar originality of Bentham's ideas, and the oddity of his language, held little attraction for contemporary lawyers. Preoccupied as he was with the elaboration of his abstract jurisprudence, he would not cultivate the ability to compromise which was necessary to a real-life reformer. The one scheme which Bentham did persevere with on a practical level – the Panopticon, a new kind of prison based on a beehive, which could be watched by a single eye – met with failure and financial loss. Bentham himself despaired of seeing his legislative science put into practice, and contented himself with writing for future

---

[102] Not surprisingly, it was difficult to secure convictions: *Puritans and Revolutionaries* (D. Pennington and K. Thomas ed., 1978), pp. 257-282.

generations. His death came, with ironic symbolism, on the eve of the 1832 Reform Act. Yet, if Bentham's writings were esoteric, his personal influence on some of the reformers of the next generation cannot be doubted. He provided the practical men with the theoretical justifications for what they were trying to do. To Brougham, at any rate, 'the age of law reform and the age of Bentham are one and the same thing'.[103]

It was Brougham who took the lead in setting the parliamentary reforms in motion. Brought up in Scotland, arrogant and impetuous of character, Henry Brougham (1788-1868) had sufficient contempt for the English common law and its practitioners to be capable of pressing forward with drastic measures regardless of professional feeling. His boldest ideas, though not as extravagantly radical as Bentham's, must have seemed anathema to men steeped in the ancient lore and practice of Lincoln's Inn and the Temple. Brougham began his campaign as a young advocate, in the pages of the *Edinburgh Review*, and continued it in Bentham's *Westminster Review*. On coming to England, and being elected as a Whig member of parliament, he represented himself as the broom which would sweep the cobwebs from Westminster Hall. He announced his programme from the floor of the House of Commons on 7 February 1828, in a celebrated speech which lasted six hours. The learned spiders who had spent their lives spinning the threads of the old system in the dusty purlieus of the law immediately voiced their terror at the thought of impending doom. Brougham swept on, becoming Lord Chancellor in 1830, and after a mass of preliminary investigations and reports by parliamentary committees most of his proposals (and more besides) were put through in the following decades.

Dicey discerned two consecutive trends in the reforms of the nineteenth century. The first, which he assigned to the period 1825-70, he labelled 'Benthamism, or Individualism'. The reforms of this period were characterised as promoting individual liberties, or improving the means of protecting them. This was followed by a 'period of Collectivism' stretching from about 1865 into Dicey's own time. The principal objects of collectivist legislation were groups of people rather than isolated individuals, and the interests of groups were if necessary furthered to the detriment of individual freedom. Dicey's analysis represented an attempt to express in theoretical terms an obvious change in the subject-matter of legislation. In Brougham's first wave, the concentration was on the legal system – procedure and jurisdiction – rather than on the substance of the law. That could be improved

103 *Lord Brougham's Speeches* (1838), vol. II, p. 287.

without threatening common-law principles. The second wave of legislation identified by Dicey was really concerned with social reform, and with associated changes in substantive law: for instance, the improvement of factory conditions and the protection of workmen against loss from industrial injuries, the improvement of public health, the protection of the helpless and exploited, and removing the legal disabilities of the married woman. More recently this second movement has been attributed to the new middle class of businessmen and industrialists, who 'set about the creation of a wholly new kind of society in which administrative powers and processes replaced, as modes of social and economic control, the discipline of free choice and freedom of contract'.[104] There was here no obvious single programme, no theory of law to match Bentham's, but rather a series of solutions to problems brought to the fore by increasing public awareness and technical knowledge. This movement, if causally unrelated to the former, overlapped with it and depended on the same new machinery of reform, which began (in Benthamite spirit) with the search for information.[105] The parliamentary select committees and royal commissions which investigated in such minute detail the legal system could equally be employed in social enquiries, beginning (in 1832) with the condition of the poor. It was soon realised that society could not be changed overnight simply by reforming legal doctrine in accordance with the prevailing tenets of political economy. Principles gave way to pragmatism; even Bentham's utilitarianism, the greatest good of the greatest number, dissolved into political and economic disputes about what was good and how its achievement could be maximised. A major result of these changes was its neutralising effect on the judiciary. The courts felt themselves remote from such complexities of policy and incompetent to deal with them, and so they virtually gave up their law-making role; even in interpreting statutes, they took shelter behind the sovereignty of parliament and contented themselves with expounding the letter.[106] Parliament also introduced some legal solutions which operated outside the courts and depended a good deal on administrative discretion.[107] In modern times even the task of improving the common law and ironing out inconsistencies has, by the establishment of the

---

104 Atiyah, *Freedom of Contract*, p. 231.

105 The need for the fullest information, rather than received public opinion, as a prerequisite for reform was explicitly recognised in the 1830s: e.g. A. Mundell, *The Philosophy of Legislation* (1834), pp. 188-208. For the rise of the information revolution, see D. Eastwood, 62 BIHR 276.

106 See p. 242, ante.

107 See pp. 170, 171, 173-174, ante.

Law Commission in 1965, largely been withdrawn from the judges and from the adversary method of exploring problems. Law reform has itself been institutionalised.

Roman law began, and ended, with a code. However little the common law owed to Roman ideas, the example of the Romans was ever present, at least from the fifteenth century, as an inspiration to would-be codifiers of English law. The idea behind 'codification'[108] is that legal principles should be laid down authoritatively in written form, so as to dispel the doubts and uncertainties which may attend law derived from scattered cases or from juristic literature. In its most extreme form, the compilation of a code may involve rewriting the whole law, as in the case of the *Code Napoléon* (1804); at its least drastic, it is a matter of editing the existing sources of the law under legislative authority, as in the authentic collections of papal decretals found in the *Corpus Juris Canonici*. Many have been the visions of a code of English law, but little has been the practical achievement.

Two or three university men in Henry VIII's reign advocated the reduction of English law into a Latin code after the Roman example, but the only attempt at a draft chapter was not calculated to inspire confidence in the idea. A few years later Sir William Staunford, a Common Pleas judge, put forward the more attainable proposition of a digest of the common law, following the titles of Fitzherbert's *Abridgement*, but with the material so ordered that the governing principles were made apparent.[109] A generation later, Francis Bacon spent over twenty years working out a scheme for reshaping the law. In the parliament of 1593 he introduced his plan for reducing the volume of statutes, which were 'so many in number, that neither the common people can practise them nor the lawyer sufficiently understand them'. Four years afterwards, the task was committed to all the lawyer members of the House of Commons; but nothing seems to have been achieved. In 1607, James I invited parliament to scrape the rust off the laws, so that they 'might be cleared and made known to the subjects', a suggestion which he elaborated (probably at Bacon's prompting) in 1609. The idea was to reconcile conflicting decisions, discard obsolete source-material, and prepare an authoritative restatement of the law.

---

[108] The word was introduced into the English language by Bentham. For the European codification movement, see O. F. Robinson et al., *Introduction to European Legal History* (1985), ch. XVII.

[109] See p. 216, ante.

Bacon elaborated this plan in his *Proposition touching the Amendment of the Law* (1616), and called for digests of the common and statute laws, with law commissioners to revise them and keep them up to date. The prospect was daunting, and Bacon's hopes were not fulfilled. His own attempts to formulate the elements of the common law were as lacking in order and analysis as Coke's *Institutes*. Coke was against the project, because he thought abridgments only confused those who relied on them. If Coke and Bacon could not produce a code, who could?

Bacon's 'great law reform project' was very much a lawyer's scheme of the less drastic kind. He did not wish to abolish the common law and put all its principles into statutory form, because like most of his contemporaries he regarded written law as technically inferior: 'there are more doubts that arise upon our statutes, which are a text law, than upon the common law, which is no text law'.[110] He wished merely to arrange and prune the sources of the law in order to simplify research. Later projects tended to be more far-reaching. Hale, the most restrained of the Interregnum reformers, wanted to see a *Corpus Juris Communis* in the Roman manner; he alone could have written such a code, but we have seen how reluctant he was to put his learning into print even in treatise form. Less informed writers wanted a little booklet which could be carried in the pocket and read aloud in church on Sundays; none of them seems to have had the ability to prepare a draft. Bentham, as might be expected, went further than anyone. His ideal code was to be derived from the principle of maximum felicity, and was to take no account whatsoever of previous law; he thought he could as easily produce a code for Russia as for England, and very nearly did so. This was the age of codification, and Bentham lived to see the *Code Napoléon* adopted or imitated in many European countries. But he did not live to see even a draft English code, and his notions of codification, attacked in his lifetime,[111] have received no serious support since his death.

Some experiments in more modest forms of codification were carried out in the nineteenth century. Much of the common law was codified between 1830 and the 1860s for use in India, and to such good effect that the matter was reopened in England. In 1853 Lord Cranworth LC proposed a consolidation of statute law which he hoped would form a

---

110 *Life and Letters of Bacon*, vol. VI (J. Spedding ed., 1872), p. 67.
111 Notably by J. J. Park, *A Contre-Projet to the Humphreysian Code* (1828). Park (who became Professor of English Law at King's College London in 1831) attacked codification generally, but was particularly exercised by the outline code of real property law published in 1826 by James Humphreys, which had (perhaps damagingly) received Bentham's approval.

Code Victoria. The proposal foundered in a profusion of divergent ideas as to what it was meant to achieve; it was also pointed out that 'to reduce unwritten law to statute is to discard one of the great blessings we have for ages enjoyed in rules capable of flexible application'.[112] The principal outcome was the 1861 consolidation of criminal legislation; but there began in 1868 the long series of Statute Law Revision Acts, which pruned the statute book of obsolete matter, and in 1869 the office of parliamentary draftsman was created.[113] Lord Westbury C raised the question of codification in parliament in 1863, and his plea resulted in the establishment of a royal commission under the chairmanship of Lord Cranworth in 1866 'to enquire into the expediency of a Digest of Law'.[114] The commission recommended the preparation of digests of particular branches of the law, and jurists were invited to submit specimen drafts. At first it looked as though no one would be so bold or immodest as to take up the challenge, and in 1875 one writer said the scheme was universally considered worse than useless.[115] But in 1876 Sir James Fitzjames Stephen published his *Digest of the Law of Evidence*, and in the following year his *Digest of the Criminal Law*. Interest in the latter led to the appointment of another royal commission, which in 1879 actually produced a Criminal Code; but the enactment of this code was defeated after opposition from Cockburn LCJ. Meanwhile Pollock had published a *Digest of the Law of Partnership* (1877), and Judge Chalmers, acknowledging the example set by Stephen and Pollock, put out a *Digest of the Law of Bills of Exchange* (1878). The last-named was the first to reach the statute-book, as the Bills of Exchange Act 1882, followed by Pollock's work as the Partnership Act 1890. Chalmers also drew up a digest of the law of sale, which became the Sale of Goods Act 1893.[116] These digests were more in the tradition of Justinian, Staunford and Bacon than of Bentham. Their object was to restate in clear language the case-law of the time, all the texts being supportable by reference to the cases on which they were based. Chalmers believed this was the only way to start: 'I am sure,' he wrote in 1883, 'that further codifying measures can be got through Parliament if those in charge of them will not attempt

---

112 *Parliamentary Papers 1854*, vol. 53, p. 391, per Talfourd J.

113 The official title is parliamentary counsel to the Treasury. The first (1869-86) was Sir Henry Thring, who had previously drafted the Merchant Shipping Act 1854; he tried to reduce draftsmanship to scientific principles in *Practical Legislation* (1878). For the origins of the office, see B. McGill, 63 BIHR 110.

114 See T. E. Holland, 'Codification' (1867) 27 *Edinburgh Rev.* 347; *Plan for the Formal Amendment of the Law of England* (1867).

115 R. K. Wilson, *History of Modern English Law* (1875), pp. 184-185.

116 45 & 46 Vict., c.61; 50 & 54 Vict., c.39; 56 & 57 Vict., c.71.

too much. Let a codifying bill, in the first instance, simply reproduce the existing law, however defective. If the defects are patent and glaring, it will be easy enough to get them amended.'[117] Pollock took an even more conservative view of the function of a code: 'Codes are not meant to dispense lawyers from being learned, but for the ease of the lay people and the greater usefulness of the law. The right kind of consolidating legislation is that which makes the law more accessible without altering its principles or methods.'[118] There is little reason, however, why clear expositions of this nature should not remain in textbook form: what Maine called 'tacit codification'. Textbooks may guide without relying on force. Textbooks have indeed proliferated, whereas proposals for codification have abated, except in connection with specific projects for law reform. Since 1965 the Law Commission has had a standing charge to review the law with a view to its development, reform and possible codification.[119] The first fruits may be another criminal code.

Further reading

Holdsworth HEL, vol. II, pp. 299-311, 406-484; vols. IV and XI; vol. XII, pp. 146-162

Plucknett CHCL, pp. 315-350

J. W. Gough, *Fundamental Law in English Constitutional History* (1955)

C. K. Allen, *Law in the Making* (7th ed., 1964)

J. H. Baker, 'English Law and the Renaissance' [1985] CLJ 46-61 (repr. in LPCL 461-476

THE COMMON LAW

T. E. Lewis, 'The History of Judicial Precedent' (1930-32) 46 LQR 207-224, 341-360; 47 LQR 411-427; 48 LQR 230-247

J. U. Lewis, 'Coke's Theory of Artificial Reason' (1968) 84 LQR 330-342

J. P. Dawson, *Oracles of the Law* (1968), pp. 50-99

---

[117] *Digest of the Law of Bills of Exchange* (1964 ed.), p. xlii.

[118] *Digest of the Law of Partnership* (1915 ed.), p. viii.

[119] Law Commissions Act 1965 (c.22).

J. H. Baker, 'Pleading and Litigation as Sources of Law' (1978) 94 SS *142-163*; 'English Law as Case Law' in *Judicial Records, Law Reports, and the Growth of Case Law* (1989), at pp. 37-42

LEGISLATION

T. F. T. Plucknett, *Statutes and their Interpretation in the first Half of the 14th Century* (1922); 'Dr Bonham's Case and Judicial Review' (1926) 40 HLR 30-70; 'Ellesmere on Statutes' (1944) 60 LQR 242-249

H. G. Richardson and G. O. Sayles, 'The Early Statutes' (1934) 50 LQR 201-223, 540-571; *Law and Legislation from Aethelberht to Magna Carta* (1966); *The English Parliament in the Middle Ages* (collected essays, 1981)

S. E. Thorne, 'The Equity of a Statute and Heydon's Case' (1936) 31 *Illinois Law Rev.* 202-217 (repr. in EELH 155-170); 'Dr Bonham's Case' (1938) 54 LQR 543-552 (repr. in EELH 269-278); (ed.) *A Discourse upon the Exposicion & Understandinge of Statutes* (1942)

G. Barraclough, 'Law and Legislation in Medieval England' (1940) 56 LQR 75-92

C. M. Gray, 'Bonham's Case Revisited' (1972) 116 *Proc. American Philosophical Soc.* 35-58

D. E. C. Yale, 'Hobbes and Hale on Law, Legislation and the Sovereign' [1972B] CLJ 121-156

M. S. Arnold, 'Statutes as Judgments: the Natural Law Theory of Parliamentary Activity in Medieval England' (1977) 126 *Univ. Pennsylvania Law Rev.* 329-343

SEVENTEENTH-CENTURY LAW REFORM

M. Cotterell, 'Interregnum Law Reform: the Hale Commission of 1652' (1968) 83 EHR 689-704

D. Veall, *The Popular Movement for Law Reform* (1970)

B. Shapiro, 'Law Reform in 17th Century England' (1975) 19 AJLH 280-312; 'Sir Francis Bacon and the mid-17th Century Movement for Law Reform' (1980) 24 AJLH 331-362

N. L. Matthews, *William Sheppard: Cromwell's Law Reformer* (1985)

NINETEENTH-CENTURY LAW REFORM

A. V. Dicey, *Law and Public Opinion in England during the 19th Century* (1905)

C. H. S. Fifoot, *English Law and its Background* (1932), pp. 145-274;
   Judge and Jurist in the Reign of Queen Victoria (1959)

The Collected Works of Jeremy Bentham (J. H. Burns et al. ed., 1968-)

A. H. Manchester, 'Simplifying the Sources of the Law: an Essay in
   Law Reform' (1973) 2 *Anglo-American Law Rev.* 395-413, 527-
   550; *Modern Legal History* (1980)

P. S. Atiyah, *The Rise and Fall of Freedom of Contract* (1979), esp.
   chs. 8-9, 13, 16 and 20

H. Beynon, 'Mighty Bentham' (1981) 2 JLH 62-76

J. R. Dinwiddy, 'Early-Nineteenth Century Reactions to Benthamism'
   (1984) 34 TRHS (5th ser.) 47-69

G. Postema, *Bentham and the Common Law Tradition* (1986), and the
   bibliography there

B. Rudden, 'A Code too Soon: the 1826 Property Code of James
   Humphreys' in *Essays in Memory of F. H. Lawson* (1986), pp.
   101-116

D. Eastwood, '"Amplifying the Province of the Legislature": the Flow
   of Information and the English State in the Early Nineteenth
   Century' (1989) 62 BIHR 276-294

Part two
13. Real Property: Feudal Tenure

The most fundamental distinction in the English law of property was between real property (realty) and personal property (personalty). Land is a place to live for man and beast, a source of food and of all other commodities, including – if one has enough to let – money. It outlives its inhabitants, is immune from destruction by man, and therefore provides a suitably firm base for institutions of government and wealth. Control of land could not, indeed, be readily divorced from power and jurisdiction, from 'lordship'. Land for this reason became the subject of feudal tenure, which will be explained presently. Schemes of provision for the interests of successive members of landed families led in due course to an elaborate system of rules governing inheritance and estates, which will be considered in a later chapter. Personalty, on the other hand, was not subject to tenure, inheritance or future estates. We shall return to this distinction in later chapters.[1] In Roman law, and to some extent in the later common law, another fundamental distinction is that between ownership (a legal right) and possession (a fact). But the word 'owner' does not seem to have been much used by medieval lawyers: ownership is not an immutable legal idea,[2] any more than the French equivalent 'property'.[3] The Latin word for ownership, *dominium*, is particularly confusing, since in medieval times it is also the word for lordship. Certainly the starting point of our story is not ownership or property; it is tenure.

Tenure

Tenure is the name given to the relationship whereby a tenant 'holds' land of a lord. Holding, as opposed to owning, must be explained in

---

[1] Chs. 17, 21, post. The distinction between realty and personalty is not quite the same as that between land and chattels: see pp. 428-429, post.

[2] One of the earliest instances of its use in a legal text will be found in B. & M. 103 (c. 1490), where *le owner* is a person without legal title at all: the beneficiary under a use. The 'owner' of goods is mentioned in 1490: Stat. 4 Hen. VII, c.10, s.3.

[3] In medieval texts this normally denotes personalty. On these words, see further D. J. Seipp, 7 LHR 175.

terms of the 'feudal system' which was the economic basis of society at the time of the Norman conquest. Unfortunately, like many other shorthand expressions, the term 'feudal system' is an anachronism, a useful modern label for certain common features of medieval life which had no contemporary name given to them. Before historians gave it the label and started disagreeing about what it denoted, feudalism had been systematised by the lawyers, who made it into the intricate 'law of tenures' as expounded by Littleton in the fifteenth century. But Littleton was not a historian, and his system of tenures was not living feudalism; it was a legal fossil, preserved and analysed for good practical purposes far removed from those of historical understanding. The clarity of the law embodied in Littleton's *Tenures* has, in fact, proved a formidable obstacle to legal historians in trying to understand what went before. We may, however, safely start with the proposition that tenure was not in origin a legal concept at all, but a social fact, or a set of common assumptions: a state of affairs beyond precise legal definition.

We know that feudal institutions of a kind existed in Anglo-Saxon England, and elsewhere in contemporary Europe, in the sense that the occupation of land was commonly associated with vassalage, with bonds between lords and their men. Land given to reward a vassal was his 'fee'.[4] Every Anglo-Saxon man seems to have had a lord; but the seignorial relationship could nevertheless exist independently of the tenurial, by reason of 'commendation',[5] and the extent to which lordship and tenure had become entangled before the Norman conquest is an elusive question. Probably there was no theory that all land was held ultimately of the king: there could be allodial land.[6] The principal division of land-holdings was into folkland (held under custom) and bookland (held under a royal diploma varying the customary terms); but the full significance of these words is disputed, as is the extent to which they convey anything about feudalism.[7] Land 'books' may have been used at first to make grants in perpetuity to the Church; but by the ninth century they were also used for similar perpetual grants from the king to laymen, who were in return generally liable to military service.[8]

---

4   The Latin equivalent *feodum* or *feudum* is the root of the words 'feudal' and 'subinfeudation'. The French form *fief* is favoured by some English historians, but it was not used in law-French. In Scots law the form 'feu' is still used.

5   That is, by a person attaching himself to a lord with an oath of homage.

6   *Allodium* is land which is not held of any feudal superior.

7   For a summary of the lengthy controversy, see A. C. Kennedy, 14 *Anglo-Saxon England* 175.

8   Bookholders themselves made 'loans' of land to their own men in return for services. In each case performance of the services was enforced by forfeiture.

Whether or not the duty to serve was thought to arise from the tie of lordship or from the grant of land, the continuing tenure of the land depended on faithful service. It therefore seems that a kind of military tenure was already familiar before the conquest.

It is no accident, however, that feudalism suddenly comes into clear focus under William I. The conquest of England in 1066, and its ensuing occupation and settlement by a French élite, necessarily led to a renegotiation of landholding arrangements. The Normans displaced the English nobility who, having fought against the conqueror, were deemed traitors. In reallocating what had been forfeited, the important assumption was made that all land is held ultimately of the king; the possibility of *allodia* disappeared, as did commendation. The reallocation began in the 1070s, when the tenancies in chief – those held directly of the Crown – were concentrated in the hands of a few Norman families. In return for their holdings the tenants in chief owed the king loyalty and military service. These chief lords parcelled out their dominions in like manner, keeping some for themselves and distributing the rest in return for the loyalty and service of their own tenants. The transaction whereby a grantee of land was admitted to hold it as tenant of the grantor, in return for services, is now called 'subinfeudation': contemporaries called it an 'entry in the fee' of the grantor. The process of subinfeudation created a chain of tenures from the king down to the men who actually occupied the land.[9] As a matter of social history, it is unlikely that the occupation of land at the bottom end of the feudal chain was drastically disturbed by the conquest. The peasantry after 1066, the unnamed country folk of the Domesday survey (1086), kept their humble allotments and went about their daily chores much as they had done under the Saxon kings. Their immediate lords were sometimes the same Englishmen as had been their lords before 1066. The Norman feudal structure had been erected above them, and self-evidently it had no direct bearing on land ownership as now understood.

The relationship between Norman lord and tenant may be seen as contractual: and the contract was more like that for a tenured appointment than a sale of property. It was the conquest which brought this contractual aspect to the fore, since the reallocation of the 1070s

---

[9]   These last were called tenants in demesne, or terre-tenants. But free tenants in demesne might have unfree tenants below them.

and 1080s was in fact a series of bargains,[10] however unequal, whereby the duties owed by vassals became express terms. Every man's holding, except at the lowest level (where no bargaining occurred), had its fixed quota of services. The tenant bound himself to perform what had been settled as the consideration for his holding, and he forfeited his interest if he committed a fundamental breach of his contract by failing in the service, by committing an unpardonable crime, or by being unfaithful.[11] The lord in return protected the tenant as his man, guaranteed his security of tenure, and held court for him and for all his other tenants. But tenure was much more than a commercial bargain. It was a life-long bond, comparable in some respects with marriage, which also began by contract. *Glanvill* called it a mutual bond of trust.[12] The special relationship was sealed by the ceremony of homage, when the tenant knelt and placed his hands between those of his lord and swore to become his man in life and limb and earthly honour against all men except the king.[13]

A typical Norman baron would have held numerous parcels of land from the king or from other barons. Some of these would have been retained for his own use: his 'demesne land'. Most would have been subinfeudated to tenants, in consideration of services defined to meet his needs. In respect of these subinfeudated units the baron did not hold the land in demesne, but a 'seignory' (lordship) comprising the services and other profits due to him as lord.[14] The same held true of lesser landowners, except for the very poorest who had only enough land to work by themselves; these last were always tenants, never lords, the men at the end of the feudal chain.

Most of these lowest tenants held of manors. The manor had been an economic and social unit before the conquest, comprising a vill or hamlet of perhaps a hundred or so inhabitants, centred upon the mansion house or hall of a lord. In feudal legal theory the manor became a nucleus of tenants holding of the same lord and having a court

10 The mid-12th century author, R. FitzNigel, *Dialogus de Scaccario* (C. Johnson ed., 1983), p. 54, said that English tenants after the conquest held not by inheritance but by contract (*pactio*). The 13th-century canonists also analysed the feudal relationship as contractual: the fee was the consideration (*causa*) for the tenant's obligations.

11 See p. 572, post. It was on this ground that William I, claiming England by rightful succession, could displace those who had resisted his entry.

12 *Glanvill*, ix.4.

13 The similarity with the marriage ceremony was recognised in the rule that a woman could not use equivalent words, but should say 'I do unto you homage'. In Glanvill's time a woman could not do homage at all: *Glanvill*, ix.1.

14 As between the lord above him and the tenant below him he was called a 'mesne' (meaning 'intermediate').

to which they owed suit. This court controlled the agrarian activities of the manor, and often many other aspects of village life as well – from personal conduct to the manufacture of flour, bread and ale. Each manor was a little feudal state, with its own customs and legislation administered through its own supreme court. At the higher levels there were similar but larger states, called 'honours', with their customs and courts. Not until the common law took to overseeing these tribunals did the lord in his court become something less than a feudal sovereign whose decree was as good as law. And that, as we shall see, is how the common law of real property began.

THE VARIETY OF SERVICES

The nature of a lord's moral obligations to his sworn men was universal; the bond of homage and the receipt of service tied him, according to the common understanding of society, to warrant (guarantee) his men's tenancies against adverse claims and to do them justice. But the tenant's obligations were almost infinitely variable. At the upper end of the feudal order, as organised by the Normans, there were three main kinds of tenure: military, civil and spiritual. The principal military tenure was *knight-service*,[15] whereby the tenant was obliged in time of war to provide one mounted soldier in combat order for every knight's fee which he held. Other forms of military tenure were *castlegard* (garrison duty) and *cornage* (border patrol). In theory, military feudalism provided the king with a reserve army of many thousand troops. The military obligations of tenants in chief could be passed on by subinfeudation, and the under-tenants would also hold by knight-service. Civilian services were similarly provided for by feudal grants. Tenants in chief who were bound to perform personal services for the king were said to hold by *grand serjeanty*; and of this there were as many forms as there were services to be done, from looking after the king's wine to holding his head when he felt seasick. Other tenants might be required to provide things, such as horses, arrows or armour for military uses, wine or food for the king's palace, sheep-skins or wax for his bureaucracy. Such services, when due from tenants in chief, were called *petty serjeanty*. Spiritual tenure arose when grants were made to ecclesiastical bodies to hold by the regular celebration of *divine service*, or the general duty of saying prayers for the soul of the donor without any service being expressed (*frankalmoin*, free alms).

At the lower level the services were not always defined. The duties of the peasant were chiefly agricultural. If they were unfixed, so that

[15] The common lawyers sometimes called this *tenure in chivalry*.

the lord might in theory demand all manner of work, the tenure was 'unfree' and was called *villeinage*.[16] If they were fixed – for instance, helping the lord with sowing or reaping at specified times – the tenure was usually called *socage*. This was originally the tenure of socmen;[17] but it became (before Littleton's time) a generic term for all free services other than knight-service, serjeanty, or spiritual service.

Under a hypothetically perfect and complete feudal economy, the type of tenure would have denoted not merely the services due from a tenant but also his status and way of life. The king at the top had the greatest bargaining power, the peasant at the bottom none. Everyone had his place in the hierarchy: tenure, rank and economic position were interdependent. Knight-service and serjeanty denoted high rank; villeinage was the servile state of the peasant. Life was not, however, as neat as this in reality: or, if it once was, it did not long remain so. A man might hold different lands for different kinds of service, or the same land for a mixture of services. It was quite possible for a tenant to hold part of his lands by knight-service and another part by socage. Moreover, tenure by knight-service did not make the tenant a knight, any more than tenure in villeinage made him a villein.[18] When legal theory formed, there was no objection to a knight holding land in villeinage, or a villein by knight-service.

In any case, the feudal economy was not one in which land was the only medium of payment; even if it had been, the kind of bargaining which occurred under William I could not recur with every passing generation. Within two centuries of the Norman conquest, at most, the concept of buying services with land was dead. The main reason was that inheritance and alienability, both engrafted onto the system at an early stage,[19] worked against the contractual nature of the feudal relationship. The military system may have been the first to founder. Armies were only intermittently needed, and only by the king.[20] Service was normally limited to forty days in the year, with no provision for training. It is unlikely whether any army after Norman times was raised solely by the feudal levy, and the last serious levy of any kind was in 1327. Inheritance created additional problems. When

---

16 See further pp. 347, 532, post.

17 Bracton and Littleton derived 'socage' from an old word for 'plough'; but the root is soke, jurisdiction (p. 11, ante). For the transformation of socage and socmen, see S. Stoljar, 6 JLH 33.

18 For the distinction between villein tenure and villein status, see p. 532, post.

19 See pp. 264-266, 297-301, post.

20 *Glanvill*, ix.1 was written on the assumption that knights might have to fight for the lord in his private wars; but this was not the reality even in Glanvill's time.

knight's fees descended or were alienated to women, children, old men, or monasteries, personal service became impossible. The division of estates upon inheritance by coheirs or upon partial subinfeudation created fractions of knight's fees, and no tenant could be expected to find a fraction of a knight. Then again, the services fixed by an ancestor might not meet the requirements of the next generation; methods of warfare changed, and cavalry lost some of its importance to artillery. The only answer to such problems was to collect money from the tenants and use it to pay mercenaries. This was effected with respect to most knight's fees within the century after 1066. Actual knight-service was replaced by *scutage*, a payment based on the number of knights to be provided. When the king went to war, the rate of scutage was proclaimed and levied proportionately on the tenants of knight's fees. Probably these payments did not exempt tenants in chief from personal service, but if they were not inclined to the sword they could buy licences to stay at home. By the fourteenth century scutage itself had become largely obsolete, and money for wars was raised by other forms of taxation.

Similar commutations were made of other kinds of service. Hereditary servants are not necessarily the best, because even if their personal qualities are inheritable the sure expectation of an employment may remove the heir's impetus for training and self-improvement. Again, the practical solution was to commute the services to a money rent which the lord could spend on servants of his own choosing. As the need for feudal military service disappeared in the thirteenth century, lords increasingly retained men to fight in the king's courts or to manage their estates; but the growing professional classes took their fees in money, perhaps charged on land, rather than in grants of land. This pecuniary feudalism – called by historians 'bastard feudalism' – suited both parties; for reasons which will be disclosed in a moment, the lord by 1200 had less control over tenants of land than he had over men paid in cash, while the recipient often preferred the flexibility of a cash income which he could invest as and where he chose. By the middle of the thirteenth century hardly any personal services were being paid for with land, except at the lowest level. Knight-service and serjeanty were no longer exacted,[21] while most others had been commuted into monetary quit-rents which were losing value through inflation to the point where many were hardly worth collecting. Feudal

---

[21] The serjeanties which survived – a few even to the present day – were those which involved honourable services to the king (e.g. at coronations), services which *tenants* were anxious to preserve.

services, the original raison d'être of the feudal system, had therefore lost much of their economic significance two centuries before Littleton. Yet, as we shall see, the legal importance of tenure continued unabated.[22]

Feudalism and Land Ownership

If the question were posed, whether under the early feudal system the land was owned by the lord or the tenant, one could not give a direct answer without misleading. Feudal tenure was the antithesis of ownership as we know it. Before the advent of the common law, the tenant enjoyed few of the privileges which we now attribute to an owner. He could not do what he liked with the land. He could not sell it without the lord's consent. He could not pass it on to others by will, and there was no legally enforceable right of succession in his family after his death. His only protection against dispossession by the lord was the lord's moral or social obligation to protect his own men. The tenant's interest therefore stopped short at possession, which is a fact and not a legal right. The fact of being in possession as a feudal tenant was called 'seisin',[23] which originally was associated with the act of homage which clinched the lord's acceptance of his man.

For similar reasons, the interest of the lord could not accurately be called ownership, though his *dominium* certainly carries the sense of an ultimate property right: the lord had once had the land, and might have it again if the tenant's interest ceased. It may be that some lords were sufficiently heedless of their customary obligations to seize profits or dispossess their tenants when they felt like it; but that was not how the system was supposed to work, nor (as far as we can tell) was it the norm in practice. Performance of the lord's duty to guarantee his men's tenure was a point of honour; and in any case, so long as tenants performed their obligations, lords generally had no cause to unseat them. Problems could certainly arise if lords inadvertently[24] or dishonestly received homage from two men in respect of the same land. But, here again, the early solution rested on the fact of seisin. The unlucky claimant had a grievance, and was entitled (under the lord's warranty) to be compensated by the lord with land of equal value, but

---

22   See pp. 271-279, post.

23   It is probable that *seisire* was originally a transitive verb, meaning to admit a tenant. The lord seised the tenant, the tenant was seised; but only the reflexive terminology (being seised) survived.

24   E.g. if a lord received tenant *A*, and then the lord's heir (unaware of *A*'s position) received tenant *B*.

the claim was essentially contractual: there was no question of upsetting seisin by reference to some more abstract notion of title. Another kind of problem arose if the tenant failed to perform his obligations. Here the lord's court could compel the tenant to answer for his default, and in the last resort disseise him. This seems to be the earliest sense of 'disseise': to unseat by judgment, to rescind the feudal contract rather than to break it.

In this feudal world, then, we should think in terms of seisin rather than ownership. The tenant was seised of the land, and the lord was seised of the tenant's services, but neither of them 'owned' the land in any absolute sense. Even if the land came back to the lord, he was then seised of it as tenant of someone else. Only the king was not a tenant; but no king after William I had the kind of control exercised in the 1070s, and no one thought of the lord king as being in any meaningful sense *owner* of all the land in England.

This description of feudal tenure is, of course, an over-simplification. And if the pristine feudal system had once exhibited the characteristics sketched above, the legal position by 1200 was very different. Two forces combined to strengthen, and in strengthening to transform, the interest of the tenant. The first of these forces was custom. As soon as the records of manorial courts begin,[25] we see that lords did not generally act as autonomous despots, but through feudal courts. Such courts were attended by all the lord's tenants, and purported to follow the customs of each manor. Manorial customs tied the lord's hands very considerably, and most lords probably submitted to the restraint, just as kings submitted to their own law; their power was more secure for being regularised. The customs which made the most impact were those which governed the devolution of land on the death of a tenant.[26] In most places there were customs of inheritance: where a tenant held under such a custom, close members of his family had the expectation of succeeding him, and the lord was supposed to accept the heir into his homage on the same terms as his ancestor. But custom alone could not make inheritance a legal right of succession. Even if the expectation of succeeding could be described as hereditary, seisin itself – the fact of the lord's acceptance – was not. Until the expectant heir did homage he was not seised; if he was passed by, and someone else did homage and took seisin, the expectation was

25 It is true that they do not begin until after the second of our factors (the common law) has come into play; but the assumption of the 12th century writ of right and novel disseisin (discussed below) is that a lord acts 'justly' through a court. Records of superior seignorial courts have not survived at all.

26 For the variety of customs of inheritance, see further pp. 303-304, post.

effectively frustrated. A person might be passed over in favour of a more remote relative for a number of good reasons: for instance, if he was not around to make his claim, or if he was thought personally unfit, or if there was no clear rule as to the choice of heir. Some manorial courts took the trouble to formulate qualifications of their customs to meet such exigencies; some even changed their customs, with the express agreement of the tenants.[27] But whether customs were modified, reformed, reversed, or utterly disregarded, could make no legal difference within the world of the uncontrolled feudal court. The decisions of a lord's court were necessarily final; they were more administrative than judicial. A custom governing succession might be a widespread social fact and a moral influence on the court; it might encourage a strong expectation based on precedent; yet seisin was still the only fact which in practice meant anything. And seisin there could not be without a compact between two living people. Only the lord could 'seise' his tenant, and the lord was bound to honour that seisin until the tenant died.

The second, and still more effective, force restraining seignorial absolutism was the common law. At an early date the king, both as the ultimate feudal superior and as the fountain of justice within his realm, took upon himself the surveillance of all feudal authority; where lords failed to do right the king would act. It became a saying in the twelfth century that no one was bound to answer in his lord's court for any free tenement without an order from the king.[28] This meant a writ of right 'patent',[29] whereby the king ordered a lord to maintain the 'full right' of someone who claimed to hold of him as a free tenant but was being kept out.[30] It seems unlikely that when this procedure began it introduced any new thinking about property. Although it had an earlier ancestry, the background to its introduction in its classical form was probably Henry II's promise to restore the inheritances of those displaced in the civil war of Stephen's reign (1135-54). Its immediate meaning was no more than that the lord was to do the right thing, as understood in that context, and the royal command may have been necessary to authorise lords to disseise (unseat) their acknowledged men.

---

27   See p. 303, post.

28   It is so stated in *Glanvill*, xii.2, 25. Milsom says it should be read more as a statement of fact than as a rule of law: *Legal Framework of English Feudalism*, pp. 57-58.

29   Patent means 'open'. For the formula, see p. 612, post; and for some proceedings in writs of right, see B. & M. 11-21.

30   These last words excluded claims to land held by villein tenure: as to which see pp. 347-348, post.

The use of the royal writ, with an 'or else' clause,[31] also meant that the king's court could take over if the lord failed to do this, as well lords might if they took the feudal warranty seriously.[32]

The protection of this 'right' by common law brought about, perhaps unconsciously, a substantial change of thinking. Someone who was out of seisin could now claim as a right to oust someone who was in seisin. Right was 'higher' than possession. In the writ *praecipe in capite*,[33] used where the claimant sought to hold in chief of the king, the claim in the writ was worded as 'right and inheritance'. But in both types of action the right which could drive out the sitting tenant was hereditary; and the plaintiff's count had to trace it from an ancestor seised in or before the time of Henry I. No doubt the thinking behind these remedies was simply that existing customs as to inheritance should be applied, starting with an ancestor in stable times; the result of insisting on descent from a previous generation was nevertheless more profound. A right to seisin was no longer just a right to be chosen if and when a vacancy occurred; it could now be enforced immediately, at the expense of the person with actual seisin, and therefore – if less directly – at the expense of the lord who had given it to him. Where once the fact of seisin had been all that mattered, the tenant in seisin now had a precarious interest. Even a tenant who had been put in seisin by the lord's court, and had done homage, was liable to be dislodged as a result of historical enquiries into events which might have occurred before he or his lord were born, perhaps even before the writ of right had been invented.[34] The choice of an heir by the lord's court had therefore ceased to be a purely administrative act; it was a judgment subject to review if it broke the rules.

An important result of this change, and perhaps the practical intention behind the writ of right, was to give the rightful claimant to land more than just a contractual right. His right under the lord's warranty was to compensation with other land; but that was only an adequate remedy if the lord had other land. The effect of the writ of right was that he recovered the land itself, and it was the displaced

---

[31] The writ provided for the sheriff to do right if the lord refused. The procedure was to remove the case into the county court by writ of tolt, and from thence into the king's court by *pone*. Right patent, tolt and *pone* soon come to be seen simply as three steps in the process of commencing a suit in the king's court.

[32] Milsom, *Legal Framework of English Feudalism*, pp. 58-60. As to whether they did, see J. Biancalana, 88 *Columbia Law Rev.* at 454.

[33] For the formula, see p. 614, post.

[34] See the case of 1199 discussed in Milsom, *Legal Framework of English Feudalism*, p. 181; and also *De Mara v. Bohun* (1198-1207) B. & M. 11.

tenant who now had to look for compensation.[35] The lord's sovereignty was beginning to evaporate in the process. At this point we may even dare to say the law has begun to recognise something like ownership in the tenant; for the 'right' to seisin is an abstract legal concept which transcends actual seisin and can be invoked to displace it. In non-feudal language, seisin has become the bare fact of possession, as against the hereditary legal right of the owner.

Hereditary right depends on history, perhaps (in practical terms) ancient history. It is difficult to guess how far back local memory could have stretched in the twelfth century, but the reliable tracing of ancestral seisin beyond human memory must have been virtually impossible, for want of written records. The ordinary mode of trial in the writs of right was battle, which recognised that such claims could only be tested by a form of ordeal. The violence and uncertainty of battle must nevertheless have seemed a high price to pay for the new remedy: whatever the theory, a man with the means to hire a good champion could too easily abuse the system and dispossess the weak. Henry II introduced for defendants in 1179 the 'royal benefit' of choosing the grand assize, a form of jury, to enquire into the right; this concession to human reason enabled questions other than that of first seisin to be raised, such as a grant from the demandant's ancestor, and the procedure also necessitated removing a dispute into the king's court.[36] But the lingering possibility of battle, especially in cases where the demandant's claim was likely to convince an assize, was one of the reasons why claimants regarded writs of right as a last resort.

THE PETTY ASSIZES

An alternative and more direct way of controlling feudal lords was also invented in the reign of Henry II. Whereas the writ of right was designed to settle the ultimate right for all eternity, through the solemnities of judicial combat, the 'petty assizes' of Henry II were intended to produce a speedy enquiry by neighbours into more readily ascertainable questions of fact. The assizes did not go into the right, but protected the status quo against wrong.

---

[35] He could recover it in the adverse writ of right itself, by 'vouching to warranty' the lord under whom he claimed; the lord then took over the defence, and if he failed to win the action the losing tenant was given judgment to recover land of equal value against him.

[36] *Glanvill*, ii.7. The grand assize was introduced by the Assize of Windsor 1179: J. H. Round, 31 EHR 268.

The assize of novel disseisin[37] caused an enquiry to be made as to whether the plaintiff had been recently disseised of his free tenement,[38] 'unjustly and without judgment'; if it was found that he had been, he would be restored to seisin by judgment of the king's justices. A criminal procedure for investigating disseisin had been introduced in the 1150s, to deal with problems caused by the civil strife of King Stephen's reign, especially in relation to depredations of Church land; the undated assize established the private remedy soon afterwards, perhaps in the 1160s. Most probably the typical defendant at that time was not a rival tenant, but a lord acting 'without judgment'; and so the policy behind the assize may have been simply to encourage the proper use of lords' courts and writs of right patent. But the remedy could equally be used by lords against encroaching tenants.[39] The change to a wider use may have been accelerated because growing numbers of lords had no courts,[40] or did not care to use them.[41] Disseisin, by losing its feudal connotation of being removed by a lord, came to mean physical dispossession. And in the process the jurisdiction of seignorial courts to disseise tenants (for non-performance of their obligations) disappeared: lords, like tenants, were now supposed to resort to the common law to protect their interests. Once again, the lord's control was becoming less important.

Another of the petty assizes was that of mort d'ancestor, founded on the Assize of Northampton 1176. The question in this assize was whether the plaintiff's father (or other close ancestor) had been seised in fee – that is, of an inheritable estate – on the day he died, and whether the plaintiff was his next heir; if both questions were answered in the

---

37 For the formula, see p. 618, post; and for specimen proceedings, see B. & M. 30-36.

38 Again the villein tenant was deliberately omitted. In many early assizes the real question was whether the tenement was free or unfree: Milsom, *Legal Framework of English Feudalism*, pp. 21-24, 167-168. The remedy may have been most needed at lower levels, where lords continued to have more say and where customs of succession were more varied.

39 See *Glanvill*, ix.11. Professor Biancalana gives some earlier examples in 88 *Columbia Law Rev.* at 479-480.

40 Every subinfeudation created a new lordship; but the vendor, outside the manorial context, had no reason to keep court for his purchaser, and if he had no other tenants to serve as suitors he could not do so. In classical common-law theory a court could not be created merely by subinfeudation but had to be immemorial: *Clerk v. Ferour* (1320) 104 SS 25; *Anon.* (1541) Bro. N.C. 132, 178.

41 In the 13th century a new deterrent to the exercise of feudal jurisdiction was the increasing use of writs of false judgment, which might result in a lord being amerced: see J. V. Capua, 27 AJLH 54.

affirmative, the plaintiff was entitled to be put in seisin.[42] This assize also was initially aimed against lords (or their recent grantees), compelling them to admit heirs in accordance with customs of inheritance, and incidentally depriving their courts of any discretion in the matter. Mort d'ancestor could only be used by children, siblings and nephews (or nieces) of the deceased, since those were the clearest cases; it was supplemented in the early thirteenth century by writs available to grandsons, great-grandsons, and other kinsmen,[43] so that the common law gradually came to control the choice of heir in every case. The assumption, as in the writ of right, was that the heir now succeeded automatically, and did not need acceptance (other than formally) by the lord's court.[44] But, unlike the writ of right, the assize worked by investigating only a specific question of recent history.

WRITS OF ENTRY

The assizes as first conceived were concerned with recent events: the death of an ancestor in seisin, or a 'novel' (recent) disseisin. A claim which went beyond such matters of current knowledge had to be raised differently. But the writ of right did not remain for long the only alternative. In the thirteenth century a wide range of special *praecipe* writs developed, chiefly designed (it seems) for the use of lords against tenants who had been admitted under earlier grants which were either invalid or no longer availed them. These writs followed the wording of writs of right by reciting a hereditary claim of right but went on to specify some flaw in the means by which the defendant had 'entered' the land. Thus, if the defendant had entered by reason of a grant made by the plaintiff's ancestor, the plaintiff could anticipate his defence by stating in his writ that the grant was invalid, thereby forcing the defendant to take issue on that point rather than on the right at large. The additional clause asserted that the defendant 'had no entry except by' the means then set out; and this explains their collective name, 'writs of entry'. The earliest may have been the writ of gage, to recover land handed over as security for a debt which had later been paid. This led to the writ of entry *ad terminum qui praeteriit*, where a tenant had been

---

42   For the formula, see p. 616, post; and for specimens of proceedings, see B. & M. 25-30.

43   The writs of aiel (grandfather), besaiel (great-grandfather) and cosinage (any other blood relationship). These were in the form *praecipe quod reddat*.

44   According to *Glanvill* (vii.9; ix.1, 4), silently glossing the Assize of Northampton 1176, the heir may retain the inheritance but must offer to do homage and pay any dues; the lord may take the fee into his hand 'gently', without 'disseising' the heir, until the identity of the heir is settled, but is then to receive his homage at once.

admitted for a term of life or years, and the term had expired. Soon there were almost as many types as there were defects in title:[45] for example, the writs of entry *dum non fuit compos mentis* and *dum fuit infra aetatem* (where a grant had been made by an insane or infant ancestor), *cui in vita* (where a husband granted away his wife's land, and after his death she sought its return), and *sur disseisin* (where an ancestor had been disseised). At first the writs of entry were limited in their scope by 'the degrees': there could not be more than two steps (degrees) in the chain set out as the defective title.[46] But in 1267 parliament extended the scope of writs of entry so that they would lie against claimants in any degree ('in the *post*').[47]

The writs of entry went further into the past than the assizes, and were therefore concerned more with right than with protecting the status quo; and yet by confining enquiry to specific historical facts they enabled battle to be avoided. That was a major attraction for plaintiffs. Moreover the writs of entry, as was appropriate if the plaintiff was a lord seeking to remove a tenant, gave plaintiffs direct access to the king's courts.[48]

LATER HISTORY OF THE REAL ACTIONS

All these remedies were developed in a feudal context, and the initial policy behind them was probably no more profound than that, to assist recuperation from an era of anarchy, there should be some way of compelling lords to do right to the dispossessed. They were not, therefore, designed to curtail feudalism or to introduce new notions of property. That was, nevertheless, very soon their effect. The lord's court ceased to be able to remove tenants, whether to expel them for wrongdoing or to instal someone with better right, and the common law took over. The old writ of right patent, intended to make lords' courts investigate a claimant's right, then came to be simply a cumbersome way of starting an action at common law: so cumbersome

---

45 For a specimen formula, see p. 614, post; and for examples of proceedings upon such writs, see B. & M. 22-24.

46 The furthest reach was achieved in entry 'in the *per* and *cui*': i.e. the defendant had no entry except through (*per*) A, to whom (*cui*) B had granted.

47 Statute of Marlborough 1267, c.29. This said that if plaintiffs could not use an existing writ of entry, they could have a writ without mentioning the degrees. In such cases the writ stated that the defendant had no entry except 'after' (*post*) the disseisin or defective grant, omitting the links.

48 A writ of right would have had to be brought in the court of the lord's lord, and then removed by tolt and *pone*; then the demandant would have had to proffer money for a jury to consider the invalidity of the grant. (For such a proffer in 1210, see B. & M. 22.)

indeed, since it required removal from the lord's court by tolt and *pone*, that it went out of use. A less cumbrous procedure was for the plaintiff to bring a writ of right in the king's court *quia dominus remisit curiam suam* (because the lord has waived his court); already in the thirteenth century this was the usual course. But the writ of right was not as popular as the assizes, which handled more manageable questions in a more direct and expeditious way.

The history of novel disseisin between the thirteenth and fifteenth centuries was one of continuous and even strained expansion. The subject matter was extended beyond land to include such things as rent-charges and offices. The novelty required of the disseisin was relaxed, because the limitation period ran from a fixed date which was not moved forward. And the notion of unjust disseisin was extended to include the acceptance of a tortious conveyance, such as a conveyance from a minor; this enabled the assize to do some of the work of writs of entry. Then the idea of seisin was broadened from actual possession to include an attempt to gain possession by someone entitled to enter. This was an extraordinary turn; for now, if A had a right to enter on land of which B was seised, and B prevented his entry, this might be a disseisin of A by B for which A could bring the assize.[49] The assize thus ceased to be concerned purely with factual questions of dispossession, and was being used to try rights of entry. Not that everyone with a right to land had a right of entry. Originally a person who was disseised was allowed but a few days to re-enter with force, after which he was obliged to seek his remedy at law; the disseisor had gained seisin. In the fourteenth century, however, many of the restrictions on rights of entry were removed, particularly by the doctrine of 'continual claim', which enabled them to be preserved for a long time provided there was notionally a continuous claiming of the right and a keeping out. As a result of these changes, the assize became a 'droitural' action – that is, it tried right rather than recent possession – and by 1400 the writs of right and entry had been largely driven out of use, except as a last resort where the assize for some reason was not available.

From about 1400 the assize itself began to decline, and was replaced by a miscellaneous array of personal actions: replevin, detinue of title deeds, trespass *quare clausum fregit*, actions on the statutes of forcible entry, and (in Tudor times) ejectment. The feudal dimension had completely gone. In 1413 it was argued that the use of trespass to try

---

[49] E.g., *Anon.* (1334) B. & M. 36.

title was an innovation which ought to be stifled; but Thirning CJ, admitting the change of practice, defended it on the grounds that trespass could be tried in banc, whereas the assize was subject to 'great maintenance in the country'.[50] The fact that assizes were not brought in the central courts also created archival problems; although these could be solved by removing the record into the Common Pleas, this was an added expense. Another reason for the eclipse of the assize was the complexity of the rules of pleading and procedure which had been occasioned by its transformation from a simple purpose to a complex one. Trespass, in contrast, enabled a straightforward question of title to be put to a common jury. Although it was a personal action which lay only for damages, it was not beyond the ingenuity of the legal mind to escape even that difficulty. This last change, when it came in the sixteenth century,[51] enabled the law of title to real property to be freed from the shackles of medieval rules of pleading rooted in the feudalism of a distant age.

The Lord's Rights at Common Law

The principal effect of these common-law remedies was that by the thirteenth century the tenant was in reality the owner of the land. The lord's rights in his seignory were more like a charge on the tenant's property than the dominion which once they had been.

OWNERSHIP OF SERVICES

The services, as we have seen, became in many cases a rent payable to the lord. But whereas lords had under the earlier regime enforced the feudal contract in their own courts, the advent of the common law turned the entitlement to services into a common-law right. The old remedy had been to distrain the tenant, by seizing his chattels, and then his land, to make him attend the lord's court and answer, with the ultimate possibility of disseisin by judgment; but, with the decline of the court's authority, distraint became a measure of extrajudicial self-help, confined to chattels, and reviewable in the royal courts. The usual method of review by the time of Edward I was replevin. This required the lord, through the intervention of the sheriff, to restore the tenant's goods[52]

---

[50] Y.B. Hil. 14 Hen. IV, fo. 35, pl.52, at fo. 36. 'Maintenance' here means the use of improper pressure on sheriffs and jurors.

[51] For the extension of ejectment, see pp. 341-343, post.

[52] If the lord had 'eloigned' (removed) the goods, then the tenant resorted to 'withernam', a procedure under which the sheriff took other goods of equal value.

on the tenant giving surety (*plevine* in French) to bring an action and return the goods if he lost; the tenant then sued the lord for taking the goods, and the lord 'avowed' (made his claim) for the services.[53] The lord's avowry had to be based on seisin of the services: originally by performance to himself or his immediate ancestor, after 1285 by performance within a limitation period.[54] If a tenant subinfeudated, and then failed to perform his services, the lord could distrain on the under-tenant, who then had to seek his remedy (by writ of mesne) against the intermediate lord, both for restitution and to compel the latter to perform in future.

The services thus ceased to be contractual in reality or theory, and became as much a property right as the tenant's right to the land. They were themselves the subject of seisin, acquired when the tenant performed. Thus, if the lord could not use self-help – for instance, if the tenant was absent and had left nothing distrainable on the land – he was driven to use a writ of right for customs and services, or the assize of novel disseisin. These actions enabled him only to recover the services; but by a statute of 1278[55] he was given the better remedy of recovering the land itself (by writ of *cessavit*) where the tenant ceased to perform for at least two years.

INCIDENTS OF TENURE

We have seen that by the early 1200s the Norman system of feudal economy, of buying services with land, was virtually dead; existing services, if demanded at all, were mostly turned into rent and were losing value through inflation; military service had become little more than abstract theory; and yet tenure was if anything growing in legal importance. The reason is that services were not the only right which the common law gave to the lord. The casual side-effects of tenure were becoming at least as valuable as the services, and in many cases more so. Indeed, long before Littleton expounded the law of tenures, the principal attractions of being a feudal lord, at any rate a lord with numerous tenants, were neither the services nor the jurisdiction but the

---

53 For a specimen writ, see p. 612, post. After the Statute of Westminster II 1285, c.2, the proceedings were usually removed from the county into the royal courts: for the motives behind the statute, see P.A. Brand, 31 AJLH 43-48.

54 Statute of Westminster II, c.2, s.2; see P.A. Brand, 31 AJLH 48-51. Rare claims based on more remote seisin could be made by the *praecipe* writ of customs and services in the *debet* ('Command A. that he perform for B. the customs and services which he ought to perform').

55 Statute of Gloucester, c.4. Some limitations were removed by the Statute of Westminster II (1285), c.21. The legislation in effect gave back to lords the remedy they had once enjoyed in their own courts.

windfalls which might be expected from time to time as 'incidents' of the tenurial relationship.

Had feudal lords resisted the control of the common law, these incidental benefits would have been whatever they could exact from their tenants within the constraints of custom. However, a necessary result of subjecting feudalism to the control of the king's courts was that seignorial powers were restricted and defined by law.[56] The incidents of tenure as defined in the law books represented what was left to lords after this had happened: they were the vestiges of a notional suzerainty which had been cut down to a standard of reasonableness. Like the services, they became in the thirteenth century another species of property: a charge on the tenant's land, protected first by distraint and then (in the alternative) by another range of *praecipe* actions introduced in the course of the century.

1. Aids

The omnipotent lord might exact financial contributions ('aids') from his tenants to assist him in meeting any financial difficulties. Since a power of random confiscation was inconsistent with the status of free men,[57] it was curtailed by law. By Magna Carta, aids were limited to three cases: where the lord needed money to ransom himself from captivity, or to knight his eldest son, or to provide a dowry for his eldest daughter. Such aids were to be reasonable, and in 1275 the two last were fixed at twenty shillings per knight's fee or per £20 of socage land.[58] The king was not to levy other aids without the consent of the great council of the realm; but taxation by the king in parliament did not need to confine itself to feudal forms, and it was destined to outlive the incidents of tenure.

2. Fines on alienation

Because tenure was a personal relationship, alienation of the land by substitution – that is, by replacing one tenant with another – required the consent of the lord. And if real consent was required, it could be charged for: the fine for licence to alienate. The fine was not generally payable on subinfeudation, which did not disturb the relationship between the vendor and his lord.[59] Fines for alienation were abolished

---

[56] This did not happen in respect of villeins until much later. But in their case a similar restraint was imposed by manorial custom: p. 348, post.

[57] It was tolerated in relation to villeins until Tudor times: p. 533, post.

[58] Magna Carta 1215, cl.12 and 15; Statute of Westminster I 1275, c.36. Cf. *Glanvill*, ix.8.

[59] See p. 298, post. There may have been an exception in the case of tenants in chief: see the order of 1256 in B. & M. 9.

when alienation by subinfeudation was ended in 1290; but the legislation did not bind the Crown, and so fines from tenants in chief continued to add to the royal revenues until the seventeenth century. By a statute of 1327, however, the Crown was restricted to a 'reasonable' fine; and by custom this came to be settled as one third of the annual value of the land.[60]

3. Relief and primer seisin

On the death of a tenant, the land went back ('reverted') to the lord. If the tenant's interest had been merely for life, the lord was then free to choose a new tenant. But if the tenant's interest had been inheritable, the lord was bound to admit the tenant's heir in his place. Before inheritance was defined and protected by the common law, lords might seize the land and take the profits for themselves until the heir bought back the land by paying 'relief';[61] unscrupulous lords might even frustrate inheritance by demanding excessive relief. When the law began to protect inheritance, the lord might still claim to take the deceased tenant's land into his hands until the new tenant did homage; this 'primer seisin' entitled the lord to the profits during the feudal limbo, and was also a security to ensure that the tenant paid relief. The common law necessarily regulated such claims, which if abused would obstruct the heir's emergent legal rights. As early as the 1160s, the relief for a knight's fee was fixed at five pounds and other reliefs had to be reasonable; the reasonable relief for socage land was held to be one year's profits.[62] Primer seisin was abolished in 1267, except for the king's rights over his tenants in chief;[63] in the latter case it remained a valuable royal prerogative until the seventeenth century.

4. Escheat

If a tenant in fee died without leaving an heir, the land necessarily fell to the lord by way of escheat.[64] Likewise, if the tenant was convicted of felony, his land fell to the lord. This latter kind of escheat was later called 'forfeiture'.[65] Forfeiture in its original sense occurred when a

---

[60] Stat. 1 Edw. III, sess.ii, c.12; Robert Constable's reading on *Prerogativa Regis* (Thorne ed., 1949), pp. 155-156.

[61] Relief (*relevium* in Latin) was a payment for 'taking up' an inheritance.

[62] R. FitzNigel, *Dialogus de Scaccario* (1983 ed.), pp. 96-97; *Glanvill*, ix.4; confirmed by Magna Carta 1215, cl.2.

[63] Statute of Marlborough 1267, c.16.

[64] The word derives from *eschier*, to fall.

[65] The means of recovery was, nevertheless, the same 'writ of escheat' as was used in the other case.

tenant committed treason: in that case his land went to the Crown, and the rights of mesne lords were extinguished.

5. Customary dues

In many places there were customary obligations to be performed on the death of either the lord or the tenant, and the common law allowed these if they were reasonable. The most widespread was the custom of heriot, which entitled the lord to seize the best beast or chattel of a deceased tenant. Such customs, however, far more commonly affected unfree than free tenures.

6. Wardship and marriage

If a deceased tenant's heir was under age, and so unable to perform his feudal obligations, he was subject to wardship. The land came back to the lord during the infancy, so that he might be compensated out of the income for the loss of services, and the lord in return was supposed to raise the ward, seeing if need be to his military training. The common law did not suppress wardship; but some regulation was necessary. The very least requirement was that the heir should inherit all the capital that his ancestor left, and so Magna Carta forbade guardians to commit waste in their wards' lands. In respect of the income, however, a difference arose between military tenure and socage. The guardian in socage, usually a near relative of the infant heir, was effectively turned into a trustee who (after 1267) could be compelled to render an account to the heir when he came of age at 14.[66] In the case of military tenure, by contrast, the guardian was the feudal lord and there was no accountability: even when actual military service was no longer exacted, guardians unashamedly helped themselves to the profits of the land until the ward was 21.

Guardians received into ward not only the heir's land but also the heir's body.[67] Perhaps this originated as a form of protection for the ward – apologists argued that grasping relatives could not be trusted with the heir's life – but again it was exploited for profit. The guardian was entitled to select a suitable marriage for the ward, and because arranging marriages for young heirs and heiresses involved substantial transfers of wealth, this right could be highly valuable. No marriage could be forced on unwilling children, because consent was a requisite of true matrimony;[68] but if a ward declined a suitable marriage when it

---

[66] Magna Carta 1215, cl.4-5 (1225, cc.4-5); Statute of Marlborough 1267, c.17.

[67] If the heir had two or more lords, the lord of the oldest tenure took the body; but if the heir held some land of the king, the king was entitled to the body by his prerogative.

[68] See p. 546, post.

was offered, he or she had to compensate the lord to the value of the marriage. And if a ward married without the lord's consent, he or she incurred the penalty (after 1236) of remaining in ward until the lord had received double the value of the marriage. The only legal concession made to the infant was that a guardian should not disparage his ward by offering a marriage with someone who was either legally unsuitable (such as a widow, a bastard, or a villein) or physically unsuitable (such as a leper, a deformed or blind person, or a woman beyond the age of child-bearing).[69]

THE VALUE OF INCIDENTS

Those incidents which were fixed in monetary terms suffered the same economic fate as the services. But those which were tied to the value of the land, or gave a right to take the profits of the land, were inflation-proof. The most profitable for lords, and the most onerous to tenants, were therefore those incidents which attached on a descent to an heir, especially if the heir held by knight-service and (as often happened) was under age. Being casual windfalls, these death duties did not provide a regular source of income except for great lords who had many tenants. But, until means were found of avoiding descents, the incidents fell due whenever a tenant in fee died, and that was an event he could not avoid. The greatest profits of all came to the Crown, which was ultimate lord of all land in the realm and also had special prerogative rights which other lords did not possess. On the death of a tenant in chief, the king's escheator seized all his lands until an inquisition post mortem had ascertained the king's rights. In addition to the rights of a common lord, the king had primer seisin (a year's profits) and priority as to wardship before all other lords of whom lands had been held. The value of the feudal revenue to the Crown explains why the feudal system of tenures was preserved by the law long after its purpose, in terms of services, had become obsolete. It explains why, as late as 1536, when confiscated monastic lands were granted out, all the grants were made for an antiquated Norman service which no one performed; knight-service attracted wardship. The most important legislation concerning real property, from 1215 to 1540, was directed principally at the preservation of the incidents of tenure from devaluation or avoidance.

---

69   Magna Carta 1215, cl.6 (1225, c.6); reading thereon, CUL MS. Hh. 2. 6, fo. 8; Provisions of Merton 1236, cc. 6-7; Littleton, *Tenures*, s.109. For the variety of issues raised in early litigation about wardship, see S. S. Walker, 9 JLH 267.

MORTMAIN

Grants to corporations – mostly religious houses – had always been damaging to feudal lords, since corporations were immortal and had no heirs. A grant to a corporation meant putting the property into a dead hand, an 'alienation in mortmain'. It suggested an early means of avoiding incidents. The tenant alienated his land to a monastic house in order to hold it of the house, arranging to acquit the monks in respect of the services to the chief lord, and providing some other consideration; the interposition of a corporation between the tenant and the chief lord prevented the accrual to the latter of any of the incidents which would have arisen on the tenant's death. This was prevented by Magna Carta: if land was given to a religious house in order to resume it again to hold of the same house, it was forfeited to the chief lord.[70]

But even a genuine charitable gift to a monastery had the same effect on the lord's incidents, and in 1279 a more sweeping reform was introduced.[71] All alienations in mortmain were forbidden, whatever the purpose. The Crown was nevertheless understood to have the power to grant licences of exemption from this prohibition, and so gifts to monasteries remained possible after a proper composition had been made for the loss of incidents. The last vestiges of the mortmain legislation remained in the law until 1960.

QUIA EMPTORES TERRARUM 1290

Once the system of paying for services with land became obsolete, the principal feudal aspect of conveyancing was that the method chosen might affect the value of the lord's incidents. If property was sold to raise money, the vendor could either put the purchaser in his place as tenant (substitution) or make the purchaser his own tenant (subinfeudation). The latter was preferable for the vendor, because it did not require the lord's approval, and because the vendor retained a seignory which might yield occasional profits, perhaps even an escheat. The purchaser, on the other hand, lost nothing by substitution that he would have gained by substitution.[72] The only loser was the vendor's lord. When his tenant died possessed of the land in demesne, leaving an infant heir, the lord had wardship of the land and could take the full profits during the minority. But if the tenant had in his lifetime subinfeudated for a worthless service, taking payment in ready money,

---

[70] Magna Carta 1217, c.36.
[71] Stat. *De viris religiosis* 1279.
[72] Under either method, the purchaser would have to perform the services due to the vendor's lord.

the lord had wardship only of the seignory (that is, the worthless service). The true value of the land, instead of being reflected in rent-service which would benefit the lord, had been converted into cash which went into the vendor's pocket. Furthermore, the likelihood of an escheat was reduced as more tenants were inserted in the chain. Alienation by substitution could harm the lord in a different way: for instance, if an old tenant substituted a young man with a long life-expectancy. The greater evil, however, was seen as subinfeudation.

The statute *Quia emptores terrarum*[73] was passed to solve this problem, and affords clear proof that the incidents were by 1290 more important than the services. In order to protect the incidents, the statute enacted that alienation was thenceforward to be by substitution, which was to be allowed without fine. As a consequence, no mesne tenures in fee simple[74] have been created since 1290, and as mesne tenures have lapsed over the years most of the land in England has come to be held in chief of the Crown. Another consequence of the statute was the increasing use made of the husbandry lease for years, which had some of the advantages of subinfeudation without being caught by the feudal rules.[75] The statute is still of importance, because it keeps the feudal system in abeyance, and it survived an attempt at repeal as recently as 1968.

EVASION AND PRESERVATION OF INCIDENTS

An equally important legal consequence of the incidents of tenure followed from the constant attempts of lawyers to arrange their clients' property interests in such a way that they attracted the least burdens. The incidents which most needed avoidance were relief, wardship and primer seisin, all of which arose when a tenant died and the fee descended to his heir. Now, these were not simply death duties, but inheritance duties; and, if death could not be avoided, inheritance could. The essence of most feudal tax-dodges was therefore to ensure that land did not descend to an heir. Provision against descent had to be made during the tenant's lifetime, because at common law land could not be disposed of by will. We have already noticed an early device for achieving the object by grants in mortmain; but that way had been

---

[73] B. & M. 9-10. Note also the directions given in 1256 to tackle the same problem in relation to tenants in chief: ibid. 9.

[74] The statute did not extend to estates less than fee simple, and so it was held that tenants of particular estates (such as tenants for life) held of the reversioner or remainderman who had the fee simple. The meaning of these terms will be discussed in the next chapter.

[75] See pp. 339-340, post.

stopped in 1215. Another method, which generally had no legal success, was to create a succession of life interests so that the tenant and his heir and his heir's heir, and so on *ad infinitum*, each had separate life estates under the original grant and took nothing by descent.[76] Another was for a father to convey the land during his lifetime to the heir apparent, or to the heir apparent jointly with himself so that the heir would take by survivorship and not by inheritance. Few fathers thought such a course wise. A fourth device was a collusive grant to friends on condition that they would convey the land back to the heir when he attained his majority. Each form of evasion was countered at an early date by legislation[77] or by judicial decision. But all were superseded by the institution of the 'use', which enabled the real owner of land to hide behind a legal façade. To this we turn in the next chapter.

Further reading

Pollock & Maitland, vol. I, pp. 229-356; vol. II, pp. 1-6
Holdsworth HEL, vol. III, pp. 3-87
Plucknett CHCL, pp. 506-520, 531-545
Simpson, *History of the Land Law*, pp. 1-56
Milsom HFCL, pp. 99-151

ASSUMPTIONS AND WORKINGS OF EARLY FEUDALISM

C. Stephenson, 'Feudalism and its Antecedents in England' (1943) 48
    American Historical Rev. 245-265

F. M. Stenton, *The First Century of English Feudalism 1066-1166*
    (2nd ed., 1961)

F. L. Ganshof, *Feudalism* (3rd English ed., 1964), esp. part 3

S. D. White, 'English Feudalism and its Origins' (1975) 19 AJLH 138-155

J. Gillingham, 'The Introduction of Knight Service into England'
    (1982) 4 *Anglo-Norman Studies* 53-64

J. C. Holt, 'The Introduction of Knight Service into England' (1984) 6
    Anglo-Norman Studies 89-106; '1086' in *Domesday Studies*
    (J. C. Holt ed., 1987), pp. 41-64

S. L. Waugh, 'Tenure to Contract: Lordship and Clientage in 13th-century England' (1986) 101 EHR 811-839

---

[76] See pp. 321-322, post.

[77] Most were defeated by the broad construction put upon the Statute of Marlborough 1267, c.6; B. & M. 8-9.

P. R. Hyams, 'Warranty and Good Lordship in 12th Century England' (1987) 5 LHR 437-503

R. P. Abels, *Lordship and Military Obligation in Anglo-Saxon England* (1988)

THE COMMON-LAW ACTIONS AND THEIR EFFECTS[78]

S. F. C. Milsom, 'The Real Actions', introduction to Pollock & Maitland (1968 ed.), pp. xxvii-xlix; *The Legal Framework of English Feudalism* (1977)

D. W. Sutherland, *The Assize of Novel Disseisin* (1973)

R. C. Palmer, 'The Feudal Framework of English Law' (1981) 79 *Michigan Law Rev.* 1130-1164; 'The Origins of Property in England' (1985) 3 LHR 1-50

M. Cheney, 'The Litigation between John Marshal and Archbishop Thomas Becket in 1164: a Pointer to the Origin of Novel Disseisin' (1984), *Law and Social Change*, pp. 9-26

J. Biancalana, 'For Want of Justice: Legal Reforms of Henry II' (1988) 88 *Columbia Law Rev.* 433-536

INCIDENTS AND THEIR PRESERVATION

T. F. T. Plucknett, *The Legislation of Edward I* (1949)

J. M. W. Bean, *The Decline of English Feudalism 1215-1540* (1968)

P. A. Brand, 'The Control of Mortmain Alienation in England 1200-1300' (1978), *Legal Records and the Historian*, pp. 29-40

S. Raban, *Mortmain Legislation and the English Church 1279-1500* (1982)

---

[78] See also the reading at the end of ch. 15.

Table B. Types of property

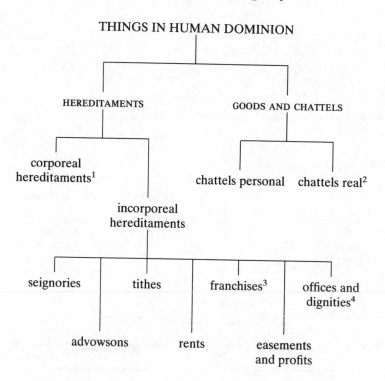

THINGS IN HUMAN DOMINION

HEREDITAMENTS — GOODS AND CHATTELS

corporeal hereditaments[1]

incorporeal hereditaments

chattels personal — chattels real[2]

seignories — tithes — franchises[3] — offices and dignities[4]

advowsons — rents — easements and profits

[1] Land, including minerals, vegetation, buildings, fixtures, wild animals, heirlooms, and title-deeds.
[2] Including terms of years, tenancies at will, and wardships severed from seignories.
[3] Including palatinates, private liberties and jurisdictions, markets and fairs, tolls, forestry rights, and rights to take royal revenues or profits (such as treasure trove, wrecks, and swans).
[4] Including peerages and baronetcies, armorial bearings, and surnames.

Table C. Types of tenure

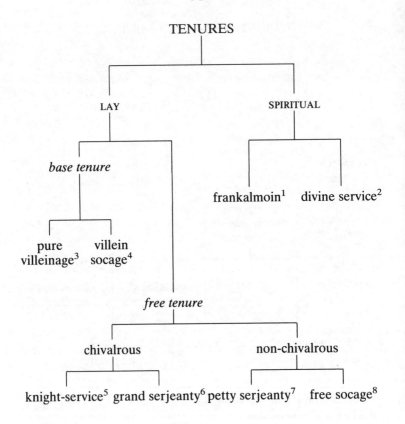

1. Tenure 'in free alms' with no specified services, but general duty of performing divine service.
2. Certain service, such as saying mass on certain days, finding a chantry chaplain, or distributing alms.
3. Uncertain villein services, e.g. copyhold, tenancy by the virge.
4. Certain villein services, e.g. tenure in ancient demesne.
5. Military service, including castlegard and scutage.
6. Certain non-military service to the king's person.
7. Service of rendering something to the king. According to some definitions it must have a military use.
8. Of two kinds: (i) common socage, the only form of tenure apart from frankalmoin and grand serjeanty remaining after 1925; (ii) customary socage, e.g. gavelkind, burgage.

14. Real Property: Feudalism and Uses

The distinction between the legal and beneficial ownership of property has become the foundation of the modern system of estates in land. But the technical distinction between legal and equitable estates could hardly have been invented, and indeed we must seek its origin not in legal thought but in a miscellany of factual situations requiring recognition in conscience if not in law. The situations arose whenever a feudal tenant was personally obliged, either by contract or by the requirements of good faith, to allow another person to have the beneficial enjoyment of land vested in himself. Such an arrangement did not in the beginning have a technical name. The nominal owner was obliged in conscience to observe the trust reposed in him, and in Latin he was said to hold the property *ad commodum* or *ad opus* (to the benefit) of the beneficiary.

That this terminology of trusteeship did not originally represent a technical concept may be seen by comparing the language used in analogous situations. Bailiffs and guardians had a trust reposed in them to look after property for the benefit of others. In their cases the property was not vested in them, and yet they were said to keep (*custodire*) the property *ad opus* of the owner. The word *commodum* is also the Latin for 'easement', a right enjoyed over another person's land, such as a right of way.[1] No doubt the case where the tenant had no beneficial interest in his own property was most easily described by analogy with these more familiar situations. But the law could only admit one 'right', and that belonged to the feudal tenant entitled to seisin. The holding *ad opus* therefore of necessity involved a separation of the title as recognised by law from the true ownership as acknowledged in fact.

ORIGINAL PURPOSES OF HOLDING LAND A: *OPUS*

The earliest known instances of land being held *ad opus* of another were of a temporary nature. Thus, if a tenant wished to alienate his land by substitution, the proper feudal procedure was to surrender his interest to his lord on trust to admit the new tenant; this remained the mode of

---

[1] See p. 484, post.

conveyancing for copyhold estates until 1925. Between surrender and
admittance the lord kept the land *ad opus* of the transferee. Another
example is provided by the case where a man wished to transfer property
into the names of himself and his wife, or to settle property on himself
and his heir; he could not grant the land to himself directly, and so he
would grant it to friends on trust to reconvey it in the required manner.
It was soon realised that arrangements of this kind could also be entered
into on a permanent basis. Grants to the Franciscans afford an early
instance. The Order of St Francis, forbidden to own land (but not to
accept hospitality), was permitted to enjoy the benefit of property vested
in others; and so a person wishing to provide a home for the friars could
grant land to a group of nominees to hold as a kind of charitable trust
for their benefit.[2] There is some evidence that the inns of court and
chancery were occupied under similar trusts in medieval times, not in
their case because of any disability but because it proved a more
convenient arrangement for a fluctuating body.

Before 1290, the lord could have refused his consent to any
feoffment[3] which prejudiced his own interests; but *Quia emptores* ended
seignorial control over such arrangements. One consequence soon
discovered was that the statutes of mortmain could be avoided by
separating beneficial enjoyment from title. Pending the issue of a
licence to alienate to a religious house, the grantor or his nominee
might hold the land for the benefit of the corporation. But, if such an
arrangement was effective, why purchase the licence at all ? Land might
just as well be held permanently for the benefit of a religious
corporation as for an unincorporated order of friars. A statute of 1391
shows that feoffments to the use of religious corporations were indeed
being resorted to 'by subtle imagination, art and scheming'; and by
stopping such schemes parliament incidentally gave legal recognition to
the use.[4] Another unworthy purpose of uses, noticed in the 1370s, was
to place land beyond the reach of creditors.[5]

The most fruitful of the devices discovered in the fourteenth century
was that which enabled a landowner to avoid the rule prohibiting wills

---

[2]   The Franciscans first came to England in 1224, and in 1225 a site was conveyed to
   the town of Oxford (a corporation) 'to the use of the friars'. Similar arrangements
   were made elsewhere. A papal bull of 1230 confirmed that the friars might use and
   enjoy, but not own, property.

[3]   A feoffment is a grant in fee simple. It is made by a 'feoffor' to a 'feoffee'.

[4]   Stat. 15 Ric. II, c.5.

[5]   E.g. *Langedon v. Stratton* (1374) *CPMR 1364-81*, p. 175. The first legislative
   measure dealing with uses was directed (in 1376) against fraudulent feoffments by
   persons who retained the profits at their will, in order to avoid execution: Stat. 50
   Edw. III, c.6.

of land. A dying tenant could grant the land to a group of friends and neighbours on trust to regrant it after his death to such beneficiary as he should name. This enabled the land in effect to be devised, and since title did not pass by descent the feudal incidents were avoided as well. But here again there was an advantage in making the arrangement permanent: the power to devise did not need to await the deathbed. It made sense for any landowner to vest his land in feoffees to perform his will: that is to carry out any immediate instructions during his life, and his last will after his death. The machinery was informal. If the feoffor made it a formal condition of the feoffment that the feoffees should perform their trust, the condition was enforced by the law with unbending exactitude; if it was unperformed, the land automatically returned to the feoffor or his heirs. Only the heir, however, could enter for breach after the feoffor's death; therefore if the condition was to convey the land after his death to someone other than the heir, this means of enforcement was useless. Moreover, if the condition was to allow someone else the full rights of beneficial ownership, it was arguably repugnant and void.[6] The solution was not to impose a condition at all, but to make the feoffment merely on trust that the feoffees would perform the will. The feoffees then held the title solely to the use of the feoffor. Whatever he directed, they were expected to obey. This was very convenient to the feoffor. He remained the absolute owner in effect, because he continued to possess the land for his own benefit and take the profits, and he could sell the fee whenever he wished by directing the feoffees to convey to his purchaser. Yet he could in addition, if he so wished, defer the selection of his successors to the point of his own death. Thus the landowner achieved the power of disposing of the land by last will or by *inter vivos* conveyance, as he pleased. It was this attribute of the holding *ad opus*, the permanent arrangement giving the beneficial owner the power to devise without impairing his other powers, which principally assured its establishment as a common institution. It also ensured that the device had to be a mere trust, because the effect of a will was necessarily to disinherit the only person capable of enforcing a condition.

THE 'USE' AS AN INTEREST IN LAND

Each of the arrangements just described began as a temporary expedient which was found to have advantageous effects if extended into a permanent state of affairs. The permanent institution which resulted was called a 'use', the law French word for *opus*; and the beneficiary,

---

6 But cf. *De St Edmunds v. Anon.* (1371) B. & M. 94.

when not the feoffor himself, was called *cestuy que use*.[7] The trusting
of feoffees with lands in use was a fact of life long before it had any
legal consequences. The common law took no notice of a mere
trusting, without a condition. As far as the common law was
concerned, the cestuy que use had 'no more to do with the land than the
greatest stranger in the world',[8] and if he remained in possession he was
technically only a tenant at sufferance of the feoffees. It was said in
1464 that the feoffees could sue the cestuy que use for trespass if he
felled timber,[9] and the proposition was often approved in later cases as a
statement of abstract theory. Yet the feoffees, being charged with a
fiduciary duty, were not supposed to obstruct the wishes of the cestuy
que use or derive any benefit from the land for themselves. By choosing
a substantial group of feoffees, usually lawyers, the feoffor ensured
against individual unscrupulousness. But difficulties were bound to
arise as such feoffments became more common, and those difficulties
required a legal solution.

The first recourse may have been to the ecclesiastical courts,
especially when wills were involved. We know, for instance, that in
1375 a group of feoffees were excommunicated for conveying land
(allegedly under duress) contrary to the feoffor's will.[10] But the
Chancery was also an obvious resort, since the feoffees were clearly
bound by ties of conscience which were not recognised in the courts of
common law. The origins of the Chancery jurisdiction over uses are
elusive,[11] but it was well established by the 1420s, and in the course of
the fifteenth century uses accounted for much of the chancellor's
business.[12]

The principles established by the courts in the fifteenth century
turned the interest of the beneficiary into a new kind of ownership,[13]

7   Probably short for *cestuy a que use le feoffment fuit fait* (he to whose use the
    feoffment was made). The word 'use' in this sense has no connection with the
    verb 'to use', but was derived from *opus* via the Old French *oeps*, the *p* becoming
    silent.

8   *Anon*. (1502) Keil. 42, pl.7, per Frowyk sjt.

9   *Anon*. (1464) B. & M. 96, per Moyle J.

10 Helmholz, *Canon Law and the Law of England*, p. 343 (case from Canterbury).

11 In 1502, Vavasour J dated it to Edward III's time: Keil. 42. He may have been
    thinking of a case in 1360 which suggests that already the *subpoena* was being
    used in connection with uses: J. Barton, 98 LQR 26. Others hold that a
    parliamentary petition of 1402 (Rot. Parl., vol. III, p. 511) assumes the absence
    of a remedy at that date.

12 For specimen cases (*c.* 1420), see 10 SS 119; *Messynden v. Pierson*, B. & M. 94.
    There is disagreement about the proportion of Chancery business which such
    cases occupied.

13 The word 'owner' was used in the 15th century for the beneficiary: B. & M. 103.

analogous to what was later called the 'equitable estate'.[14] If the feoffees died, the trust passed to the heir of the last survivor;[15] if the feoffees alienated the land, the trust passed to the purchaser, unless he bought for value without notice of the trust, in which case alone his conscience was clear.[16] A use could also be raised by implication. If the legal owner of land bargained and sold it to another, then before the conveyance an implied use was raised in favour of the purchaser, which the chancellor would protect by specific performance. And if the legal owner enfeoffed another without any consideration being given, or any express use declared, the feoffee held the land to the use of the feoffor and his heirs. The recognition of this 'resulting' use, perhaps as early as 1465, confirms how usual it had become for feoffments to be made on secret or undisclosed trusts, or to perform the feoffor's will generally.[17] By 1500 it could be asserted that the greater part of the land in England was held in use.[18]

By 1500, moreover, the law of uses was beginning to percolate into the common-law courts as a result of a statute of 1484. Since so much land was vested in people who had no visible connection with it, third parties could be at a considerable disadvantage in conveyancing. To protect those who purchased from beneficiaries in possession, the statute provided that the beneficiary could pass a title good against his own feoffors.[19] This remarkable measure enabled the beneficiary to convey something he did not in law have; he was treated by fiction as if he were the legal owner, for the purpose of conveying title. An important consequence was that the title to the use (the *jus usus*) was increasingly mentioned in common-law pleadings, so that questions relating to the transfer of uses came before the common-law judges for determination. The beneficiary's interest was in this way assimilated to legal property concepts; it could be seen as a thing, a thing which descended to heirs on an intestacy, a thing which could be bought and sold or settled on a succession of beneficiaries. Nevertheless, the new kind of ownership was inherently foreign to the common law because it conflicted with the feudal system.

---

[14] Cf. pp. 350-352, post.

[15] This rule is said to have been established by Fortescue CJ in the 1450s: Y.B. Pas. 22 Edw. IV, fo. 6, pl.18, per Hussey CJ; Keil. 42, pl.7, per Vavasour J.

[16] This rule may also belong to the 1450s: see *Cardinal Beaufort's Case* (1453) B. & M. 95.

[17] See B. & M. 97-98, 102-103.

[18] Y.B. Mich. 15 Hen. VII, fo. 13, pl.1, per Frowyk sjt.

[19] Stat. 1 Ric. III, c.1; B. & M. 101.

Evasion of Feudal Law

The main reason why so much land had come to be vested in feoffees to uses during the fifteenth century, at any rate by major landowners, was that it provided an escape from the automatic certainty of the legal rules of succession; by last will the landowner could provide for younger sons, daughters, bastards, remote relations, or charities, could vary the provision given by law to his widow, and could charge the payment of his debts and legacies on real property. These objects could be achieved either by directing the feoffees to convey property directly to the devisees, or by directing them to sell or let the property and apply the proceeds as instructed. Whichever course was taken, it was the use and not the legal title which passed on the testator's death.

The flexibility made possible by uses was accompanied by two problems. The first was that conveyancing was rendered less certain. The use could be transferred informally, without 'livery of seisin',[20] and could even pass by word of mouth. Purchasers of land might therefore find themselves adversely affected by a hidden use. This problem was eased by the statute of 1484, but other uncertainties continued to be a source of complaint well into the sixteenth century.[21]

Second, and this was the cause of all the trouble which came in Tudor times, the employment of uses deprived lords, and most of all the Crown, of valuable feudal revenues. It is unlikely that this was the prime motive behind uses, but it was their inevitable result and doubled their attraction.[22] The machinery displaced inheritance and, therefore, the incidents which attached on inheritance; even if the beneficiary died intestate, there was no descent of the land to which incidents could attach. Of course, incidents would attach if a sole feoffee died; but a plurality of feoffees, besides providing safety in numbers, also ensured that there would never be a descent. The feoffees were joint tenants, and so if one feoffee died the others absorbed his share by the *jus accrescendi*; so long as numbers were kept up, if necessary by reconveyance, there was an 'unassailable mortmain'.[23] It was unassailable because the lord had living tenants to whom the feudal rules applied; and that being so, if the lord suffered loss, it was *damnum absque injuria*. Once this became common knowledge, it was foolish

---

20   For conveyancing at law, see p. 345, post.

21   See, e.g., B. & M. 103-105. A particularly troublesome problem was whether a use in tail had the same characteristics as a legal fee tail: 94 SS *207-208*.

22   For an early recognition of the problem, see *Kyrkeby v. Salle* (1384) Y.B. Mich. 8 Ric. II, p. 99, pl.19.

23   Milsom HFCL, p. 211.

for anyone to leave land vested in his own name. By vesting it in others he paradoxically became a more absolute owner than the common law allowed: he was released from the most burdensome incidents of feudalism, and from the inflexible rules of inheritance, and the estate was also freed from claims by the widow to dower.[24] As a result of the use, feudal revenue from reliefs and wardships in chivalry was by 1500 becoming virtually obsolete. Littleton's account of feudal law might well have seemed like an obituary.

TUDOR LEGISLATION AND FISCAL FEUDALISM

In the century between 1391 and 1490 little was done to preserve the financial profits of feudalism against the encroachments of uses. Weak efforts were made in the fifteenth century by royal advisers to amplify the scope of existing legislation, and to control feoffments to uses by tenants in chief; but no king before Henry VII set about plugging the loopholes which uses had made in the earlier law. The inertia has been attributed to the turmoil of the wars of the roses, in which kings lacked the political strength to stem tax avoidance by their own supporters; but more recently it has been suggested that the problem was only of limited extent before the development of the common recovery in the 1470s.[25] When a tenant in tail suffered a recovery to uses, no fine for alienation was due to the Crown and therefore control by that means was impossible.[26] But Henry VII and Henry VIII determined to revive at least some of the feudal revenues which had belonged to their predecessors, and which they needed to defray the expense of government and of supporting themselves in royal state. Ad hoc parliamentary taxation did not have as much to commend it as a regular feudal revenue which could be collected simply by enforcing the old law of the land.

Henry VII did not tackle the main problem, the will of land, but by statutes of 1490 and 1504 the heir of an intestate cestuy que use was subjected to the same incidents as if his ancestor had died seised.[27] Just as the 1484 statute had treated the beneficiary as having the powers of

---

[24] For dower, see pp. 308-309, post.

[25] The relevance of the common recovery (as to which, see p. 319, post) is that it enabled the barring of entails; before then, most land at the level of knight-service was tied up in tail so that it could not be granted to feoffees. This was pointed out (in an unpublished lecture) by Professor J. Biancalana.

[26] A recovery was in theory a judgment in favour of the rightful tenant, not an alienation. The rule was altered in 1540 by Stat. 32 Hen. VIII, c.1, s.15.

[27] Stat. 4 Hen. VII, c.17 (B. & M. 101-102); 19 Hen. VII, c.15. The former dealt with the wardship of tenants in chivalry, the latter with relief and heriot from tenants in socage.

the legal tenant for conveyancing purposes, so the statutes of Henry VII showed how beneficiaries could be treated as having the liabilities of the legal tenant for tax purposes. They ended a glaring anomaly, and were seen chiefly as closing a gap in the Statute of Marlborough, but they were not designed to and in fact did not greatly enrich the Crown.[28] They only applied on intestacy, and perhaps served largely as a reminder to make wills. It was Henry VIII who, for revenue purposes, raised feudalism from the grave. Historians have given to this artificial revival the name 'fiscal feudalism'.

The main Tudor onslaught on the use began in the 1520s. In 1526 the king's council adopted a policy of tightening up on alienations by tenants in chief, to ensure that the Crown was compensated for any loss of incidents.[29] Then, in 1529, the king and his advisers made an agreement with a party of peers to introduce legislation whereby feudal incidents would be restored, but only to the extent of one third of the amount due at common law.[30] As mesne lords would also have had one third of their revenues restored, this seemed a fair compromise. But when the proposal was laid before the Commons in 1532 they rejected it outright. They knew that taxation could not be imposed without their consent; and uses were an established legal institution which they were keen to preserve, not least because they conferred the power to devise land. Henry VIII threatened them that if they would not accept the one-third compromise he would set in motion the full rigour of the dormant feudal law. They declined this offer, and the king kept his word.

The king's counsel were able to take advantage of two lines of thought on uses. The Common Pleas judges, in applying the statute of 1484, were coming to the view that uses were governed by the common law. If that were taken to its logical conclusion, wills of uses would be void, because wills of land were void. The other line of thought was that separating the legal and beneficial ownership was innately deceitful, and that chancellors in enforcing uses had been naively countenancing large-scale fraud and undermining the common law.[31] On this argument, uses might not be binding in conscience after all. The author

---

[28] If the 1490 statute had been promoted by the Crown, it might have been expected to mention primer seisin; but this remained avoidable by means of the use until 1536.

[29] See Guy, *St German on Chancery and Statute*, 78-79.

[30] The draft bill is printed in Holdsworth HEL, vol. IV, p. 572. The quid pro quo for the peers was that they were to be exempted from the proposed abolition of entails.

[31] Cf. the list, perhaps made for Thomas Cromwell, of 43 'mischiefs, wrongs and inconveniences' arising from uses: Holdsworth HEL, vol. IV, p. 577.

of a 'Replication' to *Doctor and Student* proclaimed uses to be an 'untrue and crafty invention' to deprive the king and his subjects of their feudal incidents. 'What a falseness,' he wrote, 'to speak and do one thing, and think another clean contrary to the same.'[32] Thomas Audley, as reader of the Inner Temple in 1526, and doubtless keen to propagate the new government policy, complained of landowners who had pursued uses 'for the evil purpose of destroying the good laws of the realm, which now by reason of these trusts and confidences is turned into a law called conscience, which is always uncertain and depends for the greater part on the whim of the judge in conscience . . .'.[33] Seven years later Audley himself became that judge in conscience, placed by the king in a position to put his preaching into practice; as indeed he did. With the assistance of the king's secretary Thomas Cromwell, appointed to sit beside him as master of the rolls in 1534, he assembled the judges to discuss a test case adjourned from the common-law side of the Chancery. The question was whether a will made by a tenant in chief, Lord Dacre, which would have deprived the king of his wardship and primer seisin, was valid. The judges, having been coerced or coaxed by Henry VIII into apparent unanimity, declared that it was against the nature of land to be devisable by will, and that a will of the use of land was just as invalid as a will of the land itself.[34] The decision flew in the face of previous learning,[35] and is perhaps the only case in English legal history in which the Crown, unable to push a bill through parliament, managed to change the common law instead. The decision accomplished more than what parliament had rejected, since there was no longer any concession as to two thirds; and within a few months the Commons were persuaded to assent to a new measure concerning uses. The reason why the Commons gave way in 1536 was not merely that their theoretical position had been undermined. If all wills were invalid in 1535, regardless of any fraud, merely because it was against the nature of land to pass by will, it followed that wills had always been invalid, and that any title dependent on a devise by will was invalid. The decision must have thrown into doubt many titles throughout the

---

[32] See p. 123, ante; Guy, *St German on Chancery and Statute*, at pp. 77, 103.

[33] Audley's reading, B. & M. 103 at 104.

[34] *Re Lord Dacre of the South* (1535) B. & M. 105. The true division of judicial opinion at first was 5 against 5, but Port J mumbled and was counted on the wrong side; the resulting 'minority' were later persuaded to give way to the 'majority' view by the king's promise of 'good thanks'.

[35] No attempt was made to explain why wills of land had always been allowed by local custom: if they were against the nature of land, such customs would be void, but this was never suggested. Moreover, when making the 1490 statute parliament had clearly assumed that wills of the use were valid.

country.[36] A significant clause in the 1536 bill provided that wills of persons dying before 1536 should be accounted as valid and effectual as they had been until recent decisions had brought their validity into doubt.[37] The effect was to reverse *Lord Dacre's Case* as to the past. Almost certainly this was the inducement which persuaded the Commons to accept without demur the sweeping legislative change which was to govern thenceforth.

The Statute of Uses 1536 carried the royal policies to the extreme of abolishing the power to devise for the future. This it achieved, without actually mentioning wills, by the neat statutory fiction called 'executing the use'. Wills had only been valid where the legal title was vested in feoffees to uses, and therefore if uses were extirpated there could be no wills. The simple abolition of uses would nevertheless have been absurd, because its effect would have been that most of the land in England would have become beneficially vested in the lawyers who happened to be acting as feoffees. The legal title had instead to be taken from those feoffees and given to the beneficiaries. The statute accordingly provided that where A was seised of property to the 'use, trust or confidence' of B, then B was thereafter to be deemed to be seised of the property 'to all intents, purposes and constructions in the law, of and in such like estates as [he] had or shall have in use'.[38] In other words, whenever A was seised of property to the use of B, the statute effected a notional or fictional livery of seisin from A to B. B, the cestuy que use, was to be statutory owner of the legal estate, and the feoffee (A) merely a channel through which the seisin passed in an instant of time to B. A similar fictional livery of seisin occurred if A covenanted to stand seised to the use of B, or bargained and sold the land to B (in which case there was an implied use).[39] The purpose and effect of executing the use was that the beneficial owner of land would always die seised, so that his last will was ineffective at common law and the feudal incidents attached on the descent to his heir. The common-law position was so completely restored that the Crown regained its prerogative rights in addition to wardship and relief.

[36] Serjeant Mountague, arguing the case for the Dacre family, said 'it would be a great mischief to change the law now, for many inheritances in the realm depend today on uses, so that there would be much confusion if [wills were treated as void]': B. & M. 109.

[37] B. & M. 114 (see s.9).

[38] Stat. 27 Hen. VIII, c.10 (B. & M. 112-113).

[39] For the latter effect, see p. 345, post. Even more strangely, if A conveyed land to B without consideration and without saying 'to the use of B', nothing passed at all, because the resulting use in favour of A was executed by the statute and the seisin which A delivered to B immediately rebounded on A.

Financially, the statute was a tremendous success. And as a piece of legal draftsmanship it was greatly admired by later generations: Francis Bacon called it the 'most perfectly and exactly conceived and penned of any law in the book'.[40] Yet at the time of its passing it aroused much popular opposition. It not only restored feudal incidents, but it imposed compulsory primogeniture on a society which had accustomed itself to wills; moreover it did so for socage tenants, who were of little interest for revenue purposes, as well as for tenants by knight-service. The Duke of Norfolk soon pronounced it the worst act ever made,[41] and it was one of the statutes attacked by the Pilgrimage of Grace in 1536. A lawyer prominent in that protest urged that landowners be allowed to leave part of their lands by will, so that they could pay their debts and provide for their children's marriages, or else lawyers would seek out loopholes in the legislation.[42] The king loftily told the protesters that the statute did not concern them, as 'base commons';[43] and yet within four years the government in effect accepted the demand, and retreated to the one-third compromise proposed in 1529. The Statute of Wills 1540 conferred for the first time the legal power to dispose of freeholds by will, save that tenants by knight-service had to leave at least one third to descend.[44] The preamble to the statute referred to the king's 'grace, goodness and liberality' towards his loving subjects; but it was a major political retreat. The retreat had little to do with the pilgrims of 1536, whose other demands had been ignored, save that their intellectual threat clearly struck home. The lawyer's pen was mightier than mere wails of protest. By 1540 the government had indeed begun to fear that conveyancers were on the verge of finding the loophole,[45] and so by an adroit manoeuvre reversed the rules.

Even after the retreat of 1540, the royal revenue from fiscal feudalism was substantial. In 1540 the Court of Wards was established, under the presidency of the master of the king's wards, an older office created by Henry VII. Its purpose was to supervise the collection of the feudal

[40] Reading in Gray's Inn (1600), printed as *The Learned Reading of Francis Bacon* (1642), p. 25.

[41] M. H. Dodds & R. Dodds, *The Pilgrimage of Grace* (1915), vol. I, p. 266.

[42] 5 EHR at pp. 563, 565; D. S. Berkowitz, *Humanist Scholarship and Public Order* (1984), pp. 228-229, 232-233. The lawyer was Robert Aske of Gray's Inn, executed in 1537. (The main brunt of the protest was religious.)

[43] Dodds & Dodds, *Pilgrimage of Grace*, p. 137.

[44] Stat. 32 Hen. VIII, c.1 (B. & M. 115).

[45] Some Crown lawyers were sent to the Tower in 1540 for advising on ways around the Statute of Uses: 94 SS 351. For the kind of device which they may have invented, see 94 SS *203*.

revenues of the Crown and to settle incidental questions of law. It enjoyed a thriving jurisdiction for one century. Yet the policy of fiscal feudalism came under constant criticism. It was suggested that if the Crown helped itself to the income of wards it ought to discharge its educational duties towards them. One Elizabethan master of the wards went so far as to plan a new university for this purpose, but nothing came of it. It was also urged, under Elizabeth I and James I, that Crown and people alike would benefit if the irregular burdens imposed by fiscal feudalism were replaced by annual composition payments or other more rational forms of taxation. This was not finally achieved until the end of Charles I's reign. Resolutions of the Long Parliament in 1645 were confirmed by a statute of 1656, and this statute was one of the few to be continued at the Restoration: the Military Tenures Abolition Act 1660 abolished tenure by knight-service, and all its incidents, and abolished the onerous incidents of grand serjeanty.[46] From that date the feudal system in England has been little more than abstract theory. Public revenue has thereafter been raised by other methods, designed to spread the burden more widely: excise duty, house tax (measured by the number of hearths or windows), purchase tax, income tax, death duty, capital transfer tax, value added tax, poll tax, and so on. Mesne lords have had no reason to maintain their claims to seignories, except where manors were preserved as units. Since there has been no new subinfeudation after *Quia emptores*, the result is that most English landowners today hold their lands of the Crown by free and common socage,[47] the only incident of which is the bare duty of fealty.

The Statutes of Uses and Wills wrought changes in jurisprudence which might never have occurred if Henry VIII's wishes had been granted without demur by the parliament of 1532. Although the abolition of knight-service and casual feudal revenue did away with the need for most of the law built on feudal foundations, the side effects of the brief conflict of 1532-40, and in particular the effects of the legislation on conveyancing and settlements, lasted for three centuries and more. These effects will be considered in a subsequent chapter.

Further reading

Pollock & Maitland, vol. II, pp. 228-239
Holdsworth HEL, vol. IV, pp. 407-480

---

[46] Stat. 12 Car. II, c.24.

[47] The common law always presumed, in the absence of proof to the contrary, a tenure in chief by knight-service: 94 SS *195* n.1. The presumption now is of a tenure in chief by socage.

Plucknett CHCL, pp. 575-587

Simpson, *History of the Land Law*, pp. 173-192

Milsom HFCL, pp. 200-222

H. E. Bell, *The Court of Wards and Liveries* (1953)

J. L. Barton, 'The Medieval Use' (1965) 81 LQR 562-577

E. W. Ivés, 'The Genesis of the Statute of Uses' (1967) 82 EHR 673-697

J. M. W. Bean, *The Decline of English Feudalism* (1968), ch. 3-6

J. H. Baker, 'Uses and Wills' (1978) 94 SS *192-203*

R. H. Helmholz, 'The Early Enforcement of Uses' (1979) 79 *Columbia Law Rev* 1503-1513 (repr. in *Canon Law and the Law of England*, pp. 341-353)

J. A. Guy, *Christopher St German on Chancery and Statute* (SS Supp. Ser. 6, 1985), pp. 75-86, 103-105, 113-114

S. W. DeVine, 'Ecclesiastical Antecedents to Secular Jurisdiction over the Feoffment to the Uses to be declared in Testamentary Instructions' (1986) 30 AJLH 295-320; 'The Franciscan Friars, the Feoffment to Uses, and Canonical Theories of Property Enjoyment before 1535' (1989) 10 JLH 1-22

15. Real Property: Inheritance and Estates

We have already seen how feudal tenure began as a contractual relationship whereby a lord rewarded a vassal with land, and how through the intervention of the common law the tenant's interest became a fully secure property right, subject to the lord's right to services and incidents. We have also pursued the history of the lord's rights down to their virtual abolition in 1645. Now we must go back to the beginning again, in order to examine more closely the changing character of the tenant's interest, particularly in terms of its duration.

Our starting point is that once a feudal contract was entered into, neither the lord nor the tenant owned the land absolutely. Each party had expectations of the other which the common law recognised and enforced: the lord was seised 'in service', and the tenant was seised 'in his demesne' (*in dominico suo*). In purely feudal terms those respective interests lasted for life: the tenant became his lord's man when he took the oath of homage and ceased to be so only when he or his lord died. This lifelong status, in the case of a free man, was called freehold. But we have seen that the common law before 1200 also recognised a more extensive kind of interest in tenants whose heirs had a right to succeed them in their holdings. That indeed became the usual arrangement at all levels of tenure. The word 'fee', the word which had originally denoted the fief itself, the consideration for the services, then came to denote this inheritable kind of tenancy. When a tenant in fee died, his heir was entitled to succeed him as the lord's man. Where there was a tenancy for life, the inheritable fee remained in the lord. In the latter case, therefore, the right to be tenant in possession was divided temporally: the tenant for life was seised in demesne and continued in seisin until his death, when the lord became seised in demesne. The notion that the right to seisin could be divided up on a time scale into present and future interests, and into interests of varying duration, was expressed by thirteenth-century lawyers in terms of the tenant's 'estate', a word derived from the Latin *status*.[1] The purpose of this chapter will be to

---

[1] Originally this referred to the person of the tenant, his estate being his own position or condition: see Plucknett, 14 *Cornell Law Qly* at 269. But in its technical sense it referred to the land: 'An estate in the land is a time in the land, or land for a time' (*Walsingham's Case* (1573) 2 Plowd. 547 at 555).

examine the development of the law relating to hereditary and life estates, and of the next chapter to show how such estates were used in planning property arrangements for families.

The notion of the hereditary fee arose from lords giving tenants their fiefs on the footing that their heirs would succeed them, by using some such words as: unto *A* and his heirs for ever.[2] In the early feudal world, the understanding of such words was not that the lord was conferring a hereditary property right on the tenant but that he was undertaking, for himself and his own heirs, an obligation to admit the tenant's heirs (and perhaps their heirs in turn) to do homage as his men.[3] Even when this obligation came to be enforced by the common law, the resulting right of inheritance need not have required any differentiation of estates in land beyond present and future interests. The right of the heir was, in feudal terms, simply a right to succeed to his ancestor's fief and become the lord's man for life. On that basis, a grant to *A* and his heirs would have been understood as creating successive life tenancies in *A* and his next heir or heirs, or perhaps an infinite succession of life tenancies in *A* and each generation of his heirs. By the thirteenth century, however, the fee had come to be understood differently; and the reason was that the settled common law allowed *A* to alienate the fee in such a way as to bar his own heirs from inheriting in demesne. It is therefore appropriate to consider next the legal effects of alienation, and how it affected the concept of inheritance.

Alienation

Alienation is the transfer of an interest in property from one person to another. There was no reason inherent in feudalism why a tenant should be accorded the privilege of free alienation, because the lord had as much right as the tenant to decide who should enter his fee. Certainly it would have run counter to the essential spirit of the feudal bond to allow a tenant unilaterally to substitute someone else in his place; the grantee would be a complete stranger to the lord, and could not become a tenant without the lord receiving him as his man. Yet the demands of a land-based economy would not have been satisfied by an absolute ban on the disposition of land, and in fact the possibility of alienation was never denied. It was always possible for the tenant to assign his interest with the lord's consent, for which he might charge.[4] But alienation did not

---

2 These remained the usual words for creating 'fee simple' until 1925.
3 See Milsom HFCL, pp. 105-107, 166-167.
4 See p. 273, ante.

necessarily require the lord's consent. One way of removing the need for consent was by prior grant from the lord: by a grant to *A*, his heirs *and assigns*.[5] The lord was then obliged to accept *A*'s substituted tenants in the same way as he was obliged to accept *A*'s heirs. There was once a view, reflected in *Bracton*, that a grant to *A*, his heirs and legatees, would similarly oblige the lord to accept someone designated in *A*'s will; but elsewhere in *Bracton* this is rejected, and it did not gain general acceptance.

Assignment, or alienation by 'substitution', was not in practice common before the statute *Quia emptores* 1290, except at the level of unfree tenures.[6] By far the more usual device was for the alienation to be effected by subinfeudation.[7] In that case the tenure between the alienor and his lord remained intact, but the alienee replaced the alienor as tenant in demesne and the alienor became his lord. It is not certain whether subinfeudation had once required seignorial consent; but by Bracton's time it did not. The lord's right to the services due from his tenant was not impaired by subinfeudation because in the event of non-performance the lord could distrain on the demesne.[8] The tenant's interest was therefore freely alienable by the middle of the thirteenth century:[9] by subinfeudation until *Quia emptores*, and by substitution thereafter.

The alienation of a seignory was subject to the same principles: the privity of the tenurial bond affected both parties, and so a lord could not by alienation impose a different lord on his tenant without the latter's submission. It was therefore requisite to the fully effective alienation of a seignory that the tenant should accept the new lord. This was called attornment, and it was effected either by words or conduct. However, there was no question of the tenant thereby obstructing, or seeking compensation for, his lord's alienations. Although the lord could not force a tenant to transfer his homage to an enemy, he could force him to

---

5   Some lawyers called this 'fee pure', and regarded it as something more absolute than fee simple: see B. & M. 52. This may have been because a fee without the words 'assigns' had once been regarded as a 'base fee': that is, one which would come to an end when the heirs of the original grantee died out.

6   For the statute, see p. 277, ante. It should be noted that even a 'substitution' was originally effected by an arranged subinfeudation: the tenant surrendered to the lord, and the lord then subinfeudated to the new tenant.

7   For this term, see p. 257, ante. For a reason why substitution was rare, see Milsom, *Legal Framework*, p. 111; HFCL, p. 111.

8   See p. 272, ante. Magna Carta 1217, c.32, provided that free men should not give or sell land without retaining sufficient to perform their services. This was aimed at grants to religious houses, which could not always be distrained: Milsom, *Legal Framework*, p. 119.

9   With the exception (at any rate after 1256) of tenants in chief: B. & M. 9.

transfer the services;[10] and by the thirteenth century that was enough to give the new lord seisin. The need for attornment was not affected by *Quia emptores*, and so tenants for life (or other particular tenants) had to attorn on the grant of a remainder or reversion. It was not abolished until 1705.[11]

EFFECTS OF ALIENATING THE FEE

Recognition of the tenant's right to dispose of his interest without the lord's consent raised a new legal problem in relation to the inheritable character of the fee. If a grant to a tenant and his heirs had been understood as conferring life interests on each tenant in succession, it might have been deduced that no tenant could alienate for a period exceeding his own life. Had that deduction become the law, the first grantor of a fee would have had the power to tie the land to the grantee's family until the end of time. Freedom of alienation would have stultified itself, because the first grant to a person and his heirs would have precluded any further grant of the same land to another person and his heirs, unless and until the heirs of the original grantee died out, which might never happen. Could any human disposition be allowed such eternal force? Could freedom of alienation include the freedom to prevent future alienation?

In the twelfth century no one asked the questions in those terms; yet it was not thought right that a man should be free to disinherit his own heir by alienation. Manorial customs surviving into the next century reflect those earlier qualms: in some places the tenant could not indeed alienate beyond his own lifetime, elsewhere he could do so only if his heir consented, and in other places the heir had the right to buy back alienated land for its full value.[12] The problem is also discussed in *Glanvill* (*c.* 1190), where a distinction is drawn between a man's acquisitions and his patrimony. What he had himself acquired he could alienate almost without restriction, provided he did not completely cut off his own issue; but what he had inherited he could alienate only in special circumstances, and even then had to leave a reasonable share to

---

[10] The method was to convey the seignory by final concord, and then the tenant could be distrained by a judicial writ (*per quae servicia*) to attorn the services.

[11] Stat. 4 & 5 Ann., c.3, s.9. It remained necessary, of course, to give notice to the tenant.

[12] See G.C. Homans, *English Villagers of the 13th Century* (1941), pp. 196-199. The last custom (of pre-emption) was more widespread on the Continent, where it was called *retrait lignager*.

the heir.[13] This approach would, however, merely have delayed the perpetuity; a single descent was effective to render the land inalienable. In any case, the heir did not suffer economically if his ancestor had subinfeudated for value; instead of land he inherited services, but the value might be the same. By the early thirteenth century, the customary restrictions had therefore – except at the manorial level – been abandoned. If land was given to *A* and his heirs, *A* received an inheritable fee which he could alienate to *B* and *B*'s heirs, or even to an immortal corporation.

The new position may have resulted from the protective force of warranties, which were guarantees of title made by grantors.[14] Around 1200 it became accepted that an alienor's obligation to warrant the title of the alienee descended upon the alienor's own heirs, so that they were barred from reclaiming the land for themselves. But this doctrine presupposed that the heirs were not seen as having a vested interest. The author of *Bracton* appreciated this point, and treated it as a substantive principle that the words 'and his heirs' in a grant gave no interest to individual heirs but merely defined as inheritable the character of the interest granted.[15] This doctrine was soon embedded in the common law. In legal language, the heir took 'by descent' and not 'by purchase'; this meant that he took his land by right of succession and not by virtue of a direct grant to himself. Unless his ancestor died seised, no one could claim to be an heir; until the ancestor's death, there was only an heir apparent.[16] If the ancestor did die seised, the heir had an absolute right of succession and neither the ancestor's last will nor the lord's disapproval could disinherit him. That is why the limitation to legatees was held not to work.[17] But if the ancestor had alienated in fee during his lifetime, the heir apparent had lost his prospect of inheritance and had no further legal standing. The contemporary explanation was that the identity of an heir could not be known until the ancestor's death; an heir apparent might die, an heir presumptive might be displaced by the birth of a brother. Heirs were made by God not man: *solus Deus facit haeredem*.[18] And since an heir apparent or

---

13 *Glanvill*, vii.1. The same distinction underlay the surviving custom of Northampton that a man could only devise what he had himself purchased: 98 SS 535.

14 See p. 262, ante.

15 *Bracton*, vol. II, pp. 66, 68. This also explained (p. 66) why the word 'heirs' extended to the heirs of heirs, and so on.

16 Or an heir presumptive: i.e. a female who might be overtaken as heir by a subsequently born male.

17 Cf. *Glanvill*, vii.1, 5, which says that one reason for not allowing a will of land was to prevent rash distribution by tenants on their death-bed.

18 *Glanvill*, vii.1.

presumptive had merely an expectation, not a vested estate, no ascertained individual was cut off by an alienation inter vivos. The conceptual change was reflected in conveyancing practice: in the eleventh century a grantor in fee often had his heirs apparent join in the grant by name, but in the thirteenth century the grantor made the warranty on behalf of his heirs in generic terms, and before long such a warranty was implied whatever words were actually used.

The tenant who was granted land 'unto himself and his heirs for ever' thus had, under the thirteenth-century common law, something quite different from a life estate. It is not improper to call it ownership, since its continuity was no longer restrained by the claims of his lord or his heirs. What he owned was an estate of infinite duration. If he wished during his lifetime he could alienate it for ever, and the grantees would remain entitled even if the grantor's own heirs later died out. If, on the other hand, he died seised, the estate did not end but descended automatically to his heir.[19] This estate was called 'fee simple', and it was the totality of ownership out of which all lesser estates were carved. Unlike lesser estates, it was as perpetual and indestructible as the land itself, subject neither to creation nor annihilation by mortal men. The fee simple, the right to land for ever, had always to be vested in someone, and if it could not be claimed by any subject it would be in the Crown. All that owners could do with it was to pass it from one to another or carve it up.

NATURE OF THE TENANCY FOR LIFE

The life estate could not be subject to the same rules as the fee simple. It was tied to the life span of the original grantee and could not be extended by alienation. This was equally true of alienation by subinfeudation and by substitution. Were it otherwise, the land might in theory be kept permanently from reverting to the grantor by a series of alienations to younger men. It was therefore axiomatic that, although a life tenant was free to alienate the whole of his interest, that interest was always determined by the death of the person for whose life the estate was originally given.

The estate which arose when a life estate was acquired from another person is still known by its French name as an estate *pur auter vie*. The tenant *pur auter vie* had an estate which lasted until some other person (the *cestuy que vie*) died. A problem insoluble by logic arose if the

---

[19] Descent vested the land automatically in the heir until 1897, when it was enacted that only the beneficial interest should descend, the legal title vesting automatically in the personal representatives of the deceased: Land Transfer Act 1897, 60 & 61 Vict., c. 65.

tenant *pur auter vie* died before *cestuy que vie*: the estate could not pass to his heirs by descent, because it was not a fee; it did not escheat, because *cestuy que vie* was still alive; and it could not be disposed of by will or by administration, because it was a freehold[20] and not a chattel. After early doubts, the estate was conceded, in default of any logical rule, to the first occupant. By 1600, however, the grantor of a life estate was allowed to specify in advance who such successors were to be, as by saying 'to *A* and his heirs for the life of *B*': in that case, if *A* predeceased *B*, *A*'s heirs would have the estate, not by descent but as 'special occupants'. The anarchic situation where there was no special occupant was not ended until 1677, when the Statute of Frauds conferred on tenants *pur auter vie* the power to devise their estate by will, and provided for the estate of an intestate tenant *pur auter vie* to be distributed by his personal representatives in the same way as a lease for years.[21]

The standard case of tenancy *pur auter vie* is where a life estate is assigned or granted by the original life tenant to another. Another common case was the lease for lives, where the estate was so made from its inception and was not derived out of another life estate. Such leases were used as an alternative to leases for years where it was desired to create an uninheritable freehold, as in the case of leases by colleges and ecclesiastical corporations who were only permitted to make short leases. The plurality of lives was a safeguard against the effect of premature death, and renewal was effected by the addition of new lives.

Because the tenant for life had always been a freehold tenant, with seisin, he was given the protection of the real actions. Nevertheless, by the thirteenth century his interest was coming to be seen as distinctly inferior to that of the tenant in fee, and closer in reality to that of a lessee for years. He was indeed called a 'lessee', and remedies were introduced to prevent him abusing his position by injuring or 'discontinuing' the inheritance. The tenant for life was made liable for waste (injuring the inheritance) in the same way as a tenant for years; after 1278, either kind of tenancy could be forfeited for deliberate waste, and the tenant sued for treble damages.[22] Discontinuance occurred when a tenant for life (or other particular tenant) with seisin made a wrongful feoffment: the feoffee acquired a fee simple, albeit precariously, and the reversioner's estate was thereby discontinued, or converted into a right of

---

[20] According to *Hengham* and *Britton*, the prevailing view. *Bracton* and *Fleta*, however, solved the problem by regarding it as a chattel.

[21] Stat. 29 Car. II, c.3, s.12.

[22] Statute of Gloucester 1278, c.5; p. 620, post (specimen writ). For the action of waste, see S. S. Walker, in *Legal Records and the Historian*, pp. 185-206.

action to recover the fee. At common law the reversioner could only 'recontinue' the alienated tenement, by bringing an action, once the tenant for life had died; but after 1285 the writ of entry *in consimili casu* was made available during the tenant's lifetime.

In later law the tenancy *pur auter vie* became increasingly different in character from a tenancy for the tenant's own life. We have seen how tenants *pur auter vie* were in some respects assimilated to lessees for years in 1677. Much later, in 1925, the commercial lease for lives was actually converted into a chattel interest by the provision that it should be treated as a lease for ninety years.[23] On the other hand, as we shall see, the tenant for life under a family settlement came to have an entirely different kind of interest, and to be given powers both to alienate or encumber the fee and to commit waste.[24]

The Law of Inheritance

The existence of inheritance as a social custom, or as a right guaranteed by a lord's grant, does not in itself necessitate fixed rules as to who should be heir. The common understanding of inheritance was that a tenant should be succeeded by close members of his family, but which member exactly it should be was determined by various conflicting factors. There were strong traditions at the time of the Norman conquest of equal partition between sons. There was also a strong tradition, where partibility was ruled out, for the ancestor to nominate his own heirs.[25] This is evident in the descent of the English Crown: for it was on this basis that William I, William II, Stephen and John all displaced nearer relatives who would have inherited under the later common law. Moreover, customs guiding lords' courts were not as permanent as law; at the manorial level, where old ways died hardest, we find that as late as the fourteenth century a manorial lord could – at the request of his tenants – replace one system by another.[26] Some of these variable traditions lived on as local customs, usually in relation to copyhold tenures, into more recent times. Coparcenary – the equal division between sons – was once very common in East Anglia; it survived as a

---

23 Law of Property Act 1925, 15 & 16 Geo. V, c.20, s.149(6).

24 See pp. 334-335, post.

25 A manorial survival has been noticed in 1317, when the lord of the manor of Ruislip granted to a tenant that she could nominate a child other than the firstborn to be her next heir: M. Morgan, *The English Lands of the Abbey of Bec* (1946), p. 71.

26 E.g., Homans, *English Villagers of the 13th Century*, p. 126 (ultimogeniture replaced by primogeniture, and vice versa).

general custom in Wales until 1536, and in Kent, where it was called 'gavelkind', until 1926. Ultimogeniture – inheritance by the last born – survived as the custom called 'borough English', which (despite its name) was prevalent in hundreds of rural manors until 1926.[27]

In the case of free tenants, however, these customs rapidly gave way in the twelfth and thirteenth centuries to the certainty of the common law. Since the common law protected inheritance as a right, by means of the writs of right and assize of mort d'ancestor, it had to define the heir. The customs adopted by the king's court therefore took on the status of rules of law: no longer mere guidance as to who should inherit, they settled who did inherit. A grantor had no say in these rules; he could choose whether to use the words 'and his heirs', but he could not choose who those heirs would be. No doubt this was a major advance in securing good order. The uncertainty of discretion begat family squabbles, of which the Battle of Hastings and the war between Stephen and Matilda were extreme examples. The scope for such disputes was greatly reduced by the orderly application of legal principle to questions of inheritance.

THE CANONS OF DESCENT

The principal canons of descent under the settled common law were as follows:

1. The parentelic scheme

Proximity of kinship for the purposes of succession was measured according to a 'parentelic' calculus. The *parentela* of a deceased person comprised all living persons who traced their blood from him: that is to say, his issue or descendants. The search for the heir went successively through the *parentelae*, beginning with that of the deceased himself, then that of his father, and so on. Each set of descendants had a better claim than those in the next degree of remoteness, so that lineal descendants of the deceased were preferred to his collateral relatives, and brothers and sisters were preferred to uncles and aunts. Only if there were no surviving children, grandchildren, or more remote issue, did the law look to siblings, cousins or other collaterals for the heir. If collaterals were considered, those on the father's side were preferred to those on the

---

[27]   It was said to take its name from the English quarter of the borough of Nottingham, where it operated. For the manorial custom, see G.R. Corner, 2 *Proc. Suffolk Inst. Archeol.* 227; 6 *Sussex Arch. Soc.* 164. For a survey of peasant inheritance customs, see R. J. Faith, 14 *Agricultural History Rev.* 77.

mother's, however remote.[28] Moreover, if the land had descended from the father's side, the mother's side was totally excluded and in the absence of heirs on the father's side the land would escheat. Similarly, if land descended through the mother, the father's side of the family was excluded by the same right of return (*jus recadentiae*); in this case the search for the heir went through the mother's male line ascending, according to the above principles.

A second aspect of the parentelic scheme was that a deceased person was 'represented' by his own issue, however remote. Thus if *A* has an elder son *B* and a younger son *C*, and *B* dies in his father's lifetime leaving a son *B*1, and then *A* dies; *A*'s heir is *B*1 and not *C*, because *B*1 represents his father. This rule was not clear at the time of *Glanvill* (which calls it *magna juris dubitatio*) or *Bracton*, and was only established after bitter struggles between grandchildren and their uncles; King John was such an uncle, and his accession to the throne in 1199 delayed complete acceptance of the representation principle until later in the thirteenth century. Before the rule was settled, a vestige of the older feudal world lingered on: whoever succeeded in gaining seisin kept it.[29]

2. Males preferred to females in the same degree

When it was generally taught that male superiority was ordained by God, and when men at least believed that they were more capable of managing affairs than women,[30] it is hardly surprising that land ownership was arranged on a patriarchal principle. The usual expectation was that family land would descend in the male line, together with the family name, and that if women owned land at all they would carry the title to men by marriage and motherhood. This was reflected in the legal rule that males were preferred for inheritance purposes to females of the same degree. Thus a brother was always preferred as heir to his sisters, even if they were born before him. But the common law did not exclude female inheritance, because it gave greater weight to the parentelic system than to the exclusion of females. Women were therefore allowed to inherit if there were no males in the same degree. Thus, if a deceased tenant left no sons, his daughters were

---

[28] *Clere v. Brooke* (1573) 2 Plowd. 442. In the 13th century there had been a doctrine favouring alternation from one side to the other in each degree. Even in the 18th century it was unsettled whether the preference for the 'male line ascending' applied to different parentelic degrees: whether, for instance, the brother of the paternal grandmother was preferred to the brother of the paternal grandfather's mother: Bl. Comm., vol. II, pp. 238-240 (Blackstone for the latter, Hale for the former).

[29] *Glanvill*, vii.3.

[30] See Plowd. 444-445; B. & M. 490, per Plowden.

preferred to his brother because they were lineal descendants within his own *parentela*.

3. *Primogeniture and coparcenary*

The usual custom of succession before the Norman conquest seems to have been coparcenary, or inheritance by all the sons or daughters of the deceased. The custom was recognised in the twelfth century, when we hear of coparceners taking as one heir but holding their shares 'in parage'. This meant that the eldest only was tenant *quoad* the lord, but his brothers held their shares of him by a strange form of tenure in which there were no services or incidents and the tenant was somehow a peer of his lord. The change to primogeniture, inheritance by the firstborn to the exclusion of his brothers, may have been connected with the precariousness of the younger brothers' holding in parage; they had no seisin which the law could protect, and having dropped first from legal notice they soon dropped from moral notice also. Primogeniture seems to have started with military tenure, and with the Crown and great offices of state (which were indivisible). By Glanvill's time (*c.* 1190) knights' fees had ceased to be partible and all went to the firstborn, but land held in socage was still partible if it had been so of old. During the next century primogeniture spread to most free tenures, and enabled great landowners to keep their estates intact, whatever the form of tenure; it was far from universal at the manorial level.

Primogeniture seems to have been applied by the Normans to women as well as men, if they succeeded to baronies or knight's fees. This was changed by a 'statutum decretum' of Henry I,[31] which provided that if there were no sons the daughters all inherited equally as parceners. That stood as law ever after, except in relation to the Crown. However, the notion developed during the twelfth century that the sisters held in parage, so that only the eldest (or her husband) did homage. The reason here was not to diminish the status of the younger sisters but to deprive the lord of their wardships. When, therefore, the parage doctrine disappeared in or before the following century,[32] sisters thereafter took equally and in parallel. It was uncertain early in the thirteenth century whether they nevertheless took as 'one heir', with survivorship as in the case of joint tenancy; but the settled law by the end of the century was that female parceners were considered as analogous to tenants in common, with undivided shares. The shares could be separated by

---

[31]　Stenton, *English Feudalism*, 39-40; J.C. Holt, 35 TRHS (5th ser.) 9 et seq.

[32]　It was taken to have been settled by the 'Statute' of Ireland *de coheredibus* 1236, which was not a statute but a writ explaining the law for the justices in Ireland.

'partition', and if the parceners could not agree on the shares there was an action *de partitione facienda* to compel a fair division by the sheriff.

4. *Exclusion of collaterals of the half-blood*

When an heir was sought among *A*'s issue, it mattered not whether the issue had been born of one marriage or another, because all *A*'s issue were descendants of the whole blood. Thus a son by a second marriage would be preferred to a daughter by the first. Half-sisters could be coparceners as heir to their father. If, however, a tenant died seised without issue, having a half-brother (that is, a brother by a different marriage) and a sister by the same marriage, the brother could not inherit because he was not related by the whole blood, and so the sister was heir. If there was no sister, the land would escheat. The reason for this artificial rule was the subject of much speculation and controversy until the rule itself was abolished in 1833.[33]

Provision for Spouses and new Families

These rules of inheritance lasted, with few alterations, until 1926, when inheritance as a principle of succession to land was virtually abolished.[34] Their endurance may be attributed less to their intrinsic merit than to the freedom with which, in later times, they could be modified. The common law ensured that unless land was disposed of or settled inter vivos, it would benefit a family only in a lineal, dynastic sense. Spouses, parents, younger sons, daughters having brothers, and illegitimate children, could not inherit on the owner's death. The dynasty was nevertheless unprotected against disherison by a conveyance made during the owner's lifetime. Inheritance, from being the only kind of protected succession recognised by law, came to operate as the default-mode of devolution when a tenant died seised in fee without having made any alternative provision.

The owner of land might attempt to circumvent the fixed laws of succession by making an express provision to govern the devolution of the land in the future. He could withdraw parcels of land from the patrimony to make gifts to members of his immediate family,

---

[33] Inheritance Act 1833, 3 & 4 Will. IV, c.106. The rule did not apply if the elder brother predeceased the father, because the half-brother then inherited as heir to the *father*. Nor did it apply in the case of an entail, because descent was always traced from the first donee and not from the deceased.

[34] Administration of Estates Act 1925, 15 & 16 Geo. V, c.23, s.33(1). The devolution of land on intestacy was thereby assimilated to that of personal property.

especially on marriage; or he might tie up the patrimony in such a way as to restrict the dispositive powers of his descendants. In deciding whether, and to what extent, to give effect to such arrangements, the law had to resolve the conflict between the interests of the living family in an extended sense and the dynastic instinct to preserve the unity of the patrimony in the male line. There was a similar tension between the social desirability of ensuring that land remained freely marketable and the paternalistic concern to restrain the rash prodigality of youthful heirs. The law therefore had to hold a balance between the living, the dead, and the unborn.

DOWER

The wife was not a descendant of her husband, and so she was outside the scope of inheritance. Husband and wife were accounted one person in law,[35] and grants from one to the other were generally void, but with one important exception. A husband could make a gift to his wife on the day they were married, at the church door, and this would take effect on the husband's death if the wife survived him. This was called 'dower', and under the supervision of the Church the endowment of wives at the church door became a regular feature of the marriage service. The lands to be assigned as dower were nominated before the nuptials, after negotiation between the families. When the wedding took place, and the husband had given his wife the ring (saying, 'with this ring I thee wed'), he gave her tokens symbolising dower, adding 'and with this dower I thee endow'. This symbolic livery gave a widow the right to an estate for life in the lands so nominated, an estate which the husband's heir was obliged to warrant. Disputes about dower were very common in the early royal courts, especially where there had been successive marriages. To protect the heir, the common law forbade the assignment of more than one third of the husband's lands as dower, and the heir could have the widow's allotted share reduced by a writ of admeasurement if there was any dispute. An alternative arrangement was for the husband to endow his wife generally of all his lands, without nominating any specific property. The widow was then entitled to claim a life estate in a reasonable share of her husband's land, which the law fixed as one third;[36] in Glanvill's time it was a third of the lands owned in fee by the husband at the time of the marriage, but the law soon allowed the widow to have the like share of land acquired or

---

[35] See pp. 550-557, post.

[36] *Glanvill*, vi.1, 2. Custom might allow more: gavelkind custom gave the widow one half.

disposed of during the marriage. Under Magna Carta this entitlement became a common-law right, independent of any agreement or formality at the time of marriage, though it could be overridden by an express assignment of less.[37] Later in the century the qualification disappeared, and a widow became entitled to reject specified dower and claim her common-law share. This right of election made the nomination of specific dower less advantageous, since common-law dower was by definition more generous,[38] and the practice went into disuse.

Dower was an estate of freehold, akin to a tenancy for life, arising by operation of law and held of the husband's heir as lord. But estates arising by operation of law have usually proved inconvenient, for men prefer to make their own arrangements. The widespread practice of vesting land in feoffees to uses rendered it virtually obsolete, except at the lowest levels of landholding where uses were inappropriate, because the Chancery did not recognise dower in respect of uses, and dower did not attach at law on the death of a joint tenant. It became usual instead to provide in a marriage settlement for some land to be settled on the husband and wife jointly for the life of the survivor, so that a widow would have the land until her death in lieu of dower. Such a provision was called a 'jointure'. The Statute of Uses 1536, by executing uses, would have revived dower generally; but it was enacted that this should only avail wives who had no jointures, so that jointresses should not become entitled to dower as well.[39] The possibility of dower being claimed by a vendor's widow was always an anxious consideration for purchasers, but the problem was aggravated after 1536 since the claim might turn on the legal efficacy of the jointure arrangements; various devices to bar dower were therefore invented, so that an unfettered title could be passed. Such problems were ended by the Dower Act 1833, which empowered husbands to bar dower by will or by alienation inter vivos;[40] in 1925 dower was abolished in respect of persons dying thereafter.

---

[37] Magna Carta 1217, c.7. It was also enacted that the widow could remain in the principal house for forty days (her 'quarantine'), during which time her dower was to be assigned.

[38] However, one advantage to the widow was that she could enter in the nominated land on her husband's death, whereas for common-law dower she needed an assignment by the heir and might have to sue.

[39] Stat. 27 Hen. VIII, c.10; B. & M. 113-114. But a widow could refuse a jointure conveyed after marriage, and take her dower instead.

[40] Stat. 3 & 4 Will. IV, c.105.

CURTESY

The man who married an heiress was in a different position. If she predeceased her husband, her land could not descend at once to her own heir, because during the marriage the husband had been seised of his wife's land and owed homage for it to her lord. The common law took the view that the husband's seisin entitled him to remain tenant of his wife's land after her death for the rest of his own life. The widower in this case was called tenant *per legem Angliae*, or tenant 'by the curtesy of England'. In fact the continuation of seisin by husbands was by no means peculiar to England, but apparently English law was thought more 'courteous' (or generous) than others in that the widower's estate was not defeated by remarriage. A mysterious prerequisite to tenancy by the curtesy was that a child of the marriage, capable of inheriting, should have been born.

Curtesy was abolished with respect to estates in fee simple in 1925, but it survives as a doctrine of equity[41] in relation to entailed interests.

THE MARRIAGE-GIFT AND THE CONDITIONAL FEE

The provision of *dos* at the time of marriage was recognised by the universal Church and was practised throughout Europe and beyond. But, while to the common lawyer *dos* meant dower, in other systems it meant dowry: a gift to the wife, or to husband and wife, by the bride's parents or other relatives. In England this was called the 'marriage-gift' or *maritagium*. Marriage-gifts were commonly made either to establish a cadet branch of a family or to assist a daughter who was not an heiress to make a good match. Since the purpose of such gifts was to provide for the couple and their progeny, the couple were not usually given an absolute fee, but an inheritance limited to their issue. Often such a gift would be in 'frank-marriage' (*in liberum maritagium*), in which case the donees held of the donor free of all feudal services for three generations. Even in cases where service was reserved, it was a usual feature of a marriage-gift that homage was not taken from the donee; the purpose of this omission was to prevent collaterals from inheriting on failure of issue. The donor remained seised, so that he could take back the land if the arrangement failed. The donee's position was in consequence weak and unstable; in *Glanvill* the arrangement is called 'a bare promise'. After three generations, however, the third heir was liable to perform services and could insist on doing homage. There was once again an ordinary fee simple. The three-generation principle apparently grew from twelfth-century custom, and recognised that the instability of the

---

[41] Equity allowed curtesy of a trust, but not dower.

gift should cease once the family was well established and the possibility of a failure of heirs had become slight.

It became common in the thirteenth century for similar gifts to be made otherwise than on marriage, or to younger sons or brothers. Homage was usually taken in such cases, but the restriction on heirs was the same. The resulting fee was called fee tail (*feodum talliatum*, meaning a cut-down fee). The typical form of words was 'to *H* and the heirs of his body begotten' or 'to *H* and *W* and to the heirs of *H* begotten on *W*'. The words of inheritance, as used to create a fee, were thus cut down by the addition of 'words of procreation' which were calculated to eliminate collateral heirs. To lawyers of the mid-thirteenth century, however, it was unacceptable that a donor should restrict the course of inheritance indefinitely; if a man gave away a fee, an inheritance, he could not restrain the donee from alienating it in fee. The words of procreation were therefore construed as a once-and-for-all condition precedent to the creation of a fee: the gift in tail was a life estate which became fee if issue was born. Thus 'to *H* and the heirs of his body' was rather artificially held to mean 'to *H* and his heirs if he has an heir of his body' rather than 'to *H* and his heirs so long as he has heirs of his body'. The same construction may have been applied to gifts in frank-marriage. The result was that the donee, on birth of issue, could alienate for ever: and his grantee's estate would endure even if the donee's issue died out, to the prejudice of the donor as lord.

This conclusion was felt to be mischievous. Family gifts of this kind removed land from the patrimony for the benefit of the donees and their issue, with the intention that it should revert to the donor and his heirs – the main family line – if the issue failed. The condition was meant to take effect as a condition subsequent; yet, because the law did not permit that construction, the land could be kept away from the donor indefinitely, either by collateral inheritance or by alienation. In 1258 the barons petitioned for redress of this grievance, and a remedy was finally provided in 1285, by the important statute *De donis conditionalibus* ('of conditional gifts').[42]

THE STATUTE DE DONIS 1285

The statute of 1285 protected the intentions of donors from frustration, in the most liberal terms. It ordained that in future when land was given to a man and wife and the heirs of their bodies, or to one person and the heirs of his body, or in frank-marriage, the 'will of the donor manifestly

---

[42] Petition of the Barons 1258, c.27; Statute of Westminster II 1285, c.1; B. & M. 48.

expressed in the terms of the gift (*forma doni*)' was to be observed. The issue and the donor were given writs of 'formedon' (from *forma doni*) to protect their statutory interests by allowing them to enforce the terms of the gift. So liberally was the statute construed that donors were able to restrict the inheritance in ways not permissible at common law but deemed to fall within the equity of the statute. Thus, a gift could be restricted to A and the heirs *male* of his body,[43] whereas a gift to A and his heirs male (without words of procreation) at common law passed a fee simple inheritable by females.

The statute produced the odd legal result that two fees could exist simultaneously in the same land; an unfeudal notion, comprehensible only in the sense that the fee had become an estate or time in the land which could vest either in possession or in the future. The fee tail (or 'tail') created by the statute was different from the common-law cut-down fee in that it was not freely alienable; if a tenant in tail alienated, his issue could recover the land by bringing formedon 'in the descender'. Moreover, it was not necessarily eternal; it was a particular estate which might come to an end on a failure of issue, in which case the donor could bring formedon 'in the reverter' against an intruder. It was therefore possible for a gift to contain successive remainders in tail to different people, each enforceable by formedon 'in the remainder'. In all these cases the fee simple stayed in the donor. This fee simple was a future estate which would not fall into possession unless the donees' issue failed, which might never happen; but it was logically necessary that it should be vested in someone, to fill the residue of eternity which would be left if and when the entails ended. In this respect the statute contributed to the doctrine of future estates, to which we must briefly turn.

Reversions and remainders

Before 1300 common lawyers had come to speak of estates in possession, in remainder, and in reversion. This tripartite classification was not based on the duration of estates but on the time of their enjoyment.

The reversion is the most natural future estate. If a tenant in fee granted a life estate or made a gift in fee tail to another, he became the grantee's lord; and when the grantee's interest ended it came back to him

---

[43] *Helton v. Kene* (1344) B. & M. 53. The losing argument was that the requirement of male issue was simply a condition precedent to the creation of a fee tail which would descend to females.

by escheat. When the feudal dimension was diluted or removed, and the same arrangement was analysed in terms of estates, the lessor for life and the donor in tail were said to have a 'reversion'; the land would revert to them when the lesser estate (the 'particular estate') ended. The reversion, viewed as an estate in the land, was an absolute fee simple, an estate of infinite duration, as freely alienable as the fee simple in possession, but with the right to possession postponed until after the particular estate. Thus, to say that a reversion is a 'future estate' is true only of the right to possession; the estate is 'vested in reversion' from the moment when the particular estate is created. Therefore, if the tenant in possession tried to alienate the fee so as to 'discontinue' the reversion, the reversioner could forthwith bring a writ of entry.[44]

If a grantor limited successive interests by the same grant, for instance 'to A for life and then to B and his heirs', the future interest given to B was not a reversion because it was to stay away from the grantor. It was therefore called a remainder, from the Latin *remanere*, to stay away. If the remainder was in fee simple, as in the example, the grantor had nothing left and there could be no reversion. But the remainder could be an estate of shorter duration than a fee simple, in which case the grantor would still have a reversion in fee simple. That is why successive remainders could be carved out of the same fee simple: for instance, 'to A for life, remainder to B for life, remainder to C for life', or 'to W for life, remainder to X in fee tail, remainder to Y in fee tail, remainder to Z in fee simple'. Provided all the remaindermen were ascertained persons, the principal restriction was that a remainder could not follow a fee simple.[45]

The law had greater difficulty accommodating the remainder than the reversion. The reversion was, in feudal terms, an escheat; and in non-feudal terms it is common sense that a man who gives away a slice of his cake keeps the cake. But a remainderman was neither lord nor heir, and was not seised of anything; he took by a form of succession unknown to feudal law, and it was not at first clear what remedy he should have to protect his interest. In *Bracton* he is a quasi-heir, to whom the land could be said to 'descend', in a loose sense, according to the *forma doni*. Perhaps the implication was that the remainderman should use a fictitious action of formedon in the descender. In fact the writ of formedon in the reverter seems occasionally to have been so used, until in 1279 the Chancery invented a new writ of formedon in the

[44] Statute of Westminster II 1285, c.24. The remedy where the prior estate ended in due course was the writ of entry called formedon in the reverter.
[45] See further pp. 321-322, post.

remainder.[46] In this action the remainderman relied on the seisin of both the grantor and the first grantee, and it came to be thought that the right to seisin passed to him via the first grantee. But this theory availed nothing if the remainder was 'contingent' and not vested.

A contingent remainder was a remainder limited to take effect upon the happening of an uncertain event, which might not happen before the determination of the particular estate or at all, or limited to a person not ascertained at the time of the grant.[47] The common example in the year-book period was the remainder to the heir of a living person: for example, 'to A for life, remainder to the heir of B'. If this contingent remainder was in fee, the location of the fee during A's lifetime was elusive. Either it stayed in the grantor until the remainder was ascertained and the remainder vested; or it stayed until the particular estate determined and the remainder vested in possession; or it just went into thin air (*in nubibus*) until it vested.[48] On any of these views, the remainder could only be valid if it vested before the particular estate ended; otherwise there would be an abeyance of seisin and no feudal tenant, a legal impossibility. Whether it was valid even if it did vest in time had been an early moot point, because on one view a remainder ought to be certain from the time of the grant; but the contingent remainder seems have become accepted in the fifteenth century, and to have been finally recognised by judicial decision in 1550.[49] Its subsequent importance grew out of the attempts of conveyancers to make perpetual settlements.

Further reading

Pollock & Maitland, vol. II, pp. 1-28, 240-356
Holdsworth HEL, vol. III, pp. 101-137, 171-197
Plucknett CHCL, pp. 521-530, 546-552, 558-570

---

[46]   *Ferlington v. Brewosa* (1279-81) 10 IJ 322. Formedon in the descender continued to be the appropriate remedy for the heir of a remainderman: *Barre v. Hales* (1329) 97 SS 459.

[47]   J. C. Gray defined a remainder as contingent when 'in order for it to come into possession, the fulfilment of some condition precedent other than the determination of the preceding freehold estate is necessary': *Rule against Perpetuities*, p. 89. A reversion could never be contingent because by definition it belonged to an ascertained person and fell into possession when the particular estate ended.

[48]   See *Blakett's Case* (1410) B. & M. 69-70.

[49]   *Faryngton v. Darell* (1431) B. & M. 70-78, esp. at p. 73, per Babington CJ ('It has been the point of a moot case'); Constable's reading on *De donis* (1489) 71 SS 179; *Colthirst v. Bejushin* (1550) B. & M. 78-84.

Simpson, *History of the Land Law*, pp. 47-80

C. M. Updegraff, 'The Interpretation of "Issue" in De Donis' (1925) 39 HLR 200-220

Milsom HFCL, pp. 166-177; 'Formedon before De Donis' (1956) 72 LQR 391-397 (repr. in SHCL 223-229); 'Inheritance by Women in the 12th and 13th Centuries' (1981) in *Laws and Customs*, pp. 60-89 (repr. in SHCL 231-260)

P. A. Brand, 'Formedon in the Remainder before De Donis' (1975) 10 IJ 318-323

J. L. Barton, 'The Rise of the Fee Simple' (1976) 92 LQR 108-121

T. G. Watkin, 'Feudal Theory, Social Needs and the Rise of the Heritable Fee' (1979) 10 *Cambrian Law Rev.* 39-62

J. S. Loengard, '"Of the Gift of her Husband": English Dower and its Consequences in the Year 1200' in *Women in the Medieval World* (J. Kirshner ed., 1985), pp. 215-255

J. Biancalana, 'For Want of Justice: Legal Reforms of Henry II' (1988) 88 *Columbia Law Rev.* at 514-534 (on dower)

Table D. Estates in land

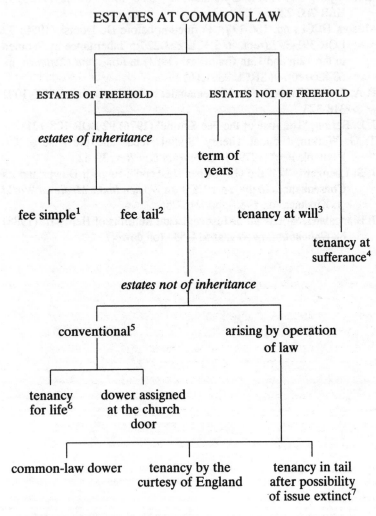

1   Absolute, conditional or qualified.
2   General or special (e.g. limited to male heirs).
3   Including the copyhold tenancy, which was at the will of the lord of the manor.
4   Including the interest of cestuy que use in possession.
5   I.e. arising by act of the parties.
6   Including tenancy *pur auter vie*, which might be an estate *quasi* of inheritance in case of special occupancy: e.g. to *A* and his heirs for the life of *B*.
7   A fee having some of the attributes of the life estate, since it cannot descend.

Table E. Modes of conveying real property

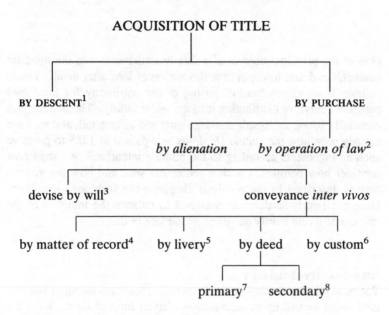

ACQUISITION OF TITLE

BY DESCENT[1]   BY PURCHASE

by alienation   *by operation of law*[2]

devise by will[3]   conveyance *inter vivos*

by matter of record[4]   by livery[5]   by deed   by custom[6]

primary[7]   secondary[8]

[1] Three modes: (i) at common law, (ii) in tail, (iii) customary (e.g. gavelkind, borough English).
[2] E.g. by escheat, forfeiture, limitation, general occupancy.
[3] Either by borough custom or (after 1540) by statute.
[4] E.g. act of parliament, letters patent under the great seal, deed enrolled, final concord, (after 1536) bargain and sale enrolled.
[5] Only appropriate to corporeal hereditaments; the livery of seisin was usually accompanied by a deed to evidence the estate granted.
[6] E.g. surrender and admittance in court customary.
[7] Creating an estate, e.g., feoffments, gifts, grants, demises.
[8] Dealing with a pre-existing estate, e.g. releases, quitclaims, confirmations, surrenders, assignments, disentailing devices.

16. Real Property: Family Settlements

One of the principal objects of a family settlement[1] was the dynastic instinct, the desire to control the devolution of land after death so as to restrain descendants from disposing of the patrimony for their own personal benefit or distributing it to the wider family. The instinct was especially strong as regards marriage-gifts and gifts in tail, and we have already seen how the statute *De donis* was passed in 1285 to preserve such arrangements according to the donor's intention.[2] We shall now consider how permanent such a settlement was, and how the various estates described in the previous chapter were fashioned into more elaborate family settlements designed to balance the interests of the immediate living family and those of the family line.

THE DURABILITY OF THE FEE TAIL

The broad draftsmanship of *De donis* raised the legal question whether land could be tied up to descendants without limit of time. Were the issue in tail to have successive life interests for ever, so that no one could alienate the fee so long as issue continued? The statute was silent as to the period for which the terms of the gift were to be inviolable. A literal reading of the statute would suggest that 'issue' meant only the issue born of the first donees,[3] so that only the donees themselves were restrained from alienating. In a case of 1312, however, Bereford CJ pronounced that the statute had failed to say what was meant: the issue were meant to be restrained from alienating until the gift became absolute in the fourth degree.[4] An anonymous lecturer at the same period explained that for three generations the donee and his issue had only life interests, and then there was fee. The old *maritagium* principle

---

[1] A family settlement was an arrangement whereby several estates in succession were created for members of a family by the same grant.

[2] See p. 311, ante.

[3] The statute spoke of issue failing 'either because there was no issue at all or because there was issue but it failed by death of such issue without an heir': B. & M. 49.

[4] *Daniel v. Bere* (1292) B. & M. 50-51; *Belyng's Case* (1312) B. & M. 52-53.

had simply been extended to all gifts in tail. But this subjective interpretation was given up before the end of the century, in deference to the words. Since the statute said nothing about three generations, and since an heir could only inherit what his ancestor had, it followed that if an inalienable estate descended once it remained inalienable for ever. Each successive heir in tail, until the end of the line, could bring formedon in the descender to thwart any attempt to discontinue the tail.

This logical but unattractive conclusion gave the fee tail almost opposite characteristics from the fee simple. It was a rigid, unalterable, inalienable perpetuity: a 'juridical monster'.[5] No one could 'own' entailed land beyond his own lifetime. Unless some escape could be found, vast quantities of land would be tied up indefinitely. But the pressures in favour of free alienation inevitably prevailed, and ways were soon found of 'barring' the entail and converting it into a fee simple.

If the tenant in tail conveyed the land to a stranger in fee simple with warranty, the issue in tail would be bound by the warranty if they had land of equal value ('assets') descending to them from the same ancestor. This was the first means of barring the entail, though the requirement of assets made it a precarious device, and it did not bar the remainderman or reversioner. In the later fifteenth century a more effective means had been found, by combining the warranty with a collusive real action called a 'common recovery'. In its simplest form, an accomplice[6] brought a real action against the tenant in tail on an imaginary title in fee simple; the tenant vouched a third party to warrant his title; the vouchee defaulted; and judgment was given for the accomplice to recover the fee simple against the tenant in tail. Of course, if the claim had been genuine, the tail would necessarily have been barred; the right in fee simple could hardly be destroyed by a usurper giving the land away in tail. The effect of the warranty, however, was to give the barred issue a right to recover land of equal value against the warrantor who defaulted. And this right to assets made the recovery effective even where the title was fictitious. The trick, established by about 1474, was for a humble, landless official of the Common Pleas to lend his name to all comers (for a fee of four pence) as the 'common vouchee'. The common vouchee would always default when his name was called, and (since the assets could only be recovered in land), the issue in tail were thereby cut off with a worthless right to execute judgment against the

---

5 Milsom HFCL, p. 177.

6 Often a group of lawyers, who upon the recovery became seised of the fee simple to the use of the former tenant in tail.

lands of a landless nobody.[7] This legal trick could not be faulted, since
in theory the issue were not injured, and by 1500 the common recovery
had made the fee tail freely convertible into a fee simple. St German
raised the moral question whether it was consistent with conscience to
allow the defeat of entails by untrue fictions; but the Student doubtless
reflected professional opinion in answering that the device was too
common to be overturned, and that the policy of *De donis* in
'magnifying the blood' deserved no support.[8] There were doubts at first
whether the recovery barred remaindermen and the reversioner as well as
the issue; but from 1484 they could be barred by final concord (or 'fine')
with proclamations, and by the end of the sixteenth century the common
recovery could be used to bar them effectively as well.[9]

Even before the common recovery was established, conveyancers had
begun to experiment with conditions to prevent barring. In an early
example of 1360 a manor was given in tail on condition that if the
donees or their heirs should alienate in fee, or lease beyond their own
lives, the donor should have a right of re-entry. It was not until 1493
that the device was questioned; and it was accepted.[10] But this was rather
a drastic remedy, because it brought the whole settlement to an end.
Attempts to restrain alienation without destroying the rest of the
settlement were initially unsuccessful: one or two judges around 1400
are said to have experimented with gifts to a son in tail, with remainder
if he attempted to alienate to the next son, and so on, but these failed
because conditions could only be enforced by the donor and his heirs.[11]

Uses and devises gave the conveyancer more flexibility: already in
1431 it had been noted that a devise had peculiar qualities for settlement
purposes.[12] An entail in use may have been unbarrable before the
Statute of Uses 1536, on the basis that the feoffees were bound in
conscience to preserve the tail. By at least 1516, however,[13]
conveyancers had invented a new kind of perpetuity clause, to achieve

7   The first common vouchee seems to have been Denis Guyer (c.1474-88,
    operating for the first ten years with Robert Kyng). Thereafter a distinct line of
    succession can be traced: 94 SS *204-205*. The idea seems to have been suggested
    by *Hunt qui tam etc. v. Smyth* (1472) Kiralfy SB, pp. 86-99, traditionally known
    as *Taltarum's Case.*
8   *Doctor and Student* (91 SS), pp. 156-159; B. & M. 61-64.
9   *Capel's Case* (1581) 1 Co. Rep. 61. The 1484 statute is 1 Ric. III, c.7; the fine
    was only operative if no claim was made within five years.
10 *Hulcote v. Ingleton* (1493) B. & M. 57-61.
11 *Rikhill's Case* (c. 1395) B. & M. 67-68; *Thirning's Case* (c. 1400) B. &M. 68-69.
12 *Faryngton v. Darell* (1431) B. & M. 70 at 74, per Paston J.
13 See 1 Leon. 256 (will of Richard Hart).

with uses and devises what had previously been impossible at law, by using a limitation in the form: to *A* and the heirs of his body until he alienated, or attempted to alienate, and then over to another. We shall see that eventually these clauses were struck down by the courts.[14] It was 'against the reason and policy of the common law' to create perpetuities, notwithstanding *De donis*, and therefore an entail was in law inherently barrable. The judges thus contrived, first by fiction and then by judicial legislation, to circumvent the unforeseen consequences of a loosely drawn medieval statute. Thereafter it could be said with some truth that the most practicable difference between the fee tail and the fee simple was the mode of conveyance.[15] Nevertheless, entails were not barrable until the issue was of full age; and, as we shall see later in the chapter, they remained the basic ingredient of family settlements for centuries.

Remainders and Executory Interests

Behind these developments may be detected the recurrent theme that the owner of land in fee, be it fee simple or fee tail, is the absolute owner and must have the power to alienate the land for a period exceeding his own life. The way to avoid such alienations, if it could be done at all, was not to impose a restraint on the fee – which was repugnant to the very idea of fee – but to postpone the fee in such a way that the tenant in possession of the land for the time being had only a life interest. If the fee could be kept always in remainder, no tenant in possession would be able to alienate more than a life estate without securing the concurrence of the remaindermen in fee.

Remainders could not be used, however, simply to split up a fee between a person and his own heirs so that the heirs took by way of remainder and not by descent from their ancestor. Thus, if land were granted 'to *A* for life, remainder to *A*'s heirs', this gave the fee simple at once to *A*. If *A* died seised, there would be a descent to his heir and the incidents would fall due; the lord would otherwise be defrauded of his incidents.[16] This construction also meant that *A* could alienate the fee, because his heirs had no estate by purchase. For the same reason, a grant 'to *B* in tail, remainder to *B*'s heirs in fee simple' gave *B* a fee simple forthwith. To have held otherwise would have enabled the creation of a fee simple which could not be alienated by lineal heirs.[17]

---

14 See pp. 325-326, post.

15 D. Barrington, *Observations on the Statutes* (4th ed., 1775), p. 132.

16 *Sutton's Case*, alias *The Provost of Beverley's Case* (1366) B. & M. 65-66.

17 *Anon.* (1320) 104 SS 114.

Another possibility was to attempt to create a perpetual succession of remainders. But the efficacy of such a settlement depended on the extent to which the law would permit contingent remainders. It was settled in 1550, after some doubts, that 'everyone who is the lawful owner of land may give it to whatever person, in whatever manner and at whatever time he pleases, so long as his gift is not contrary to law or repugnant'.[18] But, as we have seen, the law required the remainder to vest at the latest by the time the particular estate came to an end. Moreover, until vesting, the remainder had no legal existence; it did not belong to anyone, and was not property. Therefore, as a corollary to the principle that the remainder had to vest before the determination of the preceding estate, the remainder could be destroyed by the ending of that estate before the remainder vested. For example, if land were granted to *A* for life, remainder to the heirs of *B*, and *A* made a grant in fee to *C* during *B*'s lifetime, the remainder was destroyed; by the time *B*'s heir was ascertained, there was no precedent life estate to support his remainder.[19] It follows that the common law brooked no substantial risk of perpetuities once the entail became barrable. The usual settlement before 1536 was in the form of successive entails to named sons, who took not as heirs but as named living persons with vested remainders. A remainder in tail after another entail might, of course, come into possession at a remote time; but there was no perpetuity, because it could be barred by common recovery. The conveyancer could only give secure interests to living persons, because remainders to unborn persons were by definition contingent and as such liable to destruction.

The Statutes of Uses and Wills shook this common-law system to the foundations, by raising new possibilities which for a century and a half threw the land law into turmoil.

EXECUTORY INTERESTS

Before 1536 there had been little occasion to create permanent settlements in use. Most uses were passive uses in fee simple, though settlements of the use were sometimes made by will. The 'use in tail' had been a topic of debate in the years leading up to the statute, and had given lawyers nightmares. *De donis* did not, of course, contemplate equitable interests; but if it could be construed to extend to uses, it

---

18 *Colthirst v. Bejushin* (1550) B. & M. 78 at 82, per Mountague CJ.

19 See 1 Co. Rep. 135v-136 (1595). The year-book opinions conflicted: Plucknett CHCL, pp. 562-564.

would have been impossible to bar the entail by common recovery.[20] No discussion of the status of remainders in use has come to light; but there would have been no reason to subject them to the nascent legal principles governing the vesting of the legal estate. So long as the feoffees' estate conformed to the legal rules, the seisin would never be in abeyance, and the feoffees would be obliged in conscience to hold the land to the use of the remainders. The problem here began with the Statute of Uses. The statutory magic of 1536, whereby the interest of cestuy que use was transubstantiated into a legal estate, gave rise to two bewildering conundrums.

The first conundrum was whether the statute executed future interests at all, and if so how. Let us suppose a grant 'to A to the use of B for life, and after B's death to the use of C'. The statute executed the use by giving seisin to B. But what happened on B's death? The statute only operated where someone was seised to the use of another; but B had not been seised to the use of C. If the 'remainder' was to be executed by the statute, it had to be supposed that A was somehow still seised to the use of C on B's death. The theoretical obstacle was that the statute had already taken A's seisin and given it to B, and there was nothing in the statute to say that B's seisin could go back to A. Legal ingenuity solved the puzzle by supposing that, when the use was executed in B, a spark of title (which Dyer called the *scintilla juris*) nevertheless remained in A for the purpose of igniting the estate expectant on B's death.[21] C's interest was called an 'executory interest'; it was due to be executed, or turned into a legal estate, upon some contingency, but until that happened it was a mere expectancy. Similar, if not worse, problems arose under the Statute of Wills 1540, because there might not even be feoffees in whom the spark could be kept alight. The courts dealt boldly with such nice problems, and by the end of Elizabeth I's reign it was quite clear that future interests in use had this property of being 'executory': that is, subject to the statutory magic only when the time came for them to be executed.

The second conundrum followed from the solution to the first. Executory interests became legal interests when executed, but did this make them subject to the legal rules about remainders? Strict logic at first denied it. There had been no restriction on future interests in use before 1536: 'uses are not directed by the rules of the common law but

---

[20] See 94 SS *207-208*.

[21] *Brent's Case* (1575) B. & M. 140 at 141, per Dyer CJ. Peryam CB commented 20 years later that the *scintilla juris* was as real as Sir Thomas More's Utopia: B. & M. 152. Whether the doctrine was really necessary remained a topic of debate until its abolition in 1860.

by the will of the owner of the lands; for the use is in his hands as clay is in the hands of the potter, which he in whose hands it is may put into whatever form he pleases'.[22] Then came the Statute of Uses which decreed that beneficiaries should be deemed to be seised 'of and in such like estates as they had in use'; and the Statute of Wills gave full liberty and authority to a freeholder to devise the legal estate 'at his free will and pleasure'. The courts therefore drew the conclusion that, however the clay was moulded, the legislation fired it into legal solidity.[23]

Within a few years the courts were regretting the consequences of this logic, and were slowly but surely abandoning it. If the statutes of Henry VIII had really been intended to render the legal rules obsolete, conveyancers could achieve whatever they wished by adding the magic words 'to the use of' in their settlements. Seisin could be made to skip and jump as never it could before, or even put into cold storage to await future contingencies.

The first clear indication that executory interests should be governed by the legal rules came in *Shelley's Case* (1581), in which Coke made his legal reputation by persuading the King's Bench that a grant 'to the use of X for life, remainder after 24 years to the heir male of the body of X in tail male' gave X a fee tail at once and not a life estate.[24] There was no discussion of perpetuities; but what in medieval times had been a feudal rule was now turned into a rule of construction applicable to uses, that where an ancestor is given an estate of freehold, and in the same conveyance an estate is limited to his heirs, 'the heirs' are words of limitation of the estate and not words of purchase. No full reasons seem to have been given; but it is significant that the judges rejected the defendant's argument that it was simply a matter of giving effect to the settlor's intention. The year-book rules were being extended to executory interests as a matter of law, in the interests of certainty.

Soon after this, in the mid-1590s, the spectre of perpetuities haunted the courts again. The search for the unbreakable settlement, following the success of the common recovery in the fifteenth century, had led Tudor conveyancers to experiment with the new-found statutory magic and to invent (in Coke's words) 'upstart and wild provisoes and limitations such as the common law never knew'. One approach was to revive the attempt to create a succession of life interests, so that in

---

[22] *Brent's Case* (1575) B. & M. 135 at 137, per Manwood J.

[23] Ibid. For doubts in the 1560s and 1570s, see Henderson, 26 AJLH 110-114.

[24] *Wolfe v. Shelley* (1581) B. & M. 143-149. The question arose on rather unusual facts: X's heir male by descent, his grandson, was *en ventre sa mère* at X's death; a remainder, if it were so, would therefore have vested in X's second son, who was the nearest male heir living at X's death.

every generation the eldest son would take by remainder and not as heir. The courts refused to allow such schemes, applying the spirit of the year-book remainder rules: although it was accepted as possible to devise a remainder to an eldest son, or an 'heir' (in the singular), if the intention was that he should not take by inheritance, this could not be done in indefinite succession because all the contingent remainders had to vest before the determination of the first particular estate.[25] The courts also ruled that the executory interest, like the contingent remainder, was destructible; if the supporting estate of the feoffees was destroyed before the interest was executed, the *scintilla juris* was snuffed out and with it the possibility of execution.[26] This was the reason for the introduction of perpetuity clauses in the form, 'to A and the heirs of his body until he *attempted to alienate*, and then over to another'; this would shift the fee before the alienation actually occurred. They were in common use by the 1560s. In one version, the estate would be made to pass to the next remainderman, cutting off A's issue; but the preferred form was simply to take out A and pass the estate to his heir 'as if A were naturally dead'. This kind of clause became well known in the time of Elizabeth I, and was for a time accepted by the courts.[27] But it caused a great deal of discontent, even in landed families: it hindered the advancement of younger sons and daughters, prevented a landowner selling land to pay debts or exchanging it for more convenient property which became available, made eldest sons disobedient to their fathers (confident that they could not be disinherited), and set close relatives against each other (watching for attempts to alienate).[28] The courts eventually succumbed to these objections and struck perpetuity clauses down: first (in 1595) those which took out the offending tenant during his lifetime so that the estate went to his issue,[29] and then (in 1613) those which shifted the whole estate tail to the next remainderman.[30] Coke hailed the 1613 decision as having buried perpetuities, 'a

---

25   *Haddon's Case* (1576) B. & M. 134; *Perrott's Case* (1594) Moore K.B. 368, in which earlier cases were cited.

26   *Chudleigh's Case, Dillon v. Freine* (1594) B. & M. 150-157; *Archer's Case, Baldwyn v. Smyth* (1595) B. & M. 84-85; Cro. Eliz. 453; 2 And. 37.

27   See, e.g., *Scholastica's Case* (1571) 2 Plowd. 403.

28   See also the hard case which persuaded Plowden never to draw such a settlement again: B. & M. 157.

29   *Cholmeley v. Humble* (1595) B. & M. 160-161; *Germyn v. Arscott* (1595) B. & M. 159; *Corbett v. Corbett* (1600) B. & M. 158-162; *Mildmay v. Mildmay* (1602) B. & M. 163-164; *Hethersal v. Mildmay* (1605) B. & M. 164-166. The last three cases all concerned the same Mildmay settlement, the Corbetts being fictitious parties.

30   *Mary Portington's Case, Portington v. Rogers* (1613) 10 Co. Rep. 35.

monstrous brood carved out of mere invention, and never known to the ancient sages of the law ... At whose solemn funeral I was present, and accompanied the dead to the grave, but mourned not'.[31]

The decisions were based more on policy than on logic, and although it was a necessary policy they were difficult to reconcile with the earlier principle that uses were infinitely flexible. It would have saved much confusion in the law if the judges at this point had felt able to abandon that original principle completely. Coke strongly recommended that course, arguing that uses should follow 'the rules of the common law, which are certain and well known to the professors of the law, and should not be made so extravagant that no one will know any rule to decide the questions that will arise upon them'.[32] But that proved an impossible aim. The difficulty was that conveyances had been drawn generations before in the belief that there was greater freedom, and there was a diversity of legal opinion as to the exact scope of the Tudor legislation; in that uncertainty, the hopes and intentions of settlors deserved some consideration. Various exceptions to the common-law rules were therefore conceded in the case of executory interests. The judges allowed shifting uses: that is, where a fee was to pass from one person to another upon a contingency. And they allowed springing uses: usually where the freehold was to commence after a term of years. Both kinds of interest had been forbidden by the legal remainder rules.[33] Then, in 1620, they reached the stunning conclusion that executory interests of this kind were indestructible, precisely because they did not depend on a prior estate of freehold. The case arose from a devise 'to *A* in fee simple, but if *A* should die without issue during *B*'s life then to *B* in fee simple'. This could not be a legal remainder, because it followed a fee simple; and its effect, if allowed, would have been to create something like an entail. *A*, thinking that he *was* tenant in tail, suffered a common recovery to his own use in fee simple. But the recovery was held ineffective to destroy *B*'s interest. The devise had therefore created a fee simple which in reality worked as an unbarrable entail during *A*'s life. Dodderidge J dissented vigorously, on the policy grounds mentioned above: 'Common recoveries are the anchor-hold and assurance which subjects have for their inheritance, and it would be dangerous to give liberty to anyone to invent such an estate as cannot be cut down by some means'. The other judges replied that there was no

---

[31] Preface to 10 Co. Rep.

[32] 6 Co. Rep. 34.

[33] In 1597 a bill 'to take away future uses creating perpetuities' was introduced to ban shifting and springing uses, but it failed; its wording shows that they were clearly established at that date. See 35 LQR 258.

perpetuity here, for two reasons: first, the contingency might never happen, and second, the fee was not inalienable because *A* and *B* together could suffer a recovery.[34] They also had in mind a common clause in a devise, whereby the devisee was directed to make payments to the executors or to younger brothers, and for default of payment the land itself should go to them; it was thought vital that this form of security, which depended on a shifting fee, should be protected.[35]

The failure of the judges to produce a coherent system from the confusion was perhaps the worst legacy of the sixteenth-century legal revolution. Even in the mid-seventeenth century the average landowner must have found the law of real property, as Oliver Cromwell did, 'an ungodly jumble'. From about that time, however, the practical difficulties were eased by the introduction of standard patterns of strict settlement which were known to achieve what they intended.[36] And the juristic confusion over the validity of executory interests was ended by the definite, if unsatisfactory, rule in *Purefoy v. Rogers*.[37] If a contingent use or devise could not be a common-law remainder on its face, it was presumed to be a valid executory interest under the Statutes of Uses or Wills. But if it could by possibility take effect at law, the legal rules were applied, and if the remainder did not in fact vest in time it failed. Other difficulties were solved by the survival of the unexecuted equitable interest in the form of trusts and powers.

Powers

Another side-effect of the Statute of Uses was the creation of legal powers. A power is an authority granted to someone to dispose of an estate which he does not himself own. Powers were not recognised at common law, except that where wills of land were permitted by local custom the testator could give the executors a power of sale; Babington CJ in 1431 thought it amazing that a man could thus transfer a freehold which he did not have, 'in the same way as a man can get fire from a flintstone even though there is no fire inside the flint'.[38] But powers to appoint, transfer or revoke uses had been used before 1536[39] and were

---

[34] *Pells v. Browne* (1620) B. & M. 166-169; Palm. 131; 2 Rolle Rep. 196, 217.

[35] See *Purslowe v. Parker* (1600) Rolle Abr., vol. II, p. 793, to the same effect.

[36] See pp. 332-334, post.

[37] *Purefoy d. Broughton v. Rogers* (1671) B. & M. 85-88.

[38] *Faryngton v. Darell* (1431) B. & M. 70 at 74.

[39] E.g. in 1505 a tenant in tail was given power to appoint remainders to any two of his kinsmen if his own issue failed: Lord Daubeney's settlement, Dyer 136.

effective in conscience. The reasoning which established the executory interest and the *scintilla juris* likewise turned these powers into legal powers: that is, when exercised they altered the legal title.[40] Legal powers were common by the seventeenth century. They came to be used in settlements for a variety of purposes: for example, the settlor might reserve to himself a power to revoke or vary some of the terms, or to appoint some of the remaindermen later; the tenant for life might be given the power to lease or mortgage beyond his own lifetime;[41] or the trustees might be given a power of sale or mortgage. Such powers were essential to the working of the strict settlement, as it developed in the seventeenth century; the effective owner under such a settlement was only a tenant for life, but for practical reasons he had to be given powers which encroached upon the inheritance.[42] Akin in importance to the power, as an essential ingredient in the strict settlement, was the trust.

Trusts

Although the Statute of Uses executed uses by turning them into legal estates, it did not abolish conscience or eradicate equitable interests in land. It certainly had a devastating effect on Chancery jurisdiction over uses, but the chancellors' jurisdiction to enforce uses and trusts nevertheless continued to be exercised in situations not covered by the terms of the statute. There were several such situations. First, if *A* made a lease for years to *B* to the use of *C*, the use was not executed because *B* was not technically 'seised' to the use of *C*. The same was true where copyholds were granted in use, because a copyholder had no seisin. Second, the 'active use' was not executed. If the feoffee had duties to perform, such as the collection and distribution of income, the payment of debts, the management of an estate, or the execution of a conveyance, the use could not be executed by operation of law, and so the feoffee had to retain the legal estate. On the same principle, a use in favour of a purpose rather than a person was not caught by the statute; a purpose could not be carried out fictionally. Thus charitable trusts in support of educational foundations or the relief of poverty were protected and enforced by the Chancery. These were called active or special

---

[40]   *Anon.* (c. 1595) Moore K.B. 608 (concerning a power in a 1577 settlement).

[41]   E.g. the 1576 marriage settlement discussed in *Whitlock's Case* (1609) 8 Co. Rep. 69, which gave the tenant for life power to lease for lives; it was held that he could reserve a rent on such a lease to his own heirs.

[42]   See pp. 334-335, post.

trusts,[43] as opposed to the passive or general use which alone was contemplated by the statute. A fourth category where the statute did not operate was that of repugnant, fraudulent or 'troublesome' uses.[44] The most important case in this category was the double use, where land was held by *X* to the use of *X* himself to the use of *Y*, or by *X* to the use of *Y* to the use of *Z*.

Where there was such a use upon a use, the statute only executed the first use and the second use was void at law because it was repugnant to the first.[45] If, however, the first cestuy que use was not intended to hold the land beneficially, it would have been unconscionable not to hold him to the second use. That was work for the Chancery; and there is evidence that, in suitable cases, the chancellor enforced such second uses from at least 1560. The earliest reported case concerned a duchess who had sold land to a lawyer, ostensibly to his own use, but in truth subject to a secret understanding that the lawyer would hold the land to the use of the duchess. This arrangement, which had been rendered necessary by the flight of the Protestant duchess to Poland to escape the Marian persecution, was enforced by Sir Nicholas Bacon LK soon after Elizabeth I's accession. The reporter noted that the equity of the Chancery differed from the common law in allowing a secret trust to be set up contrary to an express use.[46] By the time of James I, deliberately created trusts were commonplace.[47]

By enforcing the second use the Chancery was not infringing the letter or the spirit of the Statute of Uses, but was properly exercising its jurisdiction in conscience. This application of the jurisdiction was consequent upon the legal decision not to execute the second use, for the intervention of equity would have been otiose if the second use had been caught by the statute. But what began as a mere trickle of special cases grew within a century into common form, so that from the seventeenth century until the repeal of the Statute of Uses in 1926 the most usual

---

[43] 'Trust' was originally a synonym for 'use', but came to be used to denote equitable estates not executed by the Statute of Uses: see Style 40, per Twisden.

[44] *Corbett v. Corbett* (1600) B. & M. 158 at 161, per Walmsley J; *Mildmay v. Mildmay* (1602) B. & M. 163, per Warburton J. Their example of a troublesome use was: to *A* and his heirs on Mondays and *B* and his heirs on Tuesdays.

[45] *Jane Tyrrel's Case* (1557) B. & M. 120-121; 1 And. 37. Here there was an express use limited upon the implied use raised by bargain and sale.

[46] *Bartie (dowager Duchess of Suffolk) v. Herenden* (1560) 93 LQR 36; B. & M. 121. A reader in 1591 said this report was 'kept religiously, being the opinion of all the justices by the queen's command for the present Lord Willoughby': BL MS. Lansdowne 1072, fo.199.

[47] See *Sir Moyle Finch's Case* (1600) Co. Inst., vol. IV, p. 85 at 86; *Foord v. Hoskins* (1615) 2 Buls. 337, as explained at 74 LQR 554; and see *Sambach v. Daston* (1635) B. & M. 126-127. See further pp. 350-352, post.

way of creating trusts was by a conveyance 'to *A* and his heirs unto and to the use of *B* (or *A*) and his heirs in trust nevertheless for *C*'. This vested the legal estate in the first cestuy que use as trustee for *C*, the interposition of the first use being necessary to prevent the execution of the second (called for the sake of distinction the trust). Once again the courts had allowed policy to triumph over unintended legislative hindrances; and so it could be said by 1738 that 'a statute made upon great consideration, introduced in a solemn and pompous manner . . . had no other effect than to add at most three words to a conveyance'.[48]

The reasons for the creation of trusts in the sixteenth and seventeenth centuries were, nevertheless, quite different from those which had brought about uses. They had nothing to do with enabling land to be devised, since wills were now valid at law. And there was no intention of evading feudal incidents; if there had been, it is unthinkable that chancellors would have connived at it. But there were good non-feudal reasons for wishing to separate the legal from the beneficial ownership of land. The purpose might be merely temporary, for instance where the trustee was to make a conveyance at the direction of the feoffor. Or it might be more permanent, as where the trustee was required to look after the land and its revenues during the minority of a beneficiary, or during the whole lifetime of an unthrifty son,[49] or to hold the title for the benefit of a married woman.[50]

Among the chief reasons for creating trusts, however, were the technical advantages gained in settlements by the interposition of trustees to preserve contingent remainders, to bar dower,[51] and to prevent the operation of the rule in *Shelley's Case*.[52] From the mid-seventeenth century it was the usual practice to insert in settlements after a life estate to *X*, 'remainder (after the determination of *X*'s interest for any reason in his lifetime) to trustees for the life of *X* in trust to preserve

---

48 *Hopkins v. Hopkins* (1738) 1 Atk. 581 at 591 per Lord Hardwicke C. His lordship's historical sense on this occasion was as misleading as his arithmetic. The real object of the statute had been spent since the abolition of military tenures in 1645: p. 294, ante.

49 E.g., BL MS. Lansdowne 1074, fo. 312 ('to *X* for life, remainder to trustees for the life of *X*'s eldest son, remainder to that eldest son's heirs').

50 The latter device enabled a married woman to own property independently of her husband: pp. 553-554, post.

51 The following clause, said to have been perfected by Fearne in the 18th century, in effect gave the husband (*H*) a fee simple free of dower: 'to *H* for life (with unlimited power of disposition), remainder (after the determination of *H*'s estate for any reason in his lifetime) to trustees for the life of *H* on trust for *H* and to the express intent that *H*'s wife may not be entitled to dower, remainder to *H* and his heirs for ever'.

52 E.g., *Duncomb v. Duncomb* (1695) 3 Lev. 437.

the contingent remainders expectant upon his decease from being destroyed, remainder to *X*'s eldest son . . .'. This was designed to prevent *X* from destroying the settlement. There arose a doubt, however, as to whether the trustees' remainder was not itself contingent and liable to destruction. The dispute came to a head in 1740, when Willes CJ warned the House of Lords that if the trustees' estate was held contingent all settlements for the last 200 years might be questioned; 'But can we conceive, my lords, that everyone has been mistaken for these 200 years, and that this new light is just now arisen to us?' A subtle reason was duly found for treating the estate as vested.[53] Not for the first time the courts had modified the legal rules to satisfy policy; but this time it was a policy in favour of dynastic settlement.

TRUSTS AND LORD NOTTINGHAM'S DOCTRINE OF PERPETUITIES

Trusts might indeed have provided the ultimate means of establishing perpetuities. There was no reason inherent in abstract logic why they should be subject to the legal rules about remainders, because the rationale of those rules did not extend to equitable interests. Nor were trusts in theory caught in the doctrinal confusion over executory interests, since by definition they were not executed. They should therefore have continued in the supposedly uninhibited state which uses had been in before 1536. As a matter of policy, however, there was as much reason to forbid unbreakable settlements in equity as in law.

When Lord Nottingham C set about formulating and clarifying the growing body of law concerning trusts in the Restoration period, one of his concerns was the establishment of a clear doctrine of perpetuities. The doctrine which he laid down was one of his major achievements, and it offered such an acceptable solution that it was adopted by the common-law courts as well as the Chancery. It was commendable for its simplicity. Instead of testing settlements by a mass of abstract and often arbitrary principles relating to the character of each contingency, such as the rules against double or uncommon possibilities, Lord Nottingham proposed that the validity of a contingent interest should be tested by the remoteness of its time of vesting. If it would necessarily vest within the lifetime of a person or persons in being at the date of the settlement, it was valid.[54] Though later called the 'rule against perpetuities', the decision was seen by contemporaries as introducing a

---

[53] *Smith d. Dormer v. Parkhurst* (1740) 6 Brown P.C. 351; Atk. 138; B. & M. 88-93.

[54] *Howard v. Duke of Norfolk* (1682-85) 3 Cas. in Ch. 1; 79 SS 904; B. & M. 169-176.

measure of relaxation in favour of complex contingencies which were not remote in time. Sir Francis North, who succeeded to the great seal in 1682, thought the principle too liberal: 'A perpetuity is a thing odious in law and . . . is not to be countenanced in equity. If in equity you should come nearer to a perpetuity than the rules of the common law would admit, all men being desirous to continue their estates in their families would settle their estates by way of trust; which might indeed make well for the jurisdiction of the court, but would be destructive to the commonwealth.'[55] He reversed the decree, but Lord Nottingham was upheld by a unanimous House of Lords. The decision approved a particular perpetuity period (a life in being), but it did not set the outer limits of remoteness. Eighteenth-century decisions added twenty-one years plus the gestation period. It had always been acceptable to settle land on *A* for life, remainder to the heirs of *B* in fee tail. This postponed the fee during *A*'s life, and also for practical purposes during the minority of *B*, because an infant tenant in tail could not suffer a common recovery. In the extreme case that on *A*'s death *B* had just died leaving an infant heir *en ventre sa mère*, the fee might be postponed for twenty-one years and a further nine months or so beyond the life of *A*. That was therefore adopted as the maximum period that the law would allow; but it came to be regarded as a period 'in gross', so that it did not have to be related to an actual beneficiary's life, or a minority, or a period of gestation, in a settlement of the kind just mentioned.[56]

The Strict Settlement

The kind of family settlement which was perfected between 1640 and 1700, and remained in use for three hundred years, was essentially the common-law arrangement which gave only a life estate to the owner of the land for the time being, and successive remainders in tail to each of his children in order of seniority. This was protected against destruction by the insertion of trustees to preserve the contingent remainders, and trustees were also appointed to raise various sums of money for the maintenance of members of the family. Such an arrangement was called a 'strict' settlement.[57]

Strict settlements were most frequently executed on marriage, and would regularly make provision for the bride's jointure and pin-money (an annuity for her personal use during the marriage). The settlement

55   1 Vern. 162 at 163; B. & M. 175.
56   *Cadell v. Palmer* (1833) 1 Cl. & Fin. 372.
57   The expression is found in 1715: 1 P. Wms 291.

would be set out in a conveyance to the trustees of the settlement; the uses in favour of the life tenant, the trustees, and the remaindermen, were turned into legal estates by the Statute of Uses, while the trusts imposed on the trustees (being expressed as trusts upon uses) subsisted in equity. A typical settlement on marriage might be in the form:

1) To the intended groom (*H*) in fee simple until the solemnisation of the marriage, and then to *H* for life, subject to a rent-charge to provide *H*'s wife with pin-money during *H*'s life. If any land was to be assigned as jointure, this was settled on *H* and his wife jointly.

2) Remainder to trustees during the life of *H*, to protect the contingent remainders expectant on his decease from destruction in the event of a premature determination of his life estate.

3) Remainder to trustees for a long term of years (say, 500 years from the death of *H*), to raise a jointure for *H*'s widow, and portions (lump sums by way of advancement) for his daughters and younger sons.[58]

4) Subject thereto, remainders to each of *H*'s unborn sons severally and successively in order of seniority, in tail male; followed (sometimes) by successive remainders to each of the same sons in tail general, so as to let in a grand-daughter on failure of *H*'s male issue. The first remainder in tail vested on the death of the life tenant, but it was subject to the portions term.

5) Subject to all the foregoing (including the portions term), remainder to *H*'s daughters as tenants in common, in tail male, with cross remainders. The effect of cross remainders was that on the death of any one daughter without male issue (or on the failure of her male issue) her share remained to the others as tenants in tail in common. An alternative formula was to give successive remainders to the daughters in order of seniority, as in the case of the sons, so that the eldest would take before the rest.

6) Remainder or reversion in fee simple, usually to *H* and his heirs for ever.

This type of settlement was intended to last only for one generation. It was binding on the life tenant, since if he attempted to break the

---

58 For the mechanics of these trusts, see further p. 344, post. They became common after the recognition of the equity of redemption around 1620 (p. 356, post). In the 18th century, the life tenant was frequently given power to fix the portions later.

settlement the trustees' estate came into effect to prevent it. And it was binding on the eldest surviving son as tenant in tail until he came of age, because until his majority he could not bar the entail. In each generation there would be a new settlement, reducing the estate of the tenant in possession to a life tenancy and postponing the fee for another generation. If the eldest son came of age during his father's lifetime, he would of course be able to break the settlement as soon as he succeeded; but this could be prevented if his father persuaded him to co-operate in a resettlement, achieved by means of a common recovery to bar the entails of the old settlement. The son might be induced to agree to this by the grant of an immediate income charged on the land. In reality, it was relatively uncommon for sons to reach the age of majority in their father's lifetimes and most resettlements were made voluntarily when they came to marry. This would be insisted on by the bride's family, to ensure that provision was made for her pin-money and a jointure (if not provided in land). It was also necessary to rearrange the remainders so as to advance the groom's own daughters in the line of succession before his uncles and aunts, and to provide portions for his own younger sons.

The widespread employment by the landed classes of the strict settlement, with resettlement in each generation, shackled much of the land in England to the same families until Victorian times and beyond. Economic historians dispute the extent to which strict settlements balanced the primogenitive dynastic spirit against a feeling for the extended family.[59] Certainly the effect was to tie the land itself dynastically; the land was transmitted intact in the main line, subject to the economic interests of the various other members of the family charged upon it, rather than divided up among them. The economic undesirability of tying up so much land in settlement was widely felt, especially in the nineteenth century. It was not simply that the land could not be prised out of the landed families, so that *nouveaux riches* could not acquire real property. Nor was it merely that the 'great estates' were slowly swallowing up the lesser, so that the number of landowners in the country was diminishing. Even from the point of view of the solvent landed family, there were management problems. The 'owner', being only a tenant for life, could not without special powers exercise the necessary functions of leasing and mortgaging, felling timber and mining that belonged to an absolute owner. Without ways of raising cash, improvements could not be carried out; without the means of exchanging one piece of land for another, estates could not

---

[59] For this debate, see E. Spring, (1983) 18 *Canadian Jl Hist.* 379; (1984) 16 *Albion* 1; (1988) 41 *Econ. Hist. Rev.* 454; L. Bonfield, (1984) 1 LHR 297; (1986) 39 *Econ. Hist. Rev.* 341; (1988) 41 *Econ. Hist. Rev.* 461.

be consolidated. The requisite powers could be conferred on the tenant for life by each individual settlement, according to the foresight of the settlor and his counsel; even so, many landowners were compelled to seek private acts of parliament as the only escape from unforeseen problems. Eventually, in Victorian times, the most commonly needed powers were conferred by public general statutes on all tenants for life of settled land.[60]

The final stage in the development of the law of settlements realised the economic fact that, local sentiment apart, a settlement of family wealth did not need to be tied to specific pieces of land. There was no economic reason why a tenant for life should not be permitted to exchange settled land for other land, or indeed for other forms of capital. This was suggested by the law reformer James Humphreys as early as 1826, but such a bold reform was postponed. The reform came in the 1880s, when the great agricultural depression gave rise to strong desires among landowners to be able to convert land into more profitable investments. Legislation was passed to give every tenant for life under a settlement the power to sell the land in fee simple. On his doing so, the settlement was not destroyed but attached itself to the proceeds of sale.[61]

Since Victorian times, strict settlements have for various reasons become unsatisfactory ways of arranging the devolution of property in a family. They survived as a means of ensuring that the estates of the nobility followed the peerage titles, which are usually limited in tail male, but for most purposes the devolution of wealth could be managed with less liability to tax. Between 1900 and 1970 the rate of death duties increased about a hundred-fold, and many settled estates were so badly hit by the burdens of taxation – especially during the carnage of the Great War, when father and sons might be slain in rapid succession – that they had to be sold. As in all periods, the conveyancer has sought ingenious ways of reducing the incidence of taxation; but the old law of settlements, enshrined in the pages of Littleton and Coke, has faded away with the landed gentry whose fortunes it governed for so long.

Further reading

Holdsworth HEL, vol. VII, pp. 78-238
Plucknett CHCL, pp. 552-557, 588-602

---

[60] Settled Estates Act 1856, 19 & 20 Vict., c.120; Settled Estates Act 1877, 40 & 41 Vict., c.18; supplemented by the Settled Land Act 1882, 45 & 46 Vict., c.38.

[61] Settled Land Acts 1882 (ante), 1890, 53 & 54 Vict., c.69, and 1925, 15 Geo. V, c.18.

Milsom HFCL, pp. 178-199, 225-239

Cornish & Clark, pp. 123-132, 166-172

Simpson, *History of the Land Law*, pp. 81-102, 119-138, 208-241

J. C. Gray, *The Rule against Perpetuities* (4th ed., 1942), pp. 126-190

D. E. C. Yale, [on the perpetuity doctrine] (1954) 73 SS lxxiii-xci; 'Equitable Estates in the 17th Century' [1957] CLJ 72-86

E. Spring, 'The Settlement of Land in 19th-Century England' (1964) 8 AJLH 209-223; and see p. 334, ante, note 59

J. L. Barton, 'The Statute of Uses and the Trust of Freeholds' (1966) 82 LQR 215-225; 'Future Interests and Royal Revenues in the 16th Century' (1981), *Laws and Customs*, pp. 321-335

G. L. Haskins, 'Extending the Grasp of the Dead Hand: Reflections on the Origins of the Rule against Perpetuities' (1977) 126 *Univ. Pennsylvania Law Rev.* 19-46

J. H. Baker, 'The Use upon a Use in Equity 1558-1625' (1977) 93 LQR 33-38; 'Family Settlements' (1978) 94 SS *204-209*

L. Bonfield, *Marriage Settlements 1601-1740: the Adoption of the Strict Settlement* (1983); and see p. 334, ante, note 59

B. English and J. Saville, *Strict Settlement: a Guide for Historians* (1983)

17. Other Interests in Land

Not all interests in land were subject to the developments described in the preceding chapters. Several important kinds of interest grew up outside the common-law scheme of real property, but since they did so for different reasons they are a miscellaneous collection. The kind of property which was the subject of seisin, and was protected by the real actions, was known as real property (realty), because there was a remedy *in rem*: that is, an action to recover the property (or *res*) itself. Real property in this sense was not limited to land.[1] Some kinds of property which did not fit into this scheme, such as leases for years, were distinguished as 'personal property' (personalty), because the remedy for infringement lay *in personam*: usually an action for damages. Other kinds of property were outside the common law altogether, and came to be classified as equitable estates and interests; the remedy was by *subpoena* in Chancery.

Classifications are only as good as the purpose they serve, and these classifications of property have been only partly successful. One difficulty was that some forms of personalty came eventually to achieve substantial protection *in rem* while retaining some of the characteristics of chattels (such as being uninheritable). They became known as 'chattels real'. The prime example is the term of years.

The Term of Years

A term, or lease for years, is an estate in land for a fixed period of time, usually but not necessarily a number of years. Such a term was not a freehold interest and was therefore exempt from the feudal notions of seisin and tenure, inheritance and future interests. It may surprise today's student to learn that an estate in land for nine hundred and ninety-nine years is a chattel, whereas an estate which lasts only for one man's lifetime is a freehold. The distinction obviously does not represent the quantity of an estate, as measured in terms of duration; it is a distinction of quality which lost its rational basis many centuries ago.

The classification of the lessee's interest as a chattel is usually accounted for by its not having been protected by the writ of right or the

---

[1] For examples, see 'hereditaments' in Table B at p. 281, ante.

assize of novel disseisin. If the lessee had no protection *in rem*, his property was not real but personal. *Bracton's* explanation for the denial of these remedies to the lessee was that the possession of land for a certain period could not be called a 'free tenement' or freehold (*liberum tenementum*), the only subject-matter of such actions. Both explanations are circular. The true reason for the lessee's exclusion must be sought in the feudal context. The freehold tenant who made a lease for years did not mean to part with his seisin or fee, but merely handed over the possession of the land without any 'right'. If the lessee was ejected, that was a disseisin not of the lessee but of his lessor. Maitland criticised Bracton for drawing an analogy with the Civil law usufruct, an arrangement whereby ownership was separated from enjoyment of profits, and said that 'English law for six centuries and more will rue this youthful flirtation with Romanism'.[2] But it seems that the author of *Bracton* was simply borrowing Roman terminology to explain an existing English state of affairs. The lessee in fact had no feudal existence, because he was not meant to become the owner, and so in law he could not be seised of a free tenement.

The question why the lessee had no place in the feudal framework cannot be answered by the application of abstract theory. The answer is to be found in the original purpose and function of the term of years. Whereas the unit of feudal ownership was the holding for life, and the hereditary fee was of perpetual or indeterminate duration, the letting for years began not as a family interest but as a temporary financial interest. Its principal use was to secure a loan of money.[3] This was a matter of commercial contract, not of subinfeudation, because the lessee was more interested in the money than the land, and so the natural legal remedy of the lessee against the lessor was the writ of covenant rather than a real action. The lessee's security was, however, protected against third parties. As against those claiming as grantees from the lessor, he was given the writ *quare ejecit infra terminum*, invented in the 1230s by William Ralegh. Against the rest of the world his remedy was in damages for trespass: by the 1360s the species known as *de ejectione firmae*, the action of ejectment.[4] Ejectment could also be used against the lessor himself, a remedy which might be needed if the lease was not by deed. Yet the freehold remained in the lessor, and he alone could bring the assize.

2   Pollock & Maitland, vol. II, p. 115.
3   See further p. 353, post.
4   For the form of the writ, see p. 618, post. For the date, see 100 SS lxxiii.

The tenant for years enjoyed a capital interest which before 1300 was characterised as a 'chattel' rather than as an estate in land.[5] It could be bought and sold, but not entailed or settled, and on the death of the lessee it passed to his personal representatives along with his movables. The tenant could not alienate more than the term: if he purported to do so, it was a disseisin of the lessor, who could bring an assize against the alienee. Most of these rules remained inviolate for centuries; but there occurred nevertheless a fundamental change in the term of years.

CHANGE IN NATURE OF TERM OF YEARS

Most leases at the present day involve letting the beneficial enjoyment of land at a rent. The lessee is regarded as the owner of the land for many purposes, and the lessor as the owner of a reversion which entitles him during the term to the rent. Here is a parallel with the sort of arrangement achieved before 1290 by subinfeudation at a rent, which was called 'fee farm' (from the Latin word *firma*, rent). The purpose of the fee farm was usually to produce a regular periodic income for the feudal lord. The farmer (*firmarius*), though he might have paid a premium, was primarily a rent-payer; like the lessee of today he wanted possession of land for his own use, and that is what he was paying for. He had no funds to buy the fee outright, so he bought it for a rent and became a tenant farmer.

When the statute *Quia emptores* ended subinfeudation in 1290,[6] it incidentally deprived landowners of this method of securing an income. They could still alienate their property in fee farm by substitution, reserving the rent as a charge on the land rather than as a feudal service; but they would then have to part with their property permanently, so that their manors would be diminished. A similar effect to subinfeudation could, however, be achieved by leasing the land for years to a rent-paying tenant; and within a century of *Quia emptores* the husbandry lease to farm (*dimissio ad firmam*) became very common.

At the same time as the husbandry lease grew in popularity, the mortgage by way of a term declined.[7] By the fifteenth century the typical lessee for years was not a money-lender but a farmer in the later sense, a husbandman with insufficient capital to buy an estate in fee but able to pay rent out of the fruits of his labour. The lease for years had thus come to do some of the work of feudalism; the lessor began to be

---

[5] Herle CJ even said that it was not an estate in law: *Anon.* (1333) Y.B. Mich. 7 Edw. III, fo. 45, pl.8.

[6] See p. 278, ante. For the implications in this context, see Milsom HFCL, pp. 116-117.

[7] See pp. 353-354, post.

called the landlord, the landlord could distrain, and it was said that the lessee owed him fealty.[8] The farmer tenant needed legal protection as much as the freehold tenant, and the fact that the subject of his ownership was classed as a chattel was an historical accident which seemed to deny him a just remedy. He had the action of ejectment; but that, being a form of trespass, properly lay only for damages. Although a precedent has been found as early as 1390 in which a lessee recovered his term in such an action,[9] a technical objection to such recovery was that a trespass action was concerned only with past wrongs and not with continuing rights; inability to recover seems therefore to have been the orthodox view until 1500.[10] The reversal of this orthodoxy may have resulted from confusion with *quare ejecit,*[11] or with the specific recovery available in the early action of covenant; and it may have been accelerated by knowledge that the fifteenth-century Chancery was giving protection to the lessee. Whatever the explanation, the reversal is taken to have been settled by a King's Bench decision of 1500.[12] The form of judgment in the action of ejectment, where the term had not expired, was that the plaintiff recover his term as well as damages for the trespass. The award of possession could be enforced by the judicial writ *habere facias possessionem*, giving the plaintiff the effect of a real action. The result was to transform the character of the term of years. It had become real property: a chattel still, but a chattel real.

FURTHER SECURITY OF THE TERMOR

The judges and the legislature took further steps to protect the termor in the first half of the sixteenth century. There were two common situations in which the term of years was liable to destruction without the consent of the termor, and if the termor was to be treated as a property owner these had to be remedied. The first problem was that a lease was precarious as against the lessor's lord: if the lessor died leaving an infant heir in ward, the guardian could evict the lessee during the wardship, on the ground that the seignory existed before the lease and therefore the lord's rights took priority. This harsh rule was reversed by the King's Bench in 1514, then restored (at least in the

---

8   Littleton, *Tenures*, s.143.

9   Plucknett CHCL, p. 373 n.5; Arnold, 100 SS lxxiii n.560.   A later example is *Pynchemore v. Brewyn* (1481) Kiralfy SB, p. 110.

10   Belknap CJ ruled in 1382 that the term could not be recovered in ejectment: Pas. 6 Ric. II, Fitz. Abr., *Ejectione firme*, pl. 2; [1976] CLJ 325 n.40.   For later statements to the same effect, see B. & M. 179; Port Nbk (102 SS) 127.

11   See Milsom, 74 LQR 200-201; B. & M. 178.

12   *Gernes v. Smyth* (1500) B. & M. 179-180 n.2.

Common Pleas) by the opinion of Fitzherbert J and others, until finally laid to rest in the 1540s.[13] The second problem was that a lease could be destroyed by a common recovery of the reversion. If the lessee knew that a recovery was under way, he could intervene to protect his interest; but if the lessor suffered a recovery without the lessee's knowledge, it was too late to help the latter. The remedy in this case came from parliament, which passed a statute in 1529 enabling a lessee to 'falsify' such a recovery by bringing *quare ejecit* or ejectment.[14]

USE OF EJECTMENT TO TRY FREEHOLD TITLE

The action of ejectment gave the leaseholder a remedy superior in practice to anything available to the freeholder. He could recover possession by a form of action free from the technicalities of the writs of entry and the possessory assizes, and in which trial was by jury. The lessee's position in litigation therefore excited the envy of freeholders, and by about 1565-70, through a simple expedient, they had adopted ejectment as their own standard remedy. Within a few years this innovation rendered it unnecessary for plaintiffs to resort to the Chancery to try title, and according to Lord Ellesmere it also caused 'a great decay of the true knowledge and learning of the law in real actions': indeed it had 'almost utterly overthrown' the assizes and writs of entry.[15]

The trick was as follows. The freeholder would lease the land in question to a friend for the purpose of bringing the action, and would contrive to put him in possession so that he would be ejected by the defendant. The nominal lessee would then bring ejectment against the ejector, who would plead his title, and so the question of title would be tried by jury. If the plaintiff succeeded, he would surrender to his lessor, who thereby obtained possession of the land. This procedure was so much more convenient than the older actions that the courts facilitated its use by refusing to allow defendants to evade the issue of title by disputing the details of the lessee's entry and physical ejectment. As a result, the whole process became by the latter part of the seventeenth century the subject of a remarkable fiction.

In its perfected form, the action of ejectment to try freehold title was brought by a wholly imaginary lessee (usually called John Doe) against an equally imaginary person (often called Richard Roe, or given a

---

[13] B. & M. 183-185; *Corbet's Case* (1599) 4 Co. Rep. 81. See also Arnold, [1976] CLJ at 326; 94 SS *182*.

[14] 94 SS *182-183*; Stat. 21 Hen. VIII, c.15.

[15] B. & M. 180.

pejorative name such as Shamtitle) who was supposed to be the lessee of the person in possession and to have ejected John Doe. These fictitious creatures were puppets of the real claimant, who could pull their strings without incurring the trouble, and possible danger, of making a physical entry, putting the lessee in possession, and waiting for him to be personally ejected by the real defendant. The real plaintiff could at the same time avoid the expense of a writ and of process to procure the fictitious defendant's appearance. Since he controlled the fictions, he could make the defendant enter an appearance. His attorney then wrote a letter from the fictitious defendant to inform the real defendant that an action had been commenced against him, enclosing a copy of the declaration, and inviting him to come and defend his title. This was the point where the real litigation began. The court allowed the real defendant to intervene as reversioner, but only on condition that he signed the 'consent rule'. This was an order of court which obliged the defendant to accept the fictions and to enter a plea of Not guilty. As a result, questions of title were raised in evidence to the jury on the general issue, and the more slippery technicalities associated with the pleading of title were eliminated.[16]

Ejectment replaced the old real actions and assizes in all the cases where it would lie, but it was not quite universal because the fictions enabled the plaintiff to take a short cut only where he could have gone the long way. Since a valid lease could only be granted by a person entitled to enter, the fictitious apparatus could not be set up if the real plaintiff had no right of entry. The action was therefore not available if the plaintiff's right of entry had been 'tolled' (lost in law) through failure to exercise it in time; for instance, after a descent from a disseisor to his heir, or after the expiration of the twenty-one year limitation period ordained in 1624.[17] Furthermore, ejectment would not lie for those types of property which in their nature could not be entered upon and leased: for instance, advowsons, rights of way, and unassigned dower.

For nearly three centuries from Elizabeth I to Victoria the usual action to recover real property thus involved two non-existent parties. The very title of an ejectment action – for example, *Doe d. Smith v Roe*[18] – concealed the truth. In 1833 ejectment was raised to the status of being the only permissible real action, except for the writ of right of dower and the action of *quare impedit* for advowsons. John Doe and

16 For the forms used, see B. & M. 180-182.
17 Statute of Limitations 1624, 21 Jac. I, c.16.
18 I.e. Doe (nominal plaintiff) on the demise of Smith (real plaintiff) against Roe (casual ejector).

Richard Roe were finally retired in 1852 when fictions were abolished.[19] The present action to recover possession of land is nevertheless the direct successor of ejectment, and the rules about proof of title are, with statutory alterations, those developed in that action rather than in the old real actions.

LEASES AND SETTLEMENTS

The usual husbandry lease was not for a long period; twenty-one years would have been normal. The ninety-nine year building lease was the longest beneficial term created in the ordinary course of events. In medieval times longer leases may have been regarded as unsafe because they were precarious; but the protection extended to the lessee in the first third of the sixteenth century opened the way to using long leases as a conveyancing device. The lease was now an estate in land with many of the attributes, and none of the burdens, of feudal tenure. Leases for as long as a thousand years began to appear, perhaps with the intention of avoiding feudal incidents.[20] It also occurred to conveyancers that if long leases could be used in creating settlements, there might be a way of avoiding the rules about contingent remainders and executory interests. Moreover, the splitting of ownership between a long-term lessee and a reversioner, neither of whom could convey the freehold in possession, brought perpetuities again within reach.

An obstacle in the way of using leases as the basis of family settlements was that estates could not be created in chattels.[21] It was, however, possible to settle the use of chattels, and such uses were not executed by the Statute of Uses.[22] The widest possibilities were those opened up by the Statute of Wills 1540, which empowered a testator to dispose of his real *and personal* property 'at his will and pleasure'. Soon after the statute it was held that a testator could in consequence devise a term of years to X, and if X should die during the term then to Y.[23] Y's interest could not technically be a remainder, since at law there could be no remainder in a chattel; it was a quasi-remainder or 'possibility of remainder'. If and when the time came, the whole of the remaining term passed from X to Y. The exact nature of a devise of a

---

19 Real Property Limitation Act 1833, 3 & 4 Will. IV, c.27; Common Law Procedure Act 1852, 15 & 16 Vict., c.76.

20 See *Risden v. Tuffin* (1597) Tothill 122; *Anon.* (1599) Cary 9.

21 See p. 439, post.

22 *Mayntell's Case* (a. 1553) cit. in BL MS. Harley 1691, fo. 91v. See also p. 328, ante; and p. 440, post.

23 *Anon.* (1550) B. & M. 186; *Anon.* (1553) BL MS. Harley 5141, fo. 6v; *Anon.* (1572) B. & M. 187.

term was much in doubt in the later sixteenth century. The better opinion in the 1550s was that the first devisee took the whole term and could therefore destroy the executory devise,[24] but it was settled in 1578 that the second devisee had more than a mere possibility and that his interest could not be destroyed by the first devisee.[25] In 1583 the distinction between the property in the lease and the 'use and occupation' was abandoned by a majority of judges in the Exchequer Chamber, and thereafter executory devises of terms were generally upheld and the future interests protected from destruction.[26]

Since the executory devise was now indestructible and inalienable, and since the carving up of leases was not subject to the rules about the abeyance, postponement or shifting of the freehold, these developments seemed to open the way to effective perpetuities. A perpetuity for a thousand years would have been as mischievous as a perpetual fee, and an entailed lease would have contravened the policy of the law since it would not have been barrable by common recovery. The judges recognised these problems and refused to allow a term to be devised in tail,[27] or in any way which tended to create a perpetuity. The most extreme reaction occurred in *Child v. Baylie* (1623),[28] where a 76-year lease was devised to *A* and his assigns, but if *A* should die without issue then to his brother *B*. This was not a perpetuity in the later sense, but the court said that it 'tends to create a perpetuity' and declined to uphold the limitation to *B*. The decision of the Exchequer Chamber in that case had to be abandoned when the perpetuity doctrine was formulated later in the century by Lord Nottingham.[29]

Although they were outlawed as a means of creating perpetuities, leases served a number of legitimate purposes in settlements. In particular, they were used in the classical strict settlement as a means of raising money for portions and other purposes incidental to the transmission of the inheritance,[30] the advantage being that a lease for

---

24   *Anon.* (1541) B. & M. 185; *Anon.* (1552) Dyer 74, B. & M. 186 n.18; *Foster v. Foster* (1572) B. & M. 185.

25   *Weltden v. Elkington* (1578) B. & M. 188.

26   *Amner d. Fulshurst v. Luddington* (1583) B. & M. 191; *Clarke v. Manning* (1608) B. & M. 192; *Lampet d. Lampet v. Starkey* (1612) B. & M. 193.

27   *Peacock's Case* (1576) cit. 10 Co. Rep. 87; *Lovies's Case* (1613) 10 Co. Rep. 78; *Leventhorpe v. Ashbie* (1635) Rolle Abr., vol. I, p. 611.

28   *Child d. Heath v. Baylie* (1623) B. & M. 195.

29   See p. 331, ante. Lord Nottingham expressly overruled *Child v. Baylie*: B. & M. 174.

30   See p. 333, ante.

years did not disturb the remainders in tail.[31] The technique was for the settlor to limit a long lease to trustees, who were empowered to raise the money by way of sale, subdemise or mortgage of the term. When the debt was discharged the term was said to be 'satisfied', and the settlement might provide for the term thereupon to cease. It was common, however, for the equitable interest in the term to be directed to 'attend the inheritance', so that it devolved as if it were realty. The equitable term could thus do what a legal term could not, and follow the entails of a settlement. The advantage of keeping satisfied terms on foot in this way was that they prevented the freehold from being covertly encumbered; a lessee was protected against estates and charges on the land created subsequent to the lease. Since a purchaser might well insist on such protection, it was a prudent precaution in case sale was contemplated. For these reasons, the insertion of long terms in settlements became the usual practice from the mid-seventeenth century onwards.[32] And so important was it that the beneficial interest in a satisfied term should be annexed to the realty, that the Chancery decided in the same period that attendancy on the inheritance would be implied in equity even if no express provision were made.[33]

LEASES AND CONVEYANCING: LEASE AND RELEASE

Another appendix to the history of leases for years is the story of the replacement of livery of seisin as the only method for conveying a freehold estate in possession. In the later common law seisin was transferred without reference to the feudal lord, but the ceremony of transfer still required physical presence on the land, and was often accompanied by the symbolic delivery of a clod of earth. The Statute of Uses introduced by a side-wind a second mode of legal conveyance, by virtue of the constructive transfer of seisin which occurred whenever a use was executed. Since an implied use was raised in favour of the purchaser under a contract to sell land, the statute would have produced the result that when *A* bargained and sold land to *B* the implied use was executed in *B* and the legal title effectively conveyed by operation of law. Now, simultaneous contract and conveyance would have been very

---

[31] The remainderman took his estate subject to the term, but the expectation was that the capital sum would be raised at once (e.g. by mortgage or a sale of timber) so that the remainder could take effect in possession free of the term (but subject, of course, to any mortgage).

[32] A precedent of 1647, with an express direction to attend the inheritance, will be found in *Howard v. Duke of Norfolk* (1682) B. & M. 169.

[33] For the establishment of this doctrine, see Yale, 79 SS *150-160*. It was abolished by the Satisfied Terms Act 1845, 8 & 9 Vict., c. 112.

inconvenient in practice, an interval being necessary for searches into title, the preparation of documents, and payment of the purchase money. It was therefore enacted by the same parliament that a bargain and sale should not be automatically executed unless it was enrolled in the records of one of the courts at Westminster.[34] From 1536, the 'bargain and sale enrolled' could thus be used to convey the legal title as an alternative to livery of seisin. But livery continued for a while to be the more usual.

Livery was nevertheless inconvenient, and a loophole in the 1536 legislation provided a way of avoiding it without using the equally inconvenient registration procedure or falling into the problem of instantaneous completion. The Statute of Uses executed a contract by a freeholder to grant a lease, because by implication the freeholder was seised to the use of the intended lessee by virtue of the contract. The Statute of Enrolments, however, did not extend to contracts for leases. Therefore if *A* contracted to make a lease to *B*, and then granted ('released') the reversion to *B* by deed,[35] the freehold would have passed from *A* to *B* in two stages without any livery or enrolment being necessary. This was probably discovered in genuine cases, but in the seventeenth century a nominal lease followed by a release became a deliberate mode of conveying the fee.[36] The device was traditionally attributed to Sir Francis Moore (d. 1621), a celebrated Chancery practitioner; it was certainly in general use soon after his time.[37] During the seventeenth century it became the common form. In making a settlement, for instance, a settlor would enter into a bargain and sale to trustees for a short term at a nominal premium and then execute a deed releasing the reversion to the trustees upon the trusts of the settlement. In the course of time, the release became the only deed actually made, since the recital of a previous bargain and sale in the deed would estop both parties from denying it. This fiction by estoppel was given the force of law in 1841, but practice was simplified four years later by a statute which enabled corporeal hereditaments to be transferred by grant.[38]

---

[34] Statute of Enrolments 1536; B. & M. 115.

[35] Future estates could be granted by deed, because livery of seisin was impossible.

[36] One limitation was that it could not be used for conveyances by corporations, since corporate bodies could not be seised to uses.

[37] It was recognised in *Lutwich v. Mitton* (1620) Cro. Jac. 604.

[38] Conveyance by Release Act 1841, 4 & 5 Vict., c.21; Real Property Act 1845, 8 & 9 Vict., c.106.

Tenancy at Will

Sometimes the occupier of land has a beneficial interest and yet has no recognisable estate, because he does not hold the land for any defined period. Examples are where a lessee for years 'holds over' after the end of his term, or where cestuy que use is in possession of land belonging in law to his feoffees. In the sixteenth century these were classified as 'tenants at sufferance' because, although they were not trespassers, they had no legal rights in the land at all.[39] Then there were cases where a person was deliberately given an interest in land to last only as long as the grantor liked: this was called 'tenancy at will'. Such a tenancy would arise if a lease were made without a term being fixed; the lessee could be given notice to quit at any time, but the law gave him a reasonable time to leave and also the right to any crops he had sown during the tenancy (his *emblements*). Quite common by Tudor times was the periodic tenancy, a tenancy from year to year at the pleasure of the parties; the courts inclined to the view that this took effect as a lease for one year (or two, depending on the words used) followed by a tenancy at will.[40] In later times, however, the precarious position of a tenant at will was avoided where possible by construing demises for uncertain terms as successive yearly leases.[41]

The most important kind of tenant by will in medieval times, and the principal example discussed in *Bracton* and Littleton's *Tenures*, was the unfree tenant who held at the will of his lord.

Villein Tenure and Copyhold

Much of the land in medieval England, especially that comprised within manors, was held by 'base', 'unfree' or villein tenure. The distinguishing mark of such tenure, for lawyers, was that the services were uncertain: the unfree tenant did not know, when he went to bed, what work he would have to do in the morning.[42] The separation of villein tenure from villein status[43] raised briefly the possibility that the freeman who held in villeinage might be able to sue for his holding in

---

[39] Cf. licensees, pp. 357-358, post.

[40] The leading case is *Burgh v. Potkyn* (1522) Spelman Rep. (93 SS) 136; 94 SS *183-184*. A lease for a year, and then at the will of the parties, was considered in *Watno v. Page* (1489) CP 40/909, m.254 (demurrer).

[41] *Right d. Flower v. Darby* (1786) 1 Term Rep. 159; Bl. Comm., vol. II, p. 147.

[42] *Bracton*, vol. II, p. 89; vol. III, p. 131.

[43] See pp. 532-533, post.

the royal courts; but by Bracton's time free status and freehold were distinct legal entities. The legal analysis was that a tenant in villeinage did not hold in his own name, but in the name of his lord: if a stranger evicted him, this was a disseisin of the lord and not of the unfree tenant. The tenant, though free in status, was therefore not seised of freehold; and it followed that he was not protected by the real actions or assizes. The most accurate legal description of his status was that he was tenant at the will of the lord. If the lord evicted him, this was a determination of the lord's will and the tenant could hope for no more than his emblements in an action at common law.[44] Since the tenant had no seisin, he could not make a feoffment without disseising his lord; the only way in which his tenancy could be alienated was by surrendering to the lord on trust to admit the alienee as a new tenant. The situation was a survival of pre-common-law feudalism, in which the lord's court is sovereign.[45]

The tenant was not, however, entirely without protection. His tenure, though legally at the will of the lord, was 'at the will of the lord according to the custom of the manor', and this custom was enforceable in manorial courts. The rolls of manorial courts, which exist in great profusion after the thirteenth century, show that in reality unfree tenants enjoyed heritable and alienable estates analogous to those of the common law and restrained only by analogous incidents of tenure. Indeed, manorial entails are almost as old as entails at common law.[46] A tenant's title was secured by recording the surrender and admittance on the court roll, and more often than not the tenant was given a copy of the court roll recording the admission, as his record of title. This practice accounts for the name 'tenant by copy of court roll', which came into use in the fourteenth century.[47] The admittance was sometimes symbolised by the delivery of a rod: the tenure was then called 'tenancy by the virge', and it survived in many places until 1925.

Social and economic changes – the effect of the Black Death on the labour supply and peasant mobility, the commutation of unfree services for fixed payments, and the widespread acquisition of base tenements by men of substance – all combined to make the notion of villein tenure an anachronism before 1400. The term 'villeinage' was increasingly reserved for servile status, and in the context of tenure it gave way in the

---

44   *Anon.* (1368) Y.B. Mich. 42 Edw. III, fo. 25, pl.9.
45   See p. 264, ante.
46   [1988] CLJ 411.
47   Tenancy 'per copy de court rolle' is mentioned in a special verdict in the case of 1368 (note 44, above).

fifteenth century to the socially neutral 'copyhold';[48] but the change of attitude required also a legal change. The decline of feudal reality had long since made the freehold tenant the legal landowner vis-à-vis his lord, and reason now demanded that the same should happen to the copyholder.

LEGAL RECOGNITION OF THE COPYHOLDER

The common law hardened too early for the copyholder to be accommodated directly: as a tenant at will he could not have an action against his lord, or any action based on seisin. An attempt by a copyholder in 1390 to obtain judicial review of a manorial judgment for error was thwarted on the same ground: the freehold was in the lord.[49] There were, nevertheless, two means of protection which began to be used in the fifteenth century. One was the Chancery: since it was unconscionable for a lord to flout the customs of his manor, a copyhold tenant might complain to the chancellor if the lord failed to do right.[50] The second was the fact that the tenant, though not seised, had possession; he was therefore allowed to bring trespass against third parties who evicted him.[51] By 1500 it seems to have been thought arguable that the tenant could set up his copyhold estate even against his lord, if sued by the latter in trespass, though such a plea was probably open to demurrer.[52] The better view remained that trespass could not be brought by the tenant *against* the lord; but the fact that several judges were prepared to lay such a clear rule aside is valuable evidence of the changed perception of the copyholder's position.[53]

The common law eventually solved the problem by allowing the copyholder's lessee to bring ejectment, so that the land itself could be recovered if title was established. The new remedy was established in

[48] The word is used in a statute of 1484, which recognised copyhold as a qualification for jury service in the tourn: Stat. 1 Ric. III, c.4.
[49] *Philippot v. Wade* (1390) Y.B. Hil. 13 Ric. II, p. 122, pl.8 (writ of false judgment).
[50] *Anon.* (1453/54) B. & M. 200.
[51] *Rikhill's Case* (1400) Y.B. Mich. 2 Hen. IV, fo. 12, pl. 49.
[52] There are several inconclusive cases in the plea rolls. A reported example is *Tropnell v. Kyllyk* (1505) Keil. 76; CP 40/974, m.445 (demurrer but no judgment). A similar plea was decided against the tenant, on demurrer by the lord, in *Saye v. Penreth* (1516) CP 40/1016, m.517d.
[53] The point remained in doubt for at least 80 years, and seems not to have been settled till the 1550s: see the cases in B. & M. 201-202.

the middle of Elizabeth I's reign,[54] though it gave rise to some nice legal questions. In theory, estates in copyhold were not subject to common-law rules but to the customs of each manor, which had to be proved as facts. Increasingly, however, the royal courts assimilated copyholds to freeholds by applying the same rules in the absence of proof of usage to the contrary. Remainders were recognised, the admission of the particular tenant somehow extending to the remaindermen as well. Entailed copyhold was also recognised, at any rate if there was a custom of bringing formedon in the manorial court; but this required the utmost ingenuity, since the equity of *De donis* (1285) had somehow to be coupled with notionally immemorial custom.[55] Such entails could be barred by recovery in the manorial court. All in all, as Coke remarked, time had dealt very favourably with copyholders. But some of the distinctions between copyhold and freehold, including for the former the necessity of conveyance by surrender and admittance, remained embedded in the law until 1926.

The Trust as an Interest in Land

The survival of equitable interests after the Statute of Uses, and the emergence of the trust, have already been mentioned.[56] Although the trust was not introduced into conveyancing practice for the same reasons as the medieval use, its development mirrored that of the use, in that equitable relief began in individual cases of mistake or unconscionable behaviour and then became a matter of course: when that occurred, the beneficiary came to have a distinct interest in land, governed by known rules. This feat was perhaps easier to perform the second time, because many of the rules established for uses could be reused for trusts; but the old rules were not always best suited to their new role. The achievement of creating a coherent body of trust law, and freeing it from the unsuitable aspects of the old law of uses, is generally credited to Lord Nottingham C (d. 1682).

In Coke's time the trust had been regarded as a mere unassignable personal right of action, rather than as an interest in land.[57] Lord Keeper Egerton was even unwilling to enforce a trust against a purchaser of the

---

[54] The possibility was denied as late as 1573 by the Common Pleas: B. & M. 202-203. A clear example in the Queen's Bench is *Melwich v. Luter* (1588) 4 Co. Rep. 26.

[55] *Dell v. Hygden* (1595) B. & M. 203-207. Cf. *Anon.* (1523) Bro. N.C. 175.

[56] See pp. 328-332, ante.

[57] Co. Inst., vol. I, fo. 272b; vol. IV, p. 85. See also *Wytham v. Waterhowse* (1596) B. & M. 124; Cro. Eliz. 466.

legal estate, without clear evidence of express notice.[58] Greater hostility is evident from a Lincoln's Inn reading of 1623, in which trusts were attacked as introducing yet more uncertainty into the law, so that legal estates ('the ancient darling of the common law') had become 'as shadows'. The reader advocated complete extirpation.[59] Lingering suspicion of the trust is even found sixty years later.[60] By the time of Lord Nottingham, however, the trust was treated as an inheritable equitable estate, more closely analogous to a legal estate in land than to a chose in action. In achieving this position several basic principles applicable to uses were laid aside.[61] The artificial trust was not the same as a personal confidence reposed in a human conscience, and so a corporation could be a trustee.[62] The beneficial interest was held to prevail over claims against the trustee's legal estate by third parties, such as a widow claiming dower, or a judgment creditor.[63] On the other hand, after 1677, a trust was regarded as part of a deceased beneficiary's assets for the purpose of administering his estate, and even the legal estate of the trustees could be taken in execution to satisfy claims against the beneficiary.[64] The trust was assimilated to the legal estate in other respects: for example, so far was the beneficiary regarded as the real owner of the land that the common-law rules against restraints on alienation were applied to his equitable estate.[65]

By these means, as Lord Mansfield put it in 1759, the trust had become in Chancery the same as the land itself and the trustee 'merely an instrument of conveyance'.[66] The beneficiary was the owner, and his estate was subject to rules of property as definite as those which governed legal estates. The old problem caused by the informality with which equitable interests could be conveyed, and which had been one of

---

[58] *Wildegoose v. Wayland* (1596) B. & M. 125.

[59] Henry Sherfield's reading (1623) B. & M. 125-126. This was an unconscious echo of Audley's attack on uses in 1526: p. 291, ante; B. & M. 103-105.

[60] See *Howard v. Duke of Norfolk* (1683) B. & M. 175, per North LK.

[61] See Lord Nottingham's essay on this subject, B. & M. 129-131.

[62] So also could the king. Neither could be seised to uses.

[63] *Medley v. Martin* (1673) Rep. t. Finch 63 (creditor); *Tassel v. Hare* (1675) 73 SS 230, no. 339 (doweress); *Finch v. Earl of Winchilsea* (1715) 1 P. Wms 277 (judgment creditor).

[64] Statute of Frauds 1677, 29 Car. II, c.3, s.10. This was penned by Lord Nottingham. For the trust as assets, see B. & M. 130. Note also *Sympson v. Turner* (1700) B. & M. 132.

[65] Excepting the case of the married woman, where the restraint was allowed in her own interest: p. 553, post.

[66] *Burgess v. Wheate* (1759) 1 Eden 177; 1 Wm Bla. at 162.

the objections to uses, was tackled in the case of trusts by legislation: after 1677, a declaration of trust in land was void unless 'manifested and proved' by writing.[67] Trusts could arise, however, without such formality by implication of law; and the basic principles of implied and constructive trusts were another legacy of Lord Nottingham's chancellorship.[68] From this period also the courts of equity developed distinctions between the rules governing trusts and other equitable interests (such as the equity of redemption). One important distinction was that between trusts and powers.[69] A bare power of appointment carried with it no duty, and so there was no need (as with the trust) for named or ascertainable beneficiaries. Most powers were personal and could not be assigned.[70] The court was unable to remedy the non-execution of such a power, though it could set aside improper appointments and would sometimes remedy formal defects in proper appointments. If the power was coupled with a trust, however, there had to be ascertainable beneficiaries so that the court could decree equal distribution among them if the trustee failed to appoint; if there were not, the trust itself would fail.

The trust thus joined contract and tort as one of the major conceptual categories of English law, and its importance extended beyond the area of landed property.[71] This is reflected in the nineteenth-century treatises on 'trusts and trustees',[72] which treated the subject autonomously and not merely as a branch of conveyancing. Trusts of personal property are in modern times at least as common as trusts of land; and to a large extent the same rules govern both. Under the scheme of estates introduced by the legislation of 1925, the trust became the only medium for creating an interest in real property other than a term of years or a fee simple absolute in possession.

---

[67] Statute of Frauds 1677, 29 Car. II, c.3, s.7; B. & M. 131.

[68] See Yale, 79 SS *101-160*. For the attendancy of trust terms, see p. 345, ante.

[69] For powers, see pp. 327-328, ante.

[70] *R. v. Englefield* (1591) 7 Co. Rep. 11; 4 Leon. 135, 169 (power to revoke uses, not forfeitable for treason).

[71] E.g., in the 18th century it is common to encounter trusts of stocks and other funds. Cf. the common-law 'trust' of money, enforced by *assumpsit* for money had and received: p. 409, post.

[72] E.g., Thomas Lewin, *A Practical Treatise on the Law of Trusts and Trustees* (1837); Henry Godefroi, *A Digest of the Principles of the Law of Trusts and Trustees* (1879).

Mortgages

From the earliest times, debtors have used property as security for loans of money; this was known as a 'gage'. Whether the gage was a chattel[73] or land, possession had to be handed over to the lender, to be returned on payment. In some early forms of gage no term was fixed: the gagee held the property until he was satisfied. Another early form, as we have seen,[74] was a lease for years to the gagee, the term being the period of the loan. If the gagee took the profits in reduction of the loan, this was known in early times as a living gage (*vivum vadium*),[75] apparently because the property continued to work for the borrower; but if the lender took the principal as well as the profits, it was a dead gage ('mortgage'), and the arrangement, though sinful as giving the lender a usurious return, was legally valid.[76] By the fifteenth century, however, the name 'mortgage' had apparently come to be used for any arrangement whereby a loan was secured by a conveyance of real property. The self-redeeming living gage had long since gone into disuse: it cast on the lender the responsibility of refunding himself, perhaps without profit, and it was less attractive than a passive security in the form of land which would become the lender's absolutely if the borrower failed to pay on time. Two new ways of effecting such security were developed in the thirteenth century: either the mortgagor leased the land for years to the mortgagee, with the proviso that if the debt was not paid by a certain date the mortgagee would have the fee, or the mortgagor conveyed the fee to the mortgagee forthwith, on condition that he might re-enter (and regain the fee) if he paid by a certain date. The first form had the disadvantage that the mortgagee was not seised and therefore had no security if the mortgagor wrongly regained possession; it also fell foul of the emerging doctrines of estates, under which a term of years could not be enlarged into a fee without a transfer of seisin. The second form gave the mortgagee a fee simple defeasible by condition subsequent (that is, payment). One advantage

---

[73] By Tudor times the law distinguished a pawn of a chattel (which gave the lender possession but not ownership of the thing) from a gage (which transferred title in the chattel to the lender). In medieval vocabulary a 'pledge' was usually a *person* who gave surety (e.g. by executing a bond).

[74] See p. 338, ante.

[75] The French form 'vifgage' is found in Norman law, but was not used in England.

[76] The Canon law regarded it as a sin ('usury') to take interest on a loan, and usurers were liable to punishment in the medieval church courts. The common law took a more worldly approach and did not invalidate usurious agreements, though penalties were introduced in 1495, and in 1545 parliament set an upper limit of 10% on lawful interest: Stat. 11 Hen. VII, c.8; 37 Hen. VIII, c.9. (The limit was later reduced to 5%, where it remained until the repeal of the usury laws in 1854.)

of the fee-simple mortgage was that it was arguably non-usurious. A disadvantage was that, if the mortgagee died before being paid, the fee descended to his heir and therefore attracted dower and feudal incidents, whereas the debt which it secured devolved as personal property on his executors. One way of avoiding this problem was to convey land to feoffees, on the terms that if the money was paid they would hold to the use of the mortgagor and if not to the use of the mortgagee.[77] In the seventeenth century a further alternative device came into widespread use, the long term of years with clause of defeasance.[78] This was much used in raising money under the terms of strict settlements, since the estate to be mortgaged was commonly a term of years.[79]

A popular form of security after 1285, which also avoided the legal problems, was the 'statute merchant' – and (after 1353) its analogue the 'statute staple' – whereby the borrower could by means of a registered contract charge his land and goods without giving up possession; if he failed to pay, the lender became a tenant of the land until satisfied, under a special kind of tenancy which was treated as a chattel for succession purposes but protected by the assize.[80] At first these devices were only for merchants – and they were the only kind of mortgage available to alien merchants (who could not own land) – but in 1531 a 'recognizance in the nature of a statute staple' was introduced for non-mercantile parties; the recognizance was registrable in one of the central courts or in the city of London.[81] Statutes and recognizances were still used in the eighteenth century, but had become obsolete before they were abolished in 1863.

The borrower under a statute or recognizance remained in possession of his land, and it later became a common practice under the common-law forms of mortgage likewise to allow the mortgagor to remain in possession as a tenant at will or at sufferance of the mortgagee. After

---

[77] E.g. *Sir William Capell's Case* (1494) 102 SS 12; *Anon.* (1552) B. & M. 134.

[78] See 79 SS *45, 151*. It was sometimes strengthened by a covenant to convey the reversion to the mortgagee in case of nonpayment. During the 18th century the fee-simple mortgage came back into fashion, but with the condition of defeasance replaced by a covenant to reconvey on payment; the advantage of a formal reconveyance over a re-entry was that it made the title easier to prove.

[79] See pp. 333, 344, ante.

[80] Cf. tenancy by elegit (pp. 78-79, ante), which was a security for the judgment debtor.

[81] Statute of Merchants, 13 Edw. I, stat. iii; Statute of the Staple, 27 Edw. III, stat. ii, c.9; Stat. 23 Hen. VIII, c.6. The mortgage by way of charge was revived, in a different form, in 1925.

1600 the mortgage deed might contain express provision for this,[82] but the practice is probably older. The mortgagor who stayed in possession was legally in a similar position to the cestuy que use: at law he could be evicted at will, though he might (as we shall see) expect protection in Chancery.

The mortgagor could redeem his land by discharging his debt according to the bargain; but the condition had to be performed according to its true meaning, with the result that if the mortgagor defaulted even in a minor way the land passed absolutely out of his hands. If the debtor died before payment, there was a view in the thirteenth century that the heir could not redeem the inheritance; strict performance had become impossible, and there was no room for 'equity'. In this one case the common law did come round to a more equitable doctrine; according to Littleton (*c.* 1460-70), the heir could redeem because of his interest in the land.[83] But that was the limit of common-law equity. The date of payment had to be adhered to strictly; if the money was not tendered in time for it to be counted out before sunset of the appointed day, the land was lost.[84] As in the case of the penal bond, this gave the moneylender more security than he needed; and the harsh consequences of the common law required softening in Chancery.

THE EQUITY OF REDEMPTION

The equitable doctrine of mortgages grew from the same root as the doctrine of penalties.[85] The moneylender was morally entitled only to the debt, and perhaps some reasonable profit, but ought not to profit unconscionably from a penal arrangement. No doubt relief in Chancery was first given on the hard facts of particular cases, as where the penalty was grossly excessive,[86] or where punctual payment was prevented through misfortune or sharp practice;[87] but in the early seventeenth century it became an established doctrine that in equity the mortgagor

---

[82] See, e.g., *Powseby v. Blackman* (1623) Cro. Jac. 659. Another device, where the mortgage was by way of demise for (say) 500 years, was for the mortgagee to subdemise to the mortgagor for 499 years, without reserving rent, the subdemise to be void in the event of nonpayment.

[83] *Britton*, vol. II, p. 128 (using the word *equité*); Littleton, *Tenures*, s.334.

[84] *Wade's Case* (*c.* 1602) 5 Co. Rep. 114.

[85] See p. 370, post.

[86] E.g. *Bodenham v. Halle* (1456) 10 SS 137; *Sir William Capell's Case* (1494) 102 SS 12.

[87] So the doctrine is stated in Cary 1; Co. Inst., vol. IV, p. 84.

was the true owner of the land.[88] The new doctrine meant that if the legal estate passed to the mortgagee for non-payment, the mortgagor was nevertheless always entitled to a reconveyance, on tender within a reasonable time of the principal sum and 'damages' (representing interest and costs). On being paid, the mortgagee was considered a trustee for the mortgagor. And while the debt remained outstanding only the court, by a decree of foreclosure, could give the beneficial interest to the mortgagee if payment was unreasonably delayed.[89]

The mortgagor was said to have an 'equity of redemption'. This was held to be so inseparable from a mortgage that the parties could not contract out of it, and the mortgagee could not by his conduct 'clog' the equity.[90] Even if the mortgagee forfeited his land for treason, the mortgagor's equity was safe.[91] The equity of redemption had thus become a right inherent in the land, and the mortgagor had acquired real protection. Just as the typical fifteenth-century landowner had not been seised of his own land, but was in possession as a cestuy que use, so the great landowner of the seventeenth, eighteenth and nineteenth centuries was commonly in possession of his land (or some of it) only as the owner of an equity of redemption. The equity could be bought and sold, settled in tail, and even mortgaged; like the trust it had become an equitable estate, and was open to the same objection that it made the law of property less certain. Hale CJ said in 1673 it had 'received too much favour', and that 'by the growth of equity on equity the heart of the law is eaten out'.[92] Like the trust, however, it became a settled feature of English property law; and already by the end of Lord Nottingham's chancellorship (1673-82) it was the subject of a sophisticated body of principles concerning priorities.[93]

---

88 See *Emmanuel College, Cambridge v. Evans* (1625) 1 Ch. Rep. 18. There is some contemporary evidence that the change of practice occurred during Bacon's chancellorship (1617-21).

89 The mortgagee could take possession without going to the court, but he remained a trustee and was strictly accountable for the profits.

90 E.g. by spending money on improving the land: *Bacon v. Bacon* (1640) Tothill 133.

91 *Pawlett v. A.-G.* (1667) Hardres 465. The mortgagee's heir (Edmund Ludlow of the Inner Temple) had been attainted by parliament as a regicide.

92 *Roscarrock v. Barton* (1672) 1 Ch. Cas. 217 at 219; Nottingham, *Prolegomena* (Yale ed.), pp. 284-286. Even Nottingham thought equitable relief had the 'ill consequence' of making it harder to borrow money on mortgage: *Manual of Chancery Practice* (Yale ed.), p. 165.

93 See Yale, 79 SS 62-87. The Chancery by this time also recognised the equitable mortgage, where title-deeds were deposited with the lender as security: 73 SS ciii-civ.

Licences

A licence to go upon or use land, being merely an authority to do what would otherwise be a tort, does not possess the characteristics of a property right. It is inalienable: if I license A to visit my house for dinner, he cannot substitute B.[94] It is not enforceable *in rem*: a countermand is effective, though it may be a breach of contract, and so the licensee who ignores a countermand becomes a trespasser.[95] A fortiori, a licence cannot be invoked against a purchaser from, or lessee of, the licensor. Licences are not much mentioned in the common law before the fifteenth century. Their only effect, outside the law of contract, seems to have been to provide a defence to an action in tort.

Nevertheless, just as the use and lease for years turned from being mere personal arrangements into property rights, so even licences appear to be susceptible to a similar transformation. In the later year-books there are said to be limits to the power of countermand. For one thing, a licence might amount to a lease for years. A licence to occupy land for a fixed term was not necessarily a lease, because it might not give the licensee exclusive possession; but this was a matter of construction.[96] Then again, a licence could not be revoked if it was coupled with a grant of an easement or profit. Moreover, if it were to take a profit, the licensee could assign it, or could at least exercise it through agents.[97] The medieval explanation for this distinction was that things of pleasure were purely personal and could be revoked without substantial loss, whereas things of profit were more highly regarded by law. In later times, however, the explanation advanced was that, whereas a bare authority was inherently revocable, a grant of property was not. The critical distinction was between a bare licence and a grant.[98] A grant of an easement or profit required a deed; a lease did not, but it required an intention to confer the right of exclusive occupation for a fixed period. With this distinction the common law rested; despite contrary rumblings from time to time, the law could not confer the attributes of real property upon a bare licence. However, by the nineteenth century it was

---

94 Y.B. Mich. 18 Edw. IV, fo. 14, pl. 12, per Choke J.

95 Y.B. Mich 39 Hen. VI, fo. 7, pl. 12; Trin. 20 Edw. IV, fo. 4, pl.2, per Wode sjt. The later cases are reviewed in *Wood v. Leadbitter* (1845) 13 M. & W. 838.

96 *Prior of Bruton v. Ede* (1470) 47 SS 31.

97 *Duchess of Norfolk v. Wiseman* (1497) Y.B. Trin. 12 Hen. VII, fo. 25, pl.5; Hil. 13 Hen. VII, fo. 13, pl.2. Cf. Port Nbk (102 SS) 37.

98 *Note* (*c.* 1520) Spelman Rep. (93 SS) 161, per Broke sjt; *Webb v. Paternoster* (1619) 2 Rolle Rep. 143, 152; Poph. 151; Palm. 171; Godb. 282; Noy 98. The same distinction could be applied to personal chattels: *Bringloe v. Morrice* (1676) 1 Mod. Rep. 210.

settled that equity would restrain the revocation of a licence if the licensee had been allowed to improve land on the understanding that it would not be revoked, or if the licensee had given consideration for a 'contractual licence'. It has since been maintained that, as a result of the Judicature Acts, the equitable doctrine prevails over the law to the extent that a contractual licensee may persist in exercising a countermanded licence without becoming a trespasser.[99] But the most remarkable development has occurred within the last few decades, when it has been held that an irrevocable licence to occupy land may give rise to an 'equity' or constructive trust which binds purchasers with notice.[100] The precise characteristics of this new species of interest are still a matter of controversy. It is not yet technically an 'interest in land'; but it does seem that something very like it is being elevated from the realms of contract into those of status, in order to protect the position of those who have bargained for the use or occupation of real property without becoming tenants. The historical parallel with the recognition of the use and of the lease for years is obvious.

Further reading

Holdsworth HEL, vol. III, pp. 198-217
Simpson, *History of the Land Law*, pp. 71-77, 141-143, 242-269
Milsom HFCL, pp. 101-102, 152-157, 161-165, 224-225, 230-231
Cornish & Clark, pp. 132-136
J. H. Baker, 'Agrarian Changes and Security of Tenure' (1978) 94 SS
    180-187

LEASES FOR YEARS
Pollock & Maitland, vol. II, pp. 106-124
P. Bordwell, 'Ejectment takes Over' (1970) 55 *Iowa Law Rev.* 1089-1147
W. M. McGovern, 'The Historical Conception of a Lease for Years' (1976) 23 *UCLA Law Rev.* 501-528
M. S. Arnold, 'The Term of Years' in [1976] CLJ at 323-330

---

99   *Winter Garden Theatre (London) Ltd v. Millennium Productions Ltd* [1948] A.C. 173, [1947] 2 All E.R. 331.
100 *National Provincial Bank v. Ainsworth* [1965] A.C. 1175, [1965] 2 All E.R. 472; *Binions v. Evans* [1972] Ch. 359, [1972] 2 All E.R. 70. Cf. the Housing Act 1980, s.48, under which a licensee from a local authority may have a statutory 'secure tenancy'.

J. M. Kaye, 'A Note on the Statute of Enrolments 1536' (1988) 104
    LQR 617-634

VILLEIN TENURE AND COPYHOLD

Pollock & Maitland, vol. I, pp. 356-383

F. W. Maitland, *Select Pleas in Manorial Courts* (2 SS, 1888); *The
    Court Baron* (4 SS, 1890)

G. C. Homans, *English Villagers of the 13th Century* (1941)

Simpson, *History of the Land Law*, pp. 144-172

C. M. Gray, *Copyhold, Equity and the Common Law* (1963)

R. M. Smith, 'Some Thoughts on "Hereditary" and "Proprietary"
    Rights in Land under Customary Law' (1983) 1 JLH 95-128

L. A. Slota, 'Law, Land Transfer and Lordship on the Estates of St
    Albans Abbey in the 13th and 14th Centuries' (1988) 6 JLH 119-
    138

TRUSTS AND MORTGAGES

R. W. Turner, *The Equity of Redemption* (1931)

D.E.C. Yale, 'An Essay on Mortgages and Trusts and allied Topics in
    Equity', in *Lord Nottingham's Chancery Cases*, vol. II (1961), 79
    SS 7-207

J. L. Barton, 'The Common Law Mortgage' (1967) 83 LQR 229-239

G. S. Alexander, 'The Transformation of Trusts as a Legal Category,
    1800-1914' (1987) 5 LHR 303-350

18. Contract: Covenant and Debt

From the law of real property we now turn to the law of obligations, which comprises the law of contract, of quasi-contract, and of torts. The law of torts governs infringements of interests protected by the law independently of private agreement, whereas the law of contract governs those expectations of good faith which arise out of particular transactions between individual persons. The latter type of obligation may be analysed in terms either of the *right* to performance of the contract, or of the *wrong* of breaking the contract and thereby causing loss. The modern common law knows only the latter aspect; it provides for damages to compensate for breach of contract, but to compel the specific performance of a contract in the future recourse must be had to equity. This is somewhat remarkable when one learns that the earliest form of action concerning contractual obligations was designed to compel performance. Moreover, the story begins, rather than ends, with an apparently comprehensive contractual remedy. But the English law of contract has not evolved lineally from a single starting-point. Its history has been affected by evidential problems, jurisdictional shifts, and the extension of trespass actions to remedy the deficiencies of the *praecipe* writs.

Before embarking on the story, it is necessary to understand the terminology of the medieval common lawyers. The word 'contract' possessed a more confined meaning for them that it now does. It denoted a transaction, such as a sale or loan, which transferred property or generated a debt; it did not mean a consensual contract, an exchange of promises. The modern sense of 'contract', as a legally binding agreement, was conveyed by the word 'covenant' (*conventio*). 'Covenant', as we shall see, was to acquire a restricted technical meaning because of the limited way in which actions of covenant were allowed to work in the central courts, and it then became necessary to find a general word to replace it. 'Contract' would not at first do, because of its special connotations. Pleaders, borrowing from the French, sometimes used Latin neologisms corresponding with 'agreement' (*agreamentum*) and 'bargain' (*bargania* or *barganizatio*), but the word which ultimately prevailed was 'undertaking' (*assumptio*).[1]

---

[1] For its shift from a factual to a promissory meaning: see p. 375, post.

We shall see in the next chapter how this was brought about by the development of forms of action designed to remedy wrongdoing, by in effect making it a tort to damage someone in breach of an undertaking. By about 1600 the action of *assumpsit* ('he undertook') had expanded to take over the work of the older actions based on covenants and contracts, and then the word 'contract' began to acquire its looser modern sense of 'agreement'. Serjeant Sheppard noticed this shift of meaning in 1651: 'a contract, taken largely, is an agreement between two or more concerning something to be done, whereby both parties are bound to each other, or one is bound to the other. But more strictly it is taken for an agreement between two or more for the buying and selling of some personal goods whereby property is altered.'[2] It will be noted that even the stricter sense now incorporated the notion of an agreement: 'contract', however defined, had taken on the meaning formerly borne by 'covenant'. By the end of the seventeenth century the modern distinction between contract and tort was in place.[3]

Our main historical questions are nevertheless not so much questions of terminology or classification as of remedies. What agreements or undertakings were to be enforced, and where? What remedies were available to enforce them? In respect of the ancient communal assemblies, and in the medieval town courts where mercantile litigation was mostly conducted, the answer seems very simple. The plaintiff made complaint in some standard form, and proof was by oath; everyone knew that contracts ought to be performed, and no more law than that was needed. In the royal courts – that is, at common law – the answer was governed by the writ system.

The Action of Covenant

Before 1200 there was a royal writ in the form *praecipe* to enforce covenants, and the formula settled in the thirteenth century was: 'order the defendant to keep the covenant' made between him and the plaintiff (*praecipe D quod teneat P conventionem inter eos factam*).[4] This writ was usually brought to enforce covenants concerning land, such as leases, but its wording comprehended all sorts of agreement. According

---

2 W. Sheppard, *Faithfull Councellor* (1651), p. 93.

3 See pp. 454-455, post.

4 For the full form, see p. 616, post. For a 12th-century prototype, see 77 SS 493, no. 154.

to a statute of 1284, the variety of writs of covenant was infinite.[5] The form of action was applicable in theory to all consensual contracts; it gave specific performance where appropriate, damages where not. But history did not stop in the thirteenth century, and the seemingly comprehensive action of covenant was soon reduced to playing a very minor role in the history of contract.

A covenant relating to land was usually in a charter, sealed and witnessed. Most agreements were not so formal; but the early royal courts did not think it their function to hear minor disputes. *Glanvill* and *Bracton* both say that the royal courts had little to do with 'private' agreements, apparently meaning agreements not of record. Oral agreements were best left to the local courts, where proof by compurgation was used. At first this was not a rigid rule. We find occasional covenant cases in the thirteenth-century eyre rolls in which the plaintiff has no written evidence, and this is fatal only if he has no suit (transaction witnesses) either;[6] provided the plaintiff produced suit, the defendant was put to answer, and could either wage his law[7] or put himself on a jury.[8] In 1292 the justices in eyre at Shrewsbury overruled an objection by counsel that the defendant need not answer an action of covenant without writing,[9] and this position seems to have held into the next century. By 1321, however, the royal judges had decided that the only acceptable evidence of a covenant in the royal courts was a deed, a written document under seal. In the London eyre of that year a bill of covenant was brought against a carrier who had covenanted to carry a load of hay from Waltham to London and failed to do so. The action failed for want of a deed. Counsel protested that it was not necessary to have a deed for a cartload of hay; but Herle J retorted that the judges

---

5   Statute of Wales 1284, c.10; B. & M. 281. Dr Ibbetson cites a building case in 1226: 4 JLH 72.

6   In *Dun v. Basset* (1234) Fifoot HSCL, p. 261, the plaintiff loses because he 'produces no suit save his own single voice nor shows a charter'. In *Cadigan v. Say* (1256) B. & M. 280, the defendant complains that he need not answer the plaintiff's bare or sole word (*simplex dictum*) without writing; but this again probably refers to the lack of suit. For 'suit', see p. 5, ante.

7   E.g. *Esthanney v. Drayton* (1248) B. & M. 279 (covenant denied); *Syfrewast v. Syfrewast* (1248) ibid. (breach denied).

8   4 JLH at 77, 87. The Statute of Wales 1284 (B. & M. 281) speaks only of jury trial. When the plaintiff had a deed, a plea of performance had to be tried by jury: *Aubrey v. Flory* (1321) 86 SS 235.

9   *Corbet v. Scurye* (1292) B. & M. 282.

would not 'undo the law for a cartload of hay'.[10] The policy of
excluding minor cases had become an absolute rule, the test of
jurisdiction being the ability to produce a deed. The rule could not be
displaced for a particular county by showing that it had never been
applied there in previous eyres; it had become common-law procedure,
binding eyres as well as central courts.[11]

It is clear that the rule did not imply a narrow understanding of what
a covenant was: a covenant was simply an agreement, and a deed was
evidence of an agreement.[12] What is still unclear is how the rule came
into being and how it was justified at the time. It is likely that it came
in by degrees, starting with leases;[13] and that it was resisted longest and
with some success in cases where a breach of covenant was associated
with physical harm.[14] It seems that it was not a rule confined to
covenants, but was a rule of evidence applied to any interest based on a
mere word, such as a rentcharge, an assignment of a reversion, a
remainder, or a warranty.[15] No doubt it was also influenced by the
fictionalisation of suit; whatever a plaintiff said in his count, an action
on an unwritten covenant had come in reality to depend on the plaintiff's
own bare word.[16]

Once the rule was established, it could still be said that any kind of
agreement was enforceable by the writ of covenant; but now the plaintiff
would only succeed if he had a deed to prove the agreement. The result
was that informal agreements had been shut out from the central courts,
and the development of a law of consensual contracts stifled by the

10 *Anon.* (1321) B. & M. 285 at 286. A possible interpretation of this interchange
    is that it was concerned not with the smallness of the matter but with the
    resemblance to detinue (in which a deed was not needed): D. Ibbetson, 4 JLH at
    89.

11 *Wetenhale v. Arden* (1346) Kiralfy SB, p. 181.

12 *Anon.* (1304) B. & M. 284, per Est sjt ('the writing would only have provided
    evidence of the covenant'); *Anon.* (1321) B. & M. 285 at 286, per Herle J.

13 The rule is stated as applying to leases in the tract *Exceptiones contra brevia* (c.
    1280): Ibbetson, 'Words and Deeds', pp. 81-82. Dr Ibbetson suggests this was a
    borrowing from the Civil law, which required writing for the analogous contract
    of *emphyteusis*.

14 E.g. *Corbet v. Scury* (1292) B. & M. 282 (damaged horse); *Anon.* (1311 or 1312)
    B. & M. 285, Fifoot HSCL, p. 263 (waste by lessee); *Warner v. Leech* (1330)
    Kiralfy SB, p. 184 (surgeon not treating arrow wound). In the London eyre, too,
    the justices hesitated over the surgeon: *Anon.* (1321) 86 SS 353.

15 Reversion: *Anon.* (1310) 22 SS 145; *Lucy v. Plukenet* (1312) 38 SS 92 at 93, 94.
    Remainder: *Anon.* (1341) Y.B. Trin. 15 Edw. III, p. 201, pl. 19, per Basset J.
    Warranty: *Falston v. Falston* (1370) Y.B. Mich. 44 Edw. III, fo. 27, pl.1 (rule
    compared with that in covenant).

16 For the fictionalisation of suit, see *Canon Warren's Case* (1343) B. & M. 212 (in
    debt); and for its relevance here, Milsom HFCL, pp. 247-248.

formal requirement of a seal. Contemporaries would not have viewed this as a drastic denial of justice, when local courts were quite competent to deal with informal agreements. It was true that one could not put every covenant into writing; but then one should not be able to bother the king's central courts with every unwritten covenant. The hardship in the case of the Waltham carrier was a temporary misfortune, since the plaintiff would have succeeded without question had no eyre been then sitting at the tower of London. In the mayor's court of London, and probably in all other local courts, covenants continued to be actionable without a deed; and this was as much the law of the land as the stricter evidential rule of the central courts.[17] It was also a geographical problem: the plaintiff would probably have succeeded had he brought detinue in Waltham. The change was not, therefore, a change in the law so much as a demarcation of jurisdiction. Its restrictive character made excellent sense in the eyres, which were unable to cope with the volume of business brought to them. But the central courts came rapidly to regret the policy, and by 1374 the argument that one could not make a deed for every little agreement was already being used to justify alternative remedies.[18] The consequences of the change of policy will be considered in the next chapter.

The fate of the action of covenant was not merely to be restricted to plaintiffs blessed with deeds; even for them, covenant ceased to be the usual remedy. In the fourteenth century the possibility of specific performance disappeared, so that plaintiffs who sought to compel defendants to hand over, or permit them to enjoy, property were driven into the Chancery. Unliquidated damages were an unreliable remedy in other cases, and so when parties chose to make contracts under seal it became usual in the fourteenth century and after to use the formula of the conditional bond, which gave a more secure remedy in debt.[19] Then, in the fifteenth century, when covenant had become more peripheral to the law of contract, the nature of the action was artificially constricted. It was said that the formula *praecipe quod teneat conventionem* was appropriate only for defendants who were still able to keep their covenant, and not as a means of obtaining compensation for imperfect or tardy performance.[20] If a builder constructed a house so badly that it

17   *Welshe v. Hoper* (1533) B. & M. 286 (not the law of England, as far as borough courts are concerned, that a covenant must be in writing). For London, see 102 SS 10.

18   *Stratton v. Swanlond* (1374) B. & M. 360 at 361-362, per Cavendish CJ.

19   See pp. 368-369, post.

20   This is an example of the unintended consequences of freezing a particular formula. In the 12th century there were precedents for a writ *quare non tenet conventionem*, which would have avoided the 15th century construction.

collapsed, it was futile to order him to keep the covenant – the plaintiff wanted compensation for the damage; likewise if the building were completed late, thereby putting the plaintiff to inconvenience and expense; so also if a man sold goods which turned out to be defective. There is no reason to suppose that in the thirteenth century there was any difficulty about giving damages in covenant in such cases; indeed, they were the very cases in which damages, as opposed to performance, were appropriate.[21] The reason for introducing the new learning, as we shall see, was to justify the use of actions on the case (which did not require a deed) instead of covenant.[22]

The Action of Debt

At least as old as the writ of covenant was the writ of debt, whereby the defendant was to be ordered to render or yield up a sum of money, or a quantity of fungibles,[23] which he owed to and unjustly withheld from the plaintiff (*praecipe D quod reddat P £n quas ei debet et injuste detinet*).[24] There was no theoretical overlap with covenant, because medieval lawyers saw a debt as more like property than breach of promise. The *praecipe quod reddat* formula was also used for land and chattels; debt was indeed scarcely distinguishable from detinue, which lay for personal property.[25] The difference between detinue and debt resulted from distinguishing specific chattels, which were owned, from money or fungibles, which were owed. If *D* owed *P* a quarter of barley, this was a debt because *P* could not assert property in any identified barley. But if *D* detained a specific sack of barley which belonged to *P*, then *P*'s remedy was detinue.[26] Again, if *P* lent *D* £10, this was a debt because the actual coins became *D*'s property and his duty was to render the sum of £10 in whatever lawful coin he chose. But if *P* delivered to *D* a bag of coins to the value of £10 to look after for him, the property in the coins remained in *P* and he could sue for them by writ of detinue. Covenant would only lie in such cases if *D* promised to pay *P* the £10;

---

21 Statute of Wales 1284, c.10; B. & M. 281.

22 See pp. 383-384, post.

23 Goods defined by weight or measure and generic character, but not identified in particular. Fungibles are interchangeable, so that a loan is paid in kind. The term *res fungibilia* is Roman; there was no technical term in English law.

24 For the full form, see p. 614, post. For 12th-century precedents: *Glanvill*, x.2; 77 SS 254.

25 See p. 441, post.

26 The same distinction was drawn in criminal proceedings: 97 SS 194 (1329).

and where there was a promise, or covenant, the two actions overlapped.[27]

The existence of a debt, as of a covenant, might depend on private transactions and thus present difficulties of proof. But the royal courts did not here insist on a deed as the only mode of proof. Certainly a deed was acceptable as a superior way of proving a debt, and it was necessary in the case of a mere grant to pay; but if the debt arose from an informal transaction the central courts continued to allow an action based on suit, against which the defendant could wage law. This difference of approach between the two actions to some extent clarifies the evidential rule itself. A covenant or grant consisted in fleeting words, and no action was allowed in the royal courts for mere breath. A sale, a loan, a hiring, on the other hand, were all visible conduct 'of which knowledge may be had'; the act generated the duty to pay, which therefore did not depend merely on words.[28] The deed likewise was an act (*factum*), in that the specialty was sealed and delivered before witnesses as an 'act and deed'. The distinction between words and deeds ran deep in English law.[29]

DEBT ON A CONTRACT

If he had no deed, the creditor had to show in his count some *causa debendi*, that is, a transaction or 'contract' which was the reason for the owing. The authors of *Glanvill* and *Bracton* theorised about *causa* in the language of Roman law, but in the year-books it is explained in terms of *quid pro quo*. A plaintiff could maintain an action of debt if he had conferred some valuable recompense upon the defendant in return for the duty; the furnishing of this *quid pro quo* executed the contract on his side and created the relationship of creditor and debtor. The borrower of money had *quid pro quo* in the use of the money, the buyer in the goods bought, the hirer in the use of the thing hired, the employer or client in the services rendered, and so on. Performance of a covenant could also generate a duty to pay. If a carpenter were retained to build a house for £100, there was a covenant which bound him to perform; but not until he built the house was there *quid pro quo* which entitled him to bring debt for his £100.

---

[27] *Anon.* (1292) B. & M. 225 at 226; *Anon.* (1293) B. & M. 226; *Franssey's Case* (*c.* 1294) B. & M. 227. For earlier examples, see Ibbetson, 4 JLH at 73 n.14. There remained an election in later law also: *Sicklemore v. Simonds* (1600) Cro. Eliz. 797.

[28] *Loveday v. Ormesby* (1310) B. & M. 250; *Anon.* (1338) B. & M. 228 at 229, per Shareshull J. On the same principle, debt did not lie without a deed against a surety: *Anon.* (1344) and *Anon.* (1369) B. & M. 229. Cf. *Anon.* (1330) 98 SS 743 (action allowed on a 'grant' by a surety to pay, though no 'cause').

[29] See pp. 474, 495-496, post.

The rendering of *quid pro quo* justified proof of the debt by suit rather than by deed. But in such cases the defendant had the option of waging his law that he did not owe the money. The effect was that no enquiry was made into the facts; the suit was not examined, and the oath-taking was a formality not subject to cross-examination.[30] In practice many defendants, even as late as 1500, chose jury trial rather than wager of law; they doubtless wanted more time, and were perhaps unable to pay oath-helpers. Nevertheless, from the plaintiff's point of view the mere availability of the procedure was a deterrent; and it became most unwise to give substantial credit without formal security.

Most actions of debt were in common form, since most debts fell within a few well-known categories; their object was debt collection rather than dispute resolution. If the parties pleaded to issue it was invariably the general issue, 'He owes nothing' (*Nil debet*). The prevalence of the general issue in debt effectively prevented the development of a law of contract in the medieval period. There was no way in which detailed questions could arise, unless a defendant enquired informally whether he could safely wage law on the facts which he disclosed;[31] even then the defendant acted as his own judge and the decision was off the record. *Quid pro quo* might sound like a learned doctrine; but in truth it was just a name for the recompense found in all the common debt counts. Doctrinal discussion could occur only if a new form of count was tried out. When one such discussion took place in 1458, however, there was manifestly no consensus as to what the law of contract was. Some thought *quid pro quo* had to be a benefit conferred on the defendant. One judge thought it extended to the conferment of a benefit on a third party, or an act of charity. Another thought that it was not always necessary anyway, provided there was an act done at the defendant's request. And it was doubted whether it could include spiritual matters, such as marriage. No final decision is recorded.[32] In time something like the doctrines of consideration and privity might have been developed in the action of debt;[33] but the opportunity did not arise, because (for reasons which will be disclosed in the next chapter) debt on a contract went out of use.

---

30 See p. 363, ante.

31 Reported examples of such questions are not found until the 16th century: e.g. B. & M. 218-221.

32 *Anon.* (1458) B. & M. 236. The action was for money promised by a bride's father to the groom. The objection that such a *causa* was 'spiritual' was raised inconclusively by demurrer in *Elys v. Hoberd* (1480) Y.B. Hil. 19 Edw. IV, fo. 10, pl.18; CP 40/871, m.136. See also the question of 1477 in B. & M. 242.

33 For a later discussion, see *Lady Chandos v. Sympson* (1602) B. & M. 246 (retainer to embroider gown for maid).

DEBT ON AN OBLIGATION

More important in practice was the action of debt founded on document under seal. This was a very common action in the central courts until the nineteenth century, and its popularity derived from the widespread use of the conditioned bond.

A bond (or 'obligation') was a deed[34] containing an acknowledgment that a sum of money was owed by the 'obligor' to the 'obligee'. It was usually in Latin, in the form: 'Know all men etc. that I, *AB*, am firmly bound to *CD* in £*n* to be paid at Michaelmas next following'. When it was desired to draw up an important written agreement, a common practice was for one or both of the parties to make a bond to pay a sum of money to the other unless a certain condition was performed. If the condition was broken, the bond was forfeited and the penalty became due.[35] The condition, usually endorsed on the bond in English, either set out the terms of the agreement or (if they were complex) referred to the terms in a separate indenture. The wording of a performance bond was usually in the form: 'The condition of this obligation is that if *AB* shall build a house according to specifications [*or*, perform the covenants in an indenture dated . . .] then this obligation shall become void, or else it shall stand in full strength.' The principal advantage which this device had over a straightforward covenant was that a certain sum of money, fixed in advance as a liquidated debt, could be obtained for any non-performance of the condition. Even an agreement to pay money could be strengthened by making a bond to pay a larger amount (often twice the debt) in default of payment on the day; this was later known as a 'common money bond'. Another familiar form was the arbitration bond, designed to enforce with penalties the submission of any dispute to the award of arbitrators.

So popular were conditioned bonds that by Tudor times actions of debt on an obligation were the commonest single class of actions in the Common Pleas rolls; and so they remained for three centuries. They hindered the development of a law of consensual contract. Since the action of debt was brought to enforce the penal obligation and not the underlying agreement, many of the later problems in the law of contract did not arise; they were hidden on the back of the bond. The relationship between the parties was ruled not by contractual principles but by the law of deeds and conditions. Indeed, in debt on an obligation

---

[34]   A sealed tally did not qualify, unless words were written on it: *Anon.* (1320) 104 SS 87 and note; *Anon.* (1378) B. & M. 254.

[35]   The formula came into standard use in the 14th century. A back-to-front form, with the penalty in the condition, is found in *Warren v. Poyle* (1320) 104 SS 59 (bond conditioned to deliver grain or pay a penalty).

the true circumstances of that relationship were of subsidiary importance to the document under seal. A deed was of such a 'high nature' for evidential purposes that few parol[36] defences were allowed against it. One defence generally open to the defendant was to show that the proffered document was for some reason invalid as a deed. The plea that the writing was not his deed (*non est factum suum*) enabled him to show that it was not a deed at all, or that it was a forgery, or that he had been tricked into executing it because he was illiterate and the contents had been misread to him. The deed could also be invalidated for duress, incapacity (such as infancy), or 'suspicion', where it appeared to have been tampered with after execution. In the case of a conditioned bond, it was alternatively open to the defendant to plead performance or discharge of the condition. Here parol evidence was admitted of the condition and its discharge, because the condition was not part of the deed itself but went in defeasance of it. Thus, in the case of a common money bond, parol evidence could be given to show payment of the sum mentioned in the condition. All these defences were aimed at destroying, rather than contradicting, the deed. Where, however, the defendant admitted the validity of the deed, he could not without the aid of another deed plead such defences as payment of the sum mentioned in the bond itself. The deed stated that he owed the money, and therefore parol evidence was inadmissible to show that he did not.[37] Hence an obligor might be forced to pay twice on the same bond; the law said it was his own folly not to have had it destroyed or to have obtained an acquittance under seal. Even if the debtor paid, and the bond was returned, there was no defence if the obligee wrongfully stole it back and sued on it; there was no way in the world that a valid deed could be contradicted by oral evidence.[38] Under the harsh logic of the common law it was 'better to suffer a mischief to one man than an inconvenience to many, which would subvert the law. For if matter in writing could be so easily defeated and avoided by such a surmise, by naked breath, a matter in writing would be of no greater authority than a matter of fact.'[39]

---

[36] 'Parol' means word, as opposed to deed; but it includes the written as well as the spoken word if the writing is unsealed.

[37] Cf. the action of covenant, where the deed evidenced only the agreement and not its breach, so that performance could be proved by parol: *Eden v. Blake* (1605) B. & M. 287 at 288.

[38] *Glaston v. Abbot of Crowland* (1330) B. & M. 252; *Donne v. Cornwall* (1486) B. & M. 255. The remedy was to bring a writ of trespass for taking the bond, and hope that the damages would compensate for the overpayment.

[39] *Waberley v. Cockerel* (1542) B. & M. 257 at 258.

BONDS AND RELIEF AGAINST PENALTIES

Debt on an obligation remained in use until the nineteenth century, since it was the only form of action which could be used to enforce a debt evidenced by a bond. The reason for the longevity of bonds is worth a brief excursus. When they first developed, the main advantage of conditioned bonds was the provision for a penalty; and this, after some early qualms,[40] the common law allowed to be recovered in full. By the end of the fifteenth century, however, the Chancery had adopted the view that to recover more than a creditor had actually lost was unconscionable. If a creditor tried to extract more than the principal debt or actual damages, with reasonable costs, relief was available.[41] Statutes of 1696 and 1705 made recourse to the Chancery unnecessary, by enabling the defendant to discharge his liability by paying into court the sum to which the creditor was entitled in equity; the creditor could only sue execution for this sum.[42] However, these equitable restraints had little effect on the popularity of conditioned bonds, which remained in widespread use until the last century. They still gave procedural advantages, in that judgment was formally entered for the penalty and this stood as security in case further damages or costs were incurred. And the use of a deed continued to have other advantages, such as a more favourable limitation period[43] and the preference sometimes given to specialty debts over simple debts on insolvency.[44] But the last two advantages stemmed from the seal rather than the penalty, and the procedural advantages disappeared with the reforms which made equitable relief available in any action.[45] The use of penal bonds could then have effects more adverse than beneficial, since the penalty could serve only to limit the damages, which might in the event turn out to be greater than the penalty; they generally gave way in Victorian times to simple bonds, covenants, debentures, and other non-penal instruments. Penal

---

40 E.g. *Umfraville v. Lonstede* (1308) 19 SS 58, per Bereford CJ (referring to equity); *Scott v. Beracre* (1313/14) 27 SS 27 (referring to usury). Usury was tentatively raised, but not pursued, in *Anon.* (1346) Y.B. Pas. 20 Edw. III, p. 323, pl.46.

41 *Capell v. Scott* (1494) 102 SS 13; and, for the 16th century, see E. G. Henderson, 18 AJLH 298.

42 As to performance bonds: Administration of Justice Act 1696, 8 & 9 Will. III, c.11, s.8 (real damages to be assessed at trial). As to money bonds: Administration of Justice Act 1705, 4 & 5 Ann., c.3, ss.12-13.

43 There was no limitation period for actions on bonds before 1833, but payment was presumed after 20 years. The 20-year period was reduced to 12 years in 1939.

44 E.g. until the Administration of Estates Act 1869, 32 & 33 Vict., c.46, executors were bound to pay bonds before simple debts.

45 The result was that judgment could no longer be given for the penalty. The 1705 Act was belatedly repealed in 1948, and the 1696 Act in 1957.

bonds are now used only for building contracts, in certain cases where they are required by law, and in a few other cases where traditional practices have lingered.

Gaps in the Medieval Law

As we have seen, the medieval royal courts played only a limited part in the enforcement of contracts. Actions of debt, though numerous enough, were subject to wager of law; and, however well this may have worked in the country, it seemed an artificial obstacle at Westminster. Wager of law was restrictive not merely because of the obvious dangers of misuse once oath-helpers could be hired. One could not wage another's law, and so if a debtor died his simple debts died with him;[46] the debtor's executors could not wage his law, and jury trial apparently could not be forced on them. Debt had other limitations. It could only be brought for a sum of money fixed at the time of the contract. If a house were built, but no price fixed beforehand, nothing could be recovered for work and materials even if a sum were subsequently agreed. Neither could debt be brought on a sale of goods which had no existence at the time of the sale; for instance, the sale of a crop not yet grown, or of all the butter to be produced in a year from a herd of cows. The doctrine of *quid pro quo* may also have prevented a contract being formed by mutual promises; if *D* promised *P* £10 in return for *P* promising to do something, the contract was wholly executory and *P* had no action for the £10.

Some claims that we would today consider contractual could be framed by using actions other than debt and covenant: for instance, waste against a lessee for not repairing, or account against an agent.[47] Otherwise the plaintiff would only succeed if he could show a deed. The wise course was to use deeds, and the rise of the conditioned bond shows that the lesson was widely learned. But this was not a wholly adequate solution. Even if laymen were conscious of the magic of parchment and wax, they often trusted the words of others without further security. They saw no reason why a man's word should not be as good as his bond.

---

[46] This was the explanation in the 15th century: Milsom, 77 LQR at 264. It followed that executors could be sued in debt on an obligation, or on contracts where wager of law did not lie. Cf. the argument in *Anon.* (1330) 98 SS 743 at 744 (executors not privy to the *causa*).

[47] For the writ of account, see p. 410, post.

CONTRACT SUITS IN CHANCERY

The restrictive attitude of the early common law towards contract litigation was calculated to drive plaintiffs elsewhere, to the hundred courts and to the borough and city courts. We know that many also went to the Church courts.[48] Nevertheless, the royal courts soon discovered that they could not continue to wash their hands of informal contracts on the supposition that relief was available elsewhere. As many local courts decayed, and the ecclesiastical courts were effectively prohibited from meddling with contract, so practical justice in all but very minor matters became coterminous with the law of Westminster Hall. And, if the common law remained inflexible, the Chancery was an obvious forum for redress. It could give specific performance, when it ceased to be available in covenant, and could also give remedies where the common law gave none. The creditor who lost his deed might yet enforce his debt or covenant, while the debtor who had paid would be relieved from paying again. Sometimes petitioners sought relief simply on the ground that if they brought debt in the Common Pleas they would be barred by wager of law, contrary to good conscience. Claims were entertained in Chancery for just rewards for services, where no certain sum had been fixed, and for the enforcement of wholly executory contracts. By 1500 the chancellor had assumed a general jurisdiction in contract, and it was said that 'a man shall have remedy in the Chancery for covenants made without specialty if the party have sufficient witnesses to prove the covenants'.[49]

The intervention of the Chancery was no slight factor in influencing the common-law judges to recognise new or better remedies than those obtainable through the *praecipe* writs. Equity, in the widest sense of the word, was not the sole prerogative of chancellors. The Chancery, moreover, was not the ideal forum for commercial cases, since it had no juries and lacked the common-law writs of execution for recovering money. The pressure for admission to the two benches therefore continued. For the purpose of meeting the demand, the nearest common-law equivalent of the Chancery subpoena was the writ of trespass, complaining of a wrong done. Yet, whereas the chancellor could in each case act upon free-ranging principles of conscience and equity, the common lawyers in turning to a different form of action were compelled to dress up contractual causes of action as trespasses. The earliest cases involved no real distortion; but by 1602, as we shall see in

---

48   See p. 149, ante.
49   *Diversite de courtz et lour jurisdictions* ('1523'), sig. Avi. This was first printed in 1526, but may have been written before 1500.

the following chapter, the whole law of contract was to be subsumed under the law of tort.

Further reading

Pollock & Maitland, vol. II, pp. 184-227

Holdsworth HEL, vol. III, pp. 412-424

Fifoot HSCL, pp. 217-267, 289-329

Milsom HFCL, pp. 243-282

W. T. Barbour, *History of Contract in early English Equity* (1914)

W. M. McGovern, 'Contract in Medieval England' (1968) 54 *Iowa Law Rev.* 19-62; (1969) 13 AJLH 173 at 173-190; 'The Enforcement of Oral Contracts prior to Assumpsit' (1970) 65 *Northwestern Univ. Law Rev.* 576-614

A. W. B. Simpson, 'The Penal Bond with Conditional Defeasance' (1966) 82 LQR 392-422 (repr. in LTLH 111-141); *History of the Common Law of Contract: the Rise of Assumpsit* (1975), pp. 1-196

M. S. Arnold, 'Fourteenth Century Promises' [1976] CLJ 321-334

D. J. Ibbetson, 'Words and Deeds: the Action of Covenant in the Reign of Edward I' (1986) 4 LHR 71-94

R. C. Palmer, 'Covenant, *Justicies* Writs, and Reasonable Showings' (1987) 31 AJLH 97-117

19. Contract: Assumpsit and Deceit

In the writs of covenant and debt, the plaintiff demanded the performance of a contract as a right. It is true that a breach of covenant was a wrong;[1] but to turn from the *praecipe* writs to trespass a plaintiff had to present his case in a different light. Trespass writs were not designed to compel performance, and if a medieval plaintiff brought such a writ simply for failing to perform a covenant, he would be met by the argument 'this sounds in covenant' and the action would fail. The *ostensurus quare* formula of the trespass writ required the defendant to come and explain why he had done something wrong. That, to a medieval lawyer, seemed fundamentally different from a truly contractual action, the object of which was to give effect to what the parties themselves had agreed.[2] By 1600 this distinction would lose its meaning, but even in the year-book period there was no dramatic leap from contract to tort. The extension of trespass was slow, and was resisted at every step. Moreover, the first step was taken into territory where the boundary marks were indistinct.

Breach of Covenant as Trespass

MISFEASANCE

A breach of covenant which caused physical damage, as where a carrier damaged goods or a surgeon mishandled an operation, looked like a trespass. There was a wrongful act ('misfeasance') which needed explaining; and since the complaint was of an act rather than of a failure to keep one's word there was no need for a deed.[3] It was not, however, an act of force against the king's peace;[4] the surgeon could not therefore be sued for battery, nor the bailee for trespass to chattels. The possibility of using trespass in such cases was opened up by the decision in the middle of the fourteenth century to admit actions of

---

[1] See p. 454, post, note 1.

[2] See Vampage's remarks in *Somer v. Sapurton* (1428), p. 389, post.

[3] For the doubt whether a deed was needed in covenant in such cases, see p. 363, ante.

[4] *Anon.* (1390) B. & M. 305 (horse overworked by bailee). Cf. p. 73, ante.

trespass in the central courts where no force and arms were mentioned. There was then no difficulty in allowing actions in which the plaintiff's special case was that the defendant had caused damage while carrying out an undertaking. Such cases were already known in London and other local courts; the change was not in reality a change in substantive legal thought but simply an enlargement of royal jurisdiction. By the fifteenth century the key phrase used in writs on the case based on undertakings was that the defendant 'took upon himself' (*assumpsit super se*) to do something, and then did it badly to the damage of the plaintiff. The word *assumpsit*, which gave its name to the new action, was soon inseparably paired with *fideliter promisit* (faithfully promised);[5] but in origin it need not have had a promissory connotation. Like the English word 'undertaking', it also had the primary meaning of taking something on; and this purely factual assertion was necessary to show why the writ was brought on the case rather than for a forcible breach of the peace.

The first known case in the superior courts where liability was imposed on someone who had undertaken[6] to do something and done it badly is the *Humber Ferry Case* of 1348.[7] The plaintiff complained by bill of trespass in the King's Bench that the defendant, a ferryman, had received his mare to carry across the River Humber and had so overloaded his ferry that the mare perished. Counsel for the defendant argued that the action should have been covenant. His reasons are not reported, but it is obvious that if he had succeeded the plaintiff would have been without a remedy. Covenant did not then lie in the King's Bench, and in any case no one used deeds when taking ferries. But the argument failed. The court said that overloading the ferry, so that the mare perished, was a trespass. Again the report omits the reasoning, but the decision is comprehensible enough; unlike the Waltham carrier of 1321, who had done nothing, the ferryman was guilty of a wrongful act which would have been wrong even if there had been no agreement between the parties.

The second reported case was an action on the case against a veterinary surgeon who had killed a horse by his negligence. This time the word used for the undertaking was *manucepit* (he took in hand), a word familiar to pleaders in London. As in the previous case, it was

---

5   The words 'had faithfully promised' (*fideliter promisisset*) occur independently in the earliest known precedent (1364): 103 SS 422, 74 LQR 571. *Assumpsit* is found in the first Common Pleas case proceeding to issue: [1976] CLJ 330.

6   Here the wording of the record is 'received to carry safely' (*recepit ad salvo cariandum*); but the report says *emprist*, the French for *assumpsit*.

7   *Bukton v. Tounesende* (1348) B. & M. 358; record in 82 SS 66.

argued that the action should have been covenant. Serjeant Belknap
frankly submitted in reply that the plaintiff could not bring covenant
because he had no deed, and so it was reasonable to bring this action on
his case. The defendant then argued, somewhat desperately, that the writ
should have been for trespass *vi et armis*; but this was soon dealt with,
since in law negligent treatment was not 'force'. The writ was upheld.[8]
A few years later, in a similar action against a fashionable London
surgeon for negligently maiming the hand he had undertaken[9] to heal,
the writ was quashed because it omitted to name the place where the
undertaking was made. The undertaking was evidently seen as the basis
of the action. Cavendish CJ significantly called it an action of
'covenant', and said that it could be maintained without a deed, 'because
a man cannot always have a clerk to make a specialty in respect of such
a small matter'.[10] In 1388 the Common Pleas settled that the writ could
be brought either in the county where the undertaking was made or in
the county where the damage was done.[11]

Numerous cases of a similar nature followed. It was no distortion of
language to regard misfeasance in performing an undertaking as a
trespass; but everyone knew they were beginning to encroach on the
action of covenant. The cases of 1374 and 1388 show that, although
the action lay for the wrong, the undertaking was recognised both as a
covenant and as being part of the cause of action. Nevertheless, where
trespass was brought for an act of misfeasance, no one suggested there
should be a deed. The law that could not be undone for a cartload of
hay[12] could at least be circumvented.

TRESPASS ON THE CASE FOR DECEIT

The introduction of actions on the case in the later fourteenth century
also brought into the central courts an action for deceitful contract-
making, primarily for use against sellers who made a false warranty of
the goods sold.[13] The formula was: 'whereas *P* had bargained to buy

8 *Waldon v. Mareschal* (1369) B. & M. 359.
9 The record says *manucepit sanare*, but the year-book has *emprist*. A similar case,
   using *assumpsisset*, is *Birchester v. Leech* (1390) 88 SS 63 (£10 recovered).
10 *Stratton v. Swanlond* (1374) B. & M. 360 at 362. John Swanlond was one of the
   court surgeons. A similar case, alleging a promise, is *Bradmedewe v. Rushenden*
   (1364) 103 SS 422.
11 *Skyrne v. Butolf* (1388) B. & M. 362 at 364, per Thirning CJ.
12 See p. 363, ante.
13 The first known example is *Aylesbury v. Wattes* (1382) Y.B. 6 Ric. II (soon to be
   published by the Ames Foundation); record in 103 SS 447 (sale of blind horse
   warranted sound in eye and limb). The action was used by a *hirer* in 1396: 103 SS
   451.

from *D* a horse, *D*, knowing the horse to be lame, falsely and deceitfully sold it to *P* by warranting it sound'. The 'deceit' lay in persuading the buyer to buy something which he would not have bought had he known the truth. Despite the language of the writ, which usually alleged knowledge on the part of the seller that the warranty was false, it seems that the seller's state of mind was never much regarded and that by the sixteenth century (at the latest) it was irrelevant.[14] The essence of deceit for this purpose was not the defendant's deceitfulness, but the plaintiff's having been deceived.

In 1383, in the second earliest reported case of this kind, the defendant objected that the action was 'in the nature of an action of covenant' and that the plaintiff showed no proof of the covenant 'except bare word'. The objection failed.[15] In suing for breach of warranty, the buyer was not seen as enforcing the bargain or warranty as such, but as claiming damages for having been deceived into a bad bargain. The distinction may be illustrated by an example. If *D* promised to deliver to *P* ten yards of blue cloth, and sent ten yards of red cloth, *P*'s complaint was of failure to perform the promise;[16] but if *D* sold *P* a specific bale of cloth and asserted that it contained ten yards, whereas it only contained five, *P* had in law bought the cloth and his complaint was that he had been misled. The buyer's complaint in the latter case was not that the contract remained unperformed, but that he had suffered from its performance, being now stuck with good title to a defective or unwanted chattel.

A warranty was generally essential to an action for deceit, for without one the rule was *caveat emptor*; if a man sold wine or a horse without warranty, 'the other must buy it from him at his own risk, and his eyes and taste should be his judges in that case'.[17] Most of the pleadings in such actions therefore involved denials of warranty, or assertions that the defendant bought at his own risk or by using his own judgment.[18] In the fifteenth century it was agreed that the action would not lie even on

14 100 SS lxxxiv (issue always taken on warranty, not on knowledge); *Note (c.* 1505) B. & M. 516, per Frowyk CJ.
15 *Rempston v. Morley* (1383) Y.B. Trin. 7 Ric. II, p. 30, pl.11. The only reason given is 'because this is a writ of trespass'.
16 E.g. *Carowe v. Newman* (1527) CP 40/1056, m. 127 (*assumpsit* to deliver merchantable malt, but delivered unmerchantable malt unfit for brewing ale; issue on the quality).
17 A. Fitzherbert, *Natura Brevium* (1534), fo. 94C, translated in B. & M. 344. There was an exception in the case of food or wine which made the plaintiff ill: pp. 382-383, 402, post.
18 E.g. *Fitzwilliam's Case* (1406) B. & M. 508 (wine tasted before purchase). For 14th-century examples, see 100 SS lxxxiv.

a warranty if the untruth of the statement was evident to the senses. Thus, if *D* in the previous example warranted the cloth to be blue, when it was red, *P* could not complain of deceit unless he was blind or the cloth was stored in another place.[19] Nor would the action lie in respect of statements relating to the future; for instance a 'warranty' that seeds would grow, or that a horse could be ridden so many miles a day without collapsing. Such things were either outside human control, and therefore inherently unpredictable, or they were promises which sounded in covenant; but they were not statements about the present condition of the goods when sold, and so they could not deceive.[20]

The burden of this learning was that a warranty is not the same as a promise or covenant; it is a statement of present fact. But the main reason for drawing the distinction was to justify the use of an action on the case without a deed; in reality the distinction between promise and warranty may not have been as clear as some lawyers tried to make it. Certainly the word 'warranty' was not always used as precisely as 'misrepresentation'. A warranty that fungible goods would be equal to sample might be seen as a promise *de futuro* rather than a misrepresentation.[21] In the context of land law, a warranty was thought of in contractual terms; a deed was accordingly necessary to its enforcement.[22] And it was sometimes said in the fifteenth century that if a warranty were put into a deed an action of covenant would lie upon it.[23] This conceptual indistinctness may explain why, as we shall see presently, deceit became an important element in *assumpsit* cases as well.

ACTIONS ON THE ORDINANCE OF LABOURERS

Another way in which contractual actions reached the fourteenth-century royal courts in the guise of trespass was a result of the construction placed on the Ordinance of Labourers (1349). The ordinance, and the Statute of Labourers (1351), were passed to deal with fluctuating labour conditions after the Black Death, and made workmen compellable to remain with and serve their masters on pain of criminal punishment. It

---

[19] *Drew Barantine's Case* (1411) B. & M. 509; *Anon.* (1471) B. & M. 511 at 513; Hales' reading (1537) B. & M. 345 at 349.

[20] *Anon.* (1471) B. & M. 511 at 513; Hales' reading (1537) B. & M. 345 at 349. Cf. *King v. Braine* (1596) B. & M. 517.

[21] See, e.g., the two cases of 1317 from St Ives fair court in 23 SS 102, 105.

[22] See pp. 257-258, 363, ante.

[23] *Somerton v. Colles* (1433) B. & M. 385 at 388, per Cottesmore J; *Shipton v. Dogge* (1442) B. & M. 391 at 394, per Paston J; *Anon.* (1471) B. & M. 511 at 512, per Choke J.

was held during Edward III's reign that an action lay on the 'statute' against a servant who failed to serve; and such an action, though of the trespass type, was regarded as depending on the agreement to serve, so that issue could be joined on the covenant.[24] Yet, although the relationship of master and servant sounded in covenant, the statutory action did not require a deed, presumably because the duty to serve was a public duty imposed by law.[25] The action went further than *assumpsit* for misfeasance, because it lay for a mere failure to serve, and therefore represented a major departure from the older law; the covenant itself was enforceable without a deed. But it was confined to labourers and servants of the inferior sort, and did not extend to craftsmen retained to do piece-work[26] (independent contractors) or professional men, such as chaplains retained to sing mass,[27] because they were not compellable to serve. Against them a writ of covenant was still needed, unless they committed misfeasance. But the distinction gave rise to difficulties. A 'carpenter' might be a labourer who sawed and joined under orders, or he might be the builder who employed the labourers.[28] This is doubtless why actions against carpenters provided the next battleground for the action on the case.

Assumpsit for Nonfeasance

Actions of *assumpsit* against carpenters, for failing to build, are found from the 1390s; and the earliest cases raise some interesting points about the interdependence of craftsmen retained to work on different aspects of a building.[29] In 1400, and again in 1409, actions of this kind were challenged on the ground that the plaintiff had no deed; it was agreed in both cases that an action would lie on the Statute of Labourers

---

[24] B. & M. 379 n.3; *Thelnetham v. Penne* (1378) 88 SS 7 ('plea of trespass', but issue on 'covenant').

[25] *Mussenden v. Thomas* (1371) Y.B. Mich. 45 Edw. III, fo. 15, pl.15; CP 40/443, m.371; Putnam, *Statute of Labourers*, p. 448; B. & M. 379 n.3. Cf. *Berford v. Balard* (1389) 88 SS 60, where an unemployed defendant was compelled to serve without even a covenant.

[26] *Creting's Case* (1373) Y.B. Mich. 47 Edw. III, fo. 22, pl.53 (embroiderer).

[27] *Parson of Abbots Ripton v. Can* (1376) Y.B. Trin. 50 Edw. III, fo. 13, pl.3; CP 40/462, m.100d (decided on demurrer); Putnam, *Statute of Labourers*, p. 432.

[28] The distinction is recognised in Stat. 34 Edw. III, c.9 (1360). In *Pecche v. Otteford* (1364) Y.B. Pas. 38 Edw. III, BL MS. Add. 32087, fo. 59; CP 40/417, m. 142; Putnam, *Statute of Labourers*, pp. 184, 419, an action was allowed against a carpenter despite the argument that the statute extended only to labourers. See also B. & M. 380 n.7.

[29] *Nothonby v. Wryght* (1394) 103 SS 431; *Mundevyle v. Rouhevede* (1398) 103 SS 434.

without a deed, and that an action on the case would lie for misfeasance, but that the present action for nonfeasance would not lie.[30] In some of the year-books the actions are actually called 'covenant'; there was nothing to take them outside the scope of the older action or the rule of evidence associated with it.

In these first two cases the objection was put in terms of the lack of writing rather than in terms of the choice of writ; but in the course of the fifteenth century the objections shifted to the form of action. There is all the difference in legal theory between misfeasance and nonfeasance. Misfeasance is often legally wrong in the absence of contract, whereas nonfeasance is not. In the misfeasance cases, the 'undertaking' had not necessarily been promissory; it was the taking on of a task. But the notion of an undertaking to do something in the future reflected a subtle difference of meaning which alert lawyers had already foreseen in the fourteenth century. Undertaking in that sense was the same as promising or covenanting; and, since that was the only sense possible in the case of nonfeasance, an action for merely failing to perform an undertaking 'sounded in covenant' rather than trespass. Not doing could not naturally be called trespass.[31] A benevolent promise to build a house, followed by inaction, was not more obviously a legal wrong than a malevolent promise to knock a house down, followed by inaction; and the latter was no tort, because a man was not liable for his intentions without an act done.[32] Unreal though the distinction sometimes seemed, lawyers are retained to present arguments which have a chance of success; and so whenever in the fifteenth century an action on the case was brought for breaking a promise, it was a standard objection that it was nonfeasance and therefore did not sound in trespass. As late as 1493, when a barge owner was sued for the loss of a cargo of malt in the River Thames through negligent steering, the defendant's counsel thought it worth arguing that this was only nonfeasance; but the court, viewing the facts differently, held it to be 'a great misfeasance'.[33]

The year-book discussions, inconclusive as they are, suggest that the objections to bringing *assumpsit* for nonfeasance prevailed until the end of the fifteenth century. The plea rolls, on the other hand, contain many undetermined actions based on nonfeasance dating back to the fourteenth century. It is unlikely that many of these cases came before the court

---

30 *Watton v. Brinth* (1400); *Anon.* (1409) B. & M. 379.

31 For a modern instance, see *Fagan v. Metropolitan Police Commissioner* [1969] 1 Q.B. 439. See also p. 483, post.

32 *Haukyns v. Broune* (1477) B. & M. 629 at 630, per Wode.

33 *Johnson v. Baker* (1493) B. & M. 399, 400 n.2.

judicially, but obviously the clerks of the court were happy to issue mesne process upon writs alleging nonfeasance, and presumably most of the cases were settled without recourse to legal argument. That it was so often ignored in practice may have been one reason why the distinction between misfeasance and nonfeasance broke down. It was also rather a last-ditch measure to rely on a distinction which was so difficult to apply. If a doctor gave inert medicine, or treated the wrong part of the body, so that the patient's health declined, was that misfeasance or nonfeasance? Even if we regard it as nonfeasance, it had contributed to the physical deterioration because of the patient's reliance; and that may be why the nonfeasance point was not much pressed in medical cases.[34] Nonfeasance by a bailee could likewise cause physical damage, as where a bailee of sheep did nothing to stop them drowning, though here perhaps the taking control of the sheep could be regarded as an act.[35] Nonfeasance by a carpenter could equally cause physical damage, given that medieval carpenters usually worked on materials provided by the client. If a carpenter undertook to roof or repair a house, and did nothing at all, the contents might be spoiled or the timbers of the house rotted by rain; such nonfeasance could reasonably be called trespass.[36] Now, if such physical damage was actionable, might not the courts take the next step and recognise economic loss? For instance, if the carpenter failed to build or repair a mill, the miller's livelihood might be ruined. That very case was discussed in the Common Pleas in 1425, and the problem was treated not as a scholastic problem about misfeasance and nonfeasance but as a problem of causation: whether the defendant's failure had caused the plaintiff damage.[37] Martin J remarked ominously in the course of argument that, if this approach were adopted, 'then a man would have an action of trespass for every broken covenant in the world'. That is almost what happened.

However difficult or irrational the distinction between misfeasance and nonfeasance proved on further acquaintance, and however galling the courts may have found the competition from the Chancery, there was still the fundamental objection to be overcome. Inaction was not a

---

34 See *Anon.* (1435) B. & M. 383 at 384, per Newton sjt; *Anon.* (1441) B. & M. 367 at 369, per Newton CJ (applying cure to heel instead of hand); *Tailboys v. Sherman* (1443) B. & M. 395 at 397, per Ayscough J.

35 *Anon.* (1487) B. & M. 398.

36 *Watkins' Case* (1425) B. & M. 380 at 381, per Babington CJ. Just such a case was made in *Rokeby v. Huntyngton* (1387) 103 SS 428, though the undertaking to roof was apparently made by a lessor rather than a contractor.

37 *Watkins' Case* (1425) B. & M. 380.

trespass.[38] If only some other source of liability could be found besides the agreement, which (without more) sounded in covenant, the difficulty would vanish.

1. Status

We have already seen that servants could be sued in trespass on parol retainers; here the duty to serve, though partly founded on covenant, was also founded on status. Status may also have played a part at common law, in that certain occupations were regarded as carrying public duties as well as private.[39] Attorneys and legal officials were obliged to serve litigants, and were under the control of the courts; fraudulent action or inaction was punishable, or actionable by the writ of deceit. It would therefore have seemed straightforward that an attorney should be sued in trespass for failing to continue an action.[40] In 1455, when *assumpsit* was brought against the clerk of the juries for failing to make an entry in his roll as promised, it does not seem to have occurred to anyone to object that this was nonfeasance.[41] The same liability for nonfeasance was thought to attach to counsel, who were likewise compellable to act for all who retained them.[42] Medical men were perhaps regarded in a similar way; in London an action against a surgeon might result in professional discipline as well as damages.[43] That may be another reason why the nonfeasance disputes seem not to arise in medical cases.

2. Deceit

The second idea which may have facilitated the use of actions on the case for nonfeasance was that of deceit. We have seen that the action on the case for deceit arose in the context of warranties by sellers. Here, too, status could impose liability in the absence of contract; purveyors of victuals, who had long been subject to statutory regulation and communal control, were made liable to an action on the case for selling

---

38 Cf. *Anon.* (1487) B. & M. 398, per Rede sjt ('An action on the case does not lie for nonfeasance, because for that the party shall have a writ of covenant'); *Johnson v. Baker* (1493) B. & M. 399 at 400, per Rede sjt.

39 For the 'common callings' of innkeeper and carrier, see pp. 461, 462, post.

40 E.g. the case of 1387 noted in 100 SS lxvi n.584. For an earlier example in London, see *Gardiner v. Bury* (1345), p. 383, post, note 45. Both examples speak of deceit.

41 *Holt v. Chevercourt* (1455) Y.B. Mich. 34 Hen. VI, fo. 4, pl.12 (where the argument is chiefly about causation), CP 40/778, m. 432.

42 *Anon.* (1435) B. & M. 383 at 384, per Paston J; *Shipton v. Dogge* (1442) B. & M. 391 at 392, per Stokes.

43 Milsom HFCL, pp. 318-319.

unwholesome food even if they made no warranty.[44] The liability of lawyers began with the old writ of deceit, which lay for fraudulently acting in someone else's name. But lawyers were also amenable to trespass on the case for deceit, for instance if counsel dishonestly revealed information to the other side.[45] Such a broad notion could be put to wider use.

The sphere where deceit played a significant part was that of land purchasing. The first reported case, in 1401, concerned a manorial steward who 'covenanted' in return for 5s. to obtain a copyhold estate for the plaintiff, and then deceitfully procured the lord to admit a third party; the Common Pleas allowed an action on the case for deceit, without the nonfeasance point being taken.[46] Then came *Somerton's Case* in 1433,[47] where an adviser who had been retained to purchase the manor of North Aston for Somerton, 'scheming wickedly to defraud [Somerton], maliciously revealed all his counsel' to a third party, whom he then helped to buy the manor. There was discussion of nonfeasance, but in the end the court held that the action lay because of the deceit in disclosing secret information; if the defendant had simply done nothing, he would not have been liable without a deed, but the additional deceit entitled the plaintiff to bring an action on his case. Nine years later, in *Doige's Case*,[48] a 'plea of falsity and deceit' was brought by bill in the King's Bench against a vendor who had prevented herself from performing the contract of sale by conveying the land to a third party. The defendant felt sufficiently sure of her ground to demur specially to the bill, on the ground that the facts amounted to a covenant, and the point was debated by all the judges of England in the Exchequer Chamber. Much was made of the disablement, the common link with *Somerton's Case*; it ruled out specific performance, and (according to the new doctrine of covenant) an action of covenant could not be brought to

---

44 *Anon.* (1430) B. & M. 509 at 510, per Martin J and Babington CJ; *Anon.* (1471) B. & M. 511 at 513, per Bryan CJ and Neele J; *Anon.* (1491) B. & M. 515, per curiam; *Note* (c. 1506) B. & M. 516, per Frowyk CJ; Hales' reading (1537) B. & M. 345 at 350.

45 E.g. MS. register quoted in Kiralfy, *Action on the Case*, p. 219 (counsel in an assize who, after retainer by *P* and after seeing *P*'s deeds, advised *P*'s adversary). This was another remedy foreshadowed in the London courts: *Gardiner v. Bury* (1345) *CPMR 1323-64*, p. 218 (attorney failing to plead).

46 *Anon.* (1401) Y.B. Mich. 3 Hen. IV, fo. 3, pl.12.

47 *Somerton v. Colles* (1433) B. & M. 385. Although the writ speaks of 'counsel', there is no suggestion that Colles was acting as a lawyer; he was an inhabitant of North Aston.

48 *Shipton v. Dogge* (1442) B. & M. 391 (and cf. first action on p. 390), 51 SS 97. The defendant is traditionally known by the spelling 'Doige' found in the black-letter year-books.

compel someone to keep an agreement which could no longer be kept. The plaintiff eventually succeeded, and the decision stood as law thereafter.[49] *Assumpsit* could thus be brought for nonfeasance, at any rate if there was deceitful disablement from performance. By the sixteenth century it was usual to insert a 'craftily scheming to defraud the plaintiff' clause in every *assumpsit* action, even when there was nothing in the facts to justify it; the allegation itself helped to dispose of the technical objection about nonfeasance, and the substance ceased to matter.[50]

ASSUMPSIT AS A CONTRACTUAL REMEDY

Although *Doige's Case* was framed as a bill of deceit, and the plaintiff's recovery justified on the ground of the act of disablement, contemporaries did not deceive themselves about what was thereby achieved. The plaintiff had paid in advance, and it has sometimes been suggested that the deceit lay in tricking him out of his money; but he had himself reworded his deceit allegation so as to make it clear that he was complaining of the loss of bargain.[51] And the prevailing judicial opinions stressed the reciprocal nature of a bargain. If Mrs Doige had conveyed the land and had not been paid, clearly debt would have lain against the purchaser; and it would have been 'amazing law' if the bargain did not bind the other way as well.[52] This is contractual language, the language of *quid pro quo* turned around to avail the payer; and it applied regardless of disablement. It had been put very well in 1440 in a similar case, by Thomas Browne, one of the prothonotaries of the Common Pleas: 'If a man pays a sum of money to have a house made for him, and it is not done, he shall have an action of trespass on his case because the defendant has *quid pro quo* and the plaintiff is damaged.'[53] The reporter added that this was 'privately denied to him'.

Browne was indeed ahead of his time in recognising something very like the Tudor doctrine of consideration; but by the end of the century it was orthodox learning that a person could bring *assumpsit* for nonfeasance when he had paid for something and it had not been done. The last word on the subject in print was a dictum of Fyneux CJ in

---

[49] See the cases in B. & M. 395, endnote.

[50] See 94 SS 274-275.

[51] He had sued first in the Common Pleas, alleging deceit in general terms; but the King's Bench bill said 'craftily scheming to defraud the plaintiff *of the land*': B. & M. 390, 391.

[52] *Shipton v. Dogge* (1442) B. & M. 391 at 393, per Newton CJCP. The reasoning is accepted by Fortescue CJKB (on p. 394) and Paston JCP (on p. 395).

[53] *Anon.* (1440) B. & M. 389 at 390.

Gray's Inn in 1499. He said that a purchaser who had paid for land could bring *assumpsit* against the vendor for failing to convey, and likewise that a man could sue a carpenter for failing to build a house.[54] Fyneux was something of an innovator, and in his thirty years as chief justice prepared the way for the King's Bench to restore its fortunes by developing new remedies; that a jurisdictional policy may have underlain his remark is evident from the last line, that the plaintiff 'need not sue a subpoena'. But the use of *assumpsit* as a substitute for covenant and the subpoena was never challenged by the other courts in any subsequent case.

It did not follow that *assumpsit* would lie in every case where covenant lay.[55] All the early statements on the subject stressed the prepayment: according to Frowyk CJ in 1505, 'if I covenant with a carpenter to make me a house, and pay him £20 to make the house by a certain day, and he does not make the house by the day, I shall have an action on my case because of the payment of my money; and yet it sounds only in covenant, and without payment of the money in this case there is no remedy.'[56] Frowyk CJ did not spell out why the prepayment was vital. But the remark shows that the common law did not fully accept that failing to perform a promise was actionable in trespass on the case. There had to be something more than nonfeasance: it might be misfeasance, it might be deceit, or it might be injurious reliance, for instance by entrusting goods to someone or paying someone in advance. All these elements would turn a breach of covenant into a trespass. No single concept of contractual liability underlay *assumpsit*; just a miscellany of diverse formulae.

The insistence on prepayment, a requirement which was not new in 1505, or even in 1440,[57] is the closest we come to a glimpse of contractual theory in these cases. But the reason for the requirement is not spelt out, except in Browne's brief remark. As Browne hinted, it seems to reflect two different notions. One of them, encountered in *Doige's Case*, was that bargains ought to be reciprocal: *quid pro quo* was not simply a technical requirement in debt, but the substantive

---

54 B. & M. 401. Though interpolated in the year-books for 1505, the passage was taken out of Fitz. Abr., where it is dated 1499 and marked 'In greis Inne'. (Gray's Inn had nevertheless not fully digested the lesson in 1516: B. & M. 401-402.)

55 Except, perhaps, during the period of greatest uncertainty: e.g. *Gybbes v. Wolston* (1483) CP 40/883, m. 355 (*assumpsit* to hand plaintiff's money to a creditor, which he failed to do; no *quid pro quo* or deceit is alleged, but damages are recovered).

56 *Orwell v. Mortoft* (1505) B. & M. 407 at 410 n.12; Keil. 78.

57 See *Watkins' Case* (1425) B. & M. 380 at 381; *Somerton v. Colles* (1433) B. & M. 385.

principle behind bargains. The second was that if someone made a promise on which the promisee relied to his detriment, the promisor ought to make good the resulting loss. The notion here was not so much that the promise should be enforced, for the promise in itself was not actionable, but that the damage incurred in reliance on the word of another should be restored. This squared very comfortably with the reasoning which had for a time prevailed against actions for nonfeasance: *assumpsit* did not lie to enforce the covenant, which required a deed and perhaps a different writ, but redressed the injury suffered by acting or reposing in the belief that it would be kept. It was also a principle of moral philosophy, closely akin to the modern doctrine of promissory estoppel. It could be said that a broken promise to build a house was not a legal wrong, because the promisee was in no worse position than if the promise had never been made; he had no house yesterday, and he has no house today. If, however, the promisee was put in a worse position by relying on the promise – for instance, by loss of the advance payment, or because the failure to build left him without a home[58] or a business – then an action on the case was the only remedy.

THE DOCTRINE OF CONSIDERATION

The two notions may have become confused in lawyers' minds before any attempt was made to explain them in doctrinal terms. The first attempt to supply the missing doctrine was by an early Tudor lawyer who drew on his acquaintance with the Canon law notion of *causa*. Morally was one bound by all one's promises, but in law one was bound only by those made seriously and upon good cause.[59] A promise made without cause was a naked pact (*nudum pactum*), and *ex nudo pacto non oritur actio*.[60] Cause was not a concept familiar to English lawyers in any technical way. In 1565 Plowden explained that 'because words are often spoken or uttered by a man without great advisement or deliberation, the law has provided that a contract by words shall not bind without consideration.'[61] By that date, but not for very long before, 'consideration' had become the common-law equivalent of 'cause' and the key to liability in *assumpsit*.

---

58   See *Pykeryng v. Thurgoode* (1532) B. & M. 411, per Spelman J.

59   C. St German, *Doctor and Student* (1531) 91 SS 228-233; abstracted in B. & M. 483. Cf. Y.B. Mich. 16 Edw. IV, fo. 9, pl. 5, per Jenney sjt ('parols sans reason ne liera nulluy').

60   The maxim was known to 15th-century common lawyers: see Y.B. Mich. 9 Hen. V, fo. 14, pl.23, per Cokaine J; B. & M. 242 (1477), per Townshend. It remained in common use until the 17th century.

61   *Sharington v. Strotton* (1565) B. & M. 488 at 490.

The word 'consideration' began life as a word not merely ordinary but ambiguous. The consideration for a promise was that which was given in return for it, or (more largely) the reason why it was made. In the context of contract it was the element of exchange which effected the passing of property, and this sense is encountered in the fifteenth century: 'a consideration', said Gregory Adgore in about 1490, 'may change the use'.[62] But consideration could also mean cause of action, the reason why a promise was actionable: 'if I promise to make you a house by a certain day, and do not do so, this is only *nudum pactum* on which you shall not have an action on the case [for] you are not wronged as a result of this nonfeasance . . . [but] if I give certain money to someone to make me a house by a certain day, and he does not make it by the day, there this is a consideration why I shall have an action on my case for the nonfeasance.'[63]

In the sixteenth century both senses came together. The cause or consideration for the promise was the cause of action in *assumpsit*. It therefore had to be shown in pleading; the King's Bench held in 1539, and again in 1563, that *assumpsit* was not actionable without *causa* or consideration.[64] From about 1539 onwards pleaders accordingly began to insert in *assumpsit* declarations an *in consideratione* clause setting out the prepayment, or *quid pro quo*, or some act done in reliance on the undertaking. Thus the miscellaneous elements which had been recognised as making nonfeasance tortious all came to be associated with the word consideration as an indispensable requirement in *assumpsit*. Not only must a consideration be expressed in the declaration, it must be a 'good' consideration. Consideration had to be of some value, though the courts would not investigate its adequacy: 'a penny or a jug of beer is as much obliging in a promise as £100.'[65] So long as the parties made their agreement in binding form, they were treated as being the best judges of their own bargains. But it was necessary that the consideration be present or future; something already done could not 'move' the promise, and therefore a promise to pay for

---

62 Reading on uses (Inner Temple): CUL MS. Hh. 3. 10, fo. 22v. His analysis of bargains (B. & M. 482-483) shows some borrowing from *Bracton*; by consideration he apparently meant *quid pro quo*.

63 *Anon.* (c. 1530) B. & M. 402 at 403. Cf. *Lucy v. Walwyn* (1561) B. & M. 485 at 486, per Nicholls (who speaks even of consideration for an action in tort).

64 No *causa: Marler v. Wilmer* (1539) KB 27/1111, m. 64; *Laws and Customs*, p. 339 (= LPCL 372); Ibbetson, [1982] CLJ at 142. No consideration: *Isack v. Barbour* (1563), *Laws and Customs*, p. 353 n.61.

65 W. Sheppard, *Grand Abridgment* (1675), vol. I, p. 64. A penny was said to be valid consideration for a conveyance of land: J. Rastell, *Expositiones Terminorum* (c. 1525) B. & M. 483; Inner Temple moot (1562) B. & M. 487.

something past was gratuitous and unenforceable.[66] By 1598 a binding
contract could be defined, in terms still acceptable today, as 'a mutual
agreement between the parties for something to be performed by the
defendant in consideration of some benefit which must depart from the
plaintiff, or of some labour or prejudice which must be sustained by the
plaintiff.'[67]

If we ask whether the Tudor doctrine of consideration was based on
contractual rather than tortious theory, the principal test might well be
the case of executory mutual promises. If *D* promised to perform a
service for *P* in return for *P*'s promise to remunerate *D* if he performed
the service, the only consideration for *D*'s promise was *P*'s promise.
For this consideration to be of value, the law had to treat *P*'s promise as
binding; but *P*'s promise was supported only by *D*'s and was also
conditional on *D*'s performance. There was no logical way of breaking
the circle, unless it was accepted that mutual promises could make a
binding contract by supporting each other. If the problem was never
raised in the earlier cases, it may have been because the plaintiff's
promise would have been caught by the evidential rule requiring a deed.
But we know that the possibility of an action on mutual promises had
occurred early in the sixteenth century, because Fyneux CJ himself
brought an action on facts very like those of *Doige's Case* except that
he had made no prepayment.[68] The first reported discussion is not found
for another forty years; it happens to be the very first reported argument
about consideration by that name, *Lucy v. Walwyn*. Walwyn had
promised Lucy to do his best to obtain two manors for him, in
consideration that the plaintiff would pay his expenses and give him £5
on completion; in the event Walwyn bought the manors for himself.
Unlike the earlier precedents, there was here no prepayment. Yet,
despite the argument that there was no consideration, no *quid pro quo*,
the court gave judgment for the plaintiff.[69] A counter-promise was as
good a consideration as an executed act.[70] From this point the English
law of contract might truly be said to be consensual; despite its
trespassory guise, liability was based on reciprocal agreement.

66   St German, *Doctor and Student* (1531), B. & M. at 485; *Sharington v. Strotton*
(1565) B. & M. 488; *Hunt v. Bate* (1568) B. & M. 494. Cf. *Sidenham v.
Worlington* (1585) B. & M. 495.

67   *Slade v. Morley* (1598 hearing) B. & M. at 429, per Tanfield. Cf. Coke's
formulation in *Stone v. Withipole* (1589) B. & M. 499 at 500.

68   *Fyneux v. Clifford* (1517) 94 SS 268; *Laws and Customs*, p. 346 n.42 (= LPCL
379).

69   *Lucy v. Walwyn* (1561) B. & M. 485. The MS. is now in the Derbyshire Record
Office.

70   See *West v. Stowell* (1577) B. & M. 494 at 495, per Mounson and Manwood JJ.

Assumpsit in Lieu of Debt

Assumpsit for nonfeasance was not in practice very common, at least in medieval times. The principal importance of its establishment was that it prepared *assumpsit* to storm the great citadel of debt. The failure to pay money owed is a particular species of nonfeasance, sounding in debt. Perhaps it is not an abuse of language to speak of debt as a wrong. The thirteenth-century treatise *Fet Asaver* treated debt 'a tort detenue' as a species of trespass, and the variant English versions of the Lord's Prayer use the words 'debt' and 'trespass' interchangeably.[71] Yet the lawyer sees a difference between a wrong, which is a spent act requiring redress, and a continuing duty such as a debt, which requires enforcement. '[Debt] begins by contract and consent of the parties, and the basis of the action is an indebtedness (*dutie*); and [trespass] begins by a wrong (*tort*) and without the consent of the parties, and the demand is to have a wrong punished.'[72]

The reasons for wishing to extend *assumpsit* to money claims were not the same as those for extending it to breaches of covenant. There was already a remedy in the royal courts, and a deed was not required. Simple debts could be recovered at common law, and the action of debt had lived on while covenant faded into relative unimportance. But the disadvantages of debt on a contract were outlined in the preceding chapter: wager of law, the uncertain scope of *quid pro quo*, the need for a sum certain, and the lack of a remedy against executors. Thoughts began to turn to *assumpsit* as a means of avoiding these problems in the first decade of the sixteenth century. The first reported case was an action in the Common Pleas in 1505 for non-delivery of sixty quarters of barley bought by the plaintiff. Instead of bringing debt, which would clearly have lain on the facts, the plaintiff argued that 'scheming fraudulently and craftily to defraud' him the defendant had converted the barley to his own use and failed to deliver it. The propriety of using case was raised by a demurrer to the evidence; and most of the judges were hostile. The plaintiff had made the mistake of alleging conversion; doubtless he wished to show a disablement, but since no particular sixty quarters had been set aside there was nothing of the plaintiff's to convert. Frowyk CJ, however, saw that the gist of the action was the same as in the nonfeasance cases; there was no need for a change of property, because the prepayment and the deceit met the requirements for

---

[71] G. Woodbine (ed.), *Four 13th Century Law Tracts*, p. 112; Matthew, vi.12, 14.

[72] *Somer v. Sapurton* (1428) B. & M. 234 at 235, per Vampage.

an *assumpsit* action.[73] Though no judgment seems to have been given, later generations seem to have treated Frowyk's dissent, rather than the majority opinion, as settling the matter.

Most of the development from this point was the work of the King's Bench, eager to furnish litigants with an alternative to debt. From the 1510s there was a steady flow of actions of *assumpsit* for money or fungibles. Many of the earliest actions were to enforce payments which could not be recovered in debt: actions by or against sureties, actions against executors,[74] cases where the sum was not fixed in advance, and so on. But in many cases the declaration merely showed that the parties had entered into some specified transaction which resulted in a debt, that the defendant undertook to pay the debt, and that the defendant 'little regarding his promise but craftily scheming to defraud the plaintiff' had failed to pay; the plaintiff went on to allege consequential loss in being unable to pay his own debts, or in losing the profits of further bargains which he could have made with the money. These actions were resisted, from at least 1521, on the ground that the facts sounded in debt.[75] But in 1532 the King's Bench decided that the plaintiff could elect whether to bring debt on the contract or *assumpsit* on the breach of promise. According to Spelman J, 'the action of debt is founded on the *debet et detinet*, whereas this action is founded on another wrong, namely the breach of the promise.'[76] The plaintiff in the 1532 case alleged deceit, and consequential loss in his trade; but the court laid no stress on these trimmings. It now seemed that there was a general remedy in case for any breach of promise causing damage. The possibility of suing for debts without wager of law attracted creditors to the court in droves. By the middle of the sixteenth century *assumpsit* for money was becoming the principal action on the case; and the King's Bench, now able to entertain suits on charterparties, insurance contracts, partnerships, and bills of exchange, was rapidly becoming a commercial court for the city of London.

---

73 *Orwell v. Mortoft* (1505) B. & M. 406. Cf. *Tailboys v. Sherman* (1443) ibid. 395 (*assumpsit* for not delivering wine).

74 Upheld in *Cleymond v. Vincent* (1520) B. & M. 446, Port Nbk (102 SS) 10; followed in *Norwood v. Norwood and Rede* (1557) B. & M. 448.

75 Two demurrers appear in the plea rolls: *Cremour v. Sygeon* (1521-25) and *Haymond v. Lenthorp* (1528-31) 94 SS *283*. The long continuances suggest that the point was in debate throughout the 1520s.

76 *Pykeryng v. Thurgoode* (1532) B. & M. 411. A fortiori, the action lay against sureties: *Squyer v. Barkeley* (1533) Spelman Rep. (93 SS) 7; *Holygrave v. Knyghtysbrygge* (or *Jordan's Case*) (1535) B. & M. 413. The 1535 case was the only case in the series to reach the printed year-books.

As with the other forms of *assumpsit* for nonfeasance, it became necessary by the mid-sixteenth century to show some consideration for the promise to pay. Various usages developed by Elizabethan times, some of which obviously rested on fictions introduced for the sake of preserving a trespassory formula which did not quite fit the facts. If the jury found for the defendant, that was usually an end of the matter; while, if the jury found for the plaintiff on the general issue *Non assumpsit*, it was impossible to go behind the verdict into the details. The facts could not, of course, be disputed on a demurrer. Therefore the records tell us only the formulae which were acceptable, not the true facts of cases.

One way of framing the action, appropriate where tradesmen or merchants had entered into an account with each other or with customers, was to lay the *assumpsit* 'in consideration that the parties had accounted together' (*insimul computassent*) and that the sum was found owing.[77] Another formula was to allege a pre-existing debt and a subsequent promise to pay it (*indebitatus assumpsit*). Without more, both forms were open to the objection that the consideration was past, and that the promise was to do no more than the defendant could be compelled to do by writ of account or of debt. These objections could be met by stating that the account or the contract was entered into at the request of the defendant, and by alleging a consideration over and above the debt itself. For example, the plaintiff might allege a promise by the debtor in return for a forbearance to sue for a certain time. By Elizabeth I's time pleaders were alleging nominal forbearances of a day or so in order to put their cases into this form; the King's Bench accepted this minimal consideration, though the Common Pleas did not. Another device was to show that the plaintiff paid for the promise; and here again pleaders without blushing alleged as common form the payment of a few pence as consideration. Sometimes consequential loss was added in the declaration, such as a rise in the price of grain, or even starvation, as a result of the non-delivery of grain.[78] Deceit was also alleged routinely: every debtor was 'craftily scheming to defraud' his creditor.

From the end of Henry VIII's reign the King's Bench invention came under fire from the Common Pleas. As early as 1535, Fitzherbert J told counsel to take a King's Bench report out of their books, because it wrongly upheld *assumpsit* against executors for a simple debt;[79] and by 1542 the court seems to have been against *assumpsit* for money in other

[77] See p. 416, post.
[78] *Norman v. Some* (1594) and *Anon.* (1596) B. & M. 417.
[79] *Anon.* (1535) ibid. 447 at 448, referring to *Cleymond v. Vincent* (1520), p. 390, ante, note 74.

392 Assumpsit and Deceit

cases on the ground that it would deprive defendants of wager of law.[80]
The pleading devices were rejected if they smelt of fiction, albeit that the
court did not theoretically know the facts; it was not fraud, they said, to
fail to pay simply for want of money.[81] Forbearance for a few hours
was not consideration, because one could not recover a debt in a few
hours anyway. And was not the *assumpsit* itself often fictitious? There
was usually only one contract, not a debt-creating contract followed or
accompanied by a collateral promise with separate consideration. Then
again, quite apart from the fiction, there was an objection to the
'general' *indebitatus assumpsit* formula, which did not set out the reason
for the indebtedness; this put defendants at an unfair disadvantage, since
they did not know the nature of the alleged contract until the trial. And
finally, in strictness, even if a plaintiff overcame all these hurdles, he
ought not in *assumpsit* to recover the debt as part of his damages, but
only the additional loss which could not be recovered by writ of debt.

SLADE'S CASE

These differences between the two benches were intolerable for litigants.
The King's Bench welcomed *assumpsit* in lieu of debt, the Common
Pleas made its use almost impossible. The practical problem was that a
plaintiff could not tell what kind of judge would try his case at nisi
prius. A King's Bench judge would direct the jury simply to enquire
into the debt, a Common Pleas judge would require proof of a collateral
promise and consideration.[82] And since the direction was not of record,
there could be no subsequent redress in banc at this period. When the
statutory Exchequer Chamber[83] started to reverse King's Bench
judgments in *assumpsit* in the 1590s, the matter came to a head. The
Common Pleas judges sitting in the Exchequer Chamber treated their
King's Bench brethren with open contempt, refusing even to allow
argument in support of the King's Bench judgments.[84] Popham CJ, of
the King's Bench, reacted by convoking all the judges of England, to try
to end the dispute, in *Slade's Case*.[85]

Slade had bargained and sold a crop of wheat and rye to Morley, who
(according to the declaration) undertook and then and there promised to
pay £16 for it. Slade brought *assumpsit* for non-payment, Morley

80 *Anon.* (1542) B. & M. 415, per Shelley J.
81 See *Duppa v. Jones* (1602) B. & M. 419.
82 *Edwards v. Burre* (1573) B. & M. 416.
83 Introduced in 1585: p. 158, ante.
84 *Turgys v. Becher* (1596) B. & M. 418, per Anderson CJ.
85 *Slade v. Morley* (1597-1602) B. & M. 420. See also Ibbetson, 4 OJLS at 299-302.

9

denied the promise, and the jury found a special verdict that the sale had taken place as alleged but that there was 'no promise or undertaking besides the bargain aforesaid'. This special verdict was no doubt directed in order to compel the court in banc to face the controversial issue whether case would lie on the very contract which generated the debt, or whether (as the Common Pleas held) a separate express promise was needed. The King's Bench had no doubts about this, but if they gave judgment for Slade they would certainly be reversed and the battle would be lost. That is why Popham CJ decided to refer the question to all the judges – the procedure used in *Doige's Case* – so that the King's Bench judges would have a voice. The case was argued by the best lawyers of the day, including Coke and Bacon, on several occasions over a period of five years. No real agreement was reached, but in 1602 the King's Bench entered judgment for the plaintiff on the strength of a straw vote.[86] The Common Pleas judges were incensed that they were not allowed to deliver arguments, as was usual in such cases, especially since the majority was probably no better than six to five; but Popham CJ's tough policy ensured that the dispute remained settled for practical purposes. No detailed reasons were given, even in the King's Bench, but it was stated that two questions had been resolved. First, that actions on the case could sometimes be brought where older actions were available; the duplication of remedies was not in itself an objection to the newer action. Second, every executory contract 'imported' in itself an *assumpsit* to pay what was due under it; the man in the street could not be expected to use the precise words 'I assume' or 'I undertake' when making bargains, but the law would treat the bargain as including a promise. The combination of these two principles rendered a separate promise unnecessary, and so the special verdict entitled Slade to succeed.

Slade's Case thus established the right to recover debts by the action of *assumpsit*, and thereby practically put an end to wager of law. The argument that the damages in *assumpsit* should not include the debt seems to have been given up at the same time. A judgment in *assumpsit* would bar an action in debt on the same contract, and vice versa. Indeed, *indebitatus assumpsit* was treated as so like debt that upon a default by the defendant the court could award liquidated damages without the need for an inquest. One question which the judges expressly left open was whether *assumpsit* would lie against executors to recover their testator's debts. But in 1611, by another meeting of all the judges, it was resolved that it would. Although the general rule for

86 The nature of the vote is indicated by the recollections of Walmsley J in *Wright v. Swanton* (1604) B. & M. 441. The reason for his outburst was the recent publication of Coke's report of *Slade's Case*.

torts was that *actio personalis moritur cum persona*, the action of *assumpsit* was by 1611 sufficiently contractual in nature to constitute an exception to the rule.[87]

A Unified Law of Parol Contracts

Slade's Case marked the final stage in the unification of the law of parol contracts through the action of *assumpsit*. Deeds apart, the subject-matter of the old actions of debt and covenant had been fused. Of course, there were protests. Vaughan CJ objected to the confusion of debt and covenant, and ventured to deny the authority of *Slade's Case*.[88] Nevertheless, 1602 may be regarded as the date whence the modern law of contract traces its life as a single entity.

It must not be thought, however, that all actions of *assumpsit* were the same in form. The historical differences lingered in the pleadings until the procedural reforms of the last century. *Assumpsit* for misfeasance continued to be brought as an action in tort, without the need for consideration in the contractual sense;[89] and to this day a negligent private surgeon may be sued in tort or contract at the plaintiff's election. *Assumpsit* for breach of covenant, for not performing an act as promised, varied from case to case and was therefore labelled 'special *assumpsit*'. *Assumpsit* to recover money separated out into several forms; the principal type was *indebitatus assumpsit*, which itself divided into a number of standard forms known as the 'common counts'.[90]

THE COMMON *INDEBITATUS* COUNTS

The objections to the general form of declaration did not arise in *Slade's Case*, because the transaction of sale was there set out in detail and the undertaking was imported into that transaction by the court. It was decided soon afterwards, by the Exchequer Chamber, that a general statement of indebtedness coupled with a promise to pay was insufficient.[91] It was nevertheless so advantageous not to have to tie oneself, or give away too much in advance, that pleaders soon found a compromise. The *indebitatus* formula would be used, but with just

---

[87] *Pynchon v. Legat* (1611) B. & M. 455. The Common Pleas resisted this to the last: *Maine v. Peacher* (1610) B. & M. 454.

[88] *Edgcomb v. Dee* (1670) Vaugh. 89 at 101; *Anon.* (1673) 1 Mod. Rep. 163.

[89] See p. 447, post.

[90] For some others, see pp. 417, 418, post.

[91] *Woodford v. Deacon* (1608) B. & M. 464, and the cases in the note there.

enough of the nature of the contract indicated to avoid the objection to generality. Thus, the seller of goods counted that the purchaser was indebted to him in £*n* 'for goods sold and delivered at his request', and being so indebted he, in consideration thereof, promised to pay the £*n*. He did not say what the goods were, or when he bought them, but the formula was accepted as putting the defendant on notice as to the type of claim being made. By the mid-seventeenth century this version of the *indebitatus* formula had become standard. The seven main species, in use as common counts until 1852, were those for goods sold and delivered, or bargained and sold, for work done, for money lent, for money laid out to the plaintiff's use at his request, for money had and received to the plaintiff's use, and for money due upon an account stated.[92]

The subsequent promise on which these actions were founded was fictitious, in the sense that there was no need to prove it; and the consideration seems to have been almost equally fictitious, since it was an existing duty incurred in the past.[93] No one was in any doubt that the courts had allowed the forms of action to be beneficially twisted so that the transactions represented by the common counts, which matched the common counts in debt, could be enforced without fear of the defendant waging his law. That had been the object of the prevailing side in *Slade's Case*. But the means established were different from those considered in *Slade's Case*, and the effects of the fiction were to be more far-reaching, because they enabled the use of the action to enforce non-contractual obligations to pay, obligations sometimes which had never been actionable in debt or in any other form of action.[94]

PAROL CONTRACTS AND PERJURY

A direct consequence of *Slade's Case* was the complete replacement of wager of law by jury trial in disputed actions to recover debts. Soon practitioners could not remember how to wage law, and if occasion arose no one could be found in the streets to act as oath-helpers.[95] Coke had made this a positive argument in favour of Slade, 'for experience now proves that men's consciences grow so large that the respect of their private advantage rather induces men to perjury'.[96] Unfortunately, the

---

[92] They were sometimes used in the alternative. For illustrations, see B. & M. ch. 18.

[93] See *Lord Grey's Case* (1567) B. & M. 492 (consideration not traversable); *Hodge v. Vavisour* (1616) B. & M. 504 (consideration treated as continuing).

[94] See ch.20. Holt CJ tried unsuccessfully to restrain the fictions within the ratio decidendi of *Slade's Case*: p. 420, post.

[95] *Cristy v. Sparks* (1680) B. & M. 223; p. 88, ante.

[96] B. & M. at 441.

jury, given the limitations of the seventeenth-century law of evidence, was not wholly equal to the new task. Wager of law, for all its defects, had protected the innocent defendant from fraudulent claims by unscrupulous tradesmen in cases where there was no evidence of contract or payment to leave to a jury. After 1602 there was no protection against such claims but the instincts of the jurymen. The parties themselves were excluded from the witness box until 1851;[97] if, therefore, the professional perjurer changed his occupation from wagerman to hired witness, the jurors might have nothing to salve their own consciences but perjured evidence. However, the loss caused by perjury now fell on defendants rather than plaintiffs, and this bore harder on the consumer sued by the tradesman. The perjury problem may have been exacerbated by the abolition of the Star Chamber in 1641.[98] Certainly in the Restoration period the problem was keenly felt.[99] Hale CJ remarked in 1671 that two men could not safely talk together 'but one fellow or other who stands in a corner swears a promise'. The worst fears of the Common Pleas judges had been realised, and Coke had it all to answer for: 'the common law was a wise law, that men should wage their law in debt on a contract . . . that so things might be reduced to writing.' *Slade's Case* had 'done more hurt than ever it did or will do good'.[100]

It was too late to undo *Slade's Case*, except by legislation, and so it was to a legislative solution that Hale and his colleagues looked. Hale's original idea was to reintroduce wager of law, or to require some other ceremony to bind the parties in the absence of writing. The reintroduction of wager of law was not in the event pursued, but the requirement of writing for certain types of contract seemed to provide a convenient solution. It was almost as if the history of covenant were repeating itself, save that the revival of writing did not include the seal and that it did not extend to every class of contract. The first draft of the Statute of Frauds, believed to have been written by Sir Heneage Finch (later Lord Nottingham) in 1674, adopted a simple solution. Its main object was to provide that transactions concerning land should be in writing, but it also provided that in actions upon parol contracts whereof there was no written memorandum no damages were to be recovered

97 See p. 108, ante.
98 Dr Ibbetson's suggestion, 4 OJLS at 313.
99 The taking away of wager of law on contracts is listed as one of the 'Abusions del Ley' ripe for reform, in D. Jenkins, *Rerum Judicatarum Centuriae Octo* (1661), sig. A2.
100 *Buckeridge v. Sherly* (1671) and *Anon.* (1672) B. & M. 444.

beyond a stated amount.[101]   This policy of restricting the damages recoverable for breach of oral contracts was copied from earlier Continental legislation, which had been re-enacted in 1667 by Louis XIV of France.[102]   Finch's preliminary draft was not concerned with debts and the problem left by *Slade's Case*, but with the wider problem of perjury in the proof of oral contracts.   The bill was drastically altered, by Sir Francis North, Sir Matthew Hale, and others, before it became law.   In place of the limited damages principle, the new plan was to make certain classes of oral contract completely unenforceable without evidence in writing.   These were: a promise by an executor to answer for damages out of his own estate, a promise to answer for the debt, default or miscarriage of another (a guarantee), an agreement in consideration of marriage, a contract for the sale of land or any interest therein, and any agreement which was not to be performed within one year.   No action was to be brought upon such contracts unless there was a memorandum in writing signed by the party to be charged.   It was also provided that no contract for the sale of goods for more than £10 should be good unless the buyer accepted part of the goods and actually received them, or gave something in earnest to bind the payment or in part payment, or there was writing.   All this was enacted in the Statute of Frauds 1677.[103]

The subsequent history of the statute was not entirely happy.   Strict enforcement of its terms could easily have protected more frauds than it was designed to prevent.   Courts of law and equity therefore took every opportunity of construing it in such a way as to promote the policy of inhibiting frauds;[104] but this policy only deepened the obscurity of some of the provisions.   The complex section dealing with sale of goods was an attempt to change the trading habits of the nation; yet, two hundred years after its enactment, it had made little difference to the habits of buyers and sellers and had become a dead letter, repudiated in practice by mercantile men.[105]   It was, nevertheless, incorporated in the Sale of Goods Act 1893 and survived until 1954.[106]   The requirement as to contracts for the sale of land proved generally desirable, and was incorporated into the property legislation of 1925;[107] but it remained the subject of an important equitable gloss which permitted an action to be

---

101   Holdsworth HEL, vol. VI, Appendix I.

102   See E. Rabel, 63 LQR 174; and [1984] CLJ 307 n.7.

103   Stat. 29 Car. II, c.3, ss.4, 17; B. & M. 445.

104   See *Simon v. Metivier* (1766) 1 Wm Bla. 599.

105   See J. F. Stephen, 1 LQR at 24 (1884).

106   Sale of Goods Act 1893, 56 & 57 Vict., c.71, s.4; Law Reform (Enforcement of Contracts) Act 1954, 2 & 3 Eliz. II, c.34.

107   Law of Property Act 1925, 15 Geo. V, c.20, s.40.

brought – not on the contract, but on something like an equitable estoppel – where an oral contract had been partly performed. In 1989 parliament introduced a far more drastic reform: 'A contract for the sale or other disposition of an interest in land can only be made in writing'.[108] Form is no longer a matter of evidence, but is of the essence.

ELABORATION OF CONTRACT LAW

Even as late as 1800, the content of the law of contracts was slight by comparison with the position in 1900. There were a good many old cases on consideration, and a great deal on pleading: material enough for handbooks on nisi prius practice, but not for scientific analysis. Nothing was yet heard in the common-law courts of offer and acceptance, mistake, or principles of remoteness of damage, though there had been murmurs in Chancery.[109] The reason for the absence of detailed rules was that in most *assumpsit* cases the defendant pleaded *Non assumpsit* and the merits were left to the jury as questions of fact. The change from this age-old system seems to have begun fairly suddenly, and was probably a result of Lord Mansfield CJ's response to pressure from the City for the formulation of clear rules of commercial law. Much new law was formulated by Lord Mansfield in the third quarter of the eighteenth century, by presiding at trials in the London Guildhall and developing techniques for referring detailed questions to the court in banc.[110] In 1787 a judicial colleague recalled that, 'Within these thirty years ... the commercial law of this country has taken a very different turn ... Before that period we find that in courts of law all the evidence in mercantile cases was thrown together; they were left generally to a jury, and they produced no established principle. From that time we all know the great study has been to find some certain general principles, which shall be known to all mankind ... Most of us have heard these principles stated, reasoned upon, enlarged, and explained, till we have been lost in admiration at the strength and stretch of the human understanding.'[111] Lord Mansfield consulted with the city merchants before reaching decisions; but he was also anxious to secure a uniform commercial law throughout Europe. He encouraged the citation

---

108 Law of Property (Miscellaneous Provisions) Act 1989 (c.34), s.2.

109 Lord Nottingham in 1675 said that offer and acceptance were requisite to an agreement: 73 SS 241. And mistake had long been a ground for rescission of contracts. The first coherent English treatise on contract was in vol. I of Henry Ballow's treatise on equity (1737).

110 See pp. 59-60, 101, ante.

111 *Lickbarrow v. Mason* (1787) 2 Term Rep. 63 at 73, per Buller J.

of writings current on the Continent, the works of natural lawyers such as Grotius, Pufendorf, Heineccius and Vattel, and the standard international textbooks on commercial law. Bench and bar became imbued with a new European spirit.

ATTEMPTS TO RATIONALISE CONSIDERATION

The notion of consideration had grown into a legal doctrine in a haphazard way in the Tudor period, but it could be seen as performing a single function: it was the vital element which caused parol promises to be legally binding. Little effort was made to identify or express the underlying principle until the eighteenth century, and lawyers managed with the lists of cases gathered on one side or the other in the abridgments. In an early treatise on the law of contracts, Sir Jeffrey Gilbert (1674-1726) explained that English law had adopted the middle course between holding men to a rigid fidelity in all their promises, and only enforcing pacts supported by *quid pro quo* or recompense. If a party used the formality of a writing under seal, then his contract was taken to be binding without more ado, for it would be 'downright madness to trifle with the solemnity of law and pretend after the sealing that there was nothing seriously designed'. Where, however, the contract was merely by parol it needed consideration to clothe it with binding force; 'otherwise a man might be drawn into an obligation without any real intention by random words and ludicrous expressions, and from thence there would be a manifest inlet to perjury, because nothing were more easy than to turn the kindness of expressions into the obligation of a real promise.'[112]

Lord Mansfield sought to carry this approach further in the case of *Pillans v. Van Mierop*,[113] where he refused to accept the proposition that a parol written contract without consideration was *nudum pactum*, at any rate in a commercial case. Mercantile men expected written contracts to bind. 'I take it,' he said, 'that the ancient notion about the want of consideration was for the sake of evidence only; for when it is reduced into writing, as in covenants, specialties, bonds, and so on, there was no objection to the want of consideration.' This was not a sound historical argument, but a deliberate attempt to reject the magic of the seal. Wilmot J, concurring, said that the theory of consideration had been 'melting down into common sense of late times'. He thought that the purpose of consideration, in both the common law and the Civil law, was to guard against rash undertakings made without due reflection.

---

[112] *Of Contracts* (c. 1720) BL MS. Hargrave 265, ff. 75-77.
[113] *Pillans and Rose v. Van Mierop and Hopkins* (1765) 3 Burr. 1664.

Writing supplied that purpose as well as parchment and wax. However, when Lord Mansfield reiterated his point of view in 1778, it was reversed on error. Counsel argued in the House of Lords that sealing was no more than a ceremony, and that a parol writing should displace the need for consideration in the way that a deed had always done. But Skynner CB delivered the unanimous opinion of the judges to the effect that, whatever the Civil law meant by the maxim *ex nudo pacto non oritur actio*, the common law clearly meant that an action could only be founded on a parol promise if it was supported by consideration. There was no difference in English law between written and oral contracts, only between deeds and parol contracts. The House of Lords gave judgment accordingly,[114] and the decision has been treated as law ever since. As most contracts which give rise to litigation are in writing, the decision practically ensured the survival into modern times of the Tudor doctrine of consideration.

THE NINETEENTH CENTURY

In the first half of the nineteenth century the courts were given the opportunity to formulate the classical law of contract, as counsel increasingly took advantage of the procedures for raising detailed questions of law in banc. The courts took the opportunity and, following Lord Mansfield's example, sought guidance outside the black-letter texts of the common law. The most influential sources of ideas, though not always followed slavishly, were the *Traité d'Obligations* (1761) by the French jurist Robert Joseph Pothier (1699-1772), published in English in 1806, and the university textbook *Principles of Moral and Political Philosophy* (1785) by William Paley (1743-1805), archdeacon of Carlisle. Both works included discussions of elementary contractual ideas so long absent from the common law. In them we find the seeds of the English law of offer and acceptance, mistake, frustration, and damages.[115] Ironically, it was only after Britain's admission to the European Economic Community that Pothier's authority was emphatically rejected.[116]

---

114 *Rann v. Hughes* (1778) 4 Bro. P.C. 27; 7 Term Rep. 350n.

115 See *Hadley v. Baxendale* (1854) 8 Exch. 341 (damages); *Offord v. Davies* (1862) 12 C.B.N.S. 748 (formation of contract); *Taylor v. Caldwell* (1863) 3 B. & S. 826 (frustration); *Smith v. Hughes* (1871) L.R. 6 Q.B. 597 (cross purposes); *Phillips v. Brooks* [1919] 2 K.B. 243 (unilateral mistake).

116 *Lewis v. Averay* [1972] 1 Q.B. 198 at 206, per Lord Denning MR.

Contractual Terms

We have seen, earlier in this chapter, how the common law began in the late fourteenth century to remedy false warranties made by suppliers of animals or goods. The disgruntled buyer did not bring an action on the contract, which was valid and served to pass the property, but an action on the case for deceit. Thus the warranty, though an integral part of the bargaining process,[117] was not thought to be a 'term of the contract' but something outside it, a collateral guarantee. The original reason for this, as we have seen, related to the distinction between present fact and future promise. It was not within any seller's competence to promise that goods would last or that seeds would grow; if they were defective, no effort spent on his part would enable him to keep his word. It was therefore necessary to treat such an assertion as a factual statement as to the present quality of the goods.

In the eighteenth century, pleaders nevertheless began to treat warranties on a sale as promises or contracts that the facts stated were true. The objection that such a contract was impossible ab initio was somehow laid aside,[118] in order to achieve a practical end. The motive was to enable the joinder of actions on warranties with common money counts. If an action on a warranty could be framed in *assumpsit*, it could be joined with an alternative count to recover the price for a total failure of consideration. The change occurred largely without challenge in the courts. When, in 1778, it was argued that a promise could only relate to future performance, and not to past or present facts, the practice of using *assumpsit* for breach of warranty was too well established to change. As Grose J remarked eleven years later, 'All the cases of deceit for misinformation may be turned into actions of *assumpsit*.'[119]

One consequence of the change of practice was that the tort of deceit grew more distinct from contract, and was held to rest on fraudulent misrepresentation.[120] The word 'warranty' lost its strict meaning, and was applied both to representations of fact (affirmative warranties) and to promises (promissory warranties). The bifurcation of the action for deceit left an unfortunate gap once the forms of action were abolished, in

---

117 The writ said *warrantizando vendidit*; the warranty therefore had to be contemporaneous with the contract, so as to induce reliance. Deceit would not lie on a later warranty (*Andrew v. Boughey* (1552) Dyer 76) or on pre-contractual discussions (*Lopus v. Chandler* (1606) B. & M. at 521, per Tanfield J).

118 It had been rejected by two judges in *Kinge v. Braine* (1596) B. & M. 517.

119 *Stuart v. Wilkins* (1778) 1 Doug. 18 at 20; *Pasley v. Freeman* (1789) 3 Term Rep. 51 at 54.

120 *Pasley v. Freeman* (1789) 3 Term Rep. 51; *Derry v. Peek* (1889) 14 App. Cas. 337.

that it was interpreted to mean that no action for damages would lie on a misrepresentation unless it was made fraudulently or became a term of the contract.[121]   Another consequence was that contracts ceased to be regarded as single and indivisible, and came to be seen as bundles of stipulations on both sides, of varying degrees of importance: the terms of the contract. Some terms were so fundamental to the contract that if they were broken the other party could repudiate his own obligations; these were conditional promises, or conditions, because their fulfilment was a condition of the other party's liability. For breach of a warranty which did not amount to a condition, the other party was entitled to sue for damages, but not to escape from his own obligations.

IMPLIED TERMS

Generally speaking, the common law did not impose liability on a seller, in the absence of a warranty, if his wares turned out to be of poor quality. Since in such a case there was no deceit, the rule was *caveat emptor*. From the early fifteenth century, the law admitted an exception in the case of a seller of food and drink, since he was bound by law to provide wholesome victuals.[122] Some casual dicta in the year-books were turned by Frowyk CJ into a more extensive but mischievous new theory that a seller was liable, even in the absence of a warranty, if he knew that what he was selling was not what it seemed; the deceitful concealment was thought to override the usual requirement that the buyer should have relied on a warranty.[123] The remark remained in manuscript until it was printed (in 'Keilwey') in 1602; and this bibliographical accident seems to account for a leading case a few years later. Jerome Lopus, a foreign merchant, had given a diamond ring worth £100 to a London goldsmith in exchange for a stone falsely asserted (but not warranted) to be a 'bezoar stone', an oriental rarity believed to have special medical properties. Lopus obtained judgment in the King's Bench, but it was reversed in the Exchequer Chamber on the ground that a mere assertion (or 'affirmation') was not actionable without a warranty. Lopus then brought a second action in the King's Bench, alleging that the goldsmith *knew* the stone was not a real bezoar

121 *Heilbut, Symons & Co. v. Buckleton* [1913] A.C. 30. The gap was filled by the Misrepresenation Act 1967 (c.7), s.2(1). Until the pleading reforms, however, an action on a warranty of goods could still be framed in deceit without proof of fraud: e.g. *Jones v. Bright* (1829) 5 Bing. 533.

122 See pp. 382-383, ante.

123 *Note* (c. 1505) B. & M. 516, per Frowyk CJ. Cf. *Anon.* (1430) B. & M. 509 at 510, per Godered sjt; *Shipton v. Dogge* (1442) B. & M. 391 at 394, per Paston J.

stone, and relying on Frowyk's newly printed remark; the defendant demurred. Popham CJ 'thought it good that it should be considered by all the justices of England; for if it were found in favour of the plaintiff it would affect all the contracts in England, which would be dangerous.' No trace of a final decision has been found, and only the first decision was transmitted to posterity in print.[124] It was agreed that no warranty was necessary on a sale of victuals, and also that there was an implied warranty of title on a sale of goods; but in those cases an intention to deceive was probably not necessary either.[125] No general doctrine of implied warranties emerged from Lopus's case.

The reason why the history of the implied warranty is difficult to pursue from this point is not that there was any legal doubt whether implications could be made, but that a plaintiff was required to plead an implied warranty as if it were express. This had always been so; even in actions against victuallers, an express warranty was alleged.[126] If the jury found for the plaintiff, questions about the implication of warranties by law could not come before the court in banc until the development of the special case and new trial procedures. The same is true of implied undertakings.[127] The working of implied terms was therefore chiefly a matter of nisi prius practice, and comes to light for us only when reports of circuit cases begin to appear at the turn of the nineteenth century. We then learn explicitly what we had guessed with respect to the previous four centuries, that the knowledge laid in the deceit declaration was fictitious.[128] And we learn that certain formulations by pleaders of what appear to be express undertakings were in truth intended to support implied terms. The practice was inconvenient and risky, for it cast upon the pleader the necessity of framing in alternative counts all the possible forms which an implication might take, in the hope that one of them would be upheld on the evidence; if there was no suitable formulation on the record, there was no way a term could be implied.[129] These reports also reveal the situations in which terms were implied by law. Although *caveat*

---

[124] *Chandelor v. Lopus (No. 1)* (1604) and *Lopus v. Chandler (No. 2)* (1606) B. & M. 518.

[125] The implied warranty of title was controversial: *Dale's Case* (1585) Cro. Eliz. 44 (court divided as to need for knowledge); *Sprigwell v. Allen* (1648) Aleyn 91 (knowledge needed); *Cross v. Gardner* (1689) Comb. 142, 3 Mod. Rep. 261, 1 Show. K.B. 68, Carth. 90 (knowledge not needed).

[126] For the 15th century, see Milsom, 77 LQR at 279.

[127] For the implied undertaking in the *quantum meruit* count, see p. 415, post.

[128] *Williamson v. Allison* (1802) 2 East 446 (motion for new trial).

[129] See *Gray v. Cox* (1825) 4 B. & C. 108.

emptor remained the general rule,[130] it was not applied where the buyer had no opportunity to inspect the goods. In such cases the seller was deemed to undertake, at the least, that the goods were of merchantable quality.[131] And if goods were sold by description, there was an implied warranty that the goods answered that description.[132] Best CJ explained in 1829 that the doctrine *caveat emptor* had been convenient in relation to horses; 'no prudence can guard against latent defects in a horse', and so in the absence of fraudulent concealment no more is implied on the sale of a horse than that the creature sold is a horse. A manufacturer of goods, however, bore more responsibility for the condition of articles which he had brought into being; and so he was taken to contract not only that his goods were merchantable but also, if he knew the purpose for which they were intended, that they were fit for that purpose. The general principle was, 'If a man sells generally, he undertakes that the article sold is fit for some purpose; if he sells it for a particular purpose, he undertakes that it shall be fit for that particular purpose.'[133] The same implication was later extended to vendors other than manufacturers, the deciding factor being the vendor's knowledge of the buyer's purpose.[134]

These implied terms were not merely warranties, but 'conditions precedent' to the buyer's obligation to accept and pay for the goods. The buyer was therefore usually able to reject the goods if they were not of the quality impliedly contracted for. When the law relating to the sale of goods was codified in 1893, the draftsman, Judge Chalmers, classified terms in a contract of sale as being either conditions, breach of which entitled the buyer to reject, or warranties, which did not; and he framed the implied terms as to merchantability and fitness for purpose as conditions.[135] Under the 1893 Act, as at common law, the implication of terms could always be excluded by explicit language. In the twentieth century, however, parliament has increasingly taken to imposing unexcludable 'implied terms' in order to ensure minimum standards in certain kinds of contract. Of course, such terms are fictitious. The object of implying them is to protect classes of persons

---

130 *Parkinson v. Lee* (1802) 2 East 314 (no implied warranty where goods equal to sample); *La Neuville v. Nourse* (1813) 3 Camp. 351.

131 *Gardiner v. Gray* (1815) 4 Camp. 144; *Laing v. Fidgeon* (1815) 4 Camp. 169 (at nisi prius), 6 Taunt. 108 (in banc).

132 *Bridge v. Wain* (1816) 1 Stark. 504.

133 *Gray v. Cox* (1824-25) 1 C. & P. 184 (at nisi prius), 4 B. & C. 108 (in banc); *Jones v. Bright* (1829) 5 Bing. 533.

134 *Brown v. Edgington* (1841) 2 M. & G. 279.

135 Sale of Goods Act 1893, 56 & 57 Vict., c.71, ss.11-14.

deemed incapable for economic reasons of protecting themselves through the bargaining process. Such protection was extended first to leasehold tenants, then to employees, and then to 'consumers' of goods and services. The result is that many important transactions entered into by non-commercial men are governed not by the individual bargain but by the statutory law of landlord and tenant, labour law, or consumer law. There has in that respect been a partial movement from contract to status.

STANDARD-FORM CONTRACTS AND EXCLUSION CLAUSES

The growth of large-scale manufacturing, trading and public utility companies after the Industrial Revolution inevitably brought changes in contract-making practices. It is convenient and time-saving for a business which deals with the public to make the same form of contract with all its customers. The terms are contained in a standard-form notice or printed document, on which the business has had the benefit of legal and business advice; there is no room for negotiation. As more and more everyday commodities came to be available only from large organisations, the consumer was in practice under considerable economic pressure to submit to such standard-form contracts, however one-sided they might be. It is true that the man who submits to a standard form is not under legal duress, and must be taken to have assented to the terms as a free bargain. Everyone is equal before the law, and equally free to reject proffered contracts, be he a pauper or an international organisation. Could the common law nevertheless take notice of economic pressures, or should the matter be left to the discretion of parliament?

The aspect of standard-form contracts which gave the most difficulty was the use of clauses excluding or limiting liability. General attempts to cut down or negative liability seem to have been introduced in the first place by carriers; since the law imposed on them a strict liability for the goods in their keeping, they took to giving notice that they did not accept liability for specified kinds of valuables, or goods over £5 in value, unless the consignor paid an additional sum to cover insurance. The courts regarded such notices as reasonable, although there was some doubt in the early nineteenth century whether they covered negligence;[136] at any rate they did not protect a carrier who was grossly negligent or who went outside the terms of the bailment.[137] Under the Carriers Act

---

[136] The first reported case is *Gibbon v. Paynton* (1769) 4 Burr. 2298. For the 19th century cases, see J. N. Adams, 7 *Anglo-American Law Rev.* at 140-143.

[137] *Lyon v. Mells* (1804) 5 East 428.

1830, carriers were generally exempted from liability for certain kinds of valuables worth more than £10 unless the consignor paid at a higher rate; and this statutory exception was held to cover negligence.[138] Exclusion and limitation clauses came further into prominence with the expansion of the railways in the 1840s. By 1850 the railway companies were using a clause which exempted them from 'responsibility for any damage, however caused' in respect of goods; this was intended to exclude liability for negligence in tort as well as for breach of contract. The Victorian courts were sympathetic to these clauses, because the invention of the railway had conferred new benefits on the public, and so the proprietors who exploited the invention were entitled to protect themselves against the unprecedented risks inherent in rail transport.[139] The clauses were not so welcome to the travelling public, who were rapidly coming to regard rail transport as a natural right. When the Railway and Canal Traffic Bill was passing through parliament in 1854, the subject of exclusion clauses was fully debated in the House of Lords, and strong criticisms of the law were advanced from opposite political sides by Lords Lyndhurst and Brougham. The latter, in characteristically forthright language, said that the railway exemption clauses ought in justice to be void for duress, since the public had no freedom of choice; either they agreed to the terms or they could not use the railways. A clause was therefore added to the bill to impose liability for negligence in respect of goods consigned by rail, notwithstanding any condition limiting or excluding their common-law liability, unless the condition was held by the trial judge to be 'just and reasonable'.[140] This reform attempted to strike a convenient balance between the functions of the legislature and those of the judiciary. The courts were to enforce reasonable contracts to the letter, but had a power to review exclusion and limitation clauses in railway cases if freedom of contract was missing in reality. But the principle of reasonableness proved difficult to apply in practice, and was not adopted in subsequent legislation. As exclusion clauses spread to other kinds of contract, the courts themselves endeavoured to reduce their effects. They were construed *contra proferentem* and given the narrowest effect consistent with the words used. In the absence of clear language, a clause would not protect a party who acted outside the terms of the contract, and if the contract as

---

138 Stat. 11 Geo. IV & 1 Will. IV, c.68; *Hinton v. Dibbin* (1842) 2 Q.B. 646.

139 See *Carr v. Lancashire and Yorkshire Rly Co.* (1852) 7 Ex. 707; *Peek v. North Staffordshire Rly Co.* (1863) 10 H.L.C. 473 at 556, per Cockburn CJ.

140 *Parliamentary Debates* (H.C.), Vol. 133 (3rd ser.); Railway and Canal Traffic Act 1854, 17 & 18 Vict., c.31, s.7. There were, however, statutory upper limits on compulsory liability.

a whole manifested an intention that a party be legally bound a clause purporting to exclude his liability might be rejected as repugnant. From these general principles of construction, some of the common-law judges of the 1950s, notably Lords Devlin and Denning, attempted to extract a rule of law that a party who committed a 'fundamental breach' of contract could in no circumstances retreat behind the shelter of an exclusion clause. In 1966, however, the House of Lords decided that there was no such rule of law; and a confusing rearguard action by the Court of Appeal was defeated by a further decision of the Lords in 1980. The courts would lean against construing a clause to cover a serious breach if at all possible, but there was no principle of construction which could prevent parties from making a contract in whatever terms they chose if they did so in clear terms.[141] The remedy in the end came from parliament, and was achieved by breaking with traditional principles of contract. Some liabilities cannot be limited or excluded; some limitation or exclusion clauses are subjected to judicial review to establish their 'reasonableness'; and it is even possible to enforce a 'reasonable expectation' contrary to the express terms of a contract.[142]

Further reading

Holdsworth HEL, vol. III, pp. 428-454

Fifoot HSCL, pp. 330-360, 368-371, 393-443

Milsom HFCL, pp. 314-360

Manchester MLH, pp. 264-280

Cornish & Clark, pp. 197-226

B. H. Putnam, *The Enforcement of the Statute of Labourers 1349-1359* (1908)

W. Friedmann, *Law and Social Change* (1951), pp. 34-72

A. W. B. Simpson, 'The Place of Slade's Case in the History of Contract' (1958) 74 LQR 381-396; 'Innovation in 19th Century Contract Law' (1975) 91 LQR 247-278 (repr. in LTLH 171-202); *History of the Common Law of Contract: the Rise of Assumpsit* (1975); 'The Horwitz Thesis and the History of Contracts' (1979) 46 *Univ. Chicago Law Rev.* 533-601 (repr. in LTLH 203-271)

H. K. Lücke, 'Slade's Case and the Origin of the Common Counts' (1965-66) 81 LQR 422-445, 539-561; 82 LQR 81-96

---

141 *Suisse Atlantique Société D'Armement Maritime S.A. v. N.V. Rotterdamsche Kolen Centrale* [1967] A.C. 361, [1966] 2 All E.R. 61; *Photo Production Ltd v. Securicor Transport Ltd* [1980] A.C. 827, [1980] 1 All E.R. 556.

142 Unfair Contract Terms Act 1977 (c.50).

W. M. McGovern, 'The Enforcement of Informal Contracts in the later Middle Ages' (1971) 59 *California Law Rev.* 1145-1193

J. L. Barton, 'The early History of Consideration' (1969) 85 LQR 372-391

J. H. Baker, 'New Light on Slade's Case' [1971] CLJ 51-67, 213-236 (repr. in LPCL 393-432); 'Origins of the "Doctrine" of Consideration' (1977), in *Laws and Customs*, pp. 336-358 (repr. in LPCL 369-391)

G. Gilmore, *The Death of Contract* (1974)

M. Horwitz, 'The Historical Foundations of Modern Contract Law' (1974) 87 HLR 917-956 (cf. Simpson, ante)

S. J. Stoljar, *A History of Contract at Common Law* (1975)

P. S. Atiyah, *The Rise and Fall of Freedom of Contract* (1979)

D. J. Ibbetson, 'Assumpsit and Debt in the early 16th Century: the Origins of the Indebitatus Count' [1982] CLJ 142-161; '16th Century Contract Law: Slade's Case in Context' (1984) 4 OJLS 295-317

J. Oldham, 'Reinterpretations of 18th Century English Contract Theory' (1988) 76 *Georgetown Law Jo.* 1949-1991

20. Quasi-Contract

There are various situations in which, independently of any contract, a person may be obliged in justice or in good faith to pay over money or hand over personal property to another. The beneficiary of such an obligation has an interest closer in nature to property than to a contractual right, and its greatest affinity is with the fiduciary obligation of a feoffee to uses of land: the legal ownership is in one person, but the beneficial ownership or right to enjoyment is in another. It was not impossible to conceive of an action of *assumpsit* to enforce a use of land,[1] but for reasons of convenience and historical accident the fiduciary obligation in relation to land was in practice enforced solely in Chancery,[2] while that in relation to money came to be enforced principally at common law. The means whereby the later common law recognised the use or trust of money was a fictitious extension of *indebitatus assumpsit*. Since the essence of the fiduciary obligation was that it was not contractual, the fiction was no slight one; now not only the tortious dressing but the promise itself had to become a figment of the legal imagination. However, such was the dominance of the forms of action that it became customary to treat such obligations as arising from 'contracts implied by law' or 'quasi-contract', and therefore as belonging in an appendix to the law of contract rather than to the law of trusts. There is perhaps an analogy between quasi-contract and the real thing, in so far as one of the justifications for allowing *assumpsit* against a genuine promisee had been that his receipt of a benefit obliged him to give recompense. But it is necessary to remember, as we trace the history of fiduciary money claims, that in these cases *indebitatus assumpsit* came to be independent of bargain or reliance; its object was not performance of an undertaking, but restitution of benefits. The growth of quasi-contractual obligations is another striking example of the way in which the common law could be developed, whatever the formal restraints and however devious the subterfuges needed to evade them, in order to achieve equity.

---

[1] 94 SS *197-198*; *Megod's Case* (1586) B. & M. 497. Cf. Hales' reading (1537) B. & M. 345 at 347, contra.

[2] The reason why the common law did not develop a remedy is doubtless that *assumpsit* gave only damages, whereas Chancery could decree possession.

The Action of Account

Although the quasi-contractual possibilities of *assumpsit* were not explored until the Tudor period, there was a medieval foundation for many of the later developments in the action of account. An accounting between two parties, either before auditors or by mutual reckoning, was itself a cause of action in debt; and by 1370 an action of debt on an accounting (later called 'account stated') lay to recover the sum agreed to be outstanding.[3] The action of account was not concerned with the obligation to pay this sum, which sounded in debt, but with the antecedent obligation to enter into an account in order to discover what, if anything, was owing. The writ, which is coeval with debt and covenant, was in the *praecipe* form: 'command the defendant that he render a reasonable account' (*praecipe quod reddat rationabilem compotum*). If the court decided that he should account, the defendant was committed to prison and auditors were assigned to hear the account. The imprisonment could be continued until the account was settled, but it was no part of the judgment that any sum should be paid; in later times it was necessary to bring an action of debt if the defendant declined to pay what was found due.

At first the only recognised duty to account arose where the parties enjoyed a relationship akin to what we now call agency. The early actions were all brought against bailiffs (estate managers) of land.[4] By the early fourteenth century, perhaps as a result of legislation of 1285, the duty was extended to commercial relationships by admitting a count against someone who had received money on the plaintiff's behalf: usually against those who had received money from the plaintiff to trade with (*ad mercandizandum*), or had sold goods belonging to the plaintiff and received the proceeds.[5] But the recognition of the count against a receiver opened up the possibility that account would lie even where there was no prior relationship of agency between the parties; for instance, where *A* paid money to *B* for the benefit of *C*. In the first two decades of the fourteenth century, the courts denied that *C* could bring

---

3   See S. F. C. Milsom, 82 LQR 534 (repr. in SHCL 133). The count was that the defendant accounted with the plaintiff and was found in arrears; in *Humberstone v. Hertfeld* (1389) Y.B. Trin. 13 Ric. II, p. 20, pl.7, it was argued unsuccessfully that this made the plaintiff a judge in his own cause. See also B. & M. 232-233.

4   A statutory action of account was available from 1267 against guardians in socage: see p. 275, ante.

5   In the second case it was at first doubted whether the receiver should not be called a 'bailiff': *Anon.* (1308) 19 SS 34. But the 'receiver' count stuck: *Perton v. Tumby* (1317) B. & M. 289 (cf. 41 SS 59); *Euges v. Spyk* (1317) 54 SS 138. In *Anon.* (1311) 26 SS 3, the action against a receiver was expressly attributed to the Statute of Westminster II 1285, c.11.

account against *B* unless *B* commonly acted as his receiver, so that there was a privity between the parties;[6] but in 1320 this restriction was abandoned, and account was allowed against a trustee of money who had received it to invest for an infant plaintiff's use.[7] After 1320, therefore, *B* was obliged to pay over money to *C* even though he was not in any prior relationship with him; in such cases *C* alleged that *B* received the money to the use or profit of the plaintiff 'in an accountable way' (*ad compotum reddendum*). In the example given, it was also possible for *A* to bring account against *B* if *B* failed to pay *C*; *B* had no more contracted to pay *A* than to pay *C*, but he was accountable for the money. It was by this means possible for a party to a failed transaction to recover back a deposit, and thus to obtain rescission for failure of consideration.[8] Much later, in the 1590s, it was decided that account would lie where *A* paid *B* by mistake; *B* was not in that case a debtor, but he could be said to have received the money to the use of *A* since *A* had not parted with the beneficial ownership.[9] The action was never extended, however, to tortfeasors. If a disseisor of land took the profits, or a stranger took someone else's crops, or a bailee sold the bailor's goods and appropriated the purchase money, there could not in such cases be said to be a taking to the use of the owner because the wrongdoer had received and converted the money to his own use;[10] the remedy was therefore novel disseisin or trespass.[11]

These developments split the cause of action in account into two species. Account against a bailiff, guardian, common receiver, or other agent, was intended primarily to secure an enquiry by way of audit into a series of transactions over a period; some of the individual transactions might have been contracts between the parties, others not; there might be set-offs and allowances: all the individual items merged in the finding of the auditors, who were supposed to follow equity as much as law. Account for money received to the plaintiff's use, however, lay against the receiver of some specific sum of money which could not be

6   *Anon.* (1318) B. & M. 289; *Bastenthwayt v. Lenebane* (1319) 81 SS 53. Cf. *Reppes v. Reppes* (1315) 45 SS 71, Fifoot HSCL, p. 282, where the point was not taken.
7   *Taillour v. Medwe* (1320) 104 SS 39; identifiable as the case in *Novae Narrationes* (80 SS), p. 293, no. C266B. See also *Anon.* (1367) B. & M. 291; *Hastynges v. Beverley* (1379) B. & M. 292.
8   *Anon.* (1367) B. & M. 290.
9   *Framson v. Delamere* (1595) Cro. Eliz. 458; *Hewer v. Bartholomew* (1598) Cro. Eliz. 614.
10 *Tottenham v. Bedingfield* (1572) B. & M. 295.
11 For the assize, see p. 266, ante; for the action for conversion, see pp. 449-451, post.

recovered in debt; there was no dispute as to the sum, and no question of claiming allowances or adjusting mutual claims. It is this latter species which may be called quasi-contractual. But the development from this point was not continuous. By the sixteenth century it was becoming apparent that the action of account was not the most convenient method of achieving either of the objects.

DECLINE OF ACCOUNT

In the middle of the fourteenth century account was one of the most frequently used personal actions, more common (according to some estimates) than debt. A century later it was far less common, and was beginning a gradual decline into oblivion. The reason usually given is that the defendant could wage his law. But this was not the major obstacle that it was in debt and detinue. Wager of law was not permitted where the defendant received money from a third party to the use of the plaintiff,[12] and most actions of account were of this kind. By 1600 wager of law had also been denied to the bailiff.[13]   There were nevertheless procedural disadvantages, in the process of imprisonment and of hearing the account before auditors who had no powers to compel discovery and (according to some writers) could not take evidence from the parties. In an embarrassing case of the 1520s, a defendant was incarcerated for five years without an account being taken.[14] Parties faced with a cumbersome procedure might just as well submit voluntarily to an accounting; and this explains why debt on an account stated became more common as account declined. A voluntary accounting barred the action of account.

In the quasi-contractual kind of case, it is difficult to see what possible function the auditors could have had. The count alleged the receipt of a specific sum or sums by the hands of a named person or persons, and the defendant could plead before the judges that the sum was received for a specific purpose and not *ad compotum reddendum*.[15] The judgment 'that the defendant do account' ended the suit, and yet it brought about only the appointment of auditors, not payment. Here

---

12   *Perton v. Tumby* (1317) B. & M. 289; *Huntley v. Fraunsham* (1560) Dyer 183; Coke's *Entries*, fo. 47v.

13   *Shyfield v. Barnfield* (1600) Cro. Eliz. 790.

14   *Earl of Northumberland v. Wedell* (1523-27) Spelman Rep. (93 SS) 9; Y.B. Mich. 18 Hen. VIII, fo. 2, pl.13.

15   Y.B. Mich. 19 Hen. VI, fo. 5, pl.10, per Newton CJ. E.g. *Clerk v. More* (1452) Y.B. Trin. 30 Hen. VI, fo. 5, pl.4 (money received to obtain a patent, not to trade with and account); *Earl of Worcester v. Bodringan* (1469) CP 40/830, m. 403 (money received to pay over to the master of two ships for victualling purposes, not to trade with and account).

there must have been a strong temptation to bring debt instead, and (at least by Tudor times) the courts were indulgent. It was said that debt would lie if A paid B money for a purpose which was not carried out.[16] Accordingly, in a leading case of 1536, it was held that where a grocer had paid money to be invested in prunes, and the payee died before buying any prunes, debt could be brought against his administrator. Wherever money was paid on trust, and the trust was not observed, the payer could elect to bring account or debt.[17] Soon afterwards it became accepted that where A paid money to B to pay to C, C could bring debt against B if the money was not paid over.[18] These decisions virtually put an end to the quasi-contractual use of account. The action continued to be used for its older purpose, where debt was precluded because of uncertainty as to the balance between the parties, until the seventeenth century; but from the middle of that century it collapsed in the face of the more efficient Chancery procedure for taking accounts. If accounts were needed in common-law litigation they were referred either to arbitration or to a master of the court. The action of account was obsolete.

Actions on the Case

The substitution of debt for account was not to be a lasting solution to the problems of quasi-contract. Debt, as was seen in the previous chapter, had too many shortcomings of its own. Therefore, just as debt on a contract was replaced by *assumpsit*, so debt in lieu of account was replaced by various actions on the case.

The first possibility which occurred to lawyers was to treat the failure to account for money as a conversion. In a case of 1530, a plaintiff (P) showed that he had bought pieces of camlet (cloth) from X, that at his request the defendant (D) had received them from X to resell at a higher price and pay P the proceeds, and that D undertook to do this but instead converted the proceeds to his own use. P recovered in damages somewhat more than the price paid to X, presumably the higher sum he

---

16   See *Orwell v. Mortoft* (1505) B. & M. 406 at 409, 410, per Frowyk CJ; *Bretton v. Barnet* (1599) Owen 86. An early mention is *Fransseys' Case* (1294) B. & M. 227.

17   *Core v. May* (1536) B. & M. 243, Spelman Rep. (93 SS) 132. (There was a deed, and so the objection that personal representatives could not wage law did not arise.) Cf. detinue to achieve rescission of a void contract: *Millington v. Burges* (1587) B. & M. 219 at 220.

18   Bro. Abr., *Dette*, pl. 129 (citing 15th-century cases); *Shaw v. Norwood* (1600) Moore K.B. 667. The proposition is expressly denied in Spelman Rep. (93 SS) 132, and in *Brigs Case* (1623) Palm. 364.

expected from the resale.[19] The difficulty with the conversion approach, however, was that the money so received was not specific property; and so the agent who appropriated money was not converting property belonging to the plaintiff.[20] In 1600 the Exchequer Chamber put a temporary stop to the idea of using trover and conversion for money claims. The King's Bench had given judgment against a factor alleged to have converted the proceeds of corn sold on behalf of the plaintiff; but the judgment was reversed, first, because the purchase money did not belong to the plaintiff *in specie*; and, secondly, because the plaintiff had alleged (albeit fictitiously) a loss of the money, and thereby in law admitted that he could not claim any identifiable coins.[21] The actual coins belonged to the factor, whose obligation was to account for the sum received and not to keep the coins aside as a bailee.

According to the Exchequer Chamber in this last case, the proper remedy was account. But there remained the alternative of *assumpsit*. The objections to a trover count could not apply to an *assumpsit* count. The plaintiff in the 1530 case had alleged an undertaking, but at that date there was no formal doctrine of consideration. As *assumpsit* became a distinct action on the case, in which the plaintiff was required to show consideration, this placed a hurdle in the way of using the action in place of account. But the King's Bench proved as helpful to plaintiffs in this regard as in others. The question arose in 1591, in an action against someone who been paid money by the plaintiff to pay over to the plaintiff's debtor, and had undertaken to do so. The defendant argued that the proper action was account, and that *assumpsit* did not lie because there was no benefit to the defendant; but the court held that the action lay, to recover the damages which were not recoverable in account, and that there was sufficient consideration in the defendant's having the money temporarily in his hands.[22] We shall see that in such situations a further development would enable the receiver to be sued on a fictitious undertaking. The action on a genuine *assumpsit* remained of use only in situations where there was a contractual nexus between the parties, a true agency. But this was precisely the kind of case where auditors were needed to go over the items of account, and Hale CJ is known to have rejected the use of such actions because of the

19 *Miller v. Dymok* (1530) KB 27/1077, m. 72A; 94 SS 250 n.4.
20 See *Orwell v. Mortoft* (1505) B. & M. 406 at 408, per Kingsmill J.
21 *Halliday v. Higges* (1600) B. & M. 539. The second reason was overruled in *Kynaston v. Moore* (1627) B. & M. 545. But little more is heard of trover against agents. In *Orton v. Butler* (1822) 5 B. & Ald. 652, an attempt to bring trover for money had and received to the plaintiff's use was rejected with scorn.
22 *Retchford v. Spurlinge* (1591) B. & M. 500.

inconvenience of unravelling accounts before juries. By 1689, nevertheless, it was established that *assumpsit* could always be used as an alternative to account against an agent, because by acting as an agent a receiver of money was understood to promise an account.[23] It was around this time, however, that the Chancery remedy effectively removed the incentive to seek such a remedy at law.

IMPLIED AND FICTITIOUS UNDERTAKINGS TO PAY

Slade's Case decided, amongst other things, that a promise to pay could be implied in any contractual debt. Such an implication was not a fiction, but a recognition that a contract requiring the payment of money amounted to an undertaking to pay it, even though the words 'I promise to pay' were not used. The promise was too obvious to be expressed. This may have set lawyers wondering whether similar implied promises could not be read into contracts which did not create debts, or into debts which did not arise from contracts. One could safely allege an *assumpsit* in pleading if the trial judge could be relied upon to tell the jury that in certain situations they could imply or presume an undertaking from the circumstances. Since the proceedings at nisi prius were not reported, it is very difficult for the historian to trace the steps by which the judges came to permit an *assumpsit* to be raised, first by genuine implication and then by pure fiction. But there are two common cases in which the process seems to have occurred just after *Slade's Case*, and it is likely that these paved the way for bolder extensions later in the century.

The first was the *quantum meruit* count. If a person ordered goods or services without first fixing the sum to be paid for them, he could be sued upon an *assumpsit* to pay what the goods were worth (*quantum valebant*) or what the performer of the services deserved (*quantum meruit*).[24] Of course, there may in some cases have been an express promise to pay whatever was deserved; but this seems inherently unlikely. When we see a *quantum meruit* count it is a fair guess that the undertaking was to be implied from the circumstances. This was openly stated to be so in 1609, and in 1632 the judges decided that whenever 'I bid one do work for me, and do not promise anything, the law makes it'.[25] Here we are well on the way from implication to fiction. There is doubtless an understanding that the party is to be

---

[23] *Wilkins v. Wilkins* (1689) Comb. 149; Carth. 89; 1 Salk. 9.

[24] See *Shepherd v. Edwards* (1615) B. & M. 463 (declaration upheld despite uncertainty).

[25] *Warbrook v. Griffin* (1609) 2 Brownl. 254; Yelv. 66; *The Six Carpenters' Case* (1610) 8 Co. Rep. 146; *Anon.* (1632) Sheppard's *Marrow*, p. 125.

remunerated, but the promise to pay a reasonable sum is inferred as a matter of law.

The second case was the *insimil computassent* count, the direct successor to debt *sur insimul computaverunt*. The form was to recite that the parties had accounted together and that the defendant had been found in debt to a specific amount, and then to allege that in consideration thereof the defendant undertook to pay the sum found owing. Actions of this type were in use by the mid-sixteenth century, but in Elizabethan times they met the stumbling block of consideration. The King's Bench held in 1587 that a deferment of payment for a short while was sufficient consideration for the promise to pay the outstanding balance, and in 1605 it went further and held that the debt itself was sufficient consideration.[26] By the latter date, at least, both the promise and the consideration had clearly become legal fictions; being found in arrear upon an account raised an undertaking in law to pay the debt. This ensured the survival into modern law of the concept of an 'account stated' as a cause of action sui generis, independent of contract. The modern importance of this concept grew from the use of *insimul computassent* in Georgian times to recover money due under contracts rendered unenforceable by the Statute of Limitations or the Statute of Frauds. It was established for this purpose that an acknowledgment of the existence of a debt arising from a single transaction was a cause of action separate from the contract, because it is tantamount to an accounting together and the law will imply a subsequent promise to discharge it.[27]

Indebitatus Assumpsit

The action of *indebitatus assumpsit* as it developed in the seventeenth century always rested on a fictitious promise, because whenever one person was indebted to another the law implied a promise, in consideration of the indebtedness, to pay off the debt. Where the debt arose from a contract, the fictitious promise was merely a reflection of reality. Whereas in *Slade's Case* the promise to pay was implied in the contract itself, in *indebitatus assumpsit* the alleged promise was subsequent to the contract and therefore wholly imaginary; but in either case the result was the same. However, the fictitious subsequent

---

[26] *Whorwood v. Gybbons* (1587) Goulds. 48; *Egles v. Vale* (1605) Cro. Jac. 69; Yelv. 70. For earlier precedents, see 94 SS *61, 282*.

[27] E.g. *Knowles v. Michel* (1811) 13 East 249. For the survival, see *Camillo Tank S.S. Co. Ltd v. Alexandria Engineering Works* (1921) 38 T.L.R. 134.

promise soon let in an extension of *indebitatus assumpsit* beyond the realms of contract: first to indebtedness arising by custom or operation of law, and then to the kind of equitable indebtedness or accountability arising from the receipt of money which belonged beneficially to someone else.

NON-CONTRACTUAL DEBTS

Debt would lie in a number of situations where the duty to pay arose from custom or law, but in theory *assumpsit* could only perform this task if there was a promise to pay. If the law implied a promise in such a case, it was pure fiction. There are cases beginning in 1588 which raise a suspicion of fiction,[28] but the first clear decision that the law would raise such a promise occurred in a case of 1676. The City of London brought *indebitatus assumpsit* to recover a customary import duty (called 'scavage') owed by a silk importer, and the jury found a special verdict that although the money was due by the custom there was no 'actual' promise to pay it. The King's Bench held that the city could recover. The indebtedness alone was sufficient to ground an action of *indebitatus assumpsit*, and the allegation of a promise in such cases was mere form.[29] This rapidly became accepted doctrine, and *assumpsit* was used to recover a wide range of customary duties. In *Shuttleworth v. Garnett* in 1688 it was allowed even in respect of a manorial fine payable by a tenant on the lord's death; the objection that *assumpsit* would not lie for a right of inheritance was brushed aside with the response that when a particular fine fell due it was like a 'fruit fallen', or severed crops, and was to be treated as personalty.[30]

Assumpsit was never allowed to take over the work of debt on an obligation or debt on a record, because it was not thought convenient to allow jury trial on the general issue where there was a deed or record; but in the eighteenth century the fiction of *indebitatus assumpsit* was extended so far as to allow the enforcement of judgments given by foreign courts.[31]

---

28 *Lord North's Case* (1588) 2 Leon. 179 (fine *pro licencia concordandi*); *Ayton v. Van Somer* (1665) Brown's *Vade Mecum*, p. 50 (fees as Black Rod); *City of London v. Gould* (1667) 2 Keb. 295 (custom called water-bailage).

29 *City of London v. Goray* (1676) B. & M. 476; 2 Lev. 174; 1 Vent. 298; 1 Freem. 433.

30 B. & M. 480; 3 Mod. Rep. 240; 3 Lev. 261; Comb. 151; Carth. 90. For Holt CJ's dissent, see p. 420, post.

31 *Bowles v. Bradshaw* (1748) and *Crawford v. Whittal* (1773) 1 Doug. K.B. 4. Lord Mansfield doubted the propriety of this procedure in 1777, but the objection was not pressed: *Van Uxen v. Plaistow* (1777) Mansfield Notebook 480, p. 210.

'ONERABILIS' ASSUMPSIT ON BILLS OF EXCHANGE

An early and important extension of *assumpsit* to enforce customary obligations to pay was that which permitted the enforcement of bills of exchange. The doctrine of consideration, and the related notion of privity of contract, made it difficult or impossible to sue on bills of exchange by relying on an express promise between the parties; but during the sixteenth century pleaders developed a form of *assumpsit* expressly founded on customs of merchants regulating the liabilities of acceptors, indorsers and drawers.[32] It was not strictly an *indebitatus assumpsit*, because the customary obligation to pay was not in law a debt;[33] but the formula adopted was closely analogous, alleging that the defendant was 'chargeable' (*onerabilis*) under the custom, rather than indebted. The custom was usually pleaded in the early seventeenth century as a custom of London merchants;[34] and from the 1660s as a bilocal custom operating among merchants trading between two named cities.[35] But this form of pleading, while giving flexibility, seemed to restrict liability to merchants. That would have been inconvenient, since bills of exchange were by the 1660s in wide use among non-merchants, as a substitute for currency; if the law did not extend liability to non-merchants, the use of such paper might have been frustrated. In 1689 the King's Bench overcame the difficulty; anyone who drew or negotiated a bill became a 'merchant' for the purpose of the custom.[36] But the line was drawn at bills of exchange. When in 1702 the court was asked to apply the same doctrine to a promissory note, Holt CJ expressed some indignation: 'it amounted to the setting up a new sort of specialty, unknown to the common law, and invented in Lombard Street – which attempted in these matters of bills of exchange to give laws to Westminster Hall'.[37] In this case the extension was effected by parliament three years later, when notes were made negotiable and actionable in the same manner as bills.[38]

---

32 In *Maynard v. Dyce* (1542) LPCL 357, the first known instance of *assumpsit* against a drawer, the custom of merchants was pleaded by way of replication. In *Knappe v. Hedley* (1600) LPCL 358, the Exchequer Chamber upheld an *assumpsit* on the acceptance of a bill 'according to the usage and custom of merchants'.

33 *Milton's Case* (1668) B. & M. 248; *Browne v. London* (1668) B. & M. 459.

34 *Oaste v. Taylor* (1612) Cro. Jac. 306; *Woodford v. Wyatt* (1626) B. & M. 458.

35 There is a specimen of 1685 in the reports (Lutw. 885). The precedent books have examples back to the 1660s: [1979] CLJ 317 (= LPCL 363).

36 *Sarsfield v. Witherley* (1689) B. & M. 460; Comb. 152; 2 Vent. 292.

37 *Clerke v. Martin* (1702) B. & M. 461 at 462. He also expressed misgivings about *Sarsfield v. Witherley*.

38 Stat. 3 & 4 Ann., c.8/9.

MONEY HAD AND RECEIVED

The doctrine that *indebitatus assumpsit* lay wherever debt lay enabled the action on the case also to be used in place of those forms of debt which had themselves supplanted account. By 1616 the form of the remedy was established as the count for money 'had and received to the use of the plaintiff', a formula borrowed from the action of account against a receiver. It was no objection to such an action that account lay on the facts, because debt was already an alternative to account; nor was it necessary to specify from whom the money had been received.[39] Soon it could be brought in all the quasi-contractual situations where account had lain: for instance, where *A* paid money to *B* to pay over to *C*, or where *C* paid *B* by mistake or under a void contract. In all such cases *B*, being indebted to *C* for money had and received to *C*'s use, was fictitiously presumed to have promised in consideration of that indebtedness to pay *C*.

But *indebitatus assumpsit* did not stop there. The common count merely supposed a receipt of money to the use of someone else, and this wording (though borrowed directly from the action of account) could, if construed broadly, include situations not covered by account. The main extension came about, without serious opposition, in a trio of cases in the 1670s concerning the profits of contested offices. The first arose from a dispute over the office of clerk of the papers in the King's Bench; it was resolved to try the title by bringing *indebitatus* in respect of £10 fees received by the officer in possession, which the claimant regarded as having been received to his use; the arguments were confined to the question of title, and the form of action was not challenged. In the second case, the Court of Exchequer allowed a similar action, despite the objection that a usurpation of office was a tort for which the proper remedy was an assize or an action on the case for a disturbance.[40] The only reason given was that account lay for the profits of an office, and that *indebitatus* lay wherever account lay. This reasoning was false, because account would not lie against a disseisor who received income to his own use. In the third case, the court agreed that the extension had not been very logical, but considered the remedy convenient and too well settled to alter.[41] However thin the reasons behind it, this development opened up further and wider possibilities: could *assumpsit* now be

---

39 *Beckingham and Lambert v. Vaughan* (1616) B. & M. 465; Moore K.B. 854. Cf. *Gilbert v. Ruddeard* (1607) 3 Dyer 272n (special count, but *assumpsit* implied).

40 For these remedies, see pp. 489–490, post.

41 *Woodward v. Aston* (1676) B. & M. 471 n.11; 1 Mod. Rep. 95; 1 Vent. 296; 1 Freem. 429; *Arris v. Stewkly* (1677) B. & M. 466; *Howard v. Wood* (1680) B. & M. 478; 2 Lev. 245; T. Jones 126; 1 Freem. 473. In 1705 it was said that counsel had advised against using *indebitatus* in the 1676 case: B. & M. 471.

420   *Quasi-Contract*

brought whenever money was taken or detained tortiously, or whenever the profits of property were tortiously intercepted ?

SCOPE OF THE MONEY COUNTS
Sir John Holt, chief justice of the King's Bench from 1689 to 1710, answered these questions with an emphatic 'no'. He was strongly critical of the two extensions just mentioned, because they involved an undesirable distortion of the forms of action which could bear hard on defendants; and, while it had been justifiable to allow overlapping remedies to avoid wager of law, it was not necessary to allow the indiscriminate substitution of one action for another. He dissented from the decision in *Shuttleworth v. Garnett*, saying it was not axiomatic that *indebitatus* was coextensive with debt: 'where wager of law doth not lie, there an *indebitatus* don't lie, and it is mischievous to extend it further than *Slade's Case*; for an *indebitatus assumpsit* is laid generally, and the defendant can't tell how to make his defence'.[42] He also thought the office cases had been wrongly decided. Again and again he attacked the fictitious use of *indebitatus* and promised to stop its spread: 'By my consent it shall go as far as it has gone, but not a step further.'[43] There was no reason to allow this action to be brought in place of special *assumpsit*, or actions in tort, or actions of debt where wager of law was unavailable. Had Holt CJ not called a halt, there is no telling where the action might have gone; certainly it bid fair to overtake, at one time or another, most of the other forms of action.

1. Real property
The fee cases established that *indebitatus* could be used to try the title to freehold offices, even though an assize was available for the purpose. If that was so, why should not the remedy be used for land? The logical conclusion had been conceded before 1700, when it was admitted that *assumpsit* could be brought by the true owner of land against someone who had received rent without title from tenants who had attorned to him.[44] How far *assumpsit* jostled with ejectment in reality is not known, but an obvious attraction would have been that it could be brought against personal representatives and other persons against whom ejectment would not lie; moreover, the plaintiff did not need to show

---

[42] Comb. 151. Cf. B. & M. 481. The one case which Holt CJ accepted as a fait accompli was that of overpayment by mistake: B. & M. 469, 471.

[43] *Hussey v. Fiddall* (1698) B. & M. 469 at 470.

[44] 2 Mod. Rep. 262, per curiam (1677); B. & M. 470, per Northey (1699). Cf. B. & M. 479, per Bigland (1680). An example of such an action is *Hasser v. Wallis* (1708) 1 Salk. 28.

title.[45] Opinion in the eighteenth century turned against allowing *assumpsit* to be brought for accepting rent where adverse title was claimed. In such a case the proper remedy was ejectment, which was brought against the tenant; or, if ejectment was unavailable, *assumpsit* against the tenant for the 'use and occupation', supposing him to be in occupation with the licence of the plaintiff and owing him rent. If the tenant was made to pay rent a second time, in *assumpsit* for the use and occupation, it was then for him to sue the ousted landlord to recover the rent he had paid to him, as money had and received.[46] The office cases were distinguished on the ground that the fees paid to a de facto officer discharged the payer, so that the de jure officer had to sue the usurper, whereas payment of rent to a disseisor was no discharge as against the disseisee.

An attempt was once made to use *indebitatus* instead of replevin, where the plaintiff had paid the defendant to release his cattle from distress even though he intended at the time to challenge the defendant's right to distrain. Again convenience triumphed over logic. The court said that it would be prejudicial to the defendant to allow title to be put in issue in such a roundabout way.[47]

2. Contract

In the count for money had and received, there was no need to set out the circumstances in which the money was received. This gave the plaintiff a considerable advantage compared with special *assumpsit*, in which all material details had to be shown. Attempts were therefore made to use the former instead of the latter. Holt CJ opposed this where there had merely been a breach of contract. In a case where the plaintiff paid money to the defendant to perform a service, which he subsequently failed to perform, he exclaimed: 'Away with your *indebitatus*, 'tis but a bargain.'[48] Neither would he allow *indebitatus* for the purpose of recovering back money where a party had been led into a contract by a false warranty.[49] He accepted, however, that the money count was appropriate where the money was paid under a void contract or where there was a failure of consideration.[50] By the beginning of the nineteenth

---

45 *Lewis v. Wallace* (1752) B. & M. 481.

46 *Birch v. Wright* (1786) 1 Term Rep. 386; *Cunningham v. Laurents* (1788) Bacon Abr., vol. I (7th ed.), p. 344; *Newsome v. Grahame* (1829) 1 B. & C. 234. For the contrary view, see 1 Freem. 479n.

47 *Lindon v. Hooper* (1776) 1 Cowp. 414.

48 *Anon.* (1695) B. & M. 468 at 469.

49 *Anon.* (1697) B. & M. 469.

50 *Martin v. Sitwell* (1691) B. & M. 467 at 468; *Holmes v. Hall* (1704) 6 Mod. Rep. 161.

century the distinction here was regarded as one of substance: a contract could not be rescinded for mere breach of warranty, but only for a breach going to the root of the contract followed by prompt repudiation, or for frustration, or where the contract was void *ab initio*. The principles governing the discharge of contracts, conditions and warranties, and illegality, were for this reason mostly worked out in actions for money had and received and not in actions for breach of contract.

3. Tort

The office cases represented a major departure from the old law of account in that they allowed the recovery of money appropriated by wrong. In such a case the plaintiff was said to 'waive the tort'; but in so doing he was not acting from charitable motives. By suing on a contract, albeit a fictitious one, the plaintiff gained advantages in pleading, a more favourable limitation period, and the possibility of suing executors. For these reasons, waiving the tort became a common practice in the eighteenth century and was indulged by the courts. Even Holt CJ grudgingly accepted that if personal property was converted by a tortious sale, the person wronged could waive the tort by affirming the sale and bringing *indebitatus* for the proceeds.[51] This was the most frequent case of waiver, and it was extended to the conversion of negotiable bank notes (which were treated as money) and in one case to the disappearance of a masquerade ticket for which value could be presumed to have been given.[52] But there was no count for goods received, so if goods were converted without being exchanged for money then the proper remedy was still trover. Although it became possible to waive other torts, such as trespass or deceit, where money was obtained by force or dishonesty, the concept was not appropriate to torts such as assault or slander, where no money changed hands. Legal ingenuity did nevertheless stretch the notion of waiving the tort still further in the early nineteenth century, when some of the other *indebitatus* counts were used fictitiously. Thus, where *B* tortiously lured away *A*'s apprentice, *A* could waive the tort and recover the profits of his labour against *B* in a count for work done.[53] Here the fiction was to suppose that *B* had requested *A* to supply the services of his apprentice. And in the case where *B* obtained *A*'s goods by fraud, and converted them without selling them, *A* might be allowed to waive the tort and sue for

---

[51] *Lamine v. Dorrell* (1705) B. & M. 470.
[52] *Longchamp v. Kenny* (1779) 1 Doug. K.B. 137.
[53] *Lightly v. Clouston* (1808) 1 Taunt. 112. For the tort of enticing a servant, see pp. 517-518, post.

quantum valebant in an action for goods sold and delivered to *B*.[54] Here the contract of sale was fictitious. On the same principle, it was later held that where a trespasser travelled on a railway with intent to avoid paying the fare, he could be sued on a fictitious 'implied promise' to pay.[55] By this stage, the quasi-contractual claim gave more than a procedural advantage, because the sum claimed was greater than any sum which might be recovered in tort.

MONEY LAID OUT

There was one other of the common counts which did not rest on contract. Where the plaintiff had paid or 'laid out' money on behalf of the defendant and to his use, he could bring *indebitatus assumpsit* to obtain reimbursement. Already by 1626 it was accepted that the promise to reimburse might be 'implicative', or fictitious.[56] It was not necessary to allege how the money came to the defendant's use; yet, since English law was not willing to allow one person to foist good works upon another without his consent, reimbursement could only be demanded if the payment was authorised by the defendant. It was therefore necessary to allege that the money was laid out 'at the special instance and request' of the defendant. In certain cases, however, the law was willing to imply a request as well as a promise to repay, and by means of this double fiction created another form of quasi-contractual obligation. This did not occur until the late eighteenth century, and then only in two cases.

The first case established the doctrine of contribution between co-sureties and joint contractors. If several persons stood surety for a debt, or broke a joint contract, and an action was sued to execution against one of them alone, that one could sue the others for a contribution. This principle of contribution was first established in equity, but the common law came to accommodate it by supposing that the money recovered in the first action had been laid out by the one at the request of the others.[57] The element of legal compulsion overcame the objection that a person could not spend another's money without authority. But

---

[54] *Hill v. Perrott* (1810) 3 Taunt. 274; *Russell v. Bell* (1842) 10 M. & W. 340.

[55] *London & Brighton Rly Co. v. Watson* (1879) 4 C.P.D. 118.

[56] *Anon.* (1626) Sheppard's *Marrow*, p. 124. For a pleading precedent, see *Widdrington v. Goddard* (1664) B. & M. 472 at 473 (money laid out by Cambridge tutor).

[57] *Cowell v. Edwards* (1800) 2 Bos. & P. 270.

the common law stopped short of giving the same remedy to joint tortfeasors, a reform accomplished by legislation in 1935.[58]

The second case was where the plaintiff's property was distrained for the defendant's debt, so that the plaintiff had to pay off the debt to redeem his own property. Here again, because of the legal compulsion, the law implied a request to pay off the debt and a promise to indemnify.[59] The principle was later extended to analogous cases where the plaintiff conferred a benefit on the defendant under compulsion and without acting officiously.

A General Principle

In the eighteenth and nineteenth centuries, the count for money had and received became one of the most extensively used actions in the law. The reasons for its popularity, as was suggested above, were partly procedural; and the object of keeping the defendant in the dark as to the true cause of action, as Holt CJ had recognised, was not a very worthy one. But the action was also a flexible means of plugging gaps which had appeared in other actions, and Blackstone praised it as 'a very extensive and beneficial remedy, applicable to almost every case where a person has received money which *ex aequo et bono* he ought to refund'.[60] Having escaped the buffets dealt it by Holt CJ, at the beginning of the century, the remedy was carefully cultivated by Lord Mansfield CJ in the second half. Lord Mansfield favoured 'a liberal extension of the action for money had and received; because the charge and defence in this kind of action are both governed by the true equity and conscience of the case'.[61] To compensate for the generality of the plaintiff's count, the defendant could raise at the trial every legal and equitable defence or allowance open to him, without having pleaded it, because the only issue for the jury was whether *ex aequo et bono* the money ought to be deemed to belong to the plaintiff. By establishing that the basis of this common-law action *quasi ex contractu* was an obligation to refund money arising from 'the ties of natural justice' and equity,[62] Lord Mansfield began to free the underlying principles from procedural technicalities. At the end of the following century, jurists at

---

58 *Merryweather v. Nixon* (1799) 8 Term Rep. 186; Law Reform (Married Women and Tortfeasors) Act 1935, 25 & 26 Geo. V, c.30, s.6.

59 *Exall v. Partridge* (1799) 8 Term Rep. 308.

60 Bl. Comm., vol. III, p. 163, paraphrasing Lord Mansfield in *Moses v. Macferlan* (post).

61 *Longchamp v. Kenny* (1779) 1 Doug. K.B. 137 at 138.

62 *Moses v. Macferlan* (1760) 2 Burr. 1005 at 1010.

Harvard took up Lord Mansfield's approach and began to analyse what they identified as an equitable principle that a man should not unjustly enrich himself at the expense of another.[63] The principle was not peculiar to the action of *indebitatus assumpsit*, but was also found in the *condictiones* of Roman law and in the concept of *enrichissement illégitime* in French law.

Meanwhile, the principle had been virtually forgotten in England. Even though *indebitatus assumpsit* and legal fictions were abolished in 1852, the fictitious promise seemed to be immortal. Lawyers still spoke of implied promises and waiving the tort; but as they lost familiarity with the forms in which those ideas had been clothed it was easy for misconceptions to flourish. For instance, it was held in 1904 that money paid under a contract could not be recovered back on frustration, because the contract had been in force when the money was paid and frustration only discharged future obligations. When the House of Lords unanimously overruled this decision in 1943, Viscount Simon said the Court of Appeal had overlooked the distinction between *indebitatus assumpsit* for money had and received and express *assumpsit*. The action to recover back money on a failure of consideration was of the former kind, and was not brought on the contract but on the equitable obligation to restore the money. Lord Wright attributed that obligation to the principle of unjust enrichment, which was neither contract nor tort but a third category sometimes called quasi-contract which rested on an equitable foundation. Lord Mansfield's view was thus reinstated as English law.[64] Since that time, English writers have attempted to identify the applications of this principle without undue reference to the forms of action, which tied it unnecessarily to money claims, and have found parallels in the equitable doctrine of constructive trusts as developed in Chancery,[65] and in the salvage law of the Admiralty. American lawyers had already suggested the wider heading 'restitution' for the whole class of obligations of this nature, but it was only within the last thirty years that restitution began to be firmly established in England as a discrete body of principles wholly

---

[63] See J. B. Ames, 2 HLR 66 (1888); W. A. Keener, *The Law of Quasi-Contracts* (1893).

[64] *Fibrosa Spolka Akcyjna v. Fairbairn Lawson Combe Barbour Ltd* [1943] A.C. 32, [1942] 2 All E.R. 122. The overruled case was *Chandler v. Webster* [1904] 1 K.B. 493.

[65] Constructive trusts were well established in the Restoration period, though only where grafted on to express trusts: Yale, 79 SS *124-128*. But there seems to have been no cross-influence between Chancery and common-law equity.

independent of contract, and no longer confined to the 'quasi-contract' of the old money counts.[66]

Further reading

Holdsworth HEL, vol. III, pp. 425-428; vol. VIII, pp. 88-98; vol. XII, pp. 542-549

Fifoot HSCL, pp. 268-288, 360-371

J. B. Ames, *Lectures on Legal History* (1913), pp. 149-166

T. A. Street, *Foundations of Legal Liability* (1906), vol. II, pp. 199-241

C. D. Hening, 'History of the Beneficiary's Action in Assumpsit' (1909) *Essays AALH*, vol. III, pp. 339-367

E. O. Belsheim, 'The Old Action of Account' (1932) 45 HLR 466-500

R. M. Jackson, *The History of Quasi-Contract in English Law* (1936)

S. J. Stoljar, 'The Doctrine of Failure of Consideration' (1959) 75 LQR 53-76; *The Law of Quasi-Contract* (1964); 'The Transformations of Account' (1964) 80 LQR 203-224; *A History of Contract at Common Law* (1975), pp. 105-117, 181-187; 'The Account Cases' (1989) 104 SS xi-xiv

A. W. B. Simpson, *A History of the Common Law of Contract* (1975), pp. 489-505

J. H. Baker, 'Onerabilis Assumpsit' in LPCL 359-366

P. Birks, 'English and Roman Learning in *Moses* v. *Macferlan*' [1984] *Current Legal Problems* 1-28; P. Birks and G. McLeod, 'The Implied Contract Theory of Quasi-Contract: Civilian Opinion current in the Century before Blackstone' (1986) 6 OJLS 46-85

---

[66]   The turning point was the publication of R. Goff and G. H. Jones, *The Law of Restitution* (1st ed., 1966).

21. Property in Chattels Personal

The common law relating to movable property was quite separate from that relating to real property. The reason is not that movables were once of minimal importance: 'Not even in the feudal age,' jested Maitland, 'did men eat or drink land.'[1] There was, nevertheless, a marked difference in value between the economic value of land, which was a capital asset producing a permanent livelihood or income, and most ordinary chattels, such as grain or cattle, which were consumable. Until the Industrial Revolution, land was the chief source of wealth, and litigation about landed property was one of the principal concerns of the royal courts. Every piece of land was geographically a parcel of the realm, the subject of tenure, a source of authority, immovable, indestructible, and recoverable *in specie* by real action. Chattels, in contrast, could be passed around by hand, damaged, consumed, lost. The live chattel was mortal, provisions were perishable, and many commodities such as grain and wool were fungibles with no individual characteristics; recovery *in specie* was never guaranteed, and rarely important, since money would usually do as well. To such things the notion of feudal tenure was quite inappropriate, and for many of them the processes of litigation in the royal courts were too solemn and dilatory. Even while the common law was developing its complex law of real actions, most medieval disputes about chattels were heard in local courts.

The learning of real property dominated the readings and moots of the medieval inns of court, and no book comparable with Littleton was written about chattels. Lacking the degree of concentrated attention bestowed on the land law, the law of personal property was less sophisticated. It is more difficult to perceive its substantive principles in the sources, and historical change is for that reason less clearly visible. Yet it would be wrong to deduce that this branch of the law has no history worth telling. There had to be a law of personal property, however rudimentary, which could be conceived of as distinct from the forms of action. For one thing, an owner had the right to seize his property extrajudicially without recourse to any action; and questions of property could arise in less direct ways than through actions for

[1] Pollock & Maitland, vol. II, p. 149.

428 *Property in Chattels Personal*

interference or withholding.[2] What is more, it appears that the abstract principles were occasionally discussed in the inns of court.

PERSONAL PROPERTY AND CHATTELS

We have already used the terms real and personal property without defining them, and in truth the distinction is less than straightforward. It is not the same as the physical distinction between land and movable things. Some interests in land, as we have seen, were not subject to tenure or the rules of inheritance and were classed as chattels. On the other hand, some intangible interests not directly concerned with land, such as advowsons or franchises, were real property. Real property was that which could be recovered *in specie* by means of a real action, and any other kind of property was 'personal'.[3] As will be seen, movables could be claimed by a form of action (detinue) which led to judgment for the recovery of the thing or its value; this was a 'mixed' action, but since it could not guarantee recovery of the specific thing the property which it protected remained personal.

A convenient term used by common lawyers for personal property was 'chattels', a French word having the same root as 'capital'. The English equivalent 'cattle', after about 1500, was usually confined to livestock; but the legal chattel included all movable property, and also chattels real such as a term of years or a wardship severed from the seignory. 'Goods' (*bona* in Latin) was a synonym for tangible chattels, but did not include chattels real.[4]

The fact that some movables might be part of the realty for certain purposes made the line between land and chattels nebulous. Movables as various as title-deeds, door-keys, and uncollected loose minerals and windfalls, were all part of the realty for the purposes of succession. They went to the heir rather than the executors. They also passed on a grant of the freehold. Here there could be fine distinctions. Domesticated animals were personal property, whereas unreclaimed wild animals went with the land on which they lived. Ploughshares were personal property, whereas the mill-stone of a mill was regarded as part of the mill even if it was away being mended. On the other hand, things affixed to the realty might nevertheless be regarded as chattels for the purposes of succession; for instance, certain classes of fixture placed by a tenant. Even a building might not be part of the land, if it stood

---

2 It was less than clear whether battery was justifiable in defence of chattels; the first known acceptance of such a defence was in 1500 (94 SS *315* n.16).

3 See p. 337, ante.

4 105 SS 261.

on pattens.[5] The purpose and degree of annexation determined the character of fixtures; thus, as was held at a meeting of all the judges of England in 1647, dung spread on the ground was part of the realty whereas a heap of dung was a chattel.[6] To say that something was part of the realty for the purpose of succession or conveyancing was not, however, to say that a real action lay for the thing independently of the land. There was no writ of right for muck or loose pebbles, though recovery of the land in a writ of right carried such things with it. Yet the same things when reduced into possession became chattels, could be recovered by the action of detinue, and could (if of value) be the subject of larceny.

The common law did not generally allow heirlooms, in the sense of chattels destined for heirs independently of land; on death, chattels went to the executors or administrators. But ensigns of honour might pass to heirs, as in the case of the armour of a knight or the crown jewels.[7] Another kind of heirloom was the right often given to the heir by local custom to take the best utensils of the deceased;[8] this was analogous in nature to the lord's right to take heriot, in that it was a claim against the estate rather than a hereditary interest in a specific chattel.[9]

HOW PERSONAL PROPERTY ARISES

Under the feudal system all the land in England must belong to someone, for if no tenant can be found the land must be part of the demesne of the Crown. But it is not necessary to suppose that anyone owns the atmosphere, the rain, the birds of the air, the water running in streams and rivers, and other movables in their natural state. Such things, according to *Bracton* and its Roman sources, are outside our dominion (*extra patrimonium nostrum*) and common to all mankind. Ownership of them arises, in the first place, by 'occupation'; for whoever first reduces a wild thing into his possession is its owner. A man owns the air in his lungs, rainwater in a butt, birds in a cage, or fish on his dinner plate. Those are obvious cases. The distinction between the limited property of the freeholder in unreclaimed wild

[5] 105 SS 119.

[6] *Yearworth v. Pierce* (1647) Aleyn 31; sub nom. *Carver v. Pierce*, Style 66 at 73.

[7] For the general rule, see p. 435, post. For armour: 62 SS 291. For the crown jewels: *Re King Henry IV's will* (1413) Mich. 1 Hen. V, Fitz. Abr., *Executours*, pl.108.

[8] 21 SS 138-144.

[9] It was therefore enforced by debt: *Anon.* (1356) Y.B. Hil. 30 Edw. III, fo. 2. Cf. *Anon.* (1365) Y.B. Hil. 39 Edw. III, fo. 6 ('detinue', perhaps meaning debt in the *detinet*).

animals or things on his land, and the interest of the occupant or captor, was reconciled in the medieval period as follows. Birds flying in the air belonged to no one, birds nesting in trees (and their eggs) belonged to the owner of the trees, and birds in a cage were chattels personal. Likewise, fish in a river belonged to no one, fish in a pond belonged to the owner of the pond, and fish in a net or in a fishmonger's pipe were chattels personal.[10] A difficult problem arose when a bird or beast was reduced into possession by an intruder or poacher on another man's soil; eventually, after centuries of disagreement, the courts decided that it belonged to the tenant of the land.[11]

The common law prohibited the occupation of certain classes of natural resources by private subjects because they belonged to the Crown by virtue of the royal prerogative: namely, gold and silver ore,[12] swans,[13] venison in a royal forest, and certain great fish.[14] These natural 'flowers of the Crown' could be acquired by subjects only through royal grant or prescription.

Another way in which property may arise is by the creation or manufacture of a new thing. When a new thing is made by human industry – *specificatio*, in the language of Roman law – it generally belongs to the maker; but a problem arises if he uses materials belonging to another person. In the time of Edward IV it was held that the property vested in the maker if the new thing was so different from the materials from which it was made that it could no longer be demanded by an action of detinue as being in existence.[15] But the fact that goods could not be demanded in detinue did not necessarily mean that they could not be recovered at all, for instance by legitimate self-help. If goods were taken wrongfully and made into something new, the owner of the materials was entitled to seize the new article without bringing any legal action. Accordingly, the property was only changed by *specificatio* in three cases. First, if the materials were no longer identifiable; for instance, if corn was made into bread, or barley into ale, or silver was melted down and cast in a new shape. Although the reason usually given was the practical one about seizure, there may also have

---

10 For discussions in the inns of court on these subjects, see 93 SS 64; 94 SS *214, 218, 317-322*; 105 SS 83-84.

11 *Blades v. Higgs* (1862) 12 C.B.N.S. 501, and the cases cited there.

12 *Case of Mines, A.-G. v. Earl of Northumberland* (1567) 1 Plowd. 313.

13 *Case of Swans, R. v. Yong* (1592) 7 Co. Rep. 15.

14 *Bracton*, vol. II, p. 339, and the undated 'statute' called Prerogativa Regis, c.11, mention only whales and sturgeon. But other authorities mention porpoises and dolphins.

15 See *Calwodelegh v. John* (1479) B. & M. 526, p. 448, post; *Anon.* (1596) Sheppard Abr., vol. I, p. 273 (B. & M. 318 n.16).

been a more philosophical objection to treating a thing as continuing to exist when its nature had been transformed.[16] The second case was where for some reason detinue was the only remedy available, because that action presupposed the withholding of the very thing which had been in the plaintiff's possession. And the third case was where the thing was made to accede to the freehold, in which case there was neither a right of seizure nor a writ of detinue; this would be the situation if seeds were sown in the ground, or materials built into a house.[17]

An analogous problem arose where things belonging to two persons were combined. Obviously, if a tailor added his own thread to a customer's gown, the gown (including the new stitches) belonged to the customer. This was originally explained on the *de minimis* principle: the lesser acceded to the greater. But it apparently became a general principle that where A mixed his own property with B's – as, by adding his sheep to B's flock, or mixing his hay with B's – the property passed to B.[18]

A different problem arose when things became chattels personal by severance from the realty. Fruit and crops, for instance, became pure personalty when harvested. Wool and milk belong to the owner of the animal from which they are taken. A young bird or beast born in captivity belongs to the owner of the mother.[19] If a stranger took such things wrongfully, trespass would lie.[20] But if a tenant had an estate of uncertain duration, such as a life estate, which ended before he could take the produce, the law made a fair division: crops which were the product of the tenant's own industry (his *emblements*)[21] belonged to the tenant who had sown them, or his executors, whereas natural fruits and produce belonged to the reversioner. It was a moot point whether a disseisor was entitled to emblements sown by him before the disseised tenant re-entered.[22]

---

[16] *Hoode's Case* (1490) 94 SS *212-213*; *Vanellesbury v. Stern* (1490) Y.B. Hil. 5 Hen. VII, fo. 15, pl.6; CP 40/913, m.310; B. & M. 533 n.20 (leather made into shoes); *Anon.* (1560) B. & M. 318. See also 94 SS *212*.

[17] E.g. *Phylpot v. Frenche* (1480) CP 40/872, m.429 (demurrer as to leaded glass in window); *Bodon v. Vampage* (1506) Keil. 88; 94 SS *216* n.4 (sub nom. *Henry's Case*); CP 40/978, m.328 (demurrer as to oven cemented to floor). See also 94 SS *216-217*.

[18] *Anon.* (1591) Yale Law Sch. MS. G.R29.7, p. 444; *Smoote v. Futball* (1593) CUL MS. Dd. 10. 51, fo. 7v; Poph. 33, pl.2.

[19] Y.B. Mich. 18 Edw. III, p. 232; 102 SS 24 (piglets); *Male v. Hole* (1472) Y.B. Pas. 12 Edw. IV, fo. 4, pl.10; CP 40/842, m. 303 (cygnets). Where animals are leased, however, the young belong to the lessee: *Wood v. Ash* (1586) Godb. 112.

[20] *Anon.* (1560) B. & M. 318.

[21] From the law French *embler*, to sow.

[22] *Pope v. See* (1534) Spelman Rep. (93 SS) 215; Port Nbk (102 SS) 22.

Modes of Transfer

A more usual mode of acquiring personal property than occupation was by transfer from another person. There have been three principal modes of transferring property in chattels, two by consent of the previous owner and one by operation of law on the death of the owner. It was sometimes said in the old books that property could also be acquired by trespass. This may have resulted from failing to distinguish property and possession; certainly a wrongful taker acquired possession, which would be good enough title against all but the person from whom he took. The victim of the taking, however, retained a property as against the taker, which entitled him to take it back or to recover it by appeal of larceny.[23]   Nevertheless, if the victim elected to bring an action of trespass and recovered damages, he barred himself from these remedies and thereby effectively waived the property so that it vested in the wrongdoer by estoppel.[24]

GIFT

Chattels could always be transferred by manual delivery. The Civil law regarded transfer by delivery (*traditio*) as taking effect by the law of nature, and the reasoning behind it is certainly simple. If property depended on occupation, it could be transferred by changing the occupant. But delivery did not itself pass the property, because it might simply separate the property from the physical custody, as where a master entrusted his silver to a servant. Property therefore passed upon delivery only if there was the intention to give or sell it to the recipient. In the case of gift, delivery was at first the only acceptable method of transfer. There is an analogy with the insistence on livery of seisin for the conveyance of freehold; and the consequence was similar. If a person out of possession made a gift of goods, it was no more effective than a transfer of right to land by someone without seisin. This analogy with land was sometimes drawn by medieval lawyers,[25] and between the thirteenth and early fifteenth centuries we find numerous references to seisin of chattels.[26] But the analogy was never pressed too far; by the

---

23   See *Anon.* (1510) B. & M. 528; *Anon.* (1560) B. & M. 318; and, for the appeal, p. 440, post.

24   Y.B. Pas. 19 Hen. VI, fo. 65, pl.5, per Newton CJ; Mich. 6 Hen. VII, fo. 8, pl.4, per Kebell sjt.

25   See Y.B. Mich. 6 Hen. VII, fo. 9, pl.4, per Bryan CJ; *Anon.* (1492) Y.B. Trin. 10 Hen. VII, fo. 27, pl.13 (misdated in print); Port Nbk (102 SS) 151.

26   See Maitland, 'The Seisin of Chattels', 1 LQR 324; Ames, 'The Disseisin of Chattels', 3 HLR 23 (repr. in *Lectures*, p. 172). Cf. Littleton, *Tenures*, s.324, who says that 'seisin' is only used of land, and 'possession' of chattels.

end of the fourteenth century a gift of chattels could be effected by deed.[27]

The discovery of ancient coins suggests that sale, the exchange of property for money, is as old as English history. It does not follow that a sale necessarily passed any property to the buyer independently of delivery. Indeed, it is almost certain that at first it did not do so; a sale might explain why a subsequent delivery passed property, but the property did not pass by contract alone.[28] Here the law of personalty began to diverge from that of realty in the fifteenth century. The buyer who had paid for goods might well prefer to sue for the goods (or their value) rather than seek the return of his money. Legal ingenuity found the means of achieving this in the fifteenth century by treating the seller as a bailee. This sounds strange; but in its fullest form the fiction was modest. The buyer would allege that there had been a momentary delivery to him at the time of the sale, and that he had then bailed the goods back to the seller for safekeeping pending removal.[29] This does not seem blatantly untruthful; many buyers would have handled the goods at the time of the sale and then handed them back. But it was thought necessary to present the facts as a delivery, since that was the only recognised mode of transfer, and since detinue clearly lay on a bailment. If we think of abstract ownership, it seems a long mental leap from that position to the view that some 'property' or 'title' could pass independently of the physical transfer; but there was no obvious reason why a different kind of property should not arise by contract, in the sense of a contractual right to have property delivered. The idea was already present in the action of debt, in that the buyer who paid for fungibles, such as a quarter of barley, could bring debt for the goods if they were not delivered. It would have seemed strange to deny a similar remedy if the barley was in a specific sack; and, since the same writ would apply in this case,[30] there was no compulsion to avoid the same solution. In fact, the contractual claim had been available to the buyer –

---

[27] See *Pynchoun v. Geldeford* (1385) Y.B. Hil. 8 Ric. II, p. 215, pl.17.

[28] The contract might, however, permit the buyer to help himself by taking the goods before delivery: *Bakere v. Londeneys* (1384) Y.B. Mich. 8 Ric. II, p. 144, pl.31.

[29] Milsom, 77 LQR at 274, gives examples from the 1480s and 1490s; before then buyers may have got away with a simple bailment count. The device was out of use by 1511.

[30] Debt for fungible goods had the same wording as detinue. It alleged a detainer but not an owing, and was therefore said to be 'in the *detinet*'.

without distinguishing debt and detinue – since the twelfth century.[31] Three hundred years later, when the matter was analysed in property terms, it would be said that property did not pass by sale if the goods were not specific,[32] while in the case of specific goods a kind of property might be thought to pass, since detinue would lie for them.[33] However, property would only pass under an executory sale if there was payment, or part payment ('earnest'), and a day was appointed for completion.[34]

The distinction between contract and property was of little significance in this context so long as there was some remedy for the buyer against the seller; it became of practical importance only if the chattel was destroyed or stolen between contract and delivery. But it was axiomatic that a sale could not pass more than the seller had: *nemo dat quod non habet*. Sale by a non-owner passed no property. At some point it was nevertheless desirable that the claim of the original owner should give way to the demands of commerce, and to the expectations of bona fide purchasers of goods in the open market. The law therefore came, by the fifteenth century, to protect honest sales which took place openly in a market or fair, to the extent that the purchaser thereby acquired a good title against a previous owner;[35] only if the goods had been stolen could the sale be upset, and then only if the thief had been successfully appealed of larceny or (after 1529) convicted on indictment.[36] To have the effect of divesting the property from the original owner, the sale had to take place in 'market overt': that is, openly in a market or fair established by royal grant or prescription. The rationale of the doctrine was that the owner could protect himself by going to the market to see if his goods were on display; and therefore a

---

31 *Glanvill*, x.14.

32 *Orwell v. Mortoft* (1505) B. & M. 406 at 408, per Kingsmill J; p. 389, ante.

33 See *Shipton v. Dogge* (1442) B. & M. 391 at 394, per Fortescue CJ; *Tailboys v. Sherman* (1443) B. & M. 395 at 396, per Danby sjt.

34 Adgore's reading (*c.* 1490) B. & M. 482 at 483; *Southwall v. Huddelston* (1523) Y.B. Hil. 14 Hen. VIII, fo. 22, pl.6; Port Nbk (102 SS) 110. The payment of earnest to clinch a sale is mentioned in *Glanvill*, x.14; but it is not clear whether there was any remedy against a defaulting seller.

35 Recognised as a justification in trespass: Y.B. Mich. 9 Hen. VI, fo. 45, pl.6, per Paston J; *Rande v. Bothe* (1451) CP 40/762, m. 148; *Prior of Llanthony v. Courteyne* (1472) Y.B. Pas. 12 Edw. IV, fo. 1, pl.3, and fo. 8, pl.22; CP 40/842, m.401. See also *Anon.* (1471) B. & M. 511, per Fairfax sjt. Cf. *Britton*, vol. I, p. 59, who says such a sale does not divest the property.

36 Revesting of property after conviction on indictment was introduced by Stat. 21 Hen. VIII, c.11. It was abolished in 1827; but restitution orders may now be made under the Theft Act 1968 (c.60), s.28.

sale in a secret place, in or out of the market, did not work.[37] For the same reason, a sale in a shop did not have the same effect as a sale in a market, because the true owner had no right to enter the shop in search of his goods without the shopkeeper's consent. But the city of London asserted, and still enjoys, a custom that every shop within the city is a market for the purpose of the rule.[38] Similar privileges were claimed for other cities, but liberal extension was refused because of the hardship to owners. Another way of dealing with the problem of sales by non-owners was to require registration of title to certain kinds of goods. An attempt was made in 1555 to introduce compulsory registration of title on the sale of horses, but it was ultimately unsuccessful.[39] In four centuries few changes have been made in the law of market overt; but the principle of protecting those who deal in good faith with non-owners in the open market has received some statutory extension.[40]

SUCCESSION ON DEATH[41]

Before the Norman conquest, English customs of succession seem to have been designed to provide for the whole family of the deceased by dividing his estate into aliquot parts or shares, usually halves or thirds. Under the influence of Christianity, the deceased was also given a 'part' to dispose of by testament (or through his representatives) for the good of his soul; the other two parts went to the widow and children. This system survived Norman feudalism in the case of movable property, and survives in Scotland to the present day. Under the early common law there was a writ, similar to debt, called *de rationabili parte bonorum*, whereby the widow and children could claim their reasonable parts. In the thirteenth century, however, the spiritual jurisdiction won control of testate and intestate succession to movable estates. Thereafter questions about testaments and parts fell to the Church courts.

---

[37] *Sir Gervase Clifton's Case* (1600) BL MS. Add. 25203, ff. 63v, 279. Property would not pass if the buyer was privy to the wrongful taking: *Case of Thorns* (1466) B. & M. 327 at 329, per Danby CJ.

[38] *Abbot of St Osyth v. Hayford* (1447) CP 40/746, m. 323 (alleged custom of ubiquitous market every day, and sale in shop); *Mounteagle v. Countess of Worcester* (1555) B. & M. 531 at 532, per Dyer sjt; *Palmer v. Wolley* (1595) Cro. Eliz. 454; *Case of Market Overt* (Newgate, 1596) 5 Co. Rep. 83; 1 And. 344; Poph. 84, pl.11; Moore K.B. 360 (case of the bishop of Worcester's silver). Cf. *Prior of Llanthony v. Courteyne* (1472), note 35, ante (alleged custom that every *street* is a common market for all wares every day).

[39] Sale of Horses Act 1555, 2 & 3 Ph. & Mar., c.7; *Fry's Case* (1584) B. & M. 274. The statute was repealed in 1968.

[40] Beginning with the Factors Act 1823, 4 Geo. IV, c.83.

[41] Chattels could pass on death in other ways than those here described: e.g. on the death of a pawnor before redemption, the property passed to the pawnee.

The Church encouraged men to make wills, even to the extent of disposing of all their movables, no doubt because testators were likely to be more impartial than administrators. As a result of this policy, the fixed parts of the widow and children could be claimed only if the deceased died wholly or partly intestate, or if a local custom preserved the older principle restricting testation to the deceased's part.[42] Before 1600, the province of Canterbury (excepting Wales and London) came to permit complete freedom of testation, whereas the province of York adhered to the old system of parts until 1692. Freedom of testation was not universal in England until 1724, when it was extended to the city of London.[43] Probate of wills, and litigation related thereto, belonged to the Church courts until 1857.[44]

The administration of intestates' estates also belonged to the ecclesiastical authorities,[45] and in 1357 it was enacted that bishops were to commit their responsibilities in this connection to administrators, who were made capable of suing and being sued in the same way as executors.[46] In the course of time, partly through inefficiency and partly through interference from the lay courts, the Church courts lost effective control over administrators, who usually divided the property among themselves once they had paid off any debts. After a particularly scandalous case of 1666 brought the matter to the king's personal notice, a statute was passed in 1670 to end this anarchic situation by laying down a definite scheme of distribution which administrators were obliged to observe.[47] The thirds rule was incorporated into this scheme, but the dead man's part abolished. The rules for distribution have since been adjusted many times by statute, though the rules are of necessity arbitrary.   One of the most important later reforms was the reintroduction of automatic provision for close members of the deceased's family who had been cut out by will. The extension of free testation had led to the harsh result that widows and children could be

---

42   E.g. *Anon.* (1330) 98 SS 637 (custom of Northamptonshire); *Rigge v. Burgham* (1443) CP 40/730, m.416 (custom of Westmorland); *Scotsald v. Dutton* (1448) CP 40/750, m.559 (custom of Yorkshire): all actions *de rationabili parte* by children.

43   See H. Horwitz, 2 LHR 223.

44   See p. 152, ante.

45   Magna Carta 1215, cl.27. Cf. *Glanvill*, vii.16, who says that an intestate's goods go to his lord.

46   Stat. 31 Edw. III, sess.i, c.11. Administration was normally committed to the next of kin.

47   Statute of Distributions 1670, 22 & 23 Car. II, c.10.

completely cut off by their husband or father making a will in favour of someone else. It was over two centuries before the remedy was found.[48]

Termination of Private Property in Chattels

Since chattels do not necessarily have an owner, property in them may in some circumstances come to an end.

RETURN TO NATURAL STATE

Animals which are wild by nature (*ferae naturae*) belong to humans only so long as they are in human control. If they are set free, or escape, and have no inclination to return to their captor, then property in them ceases and they become no one's (*res nullius*). The same principle applies to water poured into a river, or to combustion, whereby chattels are converted into fumes which diffuse in the atmosphere. It does not, of course, follow in any of these cases that the person who allows the escape may not remain liable in tort for any damage subsequently done.

DEODAND

A strange and seemingly irrational principle which survived into the common law was that which required the forfeiture of objects which occasioned, or were the instruments of, a man's death. The rule may have originated in barbaric notions of retribution; but by the thirteenth century it was no longer so understood, and was kept up simply as a royal prerogative. Chattels seized as 'deodands' were supposed to be appropriated to charitable purposes – this was the gift 'pro Deo' – by the king's justices or the king's almoner. At its most equitable, the deodand system provided a primitive and haphazard form of insurance for the dependents of the deceased;[49] but in many cases the right to deodand was acquired by private franchise-owners, and then the loss of offending objects could be very unjust to the innocent owner. The most valuable types of deodand commonly seized were horses and vehicles involved in fatal accidents. The doctrine was not finally abrogated until 1846, when a general awareness of its absurdity was aroused by its application to railway engines.[50]

---

48 Inheritance (Family Provision) Act 1938, 1 & 2 Geo. VI, c.45.

49 For instances in 1221 of gifts 'pro Deo' to the widow of the deceased, see 59 SS 342 no. 754, 536 no. 1222.

50 See Holdsworth HEL, vol. II, p. 47; H. Smith, 11 AJLH 389; E. Cawthon, 33 AJLH 137.

ABANDONMENT AND LOSS

The common law has never clearly decided whether a person can divest himself of property by waiver or abandonment. *Bracton*, following Roman law, allowed the possibility; others denied it.[51] The question is rarely of practical importance, because the first finder of a derelict chattel may be regarded as a donee acquiring by constructive delivery; before anyone else takes it up, the first owner is obviously at liberty to retake it. A mere accidental loss, without intention to derelinquish, certainly cannot alter property; this principle was the basis of the 'trover' counts in detinue and trespass on the case. Even a deliberate waiver of all enjoyment of a thing, for instance by burying it in a grave, does not divest the owner of his property.[52]

The finder of lost goods acquired a property against all the world except the loser, because the law would not, in an action between two parties, try to discover the absolute title but only the relative rights of the parties.[53] The finder who appropriated goods was not considered a thief until the early nineteenth century, when the notion of larceny by finding evolved.[54]

Certain categories of lost property belonged to the Crown by the royal prerogative, and these could only be taken by private owners if they had the royal perquisite by virtue of a franchise. Of these it is said in *Bracton* that, although by natural law the property should go to the finder, by the *jus gentium* it went to the prince. The best known instance is treasure trove. Gold and silver artefacts, coin or bullion, if hidden by a person unknown but not abandoned, belong to the Crown unless and until the true owner makes good his claim; and they may be seized into the queen's hands by a coroner. Wreck of sea belonged to the Crown unless the owner claimed the goods within a year and a day.[55] The rhetorical Elizabethan explanation for this ancient rule was that it compensated the queen for her expensive naval obligations.[56] Estrays, which are lost cattle or valuable domestic beasts, belong to the Crown if proclamations are made in public places and the owner does not claim

---

51 *Bracton*, vol. II, pp. 41, 338; contra, St German, *Doctor and Student* (91 SS), p. 292.

52 *Haynes' Case* (1613) 12 Co. Rep. 113.

53 *Armory v. Delamirie* (1722) B. & M. 547.

54 See p. 608, post.

55 Statute of Westminster I 1275, c.4; Prerogativa Regis, c.11.

56 *Constable v. Gamble* (1601) 5 Co. Rep. 106.

them within a year and a day. Waifs – goods waived by a thief in flight – could be seized in a similar way by the Crown.[57]

Interests in Chattels

Movable wealth could not be settled on a succession of owners, because the common law did not allow future estates to be created in chattels.[58] A gift of a chattel for an hour was a gift for ever.[59] But a lesser kind of interest could be conferred by the contract of hire, as on a lease of sheep or furniture. There is an analogy here with the lease of land, which conferred possession but not freehold or seisin; and later lawyers explained it in similar terms as a separation of ownership from possession. It is unclear how far this dichotomy was known in medieval times. To some extent ownership and possession coincided in the medieval concept of 'property' (*proprietas*), a word which came to be used only in connection with movables. Property arose from occupation and was generally transferred by delivery; it went hand in hand with possession. There was no such thing as *dominium*, absolute abstract ownership or right. The most a person out of possession could claim was a better right to possession than the person in possession. Thus, if *A* lent his horse to *B* for a week, *A* retained a property which he could enforce against *B* and against anyone who took the horse from *B*; but *B* also had property, which enabled him to maintain an action against anyone other than *A*. In this example, *A*'s position is higher than *B*'s, and if the terminology of property needed an element of relativity it could be modified by saying that *B* had a 'special property'.[60]

The relationship between property and mere possession was seen most clearly where there was some dealing between two parties. There is a natural distinction between handing over a thing with the intention that all the property should pass to the recipient (gift or sale), and handing it over with the intention that the recipient should have only the temporary use or profits of the thing (loan or hire) or should hold it merely as a pawn or deposit. These latter transactions were all forms of 'bailment', the common-law name for a transaction whereby a thing is delivered (*baillé*) on the basis that the bailor shall retain his property.

---

[57] *Foxley v. Annesley* (1601) 5 Co. Rep. 109, Cro. Eliz. 693. But property did not pass before seizure: Port Nbk (102 SS) 129-130.

[58] Unless they were (like title-deeds) associated with land: p. 428, ante.

[59] *Anon.* (1548) B. & M. 185 at 186. The same expression was used by Serjeant Broke in 1519: 94 SS *218*.

[60] Y.B. Hil. 21 Hen. VII, fo. 15, pl.23, per Fyneux CJ.

But the terms property and possession were, even here, used loosely and interchangeably in the year-book period; as against the rest of the world, both bailor and bailee had a kind of property, because either could sue a stranger who took the goods. Situations can readily be envisaged where a similar separation of property and possession might occur without a bailment; for instance, where goods are stolen, or lost and then found by a stranger. Even in these cases, however, the terms 'property' and 'possession' can describe no more than the relationship between the people involved; they mean only that the proprietor has a superior right to that of the possessor.

Two refinements to this simple distinction were made in the Tudor period. First it was decided, shortly before 1500, that the physical custody of a chattel could be entrusted to another without loss of possession; the purpose and effect of this new doctrine was that a servant or personal attendant having control of his master's goods could be convicted of their theft.[61] The second refinement, which apparently arose from the interpretation put upon an inconclusive case of 1459, was that a distinction could be made between the property in a chattel and the use and occupation of it. Whereas the property could not be settled, the use of a chattel could be limited to a succession of persons, and such a settlement would bind at least the first executors of the settlor. The analogy with the use of the land is obvious. The new doctrine enabled movables to be entailed as heirlooms, by devising the use, notwithstanding that the 'property' went on death to the executors.[62] But no one could prevent the possessor for the time being from destroying the chattel, and with it the future expectations under the settlement.

Early Restitutionary Proceedings

The earliest remedy for the person who found his goods in the hands of another was the appeal of theft. Although this was a criminal proceeding, in the sense that a convicted defendant was liable to hang, it also had the effect of restoring the stolen goods to the appellor. The claimant was supposed to demand his goods from the possessor; if the latter refused, it was evidently proper to proceed against him as a felon.[63]

---

61   See p. 607, post.

62   *Glover and Brown v. Forden* (1459) Y.B. Trin. 37 Hen. VI, fo. 30, pl.11; CP 40/794, m.291 (cited Dyer 359); *Anon.* (1572) B. & M. 187 at 188, per Dyer CJ. Bequests of chattels in tail are found in the early Tudor period: 94 SS *219-220*. For the settlement of the use of a chattel real, see p. 343, ante.

63   *Bracton*, vol. II, pp. 425-426.

The appellee would be arrested together with the goods in question, and would either show that the goods had always been his or would say how he bought them. If he could prove that he bought them in open market, he would be acquitted and the goods restored to whichever of the parties established the better right. If he alleged that he bought them privately from X, X was vouched to warranty and had to take over the defence; if X denied the sale, the proceedings turned into an appeal by the original defendant against X.

In cases where goods were taken by way of distress, without any assumption of property, the proper remedy was not the appeal but the action of replevin. The effect of bringing replevin was to have the goods restored pending trial of the right to distrain.[64] There might be other reasons for not wishing to proceed criminally, not least of which was the danger of trial by battle and the possibility of losing the goods to the Crown if the appeal failed. The claimant could therefore drop the words of felony and proceed civilly. There is mention in the thirteenth century of a civil claim for a lost chattel (*de re adirata*), but no one is very sure what form it took; it may have been a petition in eyre, or even at gaol delivery, or perhaps a complaint of trespass.[65] But no proceeding of that description could be brought in the central courts by writ, and so the claim for a lost chattel was temporarily shut out from the common law.

Detinue

The remedy ordained in the register of writs for the recovery of chattels was the writ of debt or detinue. There was no distinction in the wording of the writ between debt and detinue for goods: the writ commanded the sheriff to order the defendant to yield up to the plaintiff the chattels which he unjustly detained from him (*praecipe D quod reddat P catalla quae injuste detinet*). We have already noted that the distinction between owing and owning only became important if the defendant sought to excuse himself because of some calamity. If a debtor lost his money, he continued to owe the sum because he could not identify any specific coins as representing the debt; the debt itself, unlike coins, could not be lost or stolen. The same was true of someone who 'owed' fungibles; if the vendor of unspecified wheat had his entire crop destroyed, still the debt remained, because any other wheat would do as well. On the other hand, if a borrowed horse dropped dead, ran away or was stolen, there

---

[64] See pp. 271-272, ante.

[65] *Britton* vol. I, pp. 57, 68, seems to treat it as trespass.

was some reason for the bailee (if not at fault) to claim to be discharged; he was no longer detaining the bailor's property. Such distinctions emerged in fourteenth-century pleading.[66] But even when detinue came to be thought of as a distinct legal entity, its technical name for some formal purposes continued to be a 'plea of debt'.[67] The writ itself did not indicate why the plaintiff claimed the goods, whether his claim was contractual or proprietary; and in time the form of action encompassed both kinds of claim. But, according to fourteenth-century lawyers, it was nevertheless necessary for the plaintiff in detinue to show a 'privity' between himself and the defendant, something which made the detainer wrongful. The clearest case was where the plaintiff had bailed the goods directly to the defendant.

DETINUE ON A BAILMENT

Whether the claim in detinue on a bailment was based on contract or property is perhaps an anachronistic question; it was both, the bailment being a bilateral transaction and the detinue a contractually neutral withholding of possession.[68] The more important question in practice was whether the bailor or the bailee stood the risk of loss or theft. There is less discussion of this than might be expected from the commonness of the situation, because in most cases the law was obscured behind the general plea 'He does not withhold' (*Non detinet*). We have noticed that fourteenth-century pleadings seem to have assumed a defence of accidental loss or destruction. In the fifteenth century a stricter theory came into vogue, that the bailee was only excused if the loss was caused by act of God or the king's enemies. The reason given was that the bailee in other cases of despoliation had the right to sue the wrongdoer in trespass; and, since it would have been unjust to allow him to keep the damages himself, he ought to be liable in turn to his bailor. On the same principle, it was argued that theft should only excuse the bailee if the identity of the thief was unknown, or if the thief had been hanged and his property forfeited, because then the bailee's right of action would be useless. But the better opinion was that even those circumstances provided no defence, because there had been a remedy in law if not in fact. The bailee could only excuse himself in detinue by pleading theft or loss if the bailment had been made on terms which excused him in such circumstances; for instance, if the bailment

---

[66] See *Bowdon v. Pelleter* (1315) B. & M. 265 (theft); *Anon.* (1339) B. & M. 267 (accidental destruction); *Anon.* (1355) B. & M. 275 n.7 (theft).

[67] Warrants of attorney were so entered: Milsom, 77 LQR at 273; and see 105 SS 86.

[68] See the discussion in *Mortimer v. Mortimer* (1292) B. & M. 264.

were to keep the goods with the same care as he would bestow on his own.[69]

The bailee's liability thus became so stringent that further encouragement was given to the general issue and wager of law. In all cases of theft or loss, the plea of *Non detinet* was truthful if disingenuous. Indeed, the bailee who drank up or gave away a barrel of wine committed to his safe-keeping could truthfully, though at great danger to his soul, say that he no longer detained it.[70] It is far from clear whether the common-law courts had sufficient control over the consciences of bailees to prevent them waging their law in such cases. Justice might suggest the development of a doctrine of constructive detaining, so as to prevent the bailee relying on his own wrongdoing, but there was no procedure whereby the question could be raised as a point of law; it could only be a matter of exhortation for a man about to swear an oath.[71] On any view, detinue would not lie against a bailee who had actually returned the goods, but in a damaged condition. In such cases, where the damage was irrecoverable in detinue, or where a bailee had wrongfully put himself beyond the reach of detinue, the remedy would have to be sought in trespass.

DETINUE AGAINST A THIRD HAND

The first extensions of detinue to reach defendants other than bailees were to the executors of bailees; and at the beginning of the fourteenth century this was the furthest reach of the action on a bailment, since the courts still required the plaintiff to show some 'privity'.[72] Detinue was also allowed against third parties for title-deeds, because the claim followed the real property to which the deeds related; and here it was suggested as early as 1312 that it might equally lie against a finder of the deeds as against a disseisee.[73] By the middle of the century the concept of privity seems, however, to have been abandoned. Even if the defendant was the bailee's executor, it was not necessary to say so; all the plaintiff had to show in his count was that the chattel had left his

---

[69] See *Southcote v. Bennet* (1601) B. & M. 274, Cro. Eliz. 815 (theft no defence, without special terms). Holt CJ later condemned Coke's report of this case: B. & M. 373. But it is borne out by the MSS.

[70] Y.B. Hil. 20 Hen. VI, fo. 16, pl.2, per Brown ('If you bail to me a tun of wine, and perchance I drink it up with other good companions, you cannot have detinue for it because it is not in being').

[71] The earliest reported examples are late: *Fry's Case* (1584) and *Anon.* (1595) B. & M. 274.

[72] Y.B. Trin. 16 Edw. II (1678 ed.), p. 490.

[73] *Lyndeseye v. Suth* (1312) 34 SS 167, per Scrope sjt (but denied in the headnote). Cf. *Anon.* (1339) B. & M. 267 (bailment by plaintiff's father as her guardian).

possession by bailment and afterwards came into the hands of the defendant (*devenit ad manus defendentis*).[74] The point of telling the story was to establish the relative right of the parties, and also to establish the identity of the thing claimed; there was no need to introduce any new concept of ownership, since the count showed how the thing had come to the defendant without him acquiring a better right than the plaintiff.

The details in the *devenit ad manus* count were arguably material to the plaintiff's case and could therefore be challenged by the defendant. This made it a perilous mode of pleading, since the plaintiff was not often in a position to know exactly what had happened to goods after they had left his possession, or that of his testator. It might also raise questions of law which the courts preferred to avoid. For both reasons, pleaders were eager to abandon the *devenit ad manus* count and find a less vulnerable way of making a claim against third parties.

DETINUE SUR TROVER

The solution was found by the end of the fourteenth century. The plaintiff simply alleged that he had lost the chattel, and that the defendant had found it and unjustly detained it.[75] A finder could not resist a claim by the loser; and it was not too dishonest to speak of a loss even where the plaintiff suspected a more devious history. The *trover* count perhaps consciously represented the claim for *res adirata* when the mysterious older action disappeared from use. Since it conveniently focused attention on the property, the courts would not allow the defendant to traverse the loss and finding unless he could show that he had acquired the property by a recognised means.[76] The count on a *trover* therefore became the usual form of count in detinue against anyone who was not a bailee, and was in many cases fictitious. Liability in detinue *sur trover* was less stringent than in detinue on a bailment, because there was no contract or privity to impose a strict obligation on the finder. Accidental loss of the chattel by the defendant would be a genuine defence, because the only obligation which could be imposed on a finder arose from his having possession; as soon as he

---

74   *Wagworth v. Halyday* (1355) B. & M. 267.
75   *Anon.* (1389) Y.B. Mich. 13 Ric. II, p. 56, pl.11. Cf. detinue for a stray ass: *Anon.* (1370) Y.B. Pas. 44 Edw. III, fo. 14, pl.30.
76   *Carles v. Malpas* (1455) Y.B. Trin. 33 Hen. VI, fo. 26, pl.12; CP 40/778, m.482; Fifoot HSCL, p. 42. Carles set out the details but ended with a *trover*; issue was joined on the title, but there was a nonsuit.

lost possession, for whatever reason, the nexus between the parties dissolved away.[77]

SHORTCOMINGS OF DETINUE

We have seen how a central theme in the history of contract was the supplementation, and then the replacement, of *praecipe* actions by actions on the case. The history of the law of personal property provides a close parallel, because detinue was subject to similar shortcomings. A *praecipe* action was barred by performance, even by an imperfect performance, and so in detinue damages were only awarded if the goods were not restored at all. The bailee who starved a horse to death, or who rode it further than agreed, or who returned other goods in a damaged state, was not liable in detinue. The plaintiff in detinue could not count on a bailment or loss of the thing demanded if it was no longer the same thing as he had bailed or lost, as where it had been made part of something else or fashioned into something new. And on the same principle it was arguable that he could not allege a detaining of something which no longer existed at all. Above all, the availability of the general issue, and the proof of the issue by wager of law, meant that even where legal thinking seemed to favour the plaintiff, the defendant in effect acted as his own judge. Not only was the substantive law stunted and suppressed by the archaic procedure, but plaintiffs were driven to seek better remedies.

Trespass and Case for Chattels

The solution, as in the law of contract, was found by turning to the law of wrongs. Trespass for taking away goods (*de bonis asportatis*) was the 'civil' counterpart of larceny, and although it gave damages rather than specific restitution, the difference was not likely to matter in many cases. Writs of trespass became an established remedy in the thirteenth century, and there were variant formulae for destroying or damaging goods. But, as we have seen, such writs could at first only be obtained if the interference with the chattels could be described as *vi et armis*. Merely detaining goods was not a forcible trespass.[78] The bailee who wrongly kept goods bailed to him could not be said to commit a trespass with force and arms, because he had been given possession by

---

[77] *Anon.* (1535) B. & M. 272; *Anon.* (1572) B. & M. 273.
[78] *Knoston v. Bassyngburn* (1329) B. & M. 303.

the bailor and had appropriated the goods without force.[79] Neither could a finder, unless he damaged the thing found, or knew the identity of the owner at the time of the 'finding' and took it nevertheless. In the fourteenth century, such wrongs as these may have been remedied in trespass by the expedient of bringing a *vi et armis* writ and hoping that the defendant would not object.[80] But the need for such an unsatisfactory fiction was ended in the 1360s, when it was decided that writs of trespass might be brought on a special case instead of force and arms.

The 'case' on which a plaintiff might rely in complaining of a wrong to chattels might incorporate any number of tortious concepts, such as deceit, negligence, breach of an undertaking, or conversion. Later history was to separate these out as distinct actions, according to the element which predominated as the gist of the action. But the process of separation did not occur until the sixteenth century; when it did, the rules of law concerning personal property were distributed between the law of contract and what came to be called the torts of conversion and negligence.

UNDERTAKINGS TO KEEP OR CARRY SAFELY

The commonest of the earlier actions on the case against bailees were of the kind typified by the *Humber Ferry Case*.[81] A bailor would count that he had delivered the goods to the defendant to look after (*tradidisset ad salvo et secure custodiendum*), or for some specified purpose such as carriage, and that the defendant so neglected them that they perished or sustained damage. Sometimes the pleadings alleged an undertaking (*assumpsit*) as well, but this was not essential in the case of bailees. In this context the word *assumpsit* signified the assumption of physical custody rather than an express promise, and an assertion of a bailment was synonymous. When, however, the action of *assumpsit* came to be thought of as contractual, some confusion arose as to the nature of the action against bailees. At the beginning of the sixteenth century, the courts clearly laid down that the undertaking was not the gist of the action and could not be traversed.[82] But when the doctrine of consideration evolved in the Elizabethan period, some thought a bailee could only be charged in *assumpsit* if consideration had been given for his undertaking. In order to avoid this objection, some plaintiffs relied

79 *Taumbes v. Skegness* (1312) B. & M. 299; *Toteshalle v. Orfevre* (1321) B. & M. 301.

80 E.g. *Knoston v. Bassyngburn* (1329) B. & M. 303.

81 *Bukton v. Tounesende* (1348), p. 375, ante.

82 *Bourgchier v. Cheseman* (1504) B. & M. 409 n.7; 94 SS *249*; *Rycroft v. Gamme* (1523) Spelman Rep. (93 SS) 3; *Warton v. Ashepole* (1524) ibid. 4.

on the delivery of the goods as being in itself a consideration; but this was plainly inadequate under contractual theory because the defendant derived no benefit from the mere custody, and the promise to give up the goods on demand was *nudum pactum* because it was no more than he was bound to do by law.[83] On this view, a deposit of goods was different from a loan of goods or money, for in these cases the use of the goods or money would be a benefit to the borrower and therefore good consideration for an undertaking to return or repay.

This unnecessary intrusion of the principles of contract into the matter forced lawyers to distinguish bailees for reward from gratuitous bailees. The former were liable in contract, and were therefore strictly liable unless the contract was to take no more than reasonable care. The latter were liable for negligence; and in an action for negligence, even if the word *assumpsit* was used, there was no need to show consideration.[84] The position of the gratuitous bailee was fully explained by Holt CJ in *Coggs v. Barnard* in 1703.[85] The defendant, William Barnard, had undertaken gratuitously to move some casks of brandy from a cellar in Brook's Market to another cellar in Water Street; in performing this task he so negligently set them down that one of the casks was staved and 150 gallons of brandy spilt. It was objected that no consideration was shown for the undertaking, and that *assumpsit* therefore did not lie. The King's Bench, after a full debate, dismissed this argument. First, the negligence was itself actionable since it was a deceit to the plaintiff, who had trusted the defendant to be careful. Second, the word *assumpsit* did not in this type of case denote a future promise, but 'an actual entry upon the thing, and taking the trust upon himself'. Holt CJ took the opportunity in his judgment to restate the law of bailment in Romanist terms, borrowed from *Bracton*, as a way of escaping from the effects of formalism. The result of his labour was, as he said, to stir up many new points 'which wiser heads in time may settle'. It also encouraged the view that bailment was a transaction sui generis, not dependent on the general rules of either contract or tort.

NEGLIGENCE, CONVERSION AND DETINUE

The kinds of action on the case just mentioned lay against a bailee for negligent keeping, but there were other cases where liability could be founded on a different kind of wrong. If the bailee of a deed tore off the

83 *Riches v. Bridges* (1602) Cro. Eliz. 883; Yelv. 4; *Pickas v. Guile* (1608) Yelv. 128.
84 *Powtney v. Walton* (1597) B. & M. 370.
85 B. & M. 370 at 375-376. Lord Raymond spells the name 'Bernard', but it is Barnard in the record.

seal to invalidate it, or the bailee of a horse rode it so hard that it died, or the bailee of a gown cut it into pieces, the bailor's complaint was not of carelessness but of deliberate damage, and the special case was adjusted accordingly. It was in actions of this nature that allegations of 'conversion' first made their appearance. The bailee of coins who spent them, or the bailee of goods who sold them and spent the proceeds, was liable not because he had 'so negligently kept the goods that they were lost' but because he had wrongly taken them and 'scheming to defraud the plaintiff converted them to his own use'. In 1500 this was just one of several ways of framing a complaint against someone who had undertaken to look after goods; but in the next fifty years the action on the case for conversion grew into a general remedy which replaced detinue.

The actions against bailees for damaging goods entrusted to their care filled gaps in the old action of detinue, but did not overlap with it. Their justification, indeed, was that they lay for damage which could not be recovered in the *praecipe* action. But there were compelling reasons for extending the remedy to acts of conversion, and in the earliest cases there were attempts to conceal any overlap with detinue. If a bailee destroyed the thing bailed by converting it to his own use, as by drinking a barrel of wine, he was liable in case precisely because detinue was unavailable; and, if that had not been clear law before, it was proffered as law in the later fifteenth century in order to justify the use of case and thereby oust wager of law. In 1472 a sub-bailee of gold cloth and rich embroideries cut some of them up, and was sued by the executor of the bailor both in detinue *sur trover* and in an action on the case for damaging the cloth; both actions stood undecided for three years, but the nature of the legal difficulty may be gathered from the sources. The plaintiff apparently argued that by cutting up the material and making it into clothes the defendant had altered the property by *specificatio*; therefore, since detinue was barred, an action on the case was proper.[86] Shortly afterwards, in 1479, case was brought against a sub-bailee of silver cups who had broken them up and made them into silver vessels of a different shape and converted them to his own use. Again it was argued that detinue was unavailable, and the case of gold cloth was cited. Choke J accepted the plaintiff's argument; but Bryan CJ held that detinue was the appropriate action, and that it was improper to use case in order to oust wager of law.[87] The judges agreed in the

---

86 *Rilston v. Holbek* (1472) B. & M. 524. The year-book reports only the pleading in detinue; the argument as to case appears from the citation in 1479 (B. & M. 527).

87 *Calwodelegh v. John* (1479) B. & M. 526. No judgment was entered.

abstract that the defendant was liable if the facts as stated were true; but they differed as to whether in practice the decision should be left to his conscience. The reports then fall silent on this question until the beginning of the sixteenth century; but by then the action on the case against a bailee for conversion was as firmly established as *assumpsit*, at any rate in the King's Bench. The conversion, often aggravated by an allegation of deceit, was treated as a tort distinct from the mere detaining of goods.

Trover and Conversion

The earliest actions on the case for conversion were brought against bailees, and there was no thought at first that they might be brought against finders.[88] However, the history of detinue was set to repeat itself in trespass. It is too much to suppose a coincidence: that the repetition occurred so quickly is doubtless the result of a conscious transfer of pleading formulae from one form of action to the other. In 1519 a plaintiff brought conversion in the King's Bench against a person into whose hands his goods had come. The *devenit ad manus* count caused six years of advisement, and we may guess that the reason was one of the same difficulties which had occurred earlier with detinue.[89] The analogous remedy was not long emerging: conversion, like detinue, would be brought on a finding (*trover*). In 1531 the classical trover declaration was approved in the King's Bench, in a case where the plaintiff alleged that he had lost a purse, which had come to the defendant's hands by finding, and that the defendant had refused to hand it over but, scheming to defraud the plaintiff, had taken out the contents, sold them, and converted the proceeds.[90] By the 1540s the trover in such cases was non-traversable, and doubtless usually fictitious: we find it used for a ship lost and found in London, or for long lists of utensils which seem to be the contents of houses. The action soon became common form in the King's Bench, and later in the century was even allowed against bailees. The fiction was so liberal in scope that in 1600 it was decided that a defendant who had taken goods with force and arms

---

88   See Port's question about lost money in 102 SS 80.
89   *Audelet v. Latton* (No. 1, 1519) and (No. 2, 1520-26) 94 SS 252. Cf. *Astley v. Fereby* (1510) B. & M. 528 headnote, 94 SS 251 (conversion by receiver of stolen silver).
90   *Wysse v. Andrewe* (1531) 94 SS 252.

could be sued as a 'finder': an early instance of case overtaking trespass *vi et armis*.[91]

The first reported case in which the new form of action was discussed came before the Common Pleas in 1555. The declaration reeked of fiction: a countess had 'found' a gold chain in London and sold it. Serjeant Dyer argued that the plaintiff should have brought detinue, but some of the judges approved the action.[92] Despite the inconclusiveness of this case, and of Dyer's report (printed in 1581), there does not seem to have been any further doubt about the trover and conversion formula. What did give rise to contention in Elizabethan times was the propriety of using it in cases where detinue would lie. Here the plain motive was to avoid wager of law; and, for the same reasons as they fell out over the use of *assumpsit* for debt, the Common Pleas joined battle with the King's Bench over the use of conversion for detinue.

The King's Bench had taken the extreme position that in an action for trover and conversion neither the trover nor the conversion were traversable; it therefore lay for a mere refusal to deliver, a detinue. The Common Pleas, on the other hand, refused to allow this: 'although other courts do the opposite, they themselves were not willing to pervert actions from their natural gist'.[93] As with the dispute over debt, there was no way to resolve this difference until the establishment of the Exchequer Chamber in 1585. There was a similar crop of reversals by that court in the 1590s, and at length a test case was arranged by taking a special verdict, analogous to (but slightly earlier than) that in *Slade's Case*. The jury found that the defendant had come to the goods by finding but refused to deliver them and still withheld them, and asked the court whether this 'denial and detinue' was in law a conversion. After long debates, which provided a dress rehearsal for *Slade's Case*, the majority view favoured an election between detinue and case; judgment was given accordingly for the plaintiff in 1596, and apparently not challenged by writ of error.[94] The Common Pleas do not seem to have pursued their misgivings, except to the extent of insisting that conversion would not lie for cash.[95] In 1614, however, the King's Bench qualified its earlier view that every detainer was a conversion. A refusal to deliver was equivocal, because it might be justified in cases

91 *Bysshoppe v. Viscountess Mountague* (1600) B. & M. 540.

92 *Lord Mounteagle v. Countess of Worcester* (1555) B. & M. 531.

93 *Anon.* (1579) B. & M. 533 (King's Bench); *Anon.* (1582) B. & M. 534 (Common Pleas).

94 *Eason v. Newman* (1596) B. & M. 537.

95 *Halliday v. Higges* (1600) B. & M. 539 (Exchequer Chamber). Overruled in *Kynaston v. Moore* (1627) B. & M. 545.

where it did not amount to a denial of title; for instance, if the goods were held as a pawn or lien, or if a finder simply wished to verify the claimant's identity. But in the absence of such a justification, a refusal to deliver goods on demand was itself a conversion, and therefore it was proper for the jury to find for the plaintiff even though there was no evidence of misfeasance.[96]

The result of this last development was that the tortious origins of the action for conversion faded into the background, and the action became a proprietary action used in place of detinue. The gist of the action was no longer the wrongdoing, but the denial of title. It therefore came to be the law that a voluntary dealing in good faith with the goods of another could nevertheless constitute a conversion;[97] and it could then be said that 'trover is merely a substitute of the old action of detinue ... [it] is not now an action *ex maleficio*, though it is so in form; but it is founded on property'.[98] The title which the action protected was relative, so that a finder could himself bring trover.[99] But the change of character left English law with a curious form of proprietary remedy. It lay not merely against the person who had the chattels when the action was commenced, but against any intermediate possessor who could be said to have converted them (however innocently) by dealing with them as if he were owner. And it did not enable specific recovery of the chattel;[100] for that, in the case of something of special individual value, the plaintiff needed to have recourse to equity.

REVIVAL AND ABOLITION OF DETINUE

The abolition of wager of law in 1833, and the reform of common-law procedure, had the effect of reviving detinue as a viable remedy. From then until 1978 the common law suffered two distinct causes of action for personal property to exist side by side. The precise historical differences were not revived as well, and detinue was regarded in modern times – save by purists – as a tort.[101] Yet the choice of action remained

---

[96] *Isaack v. Clarke* (1614) B. & M. 541.

[97] *Hartop v. Hoare* (1743) B. & M. 548; *Cooper v. Chitty* (1756) B. & M. 549. See also *Hollins v. Fowler* (1875) L.R. 7 H.L. 757. Cf. the earlier vacillation in *Gallyard v. Archer* (1589) B. & M. 535; *Vandrink v. Archer* (1590) 1 Leon. 221.

[98] *Hambly v. Trott* (1776) 1 Cowp. 371 at 374, per Lord Mansfield CJ.

[99] *Armory v. Delamirie* (1722) B. & M. 547; followed in *Parker v. British Airways Board* [1982] 1 All E.R. 834.

[100] This had been attempted, perhaps by mistake, in *Knight v. Browne* (1588) Cro. Eliz. 116, but the judgment was reversed. As to the effect of bringing the chattel into court, see B. & M. 534 n.3.

[101] It was indeed held to be a 'tort' for the purposes of the County Courts Act 1846: *Bryant v. Herbert* (1878) 3 C.P.D. 389.

of practical importance. Since the action of detinue lay to recover the goods or their value, the value was assessed at the date of the judgment, whereas in conversion the damages were based on the value of the goods at the moment of conversion. The plaintiff therefore elected between the actions according to whether the goods had appreciated or depreciated since the date of conversion.[102]

On 1 June 1978 detinue was 'abolished'. The precise meaning of this terse enactment is unclear. The writ of detinue had been abolished long before. The fact of detinue cannot be abolished, because people will continue wrongfully to detain other people's goods. The legal consequences of detaining (as opposed to converting) goods may certainly be abolished; but parliament went to some trouble to preserve them. The court now has the discretion to order the return of the goods, or their value, or the payment of damages.[103]

Further reading

Pollock & Maitland, vol. II, 149-182

Holdsworth HEL, vol. III, pp. 401-544

Fifoot HSCL, pp. 24-43, 102-125

Milsom HFCL, pp. 262-275, 366-379

J. H. Beale, 'History of the Carrier's Liability' (1897) 11 HLR 158-168 (repr. in *Essays AALH*, vol. III, pp. 148-160)

J. B. Ames, 'History of Trover' (1897) 11 HLR 277-289, 374-386 (repr. in *Essays AALH*, vol. III, pp. 416-445); *Lectures on Legal History* (1913), pp. 47-87, 172-209

P. Bordwell, 'Property in Chattels' (1916) 29 HLR 374-394, 501-520, 731-751

S. Stoljar, 'The Early History of Bailment' (1957) 1 AJLH 5-34

A. W. B. Simpson, 'Introduction of the Action on the Case for Conversion' (1959) 75 LQR 364-380 (repr. in LTLH 93-109)

S. F. C. Milsom, 'Sale of Goods in the 15th Century' (1961) 77 LQR 257-284 (repr. in SHCL 105-132)

J. M. Kaye, 'Res Addiratae and Recovery of Stolen Goods' (1970) 86 LQR 379-403

---

[102] *Rosenthal v. Alderton & Sons Ltd* [1946] 1 K.B. 374, [1946] 1 All E.R. 583.

[103] Torts (Interference with Goods) Act 1977 (c.32), s.2(1); S.I. 1978 No. 627.

J. H. Baker, 'Property in Chattels' (1978) 94 SS *209-220*; 'Conversion' ibid. *248-257*

J. L. Barton, 'Remedies for Chattels' (1983), *Law, Litigants and the Legal Profession*, pp. 30-38

22. Negligence

The law of torts, or civil wrongs, is extensive and its boundaries are indistinct. An understanding of the process by which a number of miscellaneous causes of action came to be classified as 'torts' must depend partly on semantics. The nearest medieval equivalent of the modern lawyer's 'tort' was 'trespass', because the old French word *tort* (*injuria* in Latin) had a wider meaning; *tort* denoted any kind of legal injury.[1] In the preceding chapters we traced the development of trespass in the areas of contract and property law, and noticed that in the early sixteenth century there was nothing incongruous about describing a breach of contract as a tort or trespass. But when the action of *assumpsit* became a truly contractual remedy, based on a promise in return for consideration, breaches of contract came to be seen as legally different in a number of ways from other kinds of trespass. One distinction, which was being drawn soon after 1600, was that actions for breach of contract (in whatever form) could be brought against personal representatives, whereas actions for personal wrongs could not.[2] Another was that the rules concerning joint and several liability were different in contract and tort.[3] By the middle of the seventeenth century contract and tort were seen as being so different that claims in tort and contract could not be joined in the same action. Thus, when an action was brought in 1665 against the hirer of a horse for misusing the animal and for not paying the hire, counsel argued that the joinder of the two causes of action was erroneous because one action sounded in tort and the other in 'breach of promise only'.[4] In another case the same year, counsel treated contract and tort as mutually exclusive: 'tort can never be done where there is a special agreement, unless there be duty by

---

1 Even in contractual *praecipe* actions, the defence was in the words *defendit vim et injuriam* (denies the force and tort). Serjeant Westcote refers to breach of covenant as *tort* in *Berenger v. Barton* (1309) 19 SS 84 at 85.

2 See *Pynchon v. Legat* (1611) B. & M. 455 at 457; *Fossett v. Carter* (1623) Palmer 329 at 330, per Jones J.

3 *Boson v. Sandford* (1689) 1 Show. K.B. 101.

4 *Golding v. Goteer* (1665) 1 Keb. 847.

statute or common law incumbent'. This is near the modern understanding of the word, although Twisden J in the same case considered that tort connoted malice, fraud or negligence and did not include trover.[5] Already by 1663 legal indexes were classifying 'tort' in the modern sense, as a sub-heading under 'actions on the case'.[6]

As different kinds of trespass action acquired separate characteristics in the sixteenth and seventeenth centuries, further subdivisions of the law of torts were made, subdivisions which survived the abolition of the writ system itself. During the last century or so, however, the law of torts has been undergoing a gradual reclassification as a result of the rapid expansion of the tort of negligence.[7] Liability for negligence alone was rarely imposed before 1700, and even at the beginning of the twentieth century Sir John Salmond was denying the existence of a separate tort of negligence. In the practitioners' book, *Clerk and Lindsell on Torts*, negligence did not reach the status of a separate chapter until 1947. It would be easy to conclude that negligence has a short history; but this would be misleading. The negligence approach of the modern law determines liability by focusing on the quality of the defendant's act rather than on the kind of harm done to the plaintiff. The rearrangement of so much of the modern law of tort around the concept of negligence is partly a result of that shift of focus.[8] But there is nothing modern about the concept of negligence in itself; what has changed is its primacy. Negligence and fault have always been familiar ideas, and for at least four centuries before 1700 they played a role in law and legal terminology; but their role was ancillary rather than primary. Negligence was something which a plaintiff might mention together with other factors in his writ, or which a defendant might raise by way of showing that he was not at fault. It was not even confined to actions in tort, in the modern sense of the term. But that is the most convenient place to begin.

5 *Matthews v. Hopping* (1665) 1 Keb. 870. Cf. 1 Sid. 244 (conversion is founded on 'tort').

6 E.g. *An Exact Table to the Three Parts of Reports of Mr William Leonard* (1663), sig. Rr1ᵛ. See also G. Townesend, *Tables to most of the Printed Presidents of Pleadings* (1667), p. 27.

7 For the expansion, see pp. 472–477, post.

8 The only comparable concepts are intention, malice, and deceit; torts of strict liability are the residuary group in which no such element is required.

Trespass vi et armis and negligence

If negligent conduct caused direct physical harm, the usual remedy was
an action of trespass alleging force and arms. Such an action was based
not on doing something negligently which would have been lawful if
done carefully, but on doing something which there was no right to do
at all: for example, hitting the defendant, or damaging his goods. So
long as there was a forcible act causing harm, the defendant's state of
mind was irrelevant to civil liability.[9] The inattentive archer who shot a
passer-by unawares, or the careless driver who ran him down, were just
as much guilty of battery as if they had injured him deliberately.
Negligence in the sense of inadvertence was irrelevant.

A wide range of accidents qualified as battery, but the range was
obscured by the sameness of the writs and counts. Whatever the real
facts, defendants in battery were always made to 'assault, beat and
wound' the plaintiff 'with force and arms, to wit with swords and staves'
so that 'his life was despaired of'. No further particulars were allowed to
be given, let alone any mention of negligence. The degree of fault
required to make the defendant liable would therefore only become
relevant if he tried to make it so by excusing himself on grounds of
accident. Yet, if he did this, he would not usually plead the accident
specially, but would plead the general issue (Not guilty) and explain the
circumstances in evidence to the jury. The reason was that accident, or
the absence of negligence, was not (in the logic of common-law
pleading) a justification or reason for doing the act complained of, and
therefore could not be raised by confession and avoidance; nor was there
anything in the count to traverse. To forbid a special plea was not to
deny a defence; it was to keep the defence off the record. As a result, the
law relating to accident and fault was suppressed for centuries, and is
beyond certain recall. The archer whose arm slipped, and the driver
whose horse bolted, might well have been able to satisfy the jury that
they were not guilty; but since the details of their defences could
nowhere be set down in writing, they raised no legal questions for the
court in banc, set no precedent for the future, and created no legal
history. To that extent it is an unreal question whether the *law*
recognised a defence of accident; the matter was relegated to the realms
of fact. The question only presented itself on the face of the record in
one or two exceptional cases, where, through a departure from

---

9 There are some 14th-century dicta to the effect that intention was necessary in
trespass as well as in felony; but it seems that in trespass intention was relevant
only to the fine, a reminder of its criminal ancestry (for which, see p. 71, ante),
and not to the damages.

convention by the pleader, accident was raised by a special plea. Such pleas were regularly rejected, but not on the grounds that fault was irrelevant.

There are a number of fourteenth-century cases in which accident was successfully raised as a defence in trespass. But they could all be described as cases where the chain of causation was broken by a force outside the defendant's control: for instance, the forces of combustion and wind (in fire cases), the perversity of animals (in running-down cases), or the plaintiff's own action (by moving in front of a horse, a moving dagger, or an arrow).[10] Where the defendant himself caused the harm, it is not clear whether he was always able to excuse himself on the grounds that he was not negligent; the slender evidence from the time of Richard II can be interpreted either way.[11] From the middle of the fifteenth century, however, the cases suggest that lack of fault afforded a defence in principle.

In the *Case of Thorns*[12] a man was sued for trespassing on his neighbour's land to collect thorns which had fallen in the process of clipping a hedge on their common boundary. He pleaded that the thorns fell against his will (*ipso invito*), and the plaintiff demurred successfully. Intention was relevant in felony, but not in an action for damages.[13] The archer whose hand swerved might not be guilty of felony, but should nevertheless compensate the victim. The decision has occasioned some controversy in relation to fault, chiefly because of uncertainty as to what was actually pleaded. All speculation as to the form[14] of the plea has now been laid to rest by the discovery of the record. The plea as pleaded went only to intention; and the remarks of the judges in rejecting it do not assume strict liability. Choke J said, 'If he wants to make a good plea out of this, he should show what he did to prevent the thorns from falling, so that we can judge whether he did enough to excuse himself'. Of course, it is not easy to find an excuse for someone clipping a boundary hedge in such circumstances; even before Newton, men knew that things fell when dropped. The only likely excuse would be a sudden gust of wind: and Choke J chose that as

---

[10] For these cases (from 14th-century rolls) see 100 SS 16-17, 18-19, 21-22, 30; 103 SS 405.

[11] *Jankyn's Case* (1378) B. & M. 322 (stones accidentally dropped on plaintiff's house during building operations); *Bridelyngton v. Middilton* (1388) ibid. (child injured in play). In both cases the defendant relied on the lack of 'malice' (intention) rather than on lack of fault.

[12] *Hulle v. Orynge* (1466) B. & M. 327.

[13] Still less was motive relevant: *Cuny v. Brugewode* (1506) B. & M. 316 (act done with good intentions).

[14] As opposed to its purpose, which is puzzling.

his example of a possible defence. Since clipping was itself a deliberate act, breaking the chain of causation was the only means of escape.

The problem occurred again in cases arising out of shooting accidents. In *Weaver v. Ward*[15] the defendant, who had shot the plaintiff while they were both taking part in military exercises, pleaded that the wounding was accidental and against his will. Again the plea was held bad; he had pleaded lack of intention rather than lack of fault, and in any case he should have pleaded Not guilty. The reason for advancing a special plea may have been that Ward thought he had some kind of justification, as a member of a trained band acting ultimately under the orders of the Privy Council; but he could not both justify an act and deny it. Although the case was decided on pleading grounds, the court intimated in passing that liability was not absolute: the defendant could excuse himself if he showed that the plaintiff ran across the musket when it was discharging, or that the injury was 'inevitable and that the defendant had committed no negligence'. The advice was adopted in 1682 by a tax-collector who pleaded that as he was discharging his pistol, no one being in sight, the plaintiff accidentally wandered into the line of fire and was shot, against the defendant's will, and that this was 'inevitable'. Again the plea was held bad, 'for in trespass the defendant shall not be excused without unavoidable necessity, which is not shown here.'[16] But the record shows that the defendant had not adequately explained why he was shooting at all, or what precautions he had taken; the bare word 'inevitable' was no substitute for facts, and if all the facts in the plea were true the defendant might still have been negligent.

These decisions were sometimes interpreted in subsequent generations as importing strict liability, but when examined in the context of the pleadings they were by no means as sweeping as some of the language suggests. None of the pleas had put the defendant's fault in issue. It was not enough to say that the damage was accidental (*per infortunium*), or against the will of the defendant (*ipso invito*), for intention as to consequences had been irrelevant since medieval times. What the judges wanted to know was whether the defendant could have taken steps to avoid the accident; in other words, whether it was 'inevitable' – not in the sense of being predestined, but in that there was no reasonable opportunity of avoidance. A man who had caused harm could not offer as a defence that he had not meant it. If he had some justification for acting as he did, he could plead it by way of confession and avoidance. If he had done all he could to avoid it, then his proper course was to

---

15 (1616) B. & M. 331; Hob. 134; Moore K.B. 864. A similar plea was entered, with no objection, in *Ustwayt v. Alyngton* (1534) 94 SS *223-224*.

16 *Dickinson v. Watson* (1682) B. & M. 334 at 335.

plead Not guilty and tell his story to the jury. This was finally made clear in 1695, when a defendant showed how he had taken reasonable precautions to warn passers by of his runaway horse, and lost on the pleading point alone. The defence was sound, but it amounted to the general issue.[17] By the early nineteenth century this pleading rule was restricted to cases of interrupted causation, and with equally harsh consequences; but the principles of liability apparently remained the same.[18] Unavoidable accident remained a defence, and it was treated at the beginning of Queen Victoria's reign as meaning simply that the defendant was not to blame.

Thus, although negligence played no formal part in the action of trespass *vi et armis*, it seems likely that a man was only considered guilty of a trespass if he was to blame for it, first in the sense that he had caused it, and secondly in the sense that with reasonable care he could have avoided it. There is no reason to suppose that the standard of liability was any different in trespass and case, since in either case it was left to the jury to decide according to current notions of culpability. The peculiarity of trespass was that, unlike most of the other actions which continued in use, its wording almost totally suppressed the real facts; questions of fault had therefore to be raised by the defendant. This formal, procedural distinction between trespass and case was engraved on the heart of the pleader, and it was not until 1959 that a plaintiff complaining of a direct trespass was held obliged to allege negligence as part of his own case.[19]

Actions on the Case for Negligence

UNDERTAKINGS AND NEGLIGENCE

The word *negligenter* (negligently), an adverb designed to indicate neglectful conduct, first appeared in writs of trespass as the antithesis of force and arms. If damage was done in the course of performing carelessly a task undertaken at the plaintiff's behest, it could not be described as having been done *vi et armis*. It was precisely for this

---

17   *Gibbon v. Pepper* (1695) B. & M. 335.
18   See *Milman v. Dolwell* (1810) 2 Camp. 378; *Knapp v. Salisbury* (1810) 2 Camp. 500 (inevitable accident a defence, but not under general issue); *Wakeman v. Robinson* (1823) 1 Bing. 213; *Goodman v. Taylor* (1832) 5 C. & P. 407 (reasonable care must be pleaded); *Pearcy v. Walter* (1834) 6 C. & P. 232 (negligence or inevitable accident must be pleaded); *Cotterill v. Starkey* (1839) 8 C. & P. 691 (lack of negligence must be pleaded); *Hall v. Fearnley* (1842) 3 Q.B. 919 (unavoidable accident must be pleaded). The matter was settled by *Stanley v. Powell* [1891] 1 Q.B. 86.
19   *Fowler v. Lanning* [1959] 1 Q.B. 426, [1959] 1 All E.R. 290.

reason that the writ needed a special case explaining why the negligence was wrongful.

In most of the early cases where negligence was made part of the special case in the writ, there was a pre-existing relationship between the parties which precluded an allegation of force against the peace.[20] The relationship was expressed as arising either from a bailment or from some undertaking which brought the defendant into physical contact with the plaintiff or the plaintiff's property; since the plaintiff had consented to this contact, the gist of his complaint was not that the defendant had done the act but that he had done it carelessly.

Some of the leading cases have already been examined in reviewing the history of contract and bailment.[21] Actions on the case for negligence were brought against bailees (including carriers), surgeons, workmen and tradesmen. They all had a common form: the defendant was alleged to have undertaken to perform some specific task, and then to have done it so carelessly that some specified harm resulted. But the undertaking was only to do the work, not to use skill or care; to that extent the obligation to use care was imposed by law rather than by contract. In some of the actions against bailees there is not even an *assumpsit*; it was the relationship which made an action on the case appropriate, not the promise.[22] The nature of the negligence relied on in these *assumpsit* actions never clearly emerged in the cases, because (as in trespass *vi et armis*) the defendant usually pleaded the general issue and the question of fault was left to the jury alone to decide.[23] Whatever it was, it found expression always in negative adverbs, such as *negligenter, improvide, inartificialiter, indebite*, and the like. But the adverb always governed a verb of positive action. The best generalisation we can make is that a person who embarked upon a requested service which brought him into contact with the person or property of another was liable if he performed the service with want of care or skill and damage resulted.

---

[20] See p. 72, ante.

[21] See pp. 374-376, 446-447, ante.

[22] E.g. 74 LQR 563, 569 (examples from 1367); *Gardiner v. Burgh* (1382) 103 SS 418; *Abbot of Forde v. Blyke* (1387) 103 SS 419; *Bluet v. Bouland* (1472) B. & M. 563. See also p. 620, post (case against a farrier).

[23] For exceptions, suggesting similar defences to those in trespass, see *Rogerstun v. Northcotes* (1366) 103 SS 423 (storm pleaded); *Abbot of Roche v. Dukmanton* (1450) CP 40/758, m.240d (sudden wind pleaded); *Terry v. White* (1528) 94 SS 226-227 (contributory negligence and transfer of risk pleaded). In much later times, it is evident that *assumpsit* for negligence required proof of fault as well as causation: *Aston v. Heaven* (1797) 2 Esp. 533 (passenger against carrier); *Searle v. Prentice* (1807) 8 East 348 (patient against surgeon).

The pleadings remained in this form long after the word *assumpsit* became associated almost exclusively with contractual undertakings. But where there was negligence, there was no need to show consideration for the undertaking, because (as we should say today) the action was founded on tort rather than contract.[24] Nevertheless, the dual sense of the word *assumpsit* has remained embedded in the law down to the present day: 'contract' and 'tort' still overlap in cases of bailees, surgeons, and others whose duties to be careful arise both by reason of their physical nexus with the plaintiff or his property and by reason of their dealings with him.

NEGLIGENCE IN THE ABSENCE OF AN UNDERTAKING

Some fourteenth-century actions on the case for negligence make no mention of undertakings. Nearly all of the actions in this class can be accounted for in terms of the other limitation of trespass *vi et armis* considered above: conduct was not a forcible breach of the king's peace if it was caused by the forces of nature or by third parties. It was all very well to excuse someone in trespass for fire damage on the ground that it was accidental and not forcible;[25] but non-forcible fire damage might still be the result of negligence, in which case it ought to be recoverable in damages. Before the end of the fourteenth century, plaintiffs were framing such complaints in case, first with simple allegations of negligence, and then (apparently following precedents from the city of London) alleging a 'custom of the realm' which required everyone to keep his fire safely so that it did not injure his neighbour.[26] The first mention of 'custom of the realm' was in a writ devised to make innkeepers answerable for the loss of goods brought in by guests, a formula approved by the king's council in the 1360s.[27] Innkeepers were probably not regarded as bailees in respect of goods kept in guests' rooms, and any other kind of action against them might well have failed on the ground that the loss was caused by unknown intruders.[28] Since a

---

24 See p. 447, ante.

25 *Anon.* (1368) B. & M. 321; *Anon.* (1374) B. & M. 304; *Elys v. Angieyn* (1390) 103 SS 405. For earlier examples, see 74 LQR 582-583.

26 *Cok v. Durant* (1377) *CPMR 1364-81*, p. 235 (custom of London expressed in similar terms to later custom of realm); *Eskhevyd v. Coldale* (1395) 103 SS 414 (negligence, not mentioning custom, by lessor against lessee); *Beaulieu v. Finglam* (1401) B. & M. 557 (first known allegation of custom of the realm).

27 See *Navenby v. Lascelles* (1368) B. & M. 552 at 554, per Knyvet CJ. Cf. *York v. Coulynge* (1368) 103 SS 437.

28 For just such a plea in *assumpsit* against the keeper of a private boarding house for loss of a horse left to graze, see *Luffenham v. Gardyner* (1395) 103 SS 432 at 433.

common innkeeper was bound to accept travellers, the effect of the custom was to restrain him from excluding his common duty.[29] Likewise in the fire cases the custom prevented the defendant from relying on act of God. In both cases, then, although the writs mentioned negligence or fault, the purpose of the alleged custom was to impose a special kind of strict liability.[30] The custom of the realm did not develop much further, however, because 'the common custom of this realm is common law' and need not be pleaded.[31] Nevertheless, when one more custom of the realm was belatedly added to the list in the seventeenth century – the duty of common carriers so to keep goods that they were not lost or damaged through their 'fault' – the purpose was once again to impose a stricter liability than would otherwise attach.[32] There is probably a similar explanation for the *scienter* action, the action for knowingly keeping animals with dangerous propensities, such as dogs accustomed to worry sheep;[33] the defendant's knowledge of that propensity fixed him with a strict liability for any damage which the animal caused, damage for which he would not otherwise be liable.[34]

The form of the earliest actions on the case for negligence is therefore no better guide to the standard of tortious liability than the form of actions of trespass *vi et armis*. Perhaps the standard varied in fact from one type of case to another; fire was particularly feared in a world of timber-framed buildings, and may have required a stricter standard of control than a horse. Between these early forms, however, most accidents thought to occasion liability were provided for. The paucity of other cases has led legal historians to the conclusion that negligence could not have been actionable per se; there had to be an undertaking or

[29] See *Waldegrave v. Thomas of Fleet-street* (1382) 103 SS 443 (demurrer to attempt to negative fault). For later exceptions, see B. & M. 555, endnote; *Thomas v. Sampson* (1384) Y.B. Mich. 8 Ric. II, p. 145, pl.32.

[30] See the later fire cases in B. & M. 559. In innkeeper cases, however, the law did come to allow a defence that the plaintiff had been given a key and had assumed the risk: ibid. 555.

[31] *Beaulieu v. Finglam* (1401) B. & M. 557 at 558. Cf. *Horslow's Case* (1443) ibid. 554, per Newton CJ.

[32] *Rich v. Kneeland* (1613) B. & M. 561 is the first known example. The analogy with innkeepers was that both had a duty to accept customers.

[33] The first *scienter* precedent so far discovered is from 1367 (74 LQR 218).

[34] For the relevance of *scienter* in an action for trespass by dogs, see 74 LQR 216-217 (1365). For a simple negligence action against a dog-owner, in London, see *Baldeswell v. Pulter* (1366) *CPMR 1364-81*, p. 68. For doubts as to liability for dogs, see *Anon.* (1369) Y.B. Hil. 43 Edw. III, fo. 8, pl.23; *Anon.* (1439) B. & M. 324 (no liability where dog breaks leash to chase deer). See also *Whitlok v. Wherewell* (1398) 103 SS 413 (rider of hired horse not liable without knowledge of vicious propensity); *Anon.* (1481) B. & M. 315(b), per Catesby J (no liability for cattle out of control).

custom of the realm to impose a duty of care. The conclusion was also drawn by an Elizabethan judge who said, 'I have never known an action to lie for negligence save where one is retained to do something for someone and does it negligently; and the reason why it lies in that case is because he has undertaken to do it.'[35]

But how many gaps would there have been between the actions already described? If an injury was caused by the defendant, it was covered by trespass unless it was non-forcible. It might be non-forcible either because of the prior relationship of the parties, in which case *assumpsit* was available, or because of the indirectness of the accident. An indirect accident usually occurred through a dangerous force getting out of control; and the usual dangerous forces were fire and animals. Those situations, too, were covered by standard forms of case. The only question therefore outstanding is whether case lay for any other kind of indirect accident caused by negligence. The situations most likely to pose the problem were negligently releasing dangerous forces in a way not covered by the actions mentioned, as by failing to control water,[36] or where a fire began through negligence;[37] or permitting a dangerous situation, such as a hazard to casual passers by.[38] Although such cases are infrequent, there seems to have been no technical reason why actions on the case should not lie; certainly such actions were brought, and are not known to have been challenged on the ground that negligence by itself was no tort. Indeed, there was no theoretical reason why an action on the case should not be brought for neglect of a non-contractual duty resulting in non-physical damage, though few such duties were recognised.[39] It was the infrequency of these exceptions, rather than any explicit legal theory, which led some later lawyers to conclude that negligence was not a tort by itself; but as a statement of the normal

---

[35] *Bradshaw v. Nicholson* (1601) Inner Temple MS. Barrington 6, fo. 127v, per Walmsley J. Cf. the different report in B. & M. 609, which shows that he was dissenting.

[36] 94 SS 229 (cases of 1508, 1520 and 1529).

[37] E.g. *Critoft v. Emson* (1506) B. & M. 566 n.13 (mill set alight by negligent lessee); *Anon.* (1582) B. & M. 569 (thatch set alight by spark from neighbour's gun).

[38] E.g. *Loghton v. Calys* (1473) B. & M. 567 (pile of logs collapsing into road); *Frankessh v. Bokenham* (1490) KB 27/915, m.27, Caryll's MS. reports (mill-stone falling into road). Cf. the cases of pits and ditches in B. & M. 571, endnote and n.4.

[39] E.g. prescriptive duties to find chaplains to sing: *Broke v. Abbot of Woburn* (1444) Y.B. Hil. 22 Hen. VI, fo. 46, pl.36; *Danvers v. Prior of Canons Ashby* (1453) CP 40/769, m. 472; *Brudenell v. Abbot of Woburn* (1504) CP 40/968, m. 490.

position before the eighteenth century the conclusion was accurate enough.[40]

The Tort of Negligence

We now know that the distinction between trespass and case was the result of the jurisdictional accident that the royal courts entertained complaints of forcible breaches of the peace before they let in other wrongs.[41] There ought, therefore, to have been no substantive gaps between the two. Any wrong which was not forcible ought to have been remediable in case. Harmful carelessness was on the face of it a legal wrong, and as we have seen there was probably no absolute rule to the effect that there could be no duty of care without an undertaking; it was just that between trespass and *assumpsit*, together with the actions on the custom of the realm and *scienter*, most accidents were provided for. The question whether there was a tort of negligence did not arise in such terms. Problems only arose, as elsewhere in the law, when attempts were made to use case instead of an existing remedy. In this sphere the competition was between case and trespass *vi et armis*.

The first signs of a tort of negligence, encompassing direct as well as indirect injuries arising from negligence, are found in a long series of running-down cases beginning in the seventeenth century. If a man negligently drove his horse and cart, or ship, into another man or his property, that was a trespass with force. But there could be many disadvantages in bringing a trespass action. For one thing, the accident might be shown to be the fault of the horse, or of the wind, and then the jury might be persuaded to find the defendant not guilty of the trespass. Also, for similar reasons, the jury might reduce the damages if the battery turned out to have been unintended.[42] A declaration in case, on the other hand, could focus the jury's attention on the fault rather than the force: that is, on the defendant's fault in failing to anticipate or deal with those extrinsic forces. Moreover, the plaintiff would often wish to sue the driver's master, and vicarious liability could only be imposed by an action on the case. Until the late seventeenth century there had been no concept of vicarious liability; even a husband was not vicariously

---

[40] In the absence of occupiers' liability (p. 473, post), most injuries of the residuary kind would occur either in a public place or on one's own land, and would later be classified as 'nuisance'. But they were framed as actions for negligence.

[41] See pp. 71-75, ante.

[42] *Angell v. Satterton* (1663) B. & M. 333.

liable for his wife's torts.[43] But a master was liable for a servant's acts
if he commanded them, for then they were considered his own acts; and
not long before 1700 it became established that he could be made
vicariously liable for acts which he did not command, provided that they
were for his benefit and in the course of employment.[44] Then there was
the serious practical danger, after 1670, that recovery of nominal
damages in trespass *vi et armis* carried only nominal costs,[45] unless the
judge could be persuaded to certify that the trespass was both wilful and
malicious.[46] In case there was also a longer limitation period.[47]

For some or all of these reasons pleaders began to contemplate the
conversion of trespass actions into actions on the case. One
seventeenth-century pleader thought it advisable to invent a new custom
of the realm to deal with negligent driving,[48] which may indicate doubts
as to how an action should be framed for negligence per se. His
experiment led nowhere. The breakthrough appeared to later generations
to have been made in 1676. But it was only a significant step to later
eyes. At the time there was no awareness that a new principle of
liability was in the making; there was just another new case which did
not quite fit into the existing formulae. *Mitchell v. Allestry*[49] was an
action against a master and servant who had broken in unruly horses in
Little Lincoln's Inn Fields, where many people were walking about,
including the plaintiff, who was kicked and injured. Now, this was not
a *scienter* action, because the horses presumably had no abnormally
vicious characteristics; and it was not an action for negligent control of
the horses, because the evidence[50] apparently showed that they had done
all they reasonably could to prevent the accident. The essence of the

---

43   See p. 557, post.

44   *Turbervile v. Stamp* (1697) B. & M. 559 at 560, per Holt CJ; *Jones v. Hart*
(1699) 2 Salk. 441. Cf. *Kingston v. Booth* (1685) Skin. 228, where vicarious
liability is not recognised. In *Mitchell v. Allestry* (1676), n. 49, post, the
master was fictitiously alleged to have been present performing the act; the
reports reveal that he was absent, but disagree as to whether he authorised the
activity.

45   Duties on Law Proceedings Act 1670, 22 & 23 Car. II, c.9, s.9 [s.136 in *Statutes
at Large*]. The connection between this enactment and the preference for case was
made by Lord Kenyon CJ in *Savignac v. Roome* (1794) 6 Term Rep. 125 at 129.

46   Stat. 8 & 9 Will. III, c.11.

47   Limitation Act 1624, 21 Jac. I, c.16, s.3 (4 years in trespass for battery, 6 years
in case).

48   *E.R. v. J.P.* (*c.* 1675) B. & M. 562. Earlier but unpublished precedents, each in
different form, were: *Colan v. West* (1367) B. & M. 303 (negligent driving *vi et
armis*); *Whitlok v. Wherewell* (1398) 103 SS 412 (negligent control of horse).

49   (1676) B. & M. 572.

50   Revealed in a previous trial between the parties: B. & M. 574.

wrong was in bringing the horses into a London square for breaking in, 'improvidently, rashly, and without due consideration of the unsuitability of the place'. The plaintiff's case on the merits was undeniably strong: the defendants could hardly deny their awareness that the horses needed taming, and it was obvious that they had chosen the wrong place to attempt it. Some rather forlorn arguments were advanced in arrest of judgment; but no one thought of arguing that negligence was not actionable without an undertaking or custom of the realm.[51] The reports suggest that the judges were conscious only of making a slight enlargement of the *scienter* principle, in the context of a public nuisance. Yet, by 1700 lawyers were beginning to perceive a new general principle: that a man was 'answerable for all mischief proceeding from his neglect or his actions, unless they were of unavoidable necessity'.[52] How rapidly practice changed as a result has not yet been discovered; but the precedent-books of the early eighteenth century certainly began to offer declarations in case not only for new situations involving negligence but also for the kinds of negligence which had formerly been actionable as trespass.[53] Subsequent writers attributed to *Mitchell v. Allestry* the opening up of this new category of actions on the case; by about 1750 a significant chapter headed 'Of injuries arising from negligence or folly' could be written to accommodate it.[54]

Towards the close of the eighteenth century numerous problems raised by running-down cases were vexing the courts. To judge from the law reports, there was a dramatic explosion in the number of such cases at this period. That is in part an illusion caused by the beginning of nisi prius reporting in the 1790s.[55] Nevertheless, there does appear to have been an increase in the number of cases, and two reasons may be suggested for it. First, there had been a surge in the number of driving accidents. The improvement of road surfaces had encouraged an increase in both the volume of traffic and its speed. By 1775 there were estimated to be 17,000 four-wheeled carriages in England, including 400

---

51 The same is true of the less discussed case of *Mustard v. Harnden* (1680) T. Raym. 390 (case for negligent control of ship).

52 *Mason v. Keeling* (1700) 1 Ld Raym. 606 at 607.

53 B. & M. 575.

54 *An Institute of the Law relative to Trials at Nisi Prius* (1768), p. 35; B. & M. 578-579. For this work and its authorship, see p. 468, post.

55 The first reports were those of Thomas Peake (1790-95) and Isaac Espinasse (1793-1810). Cf. 92 LQR at 440-441 (cases in 1760s and 1770s); *Tayler's Case* (1780) Ann. Reg., p. 199 (£150 damages against the master of a stage-coach for an injury caused by the coachman's negligence in not driving on the left side of the road).

stage-coaches.[56] Stage-coaches, driven as often as not by men undistinguished for their sobriety, competed for the fastest journeys; and during such races they not infrequently overturned, collided with other vehicles, or went out of control. It is at this period that we first hear of the rule of the road, though no doubt many roads allowed little space for overtaking. The second reason is that the litigation arising from these accidents was beset by legal wrangling over the proper boundary between trespass and case; a defendant who failed on the merits might at least follow an age-old tradition of the common law and attack the choice of writ. The test which the courts produced was that 'in trespass the plaintiff complains of an immediate wrong, and in case of a wrong that is the consequence of another act'.[57] The metaphysics of directness were a constant trouble to courts and practitioners for over thirty years. The solution was found in 1833, when it was laid down by Tindal CJ that the plaintiff had an election; he could waive the force and sue in case whenever the injury complained of was not both direct and wilful.[58]

The effect of this decision was that trespass became more and more associated with wilful injuries. Few lawyers by 1850 would have classified a road accident as an assault and battery. Accident litigation, on the other hand, became the province of the tort of negligence, and it enjoyed a further boom when the Industrial Revolution and the development of the railway contributed a new range of serious accidents. By the beginning of Victoria's reign, actions for negligence were sufficiently numerous for some writers on the law to put them into a separate compartment. The first collection of cases arranged in this way appeared in the supplement to Mr Serjeant Petersdorff's *Abridgment* in 1843. Thirty years later, in 1871, the subject acquired its first student textbooks;[59] and in the following decade a practitioners' book, Thomas Beven's *Principles of the Law of Negligence* (1889), a tome which, despite its title, provided little more than a catalogue raisonné of duties of care, many of them contractual.[60]

---

[56] *Ann. Reg. 1775*, p. 191.

[57] *Reynolds v. Clarke* (1725) B. & M. 354 at 355 n.12, per Fortescue CJ; quoted in a treatise on pleading, B. & M. 357. See also *Scott v. Shepherd* (1773) 2 Wm Bla. 892. For the application to running-down accidents, see, e.g., *Day v. Edwards* (1794) 5 Term Rep. 648; *Leame v. Bray* (1803) 3 East 593.

[58] *Williams v. Holland* (1833) 10 Bing. 112. The King's Bench recognised the plaintiff's election in *Moreton v. Hardern* (1825) 4 B. & C. 225.

[59] T. W. Saunders, *A Treatise upon the Law applicable to Negligence* (Butterworths, 1871); R. Campbell, *The Law of Negligence* (Stevens, 1871).

[60] The earlier writer C. G. Addison dealt with negligence in his book on contracts (1845-47) rather than in his book on torts (1860). The American treatise by F.Wharton, *A Treatise on the Law of Negligence* (Philadelphia, 1874), put contract and tort in separate parts.

THE NATURE OF TORTIOUS NEGLIGENCE

Negligence, or neglect, is simply the failure to exercise care; and the failure to do something is only a legal wrong if the law imposes a duty to do it. Even in factual situations involving apparently positive misconduct, 'negligence' could still be regarded as a wrong of nonfeasance, not taking care. It all depends on whether it is the misconduct or the neglect of duty which is regarded as the core of the complaint. It is a fine point, and may seem to us a semantic quibble, whether the driver of a vehicle which runs over a pedestrian is liable for misfeasance in running him down or for nonfeasance in failing to apply the brake or turn the wheel. The distinction no longer matters, since the negligence amounts in either case to a breach of the duty to take care;[61] but before the nineteenth century it could affect the choice of the writ and the classification of the wrong.

Sir John Comyns (d. 1740), in his *Digest of the Laws of England* (published in 1762), juxtaposed the headings 'Action upon the Case for Misfeasance' and 'Action upon the Case for Negligence'. The former category covered damage caused by 'misadventure', whether remediable in trespass or case, whereas the latter included the neglect of miscellaneous duties imposed by customs of the realm, local customs, or statutes, and the duties imposed by undertakings. Of the two, the former seems closer to the modern concept of negligence than the latter. In the language of today, Comyns' 'misfeasance' might be described as negligent acts, his 'negligence' as neglectful omissions. The tort of negligence was to fuse both aspects of carelessness, and to focus attention on the breach of a duty to take care, rather than upon the miscellaneous consequences of not taking care.

Leaving aside the choice of the writ, which was discussed above, the problem for the substantive law was to settle the cases in which the law imposed a duty to take care in the absence of an undertaking or custom. We have seen that the law sometimes imposed duties independently of any prior relationship between the parties. Yet duties of care cannot be imposed on everyone in every situation. At the beginning of the eighteenth century no one, it seems, could see any pattern emerging; the kinds of case were 'almost infinite, daily increasing, and continually receiving new forms'.[62] By the middle of the century, however, a general answer had been formulated in an influential treatise, printed in 1768 from a manuscript supposedly written by Lord Bathurst (1714-94) in the 1750s, which became a standard practitioners' manual in its

---

[61]   E.g. *Kelly v. Metropolitan Rly Co.* [1895] 1 Q.B. 944 (failure to shut off steam).
[62]   T. Wood, *An Institute of the Laws of England* (1720), vol. II, pp. 939-940.

subsequent editions by Buller and Onslow. The author suggested for the first time a principle which is now familiar to every English law student: 'Every man ought to take reasonable care that he does not injure his neighbour; therefore, wherever a man receives hurt through the default of another, though the same were not wilful, yet if it be occasioned by negligence or folly the law gives him an action to recover damages for the injury so sustained ... However, it is proper in such cases to prove that the injury was such as would probably follow from the act done.'[63]

The phrase 'reasonable care' pointed to the normal standard which would become the basis of the tort of negligence. We have seen that some of the early actions for negligence were designed to impose a stricter duty; and English law sometimes experimented with differing standards of negligence, such as 'gross negligence'. By 1781 it was found convenient to express the normal standard in terms of the 'generality of rational men', and in the early nineteenth century of 'the reasonable man'.[64] The reasonable man was then incorporated into some definitions of the new tort: 'Negligence is the omission to do something which a reasonable man would do, or doing something which a reasonable man would not do'.[65] In practice more care was required of people in some situations than others; but the test of reasonableness enabled the standard to be expressed uniformly. Moreover, the courts did not (at any rate by the nineteenth century) expect plaintiffs to prove matters beyond their ken; the doctrine of *res ipsa loquitur* enabled negligence to be presumed where it seemed appropriate to cast the burden of explanation on to the defendant.[66]

The 'neighbour' figure has also proved useful and enduring as a guide to the duty of care.[67] Lord Atkin, in his classic speech two centuries

63 *An Institute of the Law relative to Trials at Nisi Prius* (1768), pp. 35-36; B. & M. 578-579.

64 W. Jones, *Treatise on the Law of Bailments* (1781), p. 6; *Jones v. Bird* (1822) 5 B. & Ald. 837 at 845-846; *Vaughan v. Menlove* (1837) 3 Bing. N.C. 468.

65 *Blyth v. Birmingham Waterworks Co.* (1856) 11 Ex. 781 at 784, per Alderson B. This dictum was the starting point of both the textbooks which appeared in 1871 (p. 467, ante).

66 *Christie v. Griggs* (1809) 2 Camp. 79 (in *assumpsit*); *Skinner v. London, Brighton & South Coast Rly Co.* (1850) 5 Ex. 787; *Byrne v. Boadle* (1863) 2 H. & C. 722. The same policy underlay the strict liability of carriers: *Coggs v. Barnard* (1703) B. & M. 370 at 375, per Holt CJ.

67 It may have been suggested by the language used in fire cases. See *Turbervile v. Stamp* (1697) B. & M. 559 at 561 ('he must at his peril take care that it does not through his neglect injure his neighbour'). See also B. & M. 356 n.13 (1734).

later in *Donoghue v. Stevenson*,[68] dwelt on the problem of defining who is a neighbour for this purpose, and offered a general solution which seems to have evolved from Bathurst's concept of the 'probability' of injury; neighbours in the law of negligence are 'persons who are so closely and directly affected by my act that I ought reasonably to have them in contemplation as being so affected when I am directing my mind to the acts or omissions which are called in question'. This generalisation is not, of course, absolutely valid. A man may know that his neighbour is in distress, but he is not in law bound to go and help him.[69] A man may have an opportunity of saving his neighbour's goods from destruction; not only is he under no duty to do so, but he may be liable in trespass if he does.[70] A man may open a shop which is calculated to and does ruin the livelihood of a neighbouring shopkeeper; but it is no legal wrong.[71] The definition in advance of all the situations in which a duty of care is owed to one's neighbour is impossible; despite attempts to formulate a general rule, a policy decision has to be made whenever new cases arise. Indeed, over the course of time very different outer limits have been set to the notion of actionable wrong in the context of negligence: and so, although the 'neighbour' principle was voiced in the time of William III in words which might still be accepted today, far fewer kinds of injury were then under its ambit than now.

EXTENSIONS OF THE DUTY OF CARE

Despite the enunciation by Bathurst of a general principle of liability for negligence, until well into the nineteenth century the principle was regarded only as an explanation for the cases already recognised, and not as a basis for potentially wider claims. The principal forms of actionable negligence[72] which had come to be recognised were: careless collisions on road and water; dangerous activities, such as breaking in

---

68 [1932] A.C. 562 at 578. See also *Langridge v. Levy* (1837) 2 M. & W. 519; *Heaven v. Pender* (1883) 11 Q.B.D. 503.

69 See *Home Office v. Dorset Yacht Co.* [1970] A.C. 1004 at 1027, per Lord Reid ('when a person has done nothing to put himself in any relationship with another person in distress or with his property mere physical propinquity does not require him to go to that person's assistance. There may be a moral duty to do so, but it is not practicable to make it a legal duty').

70 *Cuny v. Brugewode* (1506) B. & M. 316. And see, as to finders of goods, *Walgrave v. Ogden* (1591) B. & M. 569.

71 See p. 510, post.

72 Putting aside liability for fire, and for breaking customs of the realm, which were essentially strict. Strict liability for domestic fires was ended by the Act preventing Mischiefs from Fire 1707, 6 Ann., c.58 [c.31 in *Statutes at Large*].

horses or handling firearms; passive dangers to the public, such as unguarded holes in or adjoining the highway; and 'negligence, ignorance or misbehaviour of a person in the duty of his trade or calling', such as incompetence shown by a farrier or surgeon.[73] The vast majority of cases were of physical damage resulting directly from some action of the defendant (or his servant) in person or from some situation under his immediate control.

When the courts were invited in early Victorian times to develop the tort of negligence beyond this stage, the invitation was greeted with little enthusiasm. The reason for the reluctance was expressed in terms of the extensive scope given to the principle *volenti non fit injuria*; this counterbalanced the general principle of liability and explained, in a manner consonant with the individualist attitudes of the age, why so many kinds of injury caused by negligence did not lend themselves to redress. In many everyday situations injured parties were supposed to accept the world as they found it. Thus it was held in 1837 that an employee could not sue his master for the negligence of a fellow employee, even though the master would have been vicariously liable to third parties for the same negligence; by entering the employment, the servant had impliedly consented to the risk of being injured by fellow employees.[74] Likewise, a servant employed on an obviously risky activity might find he had no complaint if he was injured; he knew the risk as well as the employer, and if he was unwilling to take it his remedy was to find other employment.[75] On a similar ground, occupiers of property were not liable for injuries to visitors resulting from the state of the premises, unless there was a known and serious danger of which they failed to give notice. A visitor was deemed to be in the same position as the family and servants of the occupier; 'he must take his chance with the rest',[76] and would have been regarded as rather discourteous if he complained of injury. Liability for damage caused in one's absence by chattels (other than animals) was similarly confined to

[73] These no longer required an *assumpsit*: see the precedent in 8 Wentworth 416 (action for negligence by a male midwife, 1777). For notes of a trial in such an action in 1738, see B. & M. 576.

[74] *Priestley v. Fowler* (1837) 3 M. & W. 1. The question arose, and was considered, in relation to domestic service; but the answer soon grew into the more absolute 'doctrine of common employment'.

[75] *Skipp v. Eastern Counties Rly Co.* (1853) 9 Ex. 223; *Senior v. Ward* (1859) 1 E. & E. 385. In these cases the plaintiff might himself have been regarded as negligent. Cf. *Clark v. Holmes* (1862) 7 H. & N. 937 (awareness of risk does not preclude action against master for negligence).

[76] *Southcote v. Stanley* (1856) 1 H. & N. 247 (hotel not liable to a visitor, as opposed to a paying guest).

unusual concealed dangers.[77] A second notion underlying some of these cases, if not explicitly stated, may have been that one can only be liable for behaviour, not for things.[78] In relation to premises there was yet a third problem, that of causation. For instance, if a railway passenger was injured by tripping over something in a dimly lit station, he might be regarded by the light of cold logic as the author of his own misfortune; as Bramwell LJ reportedly put it, 'If it was too dark for the man to see, he had no business to go there. If it was light enough for him to see, he had no business to tumble over the obstacle.'[79]

Another restrictive principle flowed from the long-standing association of many forms of negligence with *assumpsit*: where someone was contractually bound to take care, it was thought that he could not be concurrently liable for breach of the same duty to someone who was not party to the contract. Thus in 1842 a negligent manufacturer was held to be free from liability except to those who bought directly from him.[80] Though attributed by some modern lawyers to a 'privity of contract fallacy', the decision was less concerned with logic than with preserving the status quo; actions had not in fact previously been brought for defective products except in *assumpsit*, and it was thought that a change might bring a flood of unwelcome litigation. It should be remembered in this context that a contract could reduce liability by agreement, since the common law allowed a party to limit or contract out of liability for negligence.[81] It might therefore have seemed anomalous to recognise a greater degree of liability to a mere stranger than to a customer, at any rate in respect of something not inherently dangerous. The failure of 1842 is clear only in retrospect; it lay not in overlooking a fallacy but in waiving the opportunity to create a new duty of care.

Despite these retarding factors, the Victorian period did in the end witness a significant expansion of the tort of negligence. A wider

---

[77] Compare *McCarthy v. Younge* (1861) 6 H. & N. 329 (lender of unsafe scaffolding not liable to borrower) with *Farrant v. Barnes* (1862) 11 C.B.N.S. 553 (consignor of acid liable to consignee). Cf. *Langridge v. Levy* (1837) 2 M. & W. 519 (defective gun), and the older cases there cited.

[78] Thus Lord Abinger CB in *Priestley v. Fowler* (above) suggested that to make a master liable for a defective van would be to make him vicariously liable for the coach-builder and harness-maker.

[79] 'Lord Justice Bramwell on Actions of Negligence' (1880) 24 *Solicitors Jo.* 305. By 1880 Bramwell's approach was regarded as extremely conservative; but it was quite typical of the previous generation. See also P. S. Atiyah, *Rise and Fall of Freedom of Contract* (1979), pp. 377-379.

[80] *Winterbottom v. Wright* (1842) 10 M. & W. 109.

[81] See pp. 405-406, ante.

liability for defective premises was opened up by *Indermaur v. Dames*,[82] in which the Exchequer Chamber held that an occupier owed a duty of care to visitors, such as customers and their servants, who were expressly or impliedly invited on to the premises. The earlier decisions were not overturned, but distinguished, as denying an action only to 'bare licensees': a difficult distinction which led to many subtleties over the next century. The *volenti non fit injuria* principle was watered down in personal injury cases in late Victorian times as a result of changing attitudes towards workmen's compensation, attitudes reflected in legislation of the 1880s and 1890s which removed the common-employment barrier in the case of workmen.[83] The recovery of compensation for accidents was further assisted by the mass of regulatory legislation passed in the nineteenth century, which was held to generate new duties of care in cases where the courts thought civil liability would advance the legislative purpose;[84] and also by Lord Campbell's Act of 1846, which (following on the abolition of deodands[85]) enabled dependents to recover compensation for causing a person's death.[86]

Another large step forward was made in a different area in 1932, when the House of Lords reversed the 1842 decision and held that a negligent manufacturer could be liable in tort for injury to the ultimate consumer.[87] Behind the extension there was no doubt the consideration that manufacturers are better able to avert accidents than consumers, who know nothing of the manufacturing process and cannot practicably be expected to test goods for safety. The new duty of care was subsequently extended to repairers, assemblers and all kinds of supplier; and the action was made available not only to purchasers but also to users and other persons injured by defective products. And the subject-matter was eventually extended from chattels to buildings, the furthest point of development being that a builder might be liable not only for damage actually resulting from a dangerous building but for the expense

---

[82] (1866) L.R. 1 C.P. 274, L.R. 2 C.P. 318.

[83] *Smith v. Baker* [1891] A.C. 325 (knowledge of risk distinguished from consent to risk). The common-employment doctrine did not finally disappear until the Law Reform (Personal Injuries) Act 1948, 11 & 12 Geo. VI, c.41. See further H. Smith, 2 JLH 258.

[84] E.g. *Couch v. Steel* (1854) 3 E. & B. 402, which proved controversial but was eventually accepted; *Groves v. Lord Wimborne* [1898] 2 Q.B. 402 (unfenced machinery).

[85] See p. 437, ante.

[86] Stat 9 & 10 Vict., c.93. The action lay only where the deceased himself could have sued, had he survived.

[87] *Donoghue v. Stevenson* [1932] A.C. 562.

of repairing such a building to prevent future physical damage.[88] Most
of these extensions were judicial, though in 1957 parliament extended
occupiers' liability, in the form of a 'common duty of care' owed to all
lawful visitors.[89]

Perhaps the largest extensions of all have been made in the last 30
years, in the spheres of economic loss and negligent words. After the
emergence of the two distinct torts of defamation and deceit, the view
had emerged, and was regarded as clear law from 1893 until 1963, that
there was no liability for negligent misstatements causing economic (or
purely pecuniary) loss.[90] Generally speaking, the older law allowed
pecuniary damage to be recovered in negligence only as an adjunct to
physical damage; for instance, a person injured in a road accident had
been able to recover his medical expenses. There were a few ancient
instances of recovery for pure economic loss, as where sheriffs and court
officers were sued for negligently causing the loss of a lawsuit or legal
advantage, or in rare cases of non-contractual undertakings.[91] But the
floodgates were not opened until 1963, when the House of Lords decided
that an action lay for a negligent misstatement causing economic loss;[92]
a principle soon extended to negligent advice, or conduct, causing
economic loss. A merger of this new-found principle of liability for
economic loss with the *Donoghue v. Stevenson* 'persons in
contemplation' principle made it possible, in the late 1970s and 1980s,
for third parties to sue for economic loss resulting from their reliance on
negligent misstatements made to others,[93] from careless work done for
others and on which they placed no reliance,[94] or even (in the most
controversial extension so far) from the manufacture of an unusable,

---

88 *Batty v. Metropolitan Pty Realisations Ltd* [1978] Q.B. 554; *Anns v. Merton
L.B.C.* [1978] A.C. 728. Cf. the comments of the House of Lords in *D & F
Estates Ltd v. Church Commrs* [1988] 2 All E.R. 992.

89 Occupiers' Liability Act 1957, 5 & 6 Eliz. II, c.31. The duty did not extend to
trespassers, who were owed a much narrower duty (sometimes called the duty of
common humanity); but the position of trespassers was improved by the
Occupiers' Liability Act 1984 (c.3).

90 *Derry v. Peek* (1889) 14 App. Cas. 337 (see p. 401, ante), as interpreted in *Le
Lievre v. Gould* [1893] 1 Q.B. 491.

91 *Wilkinson v. Coverdale* (1793) 1 Esp. 75 (gratuitous undertaking to take out
insurance policy).

92 *Hedley, Byrne & Co. v. Heller & Partners Ltd* [1964] A.C. 465, [1963] 2 All E.R.
575.

93 E.g. *Yianni v. Edwin Evans & Sons* [1982] Q.B. 438 (building society's surveyor
liable to purchaser).

94 E.g. *Ross v. Caunters* [1980] Ch. 297, [1979] 3 All E.R. 580 (testator's solicitor
liable to intended beneficiary deprived of bequest through negligent
draftsmanship).

though safe, product.[95] This last extension was doubtless conceived of
as a further escape from the 'privity of contract fallacy', but it threatened
to destroy the difference between contract and tort altogether by making
the defendant liable for failing to confer a benefit on someone who had
not bargained for it. Although this remarkable proposition emanated
from the House of Lords, it was widely condemned and it is at present
unlikely that any broad new principle will be recognised as flowing
from it.[96]

The growth in personal injury litigation in the last century is
obviously explained by the proliferating dangers to life and limb in a
machine age; but an increase in litigation does not in itself determine
whether or how the law will change. The pressure to extend the scope
of liability for negligence can perhaps be attributed rather to the growing
complexity of industrial and commercial organisation. A plaintiff, in
choosing a defendant likely to be able to meet his claim, more often had
to look beyond the party with whom he came into personal contact.
And it may be supposed that a principal reason for acceding to the
pressure has been the general view that those who create risks,
especially if they do so in the course of business, ought to pay for
them. No doubt this is the explanation for the introduction, and
subsequent extension, both of employers' vicarious liability and
manufacturers' liability. A business which depends on using potentially
dangerous machinery, be it a railway company or a factory, or which
delegates its activities to employees, or which distributes its wares far
and wide, should expect to compensate those who may be injured in the
process, and provide for such liabilities by insurance and by spreading
the cost among all its customers. At first this attitude may have been
more prevalent among juries than among judges: as was observed in
1880, 'Things that no one would dream of treating as negligence in the
case of ordinary individuals are treated as negligence in the case of
companies', and the courts were powerless to correct verdicts against the
evidence.[97] But the new spirit soon moved the judiciary and legislature
as well. Of course it would be improper for a court to base liability on

---

[95] *Junior Books v. Veitchi Co. Ltd* [1983] 1 A.C. 520, [1982] 3 All E.R. 201.
[96] A retreat began in the later 1980s: see *D & F Estates Ltd v. Church Commrs*
[1988] 2 All E.R. 992.
[97] 24 *Solicitors Jo.* 305. The remedy for a verdict contrary to the evidence was a
new trial; but 'It is no use ordering new trials when the jury is sure to find the
same way, and so the whole standard of what constitutes negligence gradually
becomes warped': ibid.

its knowledge whether or not a particular litigant was actually insured;[98] nevertheless, after the introduction of liability insurance in the last quarter of the nineteenth century,[99] the assumption that a prudent business should be fully insured may have influenced the courts in extending business liability.[100] It may also explain the tendency to increase the sums recoverable in personal injury cases far beyond anything which an individual defendant could hope to pay. The notion that those who create risks should be treated as insurers would, if pursued to its logical conclusion, suggest a regime of strict liability as preferable to one based on fault. Just such a regime was recommended in relation to personal injuries by a royal commission in 1978,[101] and a step in that direction has recently been taken in relation to defective products.[102] Such notions were not wholly foreign to nineteenth-century thought,[103] and the Victorian judges themselves developed new areas of strict liability in relation to dangerous and non-natural user of property,[104] and breach of statutory duty;[105] but the courts have generally contented themselves with enlarging the scope of the existing tort of negligence.

The number and variety of the recent cases have brought about a further change of approach. The earlier twentieth-century treatises, like the abridgments of the eighteenth century and Beven's treatise of 1889, did little more than arrange lists of apparently unrelated cases in which duties had been recognised; Beven identified no less than fifty-seven

---

98   *Davie v. New Merton Board Mills* [1959] A.C. 604 at 626-627, per Viscount Simon; the denial, of course, only proves that such factors were sometimes adverted to.

99   See Cornish & Clark, pp. 512-514. Liability insurance was at first resisted, even by reformers, on the grounds that it would encourage negligence: ibid., p. 524.

100 It was an explicit factor in allowing carriers to exclude liability for valuables without extra payment: p. 405, ante. Lord Denning MR was perhaps the first to admit it openly in other cases: e.g. *Post Office v. Norwich Union Fire Insurance Society Ltd* [1967] 2 Q.B. 363 at 375. In considering the reasonableness of a limitation clause, the court must now take into account the availability of insurance: Unfair Contract Terms Act 1977 (c.50), s.11(4)b.

101 Report of the Royal Commission on Civil Liability and Compensation for Personal Injury [Pearson Report] (1978), Cmnd 7054. The commission found that the present cost to the public of collecting damages for injuries was almost as great as the damages recovered.

102 Consumer Protection Act 1987 (c.43).

103 For Edwin Chadwick's proposals in the 1830s and 1840s, see Cornish & Clark, p. 515.

104 *Rylands v. Fletcher* (1866), p. 491, post. The judges were willing to include railway engines under this head (see *Jones v. Festiniog Rly Co.* (1868) L.R. 3 Q.B. 733), though most railways could shelter behind statutory authority.

105 See p. 473, ante.

varieties of duty. It is still to some extent unpredictable whether the courts will recognise a duty of care in a newly presented situation; but now, it is said, the general 'neighbour' principle is taken to impose a duty of care unless there is some reason of policy why it should not.[106] Indeed, it has recently been suggested in the House of Lords that the courts must follow the broad principle even if they foresee undesirable consequences in a given case, leaving parliament to draw the lines.[107] That suggestion, whether right or wrong, marks the apotheosis of negligence as a basis for liability in tort.

Further reading

Milsom HFCL, pp. 305-313, 392-400

Manchester MLH, pp. 281-297

Cornish & Clark, pp. 486-541

P. H. Winfield, 'The History of Negligence in the Law of Torts' (1926) 42 LQR 184-201

C. H. S. Fifoot, *Judge and Jurist in the Reign of Victoria* (1959), pp. 31-56

M. J. Prichard, 'Trespass, Case and the Rule in Williams v. Holland' [1964] CLJ 234-253; *Scott v. Shepherd (1773) and the Emergence of the Tort of Negligence* (SS Lecture, 1976)

J. H. Baker, 'General Principles of Liability' and 'Fault in Negligence Actions' (1978) 94 SS *220-230*

M. S. Arnold, 'Accident, Mistake and Rules of Liability in the 14th Century Law of Torts' (1979) 128 *Univ. Pennsylvania Law Rev.* 361-378; 'Towards an Ideology of the Early English Law of Obligations' (1987) 5 LHR 505-521; *Select Cases of Trespass from the King's Courts 1307-99* (100 SS, 1985; 103 SS, 1987)

V. Palmer, 'Why Privity entered Tort – an Historical Reexamination of Winterbottom v. Wright' (1983) 27 AJLH 85-98

J. L. Barton, 'Liability for Things in the 19th Century' (1984), *Law and Social Change*, pp. 145-155

D. Kretzmer, 'Transformation of Tort Liability in the 19th Century' (1984) 4 OJLS 46-87

---

106 *Home Office v. Dorset Yacht Co.* [1970] A.C. 1004 at 1026, per Lord Reid; *Anns v. Merton L.B.C.* [1978] A.C. 728 at 751-752, per Lord Wilberforce.

107 *McLoughlin v. O'Brian* [1983] 1 A.C. 410 at 430-431, per Lord Scarman.

23. Nuisance

If 'trespass' proved a useful word to lawyers because it was capable of describing a wide variety of wrongs, so to a lesser extent did 'nuisance'.[1] They both began life as ordinary words with no inherent technical significance. Nuisance comprises, for legal purposes, such unlawful conduct as annoyance or disturbance in the enjoyment of property rather than forcible physical injury. It can be regarded as a species of trespass, since that is a word of even wider ambit, but it cannot usually be trespass *vi et armis*. When, in the mid-fourteenth century, the central courts began to entertain actions of trespass on the case, nuisance was indeed brought within the common-law concept of trespass; but it had already enjoyed a separate existence, both in the local courts and in a number of special real actions in the central courts. It is from these latter forms of action that the original legal character of nuisance derived; it was a disturbance of the enjoyment of real property, or of its appurtenances, falling short of a forcible trespass or ouster.

Remedies for Nuisance

The concept of nuisance grew up within the real actions because they required supplementation in two types of case. The first was an interference with a servitude over another's land, such as a right of way or pasture. The owner of a servitude had no seisin of the servient land itself. Instead, therefore, of the writ of right to recover the land he was given an analogous *praecipe* writ to recover the servitude. Such a writ instructed the sheriff to order the defendant that he permit (*quod permittat*) the plaintiff to have his pasture, or right of way, or whatever. A variant of the writ *quod permittat* lay to permit the plaintiff to abate a nuisance; for instance, to knock down a wall built across his right of way (*quod permittat prosternere murum*), or to restore a diverted watercourse. The second situation was an interference by indirect means with enjoyment of the land itself. For instance, if a neighbour stopped up a watercourse on his own land so that the adjoining land was flooded, or left his land unfenced so that cattle strayed onto adjoining land, this

---

[1] The Latin root of 'nuisance' is *nocere* (to hurt or harm), from which come also the nouns 'annoyance' and 'noise' and the adjectives 'noisome' and 'noxious'.

was neither a disseisin of the land nor a trespass *vi et armis*, but merely the indirect consequence of something done on the wrongdoer's own property. In these cases also the injured freeholder could obtain a remedy by *quod permittat*, or something analogous. The writ *de curia claudenda*, for instance, lay to compel the defendant to enclose or fence his courtyard, 'which is open, to the nuisance of the free tenement' of the plaintiff; and the writ of *reparari facias* lay to compel the repair of sea-walls or ditches.

THE ASSIZE OF NUISANCE

The lost legislation which established the assize of novel disseisin in the reign of Henry II is thought to have contained a reference to acts done to the nuisance of a free tenement. At any rate, there was from about that time a species of the assize, later called the assize of nuisance, which lay to abate a nuisance. Like the assize for land, it may have originated as a remedy against lords, in this case for refusing pasture to tenants entitled to have it.[2] But it soon became divorced from the feudal context, and the interests protected by it were to some extent assimilated to property rights. The party aggrieved by a nuisance had a limited right of self-help analogous to the disseisee's right of re-entry; he could enter the servient tenement and abate the nuisance, or exercise his servitude notwithstanding the obstruction. After the limitation period had expired, this right of self-help was converted into a bare right of action, the appropriate action being a *quod permittat*. But the de facto enjoyment of the right could be restored, in the same way as seisin of the land could be restored, by an assize. The plaintiff in the assize of nuisance complained that he had been disseised of his common of pasture, or right of way, or whatever, or that the defendant had done some act to the nuisance of his free tenement. Recognitors were then summoned to view the tenement and to enquire whether there had been a disseisin or nuisance as alleged. If they found for the plaintiff, the defendant had to abate the nuisance and pay damages. The assize lay not only for nuisances to land, but also for disturbing the franchise of market and rights of common, and by a statute of 1285 it was extended to other profits *à prendre*, tolls, and offices.[3] But the assize availed only freeholders; it lay only against freeholders; and a number of kinds of nuisance to land were arbitrarily excluded. A wider range of nuisances

---

2   Milsom, introduction to Pollock & Maitland, vol. I, pp. xlii-xliii.
3   Statute of Westminster II 1285, c.25. As to offices, see further p. 489, post.

was protected by *quod permittat*,[4] or by viscontiel writs to initiate suits in the county court which were then removable into the Common Pleas by *pone*. The viscontiel remedy extended to a wide range of nuisances, such as those caused by smithies or watermills.

Just as the assize of novel disseisin gained popularity at the expense of the writ of right and *praecipe*, so the assize of nuisance replaced the *quod permittat* for most purposes;[5] the latter remained in use only where the nuisance was no longer novel, or where one of the original parties had died, or where the subject-matter was not within the assize. By the later fifteenth century, however, both actions were virtually unheard of in practice. They had gone the way of all the real actions and were being replaced by trespass.

NUISANCE AND TRESPASS

The assize and *quod permittat* were not conceived of as comprehensive remedies for nuisance. Minor differences between neighbours were intended to go, as they always had, to local courts: to the county, to the hundred, and to the borough or manorial court. The king's justices were not to be bothered with smelly privies; but there was a remedy elsewhere.[6] When attempts were made in the fifteenth century to explain the restricted scope of the common-law remedies, 'nuisance to the person' was distinguished from nuisance to the land, smell and noise being in the former category.[7] Actions for personal nuisance, as is shown by the *audias* form of the viscontiel writ, were seen as complaints of wrongs rather than demands; in other words, they were cases of 'trespass' in the broadest sense of the term. The writ of trespass *vi et armis* was not strictly available unless the defendant forcibly impeded the plaintiff or actually invaded his close; but factual details did not have to be spelt out in the writ, and a series of fourteenth-century writs alleging forcible nuisances to watercourses may well

---

4   E.g. damage by fumes from a limekiln: *Dalby v. Berch* (1330) Y.B. Trin. 4 Edw. III, fo. 36, pl.26.

5   One advantage of the assize was that it put the cost of abating the nuisance on the defendant: *Rikhill's Case* (1400) B. & M. 581 at 583, per Skrene sjt; Richard Sutton's reading in the Inner Temple (1494), 102 SS 118. After 1382 it could be brought as an alternative to viscontiel writs of nuisance: Stat. 6 Ric. II, sess. i, c. 3.

6   *Novae Narrationes* (80 SS) xcviii, and p. 202, no. C107; *Luter v. Ware* (1341) *London Assize*, p. 88, pl.364; *Asshecombe v. Accon* (1400) ibid. 174, pl.645. See also *Yonge v. Chadenesfeld* (1378) ibid. 160, pl.617 (vibrations and smoke from armourer's forge).

7   Case at Richard Sutton's reading in the Inner Temple (1494), 102 SS 117; B. & M. 585; 105 SS 291-292 (citing a case of Edw. IV).

conceal a stretching of remedies to fill gaps.[8] Once the royal courts dispensed with the necessity to allege force and arms, the action on the case for nuisance took over this role.

One of the earliest actions on the case was brought to recover damages for flooding suffered as a result of a failure to repair a sea-wall. The nonfeasance was a legal wrong because it was in breach of a customary duty attaching to certain tenements near the sea; and the plaintiff succeeded in recovering not only damages but also an order to repair, despite the argument that the proper remedy was *reparari facias*.[9] The order of specific performance was challenged unsuccessfully by a writ of error; but it was doubtless irregular in trespass, and that aspect of the precedent was not followed. Damages would usually suffice; and if further damage was incurred, a new action could be brought. Forty years later case was allowed instead of *curia claudenda* for failing to repair a hedge in the open country.[10] Actions on the case for failing to repair roads, bridges and fences, and for failing to clean out ditches and watercourses, abound in the records and year-books after this period. Other early actions on the case were established where for some other reason the assize did not lie; for instance, where the nuisance was perpetrated by someone other than the freeholder, or where the plaintiff was a lessee for years, or where the nuisance was over and done with before the action was brought, or where the nuisance was of a 'personal' nature, such as noise or smell.[11]

The original role of actions on the case in this area, as in others, was to fill gaps in the existing remedies, and thereby to bring cases to Westminster which formerly had gone to local courts. Therefore the argument that case could not be brought where there was already a remedy by real action – the argument which, as we have seen, was raised to prevent case from doing the work of debt, detinue and covenant – was also raised as an objection to its use in place of the assize of nuisance.[12] As in the sphere of contract, the practical impact of this objection remains uncertain, because the plea rolls of the fifteenth and sixteenth

---

8 E.g. *Lowth v. Abbot of Lesnes* (1317) 103 SS 348 (diverting and polluting water); *Abbot of Louth Park v. Parson of Somercotes* (1329) ibid. 351 (villagers filling in dike and diverting water); *Prior of Hatfield Peverel v. Willynghale* (1364) ibid. 352 (diverting water from mill). See also Arnold, 100 SS lxxxvii-lxxxviii.

9 *Bernardeston v. Heighlynge* (1342-44) B. & M. 338; 32 SS 309; 103 SS 457.

10 *Newynton v. Legh* (1388) Y.B. Hil. 11 Ric. II, p. 140, pl.6. It was argued that *curia claudenda* itself lay only for hedges between houses and their courtyards.

11 E.g. the case of the dunghill in Cheapside (temp. Edw. IV), cited in 105 SS 291-292. See also 94 SS 235.

12 See, e.g., *Rikhill's Case* (1400) B. & M. 581; *Right's Case* (1455) B. & M. 584.

centuries contain numerous undetermined actions which appear to defy the theory. Moreover, the pleader often bolstered his case by alleging consequential loss of profit and even deceit. It seems to have been settled by the last quarter of the fifteenth century, in both benches, that case would lie for diverting watercourses from water-mills;[13] that was the commonest case of nuisance in the rolls, and a case where loss of profit would usually be obvious.

The reaction against the spread of the new remedy may have come, as in other contexts, during the reign of Henry VIII;[14] but there is no clear evidence of a difference between the courts until the Elizabethan period. In 1566 the Common Pleas was able to make a definite stand in a clear case: an action on the case could not be used instead of the assize where a freeholder obstructed the right of way of another freeholder.[15] The familiar story of disagreement with the King's Bench then repeated itself. From the 1580s, at the latest, a stream of pronouncements from the latter rejected the Common Pleas view and gave the plaintiff an election between case and the assize.[16] The arguments advanced in the course of the controversy closely resemble those over the expansion of *assumpsit* and *trover*. The King's Bench was content with formal propriety, ensured by the allegations of deceit and special loss, which were probably non-traversable. The common-form allegation that a defendant who committed a nuisance did so 'craftily scheming to defraud' the plaintiff of the use, enjoyment or profit of his land, has a fictional flavour when constantly repeated; though it may more often have been true in nuisance than in *assumpsit*. The Common Pleas accepted that special loss would justify an action on the case, since it could not be recovered in the assize, and here again genuine special loss (such as the miller's lost profit) was likely to be present in the commonest cases. The dispute about overlapping remedies was therefore probably at its flimsiest in the context of nuisance, and that is doubtless why it was in this context resolved the soonest. Although the Exchequer Chamber had taken to reversing King's Bench judgments in the 1590s, it decided in

---

13   *Prior of Christchurch, Canterbury v. Hore* (1492) Y.B. Trin. 13 Hen. VII, fo. 26, pl. 4; Caryll's MS. reports; CP 40/923, m. 244d; *Lord de Grey's Case* (1505) B. & M. 586, and note.

14   See *Anon.* (1522) B. & M. 587. The undetermined demurrer in *Beaumont v. Benet* (1519-25) CP 40/1024, m. 345, may reflect a difficulty; but the demurrer was to a special plea, not to the declaration. In *Dod v. Nedeham* (1525) CP 40/1048A, m. 408, the court took advisement for four terms after verdict for the plaintiff and no judgment was entered.

15   *Yevance v. Holcombe* (1566) B. & M. 589.

16   *Aston's Case* (1586) Dyer 250, note; *Anon.* (1587) B. & M. 588, and note; *Beswick v. Cunden* (1596) Cro. Eliz. 520.

1601 – with only two judicial grumbles[17] – that case would lie for enclosing a common.[18] This seems, in effect, to have put an end to the assize of nuisance.

A finer point of disagreement between the courts concerned the old subject of nonfeasance, here in a new guise: whether a landowner was liable in case for passively continuing – that is, not putting an end to – a nuisance already existing on his land. According to the Common Pleas, this was not a wrong for which the defendant should pay damages, but was remediable only by *quod permittat*.[19] That was also the view of the Exchequer.[20] But the King's Bench took the view that it was actionable in case,[21] and this view prevailed.[22] The liability, however, was confined to 'continuing' a man-made nuisance. An occupier was not considered liable for nuisances arising solely from natural causes until 1967.[23]

The Nature of Nuisance

When actions on the case supplanted the assize, both the proprietary and the personal aspects of nuisance came together under the same legal heading. This may have turned thoughts to the need for a general principle governing disputes about good neighbourliness. It was found in the maxim, borrowed from Ulpian, that a man should so use his own property as not to injure that of others: *sic utere tuo ut alienum non laedas*. But the application of so broad a principle could be a matter of grave doubt, since it suggested a balancing of interests rather than absolute rights and wrongs. A man might build on his own land according to the dictates of his own taste. But might he build so as to block his neighbour's light and air, to spy on his private life, or to

---

[17] By the arch-conservatives Walmsley J and Peryam CB; 'but they did not dissent strongly' (B. & M. at 591).

[18] *Cantrell v. Churche* (1601) B. & M. 588; Cro. Eliz. 845; Noy 37.

[19] *Beswick v. Cunden (No. 2)* (1596) Cro. Eliz. 520; Moore K.B. 353. (The plaintiff had in fact already brought *quod permittat*, but failed on technical grounds: Noy 68.) The assize would not lie for nonfeasance: Sutton's reading, 102 SS 117.

[20] *Edwards v. Halinder* (1594) B. & M. 606.

[21] *Rolfe v. Rolfe* (1582) cit. 4 Co. Rep. 101; *Beswick v. Cunden (No. 1)* (1595) Cro. Eliz. 420 (nuisance caused by defendant, but in time of plaintiff's predecessor in title).

[22] *Rippon v. Bowles* (1615) 1 Rolle Rep. 221; Cro. Jac. 373; *Brent v. Haddon* (1619) Cro. Jac. 555.

[23] *Goldman v. Hargrave* [1967] 1 A.C. 645, [1966] 2 All E.R. 989; *Leakey v. National Trust* [1980] Q.B. 522, [1980] 1 All E.R. 171.

obstruct his view? When did a bad neighbour become a legal nuisance? A convenient way of solving such problems of policy was to divide the interests protected by actions for nuisance into those which could only exist as property rights created by grant or prescription, and those which were the natural incidents of land ownership in general.

ACQUIRED RIGHTS: EASEMENTS AND PROFITS

The words 'easement' and 'profit' did not begin as technical terms, but were words used to describe the various advantages enjoyed by an owner of property vis à vis his neighbours, whether arising by grant, by prescription, or by operation of law. Thus, a plaintiff in trespass on the case for nuisance commonly alleged a loss of *proficuum, commodum et aisiamentum*, making no distinction between them; and the phrase even occurs in a contract case to denote the profit and advantage of a bargain.[24] But the word 'easement' came to be confined to such rights as could be regarded as distinct property rights in themselves, and not merely as automatic incidents to the ownership or occupation of land. Easements were then distinguished from profits *à prendre*, servitudes which include a right to take something from the servient tenement; for instance, a pasture or fishery. Examples of easements in the narrow sense are rights of way, rights to light, and rights to receive a flow of water or air. These are not profits, for nothing is taken; nor are they natural rights belonging to landowners in general, for they must be acquired by grant or prescription.

The decision as to what interests could only subsist as easements rested upon the determination of what might subsist as natural rights. Commons and rights of way were never natural rights. The receipt of daylight to illuminate a house may once have been regarded as a natural right, acquired by building a house with unobstructed windows, and the flow of sunlight to a garden may have been similarly treated.[25] The first debate about light to be reported in full occurred in 1569. The plaintiff sued his London neighbour for erecting a new building which blocked the side windows of his house; and the defendant pleaded a custom of London to build so as to stop side windows. Counsel for the plaintiff said that 'when this light and air are taken from him, his house

---

24   94 SS *234* n.8.

25   Y.B. Trin. 19 Edw. II, p. 679 (not enough light to work by); *Novae Narrationes* (80 SS), xcviii, 203, no. C108 (no light). These were viscontiel actions. See also *Hulle v. Orynge* (1466) B. & M. 327 at 329, per Danby CJ (grass and crops deprived of sunlight).

remaineth as a dungeon', and that the alleged custom was unreasonable since it would deprive the plaintiff of a necessity of life. Counsel for the defendant said that light and air received only through side windows were not necessaries; that the side windows in themselves infringed the defendant's privacy; and that new building was in the public interest, since the more populous London became the more honourable it would be.[26] It seems the plaintiff succeeded; at any rate the better opinion favoured the action.[27] The alleged city custom to allow building which obstructed lights was obviously designed to facilitate building in cities; almost all buildings would to some extent block a neighbour's light. But the courts declined to allow such customs, except in relation to rebuilding on an existing foundation: 'a man may build upon an old foundation by such a custom, and stop up the lights of his neighbour which are adjoining unto him; and if he make new windows higher, the other may build up his house higher to destroy those new windows: but a man cannot build a house upon a place where there was none before, as in a yard, and so stop his neighbour's lights.'[28] It followed that increasing the height of a building could not be prevented merely by a few years' priority in building nearby. Nor could a wholly new building be prevented by a neighbour who happened to have built first, unless he could prescribe for the lights since time immemorial. The plaintiff in the case of 1569 did rely on the immemorial enjoyment of light through specified windows; and it soon became established that such a prescriptive claim to 'ancient lights', or a grant, was necessary.[29] Light was no longer, therefore, a natural right belonging to anyone who built first. Similarly, the right to have support for a building, originally considered a natural right, could exist in later law only as an easement.[30] Some interests were incapable of being acquired even as easements: thus it was stated in 1587 that, although an action would lie for obstructing

[26] Although this was conceded by the plaintiff, unrestrained building in the metropolis was soon seen as a threat to the quality of life and not merely as a sign of progress: see T. G. Barnes, 58 *California Law Rev.* 1332, for attitudes in a slightly later period.

[27] *Hales' Case* (1569) B. & M. 592.

[28] *Hughes v. Keene* (1611) Godb. 183; also reported in Yelv. 215; 1 Buls. 115; Coke's *Entries*, fo. 120 (plaintiff prescribes for ancient lights and alleges defendant's building to be upon a new site). See also *Bland v. Moseley* (1587) B. & M. 597 (custom held bad); *Hammond v. Alsey* (1592) cit. 1 Buls. 116 (custom to build on old foundation good).

[29] *Bowry v. Pope* (1588) 1 Leon. 168; Cro. Eliz. 118 (window only 30 years old).

[30] *Palmer v. Fletcher* (1663) 1 Lev. 122; 1 Sid. 167. The right to support for the land itself remained a natural right.

ancient lights, it could not be brought for 'a matter of pleasure only', such as a pleasant view, however long it had existed.[31]

When an easement was interfered with, an action on the case lay as a matter of course. There was no need to balance the interests of the parties, or to introduce questions of policy, because the matter was one of property.[32] Such an interference is sometimes called 'cognate nuisance' to distinguish it from interferences with the personal enjoyment of the incidents of occupying the land.

NATURAL RIGHTS

The occupier of land was protected against forcible invasions of his close by the writs of trespass and forcible entry, and he was protected up to a point by nuisance actions against the disturbance of his environment. Where noxious matter came onto the plaintiff's land indirectly by reason of the dilapidated state of the defendant's premises, the collapse or putrefaction of something placed near the boundary, the flow of water, force of wind, or permeation of damp and mould, this was not a trespass *vi et armis*; but if damage resulted, such an injury was remedied by an action on the case.

Several such cases are to be found in the plea rolls from the later fourteenth century onwards. Defendants built so near the edge of their land that water dripped onto the plaintiff's house and caused damage; or put filth in a stream and polluted the plaintiff's water supply; or dumped putrid refuse so near the boundary that the plaintiff's house was infected or rendered uninhabitable. The action on the case for pollution of various kinds became one of the commonest forms of nuisance suit in times when there were minimal public health regulations and the standards of hygiene were low. It was brought against butchers who did not adequately dispose of blood, offal and carrion. It was brought against tanners and glovers whose limekilns emitted poisonous fumes which destroyed pasture and fruit and spoiled drinking water, and against dyers for corrupting the air and water with their chemicals. It was brought against private householders for keeping leaky or ramshackle latrines in inconvenient places. It seems that a nuisance might even be committed by failing to remove noxious matter from the plaintiff's

---

31 *Bland v. Moseley* (1587) B. & M. 597 at 599, per Wray CJ. The custom of London had always permitted a view to be blocked by building: *London Assize*, p. xxv.

32 It did, however, become necessary to distinguish a substantial interference from a slight infringement, lest building in towns should become impossible: *A.-G. v. Nicol* (1809) 16 Ves. 338; McLaren, 3 OJLS at 184.

property, where there was a legal duty to do so; for instance, where tithes of milk and butter were set aside and the rector did not collect them until they were mouldy. To this further species of nuisance by nonfeasance belongs, perhaps, a novel tort envisaged in 1569: 'if one who has a horrible sickness be in my house, and will not depart, an action will lie against him; and yet he taketh not any air from me, but infecteth that which I have'.[33] The remaining on the land was a trespass, but the infection of the air was a nuisance.

The 'personal' nuisances remedied by the action on the case included noise and vibrations (typically from a smith's forge) and smell, which frequently raised the fear of infection; these were recognised from the beginning, because they had earlier been remedied in local courts. In the sixteenth and seventeenth centuries there was increasing speculation about the scope of nuisance affecting the senses. Not every inconvenience could be the subject of legal redress: the law had to strike a balance between a man's freedom to do as he liked with and upon his own property, and his duty not to injure his neighbour or his neighbour's property. Noise was considered in an early Elizabethan case. A barrister brought an action against a neighbouring schoolmaster because the 'jabbering of the boys' (*le jabber de boys*) disturbed the quiet of his chambers. The action failed, however, on the ground that it was lawful to set up school anywhere; and the lawyer had to move his study to another side of the house.[34] Protection against noise was not absolute: the utility of the defendant's conduct, and the means of avoiding damage, were also relevant factors. In the case of smell, pleaders did well to emphasise the danger of infection as well as the distastefulness to the senses; fresh air was a matter of health as well as comfort or pleasure. In a leading case of 1610, the defendant had erected a pig-sty so near the plaintiff's land that 'a fetid and unwholesome stink' flowed into his house and rendered it uninhabitable without risk of infection. Counsel argued that pigs were necessary as food, and that a man should not be so tender-nosed as to object to their smell. But it was held that the action lay, not for interfering with comfort, but for infecting the air. Again the plaintiff's interest was not absolute; as Warburton J hinted, the smell of stables might be treated differently.[35]

---

[33] *Hales' Case* (1569) B. & M. 592 at 593, per Mounson. The mouldy cheese problem was discussed in *Wiseman v. Denham* (1623) Palm. 341; Ley 69.

[34] *Jeffrey's Case* (c. 1560) B. & M. 592.

[35] *Aldred v. Benton* (1610) B. & M. 599. (The plaintiff recovered only 1d. damages, with £9. 19s. 11d. costs.) On infectious smells, see also *R. v. Rockett* (1607) Exeter College MS. 93, fo. 62v, per Williams J.

Some interests were excluded altogether; there was, for instance, no right of privacy at common law.[36]

In all these cases argument turned in part on the utility or necessity of the defendant's conduct. Someone had to keep pigs, and schoolboys. The trades of butcher, tanner and dyer were well established and necessary to the common wealth, notwithstanding their unpleasant side-effects. It was unthinkable to ban such activities; yet a line had to be drawn somewhere. The problem was fully discussed in 1629, in a case where a brewhouse was erected within six feet of the office of a bishop's registrar, and the fumes of burning sea-coal not only threatened the health of the inhabitants but damaged the registrar's papers and utensils. The court considered that it was not inherently unlawful to burn sea-coal, 'though it is not as sweet as wood', and that if a neighbour was too tender-nosed to endure the smoke he ought to leave. Argument was consciously addressed to policy issues, such as the scarceness of timber for fuel. The action was allowed, nevertheless, because the fumes were excessive by reason of their continuous emission and had actually caused damage to property.[37] From this point it became clear that if an activity amounted to a nuisance, it would be actionable regardless of its utility; and this is the present law. Noxious activities must be carried out in such places and in such manner that they do not hurt individual landowners. This was partly a matter of pre-existing local amenity; as Jones J remarked in the 1629 case, a butcher's shop might be acceptable in Newgate shambles but not in Cheapside.[38] Whether an activity amounted to an actionable nuisance was thus resolved into a question whether those affected ought reasonably to be expected to put up with it. The standard of reasonableness is, of course, ever shifting. In Victorian times it was the subject of considerable debate, when attempts were made to check some of the highly unpleasant industrial processes considered vital to the nation's economy. But the problem of pollution in an industrial age was too large to be resolved by the accidents of private litigation. The most effective weapon against large-scale

---

[36] Such rights were nevertheless asserted under local customs: *Rutton v. Forbizor* (1302) Y.B. Mich. 30 Edw. I, p. 23; 80 SS 85 (custom of Ludlow against opening windows in adjoining house so that defendant could see plaintiff's 'privetez'); *Worthstede v. Bisshop* (1348) *London Assize*, p. 100, pl. 407 (similar words used in London); reading in Gray's Inn (1512) 93 SS 17, per Fyneux CJ (custom of London). In London it became the practice to allow windows over 16 feet high: *London Assize*, pp. xxv–xxvi.

[37] *Jones v. Powell* (1629) B. & M. 601; Palm. 536. Accord. *Poynton v. Gill* (1639) Rolle Abr., vol. I, p. 89 (grass damaged by smoke from lead smelting). Sea-coal was no new problem: see *London Assize*, p. 617 (1378).

[38] B. & M. at 603. Cf. *St Helens Smelting Co. v. Tipping* (1865) 11 H.L.C. 642 (fumes in Merseyside).

industrial pollution proved to be public-health legislation, such as the statute which abolished London smog overnight.[39]

DISTURBANCES

When the action on the case had replaced the assize for easements and profits, it was found convenient also to use it to replace the assize for franchises and offices. These latter seem remote from nuisance in the usual technical sense of the word, but the remedies were closely analogous and legally indistinguishable. Franchises, being mostly economic rights acquired by royal grant or prescription – such as markets and fairs – had been protected by a number of different writs. The form finally established for use against someone who set up a rival market was *quare levavit mercatum*: 'to show why *D* set up a market to the nuisance of *P*'s market'.[40] From an early date, however, trespass had also been used to protect market rights against interference falling short of setting up in competition.[41] Economic rights other than franchises, such as the manorial right of mill-suit, came to be protected by other forms of trespass.[42]

An office of profit, granted as a freehold interest, was protected after 1285 by the assize.[43] An office in this sense was not the same as any contractual employment; it was granted with words of limitation, and had to be exercised in a certain place. Most offices were of a public character, though it was possible to bring the assize for a private office provided that it involved taking profits from land.[44] Such an office was in effect a profit *à prendre*, exercisable in the place where it was performed. For example, an officer of a court of law could bring the assize against a usurper, and the proprietary nature of the claim was shown by the allegation of seisin through taking fees in the place where he sat in court.[45] The assize for an office survived into the seventeenth century: in 1608 an assize was brought by the master of the king's tennis games (*magister ludorum pilarum palmarium regis*), and the

---

[39] Clean Air Act 1968 (c.62).

[40] E.g. *R. v. Commonalty of Shrewsbury* (1314) 100 SS 108. Cf. 80 SS c-cii.

[41] See p. 511, post.

[42] See pp. 510-511, post.

[43] Statute of Westminster II 1285, c.25 ('keeping of parks, woods, forests, chases, warrens, gates, and other bailiwicks and offices in fee'). Despite the words 'in fee', this was also applied to offices granted for life.

[44] *Cut v. Preston* (1329) 97 SS 343 (keeper of park); *Wood v. FitzRichard* (1356) 30 Lib. Ass. pl.4 (bailiff and hayward of manor). Appointing a shepherd for life did not confer freehold, because it only concerned chattels: Inner Temple moot (1492) 102 SS 104; 105 SS 257.

[45] *Vaux v. Jefferen* (1555) Dyer 114 (filazership of the Common Pleas).

judgment was that he recover his seisin in the tennis courts (*in spheristiis*).[46] But where there was no complete usurpation of the office, or where the claimant had no prior seisin, an action on the case was appropriate; and, as in other contexts, case came to be regarded as a more convenient remedy even where the assize lay. However, case for disturbance in an office, modelled on case for nuisance, did not enjoy a long history; a better remedy was soon found in the form of a quasi-contractual claim for the intercepted fees, as money had and received.[47]

The disappearance of alienable and inheritable offices made actions concerning title to office obsolete. But the action on the case was not confined to the kinds of disturbance covered by the assize, and could be brought for disturbing miscellaneous interests which would otherwise go unprotected: for instance, the right to sit in a particular pew in a church, which was a kind of easement over the parson's freehold.[48] The development of this innominate class of actions for disturbances reached a high point in the important constitutional case of *Ashby v. White*, which settled the right of a parliamentary elector to sue a returning officer who wrongfully refused to receive his vote. The pleadings show an affinity to more conventional nuisance and disturbance actions, but the right to vote was not strictly a property right and the majority of King's Bench judges thought the action would not lie because it was unprecedented. Holt CJ, in a stirring judgment which was later upheld by the House of Lords, dissented on the grounds that 'if the plaintiff has a right he must of necessity have the means to vindicate it and a remedy if he is injured in the enjoyment or exercise of it'.[49] *Ubi jus ibi remedium*. The action for disturbance would not, however, avail a plaintiff who could not assert some legal right. Purely economic nuisance, in the absence of a franchise, custom or prescriptive privilege, was not actionable.[50]

Isolated Occurrences

Since the essence of nuisance was an interference with the enjoyment of property, it was usually a continuing wrong. The plaintiff's inconvenience and damage were increased by the duration of the

46   *Webbe v. Knivet* (1608) 8 Co. Rep. 45.
47   See p. 419, ante.
48   *Harvey v. Percivall* (1606) Coke's *Entries*, fo. 8, pl.7; *Dawney v. Dee* (1620) Cro. Jac. 605; 2 Rolle Rep. 139; Palmer 46.
49   *Ashby v. White* (1703) 2 Ld Raym. 938 at 953.
50   See pp. 510-512, 524, post.

nuisance; and the older real remedies depended on its continuance down to the time of the action, because their object was abatement. In the action on the case, however, it was irrelevant whether the act complained of was spent or continuing, since the object was compensation. Presumably each time rain dripped from the defendant's eaves onto the plaintiff's house there was a nuisance, and each little hurt merged in the whole continuing nuisance.

That a single unrepeated catastrophe might be actionable was confirmed in 1704. The defendant had failed to repair the wall of his 'privy house of office' (latrine), and when the wall collapsed the filth flowed into the plaintiff's cellar and contaminated his beer and coal supply. Holt CJ applied the *alienum non laedere* principle, and allowed the action; the law would be the same, he observed, if a large dung-heap collapsed onto the plaintiff's land.[51] The principle underlying that action, and also the actions for fire and animals, was reformulated in *Rylands v. Fletcher* in 1866 in terms of a general rule of strict liability for damage caused by the escape of something brought onto adjoining land which is liable to do mischief.[52] Escapes have remained a separate category in the law of torts, because liability is imposed without proof of negligence, and because the plaintiff need not be an occupier of land; moreover, since the liability is based on the escape, rather than on conduct, the defendant may be answerable for the acts of an independent contractor. Liability for 'escapes' has been extended far beyond the traditional scope of nuisance to include damage caused by sparks from a railway engine, electrical currents, and the collapse of a flag-pole in Hyde Park, though an attempt to apply it to skidding motor-vehicles failed.[53] After a period of expansion, however, there followed a reaction against imposing liability without fault; and then the judges became unwilling to extend the tort of strict liability beyond escapes, or to escapes arising from the 'natural' use of land.[54]

---

[51] *Tenant v. Goldwin* (1704) 2 Ld Raym. 1089; 6 Mod. Rep. 311; record in 3 Ld Raym. 324.

[52] *Fletcher v. Rylands* (1866) L.R. 1 Exch. 265; affd sub nom. *Rylands v. Fletcher* (1868) L.R. 3 H.L. 330 (bursting reservoir). For the context of the decision, see Simpson, 13 *Jo. Legal Studies* 209.

[53] See J. R. Spencer, [1983] CLJ 65.

[54] See *Rickards v. Lothian* [1913] A.C. 263 (escape of water from lavatory cistern); *Read v. J. Lyons & Co. Ltd* [1947] A.C. 156, [1946] 2 All E.R. 471 (explosion in munitions factory causing injury on premises).

Common or Public Nuisances

The word 'nuisance' was used in the criminal law to describe the wide
class of misdemeanours which were said to be committed 'to the
common nuisance of the king's liege subjects'.[55] The scope of common
nuisance was far wider than that of private injury to land, although there
were close parallels. The rights of the general public to use the
highway and the navigable river were analogous to easements, in that to
pollute, obstruct or encroach upon them was an indictable nuisance.
And many forms of private nuisance became public when committed in
a city or town; for example, piling rubbish in public places so as to
increase the risk of plague, setting up butcher's stalls in the street and
leaving entrails in the gutters, or generating industrial fumes.[56] The
health hazards in a large city like London were enormous.[57] But the law
of common nuisance could hardly be more advanced than the age which
it served. Public awareness of hygiene was limited, and even in the
seventeenth century it was necessary to dissuade visitors to St Paul's
from urinating in the doorways and aisles; such unseemly practices in
public places, there being no public lavatories, were complained of as
late as the 1730s.[58] The growth of industry filled the air of many towns
with sulphur and soot; already by 1750 large industrial towns such as
Sheffield were blackened with grime. These problems were not resolved
by criminal prosecutions any more than by civil suits, though attempts
were made from time to time. The law of public nuisance could also be
used to control aspects of the environment not recognised in private law:
as in the early seventeenth-century attempt to impose planning controls
on London building.[59] Common nuisance also comprehended such
diverse wrongs as keeping a dovecote, using a loud-hailer ('speaking
trumpet') at night,[60] beating feathers in the street,[61] and being a common
scold. Bawdy houses and other places of ill repute[62] were indictable

---

55 A nuisance merely to 'divers of the king's liege subjects' was not indictable: *R.
    v. Hayward* (1589) Cro. Eliz. 148.

56 See, e.g. B. & M. 603 n.1, 605.

57 See the articles by E. L. Sabine in vols. 8, 9 and 12 of *Speculum*. For frequent
    litigation about latrines and sewers, see *London Assize of Nuisance*.

58 J. Weever, *Funeral Monuments* (1767 ed.), p. 163; *An Essay on Decorations and
    Embellishments for the City of London* (1734).

59 Regulations were made by proclamation, but prosecutions (chiefly in the Star
    Chamber) were for common nuisance: T. G. Barnes, 58 *California Law Rev.* 1332.

60 *R. v. Smith* (1726) Stra. 704.

61 *Anon.* (1770) Ann. Reg., p. 74 (conviction of a featherbed-maker).

62 E.g. a place for boxing and cock-fighting: *R. v. Higginson* (1761) Ann. Reg., p.
    123.

nuisances, and even inns and alehouses could be illegal if they exceeded reasonable local requirements. In 1671 a rope-dancer in the Strand, whom the judges had espied on their way to Westminster, was convicted of creating a public nuisance; apart from blocking the highway, he had inveigled apprentices from their shops and encouraged idle persons to stand and gape.[63]

The relevance of these miscellaneous misdemeanours to the law of tort is that no private action could be brought to recover damages for a nuisance which was common to the whole locality. If it were otherwise, a wrongdoer might be subject to hundreds of actions for the same offence. The proper course was for an indictment to be preferred against the offender,[64] or – from the mid-eighteenth century – a 'relator action' in Chancery by the attorney-general to secure an injunction.[65] It was nevertheless admitted in the sixteenth century that a private action could be brought for any extraordinary damage which an individual suffered over and above that which he suffered in common with everyone else. The point was still uncertain in 1535. In that year a plaintiff complained that the highway had been obstructed with offal, and that he and his visitors had been thereby prevented from reaching his close, which adjoined the highway. Baldwin CJ thought no action would lie, and recommended an indictment for public nuisance. But Fitzherbert J said that if a particular person suffered more harm or inconvenience than the generality he could maintain an action. He gave the example of a man who fell into a ditch across the highway; he should be allowed to sue the malefactor in respect of this special loss.[66] Fitzherbert's view prevailed; but the reasoning continued to deny a private action to someone who had suffered no special damage.[67]

Some conceptual confusion has arisen from calling these private actions 'nuisance': the implication, now clearly law, is that any criminal nuisance which causes special damage is actionable in tort. But this implication is by no means to be read into the earlier cases, which seem rather to belong to the genus of negligence actions.[68] The

---

[63] *R. v. Hall* (1671) 1 Vent. 169.

[64] *Note* (1465) Y.B. Pas. 5 Edw. IV, fo. 2, pl.4, per Heydon.

[65] The attorney-general, as a trustee of the public interest, brought such proceedings on the 'relation' of persons affected. For the rise of the relator action as an alternative to prosecution, see J. R. Spencer, [1989] CLJ at 66-73.

[66] *Sowthall v. Dagger* (1535) Kiralfy, *Action on the Case*, p. 211; Fifoot HSCL, p. 98.

[67] *Serjeant Bendlowes v. Kemp* (before 1584) cit. Cro. Eliz. 664; *Fineux v. Hovenden* (1599) Cro. Eliz. 664; *Iveson v. Moore* (1699) 1 Ld Raym. 486. Cf. *Blyth v. Topham* (1607) B. & M. 570.

[68] See pp. 463-466, ante.

fact that the defendant had committed a misdemeanour was not thought of as being in itself an element in the cause of action, but rather as being a bar to a private suit in the absence of special damage, to prevent a multiplicity of lawsuits.

Further reading

Holdsworth HEL, vol. III, pp. 153-157; vol. VII, pp. 318-342

Fifoot HSCL, pp. 3-23, 93-101

Manchester MLH, pp. 297-301, 322

Cornish & Clark, pp. 154-158

P. H. Winfield, 'Interference with Public Office' (1940) 56 LQR 463-478

F. H. Newark, 'The Boundaries of Nuisance' (1949) 65 LQR 480-490

A. K. R. Kiralfy, *The Action on the Case* (1951), pp. 55-72

S. F. C. Milsom, 'Nuisances', in *Novae Narrationes* (1963), 80 SS xcvi-civ

H. M. Chew and W. Kellaway (ed.), *The London Assize of Nuisance* (1973)

J. F. Brenner, 'Nuisance Law and the Industrial Revolution' (1974) 3 *Jo. Legal Studies* 403-433

J. Loengard, 'The Assize of Nuisance' [1978] CLJ 144-166

J. H. Baker, 'Nuisance' (1978) 94 SS 232-236

J. P. S. McLaren, 'Nuisance Law and the Industrial Revolution' (1983) 3 OJLS 155-221

A. W. B. Simpson, 'Legal Liability for Bursting Reservoirs: the Historical Context of Rylands v. Fletcher' (1984) 13 *Jo. Legal Studies* 209-264

24. Defamation

Words can be more harmful than deeds, and in some circumstances honour may be more tender than personal safety. Yet the common law has always been more reluctant to provide remedies for damage caused by words than for damage caused by deeds. It was centuries before mere words were considered capable of constituting an assault or imprisonment, and only within the present generation that words causing financial loss have been brought within the scope of liability for negligence. The reason usually advanced for the lack of a common-law remedy for defamation before 1500 is that it was deemed a spiritual matter more properly within the sphere of the Church courts. Although it was not a universal feature of the spiritual jurisdiction throughout Europe, the defamation jurisdiction of the English ecclesiastical courts was not seriously denied and was in practice quite extensive.[1] Those courts entertained what were in form criminal proceedings for defamation, and could sentence the guilty party to penance. In earlier medieval times there was also a remedy to be had in some local courts; but actions of this kind died out in the fourteenth century, probably in deference to the common-law attitude that mere words were not actionable. How far the exclusion of actions for words from the temporal courts was based on jurisdictional notions, and how far on substantive legal notions, is largely a matter for speculation; but it seems likely that it was connected with the policy which delayed remedies on parol agreements,[2] and perhaps there was a prescient fear of the vexatious litigation which ill words so often generate. It was certainly wrong to tell lies about people, but the wrong was a form of immorality best left to be punished by the Church. It was wrong to provoke disorder by spreading false rumours, but that was a matter for the criminal law. The Star Chamber occasionally entertained defamation cases even in the medieval period; but, though initiated by individuals,

---

[1] See p. 150, ante, note 16. For a full survey, see Helmholz, *Select Cases on Defamation to 1600*, 101 SS xiv-xlvii.

[2] See pp. 362-364, ante; and Helmholz, 101 SS lxii. Such thinking was made explicit in *Chaplain v. Shepherd* (1315) 101 SS 33 pl.46 (plea in manorial court that no action lies for 'wind' without an act done); and cf. 101 SS lxiii n.5.

these were essentially proceedings of a public or criminal nature.[3] Harsh words also hurt feelings, but the law is not usually much concerned with feelings; the only material damage caused by words was of the indirect kind resulting from their effect on third parties.[4] Such evanescent or indirect harm was beneath the notice of the early king's courts. According to the common law of the fourteenth and fifteenth centuries, defamation, like breach of a parol promise, or a bare threat to do something unlawful, was *damnum absque injuria*: a form of damage, certainly, but not a tort.

Nevertheless, the exclusion of actions for defamatory words was never absolute. From the beginning of the fourteenth century there had been occasional actions by judges[5] and litigants[6] maliciously slandered in open court, a kind of civil action for contempt. In 1382 a married man recovered damages for a false statement that he had precontracted marriage with another woman, which he presented as an act of forgery designed to separate him from his wife and ruin him; since the defendant was a notary who had agreed to arrange a divorce for the wife, this may also have been a complaint about something done in legal proceedings.[7] Another remedy which appeared in the fourteenth century was the special action of trespass for 'lying in wait' and threatening to seize a man as a villein. Although ostensibly founded on an ambush, the essence of these increasingly common actions was the assertion of a wrongful claim of villeinage (on which the free status could be tried);[8] and in 1483, after long debate, it was held that such an action lay even if no physical threats had been made.[9] By that time several actions had also been brought on the 1378 statute of *scandalum magnatum* by peers,

---

3   E.g. *Robert Danvers' Case* (1433) 94 SS *236*; Baldwin, *The King's Council*, p. 525 (counsel accused of forgery). Cf. also *Ravensworth's Case* (1339) 76 SS 83; Co. Inst., vol. III, p. 174 (indictment in King's Bench for criminal libel).

4   Cf. the 'economic torts': ch. 25, post.

5   Thomas Seton J in 1358 recovered 100 marks from his former wife Lucy for calling him a traitor in the court of Exchequer: *Seton v. Cokeside* (1358) Y.B. 30 Edw. III, Lib. Ass. pl.19 (misdated); 58 SS cxxxvi (record). For other examples, see 86 SS 228 n.5; 94 SS *236* n.5. Criminal sanctions were also available: *Northampton's Case* (1344) 82 SS 36; Co Inst., vol. III, p. 174 (attorney committed for libel on Kng's Bench judges and their clerks).

6   E.g. *Gisors v. Rys* (1321) 86 SS 227 (malicious accusation of treason before justices in eyre); the offender was punished, but no damages were awarded. For similar suits in local courts, see 101 SS lxiv.

7   *Roshale v. Thorne* (1382) 88 SS 22; B. & M. 623. Note also a King's Bench action by a Common Pleas official accused of misconduct: *Thomas B[rowne?] v. R.S.* (1430s?) 94 SS *236*.

8   See pp. 536-537, post.

9   *Haukyns v. Broune* (1477-83) B. & M. 629.

ecclesiastical dignitaries and judges who had been defamed.[10] The policy behind the legislation (passed three years before the Peasants' Revolt) was to prevent discord between classes, but the purpose of an action on the statute was clearly to vindicate the magnate's name by recovering damages. There may have been still more cases where, as in the villein actions, wrongs essentially defamatory in nature were coloured by allegations of real or pretended violence; only if the defendant pleaded the facts specially would the real cause of action appear on the record.[11]

Actions on the Case for Words

The common-law judges changed their minds, to permit a general action on the case for defamatory words, in the first two decades of the sixteenth century; the first writ discovered is on the plea rolls for 1507, and the first judgment in 1517.[12] Although some of the early examples concern villein-claims, or the slander of lawyers and officials, the new action was not a direct development from the medieval precedents but represented a deliberate new departure. Since there is no reported case in which the innovation was contested directly, the reason for the change can only be guessed at. The wording of the declarations in case owed as much to ecclesiastical as to common-law precedents, and it seems probable that the pressure for a new remedy arose primarily from the increasing inadequacies of the spiritual remedy as a result of common-law interference in the later fifteenth century. The Church courts had never been able to award damages, and it was disputed in 1497 whether they could even award costs.[13] Since at least the 1470s their jurisdiction over accusations of temporal crime had come under attack by prohibition and actions on the statute of *praemunire*.[14] Accusations of villeinage were likewise temporal matters, since the status was triable at common

---

10 For *scandalum magnatum*, see 94 SS *244-245*; Lassiter, 22 AJLH 216. Two examples earlier than any hitherto mentioned in print are *Duke of Gloucester v. Clere* (1442) CP 40/727, m. 586d; *Duke of Exeter v. Smyth* (1456) CP 40/781, m. 450d.

11 E.g. *Prior of Canterbury's Case* (1383) Y.B. Mich. 7 Ric. II, p. 70, pl. 8. The prior brought trespass *sur soun cas* for assaulting his steward with force and arms and hindering him from holding court; the defendant pleaded that he had merely accused the steward of deciding a case contrary to law.

12 94 SS *237-238*; 101 SS lxxii, 42-45; B. & M. 632-633. Cf. B. & M. 625 (defamation still 'purely spiritual' in 1497).

13 *Anon.* (1497) B. & M. 624 (held they could, in spiritual cases).

14 *Tanner v. Cornyssh* (1472) CP 40/844, m. 574; CP 40/845, m. 340 (prohibition for accusation of theft); *Anon.* (1482) Y.B. Trin. 22 Edw. IV, fo. 20, pl.47; 94 SS 67 n.2.

law.[15] This curtailment of the spiritual jurisdiction created an obvious gap in the law, in that the most serious accusations of all – those which put a man's life or liberty in jeopardy – were not remediable anywhere. The early Tudor period was also, of course, a period of innovation; actions on the case for not paying debts, for converting goods, and for breach of promise, were all sanctioned by the King's Bench in the same thirty-year period. It was therefore an opportune time to introduce an action for words. The essence of the new action, as it seems from the bare records, was not the opprobrium in itself but the effect of the words in terms of recognisable temporal loss.

WORDS ALLEGING CRIME OR ENDANGERING LIBERTY

The first actions on the case for slander in the plea rolls concern accusations of theft. In the first thirty years of the action, over one hundred such allegations were made the basis of King's Bench actions, in addition to accusations of murder and other temporal offences, and also villein-claims made without threats or lying in wait. The common factor in these cases was an accusation which endangered the life or liberty of the plaintiff, for instance by arrest and trial for felony, or seizure by the lord; and in some cases an actual imprisonment was mentioned by way of aggravation. A smaller class of cases involved accusations of lesser offences, such as perjury or forgery; here the plaintiff ran the risk of fine or imprisonment. There is perhaps an analogy with the Canon law insistence on accusation of a 'crime' (*crimen*); but in order to justify a suit at common law plaintiffs usually made formal allegations of deceit, and of special damage through the loss of credit with persons who used to deal with them before the scandal.

WORDS ALLEGING OCCUPATIONAL INCOMPETENCE

A second situation where financial loss regularly gave rise to actions on the case for words, in the sixteenth century, occurred when the words endangered the plaintiff's income from his profession or calling. Thus, a lawyer could show that he had lost clients and fees, or a merchant his customers and their trade,[16] as a result of allegations of dishonesty or

---

15   *Prior of Launde v. Lee* (1527) Spelman Rep. (93 SS) 186; St German, *Doctor and Student* (91 SS), p. 330.

16   This category is not much in evidence before the 1530s: e.g. *Barfote v. Smyth* (1533) KB 27/1089, m. 79d (merchant accused of falseness); *Wanton v. Maydewell* (1536) KB 27/1099, m. 68 (mercer accused of wretchedness and perjury); *Yaxley v. Watson* (1538) KB 27/1109, m. 46d (innkeeper accused of keeping a bawdy-house).

incompetence. Plaintiffs sometimes mentioned their occupation merely as a way of establishing special damage, where the accusation was of a criminal offence;[17] but in some the accusation was of misconduct punishable only by virtue of the office concerned.[18] By Elizabethan times it was established that imputations might be actionable where they touched the plaintiff in his occupation, even if they would not otherwise have been actionable. Thus, it was not in itself actionable to call someone a bankrupt; but to call a merchant a bankrupt would obviously threaten his livelihood, and subject him to statutory penalties.[19] Likewise, there was no action for saying that a man was ignorant or illiterate; but the same words spoken of a barrister would be actionable, because it was necessary to his vocation to know some law, and no one would engage him if they believed he did not.[20] Here the threat was purely economic.

'SPIRITUAL' DEFAMATION
The use of actions on the case to fill the obvious void probably met with little resistance. But it was not clear at first whether the new action could also be used as an alternative to the ecclesiastical remedy where the slander was of a kind within the permitted jurisdiction of the Church. The conservative view was that there could be no overlapping, because the king's courts could not try the spiritual matter if issue were joined upon it. This explains a Common Pleas decision in 1535 that they could not entertain an action for calling someone a heretic; they could not try the heresy, and in that sensitive year doubtless had no wish to become involved in delicate theological questions. The bolder view, held by the ecclesiastical reformers and the King's Bench judges, was that 'spiritual' defamation was actionable provided it caused temporal loss. The King's Bench accordingly gave judgment in 1537 in favour of

---

[17] Thus a barrister recovered £40 for an accusation of treason and murder which lost him clients: *Woode v. Frogge* (1517) KB 27/1022, m. 67. And an innkeeper recovered £5 because fewer people stayed in his inn after he was accused of murder: *Haukyn v. Lyncoln* (1525) KB 27/1055, m. 25d.

[18] E.g. *Elyot v. Tofte* (1513) KB 27/1006, m. 62 (king's serjeant alleged to have accepted retainers against Crown); *Southworth v. Bady* (1515) KB 27/1017, m. 103 (attorney accused of deceit); *Danby v. Thwyng* (1532) KB 27/1083, m. 32 (attorney said to have been 'cast over the bar' for professional misconduct). See also 101 SS lxxxi, xcviii.

[19] *Anon.* (1575) and *Anon.* (1580) B. & M. 638-639; cf. 101 SS ciii.

[20] *Palmer v. Boyer* (1594) Cro. Eliz. 342; Owen 17; Goulds. 26 (barrister of Lincoln's Inn said to have 'as much law as a jackanapes'); *Bankes v. Allen* (1615) Rolle Abr., vol. I, p. 54.

another man falsely accused of heresy.[21] The King's Bench likewise allowed actions where an allegation of sexual misbehaviour – in itself punishable only in the spiritual courts – resulted in a lost marriage, or where an allegation of bastardy – which, though a spiritual matter, was not even defamatory – cast doubt on an inheritance.[22] As was later explained, the cause of action in such cases was not the accusation itself but the temporal damage which it caused.[23]

WORDS IMPUTING CERTAIN DISEASES

A third special category of slander actions, which has enjoyed a separate existence in the textbooks down to the present day, was that associated with the 'French pox' (syphilis).[24] It was not actionable to say that someone was ill, unless the illness affected his calling.[25] But the imputation of French pox, which became epidemic in Tudor England, was regarded as peculiarly offensive and harmful. The only other disease said to have been included in the same category was leprosy, because lepers could be ostracised by process of law (the writ *de leproso amovendo* to put them in quarantine).

Attempts to Abate the Flood of Actions

Within half a century of its first appearance, the action for words had become part of the everyday business of the common-law courts, in particular the King's Bench. In the early days there were often more slander cases in the rolls than *assumpsit*; and even in Elizabethan times, when the use of *assumpsit* increased considerably, slander came a close second.[26] The judges apparently came to regret this aspect of their increased jurisdiction, especially since juries frequently awarded sums of

---

21 *Anon.* (1535) B. & M. 626; *Howard v. Pynnes* (1536) B. & M. 627, endnote; James Hales' reading (1537) B. & M. at 348; 94 SS *238-242*.

22 *Anon.* (1564) B. & M. 634. Cf. *Pulham v. Pulham* (1523) 94 SS *241* n.2 (undetermined demurrer).

23 *Davyes v. Gardiner* (1593) B. & M. 627. Cf. *Davys v. Henbery* (1536) 94 SS *241* n.4 (similar).

24 The first instance noted in the rolls is *Thumworth v. Potte* (1543) KB 27/1127, m. 104d. It was more common in the reports than in the records: 101 SS xcvi.

25 E.g. *Housden v. Stoyton* (1568) B. & M. 636 (innkeeper said to have plague in his house); *Anon.* (1572) B. & M. 644 ('pocky merchant'); *Levet's Case* (1593) Cro. Eliz. 289 ('thy house is infected with the pox', of an innkeeper).

26 E.g. in Michaelmas term 1510, there were 6 slander actions and 5 *assumpsit*: KB 27/997. In Hilary term 1566, there were 30 slander actions and 42 *assumpsit*: A.K.R. Kiralfy, *The Action on the Case* (1951), p. 195. Thereafter the proportion of *assumpsit* to slander increased.

money quite disproportionate to the harm and to the ability of the wrongdoer to pay. Attempts were made to cut down the damages by various forms of persuasion;[27] but the principal effect of the judicial reaction was that a spirit of repression began to manifest itself.

As early as 1557, Staunford J approved a remark by Dyer J that actions on the case for words had become too common, being brought for 'every trifling thing', and that they properly lay only for an accusation of an offence or an imputation upon a person's 'mystery' or calling.[28] No doubt he should have added 'without proof of special damage', for that would render anything actionable. One reason for the increase in slander litigation which Dyer and Staunford JJ lamented was that the courts had decided early on that the damage was not traversable, which meant that it could be presumed or fictitious.[29] The newer and more restrictive approach, which is still repeated in modern textbooks, was to insist on proof of special damage in all cases except the two established categories mentioned by Staunford J, with the two further exceptions of libel[30] and allegations of French pox.

A second line of attack was directed against actions for words spoken in anger or sport. It was held in 1565 that such words were not actionable, and that the plaintiff had to allege malice.[31] This requirement made little sense where the words had caused actual damage, and so it was not developed. The allegation of malice, though it became common form, was not normally traversed, and it only remained important as a way of rebutting certain defences.

The third and most effective attack was launched in the 1570s, when the courts began the policy of construing ambiguous or doubtful words in the milder sense (*in mitiori sensu*) so that they would not be actionable. Even the King's Bench, normally keen to attract litigation, espoused this policy under Wray CJ (1574-92).[32] They did so because, as Wray CJ complained in 1585, slander actions 'more abounded than in

---

[27] See Helmholz, 103 LQR 624.

[28] *Anon.* (1557) Derbs. Record Office, Anthony Gell MS. Rep., fo. 32v; B. & M. 638 n.20; and cf. *Anon.* (1558) B. & M. 637, per Dyer J.

[29] *Old Natura Brevium* (1528), quoted at B. & M.626; *Russell v. Haward* (1537) B. & M. 633; James Hales' reading (1537), B. & M. at 348.

[30] For libel, see pp. 506-508, post.

[31] *Anon.* (1565) B. & M. 637; and cf. *Anon.* (1579) B. & M. 639 n.2.

[32] See *Anon.* (1579) B. & M. 639 n.2 ('it is good to restrict them as much as we can, and by that means to abridge the multitude of suits . . .'); *Gray's Case* (1582) ibid. 639 ('we will not favour actions on the case [for words] but will take and record them strictly against the plaintiff . . .'); next note.

times past, and the intemperance and malice of men had increased'.[33]
The policy was carried to extremes, and seemingly absurd ambiguities
were exposed where no ordinary person would have felt any doubts. One
aspect of the policy was to restrict actions to allegations of punishable
crimes, harking back perhaps to the medieval Canon law.[34] Thus, if the
defendant said that the plaintiff had stolen apples, this would be
construed to mean growing apples, in which case there was no felony
and consequently no action for the words. On the same principle it was
not even actionable to say that a physician had killed a patient with his
pills; the patient might have choked or suffered an unusual reaction, and
so there was not necessarily an allegation of medical incompetence, let
alone murder.[35] The 'pox' cases were similarly restricted, so that a mere
imputation of 'pox' would be taken to mean small pox and therefore (for
some reason now obscure) not actionable. A great deal of subtlety was
expended on expressions such as 'pocky whore', which might be taken
to carry an indication of the kind of pox intended.[36] Two cases of 1607
illustrate the absurdities of the *mitior sensus* approach at its height. In
one, the defendant had said that the plaintiff 'struck his cook on the head
with a cleaver, and cleaved his head; the one part lay on the one
shoulder, and another part on the other'. Even this graphic description
was held ambiguous as an allegation of crime; the cook might have
survived, 'and then it is but a trespass'.[37] In the other case the defendant
had said that a justice of the peace 'reported that he hath had the use of
the Lady Morison's body at his pleasure'. Lady Morison's action
succeeded, but no less a lawyer than Sir Henry Hobart A.-G. thought it
worth arguing that the words should be taken in the best sense: 'to have
the use of her body as a tailor, in measuring'.[38]

Such cases continued to exercise the ingenuity of the legal profession
until the later seventeenth century, but it is doubtful how far the
unrealistic hair-splitting did in fact deter prospective litigants. A writer
on slander in 1647 attested that actions for words continued to bring 'as
much grist to the mill, if not more, than any one branch of the law

---

[33]   *Stanhope v. Blythe* (1585) B. & M. 640 at 641. Coke said (4 Co. Rep. 20) that
he had reported this and similar cases to 'deter men from subjecting themselves to
actions . . . for words, which are but wind'.

[34]   See Helmholz, 101 SS xcii-xcv.

[35]   *Poe v. Mondford* (1598) Cro. Eliz. 620.

[36]   *Jeames v. Rutlech* (1599) B. & M. 642 ('full of the pox' not actionable, even
with an *innuendo* that this meant the French pox); and see the cases in B. & M.
643 n.11. Cf. *Anon.* (1572) B. & M. 644.

[37]   *Holt v. Astgrigg* (1607) B. & M. 643.

[38]   *Morrison v. Cade* (1607) Cro. Jac. 162; HLS MS. 105, fo. 106v.

whatsoever'.[39] The success of the exercise was in ensuring that both parties could believe they had won. Plaintiffs in slander are not always primarily interested in damages; winning the jury verdict was often enough to restore the reputation and satisfy the sense of grievance. Upsetting the verdict later, on patently ludicrous grounds, could hardly detract from the vindication of honour which it had achieved, and yet it saved the defendant from possible ruin.

The Scope of Defamation

The *mitior sensus* rule adds amusement to the older law reports, but it had little ultimate effect on the law. A reaction against it began in the mid-seventeenth century. Rolle CJ, who collected many of the ridiculous cases in his *Abridgement*, disliked strained interpretations because they enabled a man to be 'abused by subtlety'. It was said that people had taken counsel's opinion on lists of slanderous words 'in order to know which they might out with safety', and Treby CJ (d. 1700) said that 'people should not be discouraged that put their trust in the law, for if men could not have a remedy at law for such slanders they would be apt to carve it for themselves; which would let in all the ill consequences of private revenge'. The rule was finally laid to rest in 1714, when it was held that words were always to be taken in their most natural and obvious sense.[40] The rule about special damage, on the other hand, had the important effect of putting emphasis in slander actions on the kind of damage suffered rather than on the kind of words spoken. The remedy was given for the damage caused by the words, not for the words alone. In the absence of special loss, the only remedy for defamatory words continued to be that given in the spiritual courts; but that was available only if the words charged the plaintiff with a 'spiritual offence', such as fornication or drunkenness. Defamation continued to provide the consistory courts of the seventeenth century with business, even though they could not award damages; the sentence of penance, performed in a white sheet, might give the plaintiff better satisfaction than money. Nevertheless, there remained a number of cases in which there was no remedy at all, because the words were not spiritual and did not cause temporal loss.

---

[39] J. March, *Actions for Slander* (1647), p. 2.

[40] *Hamond v. Kingsmill* (1647) Style 22 at 23; *Harrison v. Thornborough* (1714) B. & M. 645 at 646. A late stand for the old view was made by Vaughan CJ (dissenting) in *King v. Lake (No. 2)* (1671) 1 Freem. 14; 2 Vent. 28; B. & M. 654.

The common law did not at first consider whether the false words
disparaged the plaintiff's character, but only whether they resulted in
special loss. A right-thinking person does not think less of another for
being poor, or illegitimate, or foreign, and yet a person might well
suffer economic loss from being wrongly so described; therefore an
action lay. It is hardly infamous to have a sweetheart; it might be
thought flattering. But if a stranger wrote to a woman calling her his
sweetheart, and the letter came to the notice of her fiancé, who as a
consequence broke off the engagement, the woman might have been able
to sue for damages.[41] If untruths caused harm, therefore, there was no
need to show that they were also defamatory in the narrow sense of the
term.   On the other hand, plainly disparaging words might be
irremediable. Thus a parson had no remedy at common law against
those who spread a 'very scandalous' rumour that he had slept with all
the women between his parish and another.[42] And until 1891 there was
no redress for calling a woman a whore, unless she could prove special
loss.[43] There is still no action for imputing unchastity to a man.

In the eighteenth century, the courts introduced the further restriction
that in order for words to be actionable they should not only cause loss
but also should be capable of bearing a defamatory meaning. The
purpose was to withhold frivolous actions from juries, particularly once
the *mitior sensus* method had been abandoned. The old word slander
(*scandalum*) may always have imported the idea of 'infamy, discredit or
disgrace';[44] but it was difficult to define a legal concept of defamation
which would also include such sinless misfortunes as poverty and
illness. The formulation which was adopted in the eighteenth century
was that the words should expose the plaintiff to 'hatred, contempt or
ridicule'[45] or tend to cause him to be shunned or avoided.[46] This remains
an essential ingredient of the tort of defamation, though it may be
unduly restrictive.

Since the basis of the action for words was the loss of credit or fame,
and not the insult, it was always necessary to show a publication of the

41   *Sheppard v. Wakeman* (1662) 1 Keb. 255, 269, 308, 326, 459; 1 Sid. 79. Cf.
injurious falsehood, pp. 521-522, post.
42   *Yates v. Lodge* (1681) 3 Lev. 18. It would have been otherwise if it had cost him
his living.
43   *Lynch v. Knight* (1861) 9 H.L.C. 577; Slander of Women Act 1891, 54 & 55
Vict., c.51.
44   *Smale v. Hammon* (1610) 1 Bulst. 40, per Williams J. This formulation was
criticised in *Holt v. Scholefeld* (1796) 6 Term Rep. 691 at 694, per Lawrence J.
45   W. Hawkins, *Pleas of the Crown* (2nd ed., 1724), vol. I, p. 193 (defining *criminal
libel*).
46   See *Villers v. Monsley* (1769) 2 Wils. 403.

words.[47] A man could not lose credit as a result of words which reached no one's ears or eyes but his own. At one time it was said that publication had to be to someone other than a friend of the plaintiff, because a friend could be relied on to discount the scandal; but in the time of Elizabeth I it was established that communication to anyone other than the plaintiff was sufficient, provided that it either resulted in actual special loss or fell within one of the categories where the formal allegation of loss was non-traversable. The one essential was that the words should have been understandable in a defamatory sense by the persons to whom they were published.[48] If that sense was not evident from the words themselves, which by the mid-sixteenth century were invariably set out in full in the declaration, it could be explained by an *innuendo* clause, a pleading device first developed in the 1540s to explain indefinite pronouns in defamatory speech.[49]

JUSTIFICATION AND PRIVILEGE

In 1535 it was held that a man could sue for defamation even if he was of bad fame already; the essence of actionable slander was not the general reputation of the plaintiff, but the untruth of the particular statement and the damage it caused.[50] Every man, however wicked, had the right to protection against false statements to his detriment; his bad reputation was relevant to the level of the damages, but not to his right of action. As a corollary, the defendant in slander could justify his words by pleading that they were true;[51] truth, though it might hurt, was an absolute defence to an action for slander. The courts were careful, however, even at the height of the *mitior sensus* cult, to prevent abuse of this defence. The defendant's words might be literally true and yet carry a defamatory meaning; for instance, 'I think X is a thief', or 'someone told me that Y stole a sheep'. The defendant was not permitted to justify such expressions by asserting that he actually had such thoughts or opinions; and, although it was for a while held on high authority that he could justify by identifying the source of his

---

47 This was not so of criminal libel, which was punished by the Star Chamber as a 'provocation to a challenge or a breach of the peace': *Edwardes v. Wootton* (1607) B. & M. 648; *Barrow v. Lewellin* (1614) Hob. 62; *Sir Baptist Hicks' Case* (1618) Hob. 215; and the cases in Hudson, *Star Chamber* (1623) B. & M. at 650.

48 See *Anon.* (1584) Moore K.B. 182 (Welsh); *Jones v. Dawkes* (1597) Rolle Abr., vol. I, p. 74 (Latin); *Price v. Jenkings* (1601) Cro. Eliz. 865 (Welsh).

49 E.g. 'he (*innuendo*, the plaintiff) is a thief'. *Innuendo* is from the Latin *innuere*, to hint or indicate. See 94 SS *246* n.5; 101 SS lxxxiii; B. & M. 642, 646.

50 *Maunder v. Ware* (1535) Y.B. Hil. 26 Hen. VIII, fo. 9, pl.1; 94 SS 247 n.5.

51 *Legat v. Bull* (1533) Spelman Rep. (93 SS) 7.

information[52] – a sort of voucher to warranty – the repetition of the rumour came to be considered a new publication to which the defence of truth was unavailable. There had been a school of thought in Henry VIII's reign that truth was not always a defence anyway, since accusations of crime should only be made in due course of justice. This was exploded at an early date, except as to libel.

The exploded view had required the concurrence of what were afterwards seen as two different defences, truth (the plea of justification) and an appropriate reason for speaking (the plea of privilege). When these defences separated, the essence of privilege came to be that it provided an excuse for speaking words believed to be true, though in fact false, on occasions when public policy encouraged openness. The defence of privilege was not known by that name in the sixteenth century; but privileged situations were certainly recognised, as ways of disproving malice. What was said in the course of prosecutions and judicial proceedings seems to have been excusable from the beginning, in the interests of justice, and a number of the early actions for making accusations of theft were answered on this ground.[53] The recognition of this privilege accounts for the beginning of actions for malicious prosecution in the 1540s, to provide a remedy in cases where the privilege was abused.[54] By Lord Mansfield's time a similar result could be achieved in a slander action, by allowing the plaintiff to rebut a defence of privilege by proving malice; malice destroyed privilege and rendered the speaker liable to an action for defamation.

Libel

Before 1660 the common law drew no distinction between written and spoken defamation: 'It matters not how the words (if they be actionable) be published or divulged, whether by writing or by speech; for the action is maintainable in both cases.'[55] The distinction was also disregarded by Blackstone a century later.[56] Written defamation (libel) was, nevertheless, treated in a special way by the criminal law, where

---

52 *Earl of Northampton's Case, A.-G. v. Gooderick* (1612) 12 Co. Rep. 132.

53 *Anon.* (1534) Spelman Rep. (93 SS) 238; 94 SS *246-247.*

54 94 SS 247. Doubts about the action were settled by *Knight v. Jerman* (1587) Cro. Eliz. 70, 134.

55 W. Sheppard, *Epitome* (1656), p. 21. Cf. *Anon.* (1562) B. & M. 647, per Dyer CJ (where the point seems to be a purely technical one about the appropriate Latin to describe publication of a writing).

56 Bla. Comm., vol. III, pp. 123, 125.

neither publication nor untruth were required to be shown.[57] The Star Chamber, in particular, sometimes punished libel with 'sharp sentences'.[58] This special treatment may account for the doctrine that words which were not actionable if merely spoken might become actionable if disseminated in writing;[59] and that truth might not be a defence even to a civil action for libel.[60] Neither view survived.

The distinction now made between libel and slander is a different one, and of uncertain origin: it is that where the defamation is in written or permanent form there is no need to prove special damage. We have seen that in the sixteenth century three categories of defamation were actionable without proof of special damage: accusations of criminal offences, unfitness for a calling, and certain infectious diseases. There was never any decision to close this list, though as a general principle 'spiritual defamation' and other harmful words were only remedied on proof of temporal loss. The distinction was not always sharp, because it might depend on whether damage could be presumed; and it was perhaps once orthodox learning that damage could be presumed in cases of 'great and malicious slander' even if they did not fall within the three common categories.[61] As a result, there was in effect an undefined fourth category of words actionable per se by reason of their being particularly malignant or widely disseminated. Public derision was an obvious case; thus, an action lay for 'riding skimmington', a rustic custom involving a procession with effigies and stag's horns, calculated to ridicule an ill-treated husband or wife.[62] Libel, at any rate when it involved distributing the printed word, also clearly fell into this category and became perhaps the paradigm case. Somehow the courts then lost sight of the wider principle, and came to regard libel as constituting the whole category. In 1812, when Sir James Mansfield CJ pronounced the rule to be clear, he could not divine the reason behind it.[63] The result is that English law draws a distinction between libel (permanent forms of

---

[57] See Hudson, *Star Chamber* (1621), B. & M. 649-652; p. 505, n. 47, ante (as to publication).

[58] E.g. *Edwardes v. Wootton* (1607) B. & M. 648 at 649. Although the Star Chamber was mainly concerned with libel, there were precedents for punishing the spoken word as well.

[59] *King v. Lake* (1667) B. & M. 652; *Austin v. Culpeper* (1683) B. & M. 654; *Bradley v. Methwyn* (1735) B. & M. 655, endnote.

[60] *R. v. Roberts* (1735) B. & M. 651 n.11, per Lord Hardwicke CJ.

[61] See *Barnabas v. Traunter* (1640) B. & M. 628 (excommunication). An earlier example is *Morrison v. Cade* (1607), p. 502, ante, where Popham CJ said the words were so foul and unclean that £100 damages were scarcely sufficient.

[62] *Mason v. Jennings* (1680) T. Raym. 401; *Mingey v. Moodie* (n.d.) B. & M. 655. For punishment in Star Chamber, see B. & M. 650.

[63] *Thorley v. Lord Kerry* (1812) 4 Taunt. 355; Fifoot HSCL, p. 149.

defamation, even if not in writing) and slander (evanescent forms of defamation, such as speech). The distinction is not very useful, nor very easy to apply in an age of gramophone records, television, and magnetic recording. Although scholars have found some diversion in its intricacies, it bears the unsightly scars of a historical accident.

Further reading

Holdsworth HEL, vol. VIII, pp. 333-378

Fifoot HSCL, pp. 126-154

Milsom HFCL, pp. 379-392

J. M. Kaye, 'Libel and Slander – Two Torts or One?' (1975) 91 LQR 524-539

J. H. Baker, 'Defamation' (1978) 94 SS *236-248*

J. R. Spencer, 'The Press and the Reform of Criminal Libel' in *Reshaping the Criminal Law* (P. R. Glazebrook ed., 1978), pp. 266-286

R. H. Helmholz and T. A. Green, *Juries, Libel and Justice: the Role of English Juries in 17th and 18th Century Trials for Libel and Slander* (1984)

R. H. Helmholz, *Select Cases on Defamation to 1600* (101 SS, 1985); 'Damages in Actions for Slander at Common Law' (1987) 103 LQR 624-638

25. Economic Torts

The actions of trespass *vi et armis*, and the actions on the case for negligence, conversion, and nuisance, all lay in respect of some interference with the person or property of the plaintiff. The action for words protected a more subtle kind of interest; we have seen that it did not lie for the insult to the plaintiff, or for the injury to his feelings, but for the economic or social damage done to the plaintiff through the withdrawal of third parties from some relationship with him. The narrowing of that action to defamatory words made it a fairly distinct legal compartment, but in its origin and in its nature it might be considered as belonging to a diverse family of actions which have never earned a comprehensive name.[1] The innominate torts which consist in the infringement of economic or social interests are coming to be known as the 'economic torts'. Of course, the lack of such a name in the past warns us that the contents of this chapter were not formerly perceived as members of one family; they were simply a miscellany. Nevertheless, they possess some common features and invite comparison.

The principal common feature of the economic torts is that they usually involve three or more parties: the plaintiff, the defendant, and a party whose relationship with the plaintiff is interfered with, or unspecified people (such as potential customers) who might but for the interference have entered into a relationship with the plaintiff. The indirectness of the harm does not diminish the wrong: one may break bones with sticks and stones, but to ruin a man usually requires the use of influences upon others. Yet the balancing of interests can be uncommonly delicate. It is not unlawful to ruin a man by fair competition, and so the mere fact that a person has caused damage to another by his activities does not give the damaged party a cause of action. Unless some legal right is infringed, the loss is *damnum absque injuria* (damage without legal wrong). Moreover, the law is loath to recognise a right to be exempt from economic rivalry, because freedom of trade has generally been considered more in the public interest than monopoly; any such right is therefore seen as an exception from general principle. Broadly speaking, there are two kinds of situation where the

---

[1] F. A. Shaw dubbed it in 1942 the tort of 'interference', but English writers now use this term in a narrower sense and it has therefore been avoided here.

law protects economic interests by actions in tort. The first is where the law allows someone to acquire a monopoly, a right to be exempt from competition. The second is where an existing de facto relationship or state of affairs, from which the plaintiff benefits, is interfered with by unlawful means.

Monopolies

It has always been a cardinal principle of the common law that a person does not, by having in fact a monopoly of a particular trade in a particular place, thereby acquire a legal monopoly which will entitle him to prevent others from setting up in competition. This was laid down in 1410 in a celebrated case which the courts have followed ever since. Two masters of the royal grammar school in Gloucester brought an action on the case against another master who had recently set up a rival school in the same town and compelled them to lower their fees in order to survive the competition. It was held by the Common Pleas that they had no cause of action, because they had no exclusive proprietary right in local education and it was lawful for any qualified master to teach children anywhere.[2] The only advantage gained by being first in the field is the goodwill thereby accumulated; but this was so little regarded before the seventeenth century that it could not even be protected by contract.[3]

It was agreed in the argument of the Gloucester school case that the same principle applied to trade: a miller had no action if he lost business through the erection of a new mill in the same vicinity. However, it was possible in the case of a mill, and also a bakery, to acquire a monopoly by showing that the defendant and his ancestors had been compelled to grind their corn only at that mill. The element of compulsion was usually derived from manorial custom, either as an obligation of the unfree tenants, or as a kind of service reserved on a grant before 1290; the plaintiff based his claim on seisin, as if it were a kind of servitude over the defendant's land.[4] The monopoly of grinding

---

2   *Hamlyn v. More (the Case of Gloucester School)* (1410) B. & M. 613; record in Kiralfy SB, p. 126. Cf. *Oursom v. Plomer* (1375) *CPMR 1364-81*, p. 206 (similar action in London, for setting up scalding-house, compromised).

3   *Dyer's Case* (1414) Y.B. Pas. 2 Hen. V, fo. 5, pl.26 (bond in restraint of trade unenforceable); approved in *Anon.* (1587) 2 Leon. 210; Moore K.B. 242; and in *Colgate v. Bacheler* (1602) Cro. Eliz. 872; Owen 143. Opinion seems to have turned in *Rogers v. Parrey* (1613) 2 Bulst. 136 (qualified restraint enforced in *assumpsit*); *Broad v. Jollyfe* (1621) Cro. Jac. 596; Noy 98; W. Jones 13 (Exchequer Chamber).

4   For mill-suit, see Milsom, 80 SS xc-xcv.

corn (known as mill-suit), and that of baking bread (called oven-suit), were protected by the real actions *secta ad molendinum*[5] and *secta ad furnum*. These lay only against the disloyal customers, and were in due course supplemented by actions on the case against rival millers and bakers.[6] But the commonest medieval monopoly was the market or fair. The lord of a market profited from the tolls, payments taken from people trading in it, and his privilege usually excluded any sales from being made without toll within a certain area. If someone set up a rival market, an assize of nuisance lay, or a writ of nuisance *quare levavit mercatum*.[7] For other infringements a variety of trespass actions were used.[8] Thus, if a tradesman sold goods outside the market but within the lord's precinct, in derogation of the lord's rights, an action on the case lay.[9] These seignorial rights did not, however, reflect any broad principle concerning monopolies. They were limited in number, were assimilated to freehold property, and the categories were not expanded. Prescription could not, in other contexts, establish a monopolistic right to exclude rivals. The schoolmasters in 1410 had claimed, through the prior to whom the school belonged and who had appointed them, a monopoly of teaching in Gloucester since time immemorial; but this prescription could not prevent others from pursuing the same livelihood.

Another, limited, way of establishing a monopoly was by grant from the Crown. Most markets and fairs were created, or confirmed, by royal charter. So also were the livery companies, which were guilds or trade associations having the privilege of being a corporation. The main object of the earlier company charters was to confer the right to associate and to set up a governing body, but in order to make such privileges more effective it was usually granted that none should follow the trade within the city concerned unless he was a member. This was a monopoly only in a limited sense, because membership of the guild was not closed, and it was intended to impose regulation and discipline upon a particular trade rather than to restrict the trade to specific individuals. In Elizabeth I's reign, however, the Crown adopted the recent continental practice of granting monopolies to individuals who

---

5   For a specimen viscontiel writ, see p. 614, post.

6   The first known precedent is in 1397: 100 SS 1 n.307 (mill). Cf. *Prior of St Neots v. Corbet* (1448) CP 40/751, m.555d (*clibanus*, or oven); *Farmour v. Brooke* (1589) B. & M. 618 (manorial bakehouse); *Hix v. Gardiner* (1614) 2 Bulst. 195 (mill).

7   See p. 489, ante.

8   For *vi et armis* actions (e.g. for impeding the toll-collector or picketing toll-payers), see 74 LQR 418-423 (and in SHCL 42-47); 100 SS xlviii-xlix.

9   *Prior of Coventry v. Grauntpie* (1309) B. & M. 611; record in 74 LQR 422 (and in SHCL 46).

introduced new inventions into the realm.[10] Thus began the history of patents for inventions. The first patents were in respect of manufactures, and conferred industrial rather than trading monopolies. Being confined to new manufactures, they could not harm any existing trade and no one could complain of damage. A third type of monopoly which the Crown began to grant with increasing frequency at this period was the exclusive right to conduct trade in foreign parts. Such a right was conferred upon the incorporation of a merchant trading company, by virtue of the royal prerogative to license overseas trade; and again no one could complain of loss, since no subject was entitled to trade overseas without a royal licence. Soon the known world had been shared out by charter: the medieval Merchant Venturers took central Europe, the Russia Company (1533) took northern Europe and beyond, the Levant Company (1581) took the mediterranean region, and the East India Company (1600) took Asia; Africa and America were shared out in the seventeenth century, though most of the American charters were for colonising bodies.

THE ATTACK ON MONOPOLIES

The Crown reaped much profit from these sixteenth-century monopolies. Not only could cash be demanded for issuing patents, but royalties could be extracted from the continuing exploitation of new inventions and explorations. By the end of the Tudor period there were so many chartered monopolies that the matter was raised as a grievance in the parliaments of 1597 and 1601. A grave constitutional issue ensued, which was eventually left to the courts to settle. In 1602 an action on the case was brought for infringing a patent granting the plaintiff the sole right to import, make and sell playing-cards. The patent clearly transgressed the principle that the Crown should not make a grant which injured others, because playing-cards were already being made and sold in England;[11] but the Crown resorted to the rather audacious policy argument that card-playing was an undesirable activity which required control. The court declared the patent void, and gave judgment for the defendant. The reason why monopolies were generally invalid was that they operated in restraint of trade and tended to cause

---

10 See J. Phillips, 3 JLH 71.

11 The *importation* of playing-cards was prohibited by Stat. 3 Edw. IV, c.4, and so the grant to Darcy also operated as a dispensation from the statute. Contrary to Coke's report, it seems that the judges did not pronounce on this aspect of the grant: Ellesmere's observations on Coke's *Reports*, BL MS. Hargrave 254, fo. 36v; L. A. Knafla, *Law and Politics in Jacobean England* (1977), p. 303.

increased prices and reduced quality.[12] The decision was not intended to affect patents for inventors; playing-cards were not a new invention. Nor did it strike at companies which existed to regulate rather than to limit trade, although it was established at the same period that a company could not use a power to make bye-laws as a means of conferring a monopoly on itself.[13] James I, though professing to dislike monopolies, nevertheless found it difficult to restrain the greed of his ministers, and in the 1620s it was felt necessary to embody the spirit of the 1602 decision in an act of parliament. The bill was promoted in 1621 by Sir Edward Coke, who regarded monopolies as the principal economic grievance of the times and had attacked many of the patents proposed during the preceding few years; it was finally enacted in 1624. All monopolies for the sole buying, selling, making or using of any thing within the realm were declared 'utterly void'; but Coke's original bill was modified by the insertion of various exceptions before it was passed, mostly designed to preserve the status quo. The exceptions were: patents for the 'sole working or making of any manner of new manufacture' granted for not more than fourteen years[14] to 'the first and true inventor', patents concerning printing and certain other trades of public importance, licensing of taverns, and charters to 'corporations, companies or fellowships of any art, trade, occupation or mystery'.[15]

The last proviso gave ministers a means of evasion. After the decision of 1602 a weird new batch of companies had appeared, such as the Pinmakers (1605), Starchmakers (1607), Gold and Silver Thread Makers (1611), Brickmakers (1614), Tobacco-pipe Makers (1619), and so on. Even after the 1624 act, this method of evasion flourished, so that instead of granting a patent to an individual, the individual and his fellow investors were formed into a company; such foundations as the Westminster Soapmakers (1631) and the Yarmouth Saltmakers (1636) were blatantly private monopolies. The arrangements by which these companies paid duty to the Crown on sales yielded a vast income, and paved the way for the excise duty of post-Reformation times. The era of the monopolistic company ended, however, with the Civil War. The merchant companies then came under attack. The prerogative power to

---

[12] *Darcy v. Allen (Case of Monopolies)* (1602) 11 Co. Rep. 84; Moore K.B. 671; Noy 173; M. B. Donald, *Elizabethan Monopolies* (1961), pp. 196-249. For discussion, see D. Seaborne Davies, 48 LQR 394; D. O. Wagner, 6 *Economic History Rev.* (1st ser.) 31; B. Malament, 76 *Yale Law Jo.* 35.

[13] *Davenant v. Hurdis* (1599) 11 Co. Rep. 86; Moore K.B. 576, 591; *Tailors of Ipswich v. Sheninge* (1614) 11 Co. Rep. 53.

[14] Or 21 years in the case of existing patents.

[15] Statute of Monopolies 1624, 21 Jac. I, c.3. The principal provisions remained on the statute-book until 1969.

create monopolies in overseas trade was vindicated in the case of the East India Company in 1683,[16] but it was also decided that the Crown could not grant the right to enforce such a monopoly by forfeiture,[17] and in fact after this period the prerogative was no longer claimed.[18]

LATER PATENT LAW

Under the later common law, the main species of monopoly created by patent was the right to exploit a new invention. The original justification for such privileges was that they encouraged the importation of foreign innovations into England and thereby increased trade and employment; it seems few inventions began at home. In the eighteenth century the number of patents increased dramatically, with the beginnings of the Industrial Revolution, from three or four a year in the 1710s to over a hundred a year in the 1810s;[19] and there was an accompanying burst of litigation. Until the mid-eighteenth century most disputes about patents had been taken before the Privy Council; but when this practice was given up, and the Chancery proved unsatisfactory, patentees began to seek redress at common law. From the 1760s actions on the case for infringing patents were of frequent occurrence and often resulted in substantial awards of damages.[20] These developments were accompanied by a shift in the theoretical foundation of patent law, for the judges began to take the view that its object was to secure the revelation of beneficial secrets which could be exploited generally when the inventor's term was up. Increasingly it was not the right to manufacture some new substance which was granted but the industrial process itself, and this no doubt because of the greater sophistication of industry and an increase in home inventions. The new theory required that the inventor should prepare a specification sufficient to enable the invention to be used by posterity. A line had to be drawn, however, at pure ideas. It was not possible to gain a monopoly in an abstract idea, or a fact of nature, since scientific truths could not be owned privately; the patent could only be granted in respect of the

16   *East India Co. v. Sandys* (1683) 10 State Tr. 371.
17   *Horne v. Ivy* (1670) 1 Sid. 441 (Canary Island Co.); *Nightingale v. Bridges* (1690) 1 Show. K.B. 135 (Royal African Co.).
18   The point was inconclusively reopened in *Merchant Adventurers Co. v. Rebow* (1689) 3 Mod. Rep. 126; Comb. 53.
19   See K. Boehm, *The English Patent System* (1967), pp. 22-23.
20   See 8 JLH 19. Lord Mansfield praised a jury who awarded £500 for infringing a patent: *Morris v. Braunson* (1776) Mansfield Notebook no. 478, p. 144. Similar remedies were given in the Common Pleas: *Dolland v. Champness* (1766) Ann. Reg., p. 67 (£250 for infringing a telescope patent).

working process, not the underlying theory.[21] The chief defect of the common law proved to be the cumbersome procedure involved in obtaining letters patent under the great seal; not only was this expensive for petitioners, but insufficient care was taken to protect the public interest. The procedure was improved by a statute of 1852;[22] but the number of patents obtained annually then soared into four figures, and since the grant of a patent did not guarantee its legal validity there was a further increase in litigation, bred by uncertainty.

COPYRIGHT

Closely analogous to rights in patented inventions are the rights of authors. The first forms of copyright, however, resulted from grants conferring on printers the sole rights to publish particular classes of book. The prerogative of the Crown to restrict the press in this way was confined to books which the Crown claimed a special interest in controlling, such as bibles, service-books, statutes and law-books. Patentees could enforce their rights by actions on the case; but since these rights prevailed over any rights of the owner of the manuscript copy[23] and extended to the restraint of new publications within the class covered by the grant,[24] they were closer to trading monopolies than to copyright as now understood.

The first suggestion that the owner of the copy had a common-law right to damages for unauthorised publication seems to have been made in an undetermined action brought in respect of Bunyan's *Pilgrim's Progress* in 1679.[25] The matter was clarified by a statute of 1709, rendered necessary by the ending of the control exercised over the press since the sixteenth century by the Stationers' Company. The Copyright Act of 1709 gave fourteen years' protection to authors of books or other writings who registered them with the Stationers.[26] Authors could seek

---

[21] *Liardet v. Johnson* (1778) 18 LQR at 285, per Lord Mansfield CJ; pleadings in 8 Wentworth 431; trial notes in Mansfield Notebook no. 481, p. 173 (stucco patent). A similar dispute concerning Boulton and Watt's improvements to the steam engine proved so difficult that no decision was reached: *Boulton and Watt v. Bull* (1795) 2 Hy Bl. 463.

[22] Patent Law Amendment Act 1852, 15 & 16 Vict., c.83. It was not until 1905 that searches were made by the Patent Office to ensure that an invention was novel before a patent could be issued.

[23] *Roper v. Streater* (1672) cit. 2 Show. 260 and Skin. 234 (concerning the publication of Croke's reports).

[24] *Stationers Co. v. Marlowe* (1680) cit. 2 Show. 261; Lilly's *Entries*, vol. I, p. 63 (printing of English almanacks).

[25] *Ponder v. Braddill* (1679) Lilly's *Entries*, vol. I, p. 67.

[26] 8 Ann., c.19. The 14 years could run again if the author survived the first term.

an injunction in Chancery, or bring an action on the case for damages, for piracy of their work within the term. In the eighteenth century a great controversy arose as to whether literary copyright existed at common law independently of the statute. Lord Mansfield CJ and the majority of the judges held that it did, but in 1774 the House of Lords succumbed to the eloquent opposition of Lord Camden C and ruled that upon publication a book became public property at common law.[27]

The judges were thus restrained from filling gaps themselves, and subsequent development of the law of copyright depended on piecemeal legislation designed to clear up specific doubts in the law or to assuage particular pressure groups. The statutory system of 1709 had only contemplated copyright in printed books. Although it had been decided in 1758 that the owner of an unpublished manuscript could restrain its publication, doubts were cast on this by the decision of 1774, necessitating a statute in 1801.[28] Works of art were given protection more belatedly; first by a series of statutes beginning in 1735 in favour of engravings,[29] by further statutes beginning in 1787 concerning fabric designs,[30] and then by statutes of 1798 and 1814 governing sculptures.[31] It was not until 1862 that copyright was extended to paintings, drawings and photographs.[32] Printed or engraved music was held to be within the 1709 Act, but the statute of Anne could hardly be stretched to deal with live performances or the production of mechanical organ-rolls.[33] Oral publication of writings raised similar problems, which were solved first in equity and then by parliament: it was established in Georgian times that a person could be restrained from publishing notes taken from the spoken word at a play or lecture,[34] and conversely a person could be restrained from performing a dramatic or musical work published in writing by another.[35] Further extensions were made by statute in 1956,

---

[27]   *Millar v. Taylor* (1769) 4 Burr. 2303; *Donaldson v. Beckett* (1774) 4 Burr. 2408; 2 Bro. P.C. 129.

[28]   *Duke of Queensberry v. Shebbeare* (1758) 2 Eden 329 (Clarendon's manuscript history of Charles II's reign); Stat. 41 Geo. III, c.107, s.1.

[29]   Stat. 8 Geo. II, c.13; enlarged by 7 Geo. III, c.38, s.2; 17 Geo. III, c.57.

[30]   Stat. 27 Geo. III, c.38; for the sequel see Holdsworth HEL, vol. XV, pp. 40-41.

[31]   Stat. 38 Geo. III, c.71 (busts or statues of humans or animals); 54 Geo. III, c.56.

[32]   Stat. 25 & 26 Vict., c.68 (reciting that authors of paintings etc. had no copyright). Cf. *Prince Albert v. Strange* (1849) 1 H. & Tw. 1; 1 Mac. & G. 25; 2 De G. & Sm. 652 (publication restrained as a breach of confidence).

[33]   *J. C. Bach v. Longman* (1777) 2 Cowp. 623; *Boosey v. Whight* [1900] 1 Ch. 122.

[34]   *Macklin v. Richardson* (1770) Amb. 694 (play); *Abernethy v. Hutchinson* (1825) 1 H. & Tw. 28 (lecture). Cf. Stat. 5 & 6 Vict., c.45 (lecture right).

[35]   *Morris v. Kelly* (1820) 1 Jac. & W. 481; Bulwer Lytton's Act, 3 & 4 Will. IV, c.15.

to cinematograph films, broadcasts, and typography (the latter to prevent the facsimile reproduction of new editions).[36]

Loss of Services

The medieval common law allowed an action of trespass for assaulting or threatening servants so that they left or were unable to perform their services for the plaintiff. This type of action belongs conceptually with the economic torts because, although force and arms were alleged, the force was not used against the plaintiff; the action lay for the loss occasioned to the plaintiff by the interference with an existing relationship of benefit to him. Since the action lay in respect of the loss of services rather than for the forcible wrong, it was natural that it should have been extended by analogy to situations where the plaintiff was deprived of benefits by non-forcible conduct. The extensions led to the diverse torts of enticement, criminal conversation, and inducing a breach of contract.

SERVANTS AND APPRENTICES

Although it is possible that the writ of trespass *vi et armis* for abducting a servant was used fictitiously for competitive retaining,[37] before 1400 a direct remedy was available. The Ordinance of Labourers (1349) imposed criminal sanctions on workmen and servants who without reasonable cause departed from their employers within the agreed term of service, and upon those who retained or harboured deserting servants. It was soon held that a master could bring actions founded on the legislation both against the servant[38] and against his new master. The gaps in this scheme were filled in Tudor times by actions on the case. By 1530 at the latest there was an action on the case for retaining apprentices and independent contractors, who were outside the scope of the statutory remedy;[39] and for procuring or enticing a servant to depart from service, a wrong which could be committed by an intermediary who did not himself retain the servant.[40] This extension engendered another. If causing a loss of service was actionable, then it ought not to matter whether it occurred because of a new retainer or for any other reason. In the sixteenth and seventeenth centuries, therefore,

---

[36] Copyright Act 1956, 4 & 5 Eliz. II, c.74.

[37] See Arnold, 100 SS xliv.

[38] See pp. 378-379, ante.

[39] Here also trespass *vi et armis* had been used in the interim: Milsom HFCL, p. 292.

[40] 94 SS *253-254.*

we find actions brought for causing loss to a master by negligently injuring his servant,[41] or even by enticing a servant to waste time and his master's money playing cards and dice.[42] The master could sue for any wrong to the servant 'whereby he lost his service' (*per quod servicium amisit*). There was also an attempt in 1529 by a master to recover compensation not merely for the loss of an apprentice's service but also for the wasted expenditure on the apprentice's education and clothing.[43]

The principle of the action *per quod servitium amisit* was not, however, extended to all relationships of dependency. Thus, 'services' for the purpose of this action did not include the benefit of an employment contract where the person injured was not a menial servant.[44] A servant could not sue for the damage to his employment by an injury to his master.[45] And a master or husband could not sue for loss caused by killing his servant or wife.[46]

WIVES AND DAUGHTERS

The servant cases were matched by similar actions in respect of wives. They are not strictly analogous, especially since the grievance was almost always an act of adultery; but they evolved in a similar way to replace earlier *vi et armis* actions founded on fiction. Pleadings in fourteenth-century actions for 'ravishing' and abducting wives, together with the goods and chattels of the husband, often reveal that the underlying complaint was of a consensual elopement; some of the actions involved disputed marriages.[47] The fiction here was not so much factual as legal: the law took the view that the wife's consent was unlawful and void, and therefore enticing her away could be treated as a forcible abduction. The personal belongings which the eloping wife took with her were in law the husband's, and so they could also be made the subject of a trespassory complaint. Therefore, even if the jury found expressly that the abduction was not forcible, the husband could

---

41   E.g. *Clerk v. Terrell* (1507) 94 SS *229* (shooting accident); *Everard v. Hopkins* (1614) 2 Bulst. 332 (negligent doctor).

42   *Walley v. Richmond* (1602) B. & M. 620.

43   *Southworth v. Blake* (1529) 94 SS *254*.

44   Counsel for the plaintiff in *Taylor v. Neri* (1795) 1 Esp. 386 (opera singer) admitted that he could find no precedent to support a wider use.

45   See the Inner Temple moot of the 1490s in 102 SS 107.

46   See 102 SS 177, pl.102 (1500), per Conyngesby. A remedy for dependents injured by a relative's death was introduced by Lord Campbell's Act 1846: p. 473, ante.

47   See Arnold, 100 SS xlv-xlviii.

recover.[48] A similar action lay for abducting a daughter, provided she was an heiress presumptive whose marriage belonged to the plaintiff.[49] In the seventeenth century it was established that if a wife or daughter were debauched on the husband's property, he could bring trespass *quare clausum fregit*, since any implied licence to be on the premises was negatived by such behaviour, and he could recover damages for the debauchery as a matter of aggravation.[50] In all these cases, however, the wrong appeared on the record as a forcible trespass to the plaintiff.

The analogy of the action on the case for causing a loss of service gave rise by the early seventeenth century to a more straightforward remedy for interfering with family relationships. The husband was permitted to bring an action for injuring his wife 'whereby he lost her help or companionship' (*per quod consortium amisit*).[51] A similar action lay for seducing a maid or daughter *per quod servitium amisit*.[52] Provided a loss of service was made out, however trivial, the courts allowed juries to assess aggravated damages for the dishonour and injured feelings.[53] Where the wife eloped with a paramour, the husband might alternatively bring an action on the case for enticement, which bears a strong resemblance to the action for enticing away servants.[54] In the later seventeenth century another kind of trespass action appeared, called the action for criminal conversation, which treated the act of adultery as a trespass in itself; the usual declaration was to the effect that the defendant with force and arms assaulted the wife, and ravished and debauched her, so that the plaintiff lost her comfort, fellowship and society. The action became a necessary preliminary to divorce proceedings,[55] but it would not lie if the spouses were already separated,

---

[48] *Upton v. Heydon* (1308) 100 SS 73.

[49] Arnold, 100 SS xlv; *Lincoln v. Simond* (1391) 100 SS 96 (plaintiff pleads betrothal to his daughter without his consent as a constructive ravishment); *Barham v. Dennis* (1600) Cro. Eliz. 770.

[50] *Cole's Case* (c. 1625) B. & M. 309 n.19; E. Littleton, *The Newe Littleton* (c. 1644) B. & M. 309.

[51] *Cholmley's Case* (1586) cit. Cro. Eliz. 502 (*per quod negotia infecta remanserunt*); *Guy v. Livesey* (1618) ibid. 501 (*per quod servitium amisit*); *Hide v. Cyssell* (1620) B. & M. 308 (*per quod solamen et consortium necnon consilium et auxilium in rebus domesticis amisit*).

[52] *Jason v. Norton* (1653) B. & M. 353.

[53] W. Selwyn, *Law of Nisi Prius* (3rd ed., 1812), pp. 1000-1002.

[54] The first case in print seems to be *Winsmore v. Greenbank* (1745) Willes 577. But cf. *Ferdinando v. Clerk* (1528) KB 27/1069, m.79 (inciting and procuring wife to leave husband and live illicitly at defendant's command); *Byard v. Bradell* (1586) Clench's MS. Rep., per Clench J (no damages for adultery itself, but for procuring wife to commit adultery).

[55] See p. 565, post.

because there would then be no loss of consortium. The action for seducing a daughter was also extended, by requiring only the slenderest of evidence to establish the performance of services for the father: a virtual fiction, which favoured the rich man whose daughter occasionally made his tea, but left unprotected 'the poor man whose child was sent unprotected to earn her bread amongst strangers'.[56] In 1857 the action for criminal conversation was replaced by a statutory action for damages, to be brought in the Divorce Court, for adultery. Both that action and the action of enticement were abolished in 1970.[57] Although the principal use made of this class of actions has ended, it remains a tort to deprive a person of services by rendering a relative incapable of continuing to perform them.

INDUCING A BREACH OF CONTRACT

In the action for assaulting a servant *per quod servitium amisit* it was not necessary for the plaintiff to allege a contract between himself and the servant. The fact that the servant was in service when the assault occurred was sufficient to ground the action, which therefore protected a status rather than a contract. In the case of departures from service, however, it was necessary to show that the defendant knew the servant had been retained for a specific term which had not expired; and it may have been this allegation which led to the notion that the tort consisted essentially in bringing about a breach of contract between the plaintiff and the defendant. The idea of an action for inducing a breach of contract, independently of the relationship of master and servant, had certainly occurred to the common-law mind by 1529, when an action was brought against a third-party purchaser of land which the plaintiff had previously contracted to buy from the same vendor; the plaintiff alleged that the defendant had maliciously procured the vendor to break his contract with him.[58] There are few reported discussions of this tort over the next three centuries, presumably because actions were rare, though Blackstone regarded the basis of the action for retaining a servant to be 'the property which the master has by contract acquired in the labour of his servant'.[59] Recognition of the more general tort of inducing a breach of contract, a term coined by Blackstone in discussing

---

[56] Serjeant Manning's note to 7 M. & G. 1044.

[57] Law Reform (Miscellaneous Provisions) Act 1970 (c.33), s.5.

[58] *Palmer v. Wryght* (1529) 94 SS 254.

[59] Bl. Comm., vol. III, p. 142. By that time it was the practice to bring an action on the case for enticing away a servant rather than an action on the ordinance of 1349: e.g. *Whiffin v. Foster* (1770) Mansfield Notebook no. 471, pp. 89-98 (recovers £250). For waiving the tort in this situation, see also p. 422, ante.

loss of services, is generally attributed to a decision of the Queen's Bench in 1853. The manager of a theatre had retained Mlle Wagner, cantatrice to the King of Prussia, as a singer. The defendant offered her more money to sing at Covent Garden instead, and she accepted. In an action for enticing and procuring her to break her engagement with the plaintiff, her counsel argued that such an action lay only for servants because it was derived from the Ordinance of Labourers. Coleridge J thought that since the only cause of damage was a breach of contract, and since that contract was not made with the defendant, the doctrine of privity precluded an action. The majority decided, nevertheless, to allow the action; it was a tort to induce another by persuasion to break a contract with the plaintiff.[60] Later decisions confirmed the law which had been anticipated in 1529, that the tort is not confined to contracts of employment.

Unfair or Deceptive Competition

As between buyer and seller, the action on the case for deceit remedied those forms of unfair or misleading conduct which were not caught by the principle *caveat emptor*.[61] The concept of deceit was wide enough to embrace also those situations where the plaintiff was hurt by reason of a deceit practised on third parties. This provides a strong analogy with defamation, because there the action on the case lay for false assertions which drew persons away from trading with the plaintiff.[62] The earliest cases of injurious falsehood were indeed cast in the form of defamation, by treating the aspersion on the plaintiff's wares or mode of doing business as being an aspersion on his personal reputation.[63] A false denial of the plaintiff's title to his property, whereby he was hindered in selling it, was actually called 'slander of title'; and this action was almost as old as the action on the case for defamation.[64] When, around 1700, the tort of defamation crystallised out of the wider action on the case for words,[65] these economic torts were regarded as having a different

---

[60] *Lumley v. Gye* (1853) 2 E. & B. 216. Cf. *Lumley v. Wagner* (1852) 1 De G. M. & G. 604 (injunction against the singer).

[61] See pp. 376-378, ante.

[62] See pp. 496-500, ante.

[63] E.g. p. 500, ante, note 25 (plaintiff's inn said to be infected with disease); *Fen v. Dixe* (1639) W. Jones 444 (coarse remarks about plaintiff's beer); *Harman v. Delany* (1731) 2 Stra. 898 (warning about gunsmith's products).

[64] Some examples from the 1510s are noted in 94 SS *244* n.2. The tort does not seem to have been extended to chattels until the 19th century.

[65] See p. 504, ante.

basis and it became necessary to show actual malice. Both slander of
title and unfair disparagement of property or wares were then seen as
species of the tort of maliciously making false statements so as to
injure another,[66] a tort which Salmond named 'injurious falsehood' and
others have called 'malicious falsehood'. Rather surprisingly,
parliament has in recent times extended to the tort of malicious
falsehood some of the accidental attributes of the tort of defamation.[67]

The second category of deceptive competition arose from the
wrongful copying of a trademark, or the trade-name or get-up of the
plaintiff's wares. This could injure the plaintiff both by attracting
customers to the defendant in the belief that they were buying the
plaintiff's wares and also by driving away customers from the plaintiff
as a result of putting around inferior wares purporting to be his. Both
types of injury were alleged in the first known case dealing with this
problem, when the Common Pleas judges were divided as to whether an
action on the case would lie for discrediting the plaintiff's cloth by
counterfeiting his trademark and selling unmerchantable cloth so
marked.[68] Two of the judges argued that it was lawful for a tradesman to
use any mark he chose; but the other two held that it was nevertheless
wrong to injure another by such means. The printed references to this
case were so inconsistent that doubts were later entertained as to whether
the action had been given to the purchaser of the goods, in which case it
was an orthodox case of deceit on a sale, or to the original user of the
mark, in which case it was the first action for infringing a trademark.
The manuscripts show it was the latter; but it seems that no judgment
was given. And the opinion continued for some time to be that a
person could not acquire a property or monopoly in a trademark, simply
by being the first to use it, any more than in his own surname or in an
inn-sign; an action would only lie if some fraudulent use was made of
another's name, mark or sign.[69] From the time of Lord Mansfield,
however, the action on the case for passing-off was established as a
remedy for imitating another's goods.[70] And from the time of Lord
Eldon the user of a trademark was treated as having in equity a species of

---

[66] The two elements were virtually indistinguishable in *Green v. Button* (1835) 2 C.
M. & R. 707 (maliciously asserting lien over goods bought by the plaintiff, so
that the seller would not deliver).

[67] Defamation Act 1952, 15 & 16 Geo. VI & 1 Eliz. II, c.66, s.3.

[68] *J.G. v. Samford* (1584) B. & M. 615.

[69] *Blanchard v. Hill* (1742) 2 Atk. 484 (injunction refused); *Sykes v. Sykes* (1824)
3 B. & C. 541 (damages for passing-off).

[70] E.g. the two actions by a London chemist for imitating his pectoral lozenges:
Greenough v. Dalmahey (1769) and *Greenough v. Lambertson* (1771) Mansfield
Notebooks no. 469, p. 140; and no. 481, p. 84. (For other cases, see 8 JLH 22.)

property akin to copyright, or goodwill. The result was a bifurcation into two remedies, which developed separately in the nineteenth century when the rise of mass-production industries gave new commercial importance to this branch of the law. Usurping a trademark was an infringement of property, actionable per se and eventually punishable as a crime,[71] whereas passing-off by other means was actionable only on showing deceit or at least a tendency to deceive. When passing-off was extended to literary property, it came close to merging with defamation.[72]

Intimidation and Conspiracy

We began the chapter by observing that the common law never allowed an action for drawing away customers by fair competition. It was another matter if the customers were harassed by violence or diverted by unlawful conduct, such as defamatory statements or deception, or by threats of unlawful conduct. The usual medieval actions for intimidation were for interfering with markets, in the ways described above,[73] or for driving away a man's tenants with threats.[74] Nevertheless, there seems not to have been any theoretical limitation; actions are found in the fourteenth century for driving away servants, and even for frightening oath-helpers so that the plaintiff could not wage his law.[75] The first reported decision to allow an action for injuring a man's business by menacing potential customers is not, however, until 1621. Subsequent cases are few; but the same principle was applied in 1793 where shots were fired at natives in the Cameroon to deter them from trading with the plaintiff.[76] On a somewhat similar but broader principle, Holt CJ in 1705 announced that an action would lie for any malicious injury of another in his trade. The plaintiff in that case owned a pond with a duck-decoy, and the defendant had fired shots on his own land to scare off the ducks. Now, it is not in itself unlawful for a

---

[71] New criminal sanctions were introduced by the Merchandise Marks Act 1862, 25 & 26 Vict., c.88; registration by the Trade Marks Registration Act 1875, 38 & 39 Vict., c.91. The equitable concept of incorporeal property was embodied in the Patents, Designs and Trademarks Act 1883, 46 & 47 Vict., c.57.

[72] *Archbold v. Sweet* (1832) 1 Moo. & R. 162 (lawyer's reputation injured by publishing inaccurate edition of law-book in his name).

[73] See p. 511, ante.

[74] E.g. *Terry v. Beverley* (1384) 100 SS 2; *Conyngesby's Case* (1493) Y.B. Mich. 9 Hen. VII, fo. 7, pl.4.

[75] 100 SS xxxii.

[76] *Garret v. Taylor* (1621) Cro. Jac. 567; 2 Rolle Rep. 162; *Tarleton v. M'Gawley* (1793) Peake 270.

man to discharge a gun on his own land. The wrong might have been treated as a nuisance by loud noise, but the court chose instead to treat it as an unlawful interference with trade: 'the decoy is in the nature of a trade, and there is the same reason that he should be repaired in damages for his decoy as for any other trade. It is true that there may be *damnum absque injuria*. If a man set up the same trade as mine in the same town, this is a damage to me, but it is *sine injuria*, for it is lawful to him to set up the same trade if he please. But this action is brought for disturbing him from exercising his trade.' The Gloucester schoolmasters would have been able to sue, on this principle, if the defendant had kept scholars away by shooting at them; that would have been unlawful, whereas offering schooling at lower fees was not.[77]

The essence of this tort obviously turned on the meaning of unlawful conduct; and its scope became a vexed question in the nineteenth century, partly as a result of its becoming entangled with the tort of conspiracy. The writ of conspiracy (an *ostensurus quare* writ) was believed to be of statutory origin, which limited its scope;[78] by later medieval times the action was only brought in practice for conspiring to indict someone for an offence of which he was subsequently indicted and acquitted. Although the combination of two or more prosecutors was essential to the action, experiments were made with actions on the case in which this element was unnecessary; these became in Tudor times the action for malicious prosecution. Conspiracy might also be alleged in other actions on the case, though it was usually combined with some other wrong. In 1662, for instance, an action was brought for conspiring to eject a fellow of a Cambridge college, and for making a false and scandalous return to the *mandamus* to restore him; the significance of the 'conspiracy' here was that the action was brought against the fellows as a combination of individuals rather than against the college as a corporation.[79] The law of criminal conspiracy was even wider in scope, and covered combinations to injure people in their trade, regardless of the means used.[80] Prosecutions for conspiracy had been brought since medieval times against workmen combining to raise

[77] *Keeble v. Hickeringill* (1705) 11 Mod. Rep. 73, 130; 3 Salk. 9; Holt 19; Holt's MS. Rep., cited 11 East 574 n.2.
[78] See G. O. Sayles, 58 SS liv-lxxi; *Goldington v. Bassingburn* (1310-11) 20 SS 193, 31 SS 42.
[79] *Widdrington v. Cudworth and others* (1662) Vidian's *Exact Pleader*, p. 3. There had been a dispute about the plaintiff's tutorial accounts: see also *Widdrington v. Goddard* (1664) B. & M. 472.
[80] *R. v. Eccles* (1783) 1 Leach 274.

wages,[81] and they became increasingly frequent after strikes became common in the 1740s.[82] There was, however, little in the way of a general principle of civil liability when the matter came to be considered by the Common Pleas in 1844. An action was brought by an actor against a duke who had hired two hundred persons to 'hoot, hiss, groan and yell at and against the plaintiff' while on stage, and so disrupt the performance that his engagement was terminated by the theatre management. The plaintiff succeeded on one count of his claim. The only precedent was an information for criminal conspiracy in 1775;[83] but the court might well have treated this as an application of Holt CJ's principle, since it is hard to see why an action would not have lain against a single person who had contrived to make sufficient noise to achieve the same result.[84] The pleadings, however, had been framed on the basis that the conspiracy was the cause of action, and that was therefore the basis of the decision.[85]

This decision led some to believe that injurious trade competition, if carried out by a combination of persons, would be actionable as a conspiracy to injure a man in his trade. On this argument, the Gloucester schoolmasters would have succeeded if the new school had been set up by two masters rather than one. This very proposition was urged on the House of Lords in 1892, in a case where a trade association had endeavoured to secure a monopoly by driving out of business other traders who refused to join them. The means used were under-cutting at a loss, and withdrawing rebates and facilities from customers who dealt with the outsiders. One of those injured by the policy sued as for a conspiracy to induce customers not to deal with him. The House of Lords decided that this was lawful competition; it was not legally wrong to aim at driving a competitor out of business in order to advance one's own business interests. The means here used were not unlawful by themselves; there was no intimidation, and no contracts were broken. The existence of a combination to effect the desired end did not make it

81 E.g. *R. v. Osprenge and others* (1349) *CPMR 1323-64*, p. 225; *Case of the Journeymen Embroiderers* (1625) LPCL 337. For the origins of the crime, see A. Harding, 13 TRHS (5th ser.), 89.

82 See C. R. Dobson, *Masters and Journeymen* (1980), pp. 21, 62. There was another crop of prosecutions in the 1760s: e.g. Mansfield Notebooks no. 458, p. 169 (1762); no. 461, p. 59 (1763); *Ann. Reg. 1765*, p. 79.

83 This was brought for conspiring to ruin the actor Charles Macklin by disrupting his performance as Shylock. Lord Mansfield CJ persuaded the defendants to pay him substantial compensation: *Ann. Reg. 1775*, p. 117; 6 Wentworth 443.

84 However, in the 1775 case Lord Mansfield CJ had distinguished the 'unalterable right' of hissing and applauding in a theatre from a conspiracy to ruin an actor.

85 *Gregory v. Duke of Brunswick* (1844) 6 M. & G. 205 (judgment for plaintiff on demurrer), 953 (verdict for defendant on other counts).

less lawful.[86] The decision was consistent with earlier law, but it introduced a new complication in treating motive as a relevant factor. If the justification for injurious competition was the advancement of self-interest, would it be a tort to injure a trader by otherwise lawful means if it could be shown to be an act of spite which did not advance the interests of the competitor? And why should motive be relevant in the law of tort?[87]

This problem soon became of crucial importance in a series of leading cases concerning the liability of trade unions for damage done by strikes or threats to strike. Under a statute of 1875, such conduct ceased to be indictable as a criminal conspiracy,[88] and the abolition of the criminal offence drove injured workmen and employers alike to seek redress through civil actions. This inevitably brought a collision with the trade unions. Unions wanted the right to put men out of work as a means of securing monopolies of labour; but, unlike the medieval craft guilds and professional bodies, their object was not to impose educational or ethical standards on their members but simply to put themselves on an economic footing with corporate or wealthy employers when negotiating terms of employment. The judges were not imbued with the spirit of trade unionism, which had for so long been regarded as criminal, and were disposed to favour the individual against the combined power of a union. Their philosophy was embodied in Erle CJ's assertion that the right to dispose of one's labour as one wished necessitated a correlative duty to permit others to enjoy the same freedom.[89] If a union deployed all its might to prevent a man from exercising his right to work, and thereby to deprive him of the means of subsistence, the common-law mind was predisposed to find him protection if possible. But there could only be a right to work if there was a remedy; and what specific remedy could the law provide? If the union persuaded the employer to dismiss his employee in breach of contract, that would clearly amount to the tort of procuring a breach of contract. But if the union simply persuaded the employer to give his employee due notice, or to refuse a renewal of his contract, the matter was more difficult. It was not easy to distinguish such situations from that of persuading a customer not to deal further with a tradesman; and

---

[86] *Mogul S.S. Co. v. Macgregor, Gow & Co.* [1892] A.C. 25.

[87] In *Bradford Corp. v. Pickles* [1895] A.C. 597, the House of Lords decided that a malicious motive could not make an otherwise lawful act tortious.

[88] Conspiracy and Protection of Property Act 1875, 38 & 39 Vict., c.86. For the introduction of this measure, by a Conservative government, see Cornish & Clark, pp. 309-323.

[89] W. Erle, *Law relating to Trade Unions* (1869), p. 12. The author was chairman of the Royal Commission on Trade Unions, 1866-69.

that was only unlawful if the means of persuasion were unlawful. This was where the notions of conspiracy and self-protecting motives became vital. In 1898 the House of Lords held by a majority, contrary to the advice of most of the judges, that no wrong was done where someone threatened to do something he was entitled to do in order to induce someone else to do what he was entitled to do. That it was done with a malicious motive could make no difference; in Lord Macnaghten's words, 'questions of this sort belong to the province of morals rather than to the province of law'.[90] The decision was taken as a victory for the trade unions over the working man, but the wide conflict of judicial opinion which it revealed did little to clarify the law, and only three years later the House felt compelled to qualify the decision. A butcher had been injured by a withdrawal of labour intended to penalise him for failing to effect a closed shop. He was allowed an action on grounds of conspiracy and threats.[91] Conspiracy had not been formally alleged in the 1898 case; the threats amounted to intimidation under Holt CJ's principle of 1705. The 1901 decision was considered by the Court of Appeal to have revived the right to work; if a man prevented another from obtaining or holding employment in his calling, either by threats or improper influence, this was actionable even in the absence of conspiracy.[92] Malice and motive continued to be irrelevant. Although a union might be under a 'duty' by its rules to protect the interests of its members, this was a duty they had conferred on themselves privately and they could not confer on themselves a right to injure others contrary to law.[93]

These latter decisions drove the trade unions to seek their ends in parliament as well as in the courts, and at their behest the new Liberal government of 1906 introduced the Trade Disputes Act. This provided that procuring a breach of contract, conspiracy, and interfering with a trade or employment or with 'the right of some other person to dispose of his capital or his labour as he wills' should no longer be actionable if done in furtherance of a trade dispute; and that actions in tort could not be brought against trade unions.[94] Confused law was thus replaced by irrational law. Certain classes of men were given the right to place themselves outside the reach of the ordinary law of the land, whatever it might be, merely by combining to further their own interests or by

---

90 *Allen v. Flood* [1898] A.C. 1. See R. F. V. Heuston, 102 LQR 90. It was the last occasion when the judges were summoned for their opinions.

91 *Quinn v. Leathem* [1901] A.C. 495.

92 *Giblan v. National Amalgamated Labourers Union* [1903] 2 K.B. 600.

93 *South Wales Miners Federation v. Glamorgan Coal Co.* [1905] A.C. 239.

94 Trade Disputes Act 1906, 6 Edw. VII, c.47. See R. Kidner, 2 *Legal Studies* 34.

involving themselves in a dispute with their employers. The self-seeking motive had been elevated into a statutory defence.

A slight but short-lived attempt was made by the courts in the 1960s to curtail misuse of the power to strike by salvaging from the 1892-1906 chaos a tort of intimidation. This tort had its origins in the cases where trade was lost because of threats of violence. If threatening a tort against a third party, to induce him to act to the detriment of the plaintiff, constituted intimidation, then so (it was now held) should threatening a breach of contract.[95] This was a different tort from those mentioned in the 1906 Act, but in the context of labour disputes it was promptly made the subject of a statutory immunity; and since then the law of intimidation has been severely buffeted by party politics.[96] However, as far as the common law is concerned, the courts in the 1980s have shown an inclination to return to Holt CJ's simple principle, and to treat the rather disjointed legal materials as representing various species of a generic tort of interfering with the trade or business of another by unlawful means.[97]

Further reading

Holdsworth HEL, vol. IV, pp. 340-354; vol. VI, pp. 360-379; vol. VIII, pp. 392-397, 425-431; vol. XI, pp. 477-501

Cornish & Clark, 267-301, 309-336

T. E. Scrutton, *The Laws of Copyright* (1883), pp. 67-116

T. A. Street, *Foundations of Legal Liability* (1906), vol. I, pp. 263-272, 322-325, 342-373, 417-434

E. W. Hulme, 'The early History of the English Patent System' (1907) in *Essays AALH*, vol. III, pp. 117-147

F. I. Schechter, *The Historical Foundations of the Law relating to Trademarks* (1925)

C. H. S. Fifoot, *English Law and its Background* (1932), pp. 211-220

D. S. Davies, 'Further Light on the Case of Monopolies' (1932) 48 LQR 394-414; 'The early History of the Patent Specification' (1934) 50 LQR 86-109, 260-274

---

[95] *Rookes v. Barnard* [1964] A.C. 1129, [1964] 1 All E.R. 367.

[96] The story in outline is: immunity was first introduced under Wilson's Labour government in 1965, removed under Heath's Conservative government in 1971, restored by Wilson's second administration in 1974, and then modified in 1980, soon after Mrs Thatcher's Conservative government came to office.

[97] See *Hadmore Productions Ltd v. Hamilton* [1983] 1 A.C. 191 at 202; *Merkur Island Shipping Corp. v. Laughton* [1983] 2 A.C. 570 at 609.

D. O. Wagner, 'Coke and the Rise of Economic Liberalism' (1935) 6 *Economic History Rev.* 30-44

H. G. Fox, *Monopolies and Patents* (1947) [with bibliography]

G. H. Jones, 'Per Quod Servitium Amisit' (1958) 74 LQR 39-58

B. Malament, 'The "Economic Liberalism" of Sir Edward Coke' (1967) 76 *Yale Law Jo.* 1321-1358

S. D. White, *Sir Edward Coke and the 'Grievances of the Commonwealth'* (1979), pp. 115-141

J. Phillips, 'The English Patent as a Reward for Invention: the Importation of an Idea' (1982) 3 JLH 71-79

H. I. Dutton, *The Patent System and Inventive Activity 1750-1852* (1984)

J. N. Adams and G. Averley, 'The Patent Specification: the Role of Liardet v. Johnson' (1986) 7 JLH 156-177

J. Adams, 'Intellectual Property Cases in Lord Mansfield's Court Notebooks' (1987) 8 JLH 18-24

C. MacLeod, *Inventing the Industrial Revolution: the English Patent System 1660-1800* (1988)

26. Persons: Status and Liberty

The treatment of status in this book after property and actions reflects the relative lack of prominence given to the matter in legal sources rather than its intrinsic importance. Status could profoundly affect property rights and contractual capacity, not to mention access to the common-law system itself.

The principal disabilities were those of married women, aliens, monks and villeins. The position of the married woman resulted from the doctrine that her legal personality merged during marriage in that of her husband.[1] Single women (including widows) were generally treated the same as men for the purposes of private law, save that the rules of inheritance favoured males before females of the same degree.[2] There were doubts in later times about the exercise of public functions by women, though the doubts arose from the rarity of its occurrence rather than from abstract legal principle.[3] In fact women did occasionally hold offices in medieval times,[4] as when a hereditary office descended to a female heir; but they usually exercised them by deputy. Infants and lunatics lacked capacity to perform certain legal acts, but this was for their own protection. Outlaws and excommunicates also suffered from disabilities, intended to be only temporary, as sanctions in legal process.

Aliens – generally those born outside the realm[5] or outside the dominions of the Crown[6] – were treated in the early common law as having virtually no enforceable rights at all. Although aliens within the realm owed a temporary allegiance by virtue of their presence, this did not enable them to own land or (at first) to bring actions in the courts.

---

[1] See pp. 550-557, post.

[2] See p. 305, ante. The principle of coparcenary, however, meant that a younger sister was more favourably treated than a younger brother.

[3] The position was clarified by the Sex Disqualification (Removal) Act 1919, 9 & 10 Geo. V, c.71.

[4] The countess of Salisbury was sheriff of Wiltshire in the time of Henry III. Elizabeth Venour was warden of the Fleet Prison in the 1460s. See also 102 SS 113 (woman justice of the peace).

[5] Children born in England to foreign parents were not aliens: *Anon.* (1544) Bro. N.C. 58. A statute of 1351 (25 Edw. III, st.i) settled that persons born abroad to English parents were not aliens either.

[6] *Calvin's Case* (1609) 7 Co. Rep. 1, established that Scotsmen born after the accession of James VI to the English throne in 1603 were subjects and not aliens. Scotsmen born before 1603 remained aliens in England.

England, however, was a trading nation, and it was commercially necessary to extend protection to aliens.[7] This protection was originally specific to individuals, and conferred by royal letters of safe conduct. The recipient of such a document was an 'alien friend' (*alien amy*), and the common law increasingly gave rights to these friendly aliens, as opposed to alien enemies. Alien merchants could find justice in local courts, such as the courts of fairs and boroughs, and in the Council, Admiralty and Chancery. Between 1450 and 1550 the common-law courts also modified their attitudes, allowing friendly aliens to bring personal actions and to own personal property (including the lease of a dwelling house), and dropping the need for letters of safe conduct. The principal remaining disability was the incapacity of an alien to own real property. If land were conveyed to an alien, the king could seize it, while in a real action a plea of alienage would abate the writ. This incapacity continued from the earliest times until 1870.[8]

Monks were in the strange position of being considered dead to the world, a Canon law concept recognised by common law for the purposes of property and contract.[9] Upon 'profession' in monastic orders, the monk's real property descended to his heir and his personal estate was subject to administration, as if he were dead. Unlike the naturally dead, however, monks could return to life by being removed from their orders. This usually happened by 'deraignment': that is, when a woman claimed a monk as having entered into a precontract of marriage with her. How common this was in reality is uncertain, but it was a situation beloved of the law schools because of the problems it caused.[10] Monks could also revive temporarily, when acting in other capacities: for instance, as an executor, or an abbot suing on behalf of a monastery. The law of profession came to an end in 1539 when, after dissolving the monasteries, parliament brought all the monks back from the dead.[11]

A more sweeping and widespread disability was that of villeinage; and to this we must give more detailed attention.

---

7   An early provision is Magna Carta 1215, cl.41 (1225, c.30): 'All merchants shall be safe and sure in leaving and entering England ...'.
8   Naturalization Act 1870, 33 & 34 Vict., c.14, s.2.
9   The monk's person was protected by the criminal law, and his behaviour subject to it. But if a monk committed a tort, or incurred a debt, the action had to be brought against his abbot.
10 See 105 SS lxxii.
11 Stat. 31 Hen. VIII, c.6. A saving clause prevented any rights of inheritance from reviving.

Villein Status

'Villein' (*villanus*) had once meant simply a villager; and villeins had sometimes been substantial villagers. The original, and more appropriate, word for unfree status was serfdom. 'Serf' derives from the Latin word for slave (*servus*), and serfs were well known by that name before the Norman conquest. The status may have originated in capture, in punishment, or sometimes from voluntary submission to bondage in desperate straits. It was no rarity: the Domesday survey of 1086 recorded more than 25,000 serfs, a category which it carefully distinguished from villeins. The Anglo-Saxon slave seems indeed to have suffered a miserable plight; he was subject to severe punishment and had few if any rights. What the status of a slave implied by 1086 is less certain, and it probably varied from place to place; but a large proportion of the native English after the conquest were effectively tied to the land and under some form of subjection. As the categories became indistinct, the more abject varieties of slavery disappeared and in the twelfth century the word 'villein' became the general term for unfree peasants. 'Serf' did not become a legal term of art, and in so far as it remained in use it did not connote a status lower than that of villein. The merger was to the detriment of the *villani*, but it ensured that full slavery was not received as part of the common law.

Villeinage came to have two meanings in medieval law: villein tenure of land, and villein status. We are concerned in this chapter with the second aspect, unfree status or villeinage *de sank* (of blood). But this distinction was not expressly stated, and may not have been clear, in the twelfth century: before the introduction of the possessory assizes it would hardly have mattered. To the author of *Glanvill*, moreover, villeinage was an indelible status; even a grant of freedom by the lord ('manumission') worked only as against the grantor and his heirs. Yet by 1250 legal thinking had brought about a significant transformation of both aspects of villeinage.

VILLEINAGE AT COMMON LAW

The treatise called *Bracton* devoted much space to villeinage. Pursuing an abstract legal logic which treated liberty as a right akin to property, it adopted what were to be the three principal characteristics of the common law of villeinage. The first was that there was only one kind of villein status: all villeins were equally unfree.[12] The second was that

---

12   The law nevertheless recognised different periods of villeinage: if a tenant for life freed a villein, the freedom arguably lasted only pur auter vie: see p. 536, post, note 22.

villeinage was relative; a villein was unfree only as against his own lord, and free as against the rest of the world. It followed that a villein of one lord could be a free tenant of another, and that manumission by the lord freed the blood absolutely. The third rule was that villein tenure of land – that is, the holding of land by 'unfree' (or undefined) services – was quite distinct from personal villein status and did not in itself provide evidence of it. A man could therefore acquire land held in villeinage without becoming personally unfree; and, conversely, a villein could be manumitted without altering his villein tenure. Moreover, a tenant in villeinage was free to give up his tenancy, whereas a villein by blood could not renounce his status. The development of villein tenure into 'copyhold' has been considered already.[13] Villein status survived as a condition which ran with the blood rather than the land, and passed by inheritance from father[14] to child, whether or not a villein tenement went with it.

Lawyers occasionally referred to villeins as chattels, but it was an imperfect analogy since they were people with rights. They could be bought and sold, usually with the tenements to which they belonged as tied labour; but what passed on sale was a bundle of rights over the villein, and such a transfer of rights was more closely analogous to the transfer of a free man's services to a new lord than to a sale of flesh and blood. Another analogy, found in *Bracton*, was with the monk; but that was also inexact, because the villein could bring actions in his own name. The unfree nature of servile status cannot be understood by such analogies. It arose from the very extensive rights which the lord had over the person and property of his bondman.

There were three principal consequences of such status at common law. The first was that whatever property the villein acquired, whether real or personal, was liable to seizure by the lord. It was a popular saying that villeins owned only what they had in their bellies; but this was an exaggeration, because until seizure by the lord any real or personal acquisitions belonged to the villein and he could pass good title to a third party. Villeins could thus own property, albeit precariously and at the will of the lord. The second rule was that the lord could exercise corporal discipline over his villein, for instance by putting him in the stocks, without being liable to an action of trespass. This did

---

[13] See pp. 347-349, ante.

[14] *Glanvill*, v.6, stated the harsher rule (taken from Canon law) that if either parent was a villein, the child would acquire villein status. Under Bractonian theory, the status would only pass from an unfree father if he was married, and only from an unfree mother if she was unmarried. Even these qualifications were abandoned in the 14th century: p. 535, post.

not, however, give him authority to maim, rape or kill; the villein was at least within the protection of the criminal law, and perhaps had an action against the lord for unreasonable treatment. The third rule – perhaps an application of the second – was that the villein could not run away from his tenement, or even work away from it without his lord's consent; escape could be prevented by force.

In reality, the villeins' lot was not normally one of total oppression. The tax laws assumed that they would have money; and they were indeed often allowed to retain earnings, even to pursue professions. The bonds which tied them to their lords were often little different in practice from those which bound low-born free men to lords or masters.[15] Most important of all, the villeins' exclusion from the common-law courts did not exclude them from manorial justice. By the customs of manors villeins enjoyed rights analogous to those of free men at common law; for instance, they might make wills of their chattels and hold lands heritably. Under manorial custom a lord's rights were typically limited to the usual services, an annual tax payment (tallage, or 'chevage' for those living away from the manor), and a payment on marriage of the villeins' children ('merchet', or 'ransom of flesh and blood'). Custom also frequently fixed the sums payable, so that, as with the regulation of the incidents of free tenure by the common law, the introduction of accepted norms gradually reduced the lord's de facto sovereignty.[16] It was, in any case, in the lord's own interests to maintain a productive workforce. Treating villeins badly, by excessive tallage or taking away their means of livelihood, was bad husbandry; and if it drove men away in times of labour shortage it could amount in law to waste of the inheritance.[17] If a villein's life was hard by modern standards, in a harsh world it was not necessarily worse than that of his free neighbour. Nevertheless, villeins were more vulnerable to exploitation than free men. The status of being free affected a person's security and sense of dignity, and claims to villeins were frequently disputed in the royal courts.

The oldest writ in which such disputes regularly arose[18] was the action by the lord to recover a runaway villein: the writ of neifty (*de*

---

15   Cf. the restrictions imposed on labourers and servants by the legislation of 1349: p. 378, ante.

16   For the regulation of incidents, see p. 273, ante. There are obvious parallels between tallage and feudal aids, and between merchet and the rights of a guardian in chivalry.

17   'Exile of men' was one of the species of waste listed in the Statute of Marlborough 1267, c.23.

18   They could also arise if a defendant in any action alleged that the plaintiff was a villein.

nativo habendo). The writ was cast in executive (*praecipimus tibi*) form, ordering the sheriff to secure the return of a 'neif',[19] and it was doubtless invented as a remedy against rival lords thought to be poaching native labour. Villeins straying from their 'nests' (places of birth) could thus be recovered, along with their 'brood' and chattels. But if an alleged villein claimed to be free, the case had to be removed before royal judges,[20] and by the thirteenth century the action of neifty was normally brought against the alleged villein himself with the object of initiating a trial of status in the royal court. Although the plaintiff counted of his 'right and inheritance', some authorities considered this a possessory action based on seisin of the villein: the uncertainty arose from the difficulty of applying the distinction between right and possession to persons. The plaintiff would assert seisin by 'tallaging high and low at his will, and taking ransom of flesh and blood', and offered as proof either a record of previous proceedings or 'suit of kin', which meant producing the bodies of at least two male villeins of the same blood, and in his power, who would swear to their status. It was the last action in which 'suit' remained a reality, and its cumbrous nature led to its decline in the later medieval period.

THE END OF VILLEINAGE

The *Glanvill* view of villeinage as a permanent and indelible status did not survive in the thirteenth century. It was established during that century that villeins could achieve their freedom in several different ways: for instance, by manumission, by estoppel (as where the lord made a grant to a villein or sued him as a free man), by residing in London or a royal borough for a year and a day, or by marriage.[21] The lawyers of the fourteenth century added another means of escape: if a villein's child could prove that his parents or ancestors were unmarried, he must be free. This conclusion followed from treating status as akin to property; status was inheritable, and a bastard could not inherit from either parent. It replaced the older rule that bastards followed the status of their mother. The new learning proved very helpful in freeing villein families, because some episcopal courts of the fifteenth and sixteenth centuries would routinely certify bastardy on request in cases of disputed villeinage; and we may guess that this was a kind of pious perjury rather

---

19 For the writ, see p. 612, post. The Latin word *nativus* (neif) means a bondman by birth. In later law French, 'neif' usually denoted a female villein.

20 This was effected either by the plaintiff (using a writ of *pone*), or the alleged villein (using a writ of *monstravit de libertate probanda*).

21 If a female villein married a free man, she was free, at least during the marriage; if a male villein married his seignoress, the villeinage was extinguished for ever.

than a reflection on the morality of villein couples, or on their legal acuity in avoiding marriage. Moreover, if some dioceses were known to be sticklers for the facts, this also could be overcome by fiction; the alleged villein would simply plead his birth in a diocese (such as Norwich) known to be more cooperative. This procedure can be shown in some cases to have been the outcome of a composition between lord and villein, and collusion may explain the predictability of the outcome in such suits: a judgment on the plea rolls was the most secure conveyance of liberty, and such security was advisable where (as must often have happened) the lord in possession was only a tenant in tail or for life.[22]

The other principal means of escape was the jury, which could give effect to popular attitudes even when they were at odds with strict law. By the fifteenth century, at the very latest, there was no socially identifiable villein class; unfree status had become more of a legal anomaly than a social reality. Both villeins and free men could be found in the same families, and free countryfolk regularly married their villein neighbours. Men of villein stock could reach high places: even the chief justiceship of England.[23] Doubtless many families genuinely did not know whether they were free or not. Villein status seemed to most people outmoded, and it had actually disappeared in many parts of the country, especially the north. Jury trial therefore offered a good chance of freedom, and there were several ways in which an alleged villein might obtain it. The most obvious was to resist the lord's demands, and thus provoke him into bringing a writ of neifty. During the fifteenth century it became more common for the alleged villein to initiate an action himself: it could be an action of trespass for lying in wait and threatening to seize him as a villein,[24] or, if the lord was actually detaining him, the writ *de homine replegiando*, which enabled him to recover his liberty and goods pending trial of the issue. This latter was an important remedy, because without it lords could effectively have prevented men from suing them by taking their substance and locking them up. By what seems to have been an act of judicial legislation in 1498 the King's Bench under Fyneux CJ decided that trespass could be used in the same way as *de homine replegiando*,

---

22 Legal opinion differed as to whether such a manumission was effective for ever: Holdsworth HEL, vol. III, p. 504 n.3.

23 John Hody, CJKB 1440-41, was the son of a villein: 18 *Somerset Notes & Queries* 127-128. For an alderman of London seized as a villein in 1308, see 17 SS 11.

24 Ante, p. 496; *Haukyns v. Broune* (1477) B. & M. 629. If actual force was used, a general action of trespass would suffice.

so that the plaintiff's goods could be replevied pending the outcome, even when the plaintiff himself was not in custody.[25] In the next two decades the nascent action on the case for defamation was also used in respect of villein claims.[26] But any action would do, since the defendant would plead villeinage, and issue would be joined on the status. Verdicts almost always went in favour of liberty, and large sums were sometimes recovered in damages;[27] this, perhaps more than any other single factor, dissuaded sixteenth-century lords from trying to preserve villeinage. Lords who insisted on their rights might cut their losses by selling manumissions and abandoning the capital asset; others just gave up their position as uncharitable and obsolete. From time to time a 'general manumission' by statute was discussed, and the Crown effected a general manumission of most of its own remaining bondmen (at a price) in the 1570s;[28] but in the event no legislative change was needed to give effect to the prevailing general sentiment. As a consequence villeinage is still, in theory, recognised by the common law, and there must be many unwitting villeins breathing English air. But, for practical purposes, villeinage *de sank* had effectively died out by the seventeenth century.

Freedom from Arbitrary Imprisonment

One of the most celebrated provisions in Magna Carta was that 'no free man shall be taken or imprisoned, or disseised or outlawed or exiled, or in any way destroyed . . . except by the lawful judgment of his peers or by the law of the land'.[29] No remedy was mentioned,[30] and that was perhaps the source of its strength; for this vague promise would become, in later centuries, a broad guarantee of personal liberty and a source of protection against the Crown itself. It was taken in the early seventeenth century, anachronistically, to entrench procedural natural

---

[25] *Thomson v. Lee* (1498) 102 SS 6; 94 SS *190* n.9. For 'replevin' see p. 271, ante.

[26] See p. 498, ante. But the courts soon had to distinguish real claims from the use of words such as 'churl' or 'villain' (derived from 'villein') as mere abuse.

[27] The damages in *Haukyns v. Broune* (1477) B. & M. 629, were £110. £120 was recovered against a peer in 1499, and £340 against a prior in 1509: 94 SS *189* n.15, *190* n.4.

[28] It was achieved by granting the profits of the enterprise to a courtier, Sir Henry Lee. Lee sought out and manumitted, for suitable composition payments, nearly 500 villeins. Poor villeins were probably passed over.

[29] Magna Carta 1215, cl.39 (1225, c.29).

[30] The question was raised in the 15th century whether an action would lie on c.29: 105 SS lxv n. 326. There are several precedents of such actions between 1500 and 1530: 94 SS *72-73*.

justice, *habeas corpus*, the grand jury, and jury trial.[31]   In medieval times it was more often cited as the warrant for trial by peers in the House of Lords. None of these was part of the original intent. Its most important role, however, was indirect. It was the first of a stream of enactments securing the importance of 'due process of law' as protection against arbitrary acts under the king's prerogative. The early due-process legislation was chiefly aimed against irregular or inferior jurisdictions. But the same principle became important in checking the claims of kings and their ministers to imprison subjects without trial, on the basis that that was equally against the 'law of the land'.

As against sheriffs and inferior ministers, persons who claimed to be wrongly imprisoned had the remedies of *de homine replegiando* (to secure release) or false imprisonment (to recover damages); and in all but the most serious cases prisoners by legal process were entitled to bail if they could produce sufficient surety for appearance.[32]   These remedies did not avail against the Crown, and the medieval law-books are virtually silent on the Crown's powers of imprisonment. It is nevertheless stated in the fifteenth-century year-books that the king could not commit a subject by word of mouth, because if he acted wrongly the subject would be without remedy.[33]   Already it seems to have been recognised that loss of liberty required legal process, which could be examined in the courts. But the principle was hard to apply if ministers sheltered behind the authority of a conciliar tribunal, which kept no record. The principal ministers of Henry VII and Henry VIII acted on the belief that they could imprison at will, in the name of the Privy Council, but the power was regarded by the courts with disfavour.[34]   In the 1530s Thomas Cromwell, as principal secretary of state, committed to the Tower someone who had the privilege of the Common Pleas; the prisoner was released by writ of privilege (a form of *habeas corpus*), and the court refused to accept the order of a privy councillor as a sufficient cause of imprisonment.[35]   In 1540 the judges held that, although the king had the same powers of imprisonment as his justices, the cause of imprisonment could be reviewed; and they attributed this to Magna

---

31   The association between the jury and cl.29 was popularised by William Lambarde: *Eirenarcha* (1581), pp. 234 (grand jury), 436 (trial jury). See also p. 580, post.

32   The principal legislation was the Statute of Westminster I 1275, c.15.

33   Trin. 16 Hen. VI, Fitz. Abr., *Monstrans de faits*, pl.182; Y.B. Mich. 1 Hen. VII, fo. 4, pl.5.

34   See p. 135, ante.

35   94 SS 74. The source does not state whether the prisoner was an officer of the court or a litigant: privilege attached to either category.

Carta.[36] Nevertheless, Elizabeth I's ministers (usually acting in the name of the Privy Council) frequently imprisoned people without express cause. In 1592 the judges complained about the practice and gave their opinion that prisoners could be removed into the courts by writ of *habeas corpus* so that, if a lawful cause of imprisonment was returned, they could be remanded. The implication was probably that prisoners could be released if no lawful cause was returned; but the judges deliberately left the matter unclear, perhaps intending that the courts should have some discretion in considering bail.[37]

The question came to a head in the time of Charles I when Sir Thomas Darnel and four other knights were committed to prison for refusing to subscribe to a loan to the Crown.[38] The five knights obtained a writ of *habeas corpus*, and the return stated merely that they had been committed 'by special command of the king' (*per speciale mandatum regis*). The case was argued in the King's Bench, where the greatest constitutional issue – the nature of English monarchical government – was treated as a question of common law, the 'law of the land' enshrined in Magna Carta. John Selden and others presented the arguments with much historical learning, but the precedents were inconclusive and the court declined to release the prisoners.[39] Many contemporaries saw a case for allowing the Crown a prerogative right to imprison suspected wrongdoers on grounds of state, and the royal prerogative was part of the 'law of the land'; but it had here been abused as a means of enforcing an unconstitutional levy. Such powers would enable the Crown to raise money without the consent of parliament, and the forced loan was another sign of growing absolutism in Stuart government. In 1628 the question was debated at a 'conference' between the House of Lords and House of Commons, after Selden had chaired a sub-committee of the Commons to marshal the historical materials.[40] Sir Edward Coke and Sir Edward Littleton, for the Commons, argued that if a man could be imprisoned without cause he would be worse than

---

[36] *Serjeant Browne's Case* (1540) Spelman Rep. (93 SS) 184.

[37] 1 And. 298; translated in Holdsworth HEL, vol. VI, p. 32. See also *R. v. Steward of Marshalsea, ex parte Howell* (1587) 1 Leon. 71; *R. v. Warden of the Fleet, ex parte Hellyard* (1587) 2 Leon. 175. In each of the 1587 cases a return 'committed by command of Sir Francis Walsingham, secretary of state, member of the Privy Council' was held insufficient.

[38] The raising of money in this way was fiercely contested. Crewe CJ was removed from office in 1626 for denying the legality of the forced loan.

[39] *Five Knights' Case: R. v. Warden of the Fleet, ex parte Darnel* (1627) 3 State Tr. 1. No formal judgment was entered, because of a dispute as to the wording of the entry drawn up by Heath A.-G.

[40] Very full texts of the debates are now available, in *Proceedings in Parliament 1628* (R. C. Johnson et al. ed., 1977-83), 6 volumes.

a villein, and appealed to Magna Carta and the statutes of due process as confirmations of the 'fundamental laws' of the realm. A compromise could not be reached, and later in the year a plea was inserted in the Petition of Right that subjects should not be detained without cause shown.[41] The political atmosphere at this period was explosive; a member of the Commons had been committed to prison during the conference for what he had said during the 'free' discussion, and a number of members (including John Selden) were committed by the Star Chamber in 1629 for seditious behaviour in the Commons. Again *habeas corpus* was resorted to, but a head-on collision with the courts was avoided by the offer of bail.[42] In 1629 the king dissolved parliament, and tried thereafter to rule without one. The country was slipping towards civil war.

When the Long Parliament abolished the Star Chamber in 1641, it took care to reverse the effect of the *Five Knights' Case* and to guarantee *habeas corpus* as a remedy in case of committal by the king or the Council. This safeguard continued after 1660, and indeed the remedy of *habeas corpus* was further improved by legislation in 1679.[43]

Colonial Slavery and the English Courts

An extensive traffic in negro slaves from Africa began in the seventeenth century, primarily to supply labour for the sugar and cotton plantations in the West Indies and North America. English merchants were prominent in the slave trade, and the wealth of Liverpool was largely built upon it in the eighteenth century. Slavery soon presented the English courts with new legal questions. By the custom of merchants, slaves were treated as chattels with few if any rights. But could English law recognise such a custom? The question arose in English courts because personal actions could be laid in England even if the causes of action arose abroad.

---

[41]   Stat. 3 Car. I, c.1, s.5.

[42]   *A.-G. v. Strode and others* (1629) 3 State Tr. 235. The Star Chamber only had jurisdiction over misdemeanours (p. 137, ante); and for misdemeanours bail was always allowed. Nevertheless Strode and Valentine refused to find surety, and remained in custody until 1640.

[43]   Habeas Corpus Act 1679, 31 Car. II, c. 2; p. 168, ante. This Act applied only to detention 'for criminal or supposed criminal matter'. Its main provisions were extended to other restraints on liberty (excluding imprisonment in civil actions) by the Habeas Corpus Amendment Act 1816, 56 Geo. III, c. 100. For the history of *habeas corpus*, see also pp. 168-169, ante.

The courts at first held that trover would lie for negroes, as if they were chattels, apparently on the ground that they were infidels;[44] but Holt CJ rejected this view[45] and also denied the possibility of bringing *assumpsit* on the sale of a negro in England: 'as soon as a negro comes to England he is free; one may be a villein in England, but not a slave'.[46] This last, however, was an admonition to careless pleaders rather than slave dealers: the plaintiff had simply overdone the fictions, and was allowed to amend his declaration to allege the sale of the slave in Virginia, where slavery was recognised by law. Slaves were regularly sold on the Liverpool and London markets, and actions on contracts concerning slaves were common in the eighteenth century. Even the trover decisions may have been directed to good pleading rather than the legality of slavery: the plaintiffs had declared on the conversion of 'negroes' rather than 'slaves', and there was no inherent reason why a negro should not be a free man.[47]

Holt CJ's decisions therefore had only a small effect. In the England of 1700 there was no extensive use of slave labour, as in the colonies. Negro servants were common as status symbols, but their treatment was not generally comparable with that of the plantation slaves. The legal problem was most likely to arise in England if a slave escaped in transit, or if a slave-owner from the colonies brought over a slave and expected to continue exercising his power to prevent the slave from leaving his service. Increasing numbers of slaves were indeed brought to England in the eighteenth century,[48] and this may explain the growing public awareness of the problems posed by the existence of slavery. Quite apart from moral considerations, there was an obvious conflict between the mercantile custom recognising property in slaves and the English tradition of freedom protected by *habeas corpus*. If the courts acknowledged the property which was generally assumed to exist in slaves in the colonies, could such property disappear if a slave was brought to England?

The cases in which the courts had recognised property in slaves had arisen from commercial disputes and did not establish any rights exercisable as against the slaves themselves, if personally within the

---

44 *Butts v. Peny* (1677) 2 Lev. 201; *Gelly v. Cleve* (1694) 1 Ld Raym. 147. Note, however, *Sir Thomas Grantham's Case* (1687) 3 Mod. Rep. 120, in which *de homine replegiando* was brought to recover a freak captured in the Indies, even though he had later been baptised.

45 *Smith v. Gould* (1705-07) 2 Salk. 666; 2 Ld Raym. 1274; HLS MS. 1109.1, p. 22.

46 *Smith v. Brown* (1702?) 2 Salk. 666.

47 See Ambl. 75.

48 In 1772 it was estimated that there were as many as 14,000 in the country.

jurisdiction. As with villeins centuries before, the analogy with chattels failed to answer the leading question whether slaves could establish their freedom by bringing suit in the courts. The writ *de homine replegiando* was outmoded, and so the usual eighteenth-century question was whether *habeas corpus* lay to free slaves from captivity. Blackstone was in no doubt: 'the spirit of liberty is so deeply implanted in our constitution' that a slave, the moment he lands in England, is free.[49] Other prominent lawyers, such as Lord Hardwicke and Lord Mansfield, felt that it was better to recogise slavery, and to impose regulation on the slave trade rather than to withdraw from it; less enlightened nations would reap the benefits of abolition, and slaves would suffer the consequences. The 'infidel' argument was soon abandoned, since many slaves had been converted to Christianity without gaining de facto freedom; and legal justifications were now sought by analogy with the old law of villeinage.

The question came before Lord Mansfield CJ and the King's Bench in 1771.[50] A writ of *habeas corpus* had issued to secure the release of James Somerset, a negro confined on board a ship arrived in the Thames from Virginia, bound for Jamaica, and the return stated that he was a slave under the law of Virginia.[51] Lord Mansfield was anxious to avoid the issue of principle, and pressed the parties to settle; but the cause was taken up by the West India merchants, who wanted to know whether slaves were a safe investment, and it became a *cause célèbre*. The law of villeinage was turned by Somerset's counsel into an argument against slavery, since the kind of proof required to establish villein status was not available for slaves. In the event the court ordered that 'the black must be discharged'. But Lord Mansfield, while stating that slavery was 'odious', did not decide that slavery was unlawful, nor even that Somerset was no longer a slave; he confined himself to the narrow point that a slave could not be made to leave England against his will.[52] The decision also left aside the problem in the conflict of laws: if a person was a slave by the law of his place of domicile, which was not disputed in the case of Somerset, a mere temporary presence in England would not free him permanently, even for purposes of English law.[53] Several contract cases concerning overseas slaves in fact came before Lord

---

[49]   Bl. Comm., vol. I, p. 123. See also *Shanley v. Harvey* (1762) 2 Eden 126.

[50]   *R. v. Knowles, ex parte Somerset* (1772) 20 State Tr. 1; Lofft 1.

[51]   Under a Virginian statute of 1705 slaves were real property and inheritable.

[52]   See *Ann. Reg. 1778*, p. 163; and Lord Mansfield's own remarks in *R. v. Thames Ditton* (1785) 4 Dougl. K.B. 300 at 301.

[53]   *The Slave, Grace* (1827) 2 Hagg. 94. This decision by Lord Stowell caused a stir in the press.

Mansfield, and no suggestion was made that the contracts were illegal or contrary to public policy.

ABOLITION

The common law would go no further. But the decision of 1771 was widely understood as freeing slaves in England, and this understanding assisted the growing abolition movement. Slavery did not, like villeinage, die naturally from adverse popular opinion, because vested mercantile interests were too valuable, and also no doubt because many white people still regarded blacks as innately inferior; nevertheless in 1792 the House of Commons voted in favour of 'gradual' abolition, and in 1807 parliament outlawed the African slave trade by legislation.[54] This prevented British merchants exporting any more people from Africa; but it did not alter the status of the several million existing slaves, and the courts continued to recognise colonial slavery. The abolitionists therefore turned their attention to the emancipation of the West Indian slaves. This was more difficult to achieve, since it required the compulsory divesting of private property; but it was finally done in 1833, at a cost of £20 million paid from public funds in compensation to slave owners. From 1 August 1834 all slaves in the British colonies were 'absolutely and for ever manumitted'.[55]

Further reading

VILLEINAGE

Pollock & Maitland, vol. I, pp. 412-432

Holdsworth HEL, vol. III, pp. 491-510

H. G. Richardson and G. O. Sayles, *Law and Legislation from Aethelberht to Magna Carta* (1966), pp. 115-116, 139-148

R. H. Hilton, *The Decline of Serfdom in Medieval England* (1969); *Bond Men made Free* (1973)

P. R. Hyams, 'The Action of Naifty in the early Common Law' (1974) 90 LQR 326-350; 'The Proof of Villein Status in the Common Law' (1974) 89 EHR 721-749; *King, Lords and Peasants in Medieval England* (1980), and the full bibliography there.

J. H. Baker, 'Villeinage' (1977) 94 SS *187-192*

---

[54] Stat. 47 Geo. III, c.36. The offences created by the Act were made felony in 1811, to discourage contraband traffic. Slaves exported contrary to the Act were forfeited to the king, for the purpose only of divesting the property; but they could be impressed into the forces.

[55] Stat. 3 & 4 Will. IV, c.73, s.12. Transitional provisions, turning the slaves into bound 'apprentices', ended in 1838.

J. Hatcher, 'English Serfdom and Villeinage' (1981) 90 *Past & Present* 1-39

D. MacCulloch, 'Bondmen under the Tudors' in *Law and Government under the Tudors* (C. Cross et al. ed., 1988), pp. 91-109

LIBERTY OF THE SUBJECT

Holdsworth HEL, vol. IX, pp. 104-125

M. Cohen, 'Habeas Corpus cum Causa – the Emergence of the Modern Writ' (1940) 18 *Canadian Bar Rev.* 10-42, 172-197

F. Thompson, *Magna Carta. Its Role in the Making of the English Constitution 1300-1629* (1948), esp. chs III, XI

J. W. Gough, *Fundamental Law in English History* (1955)

L. S. Popofsky, 'Habeas Corpus and the Liberty of the Subject: Legal Arguments for the Petition of Right in the Parliament of 1628' (1979) 41 *Historian* 257-275

S. D. White, *Sir Edward Coke and 'The Grievances of the Commonwealth'* (1979), ch.7

W. F. Duker, *A Constitutional History of Habeas Corpus* (1980), pp. 3-94

J. A. Guy, 'Origins of the Petition of Right reconsidered' (1982) 25 *Historical Jo.* 289-312

P. Christianson, 'John Selden, the Five Knights' Case, and Discretionary Imprisonment in Early Stuart England' (1985) 6 CJH 65-87

J. Reeve, 'The Arguments in King's Bench in 1629' (1986) 25 *Jo. British Studies* 264-287

ENGLAND AND BLACK SLAVERY

E. Fiddes, 'Lord Mansfield and the Sommersett Case' (1934) 50 LQR 499-511

F. O. Shyllon, *Black Slaves in Britain* (1974)

D. B. Davis, *The Problem of Slavery in the Age of Revolution 1770-1823* (1975), chs. 8-10

J. C. Oldham, 'New Light on Mansfield and Slavery' (1988) 27 *Jo. British Studies* 45-67

ALIENS

Pollock & Maitland, vol. I, pp. 458-467

Holdsworth HEL, vol. IX, pp. 72-104

MONKS

Pollock & Maitland, vol. I, pp. 433-438

27. Persons: Marriage and its Consequences

The law of marriage is the most pervasive aspect of the English law of persons, not only because of its effect on the personal lives of married couples, and on the legal capacities of the married woman, but also because the inheritance of property was always predicated on relationships brought about by marriage. Moreover, since the union of man and woman in matrimony was from early times consecrated by the Church as a 'holy estate', it has been the concern of theologians and canonists as well as secular lawyers. In England, questions of matrimony were regarded as spiritual questions as early as the seventh century, and after the separation of lay and spiritual jurisdictions was completed in the twelfth century the subject of matrimony fell exclusively within the province of the latter. Thereafter, when the existence of a marriage came in issue in the lay courts, the question was invariably referred to the bishop to be determined and certified in accordance with the law of the Church. That division of functions persisted until the middle of the last century, until when it was true to say that the English law of marriage was part of the Canon law as used in England.[1]

The Law of Marriage

The earliest canonists held marriage to be effected by the physical union of man and woman in carnal copulation. They became one flesh by *commixtio sexuum*. But, since copulation could occur outside marriage, a mental element was also necessary. There had to be an agreement to marry. According to Gratian (*c.* 1140) marriage began by agreement but became complete and indissoluble only when the agreement had been sanctioned by a Church ceremony and consummated in a physical union. There immediately arose difficulties with this approach. The requirement of formality tended to increase the subjection of young couples to pressure from parents and lords, while the notion

---

[1] In the 18th century the Church courts also recognised Jewish and Quaker marriages: *Lindo v. Belisario* (1796) 1 Hagg. Con. 216.

that physical union was essential led to embarrassing theological questions about the marital status of Christ's parents. After grappling with such problems, Pope Alexander III introduced, in the late twelfth century, a more sophisticated doctrine of marriage. Under the new rules, marriage could be contracted by consent alone, without any ecclesiastical ceremony, parental consent, or physical consummation, provided the consent was notified in words of the present tense (*sponsalia per verba de praesenti*). Such a marriage was irregular, in so far as the parties could be compelled for the sake of order and decency to solemnise the marriage publicly at the door of a church, and punished for any sinful connection they may have had before so doing. Yet it was valid and, before consummation, created an indissoluble bond which would be upheld even in preference to a subsequent church marriage with a different spouse. On the other hand, a promise to marry in the future (*sponsalia per verba de futuro*) gave rise only to an executory contract of marriage. The regular way of executing the contract was to solemnise the marriage, using present words. But the Canon law acknowledged that it could also be turned into the indissoluble bond of present matrimony by physical consummation. In this case, before formal celebration or consummation, the espousals were but an engagement to marry and could be dissolved by mutual consent.

Thus, in the absence of carnal copulation, the validity of a marriage had come to depend on whether the contract was by words *de praesenti* or *de futuro*. Maitland remarked that this distinction was 'no masterpiece of human wisdom . . . of all people in the world, lovers are the least likely to distinguish precisely between the present and future tenses'.[2] It is hardly surprising that it gave rise to much wrangling and fraud, and that the commonest species of matrimonial suit in the medieval consistory courts was to interpret and enforce 'espousals'. Despite coercive measures, medieval marriages were frequently effected at home or in the open air, using words such as 'I here take you as my wife, for better or worse, to have and to hold until the end of my life, and of this I give you my faith'.[3] The legal effect of such declarations was probably little understood, and, since no set form was necessary, difficulties of interpretation frequently arose. What was one to make of the words 'I will have you as my wife'? Was it a present marriage, or an engagement? There were four schools of thought by the sixteenth century on that phrase alone.

---

[2]   Pollock & Maitland, vol. II, pp. 368-369.
[3]   Helmholz, *Marriage Litigation*, p. 28 (quoting from a case of 1372).

Although the Canon law required the present consent of both parties for a valid marriage,[4] the contract *per verba de praesenti* was enforceable in the Church courts until 1753.[5] In practice the procedure seems to have been little used where intercourse had not occurred. The common law as an alternative, from the sixteenth century,[6] allowed an action of *assumpsit* to recover damages for breach of promise of marriage. The thinking behind it was not to compel men to go through with marriages contrary to their second thoughts, but to make them compensate women whom they had disappointed. This cause of action was not abolished until 1970.[7]

Concubinage, where there was no marriage contract of either kind, was always punishable as fornication. Medieval spiritual courts occasionally gave unmarried couples the option of marrying or forswearing each other's company: the *abjuratio sub poena nubendi* took the form of a compulsory conditional marriage by present words, that they took each other for man and wife *if* (but only if) they had further sexual relations. But this procedure was hardly consistent with the notion that marriage should be freely entered into, and it was therefore abandoned in the fifteenth century.

THE FORMAL MARRIAGE

Both the ecclesiastical and secular authorities were from an early period aware of the importance of publicity in marriage, and insisted on public ceremonies, not for validity but for the sake of regularity . Archbishop Hubert Walter promulgated an English constitution in 1200 requiring banns to be published on three successive occasions before solemnisation, and this practice was universally established by the Lateran Council in 1215. The purpose of banns was to call upon the congregation to declare any known impediment to the proposed union, such as consanguinity or precontract. In medieval times it was not unknown for rival lovers to 'make reclamation' at that stage, with the result that the question of precontract had to be referred to the consistory court. If no objection was raised, however, the ceremony took place at the church door. The priest charged the parties to declare any impediment known to them, the parties exchanged words of betrothal and present matrimony, the husband placed a ring on the wife's third finger as a token or *wed*, and delivered to her the tokens (usually coins)

---

4   See p. 560, post.

5   The sanction was removed by Stat. 26 Geo. II, c.33, s.13.

6   The validity of the consideration, however, was still problematic in the 17th century.

7   Law Reform (Miscellaneous Provisions) Act 1970 (c.33), s.1.

representing dower.[8] The ceremony would conclude with a blessing and a nuptial mass inside the church, and would often be followed by secular festivity. The purpose of the formalities was not only to impress on the parties the solemnity of what they were undertaking, but also to secure the event in the minds of witnesses; written registration of marriages did not begin until the sixteenth century. In essence, however, the church wedding was the same as the meadow wedding. The parties were not married by the priest's blessing or the other ceremonies; they married each other.

CLANDESTINE MARRIAGES

It is clear from the records of the medieval consistory courts that neither spiritual nor temporal exhortation was very successful in altering social customs. The informal marriage remained common until the fifteenth century, and indeed seems to have lasted longer in England than on the Continent. One of the least convenient results of Alexander III's marriage laws was the necessity of recognising these unions as valid. The problem was compounded in the courts by the canonical requirement of two witnesses to prove a marriage. If present words of matrimony were exchanged in private, and then a subsequent marriage with another woman took place before witnesses, the Church would have to order the man to live in adultery with the second woman. Theologians were forced into the position that such a man ought in conscience to disobey the Church and suffer excommunication on earth, safe in the knowledge that he would be absolved at the last judgment.

By the sixteenth century there was a growing social assumption that only church marriages were proper. In 1563 the Roman Church (at the Council of Trent) changed the law accordingly, requiring the presence of a priest for validity.[9] But the Church of England did not follow suit, and therefore the old law remained in force in England until it was altered by parliament. Clandestine marriages, though still punishable, were by no means unknown in late Tudor England: Sir Edward Coke, while attorney-general in 1598, married his second wife in a private house.[10] In the century after 1660 they even began to increase in frequency, the advantages being secrecy, expedition, the avoidance of parental control, and sometimes deception – as where marriages were

---

8 For dower, see p. 308, ante.

9 It nearly required parental consent as well; but this proposal was dropped.

10 He incurred the censure of the archbishop of Canterbury; but there was no question that the marriage (which Coke had cause to regret) was valid.

antedated on the register to avoid illegitimacy.[11] The first temporal sanctions were imposed in 1694, when it became a criminal offence to marry without banns or a licence; but the only purpose of this legislation was to facilitate the taxation of matrimony.[12]

Numerous bills were introduced in parliament, between the Restoration period and 1753, to end clandestine marriages. The principal argument of their promoters was that marriages which were entered into informally and hastily, especially by the young, were likely to come to grief. They might also, if poorly documented, lead to property disputes. But reform was opposed on the ground that formal marriages were too expensive for the poorer classes and that such a change would compel them to live in sin. The chief cause for official concern was the effectively 'clandestine' church marriage which could be obtained in certain privileged places outside episcopal control. The most notorious was the 'Fleet marriage'. The Fleet Prison in London, besides serving as a gaol, was an ecclesiastical liberty and something of a social centre, with coffee shops and a tennis court. Its facilities included a number of marriage shops, where seedy clerics would conduct hurried marriages for a small fee. Hundreds of thousands of couples took advantage of this service in the eighteenth century, not all of them from the lower classes. Lord Hardwicke CJ was the principal judicial opponent of these liberties,[13] and in 1753 the publicity aroused by a case in the House of Lords gave him the opportunity to reintroduce a bill to end clandestine marriages. Under Lord Hardwicke's Act, secret marriages were completely abolished; liberties such as the Fleet were swept away; and the publication of banns or purchase of a licence (which required parental consent in the case of an infant under 21), the presence of at least two witnesses, and the recording of the marriage in a public register, all became essential requirements for validity.[14]

The 1753 Act was not without its shortcomings. Its requirements proved to be in some respects too rigid: for instance, the need for parental consent (in the case of an infant marrying by licence) upset

---

11   For the social history of clandestine marriages, see the survey by J. R. Gillis in *Disputes and Settlements* (J. Bossy ed., 1983), at pp. 261-273. Some have estimated that they accounted for a third of all marriages in the early 1700s.

12   Stat. 6 & 7 Wm & Mar. c.6.

13   See *Middleton v. Croft* (1736) Ridg. t. Hard. 109, 2 Stra. 1056, where he referred to them as an 'evil' producing 'many calamities'. There was a tradition that he used to tear up Fleet registers produced as evidence: *Lawrance v. Dixon* (1792) Peake 185, per Lord Kenyon CJ.

14   An Act for the better Preventing of Clandestine Marriages, 26 Geo. II, c.33. Falsification of the register of marriages was soon afterwards made a capital offence.

some marriages on highly technical grounds.[15] The requirement of a church marriage was subject to an exemption for Quakers and Jews, but not for Roman Catholics, nonconformists and non-believers. The problems were largely removed in 1823, when bona fide marriages were protected against invalidity on the grounds of unwitting failures to comply with the law,[16] and in 1836 by the introduction of a civil marriage ceremony, in a register office or registered building (such as a nonconformist chapel), as an alternative.[17] The civil and ecclesiastical forms of marriage have existed in parallel ever since.[18]

The statutory provisions were not applicable to members of the royal family, or to marriages with the special licence of the archbishop of Canterbury,[19] or to marriages outside England and Wales. In the case of marriages abroad, the law governing their validity in England is the law of the place of celebration, which in some overseas dominions may be the common law (or the Canon law). The courts may therefore still have to pronounce on the validity of common-law marriages[20] contracted outside England and Wales. In 1843 the House of Lords was called upon to decide the validity of an Irish marriage celebrated without the presence of an ordained priest. It was decided in Ireland – by an evenly divided court in banc – that the presence of a priest was essential, and because the House was also evenly divided the 'decision' has stood since then as the law.[21] The misreading of history which this entailed was perhaps wilful, and calculated to end the possibility of informal marriage.[22]

Unity of Person

It was a common saying among canonists and common lawyers alike that in the eyes of the law husband and wife were but one person: they

---

15 E.g. in *Priestly v. Hughes* (1809) 11 East 1 (consent of parent of illegitimate child); *Reddall v. Leddiard* (1820) 3 Phill. Ecc. 256 (consent of testamentary guardian appointed by inadequately attested will).

16 Stat. 4 Geo. IV, c.76.

17 Marriage Act 1836, 6 & 7 Will. IV, c.85. Civil marriage had been briefly in use during the Interregnum (under an ordinance of 1653).

18 Marriage Act 1949, 13 & 14 Geo. VI, c.76.

19 Under the Ecclesiastical Licences Act 1533, 25 Hen. VIII, c.21.

20 This term is sometimes misused today for concubinage, which was never a valid form of marriage at common law.

21 *R v. Millis* (1844) 10 Cl. & Fin. 534. (But see *Beamish v. Beamish* (1861) 9 H.L.Cas. 274.) When a marriage is celebrated in a foreign place where priests are not available, the marriage may nevertheless be valid at common law: *Catterall v. Catterall* (1847) 1 Rob. Ecc. 580.

22 See J.C. Hall, [1987] CLJ 106.

were two souls in one flesh (*erunt animae duae in carne una*). This one person was for practical purposes the husband, since 'the very being or legal existence of a woman is suspended during the marriage, or at least is incorporated and consolidated into that of the husband'.[23] This was a legal fiction, the logic of which did not always commend itself to laymen. It prompted Bumble the beadle to utter the immortal words, 'if the law supposes that . . . then the law is a ass'.[24] Like most legal fictions it was not universally applicable: for instance, the wife was not executed for her husband's crimes, or made answerable for his debts. The origin of the doctrine, and its one-sidedness, may be found in the earlier customary treatment of women as inferiors and the power which social custom gave the husband over his wife. According to the scriptures, woman was created for man and bound to obey him. And according to the law as stated in *Bracton*, the married woman was 'under the rod' of her husband,[25] who was both her sovereign and her guardian. In the law French of the next generation she was said to be *feme covert*, as opposed to a *feme sole* (single woman), and her husband was her *baron* (lord). If she killed him it was not simply murder, but petty treason. He looked after her and her property during the 'coverture', whereas she lost the capacity to own separate property or make contracts. She could not sue or be sued at common law without her *baron*, and this prevented her from suing him for any wrong done to her. Like wardship in chivalry, therefore, the guardianship of a wife by her husband was not subject to judicial review.

The fiction has never been abolished outright by legislation, although so many of its consequences have been removed that the courts have recently declared that it no longer exists even at common law.[26]

PROPERTY OF MARRIED WOMEN

There was some possibility in the earliest days of the common law that husband and wife might be regarded as owning property in common, so that the wife could take a share on the husband's death. There was indeed a widespread custom allowing the wife a third share of goods, and an early common-law writ to recover it; but the right was overtaken by

---

23 Bl. Comm., vol. I, p.442.

24 C. Dickens, *Oliver Twist*, ch. 51.

25 Even in the 18th century, the law allowed a husband to chastise his wife. Buller J earned the nickname 'Judge Thumb' by laying down the restriction that the stick should not be thicker than the thumb.

26 *Midland Bank Trust Co Ltd v. Green* [1981] 3 All E.R. 744 (reversing the old rule that husband and wife could not commit the tort of conspiracy).

the transfer of jurisdiction to the Church courts.[27] In some boroughs a custom survived allowing a wife who traded separately to own property as if she were single.[28] The queen of England was also treated as a *feme sole* for property purposes.[29] But English law by the early thirteenth century arrived at the general doctrine that any property which a wife had owned as a *feme sole* became the husband's on marriage.

Personal property vested in the husband absolutely, since there could be no estates in chattels, and therefore he could dispose of it absolutely. If the husband died first, the widow had no right to claim back any of her personal property disposed of during coverture, though she could have what remained. Likewise upon divorce, the wife could only reclaim such of her goods as had not been disposed of in good faith while the marriage was believed to be valid.[30] If the husband died testate, the widow could only claim whatever legacies had been left her, and her *paraphernalia* (personal clothes and jewels). The wife's claim to *paraphernalia* as against a legatee was limited to necessaries and personal ornaments appropriate to her degree; but the latter were liable to the husband's debts, 'for it is not fit she should shine in jewels, and the creditors in the mean time to starve'.[31]

The wife's real property vested in the husband only during coverture, although if she died first he was entitled to be tenant by the curtesy for the rest of his own life.[32] During the marriage the husband and wife were seised in right of the wife. This meant that the husband had seisin and took the profits; but he did not acquire the wife's inheritance, and if he granted away his wife's land it could be recovered back after his death by the widow or her heir.[33] If the wife wished to alienate her own patrimony during the marriage she had to obtain her husband's consent, and they would together levy a 'fine' in the Common Pleas.[34] Before the fine was accepted, the judges questioned the wife privately to ensure that she was not acting under coercion; the fine would then bar the wife and her heirs. Already by Bracton's time the fine was the only method

---

[27] See pp. 435-436, ante.

[28] For the custom of London, see *Beard v. Webb* (1800) 2 Bos. & P. 93.

[29] *Queen Philippa's Case* (1344) Y.B. 17-18 Edw. III, p. 430.

[30] *Anon.* (1534) Y.B. Mich. 26 Hen. VIII, fo. 7, pl. 1; Dyer 13, pl. 63; Spelman Rep. (93 SS) 216, pl. 5.

[31] *Shipton v. Tyrrell* (1675) Freem. 304; 2 Eq. Cas. Abr. 155; 73 SS 150, per Finch LK.

[32] See p. 310, ante.

[33] By the writ of entry *cui in vita*.

[34] This was the most solemn kind of conveyance, in the form of a fictitious lawsuit ending in a recorded compromise (a 'final concord').

of achieving this; and another of its principal uses was to enable a husband to convey his *own* land free of the wife's claim to dower.

The doctrine of unity also meant that any conveyance *to* the wife during coverture vested the property at common law in the husband and wife, and placed it under the husband's control.[35] Even the husband could not make a grant to his wife after marriage, though he could, as we have seen, make future provision for his wife at the time of marriage, to take effect if she survived him: usually (after the medieval period) in the form of a jointure to bar dower.[36] The rule against separate acquisitions applied equally to personalty. Thus, if a wife saved a little cash out of her living allowance, the benefit of her frugality redounded to the husband; the intention was to keep her in necessaries, 'not that she should grow rich and lay up treasure for herself alone'.[37]

By early modern times some of these rules could be avoided in equity, which generally regarded the married woman as a separate person for property purposes, and allowed her to sue independently of her husband.[38] It was not unconscionable to benefit a wife independently of her husband, and if that was the intention of a transaction equity would seek to carry it out. As early as the fifteenth century, some judges regarded a use in favour of a married woman as valid.[39] And not long after the Statute of Uses, trusts of property for a wife's separate use were established and enforced.[40] The Court of Chancery thereby gave the married woman beneficiary the same independence of ownership as if she had been single.[41] In the course of time, however, it was seen that even the separate use could be circumvented, because a compliant or weak-willed wife might be induced to dispose of her equitable estate to her husband, or to charge it with the payment of his debts, contrary to the intention of the settlor. To prevent this, conveyancers in the late eighteenth century – some say it was Lord Thurlow C while at the bar[42]

---

[35] Moreover a grant to husband, wife, and a third party, gave only half to the husband and wife.

[36] See p. 309, ante.

[37] *Shipton v. Tyrrell*, ante, per Finch LK.

[38] E.g. *Sanky v. Golding* (1579) Cary 87; Tothill 95 (action without husband); *Rivet v. Lancaster* (1597) Tothill 93 (action against husband).

[39] *Anon.* (1467) B. & M. 98 at 99. Cf. *Anon.* (1478) B. & M. 99. The separate use was recognised at moots: 105 SS 209 (Inner Temple, *c.* 1496); HLS MS. 125, no. 170 (Gray's Inn, 1518).

[40] E.g. *Wytham v. Waterhowse* (1596) Tothill 91; Cro. Eliz. 466; B. & M. 124.

[41] See *Herbert v. Herbert* (1692) 1 Eq. Cas. Abr. 66. In the 18th century the Chancery would sometimes even direct a husband to settle property to his wife's separate use.

[42] 3 Bro. C.C. 340 n.1, per Lord Eldon C. See 40 LQR 221.

– invented the 'restraint on anticipation'. This was a condition inserted in a settlement to restrain the wife from alienating or charging her capital during the marriage: the wife's absolute property was thus postponed until widowhood, and she was forbidden to 'anticipate' that estate on pain of forfeiture. It was not clear at first whether the courts would accept such a total restraint, which in the case of a man or a single woman had been treated since medieval times as repugnant and void. In the case of a wife, however, though it was a restriction on her capacity, it was accepted as serving her best interests; and after 1800 clauses of this nature were inserted in most marriage settlements.

The courts were slower to recognise a separate trust of money, lest the wife misuse it for immoral purposes. The early Stuart Chancery might protect a wife's spending-money against a spendthrift husband.[43] But in 1640 it held that a woman could not save money and put it in trust: 'it would be a dangerous precedent to suffer women to have such power to collect money secretly . . . for although this wife had disposed of it honestly . . . another wife might dispose the money to her paramour or some other in an unseemly manner'.[44] Within a few generations, this position had been abandoned and a wife was then allowed in equity to save pin-money.[45]

Thus did equity protect the women of the landed classes, but it could not assist those of the middle and poorer classes for whom the machinery of a trust was unthinkable. For centuries such protection was little needed, because working married women were rarely in a position to earn money enough to save. As the social position of women began to change, and the opportunities for their respectable employment increased, the archaic rule which gave a woman's earnings absolutely to her husband became a source of loud complaint. In 1856 a number of eminent ladies, including several well-known novelists, petitioned parliament to alter the law, on the basis that modern civilisation had begun to break down the dependence of women upon men. The married woman, they said, had no more protection than a slave. They begged the legislature to consider the plight of the woman who 'worked from morning till night to see the produce of her labour

---

43 *Fleshward v. Jackson* (1623) Tothill 94. Cf. *Sanky v. Golding* (1579) Cary 87, Tothill 95 (money put in trust for wife's maintenance).
44 *Scott v. Brograve* (1640) CUL MS. Gg. 2. 5, fo. 81, per Sir John Finch LK (reversing Coventry LK).
45 *Milles v. Wikes* (1694) 1 Eq. Cas. Abr. 66; *Slanning v. Style* (1734) 3 P. Wms 334.

wrested from her, and wasted in a gin-palace'.[46] A Royal Commission was appointed, and enquiries showed that the law had already been changed in America and Canada without ill consequences. In 1870 their plea was answered by a modest reform. Instead of making the radical change of conferring upon married women the capacity to own property, parliament simply extended the equitable concept of the separate use to wages and earnings and certain other acquisitions.[47] The statute effected a fictional settlement whereby (in Dicey's words) the rules of equity, framed for the daughters of the rich, were at last extended to the daughters of the poor.[48] But it was full of technical difficulties, and in 1882 parliament introduced a more sweeping reform. The married woman was now made capable of acquiring, holding and disposing of real and personal property as if she were a feme sole.[49] However, her liability in contract and tort attached only to her separate estate, and this remaining distinction between the property of the feme covert and the feme sole was not removed until later.[50]

CONTRACTS OF MARRIED WOMEN

The wife's inability to make contracts was the direct consequence of her inability to own separate property. There was no difficulty about contracts made by her as an agent, or as a personal representative, because in those capacities she was dealing with another person's property. For the same reason, she could make contracts in relation to property which she owned separately, for instance under a local custom permitting married women to trade. Except in those cases, however, a purported contract by a married woman was merely void, and neither she nor her husband could be sued upon it.[51]

As an agent of her own husband, the wife could sometimes make contracts on his behalf. Thus, it was settled by 1300 that she could bind her husband to a sale of goods which came to his use or profit. But by 1500 it was clear that the husband was bound in such a case only

---

46 Manchester, *Sources*, 400, at p. 401. One immediate measure was the insertion in the Matrimonial Causes Act 1857 (p. 566, post) of protection for anything a *deserted* wife acquired 'by her own lawful industry' (s.21).

47 Married Women's Property Act 1870, 33 & 34 Vict., c.93. Such property was to be 'deemed' to be settled to her own use, 'independent of any husband to whom she may be married', and she was enabled to sue for it in her own name.

48 Dicey, *Law and Public Opinion during the 19th Century*, p. 393.

49 Married Women's Property Act 1882, 45 & 46 Vict., c.75.

50 See pp. 556, 557, post. Only then was it possible to abolish restraints on anticipation: Married Women (Restraint upon Anticipation) Act 1949, 13 & 14 Geo. VI, c.78.

51 The husband could, however, be sued for ante-nuptial debts.

if he had either given his wife prior authority to act for him, or subsequently ratified a contract for his benefit. He could not be held liable for his wife's prodigality or extravagance. If a wife were accustomed to order household goods on credit, an agency might be presumed; but the husband was free to revoke the presumed authority by express notice.

There was no question of the married woman making such contracts as agent for her own separate benefit, and this limitation on the agency doctrine caused injustice if a wife was neglected or evicted by her husband. Although she could sue in the ecclesiastical courts for alimony, such proceedings cost time and money which she might not have. The courts therefore began, in the seventeenth century, to find in such cases of hardship an implied authority to pledge the husband's credit for necessaries for her own support.[52] The implication would not be raised if the wife were the guilty party. And since the implication could not be raised by law if in fact the husband had warned traders not to trust the wife, it was not always helpful to wives in distress. Traders gave credit to wives at their peril, and a separated wife might in reality find it difficult to obtain necessaries without ready cash. Equity helped by encouraging loans to such a wife in distress; provided the money was actually spent on necessaries, the lender could recover it from the husband as if he had supplied the goods himself.[53] In the present century the ability of women to support themselves from their own earnings, and their right to claim maintenance by summary proceedings in magistrates' courts, assisted by legal aid, made the implied authority to pledge credit of little practical value. It had virtually fallen into disuse when it was abolished in 1970.[54]

A married woman who owned separate property in equity was able to make contracts in respect of such property, provided the property was held to her separate use at the date of the contract. But the employment of restraints on anticipation usually prevented the wife from contracting in this way. The effect of the 1870 and 1882 Acts was to enable the wife to make contracts in respect of her legal property, and render her liable to be sued separately. But the contractual liability still attached to the property and not the person: therefore a plaintiff suing a married

---

52 *Sir Thomas Gardener's Case* (1615) Rolle Abr., vol. I, p. 351; *Dent v. Scott* (1648) Aleyn 61. Cf. *Manby v. Scott* (1663) 1 Sid. 109; 1 Keb. 482; 1 Lev. 4; 1 Mod. Rep. 124; O. Bridg. 29.

53 *Harris v. Lee* (1718) 1 P. Wms 482; Prec. Ch. 502; 2 Eq. Cas. Abr. 135. The loan could not be recovered at law; but equity held the lender 'subrogated' to the position of the supplier.

54 Matrimonial Proceedings and Property Act 1970 (c.45), s.41.

woman for breach of contract had to prove that she had separate property at the time of contracting, and if he obtained judgment it could only be executed against her unrestrained separate property.[55] This gave the married woman an irrational and unnecessary privilege, and in 1935 she was finally given the same contractual capacity as a feme sole (or a man).[56]

TORTS BY AND AGAINST MARRIED WOMEN

Her inability to own property did not render a married woman less capable of committing torts, any more than it exempted her from criminal liability. But it rendered her incapable of paying compensation, and as a matter of procedure an action for a wife's tort had to be brought against husband and wife jointly. The wrong was not visited on the husband personally, even in a vicarious sense, for if the wife died his liability came to an end; nevertheless he bore the financial brunt of any successful suit. Under the 1882 Act, it became possible to sue married women in tort as if they were single; but judgment could only be executed against their separate property. Husbands remained liable as well, until they were relieved from this obsolete consequence of the doctrine of unity of person in 1935.[57]

The converse principle applied to torts committed against a wife. The husband and wife had to bring the action jointly, and the damages belonged to the husband. The husband could, in addition, claim for any loss he had suffered through the loss of his wife's services or *consortium*.[58] Since 1935, a wife has had an independent action in respect of torts committed against her.

Bastardy

Bastardy, or illegitimacy, was a condition imposed upon a child by the Church as a punishment for the sin of parents who conceived it by illicit connection. By legal fiction, a child born out of wedlock was no one's child, *filius nullius*. This condition was visited by the Canon law on children born of a single woman, of an adulterous union, of a clandestine marriage which was found to be void, or of a church marriage where both parties knew of an impediment. The Canon law,

---

55 Any property acquired during the coverture was liable, but until 1893 the liability did not extend to property acquired after discoverture: Married Women's Property Act 1893, 56 & 57 Vict., c.63.

56 Law Reform (Married Women and Tortfeasors) Act 1935, 25 & 26 Geo. V, c.30, s.1.

57 Ibid., s.3.

58 See p. 519, ante.

however, treated the children of a bona fide putative marriage as legitimate if they were born before annulment, and also allowed that a bastard born out of wedlock was legitimated by the subsequent marriage of his parents. The Church took notice of illegitimate parentage to the extent of requiring a putative father to contribute to the support of his child; but affiliation proceedings in the ecclesiastical courts seem to have been uncommon in medieval times.[59]

Under the Canon law bastardy was an inferior status, which prevented an illegitimate man from being ordained priest. In English law, however, it was not a status or condition but simply the absence of a legitimate family relationship. The bastard had the same rights as any other free man, with the single exception that he could not be heir to his parents nor have any collateral heir[60] himself. In one case, that of villeinage, this was a distinct advantage.[61] The obvious disadvantage was that the bastard could not take real property by inheritance. It was settled in the twelfth century that bastardy could be pleaded in bar of a real action, in which case the question of fact (if disputed) would be referred to the ecclesiastical court. From an early date, however, there was a conflict between the Canon law and the common law over the doctrine of legitimation by subsequent marriage and the effect of annulment of marriage. The common law took the coldly logical view that bastardy was judged as at the date of birth and was indelible: there could not be legitimation ex post facto, and therefore nullity of marriage always bastardised the issue. Since inheritance was a question for the temporal law, the king's judges felt their law should prevail; yet, on reference to the bishop, his certificate would preclude them from applying it. The judges therefore proposed in 1236 that bishops should be expressly asked whether the birth was before the marriage. The bishops reacted by suggesting the introduction of the Canon law doctrine into English law, and received a scornful rebuff from the assembled earls and barons, who 'with one voice answered, that they would not change the laws of England'.[62] It followed that, although the bishop's certificate of bastardy was conclusive, his certificate of legitimacy was not, because a person legitimate by the Canon law might yet have been born out of wedlock. The judges therefore decided that in all except the old real actions a party could plead 'special

---

59   The evidence is surveyed in Helmholz, *Canon Law and the Law of England*, ch. 10.

60   I.e. an heir traced through his parents.

61   See pp. 535-536, ante.

62   Provisions of Merton 1236, c.9. See *Bracton's Notebook*, vol. I, pp. 104-115; *Bracton*, vol. III, pp. xv-xvii.

bastardy' (that is, birth out of wedlock), which was a question of fact capable of trial by jury. This pleading device could be used to keep a matter from the Church courts where the marriage itself was not in dispute.

The common law developed one exception to its harsh doctrine of bastardy. Where the eldest son was born out of wedlock (the *bastard eigné*) and the next son was born to the same parents after the marriage (the *mulier puisné*), and upon the ancestor's death the *bastard eigné* entered as heir and remained in undisturbed possession until his own death, the *bastard eigné* was treated as if he had been legitimate with respect to the inheritance of that land. The reason given by Littleton was that a person who was legitimate by the Canon law could not be bastardised posthumously, when he no longer had the opportunity to contest the issue.[63]

The 'laws of England' which the barons would not alter were eventually changed in 1926.[64] Since 1969 an illegitimate child also takes, on the intestacy of his parents (but not other relatives), as if he were legitimate, and likewise under a bequest to 'children' unless a contrary intention appears.[65] The old law of *filius nullius* still applies, however, to peerages.

Divorce

The contract of matrimony was the most important contract two persons could make, and yet, unlike all other contracts, there was no escape from it if it proved unsatisfactory. This followed from the teaching of the medieval canonists, to whom the common law referred all matrimonial questions. Yet in Anglo-Saxon England divorce by consent was not unknown; and there is evidence that the early Church itself, while punishing divorce as a sin, had nevertheless recognised it as ending a marriage, at least when based on adultery or desertion. The canonists, however, adopted that interpretation of the scriptures which held that the bonds of matrimony were indissoluble during the lives of the parties.[66] Marriage was an holy estate, and what God had joined together no man could put asunder. The Church courts could only grant a divorce from the bond of matrimony (*a vinculo matrimonii*), on the ground that the

---

63   Littleton, *Tenures*, ss.399-401.
64   Legitimacy Act 1926, 16 & 17 Geo. V, c.60.
65   Family Law Reform Act 1969 (c.46), ss.14-15.
66   See esp. Mark, x.2-12; Luke, xvi.18. Cf. Matthew, v.31-32; xix.3-9. See also Deuteronomy, xxiv.1-2.

putative marriage had been void from its commencement by reason of a 'dirimentary impediment'. They could not break the chains, but they could declare that the chains were never there. Whether a marriage existed or not was a question for the Church and its law; but once a valid marriage was shown to have been contracted *per verba de praesenti*, or by physical union following espousals, only God could end it by extinguishing the life of one spouse. The law of divorce *a vinculo* was, for that reason, the same as the law of marriage.

NULLITY: DIVORCE A VINCULO

According to the classical Canon law, which was law in England until 1857, persons who had undergone the forms of marriage could only be divorced, in the full sense of being free to remarry, if they could establish either a want of capacity to intermarry or a want of true consent at the time of marriage. In those cases the marriage was a nullity from the beginning, and no legal proceedings were needed to make it so.[67] In medieval times divorce could therefore be obtained by self-help rather than litigation: if a party conceived that he was not lawfully married, he left his 'wife' and, if he was so entitled and so desired, married another. The Church did not interfere. If the first marriage was void, it was the parties' duty not to cohabit. There was, nevertheless, a presumption in favour of a solemn church marriage: 'even if one marry his mother, it is lawful matrimony until it is defeated'.[68] If, therefore, the question of marriage was likely to come in issue in a property suit in the royal courts, it was advisable to seek a formal divorce in the consistory court.

Consent might be negatived not only by proof of duress, or insanity, or mistake, but also by showing that the parties were of such tender age that they were presumed incapable of consenting. The age of consent for the contract *per verba de futuro* was fixed at seven, but until the age of puberty either party could avoid the marriage. The age of puberty was, however, fixed arbitrarily by the common law as twelve years in the case of girls and fourteen in the case of boys.[69] In the landed classes marriages were often arranged while the children were very young, but the practice was rarely contested by those concerned. Even if pressure from guardians or parents verged on duress, the children usually submitted. In any case, voluntary coition and cohabitation after

---

67 See *Riddlesden v. Wogan* (1601) Cro. Eliz. 858. For medieval instances, see Helmholz, *Marriage Litigation*, pp. 59-62.

68 Y.B. Trin. 9 Hen. VI, fo. 34, pl. 3, per Paston J.

69 The minimum age of consent was raised to 16 for both sexes by the Age of Marriage Act 1929, 19 & 20 Geo. V, c.36.

reaching full age purged any inherent defects of this nature. Conversely, parental consent was not itself an essential requirement under Canon law.[70] Parents having objections had to raise them when the banns were called, or else thereafter for ever hold their peace.

The other impediments to a marriage went to capacity, and were: precontract (or a previous marriage with another spouse), consanguinity (blood relationship), affinity (relationship by marriage or carnal connection), and impotence at the time of marriage. Since Christian marriage has always been monogamous, a church marriage between A and B could always be upset by proving a previous clandestine marriage between A and C; and in this case B would be free to remarry. A person could not marry a blood-relation within the prohibited degrees. Affinity was also an impediment within certain degrees; thus, a man who had fornicated with X's sister was forbidden to marry X, and the liaison with the sister was consequently a ground of divorce from X. Some of the subtleties of the canonists in this regard seem very remote from theology, morality or human feeling, and served merely to facilitate divorces on flimsy grounds, by the discovery of forgotten indiscretions or genealogical obscurities. Moreover, some of the impediments could be dispensed with in return for money paid to the Church. At the time of the Reformation in England the opportunity was taken of discarding some of this old learning in favour of a simpler statutory table of prohibited degrees, based on scripture;[71] but this strengthening of the bond of marriage gave rise to increased pressure for a method of dissolution.

A putative marriage could also be declared void if one of the parties failed to consummate it on account of incurable impotency which existed at the date of the marriage. Failure to consummate did not itself invalidate a marriage contracted by present words: it was the inability to consummate which made the marriage void *ab initio*. Impotence might arise from malformation or from invincible frigidity. Assertions of frigidity raised difficult questions of proof, which in the fourteenth and fifteenth centuries were solved by surprisingly forthright methods.[72] They were also open to abuse, especially when it was suggested that

---

[70] For the feudal consequences, see p. 276, ante. It was required by Lord Hardwicke's Act (between 1753 and 1823) in the case of a marriage by licence: p. 549, ante.

[71] Marriage Act 1540, 32 Hen. VIII, c.38. After 1835 marriages within the prohibited degrees have been absolutely void: Lord Lyndhurst's Act 1835, 5 & 6 Will. IV, c.54. Some unreasonable remaining impediments based on affinity were removed piecemeal by Deceased Wife's Sister's Marriage Act 1907, 7 Edw. VII, c.47; Deceased Brother's Widow's Marriage Act 1921, 11 & 12 Geo. V, c.24; and some later statutes.

[72] Helmholz, *Marriage Litigation*, p. 89.

frigidity might be relative: as a witty serjeant quipped in a case of 1599, 'he that is *frigidus quoad unam* and *calidus quoad alteram* is likely to prove *callidus nebulo*'.[73]

DIVORCE A MENSA ET THORO

To satisfy the feeling that spouses should be released from conjugal duties where an intolerable matrimonial wrong had been committed subsequent to the marriage, the canonists devised the compromise of judicial separation. This they called divorce from board and hearth (*a mensa et thoro*) because the parties, though indissolubly united, were licensed to live apart. Such a separation was not a divorce in the modern sense, because the parties were not free to remarry; and it was different from nullity in that the issue of partners so divorced remained legitimate. A divorce *a mensa et thoro* could be decreed by the ecclesiastical court for such misconduct as adultery, cruelty, sodomy, and heresy, or for fear of future injury; and an innocent wife could be awarded alimony for her support after such a separation.[74] There was an element of discretion, or canonical equity, in granting this kind of divorce; it could be refused if the petitioner had been guilty of 'conduct conducing' to the offence, or had condoned the offence subsequently. By the end of the eighteenth century, however, a practically effective separation by consent could be achieved by means of a deed of separation, providing for the wife's maintenance and (if appropriate) a separation of property.[75]

DIVORCE AND THE REFORMATION

One of the immediate causes contributing to the separation of the Anglican Church from Rome in the 1530s was the clash between King Henry VIII and Pope Clement VII over the matter of the king's first marriage, to Katharine of Aragon. The dispute made divorce a topic of widespread debate and provoked fresh thinking on the subject. We may also take the matrimonial history of Henry VIII as an illustration of the intricate workings of the unreformed Canon law.

Henry married Katharine in 1509. As she was the widow of his deceased brother Arthur, Henry had first obtained a papal dispensation from the impediment created by affinity. After eighteen years of married

---

[73] *Berrie's Case* (1599) BL MS. Lansdowne 1074, fo. 291. (*Callidus nebulo*, crafty rogue.) The case is differently reported sub nom. *Webber v. Burie*, 5 Co. Rep. 98.

[74] The Court of Requests may have led the way in granting alimony: *Bowdo v. Bowdo* (1542) Caesar's *Ancient State of the Court of Requests*, p.143. The jurisdiction of the ecclesiastical courts was acknowledged in *Hyat's Case* (1615) Cro. Jac. 364.

[75] Cornish & Clark, pp. 376-379.

life, and the birth of a daughter but no son, Henry wanted the marriage declared void so that he could marry Anne Boleyn. He persuaded himself that God had denied him a son as a punishment for marrying his brother's widow, and that this was an impediment which could not be dispensed with by the pope because it derived from divine law and was not merely an arbitrary rule of Canon law.[76] This being a theological as much as a legal question, it was referred to Cardinal Wolsey as papal legate. No decision was reached, because it was certain that if the decision went in favour of the king the queen would appeal successfully to the pope; and in any case the queen had complicated the issue by claiming that her marriage to Prince Arthur had never been consummated. The king's advisers instead set about collecting scholastic opinions on the proposed divorce, and in 1533 the king felt sufficiently sure of his ground in treating the marriage as void without obtaining a formal divorce. The king's foremost protagonist, Dr Thomas Cranmer, was appointed archbishop of Canterbury, the king secretly married Anne Boleyn, the archbishop delivered a judicial sentence confirming that the marriage with Katharine was contrary to God's law and void, and parliament abolished appeals to the pope. Those who spoke against these arrangements were guilty of statutory treason.

The king now had his matrimonial affairs virtually within his own control. Three years later Cranmer again exercised his archiepiscopal jurisdiction, this time to declare void the marriage with Anne. No reasons were published, though it was rumoured that a precontract had been established; more likely it was the king's prior misconduct with Mary Boleyn, the queen's sister, which was taken to render the marriage void on grounds of canonical affinity. Anne was beheaded for treason two days later, which would have enabled the king to remarry in any event; but the purpose of the divorce was to bastardise Princess Elizabeth, the child of the marriage, later Queen Elizabeth I. In the course of time Henry also divorced Anne of Cleves, on the grounds of precontract *per verba de praesenti* with Francis of Lorraine, of incapacity, and (rather surprisingly) of duress. There was no need to divorce Queen Katharine Howard, because she had given the king no children to bastardise. In fact there was evidence of a precontract with one Denham, but the king's advisers preferred to suppress this evidence in order to have the queen convicted of treason for committing adultery with Denham.

[76] Parliament did not venture to change this impediment until 1921: p. 561, note 71, ante.

These proceedings show how the old Canon law was capable of very flexible application, if not manipulation, when pressure was brought to bear. We shall not attempt to assess the sincerity of Henry VIII, Cranmer or Clement VII in these proceedings, but it seems likely that many churchmen genuinely felt the law of divorce to be in need of reform. Even in Thomas More's Utopia – admittedly not a Christian state – divorce was allowed for adultery and cruelty. Henry VIII had not gone so far; he wished to conform, or to be seen as conforming, to the old law. But Cranmer had definite views on reform. He wrote that separation *a mensa et thoro* was a travesty of Christian marriage, which was founded on the cohabitation of man and wife. In his draft code of reformed Canon law for the Church of England he proposed that full dissolution be permitted for good causes. The causes suggested were adultery, cruelty, desertion, and bitter enmity. These proposals were never fully implemented, but for a time there was a doubt whether the Reformation had somehow in itself altered the nature of divorce *a mensa et thoro*. In the time of Edward VI a precedent was set for a new approach by the Marquess of Northampton. In 1548 he divorced his wife for adultery and then sought to remarry. Cranmer, asked to pronounce on the propriety of a remarriage, procrastinated; and so the marquess remarried without archiepiscopal authority. Eventually the validity of the second marriage was upheld by the Court of Delegates and confirmed by act of parliament. The precedent was at first followed and then overruled in Elizabeth I's reign,[77] after which there was no doubt that the old law remained unaltered.

DIVORCE BY PRIVATE ACT OF PARLIAMENT

In interpreting the canonical rules to his own advantage, Henry VIII had been careful to avoid introducing a novel approach to divorce, and such statutes as he passed concerning his marriages were merely confirmations of his interpretation of the universal law of the Church. But his divorces had bastardised two future queens of England: Mary, the daughter of Katharine of Aragon, and Elizabeth, the daughter of Anne Boleyn. Needless to say, each of them upon her accession restored her legitimacy by act of parliament, and in so doing demonstrated more finally than their father had done the sovereign power of parliament to interfere with the laws of marriage. The statute passed for the Marquess of Northampton provided another example of this sovereignty. Parliament had begun to do what the medieval Church had considered the

---

[77] *Sir John Stawell's Case* (1572) 29 LQR 86; *Rye v. Fuljambe* (1602) Moore K.B. 683; Noy 100.

exclusive province of God. Even so, the legislation at first interfered only with the interpretation and application of the rules to particular cases, not with the rules themselves.

In 1670 the view that the law of God permitted divorce for adultery was given effect by statute, when the Lord Roos's marriage was dissolved and he was enabled to remarry. After this, the promotion of private divorce bills became common. What could not be done in the ecclesiastical courts could now be done in parliament, often with the votes of the bishops. But the legislature was not an ideal forum for unravelling family disputes. When the Duke of Norfolk failed to secure a divorce act in 1692 after a trial in parliament, one reason for the failure was said to be the unsatisfactory character of such a trial, which would have been better conducted before a jury.[78] The duke therefore brought an action for 'lascivious conversation', won the verdict, and eight years later presented a successful petition for a divorce statute.[79] Thereafter it became the usual procedure for the petitioning husband to start by bringing an action for criminal conversation to establish the adultery, then to obtain a divorce *a mensa et thoro* in the ecclesiastical court on the ground of that adultery, and then to present a petition to the House of Lords.[80]

In this way divorce for adultery was introduced into English law. There was no alteration in the procedure or jurisdiction of the Church courts, no abrogation of the distinction between separation *a mensa et thoro* and divorce *a vinculo matrimonii*. Although the parliamentary procedure was long-winded and expensive, it may not have been as exclusive to the wealthy as was once supposed, because the successful plaintiff in a suit for criminal conversation usually recovered sufficient damages to cover the costs of the divorce. The critical factor was the ability of the defendant to pay.

REFORM OF THE DIVORCE LAWS

An accident of politics prevented Cranmer's proposal to introduce regular divorce *a vinculo* for adultery and cruelty from becoming law for several centuries. Once the opportunity for reform after the break with Rome was lost, any further hope of change was stifled by the

[78] 12 State Tr. 948n. Another reason may have been that the bishops were then divided on the remarriage question: ibid. 883n.

[79] *Duke of Norfolk v. Duchess of Norfolk* (1692) 12 State Tr. 883; *Duke of Norfolk v. Germaine* (1692) ibid. 1283. For the action of criminal conversation, see p. 519, ante.

[80] Adultery was the only recognised ground. No such divorces were obtained by women before 1800.

conservatism of the ecclesiastical authorities. But resistance to change
was no longer the defence of an inexorable principle, since the principle
could be dispensed with ad hoc by parliament; and it bore hard on those
who could not afford the dispensation. The stand was taken on the
proposition that divorce should not be made easier, and certainly should
not be made a right, demandable as of course.

Jeremy Bentham (d. 1832) advocated a utilitarian approach to divorce
in his *Theory of Legislation*, published posthumously in 1864. He
admitted that the natural duration of marriage was life, but thought a
dissoluble marriage would be a stronger and more loving union, because
'what is now done only to gain affection, would then be practised to
preserve it'. He concluded that divorce ought to be allowed in certain
cases, at the behest of the innocent party. The introduction of civil
marriage in 1836 removed the ecclesiastical obstacle to remarriage after
divorce, but it did not facilitate divorce itself. A strong movement for
reform stirred in the early years of Queen Victoria, and according to
tradition it was brought to a head by a much publicised observation of
Maule J at Warwick assizes in 1845. A pauper, whose wife had deserted
him, had gone through a form of marriage with another woman and had
consequently been convicted of bigamy. In terms of mordant irony, the
judge told the prisoner that the proper course would have been to obtain
a divorce by act of parliament; true, it would have cost him about £500
and he had not so many pence, but the law was the same for rich and
poor alike. The sentence was four months' hard labour, which the judge
'hoped would operate as a warning how people trifled with
matrimony'.[81] During the next few years, the Society for Promoting
the Amendment of the Law worked out proposals for transferring the
divorce jurisdiction of parliament to a special court of law, with cheaper
procedure. The proposals were considerded in detail by a Royal
Commission which reported in 1853. The commission recommended
the retention of divorce *a mensa et thoro* (to be renamed judicial
separation), but urged the establishment of a divorce court with
jurisdiction to grant dissolution in cases where it could already be
obtained from parliament, but without the need for previous proceedings
in any other court. These recommendations were carried into effect in
1857, when the Court for Divorce and Matrimonial Causes was
established and the divorce jurisdiction of the Church courts abolished.[82]

The reform was modest. There were no changes in the grounds for
divorce, only in the procedure for obtaining it. The machinery was

---

81   *R. v. Hall* (otherwise *Rollins*) (1845) *Times* 3 April, p.8.
82   Matrimonial Causes Act 1857, 20 & 21 Vict., c.85.

improved and the cost reduced, but adultery remained the sole ground for dissolution; and, in the case of a wife petitioner, cruelty or desertion (or something worse) had to be proved as well. To allay fears of collusion, decrees of divorce were to be provisional, so that enquiries could be made by the queen's proctor, after which the decree *nisi* would be made absolute.[83] The court sat only in London, and its costs were still too high to bring divorce within the reach of all classes. The abuses of the Victorian divorce court by society families became a scandal: formal evidence of adultery was often 'provided' by the respondent, no defence was offered, and unless the prying nose of the queen's proctor smelt collusion the effect was virtually divorce by consent. In 1909 the government was pressed to introduce reforms; but, in the words of Judge Parry, they 'funked a quarrel with the organised priesthoods' and took refuge 'in the constitutional asylum of a Royal Commission'.[84] The commission, under the chairmanship of Sir Gorrell Barnes, reported that they could find no unanimity among theologians on the subject of divorce and no logical secular reason for confining the grounds to adultery. They recommended as additional grounds, inter alia, cruelty or three years' desertion; and also that wives should possess the same rights as husbands. The Convocations of Canterbury and York immediately declared their hostility to any proposal to facilitate divorce, and the bill to implement the suggestions of the Barnes Commission was defeated in 1914. Another attempt, by Lord Buckmaster in 1923, failed in its main object, but succeeded in giving wives the same grounds for divorce as husbands.[85]

In the twentieth century most churchmen came to reconcile themselves to a divergence between the secular law of marriage and the ideals of Christian doctrine and discipline. In 1935 a committee of churchmen recognised the validity of such a divergence, and soon afterwards the Barnes proposals were accomplished.[86] The Church of England promptly legislated that divorced persons should not be allowed to remarry with the rites of the Church. The dilemma was ended: the law of divorce and the Canon law of indissolubility of marriage were themselves divorced. After the second world war, discussion turned to the question whether it was right to make divorce depend on proof of a matrimonial offence. After a bill had been presented in 1951 to permit

---

[83] Matrimonial Causes Act 1860, 23 & 24 Vict., c.144, s.7.

[84] E. A. Parry, *The Gospel and the Law* (1928), p.238.

[85] Report of the Barnes Commission (1912) Cd 6478; Matrimonial Causes Act 1923, 13 & 14 Geo. V, c.19.

[86] *The Church and Marriage* (1935); A. P. Herbert's Act 1937, 1 Edw. VIII & 1 Geo. VI, c.57.

divorce after separation by consent for seven years, the matter was referred to another Royal Commission, which reported in favour of retaining the matrimonial offence.[87]   Lord Walker, in an impressive dissent, argued that divorce should be permitted where a marriage had irretrievably broken down; and ten years later this approach was recommended by a commission appointed by the archbishop of Canterbury.   Unless divorce was to be regarded purely as a form of punishment, it seemed irrational to permit divorce for a single act of adultery, while denying it where a marital relationship was completely dead for reasons independent of fault.   The new approach to divorce, which stresses the breakdown of the marriage rather than the commission of a matrimonial offence, became law in 1969.[88]

Further reading

Holdsworth HEL, vol. III, pp. 520-533
R. B. Outhwaite (ed.), *Marriage in Society* (1981), chs. I, II, and VI

THE MEDIEVAL LAW OF MARRIAGE
Pollock & Maitland, vol. II, pp. 364-436
M. M. Sheehan, 'The Formation and Stability of Marriage in England from the 11th to the 14th Century' (1971) 33 *Medieval Stud*. 228-263; 'Marriage Theory and Practice in the Conciliar Legislation and Diocesan Statutes of Medieval England' (1978) 40 *Medieval Stud*. 408-460
R. H. Helmholz, *Marriage Litigation in England in Medieval England* (1975)
C. Donahue, 'Marriage and Divorce' (1981) 95 SS *81-86*; 'The Canon Law on the Formation of Marriage and Social Practice in the later Middle Ages' (1983) 8 *Jo. Family Hist*. 144-158

THE MEDIEVAL LAW OF BASTARDY
F. E. Farrer, 'The Bastard Eigné' (1917) 33 LQR 135-153
N. Adams, 'Nullius Filius' (1946) 6 *Univ. Toronto Law Jo*. 361-384
R. H. Helmholz, 'Bastardy Litigation in Medieval England' (1969) 13 AJLH 360-383; 'Support Orders, Church Courts and the Role of

---

[87] Report of the Morton Commission (1955) Cmnd 9678.
[88] *Parliamentary Debates* (H.L.), vol. 250 (5th ser.), col. 1547; *Putting Asunder* (1966); *Field of Choice* (Law Comm., 1968); Divorce Reform Act 1969, c.55.

Filius Nullius' (1977) 63 *Univ. Virginia Law Rev.* 431-448 (repr. in *Canon Law and the Law of England*, pp. 169-210)

J. L. Barton, 'Nullity of Marriage and Illegitimacy in the England of the Middle Ages' (1975), in *Legal History Studies 1972*, pp. 28-49

HENRY VIII'S DIVORCE

H. Thurston, 'The Canon Law of the Divorce' (1904) 19 EHR 632-645

G. de C. Parmiter, *The King's Great Matter* (1967)

J. Scarisbrick, *Henry VIII* (1968), pp. 163-240

H. A. Kelly, *The Matrimonial Trials of Henry VIII* (1976)

FAMILY LAW AFTER THE REFORMATION

Manchester MLH, pp. 360-401; *Sources*, ch. 15

Cornish & Clark, pp. 357-410

R. Houlbrooke, 'The Making of Marriage in mid-Tudor England' (1985) 10 *Jo. Family Hist.* 339-352

J. Wolfram, 'Divorce in England 1700-1857' (1985) 5 OJLS 155-186

A. Horstman, *Victorian Divorce* (1985)

M. Ingram, *Church Courts, Sex and Marriage in England, 1570-1640* (1987)

28. Pleas of the Crown: Criminal Procedure

The history of crime has become a favourite topic of study among social historians, because the records of criminal justice are rich in details of everyday life; but the history of criminal law has proved less attractive to legal historians, because the same records are more than usually wanting in jurisprudential content. For many centuries there was little to parallel the reasoning processes which shaped the civil law. The absence of pleaders and of special pleading from the criminal courts meant that all criminal cases were tried, as they still are, on the general issue 'Not guilty'; and so the only substantive question which could arise on the face of the record was whether the accused was charged with a known crime. So long as the detailed facts which might constitute an offence, or furnish a defence, were matters purely of evidence, off the record,[1] sophisticated definitions of crimes were needless. Reason and jurisprudence, if any there were, remained irretrievably obscured behind the inscrutable and final verdicts of juries. All the prerequisites for legal development in the civil law were here lacking. Yet the criminal law does have a history. And it is not an uninteresting story, because amongst other things it shows how law can develop from common opinion, practice and professional discussion without formal judgments in the central courts to serve as recorded precedents. The emergence of legal principles will be the subject of the following chapter; but in an introductory essay the procedures deserve at least equal attention, since they show how the system functioned even in the absence of detailed principles. The administration of criminal justice was governed by a combination of strict procedure and wide discretion long after the law of property, the heart of the civil law, had been reduced from feudal discretion to intricate and settled rules.

CRIME AND TORT

The distinction between criminal and civil justice has been such a basic feature of the common law for so long that it might be tempting to regard it as eternal. Not only are there different courts and procedures,

---

[1] For a specimen record of criminal proceedings, see pp. 632-634, post.

but there is a fundamental difference of purpose. The civil law is designed to provide private redress for wrongs to individuals, whereas the criminal law is concerned with public order and the treatment of offenders against that order. Yet there was a time when the notion of public order was so undeveloped or weak that no such distinction could be made.

In early societies there is no concept of the 'state'. Both compensation and retribution for wrongdoing are exacted at the instance of the wronged individual and his kin. Either there will be a feud between one family and another until satisfaction is wrought, or the potential feud will be averted by customary arbitration processes designed to secure the payment of money by way of 'emendation' for the wrong. The purpose of emendation payments was overtly retributive, yet it was also compensatory: in modern language, it was both a fine and damages at the same time. In so far as feuds and their settlement were governed by rules about compensation, there was a law of wrongs. But there was no division of wrongs into crimes and torts. And the main purpose of introducing fixed law into the matter was to protect the wrongdoer against excessive private vengeance, rather than to punish him or deter others.

The notion of a crime as a species of wrongdoing which requires punishment at the instance of the community or the state was at first based more on procedure than on substance. It came to the fore when the responsibility for pursuing the punitive or retributive process shifted from the family grouping of the kin to the wider local community and thence (in theory) to the king. The transfer of primitive police functions from the kin to the community at large is now imperceptible, for want of records; but the acquisition by kings, and their grantees, of valuable and powerful jurisdiction over malefactors marked a new procedural era in which the kin began to lose all significance, and the fiscal profits of punishment fell into the coffers of powerful individuals – or of the Crown itself – by right of jurisdiction.

The rather different notion of crime as a species of wrong requiring punishment because it is sinful is a more substantive notion, which may have played a greater role than procedure alone suggests. Such an approach was fostered by the early Church through its teaching on the need to atone for sin by penance. Even when it was admitted that penance could be compounded for by pecuniary payments, resembling feud-compensation, the underlying penal theory was maintained.[2] Penance was punitive; wrongdoers deserved, and needed, afflictive

---

[2] See pp. 149-150, ante.

punishment. The ecclesiastical concept of infamy, exemplified by the form of the sentence of anathema, may also have contributed to the idea that 'corruption of the blood' should follow conviction of a serious crime. That doctrine also possessed a feudal dimension, in that the felon forfeited his land, and the sins of the father were until 1870 visited on his children by disinheritance.

Criminal justice in England was born of the union between these two concepts, when the blood-feud system went into disuse and the Crown assumed the power to punish those who broke the 'king's peace'. However, it was some time before crime became clearly distinct from tort, because the principal means of initiating proceedings was still the victim and his kin.

FELONY AND TRESPASS

If the wrong was particularly heinous, it was 'unemendable' and the wrongdoer suffered judgment to lose everything he had: his life, his lands, and his personal goods.[3] Wrongs of this kind were called 'felonies', from an old French word (meaning wicked or treacherous) which seems to have originated in the feudal context; a felony was an act of such wickedness that it destroyed the bond between lord and man, so that the tenant's land was forfeited to the lord.[4] By the thirteenth century the feudal connection had disappeared from the definition, but remained as a consequence; the use of 'words of felony' in making an accusation of crime indicated an offence so serious that conviction would result in forfeiture of property and life or limb. Lesser wrongs – wrongs for which the words of felony were inappropriate – merited lesser penalties, such as imprisonment, corporal punishment, or pecuniary fine. The generic word for these lesser wrongs was 'trespass', though in later times the synonym 'misdemeanour' was adopted as a means of distinguishing the criminal offence from the tort.[5] The division of wrongs into felonies and misdemeanours had important consequences in English law until 1967,[6] and is still observed in the United States. The lesser offences were themselves subdivided into those where the wrong was alleged to be against the king's peace, so as to make them pleas of

---

3   All the felon's chattels were forfeited to the Crown.

4   Subject to the right of the Crown to have them for a year and a day, and to commit waste: *Glanvill*, vii.17; Magna Carta 1215, cl.32 (1225, c.22); Prerogativa Regis, c.16. In the case of treason, lands were forfeit to the king.

5   For 'misdemeanour' used of a civil wrong, see B. & M. 408 (1505), 533 (1555), and 320 (1666).

6   Criminal Law Act 1967 (c.58), s.1. This does not explicitly abolish felonies and misdemeanours, but only the distinction between them.

the Crown, and the remainder, which were punishable only in local courts. As a general rule, only offences involving force could be treated in the former way, and the consequence was that some offences of deceit or stealth were shut out from the common law.[7] The principal exceptions were offences committed 'to the damage and common nuisance of all the king's liege subjects'.[8]

The Initiation of Criminal Proceedings

The firm rule of the Normans and Angevins has already been averted to as one of the main causes of the common-law system of judicature. It also settled that the judgment of transgressors against the king's peace belonged to royal justice. This was necessary to preserve law and order throughout the kingdom, and was incidentally beneficial to the king's purse. The association of serious criminal offences with the king's peace justified bringing all criminal punishment within the purview of the common law; but private revenge and lynch-law existed long before criminal law came to replace it, and the replacement did not occur suddenly. In Norman times felons caught red-handed could be summarily executed, and this custom survived in some places well into the thirteenth century. The common-law judges soon restricted the extrajudicial power of executing felons to those who possessed an appropriate hundredal jurisdiction, or the franchise of infangthief; and once the power became thus judicialised, at least a summary inquiry (or confession) was expected before the offender was put to death. By the fourteenth century pre-judicial execution was permitted only where a felon took flight and could not otherwise be arrested.[9] Moreover, with the development during the same period of the gaol-delivery system, the role of the franchisal and hundredal jurisdictions was in effect reduced to that of arrest and the preparation of accusations to be laid before the royal justices.[10] It thus became generally necessary that a suspect be formally accused and then tried in a regular court. Formal accusations, whether for felony or misdemeanour, could be made in two ways: either the victim could 'appeal' the accused, or representatives of the locality could make a sworn presentment of the offence. Until the fourteenth century it was also possible for a suspected thief, if taken with the

---

7 See Milsom HFCL, pp. 404-405.
8 For public nuisance, see p. 492, ante.
9 *Note* (1329) 97 SS 212, per Louth J; Pollock & Maitland, vol. II, pp. 579-580.
10 See J. B. Post, 4 CJH 1.

goods, to be arraigned without either formality;[11] but this procedure seems to have come to an end in Edward III's time.

APPEALS

The appeal was perhaps the oldest procedure; indeed, it may have been a direct judicial successor to the feud, a legal way of seeking revenge and emends. An appeal was essentially an oral accusation of crime made by someone closely affected: either by the victim[12] or by 'approvers'.[13] Approvers were accomplices whose neck was spared in return for their undertaking to prosecute some agreed number of fellow wrongdoers. As we have seen, the appeal procedure was regarded as inappropriate in the central courts for mere trespasses or misdemeanours, so that a complaint of a wrong without words of felony had to be made by writ of trespass.[14] The appeal of felony, however, continued to be a regular method of initiating criminal prosecutions throughout the medieval period and beyond; such prosecutions were 'criminal' not in the sense that they were brought by the Crown, or initiated by any form of public authority, but in the sense that their purpose was the punishment of felony by death and forfeiture. The early procedure was for the complainant to raise the hue and cry, to inform the coroner, and then to make an oral complaint (or appeal) in the county court, where the appellee would be attached to answer before the justices in eyre; but with the decline of the eyre system it became more usual to commence an appeal at Westminster by writ, with trial at nisi prius. By the late fourteenth century about half of all appeals, and by the late fifteenth century virtually all, were begun in the King's Bench.

The appeal was a strict form of proceeding which in the thirteenth century frequently collapsed on technical grounds: an appellor could be punished for trivial ambiguities in the count,[15] or for withdrawing an appeal. Moreover, the appellee could wage battle. An approver was in an even stricter position; part of the bargain for his life was that he should confess his own part in the felony, and therefore if he failed to

---

11   Late examples are *Anon.* (1321) Y.B. 15 Edw. II, CUL MS. Hh. 2. 4, fo. 180; *Sharneye's Case* (1329) 97 SS 159. In both cases there was an accusation by some kind of summary 'inquest' but not a formal indictment.

12   In the case of homicide, the appeal could be brought by the widow or by the heir.

13   So called because they were required to prove their accusations by doing battle with the appellees. For approvers, see F. C. Hamil, 11 *Speculum* 238; J. Röhrkasten, 5 JLH 14.

14   See p. 70, ante.

15   For the minute precision required in the 13th century, see *Placita Corone*.

prosecute the appeal with good effect he was hanged.[16] Nevertheless, appeals were not discouraged by the judges, who indeed actively drove battle out of use by hedging it around with restrictions. Before the middle of the thirteenth century nearly all appeals (except those by approvers) were tried by jury; and in the early fourteenth century a Newgate judge refused to allow battle in an appeal of robbery on the explicit ground that it would encourage the strong to rob the weak.[17] The extreme technicality required in counting was also modified.[18]

Although revenge may often have been the original driving force behind the appeal procedure, there were mixed motives for the survival of the system. In the case of approvers the motive was obviously the saving of one's own life, while in the case of victims of theft it was often the recovery of the stolen goods.[19] But the records of criminal proceedings show that victims' appeals increasingly served only to bring defendants before a court; the appeal was then dropped, and the prosecution taken over in the king's name, a step which precluded punishment for a false appeal. It seems almost certain that the real purpose of such proceedings was to secure compensation; the ultimate threat in the appeal was doubtless a better bargaining factor than the uncertain prospect of damages in an action of trespass.[20] As late as the time of Henry VII, several hundred appeals of felony were commenced, though the procedure had all but ceased in reality to be a means of putting an accused on trial. Even in the 1550s, Staunford's textbook on pleas of the Crown devoted more space to appeals than to indictments; but by then they had become far less common.

In its final phase, the appeal was used less as a means of forcing a compromise, in order to obtain compensation, than as a means of obtaining a new trial where an indictment for homicide had failed. This new object explains why Holt CJ as late as 1699 vigorously defended the appeal as 'a noble prosecution, and a true badge of English

---

16 E.g. *Adam of Hereford's Case* (1249) in *Crown Pleas of the Wiltshire Eyre*, p. 172, pl.105 (approver hanged for withdrawing appeal); *Anon.* (1327) Y.B. Trin. 1 Edw. III, fo. 16, pl.4 (approver hanged where appellee absconded to Flanders); *Whippe v. Hemesby* (1342) p. 632, post.

17 BL MS. Harley 2183, fo. 175 (c. 1315), per Spigurnel J ('qar issi duneyms nous ensample a les fortes de robber les autres'). Battle was usually ousted in an appeal of robbery if the accused was found in possession of the goods in question.

18 Statute of Gloucester 1278, c.9, said appeals should not be abated as readily as in the past. But the effect may not have been immediate: see 24 SS 100-101 (1313).

19 For recovery of chattels by appeal of theft, see pp. 440-441, ante.

20 It could also be used vexatiously, perhaps to the same end: see *Chamber v. Mountegomery* (1506) Port Nbk (102 SS) 137, pl. 103.

liberties'.[21] Nevertheless, it was frequently attacked as infringing the principle that one ought not to be tried twice for the same offence, and few of the last appeals were brought from the purest of motives. The appeal was effectively obsolete by the time it was abolished in 1819.[22]

INDICTMENTS

For centuries before the demise of the appeal, the indictment had been the usual way of commencing criminal proceedings. Whatever the original meaning of the word 'indictment',[23] by the fourteenth century it had become a technical expression for a written accusation which was not an appeal by an individual but the outcome of a solemn enquiry into the commission of offences. However, the practice of swearing in a body of community representatives to make presentments of crimes began long before the word 'indictment' was used for the outcome: perhaps in Anglo-Saxon times, certainly by 1166 when it is mentioned in the Assize of Clarendon. Whether an accusation came from such a body or from an appellor seems in the twelfth century to have been relevant only to the form of proof required; and even in the gaol-delivery rolls of the early fourteenth century the two species of accusation are not consistently distinguished. In the course of the fourteenth century the legal distinction between them sharpened. An indictment became the normal way of initiating a prosecution; it was much less strict than the appeal, in procedural terms, and trial was never by battle.

The accusing juries mentioned by the Assize of Clarendon were representatives of each hundred and vill summoned before the justices in eyre and sworn to report crimes and name suspects. Much the same system was used when commissions of gaol delivery replaced the eyres as the ordinary source of criminal justice. The presenting body at the assizes or quarter sessions acquired the name 'grand jury', to distinguish it from trial juries. The grand jury was charged to make presentments from its own knowledge, but the regular practice from at least the 1360s was for draft written accusations (known as bills of indictment) to be prepared in advance of the session. The grand jurors scrutinised these bills, if necessary hearing *ex parte* evidence from accusers; if they

---

21   *Stout v. Cowper* (1699) 12 Mod. Rep. 375; *R. v. Toler* (1700) 1 Ld Raym. 555 at 557. The defendant in this appeal of murder, Spencer Cowper, was acquitted and subsequently became a judge.

22   The latest reported cases are *Smith v. Taylor* (1771) 5 Burr. 2793; *Ashford v. Thornton* (1818) p. 87, ante (the case which led to abolition).

23   Some dictionaries derive the word from the Latin *indicare*, meaning to point the finger of accusation. But the true meaning may have been to write down (cf. 'indite'): J. P. Collas, 81 SS at lxi-lxvi.

considered that there was a case to answer they found the bill 'true', and it was endorsed *billa vera* ('a true bill'), but if they did not it was endorsed *ignoramus* ('we do not know') and proceedings on the bill ended. The finding of a true bill by the grand jury was not a conviction, or a finding of guilt, and it required only a majority vote of twelve;[24] it was a written accusation upon oath, the effect of which was to initiate proceedings between the king and the accused person to try the issue of guilt.[25] Indictments were also found by coroners' juries, whose principal function came to be the holding of inquests *super visum corporis*, enquiries 'upon the view of the body' of a person dying violently or suspiciously, to ascertain the cause of death; a verdict that the death was caused by a named person was, again, not a conviction, but an accusation which required trial.

Some early indictments were extremely vague in their wording; a man might be accused of being a 'common thief', without particulars, or even of being simply a suspected evil-doer, perhaps because he was found with more cash than he could explain or was lurking suspiciously in the dark. The judges in the fourteenth century put a stop to this practice, first by directing juries not to convict on such indictments unless they had knowledge of a specific offence,[26] and then by quashing the indictments themselves for uncertainty.[27] Accusations of being a 'common' offender might still be inserted as aggravation in an indictment for a specific offence; but they could no longer be treated as sufficient in themselves. The effect of this important change was that no one could be put on trial for his life except upon a specific charge, made either by appeal or indictment. This salutary rule came to be cherished as one of the greatest liberties of the subject;[28] but it did not extend to misdemeanours.[29]

---

[24] The number of jurors was usually greater than 12, and in later times it was usually 23.

[25] The opening words of an indictment (until 1915) were: 'The jurors for our lord the king on their oath present that . . .'.

[26] E.g. *Anon.* (1313) 24 SS 141 (misleadingly translated). Cf. *R. v. Braban* (1317) BL MS. Egerton 2811, fo. 121; JUST 3/41/1, m. 12d (acquittal at Newgate where the only evidence was that the accused were seen wandering by night and sleeping in an empty house).

[27] *Anon.* (1348) Y.B. 22 Edw. III, Lib. Ass. pl.73 ('common wrongdoer' too uncertain); *R. v. Gower* (1351) Y.B. Pas. 25 Edw. III, fo. 86, pl.36 (indictment bad because no place alleged); *Anon.* (1355) Y.B. 29 Edw. III, Lib. Ass. pl.45 ('common forestaller' or 'common thief' too uncertain).

[28] See LPCL at 263.

[29] Some of the vague 'common' offences lived on as misdemeanours: e.g., being a common night-walker, common barrator, or common scold (all abolished in 1967).

INFORMATIONS

In the case of misdemeanours, a third method of initiating criminal proceedings existed in medieval times, though it did not become common until the Tudor period. This was the criminal information, laid by a single individual rather than by a presenting jury. Informations by private persons were encouraged by legislation, from the mid-fifteenth century onwards, as a means of suppressing economic offences, the informer being allowed a share of the penalty;[30] a breed of 'common informers' arose, who made a living by prying for reward. The *ex officio* information by a law officer became the regular means of commencing Crown prosecutions in the Star Chamber and conciliar courts. It also proved useful as a way of bringing controversial prosecutions before the King's Bench. Its chief attraction for the law officers was that it saved the trouble and risk of first persuading a grand jury to approve the prosecution. As a result of suspected misuse, however, the procedure attracted considerable odium in the seventeenth century, and in 1690 its legality was unsuccessfully challenged in the King's Bench. Since the possibility of abuse was evident, legislation was introduced to forbid the filing of informations in the King's Bench without leave of the court, and to make the prosecutor liable to costs. Thereafter prosecutions were commenced by information in the King's Bench only for those 'gross and serious misdemeanours which deserve the most public animadversion', such as riot or sedition.[31] The information has nevertheless remained the ordinary method of initiating summary proceedings before magistrates.

The Trial

By the end of the twelfth century two modes of trial were used in criminal cases, the ordeal and judicial combat. Wager of law had also been in use for accusations based merely on suspicion; but this had disappeared from the royal courts with the provision in the Assize of Clarendon that accusations by presenting juries were to be tried by ordeal.[32] Judicial combat was originally available only where there was

---

30   An early example is in the Statute of Liveries 1468, 8 Edw. IV, c.2. Previous statutes of liveries had provided for penalties, and informers; but recovery was by action of debt.

31   *R. v. Berchet* (1690) 5 Mod. Rep. 459; 1 Show. K.B. 106; Stat. 4 Will. & Mar., c.18; Bl. Comm., vol. IV, p. 309.

32   By the custom of London freemen continued to be entitled to wage their law on charges of homicide, but since 36 compurgators were required this was more prejudicial to the accused than jury trial: *R. v. Wight* (1321) 85 SS 76.

eye-witness evidence. Although this may have become fictionalised in practice, we have already noted that the royal judges of the thirteenth century discouraged battle to the point where it remained usual only in appeals brought by approvers. When appeals by approvers themselves declined in the fourteenth century, battle became in consequence virtually obsolete in criminal cases. The obsolescence of trial by combat was directly related to the development of an alternative and more enduring method of trial.

This development was forced on the judges against their inclinations, as a result of the decision of the Lateran Council in 1215 which put paid to ordeals.[33] The end of the ordeal raised a serious practical problem, since there was no alternative method of trial available for those accused by community presentment, or by females (who could not fight battles), or in other appeals where battle was inappropriate. The royal judges were therefore placed in an awkward dilemma. They could hardly release all suspected felons in these categories on the ground that there was no way of trying them; nor could they keep them indefinitely in prison without trial. In 1219 the council was undecided what to do, and issued some rather unhelpful instructions to the justices in eyre: some prisoners were to be allowed to abjure,[34] but those suspected of serious crimes were to be remanded to prison, apparently as an interim measure; the application of these guidelines was left to the justices' discretion.[35] Many other countries in Europe, faced with the same problem, chose torture as a means of establishing guilt by confession.[36] The English judges, after a period of uncertainty and experiment, decided instead to make use of the local people already present in court as representatives of the hundreds and vills. A panel of such men, from the neighbourhood in question, could be given an oath to speak the truth on the issue of guilt. Where the accused had already been indicted by these representatives, he must have been rather at the mercy of their prejudice; and this may explain why some thirteenth-century accused paid a fine for a 'good jury', perhaps drawn from a wider field. By the end of the thirteenth century the regularisation of this procedure produced the 'petty jury', exactly analogous to that used to try civil actions of trespass, but increasingly distinct from the grand jury. It became a matter of course for the sheriff to summon potential trial jurors before a judicial session

[33] See p. 6, ante.
[34] For abjuration, see p. 585, post.
[35] *Patent Rolls 1216-1225*, p. 186.
[36] Denmark, however, provides an interesting parallel with England, since it introduced a jury of 12 soon after 1215: R. Bartlett, *Trial by Fire and Water* (1988), pp. 138-139.

began, and after 1351 at the latest they had to be different from the members of the grand jury.[37]

Trial by jury rapidly became the almost universal form of criminal trial, both on appeal and on indictment. It was revered in centuries to come as the palladium of English liberty, enshrined in the anachronistic interpretation later placed on the provision in Magna Carta that no free man should be punished 'except by the lawful judgment of his peers'.[38] Had Magna Carta in truth sanctioned criminal trials by jury, the legal problem would not have arisen. But the adoption of jury trial was an innovation forced upon the law by outside events; and, although it happened early enough to be received as common law, it remained in form optional to the accused. The uncertainty of 1219 was never lifted; unless prisoners could be persuaded to put themselves *de bono et malo* ('for good and ill') upon a jury, they had to be kept in prison for want of any other solution. In consequence, every prisoner who pleaded Not guilty to a capital charge was asked how he wished to be tried; to which the correct and only answer was, 'by God and the country' (meaning, a jury of the neighbourhood). If the prisoner declined to accept this choice, either by standing mute of malice or by rejecting three jury-panels of twelve,[39] he was sent back to prison *tanquam refutans legem communem* ('as one who refuses the common law'). The 1219 instructions made it clear that prisoners so remanded were not to be put in danger of their life; but the imprisonment was nevertheless meant to coerce defendants into accepting a jury, and parliament in 1275 expressly provided that it should be a *prison forte et dure*.[40] These words meant a harsh regime with a meagre diet, but by a grisly misunderstanding the *prison* of the statute was read as *peine*, and by the 1300s the 'hard penance' usually involved pressing the accused to death under heavy weights.[41] Some prisoners with little hope of acquittal actually chose this horrible fate rather than stand trial, and it is supposed that they did so in order to die unconvicted and thus save their dependants from

---

37   Stat. 25 Edw. III, stat.v, c.3. For a survival of the older practice in 1313, see 24 SS 140.

38   Magna Carta 1215, cl.39 (1225, c.29). Obviously this could not, in 1215, have referred to the trial jury. Cf. pp. 537-538, ante.

39   This is the origin of the entitlement to 35 peremptory challenges. Any challenge beyond 35 was taken as a refusal of trial: 94 SS *108*; 97 SS 179; 105 SS 180. In later times, however, such a challenge was merely disallowed and the jury sworn: Hale, *History of Pleas of the Crown*, vol. II, p.270.

40   Statute of Westminster I, c.12. For other expedients used before the statute, see H. R. T. Summerson in *Law, Litigants and the Legal Profession*, p. 116.

41   The form of punishment was at first discretionary: see 24 SS 112, 125; 97 SS 179; Summerson, op. cit. in last note.

forfeiture of their property.[42] Even when *peine forte et dure* was abolished – so late as 1772 – silence at first led to automatic conviction rather than the imposition of compulsory jury trial.[43]

TRIAL PROCEDURE

Little is known of the courtroom procedure used at a trial on indictment before Tudor times, because such things did not attract the attention of reporters or descriptive writers. But the procedure described in the sixteenth century had quite probably been in use for at least a century and perhaps longer.[44]

When the commissions had been read and the justices were seated, the grand jury was sworn and charged, and started to examine the bills of indictment produced by the clerk. The prisoners were then brought into court, chained together at the ankles, to await arraignment. When the indictments were produced, the prisoners named in them were brought to the bar of the court, with their shackles struck off, and asked to plead to the indictments. If a prisoner pleaded Not guilty, as most did, and put himself on the country, twelve jurors were sworn in from the panel provided by the sheriff. The clerk then called for anyone to give evidence against the prisoner. The witnesses who came forward for the Crown were sworn to tell the truth, and in telling their story might fall into altercation with the prisoner. The jury then gave its verdict, and according to its terms the prisoner was either discharged or remanded for sentence. At the end of the session, if any prisoners remained against whom no indictments had been found, a proclamation was made for evidence against them; if no one came forward, they were discharged.

The blessing of trial by jury was certainly favourable to the accused in some respects. He was able to challenge up to thirty-five jurors without giving any reason, and more with cause. The twelve who were selected had to be unanimous before they could convict him. If they acquitted him, however perversely, the verdict was final and unimpeachable. Yet the accused was, to modern eyes, at a considerable disadvantage compared with the prosecution. His right to call witnesses was doubted at common law, and if defence witnesses were allowed they

---

[42] Some, however, had little or no property. And it remains unclear why instances are found in the 18th century, when forfeiture was no longer enforced: Beattie, *Crime and the Courts*, pp. 337-338. The last instance is said to have occurred at Cambridge in 1741.

[43] Stat. 12 Geo. III, c.20. After 1827 a refusal to plead has been treated as equivalent to a plea of Not guilty: Stat. 7 & 8 Geo. IV, c.28.

[44] For a more detailed account, based on formularies dating back to about 1550, see LPCL 280-293. Slightly earlier formularies of the same type have since been found.

were not sworn. The process for compelling the attendance of prosecution witnesses, by binding them in recognisances, was not available to the defendant. The defendant could not have the assistance of counsel in presenting his case, unless there was a point of law arising on the indictment; and since the point of law had to be assigned before counsel was allowed, the unlearned defendant had little chance of professional help. This harsh rule was defended on the grounds that the evidence to convict the accused should be so clear that it could not be contradicted, and that the trial judge would both take care of that and ensure that the trial proceeded according to law.[45] Another reason, if not expressly articulated, was the fear that trials would be lengthened if advocates took part. If counsel were allowed, it was pointed out with some alarm in 1602, every prisoner would want it.[46] There was little of the care and deliberation of a modern trial before the last century. The same jurors might have to try several cases, and keep their conclusions in their heads, before giving in their verdicts; and it was commonplace for a number of capital cases to be disposed of in a single sitting. Hearsay evidence was often admitted; indeed, there were few if any rules of evidence before the eighteenth century. The judge's charge was usually short and uninformative, since there was no requirement that the judge should sum up the evidence as he now does. A trial for felony could rarely, in any period, have taken more than half an hour.[47] The unseemly hurry of Old Bailey trials even in the early nineteenth century was disgraceful; the average length of a trial was a few minutes, and 'full two thirds of prisoners, on their return from their trials, cannot tell of any thing which has passed in court, nor even, very frequently, whether they have been tried'.[48] It is impossible to estimate how far these conditions led to wrong convictions; many, probably most, trial judges took pains to see that obvious injustices did not occur, and acquittal rates were high by modern standards,[49] but the plight of the uneducated and unbefriended prisoner was grim.

[45]   Co. Inst., vol. III, p. 137. See also LPCL 286-288; J. B. Post, 5 JLH 23.

[46]   *R. v. Boothe* (1602) BL MS. Add. 25203, fo. 569v.

[47]   Similar estimates have been made for different periods: R. B. Pugh in *Law, Litigants and the Legal Profession*, p. 104 (10 to 30 minutes around 1300); Cockburn, *Assize Records: Introduction*, p. 110 (15 to 20 minutes around 1600); Beattie, *Crime and the Courts*, pp. 376-378 (30 minutes at most in 1750s).

[48]   Anon., *Old Bailey Experiences* (1833), pp. 59-60. See also *Reminiscences of Sir Henry Hawkins* (1904), vol. I, p. 33.

[49]   In property cases in Surrey between 1660 and 1800 the conviction-rate was just under 50%: Beattie, *Crime and the Courts*, p. 425. On the Home Circuit between 1558 and 1625, it was 56%: Cockburn, *Assize Records: Introduction*, p. 114. But in medieval times it might be as low as 20%: Helmholz, 1 LHR 20.

The most important reforms were put off until the eighteenth and nineteenth centuries. After the 1730s, prisoners on trial for felony were frequently allowed counsel to help them present their case, as a matter of grace; it was made a legal right in 1836.[50] Rules of evidence designed to protect the prisoner, such as the exclusion of hearsay and the need for accomplices' evidence to be corroborated, were developed by the courts in the eighteenth century. The defence was allowed sworn witnesses after 1702; but not till 1867 was it given facilities, comparable to those of the prosecution, for calling witnesses to depose evidence before the trial and having them bound over to attend the trial.[51] In 1898 defendants were accorded the dangerous privilege of giving sworn evidence themselves.[52]

SUMMARY TRIAL

Trial by jury was the only permissible method of trial upon indictment, and was therefore almost universally used after the thirteenth century for trying alleged felons. Misdemeanours could also be tried by jury, as when they were presented by indictment; but in certain cases they could be tried by the court itself, without indictment or jury. This summary procedure was permitted by the common law only in respect of offences such as contempt, committed in the view of the judges sitting in open court. The need for a jury was in such cases displaced by the judges' own witness of the facts. The idea was extended in late-medieval statutes which gave justices of the peace the power to punish offences committed in their view out of court, just as an 'on the spot fine' might be imposed today for a traffic offence.[53] Tudor statutes gave the justices similar powers in respect of offences which, though not committed in their own presence, were discovered by 'examination': this was summary trial proper.[54] The creation of powers of summary examination and conviction accelerated in the seventeenth and eighteenth

---

50 Langbein, 45 *Univ. Chicago Law Rev.* at 307-314; Beattie, *Crime and the Courts*, pp. 356-362; Trial for Felony Act 1836, 6 & 7 Will. IV, c.114. Counsel had been allowed in treason cases since 1695, and had always been allowed in cases of misdemeanour.

51 Stat. 1 Ann., sess. ii, 2, c.9, s.3; Criminal Law Amendment Act 1867, 30 & 31 Vict., c.35, s.3. The prosecution had enjoyed such facilities since at least the 1550s.

52 Criminal Evidence Act 1898, 61 & 62 Vict., c.36. See G. Parker in *Law and Social Change*, p. 156.

53 E.g. Stat. 15 Ric. II, c.2 (forcible entry); 13 Hen. IV, c.7 (riot).

54 There was a medieval precedent in the statutes concerning labourers. For the early legislative history of summary powers, see Bellamy, *Criminal Law and Society*, pp. 8-53.

centuries. Such powers were appropriate only for minor offences, but even so they infringed the principle that a man should only be judged by his peers, and they were regarded with deep suspicion by the superior judges. In the seventeenth century the King's Bench took upon itself to review summary convictions by means of certiorari, and would examine the justices' record carefully to ensure not only that they had pursued the relevant statute precisely but also that the accused had been served with a summons and given an opportunity to defend himself.[55] Some, however, saw this as an undue interference with local authority, and parliament when conferring summary jurisdiction sometimes expressly excluded judicial review; after 1670 it became common to provide for an appeal to quarter sessions, which kept the matter within the county without denying an opportunity to correct mistakes. Each summary power, therefore, depended on the wording of the particular statute which introduced it. Summary jurisdiction was not homogenised until 1848.[56]

The Avoidance or Mitigation of Punishment

The penal policy of the common law was very simple. For misdemeanours, punishment was at the discretion of the justices, provided that it did not touch life or limb, and was not disproportionate to the offence;[57] fines and whipping became the usual forms, imprisonment being relatively uncommon for this purpose before the time of George III. For felony, the convict's person was at the king's mercy. In Norman and Angevin times this notion gave the king's justices discretion to order mutilation (such as castration or blinding) instead of death; but in the thirteenth century this bloody exercise of mercy gave way to a fixed sentence of death. For treason, it was a particularly cruel death; for murder and nearly all felonies,[58] death by hanging. The fixed penalty excluded undue savagery as well as undue mercy, but it introduced excessive uniformity: the multiple murderer expected nothing worse than the accidental slayer or the petty villain who stole two shillings. Clearly this inflexibility was intolerable, and

---

55   *R. v. Dyer* (1703) 6 Mod. Rep. 41; 1 Salk. 181. And see p. 171, ante.

56   Summary Jurisdiction Act 1848, 11 & 12 Vict., c.43.

57   The qualification of reasonableness is first mentioned in relation to 'amercements' for trespass: Magna Carta 1215, cl. 20 (1225, c.14); Statute of Westminster I 1275, c.6. Cf. Stat. 34 Edw. III, c.1 (fines by justices of the peace). The Bill of Rights 1689 added the further limitation that the punishment should not be 'cruel or unusual': 1 Wm & Mar., sess. ii, c. 2.

58   The exceptions were petty larceny (treated like a misdemeanour) and suicide (forfeiture only).

it survived in theory only because of the several ways which were found of avoiding the death penalty in practice. Its survival, however, had a stultifying effect on the substantive law. The common-law felonies were narrowly confined; legal ingenuity was devoted to elaborating the evasions instead of improving the substance of the law; and legislation to fill gaps was piecemeal, ill considered and often poorly drafted.

The three principal modes of evasion were derived from the prerogatives of the Crown and the Church respectively; and the fourth from the prerogative of the jury to pronounce conclusively on the question of guilt or innocence.

SANCTUARY

In medieval England, as elsewhere in Europe, there were a number of ecclesiastical places where the king's writ did not run. The underlying theory was that consecrated places should not be profaned by the use of force, but the result in practice was that thieves and murderers could take refuge and thereby gain immunity even against the operation of criminal justice. This was the privilege called 'sanctuary'. In the case of parochial churches, the sanctuary lasted for forty days only. Before the expiration of this period, the fugitive had to choose whether to stand trial or 'abjure' the realm. If he chose abjuration, he was allowed to proceed on foot to a prescribed port and thence to leave the country for ever. This was only permitted if he made a written confession to the coroner, which resulted in the forfeiture of his property as on conviction; his life only was spared, and if he ever returned to England he could be executed on the abjuration. Abjuration was extremely common in the thirteenth century, but became largely ineffective as the machinery for ensuring that the felon reached the sea and embarked broke down. It was ended in the time of Henry VIII, who had been persuaded that able-bodied English criminals were joining the French army.

The greatest evil was the existence of private or special sanctuaries, usually in monastic houses, where criminals could take permanent refuge. Some great churches, such as Durham, Beverley and Beaulieu, had substantial communities of sanctuarymen in residence. Without threat of expulsion, criminals in these sanctuaries sometimes contrived to carry on their outside activities, and in early Tudor times there was a strong reaction against them. The judges sought to curb them by holding that sanctuaries could not be claimed by prescription or papal grant alone, without the king's consent, so that it became doubtful whether new sanctuaries could have been created after 1189; this made proof of a special sanctuary very difficult.[59] In the great case of St John's Priory in 1516-20, several suggestions for restriction and reform were put forward. Henry VIII said that the kings and popes of old, in creating sanctuaries, never intended them to become dens of thieves, and that he proposed to reform the abuses. This was agreed by the laymen present.[60] Henry later abolished most of the sanctuaries, and removed the availability of the privilege in respect of nearly all offences; the last vestiges were finally eradicated in 1624.[61]

BENEFIT OF CLERGY

The privilege of clergymen to be exempt from capital punishment was settled in the reign of Henry II, after the conflict with Becket,[62] with the result that an accused person who could prove himself to be a clerk in orders would be handed over to the ecclesiastical authorities to be dealt with according to Canon law. Many of those handed over escaped further punishment by undergoing purgation, a form of wager of law;[63] others were put in Church prisons, from which escape was notoriously easy in many cases.

The original procedure was for benefit of clergy to be claimed on arraignment, in which case there was an 'inquest of office' (a compulsory jury) to investigate guilt. The purpose was to warrant the seizure of the clerk's chattels pending his purgation, or in serious cases to warrant handing him over 'without purgation'; but if the inquest found him not guilty the handing over could be avoided.[64] This led the way to what became the invariable later practice, whereby clerks accepted jury trial and only claimed clergy in the event of conviction.[65] At every gaol delivery a representative of the bishop, called the 'ordinary', was supposed to be in attendance to claim clerks. But the judges were not at first disposed to trust these representatives. A claim

---

59 *Ex p. Stafford* (1486) Y.B. Trin. 1 Hen. VII, fo. 25, pl.1; 64 SS 115; *Rollesley v. Toft* (1495) Y.B. Hil. 9 Hen. VII, fo. 20, pl.15; Port Nbk (102 SS), 31; *R. v. Boswell* (1513) Port Nbk (102 SS), 37; Keil. 189.

60 *Pauncefote v. Savage* (c. 1519) Keil. 188; 94 SS *342*; Port Nbk (102 SS), xlv, 41.

61 Stat. 32 Hen. VIII, c.12; 21 Jac. I, c.28, s.7 ('no sanctuary or privilege of sanctuary be hereafter admitted or allowed in any case').

62 See p. 148, ante.

63 Not surprisingly, most defendants passed the test, though the medieval ecclesiastical judges had more control over purgation than their secular counterparts had over wager of law: Helmholz, 1 LHR 1.

64 E.g. *Quynzene v. Abyndon* (1317) BL MS. Egerton 2811, fo. 121; JUST 3/41/1, m.13. For a precedent (1342), see p. 634, post.

65 This practice was noticed with mixed feelings by Bereford CJ in 24 SS 119 (1313) and 85 SS 82 (1321). It did not become the regular practice till later.

would be disallowed if the prisoner was not in clerical dress, and tonsured, or if he could not read.

During the fourteenth and fifteenth centuries the judges' attitude to benefit of clergy changed completely, and they came to see it as a regular means of escape from the mandatory death penalty. Physical appearance was disregarded, and reading became the sole test of clerical status. When a man was convicted of felony, he would fall on his knees and 'pray the book'; he would then be tendered a passage from the psalter, known as the neck-verse, and if he could read or recite it satisfactorily his clergy was taken to be proved. Judges had the discretion to choose passages at random.[66] But it was customary to assign the same text, so that with a little preparation anyone of intelligence could save his life.[67] Strictly speaking, the decision whether the convict read 'as a clerk' was for the ordinary; but he was subject to the control of the judges, and could be fined for refusing to accept someone. By the end of the sixteenth century as many as half of all men convicted of felony were recorded as having successfully claimed benefit of clergy.[68]

By fiction, therefore, the judges extended the clerical privilege to laymen; but they were unable to extend it to persons who were incapable of ordination, such as women.[69] In the sixteenth and seventeenth centuries parliament cleared the fiction of its remaining ecclesiastical impediments, substituted a short term of imprisonment for delivery of the 'clerk' to the ordinary, and extended the privilege to women.[70] The restriction of the means of escape to those who could read was another peculiarity which defied rational defence, save on the dubious social grounds that it weeded out the less intelligent criminal; but reasoning of that kind might equally have suggested that intelligent people were both more to blame for criminal conduct and more dangerous to keep alive. No doubt the judges applied the reading test with considerable latitude, and we know that occasionally a judge heard a

---

66 For instances in the early-modern period, see 94 SS *329*; LPCL 293, 333.

67 The passage was verse 1 of Psalm 51: *Miserere mei Deus secundum magnam misericordiam tuam, et secundum multitudinem miserationum tuarum dele iniquitatem meam.*

68 Cockburn, *Assize Records: Introduction*, pp. 117-121 (47% of all convicts for felony between 1559 and 1624 had clergy).

69 A woman, however, could claim the 'benefit of her belly' (i.e. pregnancy); and here too some inattention to truth was practised. See J. C. Oldham, 6 CJH 1; Cockburn, *Assize Records: Introduction*, p. 121 (38% of women convicts in sample successfully pleaded pregnancy).

70 Extension to women: Stat. 21 Jac. I, c.6 (partial); 3 Will. & Mar., c.9, s.6 (general).

man read when the performance would have failed most forms of academic examination. In 1706 the pretence was abandoned; since the reading test itself had been 'by experience found to be of no use', clergy could be claimed without knowing the neck-verse.[71]

The clemency of the royal judges in extending this privilege was almost as indiscriminate as the harshness of the automatic punishment which occasioned it. It was as inconvenient that murderers and robbers should escape all punishment as it was that they should inexorably suffer death. Some means of control was needed. The first direct reform, in 1489, was the enactment that laymen should only have clergy once; to prevent evasion, convicts who were allowed clergy were branded M (manslayer) or T (thief) in the brawn of the left thumb. The next step was to reduce the number of offences for which clergy could be claimed. Treason had never been clergiable,[72] and one early proposal – actually implemented in Ireland in 1494[73] – was to make murder once again a capital offence by turning it into treason. But if that was within the province of parliament, it might as well make specific offences 'non-clergiable' without introducing unnecessarily the further pains imposed on traitors. In 1512 the experiment was attempted of removing clergy temporarily from murder and certain forms of robbery. This provoked an angry reaction from the Church,[74] but the statute was renewed and by the end of Henry VIII's reign the underlying principle was firmly established. From 1531 until the nineteenth century most penal reforms were effected by withdrawing clergy in various circumstances and thereby reintroducing capital punishment, which in some cases was commutable to transportation. After 1718, transportation to America could also be ordered for thieves who were allowed clergy, as an alternative to branding on first conviction.[75]

Even after 1718, clergy still provided an absolute discharge, subject to branding, in the case of certain offences (such as manslaughter) which were not affected by the legislative restrictions. By then, however, the branding was largely ineffective. It was usual to pardon persons of quality from such indignity, and since 1546 peers had been

---

[71]   Stat. 6 Ann., c.9 [appears as 5 & 6 Ann., c.6, in *Statutes at Large*] (extended to illiterates).

[72]   *R. v. Merks* (1401) 88 SS 102, 104; *Anon.* (1532) Spelman Rep. (93 SS) 49, pl.15.

[73]   Stat. 10 Hen. VII (Irish), c.21. An English proposal to turn sacrilege into treason had been rejected in 1467: Rot. Parl., vol. V, p. 632, no. 17. Murder by poisoning was made high treason in 1530: Stat. 22 Hen. VIII, c.9.

[74]   See *Dr Standish's Case* (1515) Keil. 180.

[75]   Transportation Act 1718, 4 Geo. I, c.11. The preamble suggested that the measure would help ease the servant shortage in America.

automatically exempted from the iron by law. In any case, the mark was useless as a record, and not intended as a punishment; therefore in many cases the iron was heated so perfunctorily that the process could be described as 'a nice piece of absurd pageantry, tending neither to the reformation of the offender nor for example to others'.[76] When in 1779 the judges were given power to award fines or whipping instead of branding, the iron went out of use altogether. The weirdly distorted benefit of clergy was finally abolished in 1827, and the wording of penal statutes thereby released from the tortuosities of the previous three centuries.[77]

PARDONS

It seems to have been recognised ever since the Crown began to intervene in the prosecution of criminals that the king enjoyed a power to grant charters of pardon for wrongs done, as a matter of grace. In the case of homicide, this prerogative was essential to justice, because the early common law failed to distinguish between intentional and accidental killing. Ironically, the existence of this merciful prerogative served to perpetuate a procedure which was far out of line with prevailing notions of criminal responsibility, so that what ought to have been a plain question of law remained for centuries at least nominally a question of favour.[78] Pardons were granted in other cases for non-legal reasons. In 1328 parliament complained that they had been given out too freely, and enacted that in future they should only be granted where a man had killed another in self-defence or by misfortune.[79] This did not, in fact, prevent the issue of pardons for money or through influence. After the disappearance of approvers another legitimate use for pardons was found, as a means of persuading accomplices to 'turn king's evidence' and tesify against their fellows at their trial on indictment.

Besides contributing directly to the law of homicide, pardoning also contributed to penal reform. Sentences of death were pronounced in many instances where there was no intention of carrying out the judgment. From the time of James I it was a common practice, usually on the recommendation of the trial judge, to pardon convicts on condition of transportation – a new form of banishment – to some such

---

[76] M. Foster, *Crown Law* (1762), p. 372.

[77] Stat. 7 & 8 Geo. IV, c.28. Branding: 19 Geo. III, c.74, s.3. In North America, benefit of clergy was abolished in the 1790s: 33 AJLH 65.

[78] See p. 601, post.

[79] Statute of Northampton 1328, 2 Edw. III, c.2.

wild and uninviting territory as Minorca, Virginia or the West Indies. If the convict refused to go, or came back without licence, he could be executed on the original sentence; but the option of transportation must have seemed to many a welcome chance to make a new start in life. Pardons might be given on other conditions, such as imprisonment or hard labour, or even unconditionally. By 1700 the process of granting pardons had come under the routine control of trial judges, who reported at the end of every circuit to the secretary of state with their recommendations for mercy; in these confidential letters may be found the first explicit judicial expressions of penal policy.[80] Despite the theoretical variety of available punishments, transportation (as a commutation of the death sentence) remained central to the penal system throughout the eighteenth century, perhaps because it was cheaper than long-term imprisonment. When the loss of the American colonies frustrated the prevailing arrangements, imprisonment with hard labour, in 'penitentiary houses' or in the 'hulks', became normal;[81] but from 1787 a new destination for convicts was found in Botany Bay. By 1868, when transportation was finally ended, over 10,000 felons had been shipped to Australia.

The pardoning procedure was also important as the means of introducing a system of informal appeal. If a trial judge doubted the legal propriety of a conviction, he referred the question to his brethren, whose decision could be given effect (if they shared the doubt) by recommending a pardon.[82] It was only in 1848 that judges were given the power to quash convictions themselves, unless for error on the face of the record. After that date, the need for pardons has greatly diminished, their last surviving use being to undo a conviction where the Home Secretary entertains a doubt as to its safety and all regular avenues of appeal have been exhausted, or where a change of circumstances after sentence is thought to warrant the exercise of compassion.

JURY MITIGATION

The fourth means of qualifying the severity of the law was unofficial. Since the jury alone could pronounce on guilt, they could with impunity ignore the evidence in order to save a defendant from the

---

[80] See P. King, 27 *Historical Jo.* at 42-51; Beattie, *Crime and the Courts*, pp. 430-436.

[81] See Stat. 19 Geo. III, c.74. On the emergence of imprisonment as a regular means of punishment, see J. H. Langbein, 5 *Jo. Legal Studies* 35; Beattie, *Crime and the Courts*, ch. 10.

[82] See p. 160, ante; pp. 595-596, post.

gallows. Such 'pious perjury' might take the form of finding a perverse verdict of not guilty or a 'partial verdict'. Only the latter is detectable on the record. A partial verdict might reduce the offence from non-clergiable to clergiable, as by finding simple larceny on an indictment for burglary, or from capital to non-capital, as by finding petty larceny on an indictment for grand larceny.[83] Sometimes this technique was used blatantly, as when a Georgian jury valued twenty-three guineas at thirty-nine shillings,[84] but all cases of material variation from the indictment raise a strong suspicion of pious perjury; the cases which cannot be counted are those of outright acquittal against the evidence. Instances of partial verdicts are found as early as the fourteenth century;[85] but they did not become common until the seventeenth century, and became most frequent in the eighteenth, when the number of non-clergiable capital offences was increased by legislation.[86] Attempts were made in the Tudor and Stuart period to curtail this liberty, either by fining perverse jurors or by binding them over to appear in the Star Chamber or King's Bench. Although this kind of pressure was complained of, it must have cowed some juries into submitting to the direction of the court; it was finally forbidden in the late seventeenth century.[87] Even Lord Mansfield, in 1784, argued that government by law could not tolerate that 'the law should be in every particular case what any twelve men . . . shall be inclined to think'.[88] Nevertheless, it is clear that the power of the jury to mitigate the law served a vital role during periods when the criminal law itself was too harsh or too unsophisticated to take account of the variety of circumstances affecting culpability.

---

[83] A bizarre consequence of clergy, however, was that petty larceny was punishable with whipping whereas (before 1718) clergiable grand larceny was not punishable at all.

[84] Radzinowicz, *History of English Criminal Law*, Vol. I, p. 95. (Stealing 40s. from a house was made non-clergiable in 1713.) A guinea was a gold coin of 21s. value.

[85] E.g. *Anon.* (1367) Fitz. Abr., *Corone*, pl.451 (value of sheep laid in indictment as 20d., found to be 10d.).

[86] Cockburn, in *Twelve Good Men and True*, pp. 171-176; Beattie, *Crime and the Courts*, pp. 424-430. For their rarity before the 17th century, see Cockburn, *Assize Records: Introduction*, pp. 115-116, 175-181.

[87] Cockburn, *Assize Records: Introduction*, pp. 70-71; Langbein, 45 *Univ. Chicago Law Rev.* at 297-300.

[88] *R. v. Shipley* (1784) 21 State Tr. 847 at 1040.

Further reading[89]

Pollock & Maitland, vol. II, pp. 448-470, 511-526

Plucknett CHCL, pp. 421-441

Milsom HFCL, pp. 403-421

Cornish & Clark, ch. 8

L. Radzinowicz and R. Hood, *A History of English Criminal Law and its Administration from 1750* (1948-86)

R. F. Hunnisett, *The Medieval Coroner* (1961), esp. pp. 37-74

N. D. Hurnard, *The King's Pardon for Homicide* (1970)

J. H. Baker, 'Criminal Justice at Newgate 1616-27' (1973) 8 IJ 307-322 (repr. in LPCL 325-340); 'Criminal Courts and Procedure at Common Law' in *Crime in England 1550-1800* (J. S. Cockburn ed., 1977), pp. 15-48 (repr. in LPCL 259-301); 'The English Law of Sanctuary' (1990) 2 *Eccles. Law Jo.* 8-13

J. H. Langbein, *Prosecuting Crime in the Renaissance* (1974); 'The Criminal Trial before the Lawyers' (1978) 45 *Univ. Chicago Law Rev.* 263-316; 'Shaping the 18th Century Criminal Law: a View from the Ryder Sources' (1983) 50 *Univ. Chicago Law Rev.* 1-136

R. D. Groot, 'The Jury of Presentment before 1215' (1982) 26 AJLH 1-24; 'The Jury in Private Criminal Prosecutions before 1215' (1983) 27 AJLH 113-141; 'The Early-13th-Century Criminal Jury' in *Twelve Good Men and True* (Cockburn & Green ed.), pp. 3-35

C. Whittick, 'The Role of the Criminal Appeal in the 15th Century' (1984) *Law and Social Change*, pp. 55-72

D. R. Ernst, 'The Moribund Appeal of Death' (1984) 28 AJLH 164-188

V. C. Edwards, 'Criminal Equity in Restoration London and Middlesex' (1984) 5 JLH 79-96

J. G. Bellamy, *Criminal Law and Society in late Medieval and Tudor England* (1984)

J. C. Oldham, 'On Pleading the Belly: A History of the Jury of Matrons' (1985) 6 CJH 1-64

T. A. Green, *Verdict according to Conscience* (1985)

J. S. Cockburn, *Calendar of Assize Records: Home Circuit Indictments, Introduction* (1985)

---

[89] For an introduction to the vast literature on the social history of crime in England, see L. A. Knafla, 'Crime and Criminal Justice: a Critical Bibliography' in Cockburn, *Crime in England*, pp. 270-298; continued in Knafla ed., *Crime and Criminal Justice in Europe and Canada* (2nd ed., 1985), pp. vii-xxix; J. Innes and J. Styles, 'The Crime Wave: Recent Writing on Crime and Criminal Justice in 18th-Century England' (1986) 25 *Jo. British Studies* 380-435.

J. M. Beattie, *Crime and the Courts in England 1660-1800* (1985) and the bibliography there

C. B. Herrup, *The Common Peace: Participation and the Criminal Law in Seventeenth-century England* (1987)

J. S. Cockburn and T. A. Green (ed.), *Twelve Good Men and True: The Criminal Trial Jury in England 1200-1800* (1988)

29. Pleas of the Crown: The Substantive Criminal Law

It was shown in the previous chapter how the criminal law, for many centuries, rested more on practice than on authoritative principles laid down by the courts or parliament. Law of that kind is, in the first place, more akin to custom, in the sense that the rules provide guidance but may be diverged from with impunity in particular cases. But it was hardly appropriate for a body of law ostensibly operating throughout the realm that it should be applied in different ways according to the vagaries of local custom or the personal preferences of judges. As principles of criminal law became part of the common learning of the legal profession, their misapplication became so insupportable that procedures had to be devised to secure compliance and to resolve doubts. When that occurred, however informally, the principles became part of the law of the land.

THE MEANS OF DEVELOPMENT

The universality of the general plea of Not guilty in criminal cases prevented any legal development through the vehicle of special pleading. Questions of law could nevertheless arise in other ways: they could be raised upon the wording of indictments, upon the wording of statutes controlling benefit of clergy or adding to the list of crimes, and (most important of all) upon the evidence given at trials.

The most formal way of raising questions of criminal law for solemn determination was by removing proceedings on indictment into the King's Bench by certiorari, and taking exception to them for some defect. Indictments could by this means be quashed, and convictions set aside, for reasons which were recorded on parchment. The procedure was common enough in the year-book period, and it enabled the King's Bench both to set the bounds of offences and to lay down some minimal rules of procedure. But it was confined to errors on the face of the record, which did not include the evidence. In practice, certiorari was chiefly employed to obtain discharges on purely technical grounds; though it is known that, in the period before other methods of reviewing convictions were developed, technical errors were sometimes used as pretexts for quashing convictions thought unsafe for reasons not overtly given.[1]

In reviewing indictments, the King's Bench could decide no more than whether the formalised phrases were in order; if the indictment was formally correct it was for the trial judge alone to rule whether the facts as proved fitted the forms. More detailed questions of criminal law could therefore arise informally at the trial, when it fell to be decided whether the evidence proffered was sufficient to support the charge in the indictment. Thus, an indictment for theft would allege taking and carrying away with force and arms; but only the trial judge could say whether a bailee or a finder who appropriated goods could be said to take them 'with force and arms'. If the trial judge directed the jury on such a question he was in a sense applying rules of law to the facts. Whether he was making law is a different matter: his opinions were neither entered on the record nor reported, and if another judge in the next county was directing juries differently nothing could be done by way of appeal. The detailed development of the criminal law thus depended on the introduction of some way of providing for centralised discussion of the kind of questions which arose at trials. This type of discussion could not take place in banc, because criminal cases began and ended in the country. But there were other mechanisms.

First, there was the discussion of abstract principle at readings and moots in the inns of court. Criminal law was the main subject of discussion next to the land law, at least in the early Tudor period, precisely because its principles could not be aired in other ways. Those who attended these discussions included most legally-qualified justices of the peace, and sometimes judges and serjeants visiting their former inns to lend the benefit of their experience to the discussion. It is probably no exaggeration to say that the inns of court in this period contributed as much to the formulation of English criminal jurisprudence as did any court of law. The cessation of these discussions coincided with the emergence of a printed literature of criminal law in the shape of Fitzherbert's *New Boke of Justices of Peas* (1538) and Staunford's *Les Plees del Coron* (1557), both of which were influenced in form and content by the learning previously handed down at readings.

The second technique, which also came to the fore in the early Tudor period, was for the trial judge to adjourn a difficult case for consultation with his brethren in Serjeants' Inn or the Exchequer Chamber the following term. By 1500 there seem to have been regular meetings at

---

[1] 94 SS *301-302*; LPCL 298-301, 315-318.

Serjeants' Inn to discuss actual cases reserved from the circuits; and it was these meetings which developed over three centuries later into the Court for Crown Cases Reserved.[2] The procedure was made slightly more formal in the seventeenth century by taking special verdicts with a view to consultation;[3] while in the eighteenth century the practice whereby the judge stated a case from his own notes became an acceptable alternative.[4] In either case, the law was not being discussed in a court: the opinion of the assembled judges took effect either as advice to the trial judge or, if conviction had already occurred, as advice to a minister on whether to grant a pardon.   Yet these discussions, which after 1500 were sporadically reported by judges or serjeants who were present, made as real a contribution to legal development as did more formal precedents in private law.

These informal means of centralisation were chiefly used for questions relating to murder and felony. For misdemeanours, a more formal central influence was provided by the Star Chamber; but it operated by experimentation and innovation at first instance, rather than by reviewing proceedings elsewhere.[5]

Criminal Responsibility

Much of the criminal law was concerned with the definition of felonies; and, since they were capital offences, the attitude of the courts tended towards restrictive rather than equitable exposition. The filling of gaps was left to parliament, which understandably shied away from broad principles of criminal liability and legislated ad hoc to counter specific evils. One matter left to the common law, however, was the extent to which moral wickedness was a necessary constituent element of criminal offences. The word 'felony' implied wickedness, and therefore ought not to have extended to blameless accident and misadventure. In the case of homicide, effect was given to this distinction through the use of pardons,[6] but it had a much broader application. When crime and tort became separate, the essence of felony was identified as a forcible

---

[2]   See p. 160, ante.

[3]   See 8 IJ at 307 n.2 (also in LPCL 325 n.2).

[4]   This was analogous to the civil procedure for stating cases to the court in banc: pp. 99, 160-161, ante.

[5]   See p. 137, ante.

[6]   See p. 589, ante; pp. 598, 600-601, post. As to whether killing by misadventure was properly called 'felony', contrast 105 SS 74 (not felony) with 105 SS 300 (felony).

criminal act done with a guilty mind (*mens rea*), whereas evil intent ceased to be an element in trespass against the king's peace for civil purposes.[7] Intent was difficult to try. But in drawing this distinction between criminal and civil wrongs the common lawyers were following the canonist teaching – traceable to St Augustine – that mental guilt was a necessary prerequisite of criminal punishment: *reum non facit nisi mens rea.*[8]

In indictments for murder, 'malice aforethought' was laid expressly; in other indictments, the *mens rea* was held to be implicit in the word *felonicè* (feloniously). What amounted to such an intent, however, could only arise upon the evidence; therefore little is known of the thinking about criminal intention until Serjeants' Inn conferences begin to be noted in the sixteenth century.[9] There are several reported examples from the 1530s: for instance, whether a suicide who cut his throat and then vainly repented and wished to live was guilty of felony *de se*,[10] or whether provocation furnished a defence to felony.[11] Most of the reported discussions, however, both before and after this period, concern not so much specific states of mind as the defendant's capacity to form a malicious intent.

It was settled in medieval times that a child under twelve could not be convicted of felony if he was too young to bear criminal responsibility.[12] Although there was an upper limit of twelve, it is far from clear whether there was a lower limit before Hale, in the seventeenth century, adopted the Civilian limit of seven.[13] In the thirteenth century the fact of infancy was usually presented specially, as in the case of misadventure, so that a pardon could be obtained.[14] In other cases, if the defendant appeared on inspection to be a child, he might be discharged without trial at the judge's discretion; and this later

7 See the case of thorns, *Hulle v. Orynge* (1466) B. & M. 327 at 328, 330, per Fairax sjt; pp. 457-458, ante.

8 Pollock & Maitland, vol. II, p. 476 n.5.

9 Here, as elsewhere, the readers in the inns of court had taken the lead: see 94 SS 304, 309-310, 323.

10 *Anon.* (1533) Spelman Rep. (93 SS) 68, 140. Cf. *Anon.* (1498) Port Nbk (102 SS) 86, pl.21 (transferred malice and misfortune coupled with malice).

11 *R. v. Parker* (c. 1530) Spelman Rep. (93 SS) 72. The question seems to have been raised here by a special indictment.

12 Children over 12 were supposed to be in frankpledge and therefore legally responsible: *Anon.* (c. 1315) BL MS. Harley 2183, fo. 175, per Spigurnel J; and cf. Y.B. 30-31 Edw. I, Appendix, pp. 511-513, per Spigurnel J.

13 Hale, *History of Pleas of the Crown*, vol. I, pp. 19-20, 27-28. Hale also (p. 25) adopted 14 rather than 12 as the upper limit, relying on authorities dating from the 1530s onwards.

14 Hurnard, *Pardon for Homicide*, pp. 152-157.

became the usual procedure.[15] The test of responsibility was whether
the child was able to discern right from wrong, which might be indicated
by behaviour indicating a sense of guilt.[16] The same test was used for
persons of unsound mind, and at least one fifteenth-century lawyer
considered automatism to be a defence as well.[17] Drunkenness, however,
was more an aggravation than an excuse, because the want of discretion
was self-inflicted; therefore, according to an old proverb, 'he that killeth
a man drunk, sober shall be hanged'.

The defence of insanity posed a more difficult practical problem than
infancy, because of what Hale called 'the easiness of counterfeiting' it.
Therefore, although the earlier procedure had been for the state of mind
to be found specially by the presenting jury and a pardon applied for,[18]
the practice by the sixteenth century was to require a plea of Not guilty
so that the matter could be tried by jury,[19] or else to impanel an inquest
of office to determine whether the defendant was fit to plead and stand
trial.[20] For six centuries the question for the jury remained the same,
namely whether the accused was unable to know right from wrong, so
that his action was more like an animal reflex than the exercise of moral
choice.[21] However, the rise of medical jurisprudence, and the inevitable
conflicts over the types and consequences of insanity, led to popular
dissatisfaction in the nineteenth century at some acquittals of the
'partially insane', even though the acquitted lunatics were locked away
in Bedlam. In 1843 the House of Lords summoned the judges to answer
certain abstract questions about insanity and criminal responsibility,
particularly in cases of 'delusion', and the answers were the basis of
subsequent development.[22] This unusual procedure was most ill advised,

15 E.g. *R. v. Peterborough* (1317) JUST 3/41/1, m.6 (age 8); reported in BL MS.
Egerton 2811, fo. 119v; *Anon.* (1456) B. & M. 326 n.5 (age 4).

16 *Anon.* (before 1313) recollected in 24 SS 148; and in Y.B. Trin. 12 Edw. III, p.
627 ('by hiding [himself or the corpse] he showed that he knew the difference
between right and wrong, and therefore *malicia supplet aetatem*'). See also 24 SS
109; Y.B. Hil. 3 Hen. VII, fo. 1, pl.4 and fo. 12, pl.8; 94 SS *309* n.3.

17 Anonymous reading, CUL MS. Ee. 5. 18, fo. 102.

18 Hurnard, *Pardon for Homicide*, pp. 159-170. An example is *R. v. Clipston*
(1329) 97 SS 215.

19 Hale, *History of Pleas of the Crown*, vol. I, pp. 32-33. Early instances of this
procedure are: *Anon.* (1505) Y.B. Mich. 21 Hen. VII, fo. 31, pl.16; *R. v.
Petewuse* (1535) Spelman Rep. (93 SS) 58 (special verdict of guilty but insane).

20 E.g. *R. v. Somervile* (1583) 1 And. 104 at 107; Sav. 50, pl.105.

21 For a clear specimen direction, see *R. v. Arnold* (1724) 16 State Tr. 695 at 754,
764, per Tracy J.

22 *The M'Naghten Rules* (1843) 10 Cl. & Fin. 200. See also R. Moran, *Knowing
Right from Wrong: The Insanity Defense of Daniel McNaughtan* (1981). (The
spelling of the defendant's name has been almost as controversial as the state of
his mind.)

since the judges' opinions were given without the benefit of argument and yet were cast in a precise form which had all the disadvantages of legislation. The story of the law of insanity provides the strongest argument for those who maintain that the substantive criminal law was unable to develop very far under the old procedures.

Some Particular Offences

TREASON

The development of treason, which is the most serious offence known to English law, belongs more properly in a constitutional history, and little will be said of its details. Since felonies also were offences against the king and public order, including in their earliest conception an element of treachery, the notion of treason as something worse than felony was inherently elastic. The essence of high treason was a treacherous usurpation of or challenge to the king's royal authority, and the consequence of conviction was not only a particularly unpleasant death but also forfeiture of the traitor's land to the king. The limits of the offence at common law were nevertheless unclear: Hale cites a case of 1347 in which a man was indicted for imprisoning another to extort money, thereby usurping or 'accroaching' the royal power.[23] An uncertain law of treason is one of the greatest possible threats to individual liberty, and that is doubtless why treason was the first major offence to be defined by statute; the Treasons Act of 1351 has provided the principal definition down to the present day.[24] The most heinous form is compassing the death of the sovereign and certain members of the royal family. It was not necessary for the king actually to be killed, or even for an attempt to be made on his life, and at times the offence was very widely construed; in 1615 it was held to include mere expressions of opinion that killing the king would be lawful. In most ages, however, the courts required proof of an overt act of preparation in addition to words, and this was laid down as a necessary element in 1628.[25] The other principal forms of high treason, and those most frequently prosecuted, are levying war against the king in his realm, and adhering to the king's enemies. The 'king' for this purpose was the de facto sovereign, so that in times of civil war allegiance was owed to the

---

[23] Hale, *History of Pleas of the Crown*, vol. I, p. 80. It seems, however, that accroaching the royal power was not high treason but a form of petty treason.

[24] 25 Edw. III, stat.v, c.2.

[25] *R. v. Owen* (1615) 1 Rolle Rep. 185; *R. v. Pine* (1628) Cro. Car. 117. Cf. Richard Littleton's reading (1493) Port Nbk (102 SS) 83-84.

600 The Substantive Criminal Law

king in possession of the Crown.[26] This rule probably operated only to excuse the adherents of a de facto king, and it was wise for an incoming king to pardon his own supporters. It was held in a number of cases from Tudor times onwards that there could be a constructive levying of war in peace-time if three or more 'arose' to alter the established religion or law, or to effect some public purpose against all opposition.[27]

Petty (or petit) treason was a lesser form of the offence, which consisted in domestic treachery by a wife, servant or monk. If a wife killed her husband, a servant his master, or a monk his superior, the offence was not merely murder; as a form of treason it was more ignominiously punished,[28] and the punishment could not be avoided by benefit of clergy.[29] But the offence was strictly confined; thus a husband did not commit petty treason by killing his wife, and parricide was only treason if the child happened to perform services for the parent.[30] Petty treason was reduced to murder in 1828.[31] Another lesser form of treason consisted in counterfeiting the great seal or any coin of the realm; this was punished in the same way as petty treason until it was reduced to felony in the nineteenth century.

HOMICIDE

Every death in unusual circumstances required investigation by a coroner, not least because any chattel which occasioned death was forfeited as deodand.[32] The same principle of automatic liability was applied to the man whose conduct killed another, even if he had no guilty mind; his property was forfeited, and he was liable to imprisonment pending a pardon. On the face of it, this was in direct conflict with the principles of criminal responsibility outlined earlier in this chapter; but the requirement of *mens rea*, as introduced through the use of pardons, went only to the loss of life for felony. It is unlikely

---

26 Stat. 11 Hen. VII, c.1, which was said to declare the common law.

27 E.g. *R. v. Damaree* (1709) Foster 213; 15 State Tr. 521 (riotous gathering to demolish Nonconformist meeting-houses). An extreme example is *R. v. Bradshaw* (1597) Co. Inst., vol. III, p. 10 (conspiracy to put down enclosures); here a mere conspiracy was treason, by virtue of Stat. 13 Eliz. I, c.1.

28 Men were drawn on a hurdle to the place of execution, and then hanged. Women were burned to death: R. Campbell, 5 JLH 44.

29 This was disputable before the point was clarified in 1496: Stat. 12 Hen. VII, c.7.

30 Parricide: *Anon.* (1553) Dalison Rep., BL MS. Harley 5141, fo. 17v. Cf. Co. Inst., vol. III, p. 20.

31 Stat. 9 Geo. IV, c.31, s.2.

32 See p. 437, ante.

that accidental or excusable killings were ever intended to attract the death penalty; the king not only could pardon such an offender's life, but was morally bound to do so. The grant of a pardon in such cases was therefore a matter of course, upon a special finding of the facts; and after 1278 the trial judge could report cases of misadventure or self-defence to the king without the need for a special commission of enquiry.[33] But the blameless killer still in theory incurred a forfeiture, because his act was considered a tort or 'contempt' to the king in depriving him of a subject.[34] This harsh theory was nevertheless felt to be anomalous, and it was not consistently put into practice: during the late fourteenth century, and again in the eighteenth, it was avoided by directing general verdicts of not guilty in cases of misadventure and self-defence.[35] Moreover, from the fourteenth century, many of those found before coroners to have killed by accident were probably not arraigned at all.[36]

The law of pardons led not only to a distinction between felonious and excusable homicide, but also to a bifurcation of felonious homicide. This resulted from a measure introduced in 1390 to reduce the scope of general pardons, such as a pardon of 'all felonies'. It was enacted that such a pardon did not extend to murder or 'killing by lying in wait, assault or malice aforethought'.[37] It therefore became important, in drawing indictments,[38] to make a distinction between murder with malice aforethought and other forms of felonious homicide (known by 1510 as 'manslaughter'[39]). The principal kind of felonious homicide other than murder was *chaude mêlée* or chance medley,[40] a killing in the course of a sudden, spontaneous quarrel. By Tudor times the law also

---

[33] Statute of Gloucester 1278, c.9.

[34] Case from a reading on Gloucester, c.9 (c. 1486) Keil. 108, pl.27; 105 SS 74. It was disputed whether a pardon was needed in the case of a special verdict of misadventure.

[35] Green, *Verdict according to Conscience*, pp. 86-93, 123-125; Beattie, *Crime and the Courts*, p. 87 (where it is noted that pardons were still being issued in the 1670s).

[36] Green, *Verdict according to Conscience*, pp. 87, 93 n.96.

[37] 13 Ric. II, stat.ii, c.1; *Anon.* (1507) Keil. 91, pl.2, per Fyneux CJ (rule of statutory origin). In the 15th century, if not before, murder had become synonymous with killing by malice aforethought: 94 SS *305* n.4. Lying in wait was evidence of forethought: ibid. n.5.

[38] In appeals of death, pardons were not allowed; but the common form was to count on a killing 'by lying in wait and premeditated assault'.

[39] Thomas Pygot's reading in the Inner Temple (1510) CUL MS. Ee. 3. 46, fo. 47v. 'Manslaughter' is simply the English word for *homicidium*; the technical sense is a result of transferring it from the genus to the residuary category.

[40] The word *chance* here reflects the Latin *ex subito casu* of the indictmen ('by sudden chance'); but the original adjective seems to have been *chaude*, indicating hot blood.

recognised that homicide by wanton negligence might be felonious.[41] After 1512 the distinction between murder and manslaughter was accentuated by statutes which removed benefit of clergy from those convicted of 'murder of malice prepensed'.[42] It was principally as a result of this legislation that the line between murder and manslaughter came to be judicially discussed and defined in the Tudor period. Parliament had thus superimposed on the common law a tripartite classification of homicides: if the killing was done out of malice, it was punished by death and forfeiture; if there was no prior malice, and it was a first offence,[43] it was clergiable and the only certain punishment was forfeiture; if the killing was accidental or excusable, it was pardonable.

Before long it was realised that the dichotomy of malice and chance medley – of cold and hot blood – was not very sound. Malice was not easy to define, and even harder to prove; often it had to be implied from the facts surrounding the killing.[44] So long as there was a general evil intent, an intent to injure someone, there was no need to prove a specific intent to kill the deceased.[45] Moreover, a chance fight, if unprovoked, might itself be murderous. In a case of 1600 a shopkeeper became so incensed by a customer who had 'flirted' him on the nose and made faces at him from the street that he came out of his shop and hit him so hard that he died. He was indicted and convicted of manslaughter; but the widow brought an appeal and the judges held it to be murder, because there was insufficient cause to start a quarrel.[46] After this, the doctrine of chance medley faded away and the test of manslaughter in such cases came to be, not the hot bloodedness, but the presence or absence of 'provocation'.[47] This development was facilitated by a statute of 1604 which took away benefit of clergy for killing by

41 E.g. throwing a stone over a house, shooting in a city: Pygot's reading, loc. cit.; 94 SS *311-312.* The Tudor distinction was between negligence in carrying out a lawful activity and wanton negligence. This was a departure from earlier law: Hurnard, *Pardon for Homicide,* pp. 99-108.

42 The earliest statutes were 4 Hen. VIII, c.2; 23 Hen. VIII, c.1, s.3. It had been suggested in the 15th century that murder was non-clergiable at common law: anonymous reading, CUL MS. Ee. 5. 19, fo. 217. The legislation shows that this view did not prevail.

43 See p. 588, ante.

44 See *R. v. Yong* (1586) 4 Co. Rep. 40; *R. v. Mackalley* (1611) 9 Co. Rep. 68.

45 94 SS *309-310; Note* (c. 1500) Port Nbk (102 SS) 86, pl.21; *R. v. Saunders and Archer* (1573) Plowd. 473.

46 *Watts v. Brains* (1600) Cro. Eliz. 778; Noy 171; BL MS. Add. 25203, fo. 216v. Cf. *R. v. Huggett* (1666) Kel. 59.

47 *R. v. Royley* (1612) Cro. Jac. 296; 12 Co. Rep. 87; Godb. 182; *R. v. Mawgridge* (1707) Kel. 119.

stabbing, where the deceased had no weapon drawn, even where at common law the killing amounted only to manslaughter.[48]

PERSONAL INJURIES

Physical assaults which did not result in death fell only partially within the range of common-law felonies. A maiming – a serious incapacitation or loss of limb – could be made the subject of an appeal of mayhem; but this form of redress gave way in practice to the action of trespass, and mayhem did not become an indictable felony.[49] Even violent assaults were therefore mere trespasses or misdemeanours until a number of offences akin to mayhem were made felonies by statute.[50] The forcible carnal knowledge of a woman against her will was treated in a similar manner to mayhem; the woman alone could treat it as unemendable by pursuing an appeal of rape, but it was not at common law an indictable felony. If the woman pressed her appeal, the offender was liable to forfeit life or limb, and down to the early thirteenth century the punishment might be castration or blinding; if, on the other hand, the offence was presented by indictment, it was treated as a misdemeanour punishable only by fine or imprisonment.[51] By a statute of 1285, rape was made a capital felony, however prosecuted.[52] Buggery was not a felony at common law, perhaps because it included an element of consent inconsistent with the notion of force and arms, but also because it came within the purview of the Church courts; it became a capital felony in 1533, and it remained a felony until 1967.[53]

ARSON

Arson,[54] the malicious burning of dwelling houses or barns, was the more serious of the two common-law felonies concerning a man's home. The criminal misuse of fire was not only destructive of the

---

[48] Statute of Stabbing 1603, 1 Jac. I, c.8. See *R. v. Lord Morley* (1666) Kel. 54.

[49] For a consequence in the law of defamation, see p. 502, ante.

[50] The first was Stat. 5 Hen. IV, c.5 (cutting out of tongues and eyes). Kaye, [1977] *Criminal Law Rev.* at 7, gives an example of a defendant who in 1336 was merely amerced 20s. for blinding someone.

[51] E.g. 96 SS 258, pl.739 (fine of half a mark, after appeal compromised, 1256). Fines of 10 marks were imposed in 1248: 90 SS 318, pl.787; and p. 351, pl.888 (Berkshire eyre).

[52] Statute of Westminster II, c.34, which speaks of *jugement de vie et de membre*, though in practice the judgment was death.

[53] Stat. 25 Hen. VIII, c.6; Sexual Offences Act 1967 (c.60). Before 1533 it had been punishable with death by burning as a form of heresy: Pollock & Maitland, vol. II, pp. 556-557.

[54] From the French *arder*, to burn.

victim's property, but also a serious threat to public safety in times when most houses were constructed of timber and thatch, and the means of extinguishing large fires were primitive. For these reasons, arson was among the earliest pleas of the Crown and was a felony. Until the thirteenth century it was punished, *jure talionis*, with death by burning, and thereafter by hanging.[55] It is easy to see why arson was so seriously regarded, but it is astonishing that until comparatively recently it was the only criminal offence of causing damage to property. If a man burned property other than a house or granary, or destroyed houses (let alone movable property) otherwise than by fire, then at common law the only remedy was a civil action of trespass. The gaps were filled piecemeal by numerous statutes which were consolidated in 1861; and in 1971 the miscellaneous separate offences were replaced by the offence of unlawfully destroying or damaging property.[56]

BURGLARY

The criminal invasion, as opposed to the destruction, of a dwelling house was known to the Anglo-Saxons as *hamsocn* or *husbryce* (house-breach), offences which apparently included an element of violence to the person, as in an armed raid.[57] In appeals and early indictments, housebreaking often appears as an element of aggravation, though perhaps not as an independent offence; it had the effect of making even a small theft into a capital felony. The essence of it, therefore, was an offence not against property but against the person. By the fifteenth century housebreaking had become an indictable felony in itself, committed even if nothing was stolen, provided there was a felonious intent; and in this form it was usually called 'burglary'.[58] According to some definitions, which seem to preserve the original character of *husbryce*, it was necessary that someone should be in the house at the time of the breaking, and this element was certainly necessary to make the offence non-clergiable under the Henrician legislation.[59] It was also settled by the 1450s that burglary was a nocturnal crime.[60] Offences

---

55 It was made non-clergiable in 1531: Stat. 23 Hen. VIII, c.1, s.3 ('wilful burning of any dwelling houses or barns wherein any grain of corns shall happen to be').

56 Malicious Damage Act 1861, 24 & 25 Vict., c.97; Criminal Damage Act 1971 (c.48).

57 See R. Colman, 25 AJLH 95. The laws of Cnut (*c.* 1020) said that *husbryce* was unemendable.

58 The word may originally have denoted breaking into a walled town to carry out a raid (*burgaria, burglaria*). Breaking town-walls was mentioned in some definitions of burglary down to the 16th century: 94 SS *325* n.1.

59 94 SS *325*.

60 John Baldwin's reading in Gray's Inn, 94 SS *326* n.2.

committed at night were regarded as more heinous than daytime offences, because all decent folk were supposed to be asleep and off their guard. The limitation had the unfortunate effect, however, that housebreaking in the daytime, or while a house was uninhabited, was no felony at common law. This shortcoming was remedied by a string of statutes beginning in 1547.[61]

Having decided that burglary could only be committed at night, the judges had to define 'night'. At first it was agreed that night began at sunset and ended at sunrise, so that burglary could be committed in the twilight periods between sunset and darkness and between daybreak and sunrise; it was said to be easier to try the setting and rising of the sun than the beginning and ending of daylight.[62] But this test was superseded by that of darkness: whether a man's face was discernible.[63] In 1837 an arbitrary definition of night was introduced by statute; but in 1968 the nocturnal element disappeared from the law altogether.[64]

The mental element in burglary was indicated in the indictment only by the words *felonicè et burglariter* ('feloniously and burglariously'). These words of art did not import the actual commission of a felony, but only a felonious and burglarious intent. Serjeant Marow (d. 1505) thought it necessary to prove either an intent to murder or the actual commission of some felony; but Fitzherbert (d. 1538) and later writers took the view that an intent to commit any felony was sufficient. The need to show a breaking into a house operated as a further restriction; but there was no need for a bodily entry, and the judges managed to squeeze within the definition the insertion of a hook through a window (after drawing the latch), or shooting through a hole made in the wall.[65]

ROBBERY AND LARCENY

Robbery, which in law denotes stealing from the person with violence or threats,[66] was an offence against the person and also against property. Like burglary, the original significance of robbery was that, as an element of aggravation, it could turn otherwise petty crimes into capital offences; and in later times it had the effect of excluding the offender

---

61 Stat. 1 Edw. VI, c.12, s.10 (housebreaking). It was debatable whether this introduced a new offence, or vainly removed clergy from an offence which did not exist.

62 *Anon.* (1506) Keil. 75, per Frowyk CJ.

63 *Anon.* (1606) BL MS. Hargrave 29, fo. 214; Co. Inst., vol. III, p. 63.

64 Stat. 7 Will. IV & 1 Vict., c.86, s.4; Theft Act 1968 (c.60), s.9.

65 *Anon.* (1584) 1 And. 114; Sav. 59; Clench MS. Rep.; *Anon.* (1616) 8 IJ 317 (and in LPCL 335).

66 It did not include purse-picking or pocket-picking, which was simple larceny.

from benefit of clergy. Yet it was a discrete felony, subject to prosecution by appeal or indictment. Secret theft, on the other hand, was more an offence of dishonesty than of violence and was not immediately recognised as a felony. But the notion of the king's peace was wide enough to accommodate 'larceny'[67] in due course as an indictable felony; it had the same ingredients as trespass *de bonis asportatis*, with the addition of *mens rea*, an intent to steal.

Because of the fixed death penalty for felony, minor thefts were excluded from the capital felony of 'grand larceny'. Petty (or petit) larceny, the theft of money or chattels below the value of twelve pence, was usually punished with imprisonment or whipping; and we have seen how benevolent jurors sometimes valued stolen property below one shilling in the exercise of mercy.[68] The judges also decided, as a matter of law, that some things were not larcenable at all. The first category to be so treated was that of things annexed to land; they could no more be stolen than the land itself, provided they were detached and taken without any interval. By Tudor times a second category had been recognised in the form of objects of sport or pleasure, such as dogs, cats, singing birds, and even diamonds.[69]

Despite this leniency of definition, larceny was unduly restricted by its trespassory character. Many forms of dishonesty could not be treated as felonious, because they did not include a taking with force and arms. Thus the bailee, agent, factor or trustee who appropriated property or funds entrusted to him could not be convicted of larceny, because the owner had voluntarily parted with possession, or had never been in possession, and so there was no taking *vi et armis*. If this gap in the criminal law needed a justification, it was that in all these cases the owner knew whom to call to account and could avail himself of detinue or conversion; the essence of larceny was a taking by stealth or force, against which it was more difficult to guard. Nevertheless, the narrow scope of larceny became less tolerable once it was a routine matter for convicts to escape death by means of clergy. In particular, the

---

67   This word is the French equivalent of *latrocinium*, though in classical Latin *latro* was a robber. In the common law, larceny meant feloniously taking and carrying away goods with force and arms. But the operative phrase in an indictment for larceny was *felonicè furatus fuit*.

68   See p. 591, ante. The rule became rather inflexible: in the eyre of Kent 1313 two who stole 12¹/₂d. between them were sentenced to death, whereas a man who stole 10d. received but 3 weeks imprisonment: 24 SS 90, 145.

69   Trees: Y.B. 12 Edw. III, Lib. Ass., pl.32; Fitz. Abr., *Corone*, pl.119. Fixtures: *R. v. Gardiner* (1533) Spelman Rep. (93 SS) 99; 94 SS 317; LPCL 320. Diamonds: *Anon.* (1553) Dalison Rep., BL MS. Harley 5141, fo. 12, per Hales J. Note also things beyond value (holy relics): 94 SS *318* n.2.

requirement of a forcible taking was regarded even in the fifteenth century as an inconvenient restriction, and various inroads were made on the doctrine. First, in 1473, a meeting of all the judges held that a carrier could be guilty of theft if he 'broke bulk' by opening the package entrusted to him and appropriating the separate contents; and this on the rather strained reasoning that he was a bailee of the whole package only, so that with respect to the contents he could be said to act with force and arms.[70] The second extension was directed against servants. It was already law that a person having merely the temporary use of a thing was not in legal possession, so that a customer who stole the cup served to him in a tavern was guilty of felony.[71] Towards the end of the fifteenth century it was held that a servant attending his master likewise did not have a separate possession of goods in his keeping; a man did not part with the possession of the wine in his cellar by giving the keys to his butler. But this was as far as the common law would go in the direction of making servants liable for theft. A servant sent on an errand away from the master's household did have possession of the goods he took with him, and therefore could not steal them feloniously except by breaking bulk. Parliament closed this gap in 1529 by making it felony for a servant to abscond with or 'embezzle' goods worth more than forty shillings which he had received from his master to look after.[72] The offence of embezzlement as now understood, where a servant appropriated money or goods received from third parties to the master's use, was a more difficult case; although judges may at times have turned a blind eye to the legal difficulty, it was not clearly recognised as a felony until 1799.[73] In the eighteenth century some further judicial extensions of larceny were made by qualifying in other ways the scope of legal possession. Possession ceased to be treated as a physical fact, and became an abstract legal concept in which there was a mental element. The origin of this new approach was again the old notion that one could hand over goods without passing possession. Possession did not pass, as we have seen, to customers in a shop or tavern who were merely using or handling goods which remained in the owner's immediate control. The next step was to reason that when physical

---

[70] *The Carrier's Case* (1473) 64 SS 30. For other cases, see 94 SS *319-321*.

[71] Guest in inn: *Anon.* (1353) Y.B. 27 Edw. III, Lib. Ass., pl. 39. Customer in shop: *Anon.* (1616) 8 IJ 313 (also in LPCL 331); *R. v. Chisser* (1679) T. Raym. 275.

[72] Stat. 21 Hen. VIII, c.7. For the common law, see *R. v. Armysby* (1533) Spelman Rep. (93 SS) 50; 94 SS 280.

[73] *R. v. Penley* (1542) 94 SS *320* (conviction); *R. v. Bazeley* (1799) 2 Leach 835 (doubts prevail); Stat. 39 Geo. III, c.85. Trustees and bailees were not reached until 1857: Stat. 20 & 21 Vict., c.54.

possession was handed over for a specific purpose, which the recipient had no intention of carrying out, true possession did not pass in law. Thus the hirer of a horse who rode off, never to return, and sold the horse, could be convicted of larceny provided he had the intention of stealing from the moment when the horse was delivered to him.[74] This was perhaps the point at which the practical requirements of the law caused it to part company with logic, because whether possession passed was made to depend not on the actual intention of the owner but on the guilty intent of the receiver; the 'taking' in such a case was constructive, or fictitious. This new idea of constructive taking, where an apparently voluntary parting with possession could be negatived, proved fertile. Now it was possible to convict of felony those who obtained goods by a trick, on the theory that if the owner did not truly consent to part with possession then it did not pass. By the early nineteenth century, even those who appropriated goods they had found could be convicted of felony, on the principle that the loser remained in constructive possession. Of course, the word 'finding' is open to considerable abuse in this context. A thief will say he 'found' goods merely because they were out of the owner's sight. An intruder who takes a coin mislaid under a bed, or a coachman who appropriates goods left in his coach, is not truly a finder. However, although it is easy to see how the owner's possession in such cases came to rest on intention, the doctrine extended even to those who came upon goods by genuine finding. In 1873 constructive taking reached its furthest point when a majority of the judges held that a man who had been overpaid by mistake could be convicted of stealing the surplus feloniously, even though the payer intended to pass the property as well as the possession and the payee practised no deceit in accepting it.[75] Meanwhile, parliament had been moving in a similar direction, by introducing various new offences of dishonesty, such as embezzlement, fraudulent conversion, receiving stolen goods, obtaining property by false pretences, and obtaining credit by fraud. Larceny was not obviously more serious in its nature than these other forms of dishonest self-enrichment, and the idea began to take root that he who was as bad as a thief should be treated as a thief. In 1968 the classical notion of larceny, as a forcible taking of possession, was laid to rest, and a broad but troublesome concept of dishonesty put in its place.[76]

---

[74]   *R. v. Tunnard* (1729) and *R. v. Pear* (1779) 1 Leach 213; E. H. East, *Pleas of the Crown* (1803), vol. II, p. 685. The other cases are examined fully in East, pp. 635-698.

[75]   *R. v. Middleton* (1873) L.R. 2 C.C.R. 38.

[76]   Theft Act 1968 (c.60).

Further reading[77]

Pollock & Maitland, vol. II, pp. 478-511

Plucknett CHCL, pp. 441-454

Milsom HFCL, pp. 421-428

Cornish & Clark, pp. 601-609

M. Hale, *History of the Pleas of the Crown* (written in the 1670s but first printed in 1736; repr., with introduction by P. R. Glazebrook, 1971), 2 volumes

J. H. Beale, 'The Borderland of Larceny' (1892) 6 HLR 244-256

F. B. Sayre, 'Mens Rea' (1932) 45 HLR 974-1026

J. Scurlock,'The Element of Trespass in Larceny at Common Law' (1948) 22 *Temple Law Qly* 12-45

J. M. Kaye, 'Early History of Murder and Manslaughter' (1967) 83 LQR 365-395, 569-601

N. Walker, *Crime and Insanity in England. Volume One: the Historical Perspective* (1968)

N. D. Hurnard, *The King's Pardon for Homicide before 1307* (1969), esp. pp. 68-170, 251-297

J. G. Bellamy, *The Law of Treason in England in the later Middle Ages* (1970); *The Tudor Law of Treason* (1979)

G. P. Fletcher, 'The Metamorphosis of Larceny' (1976) 89 HLR 469-530

J. M. Kaye and others, 'The Making of English Criminal Law' [1977-78] *Criminal Law Rev.*

J. H. Baker, 'Pleas of the Crown' (1978) 94 SS *299-350*;'The Refinement of English Criminal Jurisprudence' (1981), repr. with corrections in LPCL 303-324

---

[77] See also the list at the end of ch. 28.

Appendices

Appendix I
Specimen Writs[1]

Original Writs

A: 'PRAECIPIMUS TIBI' FORMS

i) *Writ of right patent*[2]

Edwardus Dei gratia Rex Angliae, dominus Hiberniae, et dux Aquitaniae, Edwardo comiti Lancastriae salutem. Praecipimus tibi quod sine dilatione plenum rectum teneas A. de B. de uno mesuagio et viginti acris terrae cum pertinentiis in I., quae clamat tenere de te per liberum servitium unius denarii per annum, pro omni servitio, quod W. de T. ei deforciat. Et nisi feceris, vicecomes Nottingham faciat, ne amplius inde clamorem audiamus pro defectu recti. Teste meipso apud Westmonasterium octavo die Octobris anno regni nostri duodecimo.

ii) *Replevin*[3]

Rex vicecomiti Nottingham salutem. Praecipimus tibi quod juste et sine dilatione replegiari facias B. quendam equum suum quod D. cepit et injuste detinet, ut dicitur, et postea eum inde juste deduci facias, ne amplius inde clamorem audiamus pro defectu justitiae. Teste etc.

iii) *De nativo habendo*[4]

Rex vicecomiti S. salutem. Praecipimus tibi quod juste et sine dilatione facias habere A. B. nativum et fugitivum suum cum omnibus catallis suis et tota sequela sua ubicumque inventus fuerit in balliva tua nisi sit in dominico nostro, qui fugit de terra sua post coronationem domini Henrici Regis filii Regis Johannis. Et prohibemus super forisfacturam nostram ne quis eum injuste detineat. Teste etc.

---

[1] Note that in both appendices the Latin spellings have been standardised for ease of interpretation. The diphthong 'ae' (used in some printed precedents) was always written 'e' in the original documents.

[2] Fitzherbert, *Natura Brevium*, fo. 1 G, but with royal style and *teste* from 87 SS 108. In the remaining precedents below, the full style and *teste* are omitted.

[3] Ibid., fo. 68 D.

Appendix I
Specimen Writs (Translations)

Original Writs

i) *Writ of right patent*[1]

Edward, by the grace of God king of England, lord of Ireland, and duke of Aquitaine, to Edward earl of Lancaster, greeting. We command you that without delay you do full right to A. of B. in respect of one messuage and twenty acres of land with the appurtenances in J. which he claims to hold of you by the free service of one penny a year for all service, and of which W. of T. deforces him. And if you will not do so, let the sheriff of Nottingham do it, that we may hear no more complaint about this for want of right. Witness my self at Westminster on the eighth day of October in the twelfth year of our reign.

ii) *Replevin*

The king[2] to the sheriff of Nottingham, greeting. We command you that justly and without delay you cause to be replevied to B. a certain horse of his which D. took and unjustly detains, as it is said, and afterwards cause him to be justly dealt with therein, that we may hear no more complaint about this for want of justice. Witness etc.

iii) *De nativo habendo*

The king to the sheriff of S., greeting. We command you that justly and without delay you cause A. to have B. his villein and fugitive, with all his chattels and all his brood, wheresoever he may be found in your bailiwick except in our demesne, who fled from his land since the coronation of the lord King Henry, son of King John. And we prohibit, upon our forfeiture, that anyone detain him unjustly. Witness etc.

---

[1] Cf. B. & M. 13, 16.

[2] Real writs always began with the full name and style of the king: see note 2 on opposite page.

iv) *Justicies for mill-suit*[5]

Rex vicecomiti N. salutem. Praecipimus tibi quod justicies A. quod juste et sine dilatione faciat sectam suam ad molendinum E. in C. quam ad illud debet et solet, ut dicit, sicut rationabiliter monstrare poterit quod eam ad illud facere debet, ne amplius inde clamorem audiamus pro defectu justitiae. Teste etc.

B: 'PRAECIPE' FORMS

i) *Praecipe in capite*[6]

Rex vicecomiti N. salutem. Praecipe A. quod juste et sine dilatione reddat B. unum mesuagium cum pertinentiis in D. quod clamat esse jus et haereditatem suum et tenere de nobis in capite, et unde quaeritur quod praedictus A. ei injuste deforciat etc. Et nisi fecerit et praedictus B. fecerit te securum de clamore suo prosequendo, tunc summone per bonos summonitores praedictum A. quod sit coram justiciariis nostris apud Westmonasterium [tali die] ostensurus quare non fecerit. Et habeas ibi summonitores et hoc breve. Teste etc.

ii) *Entry in the per and cui*[7]

Rex vicecomiti N. salutem. Praecipe A. quod juste et sine dilatione reddat B. unum gurgitem cum pertinentiis in D. quod clamat esse jus et haereditatem suam et in quem idem A. non habet ingressum nisi per C. cui praedictus B. illud dimisit ad terminum qui praeteriit etc. Et nisi fecerit etc.

iii) *Formedon in the descender*[8]

Rex vicecomiti M. salutem. Praecipe A. quod juste et sine dilatione reddat B. manerium de N. cum pertinentiis quod C. dedit D. et E. uxori ejus et haeredibus de corporibus ipsorum D. et E. exeuntibus et quod post mortem praedictorum D. et E. praefato B. filio et haeredi praedictorum D. et E. descendere debet per formam donationis praedicti, ut dicit. Et nisi fecerit etc.

iv) *Debt*[9]

Rex vicecomiti N. salutem. Praecipe A. quod juste et sine dilatione reddat B. centum solidos quos ei debet et injuste detinet ut dicit. Et nisi fecerit etc.

[5] Ibid., fo. 123 A.
[6] Ibid., fo. 5 I.
[7] Ibid., fo. 201 E.
[8] Ibid., fo. 212 D.
[9] Ibid., fo. 119 L.

iv) *Justicies for mill-suit*[3]

The king to the sheriff of N., greeting. We command you that you justice A. that justly and without delay he do his suit to E.'s mill in C., which he owes and is accustomed to do to it, as he says, if he can reasonably show that he ought to do it thereto, that we may hear no more complaint about this for want of justice. Witness etc.

B: 'PRAECIPE' FORMS

i) *Praecipe in capite*

The king to the sheriff of N., greeting. Command A. that justly and without delay he render to B. one messuage with the appurtenances in D., which he claims to be his right and inheritance and to hold of us in chief, and whereof he complains that the aforesaid A. unjustly deforces him. And if he will not do so, and if the aforesaid B. shall give you security for pursuing his claim, then summon the aforesaid A. by good summoners that he be before our justices at Westminster[4] [on such a day] to show why he has not done it. And have there the summoners, and this writ. Witness etc.

ii) *Entry in the per and cui*

The king to the sheriff of N., greeting. Command A. that justly and without delay he render to B. one water gulf with the appurtenances in D., which he claims to be his right and inheritance and into which the same A. has not entry except through C., to whom the aforesaid B. demised it for a term which has expired. And if he will not do so etc.

iii) *Formedon in the descender*[5]

The king to the sheriff of M., greeting. Command A. that justly and without delay he render to B. the manor of N. with the appurtenances, which C. gave to D. and E. his wife, and the heirs of the bodies of the selfsame D. and E. issuing, and which after the death of the aforesaid D. and E. ought to descend to the aforesaid B. the son and heir of the aforesaid D. and E. by the form of the gift aforesaid, as he says. And if he will not do so etc.

iv) *Debt*

The king to the sheriff of N., greeting. Command A. that justly and without delay he render to B. one hundred shillings which he owes to him and unjustly withholds, as he says. And if he will not do so etc.

---

3 This is a viscontiel writ, conferring jurisdiction on the sheriff himself.

4 I.e. in the Common Bench.

5 See the Statute *De donis* 1285, B. & M. at 50.

v) *Detinue for bonds*[10]

Rex vicecomiti N. salutem. Praecipe A. quod juste et sine dilatione reddat B. unam pixidem cum tribus scriptis obligatoriis in eadem pixide contentis sub sigillo praedicti B. consignatis, quam ei injuste detinet, ut dicit. Et nisi fecerit etc.

vi) *Account against a receiver*[11]

Rex vicecomiti N. salutem. Praecipe A. quod reddat B. rationabilem compotum [suum] de tempore quo fuit receptor denariorum ipsius [B]. Et nisi fecerit etc.

vii) *Covenant*[12]

Rex vicecomiti L. salutem. Praecipe B. quod juste et sine dilatione teneat A. conventionem inter eos factam de quodam granario sumptibus ipsius B. apud N. de novo construendo. Et nisi fecerit etc.

viii) *Quod permittat for pasture*[13]

Rex vicecomiti M. salutem. Praecipe A. quod juste et sine dilatione permittat B. habere communiam pasturam in N. et quadraginta acris bosci, quam habere debet, ut dicit. Et nisi fecerit etc.

C: PETTY ASSIZES

i) *Mort d' ancestor*[14]

Rex vicecomiti S. salutem. Si A. fecerit te securum de clamore suo prosequendo, tunc summone per bonos summonitores duodecim liberos et legales homines de visneto de N. quod sint coram justiciariis nostris ad primam assisam cum in partes illas venerint, parati sacramento recognoscere si W. pater praedicti A. fuit seisitus in dominico suo ut de feodo de uno mesuagio et una virgata terrae cum pertinentiis in N. die quo obiit, et si obiit post coronationem domini Henrici Regis, et si idem A. propinquior haeres ejus sit. Et interim praedictum mesuagium et terram videant. Et nomina eorum imbreviari facias. Et summone per bonos summonitores B. qui praedicta mesuagium et terras nunc tenet, quod sit ibi ad audiendum illam recognitionem. Et habeas ibi summonitores et hoc breve. Teste etc.

---

10 Ibid., fo. 138 B.
11 Ibid., fo. 117 E.
12 *Registrum Omnium Brevium* (1531), fo. 166.
13 Fitzherbert, *Natura Brevium*, fo. 123 G.
14 Ibid., fo. 195 E.

v) *Detinue for bonds*

The king to the sheriff of N., greeting. Command A. that justly and without delay he render to B. one box with three written bonds marked with the seal of the aforesaid B., contained in the same box, which he unjustly detains, as he says. And if he will not do so etc.

vi) *Account against a receiver*

The king to the sheriff of N., greeting. Command A. that justly and without delay he render to B. his reasonable account of the period when he was receiver of the said B.'s money. And if he will not do so etc.

vii) *Covenant*

The king to the sheriff of L., greeting. Command B. that justly and without delay he keep with A. the covenant between them made for a certain granary to be rebuilt at N. at the expense of him the said B. And if he will not do so etc.

viii) *Quod permittat for pasture*

The king to the sheriff of M., greeting. Command A. that justly and without delay he permit B. to have common of pasture in N. and in forty acres of wood, which he ought to have, as he says. And if he will not do so etc.

C: PETTY ASSIZES

i) *Mort d'ancestor*

The king to the sheriff of S., greeting. If A. shall give you security for pursuing his claim, then summon by good summoners twelve free and lawful men of the neighbourhood of N. that they be before our justices at the first assize when they shall come into those parts, ready to make recognition by oath whether W., father of the aforesaid A., was seised in his demesne as of fee of one messuage and one yard-land with the appurtenances in N. on the day he died, and whether he died after the coronation of the lord King Henry, and whether the same A. is his nearest heir. And in the mean time let them view the said messuage and land. And cause their names to be put on the writ. And summon by good summoners B., who now holds the aforesaid messuage and land, that he may be there to hear the recognition. And have there the summoners, and this writ. Witness etc.

ii) *Novel disseisin*[15]

Rex vicecomiti N. salutem. Quaestus est nobis A. quod B. injuste et sine judicio disseisivit eum de libero tenemento suo in C. post primam transfretationem domini Henrici Regis filii [Regis] Johannis in Vasconia. Et ideo tibi praecipimus quod si praedictus A. fecerit te securum de clamore suo prosequendo, tunc facias tenementum illud reseisiri de catallis quod in ipso capta fuerint et ipsum tenementum cum catallis esse in pace usque ad primam assisam cum justiciarii nostri in partes illas venerint. Et interim facias duodecim liberos et legales homines de visneto illo videre tenementum illud, et nomina illorum imbreviari, et summone eos per bonos summonitores quod sint coram praefatis justiciariis ad praefatam assisam parati inde facere recognitionem. Et pone per vadium et salvos plegios praedictum B., vel ballivum suum si ipse inventus non fuerit, quod tunc sit ibi ad audiendum illam recognitionem etc. Et habeas ibi summonitores, nomina plegiorum, et hoc breve. Teste etc.

D: 'OSTENSURUS QUARE' FORMS

i) *Trespass vi et armis, for battery*[16]

Rex vicecomiti S. salutem. Si A. fecerit te securum de clamore suo prosequendo, tunc pone per vadium et salvos plegios B. quod sit coram nobis in octabis Sancti Michaelis ubicumque fuerimus tunc in Anglia ostensurus quare vi et armis in ipsum A. apud N. insultum fecit et ipsum verberavit, vulneravit et male tractavit, ita quod de vita ejus desperabatur, et alia enormia ei intulit, ad grave damnum ipsius A. et contra pacem nostram etc. Et habeas ibi nomina plegiorum et hoc breve. Teste etc.

ii) *Ejectment*[17]

Rex vicecomiti N. salutem. Si A. fecerit te securum de clamore suo prosequendo, tunc pone per vadium et salvos plegios B. quod sit coram justiciariis nostris apud Westmonasterium [tali die] ostensurus quare vi et armis manerium de I., quod T. praefato A. dimisit ad terminum quod nondum praeteriit, intravit, et bona et catalla ejusdem A. ad valenciam [etc.] in eodem manerio inventa cepit et asportavit, et ipsum A. a firma sua praedicta ejecit, et alia enormia ei intulit, ad grave damnum ipsius A. et contra pacem nostram. Et habeas ibi nomina plegiorum et hoc breve. Teste etc.

---

15 Ibid., fo. 177 F.
16 Ibid., fo. 86 I.
17 Fitzherbert, *Natura Brevium*, fo. 220 G.

ii) *Novel disseisin*

The king to the sheriff of N., greeting. A. has complained to us that B. unjustly and without judgment disseised him of his free tenement in C. after the first passage of the lord King Henry, son of King John, into Gascony. And therefore we command you that if the aforesaid A. shall give you security for pursuing his claim, then cause the tenement to be reseised of the chattels which were taken therein and cause the same tenement with the chattels to be in peace until the first assize when our justices shall come into those parts. And in the mean time cause twelve free and lawful men of that neighbourhood to view the tenement, and cause their names to be put onto the writ, and summon them by good summoners that they be before the said justices at the said assize ready to make recognition thereon. And put by gage and safe pledges the aforesaid B., or if he shall not be found his bailiff, that he may be there then to hear the recognition. And have there the summoners, the names of the pledges, and this writ. Witness etc.

D: 'OSTENSURUS QUARE' FORMS

i) *Trespass vi et armis, for battery*[6]

The king to the sheriff of S., greeting. If A. shall give you security for pursuing his claim, then put by gage and safe pledges B. that he be before us on the octave of Michaelmas, wheresoever we shall then be in England,[7] to show why with force and arms he made assault on the selfsame A. at N., and beat, wounded and ill treated him so that his life was despaired of, and offered other outrages against him, to the grave damage of the selfsame A. and against our peace. And have there the names of the pledges, and this writ. Witness etc.

ii) *Ejectment*[8]

The king to the sheriff of N., greeting. If A. shall give you security for pursuing his claim, then put by gage and safe pledges B. that he be before our justices at Westminster [on such a day] to show why, with force and arms, he entered into the manor of I., which T. demised to the said A. for a term which has not yet expired, and took and carried away the goods and chattels of the same A. to the value [etc.] found in the same manor, and ejected him the said A. from his farm aforesaid, and offered other outrages against him, to the grave damage of the selfsame A. and against our peace. And have there the names of the pledges, and this writ. Witness etc.

---

[6] For a specimen declaration in trespass to chattels, cf. pp. 628-629, post.

[7] I.e. in the King's Bench.

[8] For the full record in such an action, see Bl. Comm., vol. III, Appendix II. For the declaration and rules, see B. & M. 180-182.

iii) *Waste against a tenant for years*[18]

Rex vicecomiti N. salutem. Si A. fecerit te securum de clamore suo prosequendo, tunc summoneas per bonos summonitores B. quod sit coram justiciariis nostris apud Westmonasterium [tali die] ostensurus quare, cum de communi consilio regni nostri Angliae provisum sit quod non liceat alicui vastum, venditionem seu destructionem facere de terris, domibus, boscis seu gardinis sibi dimissis ad terminum vitae vel annorum: idem B. de terris, domibus, boscis et gardinis in L., quae praedictus A. ei dimisit ad terminum annorum, fecit vastum, venditionem et destructionem, ad exhaeredationem ipsius A. et contra formam provisionis praedictae, ut dicit. Et habeas ibi summonitores et hoc breve. Teste etc.

iv) *Trespass on the case against a farrier*[19]

Rex vicecomiti L. salutem. Si J. fecerit te securum de clamore suo prosequendo, tunc pone per vadium et salvos plegios R. quod sit etc. ostensurus quare, cum idem J. quendam equum prefato R. ad bene et competenter ferrandum apud N. tradidisset: idem R. quendam clavum in vivo pedis equi praedicti intantum infixit quod equus ille multipliciter deterioratus fuit, ad damnum ipsius J. centum solidorum, ut dicit. Et habeas ibi nomina plegiorum et hoc breve. Teste etc.

v) *Assumpsit for negligence by a carrier*[20]

Rex vicecomiti L. salutem. Si N. fecerit te securum de clamore suo prosequendo, tunc pone per vadium et salvos plegios T. quod sit etc. ostensurus quare, cum idem T. ad quandam pipam vini ipsius N. a villa de S. usque villam de F. salvo et secure cariandam apud praedictam villam de S. assumpsisset: praedictus T. pipam illam tam negligenter et improvide cariavit quod pipa illa in defectu ipsius T. confracta fuit, sicque idem N. magnam partem vini praedicti amisit, ad damnum ipsius N. decem marcarum, ut dicit. Et habeas ibi nomina plegiorum et hoc breve. Teste etc.

vi) *Assumpsit for nonfeasance*[21]

Rex vicecomiti L. salutem. Si W. fecerit te securum de clamore suo prosequendo, tunc pone per vadium et salvos plegios J. quod sit etc. ostensurus quare, cum idem J., pro quadam pecuniae summa sibi per praefatum W. prae manibus soluta, quandam crucem de lapidibus apud R. infra certum terminem de novo construere ibidem assumpsisset: praedictum J. crucem illam infra terminum praedictum construere non

---

18 *Registrum Omnium Brevium*, fo. 73.

19 Ibid., fo. 106.

20 Ibid., fo. 110.

21 Ibid., fo. 109v.

iii) *Waste against a tenant for years*

The king to the sheriff of N., greeting. If A. shall give you security for pursuing his claim, then summon B. by good summoners that he be before our justices at Westminster [on such a day] to show why, whereas it is enacted by the common council of our realm of England[9] that it is unlawful for anyone to make waste, sale or destruction of lands, houses, woods or gardens demised to him for a term of life or of years: the same B. has made waste, sale and destruction of the lands, houses, woods and gardens in L. which the aforesaid A. demised to him for a term of years, to the disherison of him the said A. and against the form of the aforesaid enactment. And have there the summoners, and this writ. Witness etc.

iv) *Trespass on the case against a farrier*

The king to the sheriff of L., greeting. If J. shall give you security for pursuing his claim, then put by gage and safe pledges R. that he be etc. to show why, whereas the same J. delivered a certain horse to the said R. at N. well and sufficiently to shoe: the same R. fixed a certain nail in the quick of the foot of the aforesaid horse in such a way that the horse was in many ways impaired, to the damage of the selfsame J. one hundred shillings, as he says. And have there the names of the pledges, and this writ. Witness etc.

v) *Assumpsit for negligence by a carrier*

The king to the sheriff of L., greeting. If N. shall give you security for pursuing his claim, then put by gage and safe pledges T. that he be etc. to show why, whereas the same T. at the vill of S. had undertaken safely and securely to carry a certain pipe of wine belonging to the selfsame N. from the aforesaid vill of S. to the vill of F.: the aforesaid T. carried the pipe so carelessly and improvidently that in default of the selfsame T. the pipe was cracked, so that the same N. lost the great part of the aforesaid wine, to the damage of the selfsame N. ten marks, as he says. And have there the names of the pledges, and this writ. Witness etc.

vi) *Assumpsit for nonfeasance*[10]

The king to the sheriff of L., greeting. If W. shall give you security for pursuing his claim, then put by gage and safe pledges J. that he be etc. to show why, whereas the same J., for a certain sum of money paid to him beforehand by the aforesaid W., had undertaken at R. to rebuild a certain cross of stones there within a certain time: the aforesaid J. did not take care to build the said cross within the aforesaid time, to the

9 Statute of Gloucester 1278, c.5.

10 For other specimens, see B. & M. 343, 390.

curavit, ad damnum ipsius W. viginti librarum, ut dicit. Et habeas ibi
nomina plegiorum et hoc breve. Teste etc.

Judicial Writs

i) *Common Pleas mesne process: capias ad respondendum*

Rex vicecomiti W. salutem. Praecipimus tibi quod capias A. si
inventus fuerit in balliva tua et eum salvo custodias ita quod habeas
corpus ejus coram justiciariis nostris apud Westmonasterium in octabis
Sanctae Trinitatis ad respondendum B. de placito quare vi et armis
clausum et domum ipsius B. fregit et alia enormia ei intulit ad damnum
ipsius B. quinquaginta librarum, ut dicit. Et habeas tunc ibi hoc breve.
Teste etc.

ii) *King's Bench mesne process: latitat*[22]

Rex vicecomiti S. salutem. Cum vicecomiti nostro Midd' nuper
praecipimus quod caperet C. si inventus fuisset in balliva sua et eum
salvo custodiret ita quod haberet corpus ejus coram nobis apud
Westmonasterium ad certum diem jam praeteritum ad respondendum A.
de placito transgressionis acetiam separali billae ipsius A. versus
praefatum C. pro decem libris de debito secundum consuetudinem curiae
nostrae coram nobis exhibendae, dictusque vicecomes noster Midd' ad
diem illum nobis retornavit quod praedictus C. non est inventus in
balliva sua, super quo ex parte praedicti A. in curia nostra coram nobis
sufficienter testatum est quod praedictus C. latitat et discurrit in
comitatu tuo: ideo tibi praecipimus quod capias eum si inventus fuerit
in balliva tua et eum salvo custodias ita quod habeas corpus ejus coram
nobis apud Westmonasterium die Mercurii proximo post tres septimanas
Sanctae Trinitatis ad respondendum praefato A. de placito et billa
praedictis. Et habeas ibi tunc hoc breve. Teste Johanne Holt milite,
apud Westmonasterium, nono die Junii anno regni nostri undecimo.

iii) *Exchequer mesne process: quominus*[23]

Regina vicecomiti M. salutem. Praecipimus tibi quod non omittas
propter aliquam libertatem comitatus tui quin eam ingrediaris et capias
H. ubicumque inventus fuerit in balliva tua et eum salvo custodias ita
quod habeas corpus ejus coram baronibus de scaccario nostro apud
Westmonasterium in crastino Purificationis Beatae Mariae Virginis ad
respondendum W. debitori nostro de quodam placito transgressionis,
quominus praedictus W. nobis satisfacere valeat de debitis quae nobis
debet ad dictum scaccarium nostrum, ad grave damnum ipsius W. ut

[22] *Instructor Clericalis* (3rd ed., 1700), p. 39.
[23] From the writ file for Hilary term 1590, E5/39/4.

damage of the selfsame W. twenty pounds, as he says. And have there the names of the pledges, and this writ. Witness etc.

Judicial Writs

i) *Common Pleas mesne process: capias ad respondendum*

The king to the sheriff of W., greeting. We command you that you take A. and safely keep him so that you may have his body before our justices at Westminster in the octave of the Holy Trinity to answer B. in a plea why with force and arms he broke the close and house of the selfsame B. and offered other outrages against him, to the damage of the selfsame B. fifty pounds, as he says. And have there then this writ. Witness etc.[11]

ii) *King's Bench mesne process: latitat*

The king to the sheriff of S., greeting. Whereas we lately commanded our sheriff of Middlesex that he should take C., if he could be found in his bailiwick, and safely keep him so that he might be before us at Westminster at a certain day now past, to answer unto A. of a plea of trespass, and also[12] to a separate bill of the him said A. against the said C. for ten pounds of debt, to be exhibited before us according to the custom of our court; and our said sheriff of Middlesex at that day returned to us that the aforesaid C. has not been found in his bailiwick; whereupon on behalf of the aforesaid A. it has been sufficiently attested in our court before us that the aforesaid C. lurks and roams about in your county: therefore we command you that you take him, if he can be found in your bailiwick, and safely keep him so that you may have his body before us at Westminster on the Wednesday next after three weeks of the Holy Trinity, to answer to the aforesaid A. in respect of the plea and bill aforesaid. And have there then this writ. Witness John Holt, knight,[13] the ninth day of June in the eleventh year of our reign.

iii) *Exchequer mesne process: quominus*

The queen to the sheriff of M., greeting. We command you that you omit not by reason of any liberty in your county but that you enter the same and take H., wheresover he shall be found in your bailiwick, and safely keep him so that you may have his body before the barons of our Exchequer at Westminster on the morrow of the Purification of the Blessed Virgin Mary to answer W. our debtor in a certain plea of trespass, whereby he is the less able to satisfy us the debts which he owes us at our said Exchequer, to the grave damage of the selfsame W.

---

11   Name of the chief justice of the Common Pleas.

12   The *ac etiam* clause.

13   Chief justice of the King's Bench.

dicit, sicut rationabiliter monstrare poterit quod inde respondere debet. Et habeas ibi hoc breve. Teste Rogero Manwood milite apud Westmonasterium xxviij° die Novembris anno regni nostri tricesimo secundo.

iv) *Chancery mesne process: subpoena ad respondendum*[24]

Rex C.D. armigero salutem. Quibusdam certis de causis coram nobis in Cancellaria nostra propositis tibi praecipimus firmiter injungentes quod omnibus aliis praetermissis et excusatione quacunque cessante in propria persona tua sis coram nobis in dicta Cancellaria nostra a die Sancti Michaelis proximo futuro in tres septimanas ubicumque tunc fuerimus, ad respondendum super iis quae tibi objicientur tunc ibidem, et ad faciendum ulterius et recipiendum quae dicta curia nostra consideraverit in hac parte. Et hoc sub poena centum librarum nullatenus omittas. Et habeas tunc ibi hoc breve. Teste etc.

v) *Final process: ca. sa. for damages in trespass*

Rex vicecomiti S. salutem. Praecipimus tibi quod capias B. si inventus fuit in balliva tua et eum salvo custodias ita quod habeas corpus ejus coram nobis apud Westmonasterium die Lunae proximo post quindenam Sancti Martini ad satisfaciendum J. de quindecim libris pro damnis suis quae sustinuit tam occasione cujusdam transgressionis eidem J. per praefatum defendentem illatae quam pro misis et custagiis suis per ipsum circa sectam suam in hac parte appositis, unde convictus est sicut nobis constat de recordo. Et habeas ibi tunc hoc breve. Teste etc.

Prerogative Writs

i) *Error*[25]

Rex dilecto et fideli suo A.B. militi salutem. Quia in recordo et processu ac etiam in redditione judicii loquelae quae fuit in curia nostra coram vobis et sociis vestris justiciariis nostris de Banco per breve nostrum inter X. et Y., de quodam debito ducentarum librarum quod idem X. in eadem curia nostra coram vobis et sociis vestris praedictis recuperavit versus eum, error intervenit manifestum ad grave damnum ipsius Y., sicut ex querela sua accepimus: nos, errorem si quis fuerit modo debito corrigi et partibus praedictis plenam et celerem justiciam fieri volentes in hac parte, vobis mandamus quod si judicium inde redditum sit tunc recordum et processum loquelae praedictae cum

---

[24] *The Compleat Clerk in Court* (1726), p. 10.
[25] Based on Coke's *Entries*, fo. 246; Bl. Comm., vol. III, Appendix III(6).

as he says, as he can reasonably show that he ought to answer therein. And have there this writ. Witness Roger Manwood, knight,[14] at Westminster, the 28th day of November [1589] in the thirty-second year of our reign.

iv) *Chancery mesne process: subpoena ad respondendum*
The king to C.D., esquire, greeting. For certain causes set forth before us in our Chancery, we firmly enjoining command you that, laying aside all other things and all excuses whatsoever, you be in your own person before us in our said Chancery in three weeks from Michaelmas day next following, wheresoever we may then be, to answer there upon those matters that shall then be charged against you, and further to do and receive whatever our said court shall award in that behalf. And this in no wise omit, upon pain of one hundred pounds. And have there then this writ. Witness etc.

v) *Final process: ca. sa. for damages in trespass*
The king to to the sheriff of S., greeting. We command you that you take B., if he can be found in your bailiwick, and keep him safely so that you may have his body before us at Westminster on the Monday next after the quindene of St Martin, to satisfy J. in respect of fifteen pounds, for his damages which he sustained both by reason of a certain trespass committed by the said defendant against the same J. and also for his outlay and costs laid out by him about his suit in that behalf, wherein he is convicted, as appears to us of record. And have you there then this writ. Witness etc.

Prerogative Writs

i) *Error*
The king to his trusty and beloved A.B., knight,[15] greeting. Because in the record and process, and also in the giving of judgment, of the plaint which was in our court before you and your fellows our justices of the Bench, by our writ, between X. and Y., in respect of a certain debt of two hundred pounds which the same X. has recovered in our same court before you and your aforesaid fellows, manifest error has intervened, to the great damage of him the said Y., as we from his complaint are fully informed: we, being willing that the error, if any there be, should be duly corrected, and that full and speedy justice should be done to the aforesaid parties in that behalf, do command you that, if judgment has been given therein, then under your seal you do distinctly and openly send the record and process of the plaint aforesaid, with all things

---

[14] Chief baron of the Exchequer.
[15] In this instance the chief justice of the Common Pleas.

omnibus ea tangentibus nobis sub sigillo vestro distincte et aperte mittatis, et hoc breve, ita quod habeamus a die Sanctae Trinitatis in tres septimanas ubicumque tunc fuerimus in Anglia, ut, inspectis recordo et processu praedictis, ulterius inde pro errore illo corrigendo fieri faciamus quod de jure et secundum legem et consuetudinem regni nostri Angliae fuerit faciendum. Teste etc.

ii) *Certiorari to commissioners of sewers*[26]
Rex dilectis et fidelibus suis A., B., C. et D., justiciariis nostris ad wallias, fossata, gutteras, seweras, pontes, calceta et gurgites per costeram maris et marisci in partibus de M. inter aquas de E., F., G. et H. in comitatu E. supervidenda assignatis, et eorum cuilibet, salutem. Volentes certis de causis certiorari super omnibus et singulis praesentationibus coram vobis versus J.S., quocumque nomine censeatur, factis sive praesentatis ut dicitur: vobis mandamus quod tenores praesentationum praedictorum nobis in cancellariam nostram [tali die] ubicumque fuerit sub sigillis vestris vel unius vestrum distincte et aperte mittatis, et hoc breve. Teste etc.

iii) *Habeas corpus ad subjiciendum*[27]
Rex J.L. militi, gardiani prisonae nostrae de le Fleet, salutem. Praecipimus tibi quod corpus W.E. militis in prisona nostra sub custodia tua detentum, ut dicitur, una cum die et causa detentionis suae, quocumque nomine praedictus W.E. censeatur in eadem, habeas coram nobis [tali die] ubicumque tunc fuerimus in Anglia, ad subjiciendum et recipiendum ea quae curia nostra de eo adtunc et ibidem ordinare contigerit in hac parte. Et hoc nullatenus omittatis periculo incumbente. Et habeas ibi hoc breve. Teste etc.

Writ of Summons after 1834[28]

William the fourth by the grace of God etc. to C.D. of Y. in the county of Z., greeting. We command you that within eight days after the service of this writ on you, inclusive of the day of such service, you do cause an appearance to be entered for you in our court of . . . in an action on promises [*or as the case may be*][29] at the suit of A.B.; and take notice, that in default of your so doing the said A.B. may cause an appearance to be entered for you and proceed therein to judgment and execution. Witness etc.

26 *Registrum Omnium Brevium*, fo. 287.
27 Based on 3 State Tr. 11 (1628).
28 Uniformity of Process Act, 2 & 3 Will. IV, c.39, Sch. I. With slight changes, the same form was in use until 1980.
29 This statement of the cause of action was omitted after 1852. See the Common Law Procedure Act 1852, 15 & 16 Vict., c.76, Sch. A.

concerning them, and this writ, so that we may have them in three weeks from the day of the Holy Trinity wheresoever we shall then be in England, so that, the record and process aforesaid having been inspected, we may cause to be done thereupon whatever of right and according to the law and custom of our realm of England ought to be done in correcting that error. Witness etc.

ii) *Certiorari to commissioners of sewers*[16]

The king to his trusty and beloved A., B., C. and D., our justices assigned to survey the banks, dykes, channels, sewers, bridges, causeys and weirs by the coast of the sea and marsh in the parts of M. between the waters of E., F., G. and H. in the county of E., and to each of them, greeting. We, wishing for certain reasons to be informed concerning all and singular the presentments made or presented before yourselves, as it is said, against J.S., by whatever name he is charged, do command you that under the seals of yourselves, or of one of you, you do distinctly and openly send the tenors of the aforesaid presentments, and this writ, unto us in our Chancery [at such a day] wheresoever it should then be. Witness etc.

iii) *Habeas corpus ad subjiciendum*

The king to J.L., knight, warden of our prison of the Fleet, greeting. We command you that you have the body of W.E., knight, who (as it is said) is detained in our prison under your custody, by whatever name the aforesaid W.E. is charged, before us [at such a day] wheresover we shall then be in England, together with the day and the cause of his detention, to undergo and receive whatever our court should then and there happen to order concerning him in this behalf. And this in no wise omit, upon the peril that may befall. And have there this writ. Witness etc.

---

[16] This form is for removal into the Chancery, but a similar form was used by the King's Bench for reviewing summary convictions and justices' orders.

Appendix II
Specimen Entries

Not many law students will ever have occasion to consult a plea roll; but the forms of pleading used before 1852 were so different from those of today that it will be instructive to read these specimen entries from the plea and Crown sides of the King's Bench. The words have been extended from the original court-hand, and punctuation introduced.

An Action of Trespass

BELHOUS V. CLAVERYNG (1341)[1]

Essex'. Johannes filius Johannis de Claveryng, Thomas de Eppeford et Radulfus frater ejus, Johannes Munchanesy, Johannes Illeye de Wytham, Ricardus Plantyng de Hatfeld, Johannes Knyght Jonesservaunt Claveryng, et Walterus le Sadeler de Branketre, attachiati fuerunt ad respondendum Isoldae de Belhous de placito quare ipsi simul cum Roberto le Ismanger de Mymmes, Willelmo Baiser, Ricardo Baiser et Johanne Barber, clerico, vi et armis triginta et unam vaccas, octo boviculos et decem juvencas ipsius Isoldae pretii triginta librarum apud Ramesdene Belhous inventos ceperunt et abduxerunt et alia enormia etc. ad grave damnum etc. et contra pacem etc.

Et unde eadem Isolda, per Simonem de Kegworth attornatum suum, queritur quod praedicti Johannes filius Johannis de Claveryng et alii, simul cum praefato Roberto le Ismanger de Mymmes et aliis, die Sabati proxima post festum Omnium Sanctorum anno regni Regis Edwardi nunc tertio decimo, vi et armis, videlicet gladiis etc., triginta et unam vaccas, octo boviculos et decem juvencas ipsius Isoldae pretii triginta librarum apud Ramesden Belhous inventos ceperunt et abduxerunt contra pacem etc. Unde dicit quod deteriorata est et damnum habet ad valenciam sexaginta librarum. Et inde producit sectam etc.

---

[1] Public Record Office, KB 27/324, m. 22 (plea roll for Easter term, 15 Edw. III).

Appendix II
Specimen Entries (Translations)

These precedents have been taken at random from the King's Bench rolls of Edward III. Various other precedents of entries in civil and criminal cases will be found in Spelman's Reports, vol. II (94 SS, 1978), and some English translations of civil pleadings in B. & M.

An Action of Trespass

BELLHOUSE V. CLAVERING (1341)

Essex. [*Note of attachment by writ:*] John son of John of Clavering, Thomas of Eppeford and Ralph his brother, John Munchanesy, John Illey of Witham, Richard Planting of Hatfield, John Knight the servant of John Clavering, and Walter the Saddler of Braintree, were attached to answer Isot of Bellhouse in a plea why they, together with Robert the Ironmonger of Mimms, William Baiser, Richard Baiser and John Barber, clerk, with force and arms took and led away thirty-one cows, eight bullocks and ten heifers of the selfsame Isot's, worth thirty pounds, found at Ramsden Bellhouse, and other outrages [offered against her], to the grave damage [of the selfsame Isot] and against the peace [of the lord king].

[*Declaration:*] And thereupon the same Isot, by Simon of Kegworth her attorney, complains that the aforesaid John son of John of Clavering and the others, together with the said Robert the Ironmonger of Mimms and the others, on the Saturday [6 Nov. 1339] next after the feast of All Saints in the thirteenth year of the reign of the present King Edward, with force and arms, namely with swords etc., took and led away thirty-one cows, eight bullocks and ten heifers of the selfsame Isot's, worth thirty pounds, found at Ramsden Bellhouse, against the peace [of the lord king]. Whereby she says she is the worse and has damage to the extent of sixty pounds. And thereof she produces suit etc.

Et praedicti Johannes filius Johannis de Claveryng et alii, per Rogerum de Horkesleye attornatum suum, veniunt et defendunt vim et injuriam quando etc. Et dicunt quod ipsi in nullo sunt culpabiles de transgressione praedicta. Et de hoc ponunt se super patriam. Et praedicta Isolda similiter. Ideo veniat inde jurata coram domino rege in octabis Sanctae Trinitatis ubicumque etc. et qui nec etc. ad recognoscendum etc. quia tam etc.

Postea continuato hic inde processu inter partes praedictas per juratas inter eas positas in respectum usque in octabis Sancti Michaelis anno regni regis nunc quinto decimo ubicumque etc. nisi W. Scot prius die Martis proxima ante festum Sancti Michaelis apud Reylegh venisset etc. Ad quem diem venit coram domino rege praedicta Isolda per praedictum attornatum suum et praedicti Johannes filius Johannis, Thomas, Radulfus, Johannes, Johannes, Ricardus, Johannes et Walterus non veniunt. Et praedictus W. Scot coram quo praedicta jurata capta fuit tulit hic recordum veredicti juratae praedictae in haec verba:

Postea ad praefatum diem Martis apud Reylegh coram praefato Willelmo Scot, associato sibi Johanne Bray, venit praedicta Isolda per praedictum attornatum suum. Et praedicti Johannes filius Johannis, Thomas de Eppeford et Radulfus frater ejus, Johannes Munchanesy, Johannes Illeye de Wytham, Ricardus Plantyng, Johannes Knyght et Walterus le Sadeler, per praedictum attornatum suum, veniunt. Et similiter juratores veniunt qui dicunt super sacramentum suum quod praedicti Johannes filius Johannis, Thomas de Eppeford et Radulfus frater ejus, Johannes Illeye, Ricardus Plantyng, Johannes Knyght et Walterus le Sadeler culpabiles sunt de transgressione praedicta ad damnum ipsius Isoldae sexaginta librarum, et quod praedictus Johannes Munchanesy in nullo est inde culpabilis.

Ideo consideratum est quod eadem Isolda recuperet versus praedictos Johannem filium Johannis, Thomam, Radulfum, Johannem Illeye. Ricardum, Johannem Knyght et Walterum damna sua praedicta et iidem Johannes filius Johannis et alii capiantur. Et praedicta Isolda in misericordia pro falso clamore suo versus praedictum Johannem Munchanesy et idem Johannes eat inde sine die etc. Et super hoc

[Defence:] And the aforesaid John son of John de Clavering and the others, by Roger of Horkesley their attorney, come and deny the force and wrong whenever [and wherever they ought]. *[Plea and joinder of issue:]* And they say that they are not guilty of the trespass aforesaid. And thereof they put themselves upon the country. And the aforesaid Isot likewise. *[Venire facias:]* Therefore let a jury come thereon before the lord king on the octave of the Holy Trinity wheresoever [he shall then be in England], who neither [to the plaintiff nor the defendants have any affinity], to make recognition [upon their oath whether the defendants are guilty of the trespass or not], because both [the plaintiff and the defendants have put themselves upon that jury].

[Respite with nisi prius clause:] Afterwards, the process therein was continued here between the parties aforesaid by the juries between them being put in respite until the octave of Michaelmas in the fifteenth year of the reign of the present king, unless William Scot[1] should first have come to Rayleigh on the Tuesday [25 Sept. 1341] next before Michaelmas [by the form of the statute]. At which day [6 Oct. 1341] the aforesaid Isot comes before the lord king by her aforesaid attorney; and the aforesaid John son of John, Thomas, Ralph, John, John, Richard, John and Walter do not come. And the aforesaid William Scot, before whom the aforesaid jury was taken, has sent here the record of the verdict of the aforesaid jury in these words:

[Postea:] Afterwards on the aforesaid Tuesday, at Rayleigh before the said William Scot, John Bray being associated unto him, the aforesaid Isot comes by her aforesaid attorney. And the aforesaid John son of John, Thomas of Eppeford and Ralph his brother, John Munchanesy, John Illey of Witham, Richard Planting, John Knight and Walter the Saddler, come by their aforesaid attorney. *[Verdict:]* And the jurors likewise come, who say upon their oath that the aforesaid John son of John, Thomas of Eppeford and Ralph his brother, John Illey, Richard Planting, John Knight and Walter the Saddler are guilty of the aforesaid trespass to the damage of the selfsame Isot sixty pounds, and that the aforesaid John Munchanesy is not guilty thereof.

[Judgment:] Therefore it is awarded that the same Isot do recover her aforesaid damages against the aforesaid John son of John, Thomas, Ralph, John Illey, Richard, John Knight and Walter; and let the same John son of John and the others be taken. And the aforesaid Isot is in mercy for her false claim against the aforesaid John Munchanesy; and let the same John go therein without day etc. *[Nonsuit against absent*

[1] Chief justice of the King's Bench.

praedicta Isolda asserit se nolle ulterius prosequi versus praefatum Robertum le Ismanger, Willelmum Baiser, Ricardum Baiser et Johannem Barber qui nondum placitaverunt etc. Ideo cesset executio de damnis quousque etc.

Proceedings at a Gaol Delivery

DELIVERY OF THE MARSHALSEA PRISON AT NORWICH (1342)[2]

[1] Johannes Pertrik de Topcroft, indictatus coram domino rege de morte Adae de Nethergate de Shelton in villa de Biskele die Sabati in festo Nativitatis Beatae Mariae anno regni regis nunc quinto decimo felonice interfecti, venit per vicecomitem ductus. Et allocutus qualiter se velit de morte et felonia praedictis acquietare dicit quod in nullo est inde culpabilis et de bono et malo ponit se super patriam etc. Ideo fiat inde jurata etc. – Juratores de visneto de Biskele ad hoc electi et triati veniunt, qui dicunt super sacramentum suum quod praedictus Johannes Pertrik in nullo est culpabilis de morte seu felonia praedictis sibi impositis. Ideo ipse eat inde quietus etc. Catalla ejusdem Johannis forisfacta quia subtraxit se, ij s. iiij d., unde villata de Topcroft respondebit etc.

[2] Agnes de Hemesby de Lenne Episcopi, capta per appellum Ricardi Whippe de Ormesby probatoris qui coram Rogero Breton uno coronatorum comitatus praedicti devenit probator et appellavit praedictam Agnetam de eo quod ipsa scienter receptavit ipsum Ricardum Whippe apud Lenne Episcopi cum duabus supertunicis et cum una tela panni lanuti pretii viginti solidorum quas idem Ricardus furatus fuerat in villa Cantebrigiae die Martis proxima post festum Sancti Martini Episcopi anno regni regis nunc undecimo, sciens ipsum esse latronem et praedicta bona esse furata, quod quidem appellum praedictus coronator praesens hic in curia recordatur, venit per marescallum ducta. Et praedictus probator similiter venit. Et quaesitum est ab eo si prosequi velit appellum suum versus praefatam Agnetam nec ne. Qui dicit quod sic. Per quod eadem Agnes allocuta qualiter se velit de receptamento

2 Public Record Office, KB 27/328, Rex m. 33. The first three cases from the King's Bench gaol delivery at Norwich on 13 May 1342.

defendants:] And thereupon the aforesaid Isot stated that she did not wish to sue further against the said Robert the Ironmonger, William Baiser, Richard Baiser and John Barber, who have not yet pleaded etc. Therefore let execution in respect of the damages be stayed until etc.

Proceedings at a Gaol Delivery

DELIVERY OF THE MARSHALSEA PRISON AT NORWICH (1342)

[1] [*Arraignment upon an indictment for manslaughter:*] John Partridge of Topcroft, having been indicted before the lord king for the death of Adam of Nethergate, of Shelton, feloniously slain in the vill of Bixley on Saturday the feast of the Nativity of the Blessed Mary [8 Sept. 1341] in the fifteenth year of the reign of the present king, comes led by the sheriff. [*Allocutus and plea:*] And, being asked how he will acquit himself of the death and felony aforesaid, he says that he is in no way guilty thereof and puts himself for good and ill upon the country etc. Therefore let a jury thereon be made etc. – [*Verdict:*] The jurors of the venue of Bixley, chosen and tried for that purpose, come and say upon their oath that the aforesaid John Partridge is in no way guilty of the death or felony aforesaid laid against him. [*Judgment:*] Therefore let him go quit thereof etc. The chattels of the same John are forfeited because he ran away; [they are appraised at] 2s. 4d., for which the vill of Topcroft shall answer.

[2] [*Arraignment upon an approver's appeal for receiving:*] Agnes of Hemsby, of Bishop's Lynn, having been arrested by reason of the appeal of Richard Whip of Ormsby, approver, who became an approver before Roger Breton one of the coroners of the aforesaid county and appealed the aforesaid Agnes for that she knowingly received the selfsame Richard Whip at Bishop's Lynn with two surcoats and a piece of woollen cloth worth two shillings which the same Richard had stolen in the vill of Cambridge on the Tuesday [18 Nov. 1337] next after the feast of St Martin the Bishop in the eleventh year of the reign of the present king, knowing him to be a thief and knowing the aforesaid goods to be stolen, which appeal the aforesaid coroner records here in court, comes led by the marshal. And the aforesaid approver likewise comes. And he is asked whether he will prosecute his appeal against the said Agnes, or not; and he says he will. [*Allocutus and plea:*] Wherefore the same Agnes, being asked how she will acquit herself of

praedicto acquietare dicit quod in nullo est inde culpabilis et de bono et malo ponit se super patriam. Et praedictus probator similiter. Ideo fiat inde jurata etc. – Juratores de visneto praedicto ad hoc electi et triati veniunt, qui dicunt super sacramentum suum quod praedicta Agnes in nullo est culpabilis de [receptamento seu] felonia praedictis sibi impositis nec unquam ea occasione se retraxit. Ideo ipsa eat inde quieta etc. Et praedictus probator suspendatur etc.

[3] Thomas Bannes de Foxton, captus per ballivos civitatis Norwici pro suspectione latrocinii et cum manuopere trium corporalium, quinque manutergiorum et unius sudarii apud ecclesiam de Merkeshale in festo Sancti Bartholomei Apostoli anno regni regis nunc quinto decimo felonice furatorum, venit per praedictos ballivos ductus. Et allocutus qualiter se velit de felonia et latrocinio praedictis acquietare dicit quod clericus est et membrum sacrae ecclesiae et non potest sine ordinariis suis inde respondere. Et super hoc venit Robertus decanus capellae Beatae Mariae in campis Norwici gerens vices Antonii Norwici episcopi per litteras ipsius episcopi patentes quas protulit hic in curia hoc idem testificantes ad clericos petendos etc. et petit ipse tanquam clericum etc. Et ut sciatur pro quali etc. inquiratur inde veritas per patriam etc. Ideo fiat inde jurata etc. – Juratores de visneto praedicto super hoc onerati dicunt super sacramentum suum quod praedictus Thomas culpabilis sit de latrocinio et felonia praedictis sibi impositis. Ideo idem Thomas tanquam clericus convictus liberatur ordinario ad salvo custodiendum periculo quod incumbit etc. Et sciendum quod pelfrum praedictum traditur Edwardo de Cretyng vicecomiti ad sacros usus capellae domini regis infra castrum Norwici imperpetuum remanendum etc. Et idem Thomas Bannes nulla habet catalla.

the aforesaid receiving, says that she is in no way guilty thereof and puts herself for good and ill upon the country. And the aforesaid approver likewise. Therefore let a jury thereon be made etc. – [*Verdict:*] The jurors of the venue aforesaid, chosen and tried for that purpose, come and say upon their oath that the aforesaid Agnes is in no way guilty of the receiving or felony aforesaid laid against her, and that she never ran away on that account. [*Judgment:*] Therefore let her be quit thereof etc. And let the aforesaid approver be hanged etc.

[3] [*Arraignment upon an arrest for larceny:*] Thomas Bannes of Foxton, having been arrested by the bailiffs of the city of Norwich on suspicion of larceny, and with mainour[2] of three corporal cloths, five towels and one handkerchief, stolen at the church of Markshall on the feast of St Bartholomew the Apostle [24 Aug. 1341] in the fifteenth year of the reign of the present king, comes led by the aforesaid bailiffs. [*Allocutus and prayer of clergy:*] And, being asked how he will acquit himself of the felony and larceny aforesaid, he says that he is a clerk and a member of Holy Church and that he cannot answer therein without his ordinaries. [*Ordinary claims him:*] And thereupon comes Robert, dean of the chapel of the Blessed Mary in the Fields of Norwich, bearing the authority of Anthony [Bek] bishop of Norwich for claiming clerks etc., by letters of the selfsame bishop which he puts forward here in court and which witness the same; and he claims him as a clerk etc. [*Inquest of office:*] And that it may be known in what [capacity he should be delivered], let the truth thereof be enquired into by the country etc. Therefore let a jury thereon be made etc. – [*Verdict:*] The jurors of the venue aforesaid, charged upon this, say upon their oath that the aforesaid Thomas is guilty of the larceny and felony aforesaid laid against him. [*Judgment:*] Therefore let the same Thomas be delivered to the ordinary as a clerk convict, to be safely kept upon the peril which may befall etc. And it is to be known that the pelf aforesaid is delivered to Edward of Creeting, the sheriff, to remain for ever to the sacred uses of the lord king's chapel within Norwich castle etc. And the same Thomas Bannes has no chattels.

---

2 Suspected stolen goods found on the prisoner's person.

Index

Lancaster
county palatine, 32, 140 n.19
Duchy Chamber, 140 n.19
Land. *See* REAL PROPERTY
Larceny, 591, 606–608, 609R, 634–635
appeal of, 434, 440–441
common thief, 577
grand and petty, 591, 606
Lateran Council (1215), 6, 547, 579
Latin language, 67, 102–104, 117 n.16,
117, 202, 244, 505 n.48, 506 n.55
Latitat, 51, 53, 60
specimen writ, 622
Law, Edward (1750–1818, Baron Ellen-
borough, CJKB 1802–18), 193
Law
development of, 84–85, 94–96, 97–98
fact and, 6–7, 84, 97–98, 110, 111R,
122
reform of, 81, 223, 243–249, 253R
Law Commission, 249, 252
Law Reports, The, 211
See also REPORTS OF CASES
Law Society, 187, 196 n.47
Law, wager of. *See* WAGER OF LAW
Lawyers. *See* LEGAL PROFESSION
Lease and release, 346
Lease for life. *See* tenancy for life
Lease for lives, 302, 303
Lease for years, 337–346, 358R
attendant on inheritance, 345
changing character of, 278, 339–340
compared with licence, 357
deed as evidence of, 363
in settlements, 343–345
lease and release, 345–346
long leases, 343
mortgage by, 338, 353, 354
satisfied terms, 345
Lee, Sir Henry (1530–1610, Master of
the Ordinance), 537 n.28
Leets, 11, 29, 32, 33
Legal education
early, 182, 199R, 214–215
in inns, 184–185
in universities, 194–197, 199R
Legal history, in past, 1, 218–219, 222R
Legal literature. *See* formularies;
reports of cases; treatises
Legal profession
apprentices, 182, 185, 202, 205, 214
attorneys (q.v.)
barristers, 184–186, 187, 197R
civilian advocates. *See* DOCTORS OF
LAW
deceit by, 179
dress of, 180, 189 n.27
forespeakers, 178

Legal profession—*continued*
king's counsel, 187–188, 197R, 293
n.42
origins of, 177–179, 197R
serjeants at law, 180–182, 189,
197R
slander of lawyers, 498–499
solicitors, 185–186, 197R
See also COUNSEL; INNS OF COURT;
JUDGES; LEGAL EDUCATION
Legal year
Chancery always open, 119
divisions of, 77–78
Legatus juridicus, 2
Leges Henrici Primi, 15
Legislation, 234–243, 253R
Anglo-Saxon, 2–4, 234
consolidation of, 249–250
Angevin, 16, 234
equity and, 122, 126–127
Henry VIII clause, 37
interpretation of, 173–174, 239–243
judicial review of, 126–127, 173, 240–
243, 253R
texts of, 236–237
Tudor, 237
Leprosy, 500
Levant Company, 512
Levari facias, 78 n.58
Libel, 501, 506–508
criminal, 137, 505 n.47, 508R
juries and, 109
See also DEFAMATION
Liberty, personal. *See* HABEAS CORPUS;
IMPRISONMENT; SLAVERY; VILLEI-
NAGE
Licence
to alienate land, 273
to alienate in mortmain, 277
to enter land, 473, 519
to keep tavern, 513
to marry, 549–550
to occupy land, 357–358
Lien, 451, 522 n.66
Light, right to, 484–485
Limitation of actions
contract and tort, 422
debt, 370
money, 416
real actions, 342
trespass, 465
Limitation of estate, words of, 324
Lincoln's Inn, 133, 183, 197R
Lindley, Nathaniel (1828–1921, Lord
Lindley, MR 1897–1900), 181, 182
Litigation
delays in. *See* DELAYS
likened to game, 15, 91, 107, 109

Majority
 in judicial decisions, 158, 227, 291
  n.34
 in verdicts, 90, 577
Male sex. *See under* SEX
Malice
 in criminal offences, 597, 601–602
 in defamation, 501, 506
 in tort, 455, 457 n.11, 465, 526 n.87,
  527
 malicious falsehood, 522
 malicious prosecution, 506, 524
Manchester, Owens College, 196 n.48
Mandamus
 action for, 175 n.83
 writ of, 169–170, 524
Mandeville, Geoffrey de (d. 1166, earl of
  Essex), 18
Manors, 9, 10, 258–259
 courts of, 9, 10, 32, 33, 258–259, 348
 customs of. *See under* CUSTOMS
  (MANORIAL)
 steward of, 383, 497 n.10
 villeins in, 534
Mansfield, Lord. *See* MURRAY, WILLIAM
Manslaughter, 588, 597, 601–603, 632–
  633
Manufacturers
 liability in contract, 404
 liability in tort, 472, 473–474, 474–475
 new manufactures. *See* PATENTS
Manumission, 532, 533, 535, 536, 537
Manuscripts
 copyright in, 516
 legal, 222R
Marches of Wales, 37, 42R, 139–140
Mareva injunction, 233
Maritagium, 310–311
Maritime law, 142–143
Markets
 interference with, 479, 489, 511
 sale in market overt, 434–435, 441
Markshall, Norf, 634–635
Marow, Thomas (d. 1505, bencher I.T.,
  later sjt at law), 605
Marriage
 banns, 547, 549
 breakdown of, 568
 civil ceremony, 550, 566
 clandestine, 548–549
 common-law, 550
 consent, 546–547, 560
 consummation, 546, 561
 disputed in trespass action, 518
 endangered by slander, 500
 formation of, 308, 545–550, 568R
 guardian's right of, 275–276
 impediments, 561–562

Marriage—*continued*
 jurisdiction over, 149, 152
 licence for, 550
 litigation concerning, 568R
 money promised on, 367
 nullity, 560–562
 parental consent, 549, 561
 registration of, 550
 words of, 546
 See also DIVORCE; HUSBAND AND WIFE
Marriage-gift (maritagium), 310–311,
  367
Marriage settlement, 333–334, 336R
Married women. *See* HUSBAND AND WIFE
Marshal. *See* EARL MARSHAL OF ENGLAND
Marshalsea gaol, 49, 632–635
Martial law, 141 n.22
Mary I (1516–58, queen of England),
  legitimacy of, 564
Masquerade ticket, conversion of, 422
Massachusetts, province of, 167
Master and servant
 common employment doctrine, 471,
  473
 enticement of servant, 422, 517–518,
  520 n.59
 loss of services, 517–518
 theft by servant, 607
 vicarious liability, 464–465, 475
 workmen's compensation, 473
 See also LABOURERS; PETTY TREASON;
  TRADE DISPUTES
Master of the Rolls, 115, 128–129, 131
Masters
 in Chancery, 115–116, 129, 131
 of Requests, 138
 of Supreme Court, 131
Maule, Sir William Henry (1788–1858,
  JCP 1839–55), 566
Maxims and aphorisms
 actio personalis moritur cum persona,
  394
 better to suffer a mischief than an
  inconvenience, 369
 caveat emptor, 377, 403–404
 chancery mends no man's bargain,
  127
 equality is equity, 128
 equity prevents mischief, 128
 ex nudo pacto non oritur actio, 386,
  400
 executory contract imports assumpsit,
  393
 he that killeth a man drunk sober shall
  be hanged, 598
 in fictione juris semper est aequitas,
  231
 jura naturae sunt immutabilia, 242